HEARNES LRC, MWSC
1 MWS 00 0 214358.
S0-BRS-157

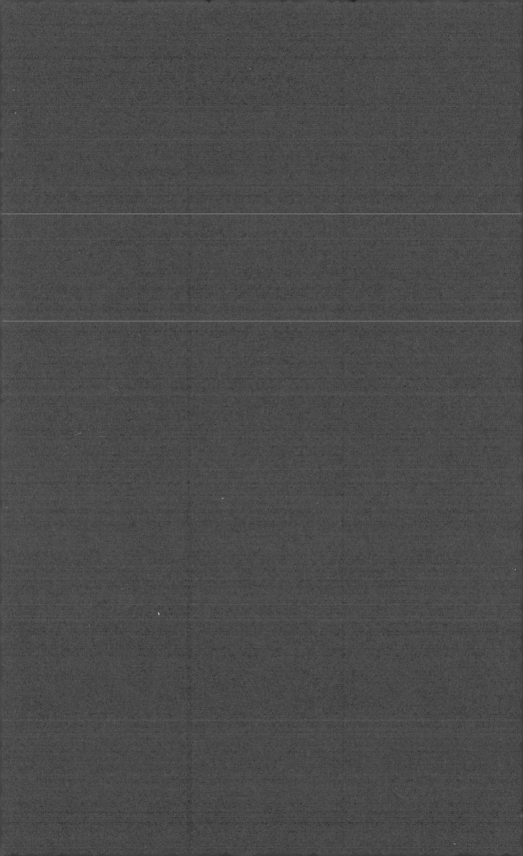

The British Library Studies in the History of the Book

THE GERMAN BOOK
1450-1750

THE GERMAN BOOK 1450-1750

Studies presented to
DAVID L. PAISEY
in his retirement

Edited by
JOHN L. FLOOD
and
WILLIAM A. KELLY

THE BRITISH LIBRARY
1995

ACKNOWLEDGEMENTS

We are grateful to the following for their kind permission to reproduce illustrations: Bayerische Staatsbibliothek, Munich (pp. 41, 255, 257); Bibliothek der Hansestadt Lübeck (p. 67); Professor M. Bircher, Zürich (pp. 287, 290, 294); Bodleian Library, Oxford (p. 17); University Library, Bristol (pp. 196–202); The British Library Board (pp. xviii, 25, 34, 37, 43, 55, 56, 58, 59, 65, 86, 87, 88, 89, 140, 141, 167, 216, 217, 218, 219, 227, 235, 238, 240, 244, 245, 252, 253, 293, 298, 348); The British Museum, Department of Prints and Drawings (pp. 86, 87, 88, 89); Deutsche Bücherei, Leipzig (p. 303); Forschungs- und Landesbibliothek Gotha (p. 17); Herzog August Bibliothek, Wolfenbüttel (pp. 132, 135, 149, 152, 155, 157, 158, 214, 215, 220, 222, 223); Österreichische Nationalbibliothek, Vienna (p. 69); Sächsische Landesbibliothek, Dresden (p. 70); Staats- und Universitätsbibliothek Hamburg (p. 66); Stadt- und Universitätsbibliothek, Bern (p. 68); Universitätsbibliothek, Tübingen (p. 311).

First published 1995
by the British Library,
Great Russell Street,
London WC1B 3DG

British Library cataloguing in Publication Data
is available from The British Library

ISBN 0 7123 0404 5

Designed by John Trevitt
Typeset in Monotype Ehrhardt by
Nene Phototypesetters Ltd, Northampton
Printed in England by
Redwood Books, Trowbridge

CONTENTS

Contents

Contents

FOREWORD

Bernhard Fabian

Antonio Panizzi, that 'Prince of Librarians', wanted the library of the British Museum to be 'as complete and as perfect' as possible. His ideal of completeness embraced not only every book printed in England or relating to England: it also included foreign books. Panizzi's aim was to build up a collection of French, Italian, Spanish and other books second only to the best collection in the respective countries. When he started he singled out the German collection of the British Museum as 'extremely incomplete in most of its branches'. When he looked back on his achievement he again singled it out, noting proudly that 'out of Germany there is no library like that of the British Museum for German books'.

When David Paisey, whom we honour with this *Festschrift*, took over responsibility for the British Library's early German holdings he inherited a great, if not daunting, tradition of collecting German books. In fact, the German section constitutes, as some other sections do, a major library in itself. It is a collection so large and so important that, if it were transferred to Germany, it would occupy a high-ranking position among the foremost libraries of the country.

A dual task confronted David Paisey. He had to round off a historical collection of outstanding quality, strong not only in 'great books' but also in minor works and ephemeral material. And he had to administer a library within a library. He had to make the German holdings readily accessible for scholarly use, and to bring its resources, conspicuous and concealed, to the notice of researchers. David Paisey has succeeded brilliantly. He has added treasures to a treasure, particularly in areas where expertise counts as much as – if not more than – purchasing power. And he has bibliographically mapped a territory notorious for traps, snares and impasses. In his own quiet way he has set new standards.

David Paisey is a reader's librarian. Those who know him find it difficult to conceive of a librarian more naturally helpful to scholars. He is always generous in providing information or offering advice from the large reservoir of his knowledge. Invariably, he gives his help as a matter of course, and he does so with a rare combination of factual precision and personal graciousness. He would inform readers of new purchases when he felt that these would be of use or interest to them. Time and again he has drawn my attention to rare items acquired in the recondite field in which I happen to be working. And occasionally a smile would reveal the satisfaction he gained from securing a book for the British Library which any librarian in Germany would have been proud to add to his collection.

Pre-eminently, David Paisey is a research librarian – a member of a species which is threatened by extinction and which we must make every effort to prevent from dying out. Libraries depend on them, as civilization depends on libraries. The task that fell to him was the compilation of the British Library's catalogue of its seventeenth-century German holdings. Though not originally a seventeenth-century scholar, David Paisey is now internationally recognized as a leading expert in the bibliography of the period. When, years ago, the Deutsche Forschungsgemeinschaft began to plan the *Verzeichnis der deutschen Drucke des siebzehnten Jahrhunderts*, the point of departure was a paper which David Paisey had been invited to submit. Work on the *Verzeichnis* is still in its initial stages. His own catalogue is completed, and it is a bibliographical triumph. There can be nothing but admiration for his achievement and his commitment.

Germany owes a debt of gratitude to David Paisey. He has for many years been an exemplary custodian of that large segment of its printed heritage which is preserved in the British Library.

Münster, 1 January 1995

NOTES ON CONTRIBUTORS

JEREMY ADLER is Professor of German at King's College London. He has published extensively on visual poetry, Hölderlin, Goethe, and many other topics. His books include *'Eine fast magische Anziehungskraft.' Goethes 'Wahlverwandtschaften' und die Chemie seiner Zeit'* (1987) and *Text und Figur. Visuelle Poesie von der Antike bis zur Moderne* (with Ulrich Ernst, 1987, 3rd ed. 1989).

NICOLAS BARKER is editor of *The Book Collector* and Libraries Adviser to the National Trust; sometime Deputy Keeper in the British Library. His many books include *Treasures of the British Library* (1992) and *Hortus Eystettensis: The Bishop's Garden and Besler's Magnificent Book* (1994).

JILL BEPLER is Head of Research Grants at the Herzog August Bibliothek, Wolfenbüttel. Her research interests include links between England and Germany in the seventeenth century, and the history of travel and collecting. Her major publications are *Ferdinand Albrecht, Duke of Braunschweig-Lüneburg (1636-1687): a Traveller and his Travelogue* (1988); *Barocke Sammellust. Die Bibliothek und Kunstkammer des Herzogs Ferdinand Albrecht zu Braunschweig-Lüneburg (1636-1687)* (1988).

IRMGARD BEZZEL is a member of the staff of the Bayerische Staatsbibliothek, Munich. Since 1969 she has headed the project for the *Verzeichnis der im deutschen Sprachbereich erschienenen Drucke des 16. Jahrhunderts (VD 16)*. Dr Bezzel's publications include *Erasmusdrucke des 16. Jahrhunderts in bayerischen Bibliotheken* (1979), *Erasmus von Rotterdam. Deutsche Übersetzungen des 16. Jahrhunderts* (1980), as well as many articles on library history and sixteenth-century bibliography.

MARTIN BIRCHER is the head of research on the seventeenth century at the Herzog August Bibliothek, Wolfenbüttel, and holds a chair at the University of Zurich. His publications include *Deutsche Drucke des Barock 1600-1720 in der Herzog August Bibliothek* (1977-) and *Im Garten der Palme: Kleinodien aus dem unbekannten Barock: die Fruchtbringende Gesellschaft und ihre Zeit* (1992). He is editor of *Librarium* and *Wolfenbütteler Barock-Nachrichten.*

MARTIN BOGHARDT is a member of the staff of the Herzog August Bibliothek, Wolfenbüttel, where he is particularly concerned with the early history of printing and with the application of the techniques of analytical bibliography to German books. His many publications include *Analytische Druckforschung* (1977) and (together with Walter Wilkes) a valuable series of reprints of German printer's manuals of the seventeenth to nineteenth centuries.

MIRJAM BOHATCOVÁ took her doctorate at the Charles University in Prague. She was a librarian at the National Museum in Prague and later at the Czechoslovakian Academy of Sciences before becoming an editor with the publishing house Artia. Her research focuses on printing and the history of the book in the sixteenth to eighteenth centuries on which she has published widely.

HELMUT CLAUS is Director of the Forschungs- und Landesbibliothek at Gotha. His research interests lie in early-sixteenth-century German printing and bibliography and focus particularly on the early Reformation period. Dr Claus's publications include studies of printing in Leipzig and Zwickau and articles on individual printers in a number of towns.

BERNHARD FABIAN, Professor of English and Bibliography at the University of Münster, was recently elected a Corresponding Fellow of the British Academy. In 1991 he delivered the Panizzi Lectures on *The English Book in Eighteenth-Century Germany*, and in 1993 he gave the Lyell Lectures at Oxford. He is General Editor of the *Handbuch der historischen Buchbestände in Deutschland* and is currently preparing a bibliographical catalogue of eighteenth-century German reprints and translations of English works.

JOHN L. FLOOD is Professor of German in the University of London and Deputy Director of the University of London Institute of Germanic Studies. He is a former Fellow in the Centre for the Book at the British Library. Much of his current research is devoted to the history of the book, particularly in fifteenth- and sixteenth-century Germany. His publications include *Die Historie von Herzog Ernst* (1992) and his many articles range over medieval literature, incunabula and sixteenth-century bibliography, humanism, the history of medicine, linguistics, and German-speaking exiles in Great Britain.

LEONARD FORSTER was formerly Professor of German at University College London and then Schröder Professor of German in the University of Cambridge. He is a Fellow of the British Academy, a member of the Royal Netherlands Academy of Sciences, and a Corresponding Member of the Deutsche Akademie für Sprache und Dichtung at Darmstadt and of the Royal Belgian Academy. His publications include *The Icy Fire: Five Studies in Petrarchism* (1969), *The Poet's Tongues: Multilingualism in Literature* (1970), *Kleine Schriften zur deutschen Literatur im 17. Jahrhundert* (1977), *Iter Bohemicum* (1980), and *Christoffel Sichem in Basel und der frühe deutsche Alexandriner* (1985).

ANTHONY J. HARPER is Professor of German in the University of Strathclyde. His research focuses on poetry and song in the baroque period. His books include *The Lyric Poetry of David Schirmer* (1977), *Schriften zur Lyrik Leipzigs 1620-1670* (1985), *The Song-Books of Gottfried Finckelthaus* (1988), *Studien zum deutschen weltlichen Kunstlied des 17. und 18. Jahrhunderts* (with G. Busch, 1992), and he has recently published an edition of Christian Brehme's *Lustige Gedichte* of 1637.

LOTTE HELLINGA FBA is a Deputy Keeper in the British Library. She has published widely on fifteenth-century printing, and early printing in Mainz is one of her areas of particular interest.

FRANK HIERONYMUS is a librarian at the University Library at Basle. His research interests include book illustration and printing in Basle down to about 1630. The most recent of his many publications is *Theophrast und Galen, Celsus und Paracelsus, Medizin, Naturphilosophie und Kirchenreform im Basler Buchdruck bis 1600* (1995).

GRAHAM JEFCOATE was appointed to the staff of the British Library in 1988, following a number of years in Germany where he helped to compile *A Catalogue of English Books Printed before 1801 held by the University Library at Göttingen*, edited by Bernhard Fabian. At the British Library he has worked on the *ESTC* project. He has written various articles on library history and on the Anglo-German book trade in the eighteenth century.

WILLIAM ASHFORD KELLY has been an Assistant Keeper at the National Library of Scotland's Department of Printed Books since 1970. His interests include printing at Helmstedt, the bibliographical control of academic dissertations, and occasional verses published in monographs. He has contributed extensively to Gerhard Dünnhaupt's *Personalbibliographien zu den Drucken des Barock* (1990-93).

MANFRED KOMOROWSKI is on the staff of the University Library at Duisburg. His special fields of interest include the history of universities (particularly Duisburg and Königsberg) and libraries in the Early Modern period and the bibliographic control of early dissertations, subjects on which he has published extensively. Dr Komorowski is also interested in German library history in the period 1933-45.

ULRICH KOPP has been working in the cataloguing section of the Herzog August Bibliothek, Wolfenbüttel, since 1974 and is a member of the Wolfenbüttel *VD 16* team. His research interests lie in the history of the book and sixteenth-century bibliography.

HORST MEYER is best known for his annual bibliography *Bibliographie der Buch- und Bibliotheksgeschichte* which has been appearing since 1982, but he has published extensively on various aspects of the history of the book.

GRAHAM NATTRASS works in the Early Collections Service at the British Library, where he has responsibility for the pre-1850 German collections. He is currently preparing a special catalogue of the Library's German holdings of the period 1701-1750.

MARGARET NICKSON was formerly an Assistant Keeper in the Department of Manuscripts at the British Library. She has published in the *British Library Journal* and elsewhere on the manuscripts of Sir Hans Sloane, and is currently working on the history of English libraries in the seventeenth and eighteenth centuries.

JOHN ROGER PAAS is Professor of German language and Literature at Carleton College, Northfield, Minnesota, USA. He is presently editing a comprehensive, multi-volume edition of German political broadsheets of the seventeenth century. His other areas of research include printed German portraiture in the Early Modern period and co-operation between poets and graphic artists in the seventeenth century.

DENIS V. REIDY taught Italian at the Universities of Sheffield and Leeds before being appointed Head of the Italian and Modern Greek Collections and he now has overall responsibility for Romance languages at the British Library. He edited *The Italian Book 1465-1800* (1993) and has published on many aspects of Italian civilization.

DENNIS E. RHODES was formerly Deputy Keeper in the Department of Printed Books at the British Library. A specialist in Italian printing, he has compiled several catalogues of the Italian holdings in the British Library (as well as the revised edition of its *Short Title Catalogue of Spanish Books*) and has published many books and articles on a wide range of aspects of early printing. His latest book, *The Silent Printers* (1995), deals with books printed anonymously at Venice.

ANNA E. C. SIMONI, who was educated in Germany, Italy and Scotland, joined the British Museum Department of Printed Books in 1950 and in due course became head of the Dutch Section at the British Library. In addition to her *Catalogue of Books from the Low Countries 1601-1621 in the British Library* (1990) her publications include *Publish and be free* (1975), *Printing as Resistance* (1990), and many articles in Dutch and British bibliographical journals.

MARIE-LUISE SPIECKERMANN is on the staff of the English Department of the University of Münster. She has published a number of articles on the reception of English authors and on various aspects of the book trade in eighteenth-century Germany.

HELEN WATANABE-O'KELLY is a Fellow of Exeter College, Oxford. Her books include *Triumphall Shews. Tournaments at German-speaking Courts in their European Content 1560-1730* (1992), and she is currently working with P. Béhar on *Spectaculum Europaeum. A Handbook of Theatre and Spectacle in Europe 1580-1750*.

ABBREVIATIONS

Adams	H. M. Adams, *Catalogue of Books Printed on the Continent of Europe, 1501-1600, in Cambridge Libraries.* 2 vols (Cambridge, 1967)
ADB	*Allgemeine Deutsche Biographie* (Leipzig, 1875-1912; reprint Berlin, 1967-71)
AGB	*Archiv für Geschichte des Buchwesens*
Benzing/ Claus	Josef Benzing, *Lutherbibliographie. Verzeichnis der gedruckten Schriften Martin Luthers bis zu dessen Tod.* Bearbeitet in Verbindung mit der Weimarer Ausgabe unter Mitarbeit von Helmut Claus. Bibliotheca Bibliographica Aureliana, X, XVI, XIX (Baden-Baden, 1966). [With supplement:] *Ergänzungen zur Bibliographie der zeitgenössischen Lutherdrucke.* Im Anschluß an die Lutherbibliographie Josef Benzings bearbeitet von Helmut Claus und Michael A. Pegg. Veröffentlichungen der Forschungsbibliothek Gotha, 20. (Gotha, 1982)
BL	British Library, London
BLJ	*The British Library Journal*
BM	British Museum, London
BMC	*A Catalogue of Books printed in the XVth Century, Now in the British Museum.* Parts I-X, XII. (London, 1908-; reprint London, 1963)
Brunet	Jacques Charles Brunet, *Manuel du libraire et de l'amateur de livres.* 5th ed. 6 vols and supplements (Paris, 1860-80; reprint Berlin 1921; New York, 1923; Paris, 1923 and 1928)
BSB	Bayerische Staatsbibliothek, Munich
BSB-AK	*Bayerische Staatsbibliothek Alphabetischer Katalog 1501-1840.* 60 vols (Munich, 1987-90)
BU	Biblioteka Uniwersytecka
CIBN	*Bibliothèque nationale de France. Catalogue des incunables* (Paris, 1985-)

Dünnhaupt	Gerhard Dünnhaupt, *Bibliographisches Handbuch der Barockliteratur.* Hiersemanns bibliographische Handbücher 2. 3 vols (Stuttgart, 1980-81). Second edition under the title: *Personalbibliographien zu den Drucken des Barock*, Hiersemanns bibliographische Handbücher 9. 6 vols (Stuttgart, 1990-93)
ESTC	*Eighteenth-century Short Title Catalogue* (London, 1990)
Ger STC	Short-Title Catalogue of Books Printed in the German-Speaking Countries and German Books Printed in Other Countries from *1455-1600 Now in the British Museum* (London, 1962)
Ger STC Suppl.	*Short-Title Catalogue of Books Printed in the German-Speaking Countries and German Books Printed in Other Countries from 1455-1600 Now in the British Library. Supplement* (London, 1990)
Ger 17th c. STC	*Catalogue of Books Printed in the German-Speaking Countries and of German Books Printed in Other Countries from 1601 to 1700 Now in the British Library.* 5 vols (London, 1994)
GJ	*Gutenberg-Jahrbuch*
GK	*Gesamtkatalog der Preußischen Bibliotheken mit Nachweis des identischen Besitzes der Bayerischen Staatsbibliothek in München und der Nationalbibliothek in Wien* (Berlin, 1931-35) [continued as:] *Deutscher Gesamtkatalog* (Berlin 1936-39)
GLL	*German Life and Letters*
GW	*Gesamtkatalog der Wiegendrucke* (Leipzig, 1925-40; Stuttgart, 1968 and 1978-)
Hain	Ludwig Hain, *Repertorium Bibliographicum, in quo libri omnes ab arte typographica inventa usque ad annum MD. typis ... expressi recensentur.* (Stuttgart and Paris, 1826-38; reprint Frankfurt am Main 1920; Berlin, 1925; Milan, 1948 and 1964)
Hain-Copinger	Walter A. Copinger, *Supplement to Hain's Repertorium Bibliographicum* (London, 1895-1902; reprint Berlin, 1926; Milan, 1950)
ISTC	*Incunabula Short-Title Catalogue:* on-line database at the British Library
Italian STC	*Short-Title Catalogue of Books Printed in Italy and of Italian Books Printed in Other Countries from 1465-1600 Now in the British Museum* (London, 1958)
Kyriss	Ernst Kyriss, *Verzierte gotische Einbände im alten deutschen Sprachgebiet* (Stuttgart, 1951-58)
LB	Landesbibliothek
Madsen	Victor Madsen, *Katalog over det Kongelige Biblioteks incunabler.* 3 vols (Copenhagen, 1935-63)

MLR	*The Modern Language Review*
NUC	*The National Union Catalog. Pre 1956 Imprints. A Cumulative Author-List* ... 750 vols (London and Chicago, 1968-81)
Panzer DA	Georg Wolfgang Panzer, *Annalen der älteren deutschen Literatur ... welche von Erfindung der Buchdruckerkunst bis 1526 in deutscher Sprache gedruckt worden sind* (Nuremberg and Leipzig, 1788-1802; reprint Hildesheim, 1961-62)
PBSA	*Papers of the Bibliographical Society of America*
Proctor	Robert Proctor, *An Index to the Early Printed Books in the British Museum ... to the Year 1520. With Notes of those in the Bodleian Library* (London, 1898-1903; reprint London, 1960).
SB	Staatsbibliothek
StB	Stadtbibliothek
STC[2]	Alfred William Pollard and Gilbert Richard Redgrave, *A Short-Title Catalogue of Books Printed in England, Scotland and Ireland and of English Books Printed Abroad 1475-1640.* 2nd ed. revised and enlarged by W. A. Jackson and F. S. Ferguson, completed by Katharine F. Pantzer (London, 1976-91)
Stevenson	Enrico Stevenson, *Inventario dei libri stampati Palatino-Vaticano* (Rome, 1886-89)
UB	Universitätsbibliothek
UL	University Library
VD 16	*Verzeichnis der im deutschen Sprachbereich erschienenen Drucke des XVI. Jahrhunderts.* Hrsg. von der Bayerischen Staatsbibliothek in München in Verbindung mit der Herzog August Bibliothek in Wolfenbüttel. Redaktion Irmgard Bezzel. I. Abt. (Stuttgart, 1983-)
VGT	*Veröffentlichungen der Gesellschaft für Typenkunde des 15. Jahrhunderts.* 33 vols (Halle, Berlin and Leipzig (1907-39; reprint Osnabrück, 1966)
WBN	*Wolfenbütteler Barock-Nachrichten*
Weimar HAAB	Herzogin Anna Amalia-Bibliothek, Weimar
Weller	Emil Weller, *Repertorium typographicum. Die deutsche Literatur im ersten Viertel des 16. Jahrhunderts* (Nördlingen, 1864-85; reprint Hildesheim, 1961)
WNB	*Wolfenbütteler Notizen zur Buchgeschichte*
Wolfenbüttel HAB	Herzog August Bibliothek, Wolfenbüttel

David L. Paisey

EDITORS' INTRODUCTION

JOHN L. FLOOD and WILLIAM A. KELLY

THE PURPOSE OF THIS VOLUME is twofold. More generally it is to bring to the attention of a wider public the extraordinary depth and richness of the British Library's holdings of early printed books from the German-speaking countries. While these have been catalogued, most conveniently in the *Short-Title Catalogue of Books Printed in the German-Speaking Countries and German Books Printed in Other Countries from 1455-1600 Now in the British Museum*, its supplement, and in the newly published *Catalogue of Books Printed in the German-speaking Countries and of German Books Printed in Other Countries from 1601 to 1700 Now in the British Library*, the collections still await full exploitation. Library collections are, in Lord Samuel's phrase, 'thought in cold storage'. Several of the essays in this book attempt to 'defrost' these thoughts and to breathe life into the dry catalogue entries by examining individual books, or groups of books, in a broader context.

The second aim and the immediate occasion of this volume is to honour David L. Paisey who, over the past thirty years or so, has done more than anyone else to investigate and interpret the British Library's holdings of pre-1750 German books. David Paisey's greatest contribution as a bibliographer is undoubtedly as a compiler of the *Catalogue of Books Printed in the German-speaking Countries and of German Books Printed in Other Countries from 1601-1700 Now in the British Library*, published in five volumes in October 1994, a labour that has occupied him for more than twenty years. This catalogue stands in the tradition of the Short-title Catalogues, a series which goes back a long way: the first was the *Short-Title Catalogue of Books Printed in Spain and of Spanish Books Printed Elsewhere in Europe before 1601 Now in the British Museum*, compiled by Henry (later Sir Henry) Thomas and published in 1921, followed by the French Short-title catalogue in 1924 and then by similar volumes for other foreign languages. But while the first two were both decidedly experimental and hurried productions, David Paisey's new catalogue of seventeenth-century German books – as indeed his supplement to the *German STC 1455-1600*, published in 1990 – was well planned and many years in the making. This new catalogue is, however, of very special importance not only on account of its scope – it lists more than 26,000 items – but also because of its pioneering role: for no German library has yet produced a full catalogue of its seventeenth-century holdings. Moreover, with its range of indexes (of subjects, printers and publishers, collaborators, and literary genres) going far beyond those in any of the earlier *STC*s, the British Library's seventeenth-century catalogue will open up hidden riches to scholars in all historical disciplines and also provide valuable input into the German national union catalogue which is now in its early stages. Another way in which the catalogue marks a major step forward is that it is due to become available on-line, to be followed, it is hoped, by a CD-ROM version. The magnificence of this new catalogue cannot be over-estimated, and David Paisey deserves full credit for it. It is of course a long-established tradition with the *STC*s that the input of their compilers is played down: their names do not feature on the title-page and, traditionally also, they are mentioned almost *en passant* in the preface. Against such a background the Director General (London Services) surpasses his predecessors in effusive praise when, in this particular case, he writes 'The catalogue is entirely the work of David Paisey, to whom grateful thanks are due, not only for the scholarship he has brought to it, but also for the great labour involved in keyboarding the text and preparing the camera-ready copy'. It is in order to give David more tangible recognition of his work that we offer him the present volume of essays as he embarks on the challenge of retirement – not that he contemplates 'retirement' at all: he has now volunteered to assist the British Museum's Department of Prints and Drawings with the identification, cataloguing and arrangement of their substantial holdings of materials of German provenance.

David Lincoln Paisey was born in Cardiff in May 1933. Though the capital of Wales still holds attractions for him, not the least of which is the Welsh National Opera, he has spent most of his life in the capital of England. He read for a degree in German at University College London, graduating in 1954, and then in 1957 took an M.A. in German there in the days when this was still a highly respectable and highly respected academic qualification, involving not only research and the presentation of a thesis but also the taking of gruelling written papers. His thesis, supervised by Professor Leonard Forster who, to our delight and despite his advancing years, has felt able to contribute to this volume, concerned the poetry of Gottfried Benn (1886–1956), a writer whom he had got to know quite well, regularly taking tea with the poet and his wife at their home in Berlin. Getting to know Benn in this way was no small achievement because he was a man who generally kept himself very much to himself, and that he was able to form a fruitful relationship with him is no doubt due in no small measure to David's modesty, sincerity, and devotion to his work. Like most men of his generation, David Paisey did National Service, serving in the Army where he learned Russian if nothing else. Following this he entered the service of the British Museum as an Assistant Keeper in 1959. After a time he succeeded Philip Harris as Assistant Secretary to the British Museum, working under the genial eye of Bentley Bridgewater for three years. In 1965 he returned to the

Department of Printed Books where, as it turned out, he was to spend the rest of his professional life, still in what – not without reason, it seems – was called the 'career grade' of Assistant Keeper in the German section. Though he deftly forewent the opportunity to become Deputy Superintendent of the Reading Room in the later sixties, he was clearly cut out to be given particular responsibility for German antiquarian books – something which must have been a real pleasure in those halcyon days when money was still amply available for new acquisitions. He also enjoyed several years as Superintendent of the North Library where he will have become a familiar figure to very many readers, and not only those who were privileged to benefit from his wise counsel and vast experience of matters bibliographical.

It would be idle to pretend that David Paisey has been a conventional colleague. His famed habitual non-wearing of a tie is a kind of sartorial manifesto, and his request on one occasion to be provided with a pair of industrial ear-protectors to cut out the noise of a busy library environment is the stuff of which British Library legend is made. Happily he has always been, as Mirjam Foot put it at his farewell party on 30 September 1994, a fish who swims against the tide:

> *Levende vissen zwemmen tegen de stroom,*
> *alleen de dooien drijven mee.*
> 'Live fish swim against the current, only dead ones go with it.'

We users of the Library, and the world of scholarship at large, have real cause to be grateful to him for the firmness of his resolve to swim against the tide, to fight for the needs of scholars and for standards of scholarship, and to persuade (perhaps 'bully' would be more accurate) the authorities to permit him to devote an ever-increasing proportion of his time to the preparation of his catalogue of the Library's seventeenth-century German holdings.

What may have passed behind the scenes is, however, of no consequence to users of the Library. What concerns them, be they regular or occasional readers or postal enquirers, all of whom were treated with great courtesy, is the qualities he has brought to his work, and among these we readily number competence, efficiency, meticulousness, and above all true scholarship and commitment. The significance of his work is displayed nowhere more effectively than in his *Catalogue of German Books in the British Library 1601-1700*, which truly sets a new standard in the tradition of the British Library's Short-title Catalogues, and assures him a secure place in the Library's long line of distinguished scholar-librarians. '*Si monumentum requiris, perlege hoc opus*' could well be his epitaph. But beyond that his *Supplement* to the *German STC* (which one contributor to this volume – against all the traditions of the British Museum and British Library – wished to insist should be referred to simply as 'Paisey' in the same way as bibliographers speak of Hain, Goff, Adams, etc.), his pioneering directory of members of the German book trade in the first half of the eighteenth century (*Deutsche Buchdrucker, Buchhändler und Verleger 1701-1750* (Wiesbaden, 1988)) – to assist him with the preparation of which the British Library granted him all of three days' research leave! – and from among his many articles particularly the seminal paper on books which failed to be listed in the German fair catalogues ('Literatur, die nicht in den Meßkatalogen steht', in Paul Raabe's *Bücher und Bibliotheken im 17. Jahrhundert in Deutschland* (Hamburg, 1980)), are cited many times over in the pages of this volume as truly authoritative contributions to bibliographical research in the period. His international standing as bibliographer and librarian was recognized when in 1976 he was appointed a Corresponding Member of the Historische Kommission des Börsenvereins des Deutschen Buchhandels, and his contribution to scholarship of the baroque period has been recognized through his membership of the committee of the Internationaler Arbeitskreis für Barockliteratur, based at Wolfenbüttel. It should also be recalled that it was on his initiative that in 1985 the British Library organized a symposium to review existing resources and future needs of scholars working in the area of German Studies, broadly defined. Efficiently and expeditiously he edited the proceedings, which were published by the British Library under the title *German Studies: British Resources* in 1986. And it is important to record that one of the immediate consequences of that symposium was the establishment of the German Studies Library Group, a thriving national association of librarians and scholars concerned with provision of library resources for research in the field.

Besides being someone who has made an immense contribution to bibliography, David Paisey is a man of many parts. As the list of his publications shows, he has a profound interest in art and in poetry. He is an expert translator, whether of bibliographical technicalities (see his English version of the introduction to *VD 16*) or of Schiller's *Kabale und Liebe* (performed at the Lyric Studio, Hammersmith in 1992); he used to play the viol and now plays the organ, and he is renowned for having a fastidious taste in opera, and he also claims an interest in football.

A measure of the great respect in which David Paisey's work as a bibliographer is held world-wide is the warmth and enthusiasm with which our proposal to prepare a volume of essays in his honour was greeted not only by his colleagues in the British Library but also by other librarians, bibliographers, and scholars in the field of German literature throughout the United Kingdom, the German-speaking countries of Europe, and the United States of America. All the contributors to the volume know David Paisey well and have benefited over the years from his expertise, knowledge and wisdom. Indeed, both the editors of this volume have even had the sobering experience but undoubted privilege of having him act as External Examiner for their doctoral theses; even in such a context we were struck by the generosity of spirit and great erudition he wears so lightly. The heart-warming response which our proposal to edit this volume received from all who were invited to contribute was a great encouragement, and many contributors – and indeed many other colleagues who for one reason or another felt unable to write for the book – were most touchingly generous in their deep appreciation of the many professional and personal kindnesses David Paisey has shown them over the years.

David Paisey's interests are so wide-ranging and varied that we could not contemplate doing justice to them all within the covers of a single volume. Instead we have chosen to focus on two: early German books, and German poetry. And even here we have felt the need to restrict coverage to that period with which he has been most closely concerned as a professional librarian, the period covered by his three most important publications: the *Supplement* to the *German STC*, the *Catalogue of German Books 1601–1700*, and his directory of German printers and publishers of the first half of the eighteenth century. This period, the three centuries from 1450 to 1750, is one of the most significant in the history of the German book trade, and yet vast tracts of it so far remain under-researched. It is our hope that the essays offered in this volume will make an important contribution, however modest, to the further exploration and elucidation of this period.

Anna Simoni, writing about a small sample of Dutch books with German connections, describes them as ranging over wide fields of interest, 'from art theory to zoology, from classical antiquity to the hottest of hot news, for the studious and the curious at home and abroad'. Virtually the same could be said about the present collection of essays which are designed to reveal to the interested reader the wealth of subjects covered by the British Library's German collections and to relate these to the wider world of current research in German bibliography.

The essays are arranged broadly following the chronology of their subject matter, beginning with incunabula and ending with the early-eighteenth-century book trade. In a number of cases the British Library's holdings have supplied the starting point or the inspiration for the essay. Thus Helmut Claus reveals how it was a plea from what was then the library of the British Museum for help with identifying the printer of some Reformation pamphlets that led him to investigate the press of Adam Dyon of Breslau, a study which, as the reader will see, has borne fruit so abundantly here. Some of them are concerned with particular books in the British Library's collections, whether Martin Boghardt's analysis of printing variants in the 1459 Mainz Psalter, John Flood's relation of the curious tale of twentieth-century 'facsimiles' of the unique copy of the 1515 edition of *Till Eulenspiegel*, Denis Reidy's investigation of links between a sixteenth-century Venetian blockbook and Albrecht Dürer's *Kleine Passion*, or Nicolas Barker's re-examination of the problem of who printed the magnificent *Hortus Eystettensis*. In his inimitable manner, Dennis Rhodes investigates two books previously believed to have been of Italian origin and shows that without doubt they are in reality German imprints. Similarly Ulrich Kopp shows that the 1576 Antwerp edition of Baptista Mantuanus, 'the Christian Vergil', has its origins in Germany. And while Horst Meyer's chief concern is to show what light the happily surviving journal of the Osnabrück printer Gottfried Kisling for the period 1713-1739 throws on the day-to-day running of his business, he tells us something about an intriguing controversy about poltergeists that was fought out in books now in the British Library.

Other contributions deal with groups of books in the British Library. Margaret Nickson and Lotte Hellinga, for instance, endeavour to trace Mainz incunabula sold in the early eighteenth century which formerly belonged to the Frankfurt Dominicans; Irmgard Bezzel examines early-sixteenth-century news booklets giving accounts of the Portuguese exploration of the East; Frank Hieronymus breathes life into the Library's rich holdings of sixteenth-century medical books printed at Basle, works which once represented the last word in science but which today, with the possible exception of Vesalius's *De humani corporis fabrica* (Basle, 1534), are totally forgotten. Mirjam Bohatcová, drawing on the *German STC 1455-1600* and David Paisey's *Supplement*, directs our attention to the British Library's significant holdings of sixteenth-century books of Bohemian interest. In a similar way, Anna Simoni points to an interesting range from the Library's collection of Dutch books with German connections printed by Henrick van Haestens at Leiden and Jan Jansz at Arnhem. Whereas many of the books described by Dr Bohatcová and Miss Simoni have long formed part of the Library's collections, others discussed here are recent acquisitions. Martin Bircher, for instance, gives an account of the library of the Counts of Auersperg in Ljubljana, from which the British Library – thanks to David Paisey's keen eye for what is significant – was able to acquire a number of important items when they were offered for sale at Sotheby's in 1982 and 1983. An even more recent acquisition is the volume of eighteen baroque sermons, mostly printed in Austria, from the first half of the eighteenth century, described by Graham Nattrass.

Recent years have seen a growth of scholarly interest in bibliographically rebarbative fields like the baroque sermon and the academic dissertation. Several of the essays in this volume show how the substantial holdings of the British Library in these areas may be brought into the orbit of ongoing European research. Both Jill Bepler, in her discussion of German funeral books, and Helen Watanabe-O'Kelly in her piece on festival books for religious occasions, demonstrate the value and significance of such research. Similarly, Manfred Komorowski describes the current state of research on early university dissertations, thousands of which lie neglected, even uncatalogued, in many libraries; as Willie Kelly tells us, the National Library of Scotland has nearly thirty-five thousand such pieces, and he amply demonstrates their importance when, in the course of compiling a checklist of the works of Konrad Philipp Limmer (1658-1730), he uncovers evidence which suggests that Limmer may have played a role in the sowing of Cartesian ideas in Germany.

One of the most important areas of research which has been opened up in recent years is that of Anglo-German links in the book trade. Not least through his Panizzi Lectures in 1991 and his Lyell Lectures at Oxford in 1993, Bernhard Fabian has drawn our attention to the growing awareness of English culture in

Germany in the eighteenth century. Here, in an essay written jointly with Marie-Luise Spieckermann, he examines the role played by the House of Weidmann in Leipzig in the importation of English books to Germany. Graham Jefcoate approaches the subject from the other end: the translating, printing and distribution of German Pietist writing in London at the beginning of the eighteenth century. (We make the acquaintance of *Estrid: an account of a Swedish maid* – not an early candidate for the notorious 'Private Case' apparently but 'an account of pubertal piety'.) Jefcoate offers an admirable demonstration of the value of the *ESTC* database, which has been developed in the British Library, for bringing together scattered information: for the first time it is possible to assemble a considerable amount of evidence for Johann Christian Jacobi's activities as owner of what was probably the first German bookshop in eighteenth-century London and his collaboration with the local printer Joseph Downing. Jefcoate's essay also brings the importance of the magnificent collections of the Franckesche Stiftungen in Halle, happily recently awakened from their enforced *Dornröschenschlaf*, to the attention of those concerned with the book trade in eighteenth-century Germany.

One of David Paisey's particular interests is poetry. By design, therefore, the volume includes a number of essays devoted to poets of the baroque period. Leonard Forster, the doyen of German baroque studies in Britain and doubtless personally responsible for having awakened David Paisey's love for the literature of this period, discusses and reproduces his own copy of Christian Cunrad's *Hirten Gespräch*, a book so rare that it does not figure in even the British Library's vast collections of seventeenth-century German books. And while Jeremy Adler focuses on the visual poetry of Sigmund von Birken, one of the 'Pegnitz Shepherds', John Roger Paas reveals a forgotten dimension of Birken's activities when he tells the story behind the publication of his historical-topographical *Der Donau-Strand* of 1664. Anthony Harper is similarly informative about the activities of another many-sided poet, Christian Brehme.

Editing this volume has been a pleasurable experience throughout. Of course, we have had our trials and tribulations – but, as the twelfth-century Austrian poet Dietmar von Aist put it, *liep âne leit mac niht gesîn* ('pleasure cannot exist without pain'). We have rejoiced over the willing co-operation and ready support of the contributors and have enjoyed and profited from their offerings. It has been a privilege to work with them and for this we owe them a profound debt of gratitude.

We are particularly grateful to those who allowed us to translate their contributions into English. In *The Age of Innocence* (1920), some readers may recall, the American novelist Edith Wharton wrote, 'An unalterable and unquestioned law of the musical world required that the German text of a French opera sung by Swedish artists should be translated into Italian for the clearer understanding of English-speaking audiences'. The world of opera is one thing, the history of the book, fortunately, is something quite different. In preparing the present volume we have not had to translate anything into Italian, but we have felt constrained to make everything accessible in English. While some contributors would certainly have preferred their pieces to remain in German, not least out of immense respect for David Paisey's superb command of the language, we have believed it appropriate that the book should be entirely in English since it is intended to appeal not just to specialists in German bibliography but also to all who have an interest in the history of the book generally or in the British Library's rich collections of early German printed books. Accordingly, we have translated the nine essays submitted to us in German. If indeed we did not do so before, we now have a keen appreciation of why, in 1530, Martin Luther was moved to utter the heart-felt sigh, *Ah es ist dolmetzschen ja nicht eines iglichen kunst*, 'translating is an art not everyone can master'. But we hope we have acquitted ourselves of the task reasonably competently. Any remaining linguistic infelicities – what, as Graham Jefcoate tells us, his Joseph Downing in 1709 called 'Teutonisms or other imperfections' – are ours, not the authors'. We thank them for their tolerance and forbearing.

Equally sincere thanks are due to Jane Carr and particularly David Way of British Library Publications for the support they have unstintingly given since this project was first proposed to them. And, as outsiders, we are indebted to friends in the British Library – particularly Philip Harris, Graham Nattrass, Denis Reidy, Dennis Rhodes, and Anna Simoni – who have supported us, indeed have conspired with us, in our endeavours to assemble this volume which, we hope, David Paisey will receive as a modest tribute and heartfelt thankyou for the immense contribution he has made to the cause of German bibliography over more than three decades.

John L. Flood — London
William A. Kelly — Edinburgh

1995

THE SECOND DISTURBANCE IN QUIRE F

An unsolved mystery in Fust and Schöffer's 'Psalterium Benedictinum' of 1459

MARTIN BOGHARDT

EARLIER INVESTIGATION of the *Psalterium Benedictinum* (Hain 13480; ISTC ip01062000), a large folio printed on vellum by Johann Fust and Peter Schöffer at Mainz on 29 August 1459, has revealed three instances of leaves being replaced; these may be considered as providing early – if not indeed the very first – exemplification of the typical reasons for the emergence of the practice.[1] The leaves in question are fol. 10, the last leaf of the first gathering which, following *BMC*, I shall call [A], fol. 51, the first leaf of the sixth gathering ([F]), and fol. 121, the third leaf of the thirteenth gathering ([N]).

Such leaves may be recognized by the following features:

1) disruption of the structure of the gatherings deriving from the substitution of leaves;
2) partial or total disruption of the *mise-en-page* resulting from changes to the setting or complete resetting;
3) typographical or textual differences between pages from different settings which may provide information about the substitution of leaves;
4) differences in the frequency pattern of original and replacement leaves, which may likewise provide a pointer to the reasons for the change.[2]

I

Sir Irvine Masson was the first to draw attention to fols 10 and 121 in what was basically a very careful study, his book *The Mainz Psalters and Canon Missae 1457-1459* (London, 1954), which, however, focused primarily on the *Psalterium Moguntinum* of 1457, rather than on the *Psalterium Benedictinum* of

1 *BMC* I, pp. 19-20. Irvine Masson, *The Mainz Psalters and Canon Missae 1457-1459* (London, 1954), p. 64.

2 Further indications which are either difficult to detect or are not relevant in the present context where we are dealing with vellum copies include changes in the constitution of the ink and different sorts of paper. See Richard N. Schwab, 'An *Ersatz* Leaf in the Doheny Gutenberg Bible Volume I', *PBSA*, 81 (1987), 479-85. Martin Boghardt, 'Die bibliographische Erforschung der ersten *Catholicon*-Ausgabe(n)', *Wolfenbütteler Notizen zur Buchgeschichte*, 13 (1988), 138-76, here pp. 155 and 174.

1459, which explains why he examined only three of the thirteen known copies of the latter.[3] These were the first copy in the British Library (IC.75) and the copies in the John Rylands University Library, Manchester, and the Bodleian Library, Oxford. Masson writes: 'Certain leaves of which the first settings were found betimes to be faulty were reset and reprinted, in particular ff. 10, 51, and [...] 121' (p. 64). Masson must have been led to notice fols 10 and 121, on which I will concentrate first of all, in Earl Spencer's copy now in Manchester by comparing the settings, for in this copy these leaves are from an entirely different setting from the London and Oxford copies although – and here Masson was mistaken – these are by no means less defective than the Manchester one. Let us examine them.

The way in which fol. 10 in gathering [A], a quinio, has been inserted cannot be determined for certain. Neither loose stubs pointing to excision nor traces of gum indicating later insertion of leaves can be observed, nor can one tell whether fol. 10 is conjugate with fol. 1 or not. The copy from the Bibliotheca Spenceriana was rebound in the eighteenth century according to the bibliophile taste of the age. It was given a red morocco binding by Dêrome le Jeune[4] and it is likely that all vestiges of a leaf having been replaced at an earlier date were deliberately removed, not least because they would have been particularly obvious in the case of the first gathering in the book.

On the other hand, fol. 121 is very clearly not conjugate with its twin, fol. 126; they are what I have called elsewhere a *Schachtelbogen*,[5] that is to say, the inner edges have stubs which are folded to interlock with one another so that they may be sewn in the usual way without any need for gum. The projecting stub on fol. 126 is located before fol. 121 and that on fol. 121 before fol. 126. This shows that one of the two leaves, which ought to constitute a single sheet, has been replaced, unless of course two smaller pieces of valuable vellum had been used from the outset instead of one larger piece.

The *mise-en-page* on fols 10^{r}, 10^{v}, 121^{r} and 121^{v} of the Rylands copy is quite different from that in the London and Oxford copies, which means that the passages of text in question must have been set up twice. This fact indicates that for some reason a supplementary printing or a replacement impression was needed for each of the two leaves.

The two settings contain the following variants:[6]

3 Details of the ownership of the thirteen copies may be found in Seymour de Ricci, *Catalogue raisonné des premières impressions de Mayence (1445-1467)*, Veröffentlichungen der Gutenberg-Gesellschaft 8-9 (Mainz, 1911), pp. 57-59, no. 55, 1-13. The Holkham Hall copy (55, 4) is now the second copy in the British Library (IC.74), the second copy in Paris (55, 6) is now in the John H. Scheide Library at Princeton, N.J.

4 See de Ricci, p. 57, no. 55,2.

5 Boghardt, pp. 154-6.

6 I have used the following symbols in the list of variants:

dots below = contraction signs	9 = abbreviation for 'com-'
overscore = nasal or combination with a nasal	& = abbreviation for 'et'
underscoring = ligature	l' = abbreviation for combinations with 'l'
| = end of line	ꝑ = abbreviation for 'par-'

Line	*London, Oxford*	*Manchester*
Fol. 10^r (Psalm 17 (18), vv. 38–51)		
3	cadēt	cadent
3	pedes meos	pedes meo^s
4	supplautasti *[m]*	supplantasti
5	insurgētes	insurgentes
7	facėt	faceret
12	non	nō
12	s'uiuit	seruiuit
19	insurgentib$_3$	insurgētibus
21	nacōnib$_3$	nacōnibus
21	noī	nomī
21 | 22	dicā Ma= | gnificās	dicā | Maġficās
22	regis eius: et	regi^s ei^9: &
Fol. 10^v	(Psalm 18 (19), vv. 1–14)	
2	firmamentū. *[p corr]*	firmamentū
3	verbū	verbū
3	scientiā	scientiā. *[p corr]*
10	eius. Et *[p corr?]*	eius Et *[p corr?]*
11	eius	ei^9. *[p corr]*
15	lucidū	Incidū *[m]*
18	p̄ciosum multū	p̄ciosū multum
19	fauū. *[p corr]*	fauū
23	&	et
Fol. 121^r	(Hymn: *Conditor alme siderum*)	
6 | 7	lā- | guidū	lā | guidū *[m]*
7	donās	donans
11	seculi: *[p corr]*	seculi
12 | 13	pa- | clito *[m]*	pa- | cleto
	(Hymn: *Verbum supernum prodiens*)	
20	ꝓ	pro
21	ꝓ	pro
Fol. 121^v	(Hymn: *Vox clara, ecce, intonat*)	
7 | 8	de- | mus	de | mus *[m]*
9	tuuc *[m]*	tunc
9 | 10	prote- | gat	prote | gat *[m]*
	(Hymn: *A solis ortus cardine*)	
15	corpus	corpns *[m]*

p̄ = abbreviation for 'pre-'
ꝓ = abbreviation for 'pro-'
^{s} = sign for 's'
s' = abbreviation for 'ser-'
$_3$ = abbreviation for '-ue' oder '-us'
^{9} = abbreviation for '-us'

Erasures and handwritten emendations have been ignored for purposes of this list.

16	celesti^{s}	celestis
17	mtrat	intrat
22	pastus est per quē	pastus est per quem
23	angeli	āgeli
23	palāq$_3$	palamq$_3$
25	secl'm. Amē· *[p corr]*	secl'm Amē

As can be seen, most of the variants are purely typographical in nature, consisting of differences in single letters, ligatures, contractions and abbreviations.[7] Then there are some punctuation variants, with the correct and incorrect readings being more or less evenly distributed between the two settings,[8] while at one point I am not clear as to which version the contemporaries would have regarded as correct.[9] Finally both settings of each of the leaves concerned contain compositors' errors of negligible significance and which again are evenly distributed between the two versions: *supplautasti* for *supplantasti*, *paraclito* for *paracleto* and *tuuc* for *tunc* in the one case,[10] *Incidum* for *lucidum, lan | guidum* for *lan- | guidum*, *de | mus* for *de- | mus*, *prote | gat* for *prote- | gat* and *corpns* for *corpus* in the other.[11] Neither the nature nor the distribution of these compositor's errors allows us to declare one of the two versions to be significantly more defective than the other and certainly neither of the two groups of errors throws any light on why the resetting was deemed necessary.

If one compares the book from the Spencer collection not only with the London and Oxford copies but also with the other surviving copies of the *Psalterium Benedictinum*, one finds that in all these other copies fols. 10 and 121 are, as far as one can tell, conjugate with their respective counter-leaves; furthermore they are printed from the same setting of type. That is to say that the new setting and the structural disruption occur just in a single copy, the one in the Rylands library. Given the absence of a major compositional error which demanded urgent correction we must, in my view, conclude that the Spencer copy contains two cancels of a special kind, with two leaves being replaced for reasons unconnected with composition: the leaves were probably reset and printed because a pull of the relevant sheet was imperfect at the relevant point, perhaps being blurred or having become dirty or damaged after printing off.

II

From *cancel light* to *cancel classic*, to adapt a phrase from a well-known drinks advertisement. As far as I am aware, the earliest classic cancellation so far found

7 Cf. fol. 10^{r}, lines 3, 5, 7, 12, 19, 21, 22; fol.10^{v}, lines 3, 11, 18, 23; fol.121^{r}, lines 7, 20, 21; fol.121^{v}, lines 7, 16, 17, 22, 23.
8 The correct readings are marked *[p corr]*.
9 Fol. 10^{v}, line 10 = Psalm 18 (19), v. 7.
10 Fol. 10^{r} 4, 121^{r} 13, 121^{v} 9. Indicated with *[m]*.
11 Fol. 10^{v} 15, 121^{r} 6|7, 121^{v} 7|8, 9|10, 15. Indicated with *[m]*.

in a printed book affects fol. 51, the first leaf of gathering [F] of the *Psalterium Benedictinum*; the case was described as long ago as 1908 in *BMC* I. It was mentioned in the incunable catalogue of the Museum Meermanno Westreenianum at The Hague, and of course Masson mentions it too.[12] It seems that this cancellation was noticed from the two settings of the two columns on this leaf of which the British Library, in addition to its complete copies, possesses two single-leaf copies. But let us examine this case, too, in the light of the features we listed above.

Fols 51 and 60, which ought to be conjugate leaves, in fact take the form of interlocking leaves (*Schachtelbogen*) in the copies in Bautzen, Berlin, The Hague, Gotha and New York. In the copy in Mainz fol. 51 has a stub gummed behind fol. 60 (not the other way about!); the Holkham (now British Library IC.74), London (IC.75), Paris and Oxford copies contain no signs of cancellation, and in the Munich copy fol. 51 is lacking, as indeed it is in the copy formerly in the Bibliothèque Nationale, Paris, and now in the John H. Scheide Library at Princeton. However, in the Munich copy fol. 60 does have a hanging stub so that one has the impression that the original fol. 51 was cut out but not replaced by the cancel, while the copy in Princeton has traces of gum in the gutter between fols 60 and 61 which could derive from an earlier gummed stub such as still survives in the Mainz copy. The Manchester copy shows no evidence of cancellation; it is, however, so tightly bound that it is impossible to determine whether fols 51 and 60 are truly conjugate or not.

As has already been mentioned, the British Library possesses two single-leaf copies of fol. 51 (IC.76 and IC.77), printed from a different setting from the corresponding leaf in its main copy IC.75. This same special setting is also found in a single-leaf copy in the Museum Meermanno Westreenianum in The Hague as well as on the corresponding pages of the copy in the Spencer collection. All three of these single leaves have a very narrow inner edge; that is to say, the text is not printed exactly in the centre of the page, but they were cut off from fol. 60 to leave a stub hanging, a fact which in itself shows that they are not to be seen as just some kind of scrap leaves; rather they are cancelled leaves, deliberately removed. The recto of British Library leaf IC.77 lacks the red versals which would be printed in a second run through the press;[13] the explanation for this is presumably that the decision had already been taken to replace this leaf.

The textual and punctuation variants between the two versions of the leaf are, with a single exception, of the same kind as on fols 10 and 121, wherefore I will not detail them here, not least because, for a reason I shall presently elucidate, they are considerably more numerous than they are there. The exception concerns the inadvertent omission of two verses caused by the break between

12 *BMC* I 20. *Museum Meermanno Westreenianum. Catalogus van de Incunabelen* (The Hague, 1920), II, pp. 250–1, no. 592. Masson, p. 64.

13 This was noted already in *BMC* I, p. 20.

the recto and verso and the actual nature of the text at this point. In Psalm 77 (78), verses 19 and 20 read, in English translation:

Yea, they spake against God; They said, Can God || prepare a table in the wilderness? Behold, he smote the rock, that waters gushed out, And streams overflowed; Can he give bread also [or prepare a table] ... for his people?[14]

In Latin, in the *Psalterium Benedictinum*, the text reads (all abbreviations and contractions have been resolved):

Et male locuti sunt de deo, dixerunt numquid poterit deus || [*parare mensam* in deserto? Quoniam percussit petram et fluxerunt aquae, et torrentes inundaverunt Numquid et panem poterit, aut] *parare mensam* populo suo?

The parallel lines (||) mark the end of fol. 51^r in its first setting. In the leaves that have almost all been cancelled, the compositor originally left out the passage marked here with square brackets, probably because he was confused by the repetition of the phrase *parare mensam* when he began the new page. This error, which seems already to have been noticed before the second run through the press for the red versals had been completed, was corrected by means of resetting both sides of the leaf, it being necessary to save space line by line on both pages in order to accommodate the missing text by inserting it at the turn of the page. The need to save space is the explanation for the unusually large number of typographical variants at this point, consisting not only of ligatures, contractions and abbreviations but also of shifts in the line-breaks.

The motivation for cancelling and resetting fol. 51 tends to be confirmed by the frequency of its survival. Whereas the two cancels of fols 10 and 121 are each attested only in a single copy, in the case of fol. 51 it is precisely the opposite: leaving aside the three single leaves in The Hague and London, which have presumably survived only by a lucky chance after having been removed from their original position, there is only one copy, Earl Spencer's, in which the original leaf with the omission of *parare mensam* still remains; in all the other copies it is either lacking (Munich, Princeton) or it has been replaced by the corrected leaf (Bautzen, Berlin, The Hague, Gotha, London (IC.74, IC.75), Mainz, New York, Oxford, Paris). This is, as I have previously mentioned, the earliest case known so far of the substitution of a leaf for textual reasons in the history of printing with movable type, the first cancel in the proper, classical meaning of the term.

III

In its collation of the main London copy IC.75, *BMC* describes the quinio [F] not as [F^{10}] but as [F^{8+2}], that is, as a quaternio to which two further leaves have

14 *The Holy Bible, containing the Old and New Testaments translated out of the original tongues ...* (Oxford, 1885), p. 441. The passage in square brackets has been added to simulate the Vulgate version.

been added. One might imagine that fols. 51 and 60 were meant with these two leaves; after all, these are not conjugate in the London copy either, because fol. 51 was cancelled. But for one thing one cannot see this directly but has to deduce it in the case of the London copy, and for another *BMC* notes on IC.76, one of the two single-leaf copies of fol. 51: 'This cancel corresponds to the first of the two disturbances of quire [F].'[15] So what is this second disturbance of quire [F]?

BMC says nothing about it, but from the copy it describes (IC.75) and which has provided the stimulus for the present enquiry, it is evident that the second disturbance occurs precisely in the centre of the quire: fols 55 and 56, which ought to constitute the innermost sheet of the gathering, are in fact not conjugate but interlocked leaves; the stub of fol. 56 protruding out from the sewing appears before fol. 55, that of fol. 55 before fol. 56. This state of affairs, which indicates that one of the leaves has been replaced, is confirmed, in various different ways, by other copies too: in the Berlin copy fol. 55 is gummed to a stub of fol. 56, in the second copy in the British Library (from Holkham) fol. 56 is gummed to a stub of fol. 55, while in the copies in The Hague and Gotha the two leaves are interlocked in exactly the same way as in the first London copy. In the Princeton copy (formerly in Paris) one cannot examine the make-up but there are traces of gum and of pressure before and after fol. 56, which indicates that stubs were once present. On the other hand, there are copies in which fols. 55 and 56 are clearly conjugate (Bautzen, Mainz, Munich, New York, Oxford) or in which one cannot detect any signs of a leaf having been replaced (Manchester, Paris).

Regarding the question of the identity of the setting of these leaves in the different groups of copies I have described, there has only ever been one library in the whole world in which it would have been possible long since to find an answer to it by examining the books in the original, the Bibliothèque Nationale in Paris. Only here were until 1970[16] copies from each of the two groups to be found, but as it turned out the proud new owner of the second Paris copy has had to have a microfilm made of the copy in the Pierpont Morgan Library in New York, with the help of which he was able to determine that there are differences on fol. 56 between that copy and the one he has recently acquired.[17]

15 *BMC* I, 20 on IC.76. The collation of IC.75 is given in *BMC* I, 19.

16 *CIBN*, Tome II. (Paris, 1985), p. 467, P-668: 'Rés. Vélins 226 (Échangé en 1970; conservé actuellement à la John H. Scheide Library, Princeton.)'.

17 This is confirmed by pencilled notes in the copy of Masson's book which I have seen in the John H. Scheide Library. There are similar manuscript notes in the Bibliothèque Nationale, but these were not made until after the sale of this copy by barter had already been agreed. As far as I know, the results of these observations have not been published. For the Bibliothèque Nationale there might have been another good reason not to give up its second copy, and this is the book's truly curious structure which de Ricci (p. 58, no. 55,6) described only in a very simplified form. In his census, in which he gives an account of the history of this incomplete copy, he says that it is made up from parts of two other copies which had been trimmed in different ways and which therefore could be distinguished by the dimensions of the pages. In

These differences are clearly the result of resetting. The text of fols 56^r and 56^v in the first group of copies generally does not align with that in the second group, and since the first group contains all the copies which display physical signs of cancellation the setting from which they were printed must be the later one. But why was it made?

The differences between the two settings are entirely similar in nature to those found on fols 10 and 121. See figs. 1-4.[18] Once again there are a number of purely typographical variants:

fact, however, the copy is not made up of fragments of two copies but from parts of five copies whose former existence it thus proves. I give below a description, taking the sequence of pages as its basis.

1. Small format (fol. 5 = 315 × 411 mm) with old arabic foliation (wrongly from fol. 70, which is foliated '71'): fols 5, 6, 8-21, 23-28, 30-50, 54-62, 64-72, 74-76, 78-80, 101-104, 108.

2. A different small format (305 × 429 mm) without old foliation: fol. 7 only.

3. Very large format (fol. 22 = 325 × 465 mm), in some cases trimmed at the foot (fols 63, 73, 106, 107), without old foliation: fols 22, 29, 63, 73, 77, 105-107, 111-113.

4. Large format but smaller than 3. (fol. 119 = 315 × 448 mm) with old roman foliation: fols 119-124, 126, 128, 131, 133.

5. Another small format (fol. 125 = 315 × 409 mm) without old foliation, but very clearly not belonging together with fol. 7: fols 125, 127.

The following are lacking: fols 1-4, 51-53, 91-100, 109, 110, 114-118, 129, 130, 134-136.

De Ricci brackets 3) and 4) together (*l'un exemplaire très grand de marges*) and does the same with 1), 2) und 5) (*l'autre plus rogné et doré sur tranches*) while wrongly assigning fols 71 and 73.

According to De Ricci, fol. 4 (possibly an error for fol. 3, of which a copy survives in The Hague) and fols 91-100 are now in the copy in the Museum Meermanno Westreenianum in The Hague, but I have not been able to confirm this since, when I was in The Hague, I had not then had the opportunity to see the copy in the Scheide Library. Fols 51-53 belonged to Group 1 and are now in the copy in the Bodleian Library, Oxford.

18 For the interpretation of the abbreviations see note 6. Erasures and manuscript emendations have again not been listed, but in order to assess the reproductions properly one should take note of the following handwritten changes to the originals:

Oxford copy

Fol. 56^r 20: The vocative *domine*, omitted in both settings, has been added by hand in most copies, though in different ways.

Fol. 56^r 21: *Beatus vir cuius est auxilium abs te;* – the semicolon after *te* was changed by hand from a printed colon which, in this book, generally serves as a comma.

Fol. 56^r 22/23: *in valle lacrimarum: in loco quem posuit* – in both settings the colon used to structure the two phrases has been overlooked; in most copies there has been an erasure to make room for it and the colon has been entered by hand.

Fol. 56^v 1: *legislator;* – the semicolon has been changed from a colon by hand;

Fol. 56^v 4: *deus::* – the second colon has been added by hand while an attempt has been made to erase the first one, which is printed.

Gotha copy

Fol. 56^r 20: *in* and *dne* have been added by hand.

Fol. 56^r 23: *rum: i* has been altered from *rum in* by erasure and addition by hand.

Fol. 56^v 13/14: The ornamentation of the initial B, which is clearly to be seen in the original, is hardly visible in the reproduction.

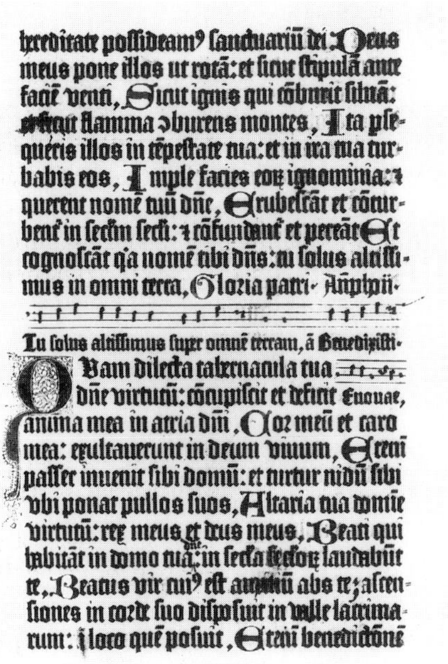

Fig. 1. *Psalterium Benedictinum*. Mainz: Johann Fust and Peter Schöffer, 29 August 1459. Fol. 56[r] in its original state. The type area measures 210 × 335 mm. Reproduced by kind permission of the Bodleian Library, Oxford.

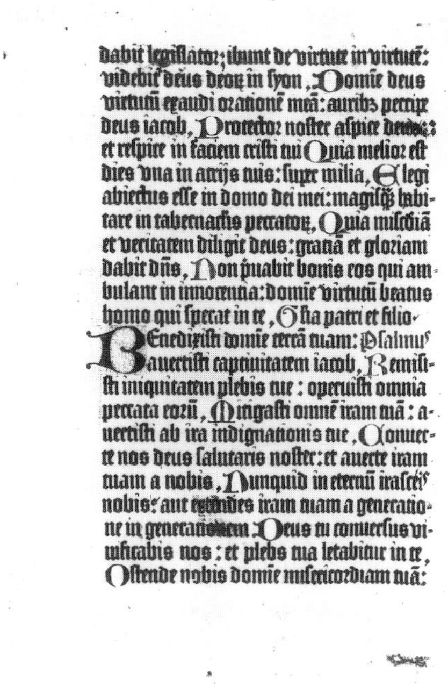

Fig. 2. Fol. 56[v] in its original state. Bodleian Library copy.

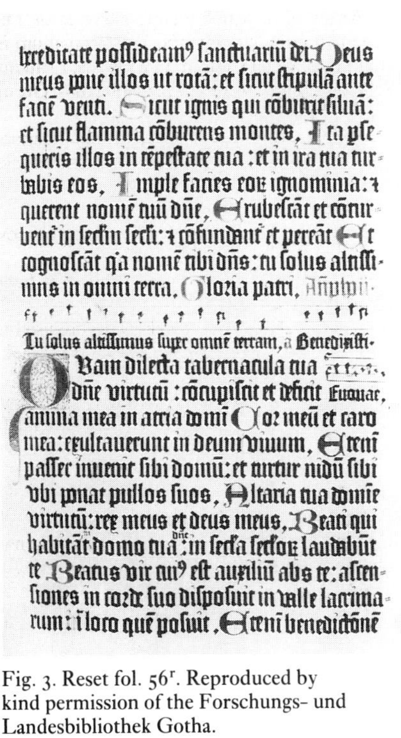

Fig. 3. Reset fol. 56[r]. Reproduced by kind permission of the Forschungs- und Landesbibliothek Gotha.

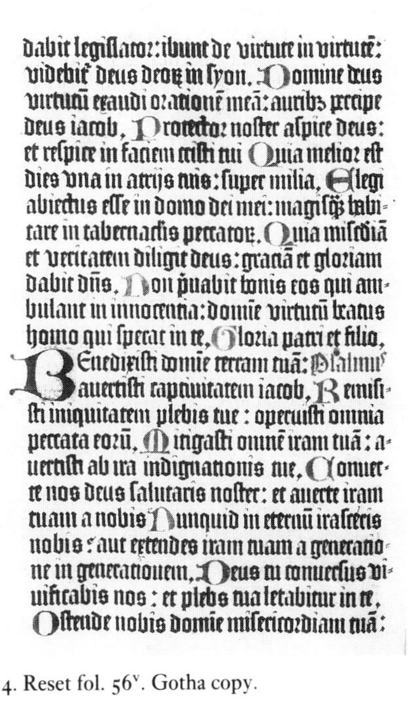

Fig. 4. Reset fol. 56[v]. Gotha copy.

Fol. 56^{r} (Psalm 82 (83), v. 13–83 (84), v. 8)

Line	*Oxford*	*Gotha*
2	pone	pone
4	9burens	cōburens
6	babis	babis
13	tabernacula	tabernacula
15	dn̄i	domī
18	ponat	ponat
19	deus	deus
20	habitāt	habitāt
22	disposuit	disposuit

Fol. 56^{v} (Psalm 83 (84), v. 8–84 (85), v. 8)

2	Domīe deus	Domine deus
3	percipe	percipe
9	gratiā	graciā
10	bonis	bonis
11	beatus	beatus
12	Gl'ia	Gloria
13	terrā tuam	terram tuā
19	irascei^{s}	irasceris

In addition there are a number of minor differences in punctuation, with the group with the substitute leaves having on the whole the worse set of variants.

Fol. 56^{r}

10	patri·	patri.
15	dn̄i.	domī
21	te. Beatus	te Beatus

Fol. 56^{v}

12	filio·	filio.
19	nobis.	nobis.
21	generationem	generatiouem.

Finally, there are three clear (though hardly serious) instances of compositor's errors, and once again in the setting of the cancels:

Fol. 56^{r}

9 | 10	altissi= | mus	altissi= | mns
20	habitāt in domo tua	habitāt domo tua

Fol. 56

21	generationem	generatiouem

If one compares these variants with those on fols 10 and 121 on the one hand and those on fol. 51 on the other, then the cancels for fol. 56 will be recognized as clearly being of the type we have referred to as 'cancel light', for one cannot identify any error in the first setting which was so serious that it was essential to cancel the leaf. Yet this is at variance with the pattern of distribution of pulls of the two settings which, given the odd number of thirteen surviving copies, could not be more even than it is: seven copies of fol. 56 contain the – slightly more correct! – first setting (Bautzen, Mainz, Manchester, Munich, Oxford, Paris, New York), and six copies have the – if anything slightly less correct! – second setting (Berlin, The Hague, Gotha, London BL IC.74, IC.75, Princeton).[19]

The contradictory nature of these findings becomes evident if we consider the circumstances during the production process which may have led to the defects which made replacement of the affected leaves by cancels desirable. What could go wrong during composing, during printing or even at a later stage? At what point could or should it have been noticed? What steps were necessary to remedy it?

In order to answer these questions one must first recall that, in the early period, folio books were printed page by page, not sheet by sheet. That is to say, in the present case, the sheet containing fols 55 and 56 went through the press four times.

When setting up the recto or the verso of fol. 56 a mistake might have been made that distorted the text or there might have been a major blunder with severe repercussions on the typography such as confusion of the ornamental initials printed in red and blue. If errors of this sort were not noticed until after all the copies required of fol. 56 had been printed off, they should be evident in the leaves that were not replaced, but there are in fact no such cases; moreover, one would have been entitled to ask why so many copies remained uncancelled. If they had occurred exclusively on the verso of fol. 56 and had been noticed when only part of the required number of copies of this verso had been printed off, only the copies so far produced would have needed to be cancelled – this would account for the equal distribution of pulls from the different settings – and it would have meant that, if the type for the recto had already been broken up, this would have had to be reset too. But why, in such a situation, would one have reset the whole of the verso, given that the type must still have been standing seeing that only part of the required number of copies had been printed off, in preference to making stop-press corrections? There must have been some reason for this which we do not know.

If, incidentally, the presumed error was not on fol. 56 but had been detected on its twin, fol. 55, only when they were printing fol. 56^{v} having printed about half the sheet, it would have been necessary to set up the type again for fols 55^{r} and 55^{v} and this leaf would then have only existed in the new setting. The pulls

19 A single leaf beginning *hereditate possideam*[9], which thus seems to have been a copy of fol. 56, is said by de Ricci (p. 59, no. 16) to have belonged to the former Royal Public Library in Dresden (pressmark: mscr. Dresd. g. 3); however I have recently been informed by the Sächsische Landesbibliothek Dresden that this formed part of its holdings outhoused during the Second World War.

for fol. 56, on the other hand, in so far as they had already been printed on both sides, could be interlocked with copies of the new setting of fol. 55, whereas the copies of fol. 56 so far printed on one side only would have been replaced by fresh whole sheets, showing the new setting on both fol. 55 and fol. 56. In this case the interlocked or gummed copies of fol. 56 would contain the first setting and the copies with a conjugate fol. 55 the second setting, though in these cases one would be entitled to ask why the remaining copies of fol. 56 were not printed from the first setting on their versos and interlocked with the corresponding pulls from the new setting for fol. 55, so that all the copies of the inner sheet of quire [F] would have consisted of interlocked leaves. Furthermore, it would be necessary to explain why not only the text for fol. 56^r but also that for fol. 56^v, which must still have been standing, was entirely reset.

It is conceivable that even during the actual printing process many mistakes and mishaps could have occurred which necessitated cancellation. If, for instance, the set-up type for the recto and verso of fol. 56 were confused and if this were noticed while printing of the recto was still in progress, this set of copies would have had to be replaced but it would have necessitated only resetting the text for the verso which had been printed on the recto page in error and which might already have been broken up. The recto text, on the other hand, which had begun to be printed on the versos by mistake, could have been used for the substitute leaves.

Another possibility might be that during printing the type for fol. 56 collapsed for some reason or other. Then, clearly, it would have been necessary to set up the type again, and though no further explanation of the same number of copies printed from the first and from the second settings would be necessary, it would be a problem to explain why both the recto and the verso type-settings for the same sheet were affected in the same way.

Finally, if an unusually large number of defective copies of fol. 56^r or 56^v had been produced without this being noticed to start with, it would be possible to account for the resetting of both pages and for a number of replacement copies, but that these should constitute approximately half the total number of copies in the edition seems most improbable.

Once the printing process was completed the music had to be entered by hand in the spaces reserved for it. This, too, was subject to possible error, and there was also the risk that individual sheets might have been dirtied or damaged during storage or when the different copies were being made up. But in my view the notes have been entered by a different hand in each of the surviving thirteen copies; one cannot assume, therefore, that they were entered in the printing shop where, if an error had been made in many copies, it would have been possible to reset the type and make replacement sheets. And if individual sheets had been spoilt or damaged at a later stage, we could account for the existence of individual cancels, whilst we simply do not know how a whole pile, half of the edition of sheet [$F_{5.6}$], with one of each of its two leaves in each case might have become unusable in such a way.

As this investigation and my conclusions show, the 1459 *Psalterium Benedictinum* provides not only early instances of the 'cancel light' (fols 10 and 121) and the first case of a classically motivated cancel but also the earliest occurrence of a problematic leaf-substitution, a cancellation for no apparent reason.[20] The reason for the second disturbance in quire [F] cannot, it seems to me, be determined for certain. Unsatisfactory as this conclusion is, it is a salutary reminder to us all that when dealing with circumstantial evidence for the reasons for bibliographical facts we are in principle always working with hypotheses which differ from one another only by the degree of probability that they contain according to our feeling for the evidence.

20 I shall be discussing elsewhere some further divergences and two further cases of interlocking cancels in the *Psalterium Benedictinum* (fols 4 and 7 in the Spencer copy, and fols. 14 and 17 in the Berlin copy), which are not relevant to the present enquiry, and compare them with similar phenomena in the 42-line Bible.

AN EARLY EIGHTEENTH-CENTURY SALE OF MAINZ INCUNABULA BY THE FRANKFURT DOMINICANS

MARGARET NICKSON and LOTTE HELLINGA

MOST OF THE BOOKS which once formed the important medieval library of the Dominicans in Frankfurt am Main survive in the Stadt- und Universitätsbibliothek (StUB) in that city. The convent, founded in the thirteenth century, flourished chiefly in the fifteenth century during the years when printing was invented and developed in nearby Mainz. It is therefore not surprising that the library of the Dominicans was particularly rich in incunabula. Dr Vera Sack gives ample space to the history of this library in her introduction to the catalogue of incunabula in the StUB,[1] for with 1097 items, well over a third of the *c.* 2700 incunabula at present in the collection, it is the largest single historical constituent.[2] In addition to the items still in Frankfurt Dr Sack lists 25 books which she was able to trace in collections elsewhere: the British Library in London, the Royal Libraries in Copenhagen and Stockholm, the University Libraries in Cambridge, Uppsala and Strasbourg, and the Bibliothèque nationale de France in Paris.[3] With further publication of catalogues and examination of copies more items can now be added to this list.

In her survey Dr Sack discusses the accumulation of printed books from a variety of sources during the half-century from the 1470s to the Reformation, but she also records losses and dispersal which can be documented from the seventeenth century onwards. The decision to dispose of books can be subject to a variety of considerations, just as the motivation for acquisition will change with time. For the seventeenth century Dr Sack quotes sales in 1628, 1650 and

1 Kurt Ohly and Vera Sack (eds.), *Inkunabelkatalog der Stadt- und Universitätsbibliothek und anderer öffentlicher Sammlungen in Frankfurt am Main.* Kataloge der Stadt- und Universitätsbibliothek Frankfurt am Main (Frankfurt am Main, 1966-67). The historical introduction is signed by Dr Sack alone.

2 There are also 200 manuscripts from the same source. See Sigrid Krämer (ed.), *Handschriftenerbe des deutschen Mittelalters, Teil I: Aachen - Kochel* (Munich, 1989), pp. 144-45, with reference to Gerhard Powitz, *Die Handschriften des Dominikanerklosters und des Leonhardstifts in Frankfurt am Main* (Frankfurt am Main, 1968). Dr Krämer adds 17 manuscripts to those listed by Dr Powitz, including seven in other libraries.

3 Ohly-Sack, p. 735.

1685, all to book binders, who were probably simply seeking to acquire strong vellum to use in bindings. The sums of money involved were low, and we can therefore consider this in every respect as a depreciation in value of the materials.[4] The next sale referred to by Dr Sack is quite different. The account books of the Frankfurt Dominicans record the sale in 1718 of four unspecified precious volumes for a price of 90 Gulden. Although very incomplete this information can help us to identify at least three of the items sold and to reveal some of the circumstances of the sale.

Generally it is not difficult to identify books from the Frankfurt Dominicans. An owner's mark 'Conventus franckfordensis ordinis predicatorum' was written uniformly in the copies, probably *c.* 1500 (fig. 1), with some variation in the abbreviations used. Many books with this mark still have an early shelf-mark, probably of the early sixteenth century, which combines a capital letter with an arabic figure (fig. 2). In the middle of the eighteenth century further ownership marks were added by the librarian Franz Jacquin, but obviously these were not present in items sold in 1718.[5]

In 1911 Seymour de Ricci noted that a two-volume vellum copy of the Mainz *Catholicon*, now in the British Library and which had belonged to the Frankfurt Dominicans, was at one time part of the Harleian library.[6] In her introduction to the catalogue of the StUB Dr Sack was able to list another book with the same provenance: a vellum copy of Clemens V, *Constitutiones* printed by Peter Schöffer in 1467, now in the Royal Library in Copenhagen (Madsen 1209).[7] She then surmised that these works were two of the four important items sold by the Frankfurt Dominicans in 1718. Neither copy contains any internal evidence of ownership by the Harleys, and their identification as Harleian copies is based on a recognition of their splendid red morocco gold-tooled bindings as the work of known Harleian binders. As a result of research published by Howard Nixon in 1975 it appears that the *Catholicon* was bound by Christopher Chapman and the Clemens by Thomas Elliott.[8] The two volumes of the *Catholicon* bear the early shelf-marks R.9 and R.10, the Clemens P.4. A neighbour on the Dominicans' shelves can now be shown to have been another item also destined for the Harleian collection. A vellum copy of the Bonifacius VIII *Liber VI Decretalium* printed by Johann Fust and Peter Schöffer in 1465 has the ownership inscription of the Frankfurt Dominicans together with the shelf-

4 Sack, p. XVI.

5 Sack, p. XVI.

6 Seymour de Ricci, *Catalogue raisonné des premières impressions de Mayence (1445-1467)*, Veröffentlichungen der Gutenberg-Gesellschaft, 8 (Mainz, 1911). De Ricci gives the subsequent provenance as Thomas Osborne (his sale catalogue of the Harleian printed books, *Catalogus Bibliothecae Harleianae*, I, 5010) – Gros de Boze – de Cotte – Gaignat – Duc de la Vallière – Count MacCarthy – Grenville – British Museum. The press-mark in the British Library is G.11966-67, BMC I, pp. 39-40.

7 *Catalogus Bibliothecae Harleianae*, II, 10193 or III, 3258 (these two entries may refer to same copy).

8 H. M. Nixon, 'Harleian bindings', in R. W. Hunt *et al.* (eds), *Studies in the Book Trade in honour of Graham Pollard* (Oxford, 1975), pp. 153-94.

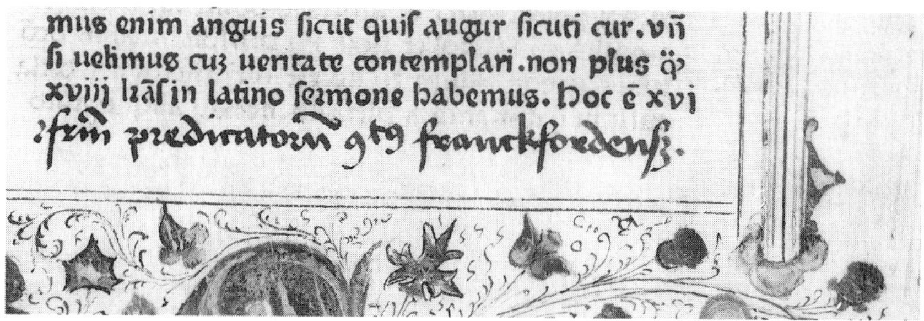

Fig. 1 Ownership inscription of the Frankfurt Dominicans in Joh. Balbus, *Catholicon*, vol. I, British Library G.11966, leaf 1 recto (detail).

Fig. 2 Shelf-mark of the Frankfurt Dominicans at the top of the same page.

mark P.3. It is now in the Bibliothèque nationale de France (Vélins 375) and is also bound by Christopher Chapman in gold-tooled red morocco, some of the tools being the same as those used for the *Catholicon*. This volume does contain an internal indication of Harleian provenance as the price of £25 was pencilled on the fly-leaf by the bookseller Thomas Osborne after he had bought the Harleian printed books in 1742.[9]

A great deal is known about the acquisition of items, both manuscript and printed, for the Harleian Library during the time that Humfrey Wanley, Harley's librarian, kept his famous Diary.[10] Unfortunately there is a gap in the entries between July 1716 and January 1720, so that the Diary cannot be used to show whether the three works of early Mainz printing listed above were acquired directly for Harley from the Frankfurt Dominicans. That this was

9 *Catalogus Bibliothecae Harleianae*, II, 10192.
10 C. E. and R. C. Wright (eds), *The Diary of Humfrey Wanley, 1715–1726* (London, 1966), 2 vols.

indeed the case, however, is suggested by the inclusion of all three in Wanley's 1721 catalogue of Edward Harley's old Latin printed books.[11] One of Harley's chief suppliers of manuscripts and printed books from abroad at this period was Nathaniel Noel, who obtained many of his prestigious offerings through the manuscript and book buying activities of a peripatetic resident on the Continent, George Suttie.[12] Suttie was described by Wanley in 1726 as Noel's agent but he issued his own catalogues and sometimes acted on his own behalf.[13] His letters and catalogues were supplied regularly by Noel to Wanley so that the latter could extract from them any items which he thought should be acquired by Harley. The letters and catalogues themselves are no longer extant but Wanley's extracts made on scraps of paper were preserved in the Harley family archives, now in the British Library (Add. MSS. 70001-70523).[14] From these extracts it is possible to piece together some of the circumstances surrounding Harley's acquisition of the three Frankfurt Dominican books.

Suttie's peregrinations in search of books in 1718 may be partly reconstructed from the dates and places mentioned in the extracted letters;[15] from 10 February to 17 March he was in Strasbourg and by 9 April he had reached Mainz. About this time he presumably made a visit to the Dominicans in Frankfurt for the books listed in his letter to Noel from Mainz dated 9 April already included the Clemens.[16] The Boniface was listed 'in some of Mr Sutties Papers communic-

11 BL Harley MS. 7627A, f.10^r ('Catholicon (liber) ... Magunt. 1460. fol. membr. 2 Voll.'); f.10^v ('Clementinae Constitutiones ... cum Gloss. Magunt. per Petr. Schoiffer, 1467. membr. fol. mag.'); f.12^v ('Decretalium Sextus Liber cum Glossa Magunt. per Petr. Schoiffer. 1465. fol. membr.').

12 For an account of the London bookseller Noel see *Diary*, *op. cit.*, p. 457, and C. E. Wright, *Fontes Harleiani* (London, 1972), pp. 253-57.

13 He sold two manuscripts originating from the Burgundian court (BL Harley MSS. 2897, 2697) to Edward Harley in 1715 (*Diary*, p. 13). Virtually nothing is known about Suttie except what can be gleaned from Wanley's correspondence (edited by P. L. Heyworth, Oxford, 1989) and the *Diary*. Dark hints by Wanley concerning his reputation raise the possibility that his long sojourn abroad may not have been entirely voluntary. In January 1725 Wanley reported to Noel that Suttie was 'said to live a vagrant & idle Life in Paris, without doing any business at all, for above a year past'. In August of the same year Noel set out for France at least partly to look for Suttie, while Wanley in London reflected that 'this Man has mended of late Years, and may, if God will give him ... Contrition, & his Saving Grace, obtain Pardon from the most High'. However on 9 November Noel had to confess to Wanley that Suttie had been 'long guilty of private Gaming, undone himself, and cannot leave Paris before his Debts are paid ...'. He is last heard of in the spring of 1726 when Noel, having extracted a promise that Suttie would give up gaming, was proposing a joint Continental tour for 'half a year'. In spite of these faults Suttie appears to have been for a considerable time a knowledgeable and industrious pursuer of manuscripts and books, sometimes producing more than twenty catalogues a year, and it was due to his efforts that Edward Harley obtained some of his most important acquisitions.

14 The scraps of paper are referred to by C. E. Wright in his edition of the *Diary* as being amongst the Welbeck Wanleyana but are now contained in BL Add. MS. 70488 (unfoliated).

15 For a reconstruction of Suttie's journeys, 1717-1721, see C. E. Wright's introduction to the *Diary*, pp. XLVIII-XLIX.

16 'Institutiones Clementinae. Mogunt. per Petr. Schoiffer de Gerentzheim. 1467. fol. max. membr. Colord Letters. fine.'

ated to me [Wanley] by Mr Noel, 13 July 1718'[17] and the *Catholicon* was referred to in a letter from Suttie to Noel dated at Würzburg, 14 July.[18] Both these latter items appeared again in a 'General Catalogue' sent by Suttie to Noel and received by Wanley on 12 September, and were afterwards recorded by Wanley as being part of a consignment of books which arrived at Harley's country seat at Wimpole on 5 February 1719. In spite of the literally fragmentary nature of this evidence there seems little doubt that Suttie had obtained the Clemens, Boniface and *Catholicon* from the Frankfurt Dominicans in the spring of 1718 and that they had been bought from him by Noel on Harley's behalf in the same year.

This enables us then to identify three of the valuable printed books sold by the Frankfurt Dominicans in 1718. Was there a fourth as recorded in the accounts? The *Catholicon* was certainly already in two volumes while in the Dominicans' library as the ownership inscriptions and press-marks show, so it is possible that these three works alone comprised the four volumes. It seems more likely, however, that Suttie had obtained a fourth treasure, most probably another early Mainz book, from the Dominicans in 1718. There was no shortage of such items in the Dominicans' library and Suttie would have been well aware of the attraction of such material for noble collectors such as Harley and the Earl of Sunderland. If so, however, it cannot yet be identified with certainty, although there are several copies with ownership marks of the Frankfurt Dominicans which could be possible candidates.

We can dismiss as a candidate for the 1718 sale the vellum Justinianus *Institutiones*, printed by Peter Schöffer in 1468, now in the Pierpont Morgan Library (ChL ff13), because it was acquired by the Frankfurt medical doctor Johann Christian Senckenberg (1707-1772). This copy can be identified with certainty since it bears the spectacular feature of the coat of arms of the Holzhausen and Glauburg family.[19] The paper copy of Thomas Aquinas, *Super IV Libro Sententiarum* printed by Peter Schöffer in 1469, in the same collection (ChL ff14), and with the early shelf-mark E.6, is still in its original binding. Apart from the late fifteenth-century note of ownership of the Frankfurt Dominicans it has a note to the same effect in a later eighteenth-century hand, which excludes it from a possible change of ownership in 1718.

A much more serious candidate is a Thomas Aquinas, *Summa* P.II.II, printed by Peter Schöffer in 1467. There is a copy on paper in the Bibliothèque nationale de France (Rés. D 2637, CIBN T-175) with the Frankfurt Dominicans' ownership inscription and their shelf-mark I.31. This copy, in a red

17 'Sextus Decretalium Liber cum Glossa D. Bernardi. Mogunt, per Jo. Fust & P. de Ger. 14654 [*sic*] Velum. fol. large. Illum.'

18 'Catholicon, on large Parchmt. 1460. 2 Voll. Illuminated. fine.' Wanley has copied the date of the letter as 1716 but this is an evident error in view of the inclusion of the same item in the 12 September excerpt.

19 Dr Senckenberg established a foundation in 1763. In 1869 a list of incunabula was published in which the Justinianus can be identified. Only part of the books in this list remain in public collections in Frankfurt. See Ohly-Sack, p. 688, and Sack, p. x.

morocco binding with gold-tooled spine decoration, is not bound by one of the binders working for the Earl of Oxford.[20] If this book had ever been offered to the Harleian collection there was a good reason for its being rejected: for by 1718 Edward Harley already owned a vellum copy of the 1467 *Summa*, which he had splendidly bound by Jane Steel, who was paid for this work in 1717.[21] The copy is now in the Royal Library in Copenhagen (Madsen 3931), donated in 1787 with the collection of Count Otto Thott (Thott VII, 404).

A further possible candidate is another early Mainz book, a copy of Peter Schöffer's Gregorius edition of 1473 printed partly on paper and partly on vellum, which was mentioned in Wanley's notes on Suttie's 1718 letters.[22] This book was listed amongst the books received at Wimpole on 5 February 1719 and must have been the part paper and part vellum copy described by Wanley in his 1721 catalogue of Harley's Latin books.[23] There are only two copies answering to this description in the *Gesamtkatalog* (*GW* 11451); one is in the Library of Congress and the other in the Library of St Mary's of the Barrens at Perryville, Missouri (formerly in the possession of Estelle Doheny). However, neither of these copies has marks of ownership of the Frankfurt Dominicans nor any indication of having once formed part of the Harleian Library. The identity of the fourth item (if there was one) therefore remains unsolved.

The reason why Wanley and Harley were eager to acquire these books for the Harleian library in 1718 is clear to us: three of them at least, probably all four, were monumental works, outstanding witnesses to the early years of printing in Mainz, preserved in a library not far from the place where they were produced. A collector in search of the origins of printing could not do better. The modern world met here the remnants of a medieval world and its way of thinking, for in the decision of the friars to sell these books we can detect, apart from need of money, a weighing of values other than those of the collector. Fortunately the collection as it is still preserved in Frankfurt allows us to perceive what they kept. In each case they had a number of incunabula editions of the same text. They owned at least five other editions of the Boniface (Ohly-Sack 666, 670, 671, 674, 676 and another copy of the latter, Ohly-Sack 677). Of the *Catholicon*

20 The binding of this copy suggests that it may have been owned by Loménie de Brienne, and is the same as appeared in 1791 in his sale (Laire, p. 65, no. 3) which was sold to Payne. The library stamp indicates that it was acquired by the Bibliothèque nationale before 1830. Apart from the early 16th-century shelf-mark I 31 the copy has a large shelf-mark 'No. A.16', which could well have been written in the 18th century, thus suggesting a later date of sale by the Dominicans. We are very grateful to Mademoiselle Denise Hillard for her opinion on this copy.

21 Probably the Thomas Aquinas bought from Pembroke Hall, Cambridge, in November, 1716 (see Wanley's correspondence, ed. Heyworth, p. 359). Jane Steel's bill was dated 30 April 1717 (see H. M. Nixon [note 8], pp. 160-63.

22 BL Add MS. 70488. It is included in the list dated 13 July and in the 'General Catalogue' received by Wanley on 12 September where an entry for the 'Decretalia Gregorii Papae ... half velum, half paper' follows immediately after the *Boniface* discussed above.

23 BL Harley MS. 7627A, f. 12v. Harley already had a copy of the Gregorius so it was described as 'aliud exemplar et membran. et chartaceum'.

they had two later editions printed in the 1480s (Ohly-Sack 354, 355), of the Clemens V, *Constitutiones*, four other editions plus a duplicate copy, all conveniently bound with Boniface (Ohly-Sack 885, 888, 676-7). And of the Thomas Aquinas of 1467, if that was the book they sold, they even had a duplicate copy of the same edition (Ohly-Sack 2763 in a Mainz binding Kyriss 160), as well as at least five other editions of the same text (Ohly-Sack 2762, 2764-6, 2768). If, on the other hand, it was the Gregorius, they would have had at least one, possibly two copies of an edition printed in Basle (Ohly-Sack 1311, 1312). In obliging the taste of noble English collectors for these handsome witnesses to the achievements of the earliest printers the friars were not substantially depriving themselves of their intellectual heritage.[24]

24 The authors are grateful to Ursula Baurmeister and Denise Hillard, Bibliothèque nationale de France, to Dr Ingrid Ilsøe, Det Kongelige Bibliotek, Copenhagen, and to the Revd. Father L. Derbes C.M., St Mary's of the Barrens, Perryville MO, for facilitating access to collections and for further information on the copies discussed in this article.

NEWS FROM PORTUGAL IN 1506 AND 1507, AS PRINTED BY JOHANN WEISSENBURGER IN NUREMBERG

IRMGARD BEZZEL

WHEN IN 1969 librarians from the Bayerische Staatsbibliothek, Munich, and the Herzog August Bibliothek, Wolfenbüttel, commenced work on the retrospective national bibliography of sixteenth-century German books, the *Verzeichnis der im deutschen Sprachbereich erschienenen Drucke des 16. Jahrhunderts (VD 16)* (the final volume of which, vol. 22, is due to appear in 1995), no German library as yet possessed a printed catalogue of its holdings. The library of the British Museum was unique in having published, a few years earlier in 1962, a catalogue of its fifteenth and sixteenth-century German books, the *Short-Title Catalogue of Books Printed in the German-speaking Countries from 1455 to 1600 now in the British Museum* (Ger STC), now augmented by David Paisey's 1990 supplement. With more than twenty thousand entries this was then the most comprehensive catalogue for the period. German bibliographers soon came to recognize this as an essential reference work providing information about many works and editions not available anywhere in Germany. Consequently *VD 16* frequently cites British Library copies as sources. For very many years we found in David Paisey, as Head of the German Section, both an expert and a helpful colleague, for which I should here like to express my gratitude.[1]

In the following pages I should like to draw attention to some pamphlets from the years 1506 and 1507 in the British Library's collections, supplemented by copies in German libraries, which give an account of Portuguese voyages and report on events in Lisbon. With a single exception, written in Latin, they all appeared without any indication of the name of the printer or of the place of publication, but typographical evidence suggests that they are the work of the Nuremberg printer Johann Weissenburger.

Johann Weissenburger was one of the many scholarly printers of the fifteenth and sixteenth centuries. In 1480 he enrolled at the University of Ingolstadt and he was later ordained priest. From 1501 or 1502 onwards he ran his own

1 David Paisey prepared the English version of the preface to *VD 16*, vol. 1 (Stuttgart, 1983), pp. XXXI–XXXVII.

printing business in his native city of Nuremberg.[2] As far as we know, the first dated product of his press was Johannes Gallinarius, *Tractatus super Salve regina* (*VD 16* G 231), completed on 16 February 1502. To begin with Weissenburger published mainly theological treatises in Latin, including three reprints of Johannes Staupitz's little *Decisio quaestionis de audientia missae* between 1502 and 1505.[3] Certainly no later than 1505 he attempted to play a part in the lucrative business of printing and distributing items of topical interest, such as news reports in German. It is likely that many of these pamphlets, consisting as they did of but a few leaves, have not survived, but those which have come down to us do provide us with some insight into Weissenburger's interests and working methods.

It cannot be purely coincidental that four of the oldest pamphlets that Weissenburger produced, in seven editions all told, deal with Portuguese affairs, for since the discovery of the new sea-route to India in 1498 and the consequent switching of the Indian trade from Venice to Lisbon Nuremberg and Augsburg merchants had established bases in the Portuguese capital. They competed with one another to secure privileges from King Manuel I (1495-1521) for the lucrative trade with India.[4] Regular reports from the representatives in Lisbon to their employers back home ensured a rapid exchange of information. Only very few of these reports, which were hand-written and generally not intended for publication, found their way into the hands of printers and were published as pamphlets. For many of the people living then these slim booklets were the only way of finding out about what was going on in the world.

I

The first of Weissenburger's 'Portuguese' pamphlets bears the title *Den rechten weg ausz zu faren von Liszbona gen Kallakuth* [= Calicut, on the Malabar Coast] *von meyl zu meyl. Auch wie der kunig von Portigal yetz newlich vil galeen* [...] *durch kallakuth in Jndien zu faren. Durch sein haubtman also bestelt als hernach getruckt stet gar von seltzsamen dingen*, probably issued in 1506.[5] The author,

2 For Weissenburger's books printed in Landshut between 1513 and 1533 see Karl Schottenloher, *Die Landshuter Buchdrucker des 16. Jahrhunderts.* Veröffentlichungen der Gutenberg-Gesellschaft (Mainz, 1930). Weissenburger's work in Nuremberg in the period 1501-1513 has not yet been investigated in detail.

3 *VD 16* S 8699-S 8701. The original edition, which Weissenburger followed, had been printed by Johann Otmar at Tübingen in 1500. The BL copy (3478.d.13.) is a copy of the 1505 reprint (*VD 16* S 8701). I am grateful to Graham Nattrass for this and subsequent information.

4 On Nuremberg and Augsburg merchants in Lisbon see Hermann Kellenbenz, 'Die Beziehungen Nürnbergs zur iberischen Halbinsel, besonders im 15. und in der ersten Hälfte des 16. Jahrhunderts', *Beiträge zur Wirtschaftsgeschichte Nürnbergs*, I (1967), 456-93; Christa Schaper, *Die Hirschvogel von Nürnberg und ihr Handelshaus.* Nürnberger Forschungen. Einzelarbeiten zur Nürnberger Geschichte, 18 (Nuremberg, 1973); Hermann Kellenbenz, *Die Fugger in Spanien und Portugal bis 1560*, I (Munich, 1990).

5 BL: C.32.g.37. Proctor 11047. Weller 305 [wrongly assigned to 1504]. Joseph Sabin, *A Dictionary of Books Relating to America*, XVI (New York, 1886), no. 68354. For a facsimile with

presumably a German merchant working in Lisbon, details the distances between the various bases that the Indian fleet would call at on its way around the African continent. He also gave details, being obviously well-informed, about a number of recent events in Lisbon. He reports that three ships had left port on 19 November 1505, that a large fleet would set sail in April 1506, and that King Manuel I had entrusted important commissions and powers to Admiral Afonso de Albuquerque.[6] This report is largely confirmed by contemporary sources published somewhat later,[7] but it also contains several errors.[8]

The letters written between 19 November 1505 and April 1506 were turned into a pamphlet and published in two slightly different editions. The place of printing is not stated but can be deduced from an intriguing addition made to the map printed on the verso of the title page in both versions: apart from Lisbon and Calicut the only geographical reference point given is Nuremberg,[9] and that the pamphlets were published there is confirmed by typographical evidence. They were printed in Nuremberg by Georg Stuchs[10] and Johann Weissenburger.

For an understanding of Weissenburger's business practices it is important to know whether someone sent the letters from Portugal specifically for publication and, further, whether it was Weissenburger or Stuchs who printed them first.

The two pamphlets both have a map on the verso of the title-page, but printed from different woodcuts in each case. The map is a crude and smaller copy of the 'Sphaera Ptolemaei' in the Rostock edition of Vespucci's *Epistola de novo mundo* (fol. 4^{v}).[11] Stuchs's woodcut is closer to the original; in Weissenburger's, which is otherwise very similar, the empty space at the top has been filled with cloud shapes. In Stuchs's edition the accompanying text has been set in type, in Weissenburger's it is xylographic.

The title-page woodcut (fig. 1), which is repeated on fol. 4^{r} in both editions, is not easy to interpret. One attractive theory describes the triangle projected on to

English translation see *From Lisbon to Calicut*. Translated by Alvin E. Prottengeier, commentary and notes by John Parker (Minneapolis, 1956).

6 Fol. 2^{v}. Curiously the admiral, who was later to become viceroy of India, is not mentioned by name.

7 Such as the account of the Venetian spy Leonardo Massari (or Cà da Massar) from Lisbon to the Signoria, first published in *Archivio storico italiano*, appendice 2 (1846), 13-48.

8 Some of the distances given are wrong (fol. 2^{r}). It is claimed that the distance from Cape Verde to the Cape of Good Hope is a mere one hundred and twenty miles and that from Melinde in East Africa and the island of Angediva off the Indian mainland it is only forty miles. Is this an error in translation from Portuguese to German?

9 This was noted already by Emil Sarnow in the introduction to his facsimile of Amerigo Vespucci's *Epistola de novo mundo [Rostock: Hermann Barkhusen, 1504/1505]*. Drucke und Holzschnitte des 15. und 16. Jahrhunderts in getreuer Nachbildung, 9 (Strasbourg, 1903), pp. 11-12. The BL possesses a copy of the original (C.20.e.18.).

10 BL: C.32.g.38. *VD 16* R 491. Proctor 10966. Weller 304. Sabin 68353.

11 See Sarnow, pp. 11-12, with a reproduction of the woodcut as used by Weissenburger. Further evidence that the two Nuremberg woodcuts are related to each other may be seen in the fact that the direction *Septentris* 'north' has been wrongly translated as *Osten* 'east'.

Fig. 1. Europeans and the 'Antipodeans' in Calicut. Reproduced from the 1956 facsimile edition. The British Library's copy (C.32.g.37) is coloured.

an island as showing the geographical position of the Europeans in relation to the Antipodeans, the peoples of the distant world.[12] The soldier with a halberd on the vertical side of the triangle is a Portuguese, the warrior with bow and arrow (turned 90°) on the horizontal side of the triangle has to be interpreted as an Indian (= Red Indian), and the ship symbolizes the voyage from Lisbon to Calicut. The woodcuts differ in various details, the most important of which for our purposes is that in Weissenburger's version there is a tree growing next to the native warrior. There can be no doubt that the two blocks are related to each other, but which is the earlier cannot readily be determined.

It may be possible to ascertain the order in which the two editions were produced by analysis of textual variants. The usual spelling variants are of no significance. It is very apparent that the printers strove to reproduce the text

12 The diagram is found with an explanatory text in several Latin and German editions of Amerigo Vespucci's famous report. See Cäcilie Quetsch, *Die 'Entdeckung der Welt' in der deutschen Graphik der beginnenden Neuzeit*. Doctoral dissertation (Erlangen, 1984), vol. I, pp. 17–18; vol. III, fig. 13, woodcut from Weissenburger's edition (reduced). Susi Colin, *Das Bild des Indianers im 16. Jahrhundert*. Beiträge zur Kunstgeschichte, 102 (Idstein, 1988), p. 185. *Die Neuen Welten in alten Büchern. Entdeckung und Eroberung in frühen deutschen Schrift- und Bildzeugnissen* [exhibition catalogue] (Bamberg, 1988), pp. 56 and 58 with illustrations from Georg Stuchs's edition (enlarged).

accurately. For example, the distances given agree, but whereas Stuchs mostly gives them in roman numerals and occasionally in words, Weissenburger almost invariably gives them in arabic numbers, which could indicate an attempt to introduce an element of systematization. In a hasty reprint it is easy for words to be omitted, and instances of this are found only in Weissenburger's edition. Thus the important word *von* is twice omitted on fol. 2^{r} where distances are being given, and at another point it is difficult to understand the text because a word has been left out.[13]

Using these same observations, which in my view tend to show that Weissenburger's edition is the reprint, John Parker concluded that Stuchs had revised the language of Weissenburger's first edition which he believed had appeared in 1505.[14] Other arguments he adduced to support his view were that Stuchs had been working temporarily in Schneeberg (where in April 1506 he finished printing missals for Havelberg and Cammin) and that he used his type 18 (as well as type 16) which is otherwise not attested prior to 1508. This led Parker to date Stuchs's edition to 1508. But such a late date would seem to be precluded by the very content of the book. Even Proctor had no doubt that this pamphlet dealing with current events which were long since *passé* by 1508 must have been printed before Stuchs removed to Schneeberg.[15] Both editions of the pamphlet *Den rechten Weg auszufahren* must have appeared soon after each other in 1506.

II

It was clearly Weissenburger who brought out the reprint in the case of the *Gesta proxime per Portugalenses in India, Ethiopia et aliis orientalibus terris* which Johann Besicken had issued in Rome on 7 November 1506.[16] The British Library possesses two copies of Weissenburger's edition, published at Nuremberg in 1507.[17] This report on the successful Portuguese voyage to India in 1505-06 had originally been written as a letter from King Manuel I to Cardinal Jorge da Costa (Alpedrinha), but the recipient then arranged for Pedro Afonso Malheiro to prepare it for publication – the Rome edition refers to Malheiro's

13 On fol. 2^{r} where Stuchs reads *ob sie funden*, Weissenburger has only *funden*. On fol. 2^{v} where Stuchs has *alle porten vom mer außfaren ob* ... Weissenburger omits *außfaren*.

14 See his commentary to the facsimile in *From Lisbon to Calicut* [note 5], p. 7f.

15 Proctor (10966) lists this as Stuchs's last book before he moved to Schneeberg. See also Walter Baumann, 'Die Druckerei Stuchs in Nürnberg (1484-1537)', *GJ*, 1954, pp. 122-32, here p. 129, no. 117.

16 The BL copy has the pressmark C.32.f.1. Besicken, who hailed from Besigheim in Württemberg, had already in 1505 published King Manuel I of Portugal's extremely interesting letter to King Ferdinand of Spain in which he gives an account of the Portuguese successes in India in the period 1500-1505. This is *Copia de una littera del viaggio e successo de India* (BL: C.32.f.19.). An English translation was published by Sergio J. Pacifici (Minneapolis, 1955).

17 C.32.f.18. and G.6958. *VD 16* P 4379. Proctor 11048. It is reproduced on microfiche in: *Flugschriften des frühen 16. Jahrhunderts*, ed. Hans Joachim Köhler (Zug, 1979f.), no. 4752.

input in terms of *industria et correctio* (fol. 2r).[18] That it was originally a letter is no longer evident: the address, salutation, and date of issue have been removed.[19] The King is always referred to in the third person. The theological reflections and the biblical quotations, which go far beyond the usual style of official letters, are presumably at least in part additions by the editor. But the contemporaries will have found the factual information useful. The letter tells how, on the orders of Manuel I, Francisco de Almeida, the commander of this impressive fleet and first viceroy of India, had established fortified bases on the east coast of Africa, on some strategically important islands, and on the Malabar Coast in order to secure the sea-route to India and to hold back the rival Arab traders.

In the space of a few months the *Gesta* had been printed in Germany in two Latin editions and one German translation.[20] They were of interest not least because (though this is not actually mentioned in the text) some Augsburg merchant-houses such as the Welsers and Fuggers and Nuremberg patricians like the Imhoffs and Hirschvogels had also been involved in the enterprise.[21] An account of the voyage, seen through the eyes of a German, eventually appeared in 1509.[22]

The Curia had sent the Archbishop of Cologne a copy of the *Gesta*. As early as 1 February 1507 the Cologne printer Johann von Landen had brought out an exact reprint, even down to the impressum, at the Church's behest, its authenticity being confirmed by the archbishop's notary, Johannes Wanloe.[23]

How Weissenburger obtained his printer's copy is not known. Comparison shows that his edition is based on the Rome original, not on the Cologne reprint. He gave his address in the colophon but not the year of publication. Weissenburger altered the wording of the text only here and there, referring to the function of the editor appropriately as *edita* on the title-page instead of as *impressa* as in the original.

Weissenburger took special care over designing the title-page. Unlike the Rome *editio princeps*, it provides information about the author, the King of

18 The letter was originally written after 22 May 1506, the day on which Fernão Soarez returned to Lisbon with some of the ships that had formed part of the fleet of 1505. He delivered Almeida's reports which formed the basis of Manuel I's letter. See Gerónimo Osório, *De rebus Emanuelis, Lusitaniae regis* (Cologne, 1581), fol. 125v.

19 Other printed letters of Manuel I, including those to Popes Julius II and Leo X, retain the traditional letter-form.

20 See Henry Harrisse, *Americus Vespuccius. A critical and documentary review of two recent English books concerning that navigator* (London, 1895), p. 30f. Sydney R. Welch, *South Africa under King Manuel, 1495–1521* (Cape Town and Johannesburg, 1946), p. 373.

21 Franz Hümmerich, *Die erste deutsche Handelsfahrt nach Indien 1505/06*. Historische Bibliothek, 49 (Munich and Berlin, 1922).

22 Balthasar Sprenger, *Die Merfart und erfarung nüwer Schiffung* [Oppenheim: Jakob Köbel] 1509. *VD 16* S 8379. Facsimile edited by Franz Schulze, in the series Drucke und Holzschnitte des 15. und 16. Jahrhunderts in getreuer Nachbildung, 8 (Strasbourg, 1902).

23 BL copy 582.e.1. *VD 16* P 4378. Proctor 10487. Information about the Cologne edition is found on fols 2r and 4v.

Fig. 2. The successes of the Portuguese crown in India (BL: C.32.f.18).

Portugal, and the editor (see fig. 2).[24] The woodcut by the Nuremberg artist Wolf Traut gives a clear indication of what the pamphlet is about: in its centre there are the arms and crown of Portugal, on the left is an Indian wearing a headdress and a skirt of feathers, on the right a naked woman, she too representing foreign tribes.[25] Thus Weissenburger deliberately made use of the title-page to promote sales, whereas his Cologne rival had used quite unspecific woodcuts of saints which simply happened to be available in his shop.[26] Johann Besicken in Rome had made do without any ornamentation. Allowing for the time taken to prepare a new woodcut, it seems that the Nuremberg edition was printed later than the Cologne one (1 February 1507) but still in the first half of the year.

24 In the Rome and Cologne editions this information is found on fol. 2^r before the report itself. It is not repeated in Weissenburger's edition at this point.

25 See Christian Rauch, *Die Trauts. Studien und Beiträge zur Geschichte der Nürnberger Malerei.* Studien zur deutschen Kunstgeschichte,79 (Strasbourg, 1907), p. 30, and Colin [note 12], pp. 190 and 395 where the title-page woodcut is reproduced. The picture of a Red Indian (= an Indian) has been influenced by a pamphlet issued in Augsburg in 1505, reproduced in [Hans Wolff], *America. Das frühe Bild der Neuen Welt.* Ausstellungskataloge der Bayerischen Staatsbibliothek, 58 (Munich, 1992), p. 29.

26 The title-page of the Cologne edition has a woodcut of Saints Anne and Mary with the infant Jesus, which is repeated on the verso, and at the end, on fol. 4^v, there are two small woodcuts depicting the Mass of St Gregory and St Jerome with the lion.

The same title-page woodcut was used for an unsigned German translation, issued under the title *Geschichte kurtzlich durch die von Portugalien in India, Morenland und andern erdtrich.*[27] Since it was only in the vernacular that accounts of new discoveries achieved the desired sales levels, we may assume that Weissenburger had arranged for the translation to be made even before he had printed the Latin edition, for the German version is based on the Rome edition, not the Nuremberg reprint, as many details reveal. Thus the phrasing of the title-page accords strictly with that of the Rome original and does not follow Weissenburger's innovations. The passage about *in terris antea incognitis* for which the Nuremberg Latin edition reads ... *aurea* ... was translated correctly (fol. A5^{v}). The year of publication, 1507, though not specified, is confirmed by an innovation on the part of the translator: the departure of the Portuguese fleet, referred to in the 1506 *editio princeps* with the words *anni praeteriti 1505*, was erroneously brought up to date when it was translated as *vorverganges jar 1506* ('in 1506, the year before last') (fol. A2^{r}).

It seems that time was short when the translation was made. Even compared with other contemporary translations, it is exceptionally clumsy, wordy, and often enough misleading, and intelligible only in conjunction with the Latin text. Whether it nevertheless came up to Weissenburger's expectations we do not know.

III

News of a completely different kind was to be found in letters from Portugal which were published in the shape of two pamphlets in Germany in 1506. Based on reliable sources and partly on his own eye-witness account, a German living in Lisbon described the bloody measures taken against the new Christians, the Jews forcibly converted, in April 1506 and the punitive measures taken by Manuel I.

The first pamphlet, entitled *Von dem christenlichen streyt geschehen im 1506. Jar zu Lißbona, ein haubtstat in Portigal, zwischen den christen und newen christen oder juden von wegen des gecreutzigisten got*, gives an account of the massacre.[28] Ever since it was analysed by Gotthelf Heine in 1848 and Meyer Kayserling in 1867 it has been regarded as an important historical source.[29] It was issued in three editions with some textual variation between them; none of them bears the name of the printer, place or date of publication. One edition has additional material at two points.

27 Imperfect copy in the Germanisches Nationalmuseum, Nuremberg (pressmark: Hist. 8224.8°); Weller 389.

28 Copy in the Bayerische Staatsbibliothek, Munich (4° Germ.g.197 g/5). *VD 16* V 2457. Reproduced in *Flugschriften* [note 17], no. 3197.

29 Gotthelf Heine, 'Die Einführung der Inquisition in Portugal', *Allgemeine Zeitschrift für Geschichte*, 9 (1848), 139-80 (with an abridged and modernized text from an unspecified source but in fact from the [Strasbourg] edition as appendix I, pp. 171-78). Meyer Kayserling, *Geschichte der Juden in Portugal* (Leipzig, 1867), pp. 146-56, with quotations from the detailed version printed by Weissenburger.

The content will be summarized here only in so far as it can help resolve problems regarding the printing. Plague had been raging in Lisbon since the autumn of 1505. The court, the nobility and well-to-do townsfolk had left the city. Suffering and fearful people walked in procession to the church of the Dominican monastery of São Domingos. The object of devotion there was a crucifix into which, in the place of the heart, a mirror had been set, in which various miracles could allegedly be seen. Only the longer version of the text contains a passage eight lines long in which the reporter gives expression to his reservations and doubts. He himself says he had not been able to see any reflection, yet more than two hundred people he knew had claimed that they had seen it, and good friends of his had assured him that there was no question of any trick on the part of the monks (fol. A2^{v}).

On Low Sunday, 19 April 1506, the first Sunday after Easter, when one of the new Christians in the crowd of devoted pilgrims expressed some scepticism about the miracle, he was seized, dragged from the church and beaten to death. Over the next few days these spontaneous riots resulted in general unrest which spread to the surrounding areas. The royal officials failed to stem the revolt. One thousand nine hundred and thirty deaths were reported, but at this point the correspondent (in the longer version) remarks that the exact figure could not yet be ascertained because many of the converts had fled and had gone into hiding. All this had taken place between 17 and 29 April. Since then, according to a second addendum, nothing worth reporting had happened.[30]

It is an obvious step for bibliographers to use these two additional passages as an aid to determining the order in which the three editions appeared. The American historian Yosef Hayim Yerushalmi regarded the long version as the latest of the three (edition C), but his arguments have not convinced me.[31] It is possible that the sixteen lines at the end of the pamphlet could represent a later addition, but one might object that the join occurs just before the writer voices his own personal opinion. Yerushalmi ignores the writer's critical comment on the miracle in São Domingos. How can one account for the later interpolation of this extremely interesting passage into a text that had already been published?

The explanation is complicated by the fact that recent studies of the types used have shown that two of the three editions – the longer version and one of the two shorter ones – were published by Johann Weissenburger in Nuremberg.[32] Only the abridged version has a title-page woodcut which has any meaningful connexion with the pogrom. This tends to point to a later date for this version, the block having been specially commissioned.

Close textual analysis likewise points to the conclusion that the longer version

30 *Von dem christlichen Streit*, longer version, fol. A6^{r}, where sixteen lines of text have been added.

31 Yosef Hayim Yerushalmi, *The Lisbon Massacre of 1506 and the Royal Image in the Shebet Yehudah*. Annual Supplements of the Hebrew Union College, 1 (Cincinnati, 1976), pp. 69–80, with an edition of the text of the longer version. Yerushalmi's analysis of the text is based solely on the interpretation of the two additional passages.

32 I am grateful to Helmut Claus in Gotha for confirming my suspicions.

was Weissenburger's first edition, the shorter version was his second, and this in turn was reprinted by Matthias Hupfuff in Strasbourg.

The letters from Lisbon were first printed in the early summer of 1506. The title-page of the first edition is adorned with a very fine but non-specific woodcut that Weissenburger already had to hand.[33] It is a Nuremberg copy, perhaps made around 1500, of one of the famous woodcuts from Stephan Fridolin's *Schatzbehalter* of 1491.[34]

It seems the pamphlet was quickly sold out, so Weissenburger was able to plan a second edition.[35] When setting up the type afresh he deleted the two passages in which the Lisbon correspondent aired his personal views. It is not impossible that he was pressurized to do this by the Nuremberg council though a search of the Nuremberg archives has not produced anything to support this. It is quite clear the attempts were made to iron out some of the linguistic imperfections in the text, as a single example will show. At one point the longer version had two lines of print more than the other editions. The formulation was too clumsy, so it was shortened and some words were omitted by mistake.[36]

For the title-page of the second edition Weissenburger had a new woodcut prepared to catch the eye of customers. According to Dodgson, this was also the work of Wolf Traut.[37] It clearly makes reference to some important features of the pogrom: in the background on the right two men are seen venerating the miraculous cross of São Domingos; on the left there is a clutch of armed men in front of a house. In the foreground a monk with a cross and several other men are approaching a fire on which two human figures are burning (fig. 3).

This second, abridged edition served as copy for Matthias Hupfuff's Strasbourg reprint.[38] It takes up most of the textual improvements which distinguish the second Nuremberg edition for the first, but the text was revised once more and recast in the form of German typical of Strasbourg books – the phonology was changed and individual words were replaced by their Alemannic equivalents. Two small textual changes on the title page and at the beginning of the text give a clue as to when the book was printed, for whereas both the

33 This is reproduced by Yerushalmi, p. 68, but his claim on p. 71 that the picture is to be linked iconographically with Isaiah 6 (the calling of the prophet) is misleading. No earlier use of this woodcut by Weissenburger or any other printer has yet been found.

34 Stephan Fridolin, *Schatzbehalter* (Nuremberg: Anton Koberger, 1491). *GW* 10329. Hain-Copinger 14507. ISTC is00306000. The woodcut in question, on fol. g1^r, shows the angels assembled before the Throne of God. The theological significance is explained in the accompanying text.

35 Copy in the Bayerische Staatsbibliothek, Munich (pressmark 4° Port.23 d). *VD 16* V 2458. Reproduced in *Flugschriften* [note 17], no. 4046.

36 The passage concerned is found at the foot of fol. A5^v in Weissenburger's longer version and in his reprint and on fol. A6^r in the Strasbourg edition. It is impossible to imagine that these lines might be a later insertion.

37 Campbell Dodgson, *Catalogue of Early German and Flemish Woodcuts preserved in the Department of Prints and Drawings in the British Museum*, I (London, 1903), p. 505.

38 Copy in the BL (pressmark 4515.b.8.). *VD 16* V 2459. Proctor 10019. Jean Muller, *Bibliographie strasbourgeoise*, II (Baden-Baden, 1985), p. 60, no. 63. Reproduced in *Flugschriften* [note 17], no. 3212. Hupfuff's non-specific woodcut is reproduced by Yerushalmi, p. 67.

Von dem christelichen streyt geschehē jm. M.CCCCC.vj. Jar zu Lißbona ein haubt stat in Portigal zwischen den christen vnd newen christen oder jüden/ von wegen des gecreutzigisten got.

Fig. 3. Scenes from the Lisbon massacre. Title-page of Weissenburger's second edition (Munich BSB: 4° Port. 23 d).

Nuremberg editions specify the year in which the massacre took place, the Strasbourg edition says that it had happened 'recently' (*kürtzlich beschehen*) or 'in recent years' (*In kurtzvergangen jaren*), which indicates that it was printed after 1506, presumably in 1507.

IV

The pamphlet ends with a formulaic promise: *Was sich weyter begibt, werdt ir zu seinen zeyten vernemen* ('What happened later, you will learn in due course') (fol. A6^r^ in the longer version). Many sixteenth-century reports end with a phrase of this kind. Often enough there is no evidence that a sequel ever appeared in print, but in this case our critical, well-informed Lisbon correspondent kept his promise. The principal themes of his later letters were the suppression of the revolt and the punitive measures taken by King Manuel I in May 1506. These reports, too, found their way into the hands of Johann Weissenburger who published them as pamphlets, once again without any indication of date or place of publication.

The title chosen by the printer or the editor (if these were not one and the same) deliberately echoed the earlier pamphlet, for whereas that had been called *Von dem christlichen Streit* the new one was called *Von der unkristenlichen handlung, so der Kunig von Portigal wider das unschuldig plut der kristen ... geubt hat.*[39]

That these two pamphlets belong together, providing an early example of the publication of a sequel, was noticed by Georg Wolfgang Panzer as long ago as 1788, though he regarded them as two parts of a single book. Appositely, with regard to the content and the formulation of the title he remarked: 'Jener Mord heißt ein christlicher Streit. Die Bestrafung der Mönche hingegen eine unchristliche Handlung. Wie verkehrt!' ('These murders are termed a Christian battle. The punishment of the monks, on the other hand, is called an unchristian act. How topsy-turvy!')[40]

Despite Panzer's note, the second pamphlet was ignored until very recently.[41] Like the account of the Lisbon massacre it is a document of historic importance which corrects and adds a number of details to what we knew before.

The first part of the pamphlet gives a precise and vivid account of the arrest and execution of the ringleaders before the King intervened on 8 May and of the punishment meted out to the Dominicans. In a second, clearly defined section the writer gives a summary of the main provisions of the royal edict of 22 May 1506, elucidating them for the benefit of German readers. Several of Lisbon's privileges were abolished, other provisions concerned the confiscation of private wealth to the benefit of the crown rather than to compensate the victims.

Johann Weissenburger seems to have underestimated the size of the edition needed for this pamphlet of three and a half pages of text, so that he soon had to

39 BL copy 4625.b.13. *VD 16* V 2640. The first line of the title-page of the only known copy is damaged but has been supplied by hand on the basis of the reprise of the title on fol. 2^r.

40 Georg Wolfgang Panzer, *Annalen der älteren deutschen Litteratur* (Nuremberg, 1788), no. 568 (no copy specified). He describes the shorter version of the earlier report and the second report, both printed by Weissenburger. Panzer probably knew a copy in which pamphlets had been combined. He states that it contained nine leaves (six and three, the last leaf of the second pamphlet being blank). It is possible that Panzer used the copy acquired by the British Museum in 1850, for the first line which had apparently already been damaged by then was incorrectly amended by hand to read *handlung die* (instead of *handlung so*).

41 See Irmgard Bezzel, 'Die Strafmaßnahmen König Manuels I. von Portugal im Jahr 1506. Nach dem Bericht eines in Lissabon lebenden Deutschen', *Judaica*, 49 (1993), 170–83. This contains an edition of the text.

Von der vnkriſtenlichen handlũg ſo der Kunig von Portigal wider das vnſchuldig plůt der kriſten/ auff die vorergangen geſchicht der ſchalckhafftigẽ newẽ kriſten ader Judẽ zu Lißwona geůbt hat

Fig. 4. Scenes from Manuel I's retribution. Title-page of the first edition (BL: 4625.b.3).

bring out a second edition, setting it up afresh. It was unusual that he altered the title: *Von dem geschicht und handlung, so der Kunig vonn Portigal* ...[42] A short anti-semitic passage is deleted, otherwise the text of the second edition is identical with that of the first.[43]

In the second edition Weissenburger reused the woodcut he had had specially made, now putting it on the verso of the title page. For the title-page itself,

42 Copy in Wolfenbüttel HAB (Th 2927). *VD 16* V 2641. *Flugschriften* [note 17], no. 2436.

43 The suggestion made in the first edition (fol. 3^v) that the king's mother was of Jewish extraction is not repeated in the second.

whose role it was to attract customers, he commissioned another woodcut from the same artist, Wolf Traut.[44] This shows King Manuel I (who had not been present in person) in the left foreground, accompanied by two officials, with two condemned men (monks?) being burnt at the stake on the right. In the background there are two men hanging from a gallows and a third, who has fallen from the gallows, lying on the ground (fig. 4).

As the reuse of the older woodcut shows, both editions of this report were printed later than the shorter version of *Von dem christlichen Streit*, presumably still in 1506.

Examination of the printing history of the text of these four pamphlets shows how successful Johann Weissenburger was in disseminating news. Some of the reports he simply reprinted; the only Latin text, Manuel I's letter, he immediately had translated into German. He knew how to gain access to interesting, previously unpublished texts. It seems likely that the accounts of the pogrom which were printed first or only in Nuremberg and which probably came from the Lisbon base of a Nuremberg merchant were given to him directly or indirectly by their Nuremberg recipient for publication. Weissenburger probably had a hand in formulating the title and in editing the text for publication. He was one of the first printers to recognize the importance of a relevant picture relating to the content. With a single exception he always had a new woodcut made.

44 See Dodgson, I, p. 505.

'CAVEAT LECTOR!'

Edward Schröder's 'facsimile' of the 1515 Strasbourg edition of 'Till Eulenspiegel' and the consequences for scholarship

JOHN L. FLOOD

ONE OF THE GREAT RARITIES among the British Library's extensive holdings of German books from the early sixteenth century is the only known copy of the 1515 edition of *Till Eulenspiegel.* Until about twenty years ago this was believed to be the earliest surviving edition of the collection of tales about the lovable rogue, but we now know for sure what had long been suspected by textual scholars, that there was at least one earlier edition. Two incomplete copies of an edition produced in about 1510 or 1511 came to light during the 1970s. The first of these, comprising only a few leaves taken from a binding, was described by Peter Honegger in 1973 in a book which revolutionized and revitalized *Eulenspiegel* studies, not least because he was able to show that the author was the Brunswick writer Hermann Bote (*c.* 1450-*c.* 1520).[1] The second came to attention briefly when it was acquired by Bernd Ulrich Hucker at auction in 1976 but has ever since remained inaccessible to scholars in a bank vault somewhere in Germany.[2]

The 1515 edition was in fact one of three editions of *Till Eulenspiegel* published by Johann Grüninger at Strasbourg. In addition to the 1510/11 edition there was also one published in 1519 (of which also but a single copy survives, in Gotha).[3] All three (known respectively as S 1510/11, S 1515, and S 1519 in the critical literature)[4] have their interest, both from the biblio-

1 Peter Honegger, *Ulenspiegel. Ein Beitrag zur Druckgeschichte und zur Verfasserfrage* (Neumünster, 1973). For the most recent substantial assessment of Bote see Herbert Blume and Eberhard Rohse (eds), *Hermann Bote. Städtisch-hansischer Autor in Braunschweig 1488-1988* (Tübingen, 1991) (Frühe Neuzeit, 4).

2 For a detailed description of the volume see Bernd Ulrich Hucker, 'Eine neuentdeckte Erstausgabe des Eulenspiegels von 1510/11. Zur Geschichte eines verschollenen Frühdruckes', *Philobiblon*, 20 (1976), 78-120.

3 A facsimile of this, together with a commentary volume, *Ein kurtzweilig lesen von Dil Ulenspiegel. Kommentar zur Faksimileausgabe*, by Anneliese Schmitt was published by Insel Verlag at Leipzig in 1979. See also the reviews by Ingeborg Spriewald, in *Deutsche Literaturzeitung*, 102 (1981), cols 228-31, and Wolfgang Virmond, in *Anzeiger für deutsches Altertum und deutsche Literatur*, 95 (1984), 130-36, especially 134-36.

4 They are listed in Jean Müller's *Bibliographie strasbourgeoise*, vol. II (Baden-Baden, 1985), under nos 82, 121, and 147 respectively in the list of books printed by Grüninger (pp. 22-50).

graphical and textual points of view, but in the present context I wish to concentrate on the unique copy of the 1515 edition, since this, preserving as it does the earliest complete text of the work, continues to be used by modern editors as the basis of scholarly and popular editions.[5]

How S 1515 came to be in the British Library is itself an interesting story which I have related in detail elsewhere.[6] Briefly, it was acquired by John Morris, a wealthy London citizen and recorded as Master of the Watermills in 1640. Morris was the son of a Dutch water engineer who established himself in England in the 1540s and who in 1580 built a large waterworks near London Bridge which supplied most of the capital and which remained in his family's hands until it was destroyed in the Great Fire of 1666. The son, John Morris, who was born some time in the 1580s, enjoyed a substantial income which enabled him to pursue his antiquarian and bibliophile interests. In the early years of the seventeenth century he travelled widely, visiting Leiden in 1608, Paris, Madrid, Genoa, Padua, Venice, Florence and Rome in 1610-11, and Lisbon in 1617. He died in 1658.[7]

Among the approximately fifteen hundred books which Professor Birrell has traced to Morris's collection there are only two in German: one is the 1515 *Eulenspiegel*, the other, bound with it, is a copy of Thomas Murner's *Schelmenzunft* (Strasbourg: Grüninger, 1516).[8] Birrell suggests that Morris, who seems at least to have had a dilettante interest in languages, acquired these to serve, together with his copy of Josua Maaler's German-Latin dictionary *Die Teütsch spraach* (Zurich 1561),[9] as 'elementary German textbooks', but this seems improbable as an explanation. If he had wanted to learn German, even though there were as yet no primers of German intended for Englishmen – Heinrich Offelen's *Double Grammar for Germans to learn English and for English-Men to learn the German tongue* did not appear until 1686-87 – Morris could surely have found something much more suitable than two verse satires that were already a century old and written in an antiquated form of German. It is more likely that Morris acquired them as examples of satirical literature – in 1608 he bought a

5 There is in fact little justification for this because at several points the 1519 edition appears to preserve the original reading of the text more faithfully, S 1515 often abbreviating the text. The three editions seem to be related to one another as follows:

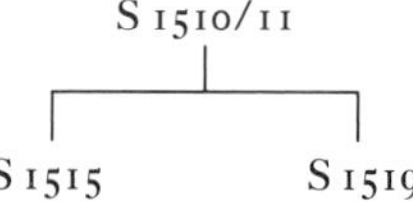

6 John L. Flood, 'Wie Eulenspiegel ins Britische Museum kam. Zur Provenienz des Londoner Exemplars von S 1515', *Eulenspiegel-Jahrbuch* 1984, pp. 133-40.

7 On Morris see T. A. Birrell, *The Library of John Morris. The Reconstruction of a Seventeenth-Century Collection* (London, 1976), and further references in my article mentioned in note 6.

8 The British Library shelfmarks are, respectively, C.57.c.23. (1.) and C.57.c.23. (2.). Though it seems the books shared a single binding in Morris's day and were probably already bound together when he bought them, the binding on them today is a nineteenth-century one, made (according to Hermann Knust, *Till Eulenspiegel* (Halle 1884), p. IV) in 1883.

9 Now British Library 628.h.1.

copy of the works of Rabelais in the 1596 Lyons edition. Nor is it impossible that Morris already knew of *Eulenspiegel*, which had been an international success in the sixteenth century, through one of the English or Dutch editions.

However Morris may have come by the 1515 *Eulenspiegel* and for whatever reason, we have good cause to be grateful to him. From him it passed through the Old Royal Library and eventually into the collections of the British Library. Because of its uniqueness it has been at the focus of attention in *Eulenspiegel* studies ever since it first became known to interested scholars. Unfortunately it was not yet known to Johann Martin Lappenberg, described by Wilhelm Grimm as a semi-Englishman[10] and the first serious student of *Eulenspiegel*, who based his edition, published under the title *Dr. Thomas Murners Ulenspiegel* (Leipzig, 1854), on Grüninger's 1519 edition. The 1515 edition, which is entered in the first printed catalogue of the British Museum under the wrong date, 1516,[11] first came to notice in Germany through an anonymous contribution in 1868 in the first issue of *Mittheilungen aus dem Antiquariate von S. Calvary & Co, in Berlin*, where – in the course of a eulogy on the British Museum for the exemplary way in which it made its treasures accessible – the book is briefly described and chapters 13-16 are reprinted.[12] The author of the piece already surmised, quite correctly, that there must have been an even earlier edition.[13] This article came to the attention of the literary historian Wilhelm Scherer who soon compared the 1515 and 1519 editions in more detail (though without seeing the former himself; he relied on information supplied by his friend Professor Karl Vollmöller) and confirmed their dependence on a yet earlier edition.[14] The text of the 1515 edition was first reprinted by Hermann Knust in his *Till Eulenspiegel. Abdruck der Ausgabe vom Jahre 1515* (Halle, 1884,

10 Quoted in 'Der antiquarische Buchhandel und die Bibliotheken. Zugleich als Prospect dieser Zeitschrift', in *Mittheilungen aus dem Antiquariate von S. Calvary & Co, in Berlin*, 1, no. 1 (1868), 1-12, here p. 3. I owe this reference to Bernd Ulrich Hucker and Wolfgang Virmond (eds), Edward Schröder, *Untersuchungen zum Volksbuch von Eulenspiegel* (Göttingen, 1988), [hereafter: Hucker/Virmond], p. 113, note 2. The jibe that Lappenberg (born 1794) was a semi-Englishman presumably alludes to the fact that in 1829 he had published a two-volume history of England up to 1153 in the series *Geschichte der europäischen Staaten*, ed. by A. H. L. Heeren and F. A. Ukert; he also wrote *Der große Brand von London* (Hamburg, 1842) and an authoritative article on Ireland in J. S. Ersch and J. G. Gruber (eds), *Allgemeine Encyklopädie der Wissenschaften und Künste*. 2. Section, 24. Theil. (Leipzig, 1845), pp. 1-103.

11 *Librorum impressorum qui in Museo Britannico adservantur catalogus* (London, 1813-23), vol. VII: Vlenspiegel 4° Strasb. 1516. The error is explained by the fact that the second item with which it is bound, Murner's *Schelmenzunft*, has the date 1516 at the end. Calvary's *Mittheilungen* compounds the error by giving the date as 1518 and stating that the work with which the *Eulenspiegel* is bound is Murner's *Geuchmatt* (p. 4).

12 See note 10.

13 '... und so lässt sich wiederum schliessen, dass es noch eine frühere Ausgabe giebt, aus welcher die spätere Ausgabe von 1519 abgedruckt ist' (p. 4).

14 Wilhelm Scherer, *Die Anfänge des deutschen Prosaromans und Jörg Wickram von Colmar* (Strasbourg and London, 1877) (Quellen und Forschungen zur Sprach- und Culturgeschichte der germanischen Völker, 21), especially pp. 26-34 and 78-92. The reference to Vollmöller is on p. 78. There Scherer points out that the book is bound with Murner's *Schelmenzunft* of 1516, not his *Geuchmatt* of 1518.

reissued 1896), published as vol. 55/56 in the series *Neudrucke deutscher Litteraturwerke des XVI. und XVII. Jahrhunderts*, still one of the most useful and highly respected series of editions of German texts of the early modern period. Dr Knust, about whom nothing is known to me beyond the fact that he died in 1889 and that, according to the British Library's General Catalogue, he edited a number of German and Spanish texts (some of them published posthumously), apparently prepared his transcription and edition in London, for his introduction ends with the dateline 'Britt. Mus., den 16. Sept. 1884' (p. XXIII). Directly or indirectly, it has formed the basis of most scholarly work on *Eulenspiegel*.[15]

Knust's edition is adequate for most purposes, even though Edward Schröder complains that it is 'neither diplomatic nor critical and therefore quite unusable for more detailed investigations'.[16] It is certainly useless for bibliographical investigations, for Knust tells us (p. V) that he has resolved all the abbreviations (which, as it happens, are more numerous in Grüninger's 1515 edition than in either the 1510/11 or the 1519 editions), except in those cases where the abbreviation is ambiguous. He has also silently corrected a large number of Grüninger's misprints (he is well known as a somewhat shoddy printer) which are listed on pp. V–VII, and amended the text at various points (listed on p. VIII) where it was clearly defective and where S 1519 offered a correct reading.

The chief drawback of Knust's edition was, however, that it contained no illustrations, even though the editor himself clearly recognised the importance of the woodcuts which he describes, albeit laconically, on pages III–IV of the introduction.[17] The *Neudrucke* series was intended to be affordable for students (my 1896 copy is priced 1 Mark 20 Pf.), so the publishers doubtless felt that reproducing the woodcuts would have been an undesirable additional expense, especially seeing that the originals were in London. But scholars soon realised that the woodcuts were an indispensable feature of the book and must be available for study if *Eulenspiegel* were to be fully appreciated. After all, one of the chief innovations of Strasbourg printers around the year 1500 was to have promoted the illustrated book – men like Johann Grüninger, Johann Knobloch and Bartholomäus Kistler made important contributions precisely in this field.

Not surprisingly, therefore, an attempt was made to produce a high-quality facsimile of the book. Photolithographic facsimiles of two other early *Eulenspiegel* editions had been published in the nineteenth century,[18] but there was as

15 Thus it was used as the basis of the text in Peter Suchsland (ed.), *Deutsche Volksbücher* (Berlin and Weimar, 1968), vol. II, pp. 5–155 (text slightly modernized).

16 Edward Schröder on p. 6 of his commentary on the facsimile of S 1515 (see note 24 below).

17 Lappenberg had at least reproduced the title page woodcut and what he calls 'the final vignette' depicting an owl and a looking glass. Lindow's edition reproduces all the illustrations but in reduced format.

18 One was made by the bookseller Ascher on the basis of two incomplete copies (one in Vienna, the other in Berlin) of the Cologne edition issued by Servais Kruffter sometime in the 1520s, published as *Tyel Ulenspiegel in niedersächsischer Mundart nach dem ältesten Druck des Servais*

yet no reproduction of the oldest of them then known, S 1515. For this we have to thank Edward Schröder (1858-1942), the eminent Professor of German at Göttingen and devoted pupil of Wilhelm Scherer since his student days at Strasbourg in 1876.[19] Schröder had bought a copy of Knust's edition as soon as it appeared[20] and continued to work on *Eulenspiegel* sporadically for more than half a century. In June 1909 he gave a lecture in Münster on the origins of *Eulenspiegel*, which came to be reported in a Berlin newspaper.[21] A few days later, on 16 June, Dr Anton Kippenberg of the Insel Verlag in Leipzig wrote to him in the following terms (my translation):

> A report in the *Nationalzeitung* on your *Eulenspiegel* lecture in Münster brings me back to a plan that I have been wanting to put into effect for years, namely to bring out a facsimile of the oldest surviving *Eulenspiegel* edition, which appears to be the Strasbourg reprint of 1515. I should be extremely grateful if you would consent to write an afterword for this edition, discussing the origin and history of the *Eulenspiegel* theme.[22]

Schröder replied the very next day: 'Your proposal accords with a plan I have long had in mind myself, and I accept it without more ado.'[23] The book appeared in 1911.[24] Schröder's 'Geleitwort' to the facsimile, dated May 1911, is in fact his most substantial published piece on *Eulenspiegel*. It should now be read in conjunction with his unpublished *Untersuchungen*, recently valuably edited by Hucker and Virmond.

In the agreement with the Insel Verlag were sown the seeds of a malignant weed whose tendrils still threaten to strangle sound scholarship today. This is the story I have to tell.

On the face of it, the auguries were good. Edward Schröder was an eminent scholar with a genuine interest in *Till Eulenspiegel*. The Insel Verlag was one of

Kruffter photolithographisch nachgebildet (Berlin, 1865) (a misleading title if ever there was one, for the dialect of Cologne is not Low Saxon!). The other, *Tyl Uilenspiegel. Antwerpen - Michiel van Hoochstraten - z.j. (1512)*, was prepared by Martinus Nijhoff on the basis of the incomplete copy in the Royal Library at Copenhagen and published at The Hague in 1898; the date which Nijhoff gives to the edition, 1512, is much too early: van Hoochstraten cannot possibly have printed it before 1519.

19 On Schröder see the monumental obituary essay by Jost Trier, 'Edward Schröder', *Jahrbuch der Akademie der Wissenschaften in Göttingen für das Geschäftsjahr 1942/43* (Göttingen, 1943), pp. 101-50.

20 Schröder's copy is still preserved in Göttingen University Library; see Hucker / Virmond, p. 113.

21 *National-Zeitung*, vol. 62, no. 263, p. 2.

22 My translation. For the original, which is now in Weimar, see Hucker / Virmond, p. 115.

23 Letter to Kippenberg, 17 June 1909. Translated from Hucker / Virmond, p. 115.

24 *Ein kurtzweilig lesen von Dyl Vlenspiegel geboren vß dem land zů Brunßwick. Faksimile des Straßburger Drucks von 1515.* Geleitwort E. Schröder (Leipzig: Insel, 1911). See Heinz Sarkowski, *Der Insel-Verlag. Eine Bibliographie 1899-1969* (Frankfurt am Main, 1970), p. 87, no. 432. This facsimile is not to be confused with *Ein kurzweilig Lesen von Till Ulenspiegel.* Ausgewählt von Christian Heinrich Kleukens, first published as vol. 56 in the Insel-Bücherei series with 57 hand-coloured woodcuts (selected from the 1572 edition) in 1913 which sold 40,000 copies by 1924, to be followed by an abridged version with only 42 woodcuts that year and selling a further 65,000 copies by 1955; on this see Herbert Kästner, *75 Jahre Insel-Bücherei 1912-1987. Eine Bibliographie* (Leipzig, 1987), p. 11.

the most distinguished publishing houses in Germany. Furthermore they were dealing with the British Museum. So what could possibly go wrong?

In fact, until a few years ago no one was aware that anything did go wrong, and indeed to this day almost all *Eulenspiegel* scholars subsist in blissful ignorance. One only becomes aware that there is a problem if one sees the original and the facsimile side-by-side. For obvious reasons this is possible only in the North Library, and even then only if one brings along one's own copy of the Insel Verlag's facsimile – the British Library does not possess its own copy, either because the Insel Verlag omitted to send a complimentary copy or more likely because the British Museum haughtily declined to accept one since it possessed the original anyway. Four hundred copies were printed, but today it is so hard to find that in 1982 Werner Wunderlich brought out a facsimile of it;[25] as the following will show, this was unwise – it would have been much more sensible to have prepared a totally new one. The importance of Schröder's facsimile is evident from the fact that Wolfgang Lindow states that he used it as the basis of his own edition, the edition which remains the most widely used today.[26]

A close comparison of the Insel Verlag's so-called facsimile with the original reveals that the photographic plates used for the facsimile have been extensively retouched. This affects not only the woodcuts; the text too has been retouched in a way which reveals a real lack of understanding of it, which is in itself perhaps an indication that the retouching was done in England by someone for whom sixteenth-century German was all Greek, though at first one might well wonder why anyone in England would have thought that the text needed any retouching and thus be inclined to suspect rather that the work was carried out in Leipzig.

The only reference to the misleading nature of Schröder's facsimile that I am aware of in the extensive literature on *Till Eulenspiegel* is hidden away in Wolfgang Virmond's rather intemperate review of Wunderlich's and Schmitt's facsimiles.[27] The details given there go back in part to correspondence and conversations I had with him and Bernd Ulrich Hucker at that time. Virmond speaks of Schröder's facsimile showing lesser or greater divergences from the original 'in every woodcut, every line, every word, every letter, every mark',

25 Werner Wunderlich (ed.), *Dyl Ulenspiegel. In Abbildungen des Drucks von 1515 (S 1515)* (Göppingen, 1982) (Litterae. Göppinger Beiträge zur Textgeschichte, 96) . It is important not to overlook the statement on the copyright page that there has been slight retouching of the illustrations, a fact not mentioned in Wunderlich's afterword. Wunderlich's facsimile was discussed by Virmond in his review mentioned in note 3 above.

26 Wolfgang Lindow (ed.), *Ein kurtzweilig lesen von Dil Ulenspiegel. Nach dem Druck von 1515 mit 87 Holzschnitten* (Stuttgart, 1966) (Reclams Universalbibliothek, 1687/88/88a/b) (frequently reprinted; reissued with minor revisions as vol. 1687 [4] in 1978). On Lindow's use of Schröder's facsimile see p. 269. The facsimile was also used in preparation of the modernized editions by Siegfried H. Sichtermann (published by Insel Verlag, Frankfurt am Main, 1978, 2nd ed. 1981) (insel taschenbuch, 336) and Günter Jäckel (published by Gustav Kiepenhauer Verlag, Leipzig and Weimar, 1987).

27 See note 3 above.

so that one could only conclude that the publishers had had the London photographs traced by hand and had used these, rather than the photographs, for the facsimile.[28] Virmond believes that, faced with the 'poor quality of the printing and the poor state of preservation' of the original, Anton Kippenberg's aestheticism left him with no choice but to produce the book in this way. There is some truth in this, but Virmond exaggerates. The book is not in a poor state of preservation at all, nor is the printing any worse than in any other of Grüninger's books. And certainly it is a gross distortion of the facts to claim that 'every woodcut, every line, every word, every letter, every mark' in Schröder's facsimile departs in some degree or other from the original. It is highly improbable that the facsimile was produced from tracings – the accuracy is too great for that – but the photographs have most assuredly been extensively retouched.

The key to the mystery is to be found in the colophon to the facsimile edition. This informs us that the photographic reproduction was carried out by Emery G. Walker in London. The zinc plates[29] used for printing were prepared by the Graphische Kunstanstalt F. Bruckmann A.G. in Munich who also did the actual printing, on paper (similar to that of the original) supplied by J. Batchelor & Son, Ford Mill, Little Chart. Four hundred numbered copies were produced, including one hundred with illuminated woodcuts (the woodcuts in the British Library's original have not been coloured).[30]

The references to Emery Walker and Joseph Batchelor make it clear that we have to see the production of the facsimile in the context of the growth of interest in the art of the book in Germany under the influence of the revival of appreciation of fine typography in England that we associate particularly with the Arts and Crafts Movement, William Morris, and the Kelmscott Press.

Briefly, Emery Walker (1851-1933) had joined the Typographic Etching Company in Farringdon Street, London in 1873, and during the ten years he spent with them he learned a great deal about a wide variety of current methods of printing illustrations. In 1886 he founded a process-engraving business in partnership with Walter Boutall and around the turn of the century he was the most distinguished practitioner in England. A lecture given by Walker on early printed books on 15 November 1888 to the newly formed Arts and Crafts

28 As note 3, p. 130 (my translation). Tracing was, of course, employed for small-scale facsimiles of individual pages, but not for whole books. See Robin Myers, 'George Isaac Frederick Tupper, facsimilist "whose ability in this description of work is beyond praise" (1820?-1911)', *Transactions of the Cambridge Bibliographical Society*, 7 (1978), 113-34.

29 It is not clear to me what precise process was involved at this time, but it seems that the photographic negatives were etched on to zinc plates (cf. the remarks in Ernst Voss (ed.), *Thomas Murner, An den grossmächtigsten und durchlauchtigsten Adel deutscher Nation* (Halle, 1899) (Flugschriften aus der Reformationszeit, 13), p. IV). Presumably the negatives would have been retouched, rather than the zinc plates.

30 A copy of the hand-coloured version and one of the non-coloured ones are listed as items 125 and 126 in Hauswedell & Nolte's auction catalogue 257 *Die Insel und die moderne deutsche Buchkunst* (21 and 22 May 1985). Other copies appeared in Hauswedell's catalogue no. 200, 1974, item 400, and Haus der Bücher, Basle, catalogue no. 52, 1976, item 903.

Exhibition Society in London and reported by Oscar Wilde in the *Pall Mall Gazette* the following day is said to have encouraged William Morris to realise his idea of printing his own books by founding the Kelmscott Press.[31] Walker acted as midwife to the whole enterprise, finding Edward Prince, a man in the first rank of punch-cutters, and he knew that Joseph Batchelor made the finest hand-made paper. After 1894 Walker produced a series of spectacular reproductions of illustrated manuscripts. When Morris died in 1896 he joined T. J. Cobden-Sanderson in a new venture, the Doves Press.

How did Walker become associated with the Insel Verlag? In 1904 he formed a friendship with Harry Graf Kessler (1868-1937), the diplomat and connoisseur, born in Paris of an Anglo-Irish mother (a famous beauty) and a German father (a wealthy Hamburg merchant, raised to the nobility in 1880). Young Kessler began his education in England, at St George's School, Ascot (where one of his fellow-pupils was Winston Churchill). During his short time there he had founded a school newspaper, *St George's Gazette*, which he had printed in Windsor. Later, in 1895, he became involved with Julius Meier-Graefe's sumptuous but short-lived German art journal *Pan* which aimed to introduce the philosophy of William Morris's Arts and Crafts Movement to Germany.[32] A merger Kessler proposed with a rival publication, the equally short-lived *Die Insel*, came to nothing. *Die Insel* transformed itself at the last gasp into a publishing house, Insel Verlag, and Kessler became associated with that. When in England in 1904 he told Walker of Insel's plans to bring out a series of German classics and got Walker interested in the typography of the series, launched in 1905. This was the *Großherzog Wilhelm Ernst Ausgabe deutscher Klassiker*, comprising the works of Goethe, Kant, Körner, Schiller, Schopenhauer and others. Walker supervised the printing and Eric Gill designed the title-pages and initials.[33] When in 1913 Kessler decided to set up his own press, the Cranach-Presse, in Weimar, Walker prepared a type for him based on Nicolas Jenson's roman, and it was cut by Edward Prince. The outbreak of the Great War must have brought many sorrows to Walker; he had a great many friends in Germany. The Leipzig 'Internationale Ausstellung für Buchgewerbe und Graphik', which ran from May to October 1914, demonstrated the typographical revival in which he, through his involvement with the Kelmscott Press and the Doves Press and his friendship with Kessler, had played such an important role.[34]

31 See now John Dreyfus, 'A reconstruction of the lecture given by Emery Walker on 15 November 1888', *Matrix*, 11 (1991), 27-52.

32 Kessler visited Morris on 20 June 1895.

33 See Sarkowski [note 24], p. 492. On the Cranach-Presse see Renate Müller-Krumbach, *Harry Graf Kessler und die Cranach-Presse in Weimar* (Hamburg, 1969).

34 For a full account of Walker see R. C. H. Briggs, *Sir Emery Walker, a memoir composed on the occasion of the unveiling by Miss Dorothy Walker of a commemorative medallion put up by the London County Council at 7 Hammersmith Terrace, London W.6., 17 October 1959* (London, 1959) (cyclostyled; BL copy 2702.ct.2.). See also John Dreyfus (ed.), *Typographical partnership. Ten Letters between Bruce Rogers and Emery Walker 1907-1931* (Cambridge, 1971), pp. vii-x.

In view of Emery Walker's immense experience with a variety of reprographic techniques (which in itself is sufficient to discredit Virmond's theory that preparation of the *Eulenspiegel* facsimile involved anything as crude as tracing) one must assume that it was not so much the quality of the plates themselves as Walker's opinion of the quality of the sixteenth-century original that dictated that some retouching should be carried out. John Dreyfus has suggested that such interference is 'quite in character' with Walker, especially given that he 'had the photographic and retouching resources within his own companies to carry out such work'; furthermore, he considers it 'probable that Walker directed an employee of his named Percy Tiffin to retouch photographic enlargements of the 1515 Strasbourg edition of *Till Eulenspiegel* in preparing the 1911 Insel Verlag edition'.[35] It is known that in preparing a roman type for the Doves Press, based on Jenson's 1476 Venice edition of Pliny's *Historia Naturalis*, Walker had his draughtsman Tiffin retouch the photographic enlargements because, by modern standards, the book looked over-inked and thus gave an imperfect impression of the type.[36]

When the extent of the retouching in the *Eulenspiegel* edition is recognised, one can only assume that Edward Schröder was never consulted about the matter, for it is inconceivable that such a discerning scholar could ever have condoned the procedure to which the *Eulenspiegel* photographs were subjected, let alone have claimed, as his does in his 'Geleitwort', that the sixteenth-century original had been reproduced 'with a degree of fidelity unique even in this age which so delights in facsimiles'.[37] Schröder never saw the original, but he did see the book in proof because, in a letter to Kippenberg written on 1 August

For a recent assessment of the role of Kessler in the German cultural revival around the turn of the century see Hildegard Nabbe, 'Mäzenatentum und elitäre Kunst. Harry Graf Kessler als Schlüsselfigur für eine kulturelle Erneuerung um die Jahrhundertwende', *Deutsche Vierteljahrsschrift für Literaturwissenschaft und Geistesgeschichte*, 64 (1990), 652-79; and also L. M. Newman (ed.), *The Correspondence of Edward Gordon Craig and Count Harry Kessler 1903-1937* (London, 1995). On the history of the Insel-Verlag see Bernhard Zeller, *Die Insel. Eine Ausstellung zur Geschichte des Verlages unter Anton und Katharina Kippenberg* (Marbach, 1965) (Sonderausstellungen des Schiller-Nationalmuseums, Katalog Nr. 15).

35 Thus John Dreyfus in a personal communication to me on 27 November 1993. Whether there is anything bearing on this in Walker's papers, which have now been deposited with Cheltenham Art Gallery and Museums, I have not yet ascertained.

36 See John Dreyfus, *Italic Quartet. A Record of the Collaboration between Harry Kessler, Edward Johnston, Emery Walker and Edward Prince in Making the Cranach Press Italic* (Cambridge, 1966), p. 7.

37 'Die Ausgabe, die wir hier bringen und die ein Werk des frühen 16. Jahrhunderts mit einer Treue, bis in das Papier hinein, reproduziert, die auch in unserem faksimilefreudigen Zeitalter einzig dasteht, tritt doch ohne den Anspruch ans Licht, Laien und Gelehrte dem alten Original näher zu bringen, als es nun einmal möglich ist' (p. 3). It is of course possible that Schröder was too preoccupied with other concerns at the time – in 1911 he was offered (but turned down) a chair at Bonn (Trier, p. 108) – but he was generally extremely conscientious (Trier, p. 114f.). On his other scholarly output at this time see Trier, p. 128. Dr Cyril Edwards has very kindly brought to my attention an interesting nineteenth-century defence of the practice of retouching, in a review by J. Kelle in *Heidelberger Jahrbücher der Literatur*, 53, 2 (1860), no. 6, pp. 81-91, here pp. 81-2.

1910, he exclaims 'Die Clichés des Eulenspiegel von 1515 sind weit schöner als die Originale des Drucks von 1519'.[38] His role consisted, as we have seen, solely in writing the introduction, and this is in essence a survey of all the early editions of *Eulenspiegel* and a discussion of problems relating to its genesis, all of which Schröder could easily have written without ever seeing the British Museum's original. Without any opportunity to observe the differences, it is no surprise that, when discussing S 1515, he can say the facsimile 'reproduces Grüninger's book so faithfully (apart from the quiring which is very irregular in the original, as can be seen from the page signatures anyway) that no further description is necessary' (p. 5). He simply thanks the British Museum for its very willing assistance, and goes on to mention merely that the *Eulenspiegel* and Murner's *Schelmenzunft* had been rebound in 1883, a fact referred to already by Knust.

Retouching is – or at least was – not unusual in the preparation of facsimiles, but I know of no case where retouching was carried out to the extent that it was in this case. It seems that Emery Walker took a dislike to the type-face that Johann Grüninger had used four hundred years before and in particular to the rather stubby ascender above the bar of the lower-case *t*. To the untrained eye the lower-case *t* was somewhat difficult to distinguish from the lower-case *r*. Accordingly, the decision was taken to go over the text (whether with pen on a positive print or with a metal point on the glass negative I do not know) and to increase the height of the ascender every time a lower-case *t* occurred – which, needless to say, was very frequently indeed, seeing that *t* in German occurs with about the same frequency as *d* in English. Precisely because of the enormity of the task it is unlikely that Walker carried out the work himself; as John Dreyfus has suggested, it was probably entrusted to Tiffin or (even more likely perhaps) to another minion whose understanding of sixteenth-century German is likely to have been even less than Walker's own. While this tedious task seems to have been performed conscientiously enough,[39] there are a number of points in the text where the ascenders were touched up even where in fact an *r* is intended and conversely where there has been no retouching even though a *t* is required. This gave rise to wrong interpretation of particular words, and this has resulted in some erroneous readings and translations finding their way into modern *Eulenspiegel* scholarship, three-quarters of a century after Schröder's 'facsimile' appeared.

Fig. 1, showing the running heading and the first seven lines of fol. B6ʳ in the original and the facsimile, will serve to demonstrate various instances of the retouching. The most important detail concerns the phrase *zwen vnd zwen* 'two by two' in line 7; the retoucher has changed this to *zwen vnd zweit*, which is quite unidiomatic. Throughout the passage the ascenders of the *t* have been

38 Cited by Virmond [as note 3], p. 131. Schröder had borrowed the Gotha copy of S 1519 so that he could make a comparison.

39 There are very few pages where there is no immediately obvious evidence of retouching; among those which appear not have been tampered with are B1ʳ, B2ʳ, C1ᵛ, C4ᵛ, D1ʳ/ᵛ and D2ʳ/ᵛ. A collating machine might be able to confirm this.

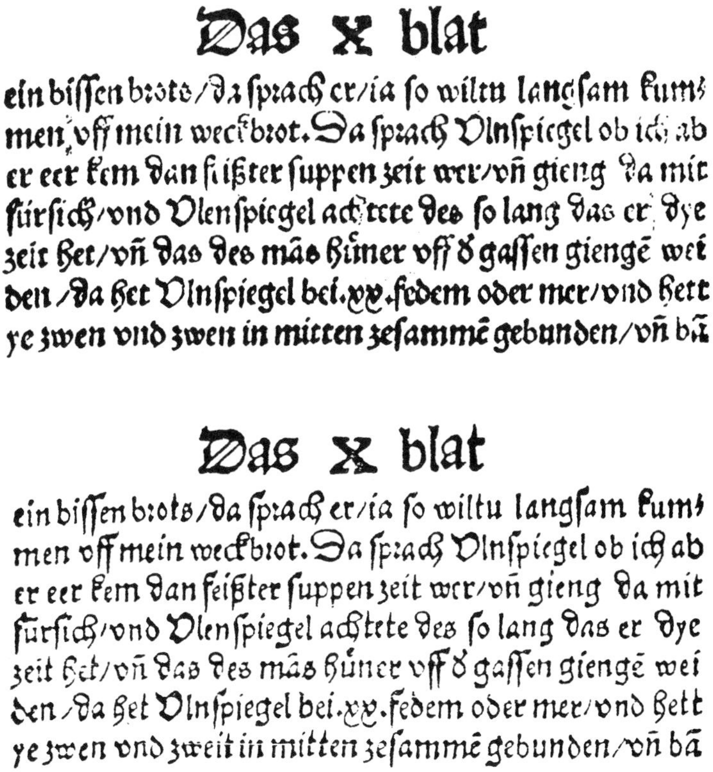

Das x blat

ein bissen brots/da sprach er/ia so wiltu langsam kum-
men vff mein weckbrot. Da sprach Vlnspiegel ob ich ab
er eer kem dan feißter suppen zeit wer/vñ gieng da mit
fürsich/vnd Vlenspiegel achtete des so lang das er dye
zeit het/vñ das des mãs hüner vff d gassen giengẽ wei
den/da het Vlnspiegel bei.xx.federn oder mer/vnd hett
ye zwen vnd zwen in mitten zesammẽ gebunden/vñ bã

Das x blat

ein bissen brots/da sprach er/ia so wiltu langsam kum-
men vff mein weckbrot. Da sprach Vlnspiegel ob ich ab
er eer kem dan feißter suppen zeit wer/vñ gieng da mit
fürsich/vnd Vlenspiegel achtete des so lang das er dye
zeit het/vñ das des mãs hüner vff d gassen giengẽ wei
den/da het Vlnspiegel bei.xx.federn oder mer/vnd hett
ye zwen vnd zweit in mitten zesammẽ gebunden/vñ bã

Fig. 1. Part of fol. B6r in the original (*top*) and the facsimile (*bottom*).

systematically lengthened, in *blat* in the running heading and in the words *brots*, *wiltu*, *weckbrot*, *feißter*, *zeit*, *mit*, *achtete*, *zeit*, *het*, *het*, *hett*, *mitten*. Elsewhere the retoucher has simply 'improved' the shape of a letter, notably by adding an upward curl to the tops of *f*, and long *s*, and *ß* in most cases: examples include *bissen*, *langsam*, *vff*, *feißter*, *fürsich*, *so*, *vff*, *Vlnspiegel*, and *federn*. One could add hundreds of similar examples from other pages.

Fig. 2, taken from fol. a2r, illustrates a particularly grotesque example of the retoucher's lack of understanding. In the original, the word *durchlüchtigen* 'illustrious' has had to be divided at the end of the line 1. Since this happens to be the first line in chapter 88 it was set in display type, so that the retoucher needed to increase the height of the ascender on the *t* by about two millimetres, producing the nonsensical *dut=* | *chlüchtigẽ*. On the same page, line 13, in S 1515 an *e* has fallen out in *der*; the retoucher did not notice or understand this, so the 'facsimile' still reads *d r*.

Das CXXII blat
V F ein zeit hieltē die dur/
chl' chtigē vñ hochgebornen fürsten von
Brunschwick ein rennē vñ stechē vñ tor/
nieren/ mit vil frembdē fürsten vñ herrē
ritter vñ knechtē/ in ꝺ stat zů Einbeck/ vñ mit irē hinꝺ
sassen. Nun wz es in ꝺē sumer/ das die pflomē vñ anꝺ

Das CXXII blat
V F ein zeit hieltē die dut/
chlüchtigē vñ hochgebornen fürsten von
Brunschwick ein rennē vñ stechē vñ tor/
nieren/ mit vil frembdē fürsten vñ herrē
ritter vñ knechtē/ in ꝺ stat zů Einbeck/ vñ mit irē hinꝺ
sassen. Nun wz es in ꝺē sumer/ das die pflomē vñ anꝺ

Fig. 2. Part of fol. a2^r in the original (*top*) and the facsimile (*bottom*).

There are numerous points where the retoucher's intervention has resulted in falsification of the actual reading of the text, and in some cases these false readings have found their way into modern standard editions like Lindow's. Examples include:[40]

fol./line[41]	S 1515	Schröder	Lindow
A2^r 25	*fabulieren*	*fabulleren*	**fabulleren* (p. 7)
B6^r 7	*zwen vnd zwen*	*zwen vnd zweit*	**zwen und zweit* (p. 26)
B6^r 15	*grősse*	*grosse*	**Grosse* (p. 26)
E2^v 18	*guldī*	*guldl*	**Guld* (p. 53)
G1^r 13	*mit*	*nut*	*mit* (p. 74)
G1^r 16	*rüpf* [= *rumpf*]	*rüpt*	**Rüpt* (p. 74)[42]
H5^r 8	*warheit*	*watheit*	*warheit* (p. 89)

40 For further examples see Virmond [as note 3], pp. 132–33. His promise (p. 133) to publish an even fuller list in the journal *Daphnis* appears not to have borne fruit.

41 In counting the line numbers I have excluded the running headings.

42 Lindow even has a footnote saying that *Rüpt* = *Rumpf*!

J4^{r} 20	*tusent*	*insent*	*tusent* (p. 104)
J4^{r} 20	*er v'koufft*	*et bkoufft*	*Er verkouft* (p. 104)
J4^{r} 20	*beer*	*beet*	*beer* (p. 104)
K1^{r} 2	*werckt*	*wetckt*	*werckt* (p. 105)
L6^{r} 1	*vff stād*	*vff stad*	**uffstad* (p. 121)
N7^{v} 7	*auch*	*anch*	*auch* (p. 147)
N7^{v} 9	*hōd*	*höd*	**höd* (p. 147)
O2^{v} 23	*hůschdet*	*huschdet*	**huschdet* (p. 153)
Q6^{v} 9/10	*ver | kydelt*	*ver | kydeit*	**verkidet* (p. 176)
Q7^{v} 5	*mēglichem*	*meglichem*	*menglichem* (p. 178)
a2^{r} 26	*schalck (der*	*schalck der*	**schalck, der* (p. 252)
a3^{v} 1	*gebůt*	*gedůt*	*gebüt* (p. 254)
b2^{r} 1	*zenen*	*zonen*	**Zanen* (p. 258)
b2^{r} 3	*ir*	*it*	*ihr* (p. 259)
b2^{r} 8	*negtē*	*negei*	**näget* (p. 259)
b2^{r} 15	*darīd'*	*darid*	*darin der* (p. 260)
b2^{r} 17	*personē*	*persone*	**Persone* (p. 260)
b2^{r} 25	*dem pfaffen*	*dein pfaffen*	*dem Pfaffen* (p. 260)
b5^{r} 7	*vigili*	*vigilt*	**Vigilt* (p. 265)
b5^{v} 4	*lag / da*	*lag da*	*lag, da* (p. 266)
b5^{v} 5	*beiden*	*beider*	*beiden* (p. 266)
b5^{v} 6	*vnnd*	*vund*	*unnd* (p. 266)
b5^{v} 14	*in den klowen het*	*in den Howen hei*[43]	**in den Clowen het* (p. 266)
b5^{v} 19	*Epithaphium*	*EpithapCium*[44]	*Epitaphium* (p. 267, line 2)
b6^{r} 4	*Johañes. Grieninger*	*Johañes, Grieninger*	*Johannes Grieninger*
b6^{r} 5	*Adolffs*	*Adolffo*	**Adolffo* (p. 267)

The asterisk before the reading from Lindow indicates those cases where he has been led astray by Schröder's facsimile. In the other cases he has used his editorial judgement to restore the correct reading. He would seem not to have consulted Knust's edition where all these passages have been correctly transcribed. To be sure, most of these points are trivial in the extreme, but nevertheless there can be no denying that the Insel 'facsimile' falsifies the text and gives a misleading impression of the British Library's original.

It might have made some kind of sense if the retoucher had interfered where there are obvious errors in S 1515. On E3^{r} line 23, for example, S 1515 reads *spiralmeister* (for *spitalmeister*), yet this has not been corrected in the facsimile. There are very many other misprints and blemishes in the original which have escaped the retoucher's attention.

Even the ornamental initial H on fol. V4^{v} has been retouched (fig. 3): it is barely recognizable as the same worn initial found in the original. The face below the bar and the wings to the left and right are quite different, and even the

43 *Howen* is perhaps the most readily observable example of retouching: the *H* has almost the thin appearance of a roman *H* instead of Grüninger's thick gothic.

44 Or *Epithaplium*. In S 1515 the second *h* is badly inked.

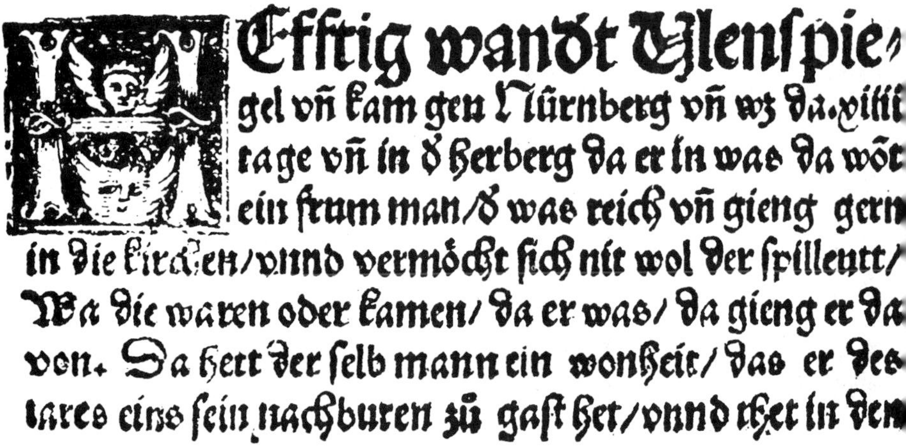

HEfftig wandt Ulenspie-
gel vñ kam gen Nürnberg vñ wz da.xiiii
tage vñ in d' herberg da er in was da wōt
ein frum man/d' was reich vñ gieng gern
in die kirchen/vnnd vermöcht sich nit wol der spilleutt/
Wa die waren oder kamen/ da er was/ da gieng er davon. Da hett der selb mann ein wonheit/ das er des
iares eins sein nachburen zů gast het/vnnd thet in den

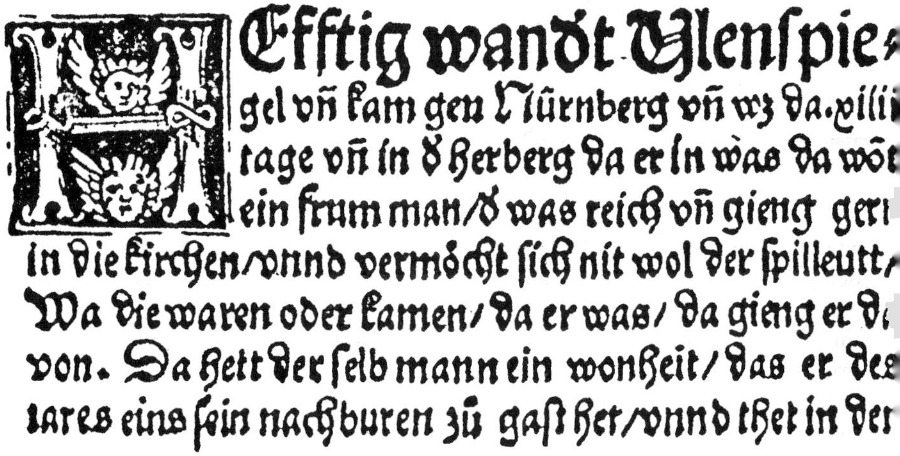

HEfftig wandt Ulenspie-
gel vñ kam gen Nürnberg vñ wz da.xiiii
tage vñ in d' herberg da er in was da wōt
ein frum man/d' was reich vñ gieng gern
in die kirchen/vnnd vermöcht sich nit wol der spilleutt/
Wa die waren oder kamen/ da er was/ da gieng er davon. Da hett der selb mann ein wonheit/ das er des
iares eins sein nachburen zů gast het/vnnd thet in den

Fig. 3. Initial H (enlarged) on fol. V4^{v} in the original (*top*) and the facsimile (*bottom*).

figure-of-eight knots on each of the uprights look different from those in the original.

As for the illustrations themselves, a number of them have been retouched, but not in any really significant way. Sometimes in S 1515 the black border around the woodcuts is incomplete, whether through damage to the block or through bad inking, and in several cases these defects have been repaired by retouching in the facsimile (e.g. on fols A4^{r}, B2^{r}, L5^{r}, R4^{v} and S2^{v}). Very few of the woodcuts fill the full width of the type-area of the page; generally, instead of

Fig. 4. Part of the woodcut on fol. N5v in the original (*left*) and the facsimile (*right*).

an oblong picture, a square block has been used, the remainder of the type-area being filled with a side-piece showing either some buildings or, occasionally, a human figure.[45] On one of the blocks showing houses, which was used some thirty-seven times (a fact which itself can tell us a great deal about Grüninger's printing procedures), a window in one of the houses is badly drawn; the retoucher has improved it on fourteen occasions, leaving it untouched on twenty-three other pages.[46] On fol. N5v the retoucher has repaired the defective window, the one on the extreme right on the lower row in fig. 4, while for some obscure reason removing the shading from the roof above it.

The Insel Verlag's facsimile, and its derivative produced by Werner Wunderlich, are deficient, indeed seriously misleading in respect of the text. The sooner they are replaced by a new facsimile of the British Library's original the better.

45 This composite use of pictures is a prominent feature of early-sixteenth-century Strasbourg books.

46 It has been improved on fols B3v, E4v, F4v, H5r, J1v, K2r, N2r, N5v, N6v, O2r, T7r, V1r, Z3r, b4v, and left untouched on fols. C2r, E3v, F7v, F8r, G2r, H1v, J2v, L3v, L5r, L7r, L8r, M4v, P3r, P4r, Q4r, Q5r, Q7r, R3v, T2r, V3r, Y2v, Z1r, and a3r.

NEW LIGHT ON THE PRESSES OF ADAM DYON AND KASPAR LIBISCH IN BRESLAU (1518-1540)

HELMUT CLAUS

IN THE MID-SIXTIES, as he was nearing the end of his work on his *Lutherbibliographie*,[1] Josef Benzing sent me a number of photocopies of rare Luther editions which he had received from the British Museum. He was busy trying to identify the printers, and he sought to enlist my opinion. Among them was what is still the only known copy of the octavo edition of the *Historie oder wahrhaftige Geschichte des Leidens und Sterbens Leonhard Keysers* (1527), an account of the martyrdom of Leonhard Käser with a letter by Luther which was printed several times.[2] Having only a fairly modest collection of material on the history of printing in the Reformation period available to me, my many attempts to identify the printer failed. Yet the book is decorated with a title-page border made up of various ornamental woodcut strips which, together with the types used, should generally offer a good prospect of identifying the printer. There was nothing for it but to make a systematic examination of all the descriptions of woodcut material known to me, of the kind provided by Arrey von Dommer in his admirable catalogue of Luther editions in Hamburg and by those who had adopted his methods.[3] This search eventually led to success in that at least I found one of the four ornamental strips used in Heyer's descriptions of Luther editions in the Stadtbibliothek at Breslau.[4] This clue suggested that the book was an imprint of Adam Dyon in Breslau, and the types confirmed this. Heyer's catalogue covers only the period up to and including 1523, but nevertheless, as this example shows, in his descriptions of ornaments he has provided us with an invaluable aid to the identification of later editions too. These descriptions of book ornaments are especially valuable for identifying the extremely rare early Breslau editions of Reformation tracts. Comparable in this respect with the

1 Josef Benzing/Helmut Claus, *Lutherbibliographie*. 2 vols (Baden-Baden, 1989-94).

2 BL pressmark 1370.a.26.; *Ger STC* 470; Benzing/Claus 2452. Adolf Laube *et al.* (eds), *Flugschriften vom Bauernkrieg zum Täuferreich (1526-1535)*. Vol. II (Berlin, 1992), p. 1509ff.

3 A. von Dommer, *Lutherdrucke auf der Hamburger Stadtbibliothek 1516-1523* (Leipzig, 1888).

4 Alfons Heyer, 'Lutherdrucke auf der Breslauer Stadtbibliothek, 1516-1523', *Zentralblatt für Bibliothekswesen*, 9 (1892), 21-29; 267-274; 403-416; 459-483. The strip in question is Heyer's Orn. 48.5. See fig. 1, vertical strip on the left = strip 4.5 in my inventory.

Königsberg imprints of Hans Weinreich, the Breslau imprints of the early Reformation period seem to have percolated westwards only in very few copies, and outside Silesia itself they may today be accounted among the greatest rarities in even the largest collections. This is confirmed by a search of *VD 16*, in which descriptions of books printed by Adam Dyon especially, which are our particular concern in the present context, have been taken over from secondary sources in the overwhelming majority of cases.

Naturally enough, not all Breslau imprints of the Reformation period have survived even in Silesia, as is evident from a comparison of Heyer's checklist of the Luther editions in the Breslau Stadtbibliothek with Benzing's *Lutherbibliographie*. And yet the holdings of the old Breslau library survived the horrors of the Second World War relatively unscathed, while Breslau University Library, founded only in the nineteenth century and whose older stock came largely from the collections of the library of the former University of Frankfurt an der Oder, unfortunately suffered immense losses during the War. As a result of a policy of centralizing valuable Silesian library collections on what is now the Biblioteka Uniwersytecka in Wrocław we still – or rather, after many decades, once again – have a collection of Breslau Reformation editions which has no equal anywhere else.

It was relatively soon after the Second World War that scholars began to turn their attention once again to the history of printing in the city. As early as 1961 Marta Burbianka published a study of Adam Dyon and Kaspar Libisch as well as one on Andreas Winkler, the Scharffenbergs and the Baumanns and their heirs.[5] The starting-point and focus for these studies were of course the Breslau holdings themselves, whereas collections outside Poland were hardly taken into account. Thus her checklist of books by Dyon and Libisch does not cover the British Library's holdings, though of course the *German STC*, which has long since become a standard work and whose value has meantime been enhanced by the appearance of David Paisey's 1990 supplement, did not come out until a year after Burbianka's work on Dyon and Libisch. It is well recognized that one of the advantages of these short-title catalogues is that the books are indexed by printers and publishers so that one can quickly access the information one needs for research of this kind.

But when one looks closer, one sees that even the British Library's holdings, excellent though they are, are not very helpful when it comes to Breslau imprints of the Reformation period. Proctor, whose *Index* of course covers only the period up to 1520, recorded only one item by Dyon, his 1519 edition of Luther's *Sermon von Ablaß und Gnade* (Benzing/Claus 108); but even the printers' index in the *German STC* records only four Dyon items from the years 1519 to 1530

5 Marta Burbianka, 'Adam Dyon i Kaspar Lybisch – wrocławscy drukarze reformacyjni,' *Roczniki biblioteczne* 5 (1961), 65-113; 'Andrzej Winkler – drukarz wrocławski XVI wieku', *Roczniki biblioteczne*, 4 (1960), 329-445 and plates; also her *Produkcja typograficzna Scharffenbergów we Wrocławiu* (Wrocław, 1968); and *Z dziejów drukarstwa śląskiego w XVII wieku. Baumannowie i ich spadkobiercy. Do druku przygotowała Helena Szwejkowska* (Wrocław, 1977).

while for Libisch at least there are eight from the years 1523 and 1524. Even today we can add only Dyon's 1519 reprint of Eisermann's *Encomium* (BL pressmark 3906.i.28 (1). *Ger STC*, p. 647; no. 3 in our checklist) and Luther's *Histori oder das warhafftig geschicht des leydens vnd sterbens Lienhart Keysers* of 1527 (Benzing/Claus 2452) (see fig. 1) which has already been mentioned.

Having once become interested in Dyon as a result of this complex process of trying to identify the books Benzing had brought to my attention and having initially relied on Heyer and Burbianka, I have ever since been on the lookout for further imprints of Dyon in particular; scarcer and more varied in their subject matter, the products of his press are more interesting from the point of view of cultural history than those of Libisch who was his rival for a time. Our knowledge of Breslau printing in the Reformation period was considerably enriched in 1967 when the renowned Luther scholar Hans Volz produced his study of the subject.[6] With his unique blend of learning and meticulousness he had brought together everything that could be found from widely scattered sources and offered a fresh picture that set new standards. The following year I had my first opportunity to work in the University Library at Wrocław for a few days and to examine its holdings for Breslau Reformation imprints. I was not disappointed in what I found.

Since then another quarter of a century has elapsed. In the interim many new studies and checklists relating to sixteenth-century printing have been published, and with the publication of *VD 16* a good start has been made on establishing a comprehensive bibliographical record of sixteenth-century printing in the German-speaking countries. Building on the work of Heyer, Burbianka, and Volz, I welcome this opportunity to report on the present state of our knowledge about the press of Dyon and his successor.

Let me first draw attention to Frieder Schanze's work on Dyon's early activities in the imperial city of Nuremberg. Schanze adds a number of books and, in particular, several broadsides to our sparse information about Dyon's work there. Moreover, he is able to show that a type used by Johann Weissenburger from his early days in Nuremberg passed from him to Dyon in 1509.[7] This change of ownership marks not only the starting point of Dyon's

6 Hans Volz, 'Die Breslauer Luther- und Reformationsdrucker Adam Dyon und Kaspar Libisch', *GJ*, 42 (1967), 104-117. The entry *Vom rechten, wahren, lebendigen und tätigen Glauben ... durch Bruder Kaspar den Blinden von Breslau, itzund Prediger zu Wohlau*, listed by Volz in the addendum on p. 117, is incorrect: it was not in the Ratsschulbibliothek Zwickau but in the Landesbibliothek in Dresden (see Clemen, *Kleine Schriften*, vol. 7, p. 467f., note 2) but has been lost since the Second World War.

7 Frieder Schanze, 'Einblattdrucke von Hans Hochspringer d.J., Jakob Köbel und Adam Dyon', *GJ*, 59 (1984), 151-56. See also Frieder Schanze (ed.), *Jörg Dürnhofers Liederbuch (um 1515). Faksimile des Lieddruck-Sammelbandes Inc. 1446a der Universitätsbibliothek Erlangen* (Tübingen, 1993), nos. 32 and 42. Schanze's observations concerning this Schwabacher text type used by Weissenburger can be supplemented with *Practica teutsch des kunfftigen Jars M.CCCCC. vñ xiij. ... durch meyster Endres vō Weinmer ...* [Nürnberg: Dyon 1512] 4° – Zinner 981. Alexander Seitz, *Sämtliche Schriften*, II (Berlin and New York, 1975), p. 438, no. 5 (copy in Coburg Landesbibliothek).

work but tellingly demonstrates how this new printer had firm roots in the surrounding typographical climate of Franconia, to which he remained indebted even during his years in Breslau.

Dyon's move to Silesia took place in stages from 1518 onwards, and even after that he probably spent several periods in Nuremberg, and not only in 1524 when he is recorded as having been imprisoned for printing one particular book.[8] But otherwise details of his life have hitherto been difficult to come by, and there is now little prospect of further discoveries being made seeing that the Breslau archives were destroyed during the Second World War. Thus he shares the same fate as many of his fellow printers whose work and achievements have mainly to be extrapolated from examination of the products of their presses.

In Breslau Dyon used just three types for all but very few of his books. There was a Schwabacher text type, a display type of medium size, and a large display type used mostly for the first line of a title. This curious monotony makes his books relatively easy to recognize. The type that Dyon had obtained from Weissenburger in Nuremberg (which Schanze, following Proctor, calls type 6) seems not to have been used again in Silesia. This is also true of the medium-sized display type (Proctor's type 1, p. 103) and the larger Schwabacher text type (Proctor's type 2). Accordingly Proctor's notes on p. 114 on the type for no. 11212 (= Benzing/Claus 108, Burbianka 7) stand in need of correction: instead of 'Types 1, 2, 3' we should now read 'Types 3, 4, 5'.

Summary of types

Type 3 (after Proctor)

Large display type. Canon type of the Upper Rhenish-Franconian kind (M^{66}), which Proctor inappropriately described as being of the 'Erfurt-Leipzig style'. For fifteenth-century examples see *VGT* 891 (Basle: Johann Amerbach) and 935 (Nuremberg: Anton Koberger). It is found in 1523 in line 1 of Libisch's *Schutzrede des Rates der Stadt Breslau* (Weller 2682; Burbianka: Libisch 15; Volz 115.17; *Ger STC*, p. 152; *VD 16* B8006). As so few letters occur, it is difficult to decide whether we may assume that Dyon was the source, which might seem plausible given that the type is rare. In central Germany it was used by Johannes Loersfeld after 1525, towards the end of his period in Erfurt.

Reproductions: figs. 1, 3, 4, 6 (line 1 in each case); Alfred Götze, *Die hochdeutschen Drucker der Reformationszeit* (Strasbourg, 1905), pl. 21, line 4.

Type 4 (after Proctor)

Medium-size display type (M^{29}): 20 lines = 136 mm. The double hyphen is regularly inverted. The comma is either small and then mostly inverted too, or larger and then correctly used.

Reproductions: figs. 1 (line 2), 2 (line 1), 3 (line 2), 4 (lines 2ff.), 5 (line 1), 6 (line 2); Götze, pl. 21, lines 5-7.

8 Volz, p. 105 and note 5. Hans-Otto Keunecke, 'Jobst Gutknecht, der Drucker des Nürnberger Rates', *GJ*, 62 (1987), 146-57, here p. 147 and note 7; see also the survey by Günter Elze, 'Von Druckern, Verlegern und Buchhändlern in Breslau', *Buchhandelsgeschichte* 1993/3. p. B 83.

Histori oder
das warhafftig geschicht/
des leydens vnd sterbens Lienhart
Keysers seligen / etwa Pfarrer zu
Weytzenkirchen / võ des heyligen
Euangelij vnd Götlicher war-
heyt wegen zu Passaw verur-
teylt / vnnd zu Scherding In
Bayern verbrãdt / am Frey
tag nach Laurentij /
im jar M. D.
xxvij.

Fig. 1. Title-page of Benzing/Claus 2452, [Breslau: Dyon 1527.] 8°.

G'Nedigeste, gnedige vnnd gün-
stigen herrē Ewer Churfürstlichen: Fürstlichen
vnd andern gnaden: vnd gunsten sey mein vn-
dertheniig dinst vnd gebet alzeit beuor Gnedi-
geste: gnedige: vnd gūstigen hern: nach dē die Ro. Kay. M.
mich auff yr freisicher vñ starck geleit gen Wuormbs berüffen
vō mir zu erkundigūg meyner bücher halbē die in meinē namē
außgegangen zuentpfahē: byn ich vndertenigster Cappellan
für Kay. May. vñ den Stenden des Reichs in gehorsam er-
schinnē. Also hat mir der K. M. erstlich lassen fürhaltē anzu-
zeigen: ob ich mich zů berüerten püchern bekenne: vñ die sel
ben widerrüffen: od dar auff beharrē wolte. Hab ich nach vn-
derthenigē bekātnuß der bücher: so vō mir gemacht vñ durch
meine mißgünstige oder in ādre wege nit verkert: vñ zu nachteil
verandert: mich vndertheniclich vernemē lassen weil meie
schriften mit dem klaren vnd lautern wort gotes bekrefftiget
seind: ist mir auff dz hochst beschwerlich: vnpillich: vñ vnmüg
lich gottes wort zu verlaugnē: vñ solche meine bücher der maß
zu widerruffen: vnd in diemut gepettē Kay. May: wolt mich
zu sollichem widerspruch in keinen weg lassen dringen: besund
mein schrifften vñ bücher durch sich sebst oder andre: auch dy
wenigesten so es vermügen beschrigē: vñ die yrtung so dar in
nen sein sollen durch gotlich Euangelisch vnnd Prophetische
schrifften zu erweisen: mit Christenlichē erpietten so ich vberwey-
set würd: das ich sol geyrret habē: wolte ich alle yrthumb wid
rüffen: vñ der erst sein: der meine bücher in das feür wolt wer
ffen: vnd mit den füessen dar auff tretten: Darauff vō mir be-
gert ist: ich wolt eyn kürtze vñ richtige antwort gebē: Ob ich
wolt widerruffen: oder auff meynē furnemē bleyben. Der hal
ben aber mals Kayserlicher Maiestat: vnd C. F. G. vndthe-
nicklich geantwort. Die weil mein gewissen durch die goet-
liche geschrifft: so ich in meinen püchern füregefangen vñ begriffen sey: so müg ich in keinē weg one weysung durch die hei
lige gotliche geschrifft etwas widerruffen. Also haben volgēt
etlich Churfursten Fursten: vnd etlich auß den Stenden des

A ij

Fig. 2. First page of the text (fol. A2r) of no. 12.

Die bekent=
nus Martini Luthers/
auff den yzigen angestelten
Reichstag zu Augspurg einzu-
legen In Sibenzehen Ar-
tickel verfasset.

Im. XXX. Jar.

Fig. 3. Title-page of Benzing/Claus 2858, Breslau: Adam Dyon 1530. 4°, with title border 2.

Deuttung der czwo
grewlichen Figuren Bapstesels czu
Rom und Munchkalbs czu Freyberg ynn Meysszen funden.

Philippus Melanchthon.
D. Martinus Luther.

wittemberg
M.D.xxiij.

Fig. 4. Title-page of no. 18.

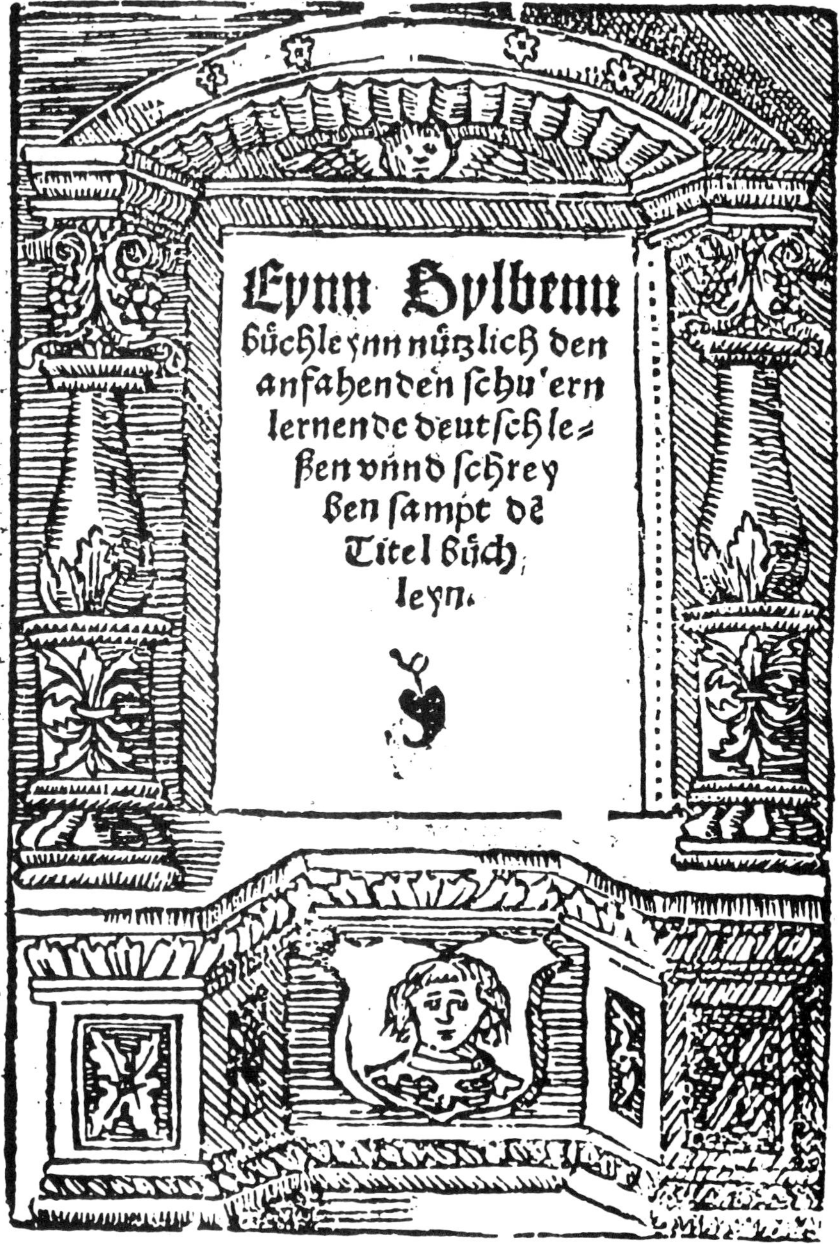

Eynn Sylbenn
büchleynn nützlich den
anfahenden ſchu'ern
lernende deutſch le=
ßen vnnd ſchrey
ben ſampt de
Titel büch
leyn.

Fig. 5. Title -page of no. 30 with title border 3.

Keyserlicher Maies-
tat eroberung des Konigreychs Tunisi/
wie die vergangener tag vonn Rom / Neapls /
vnd Venedig / ken Augspurg gelangt hat /
vnd von Genua den xij. Augusti
hieher geschriben ist.

Gedruckt in der Kóniglichen stat Breslaw
den xxviij. Augusti. 1535.

Fig. 6. Title-page of CHRISTOPH SCHEURL, *Keyserlicher Majestat eroberung des Konigreychs Tunisi* (Breslau, 28.8.1535). See p. 74, A.

Type 5 (after Proctor)
Schwabacher text type (M^{81}): 20 lines = 88/89 mm. Proctor Type 5. In the Latin books around 1520 we find a colon falling slightly below the line instead of a virgula; in the German books the virgula is small and shallow until 1523, *b* occurs with and without a loop, and ꞵ alternates with *ß*; after 1524 the virgula is large and steep, *b* has a loop, and ꞵ has been ousted by *ß*; from 1527 a number of looped forms occur as alternatives to the normal shapes (*l*; *h* in the combination *ch*, with no ligature in these cases) but these disappear after 1530. There is a bold rubrum ¶, sometimes replaced by a hand-symbol. In some books from 1526 onwards the rubrum sometimes has an x-shaped cross reversed out in white in the black loop, a feature I have not encountered elsewhere (cf. the signed book listed by Burbianka, Dyon 29, of 20 April 1526, fols a4ʳ, line 11; b1ʳ, line 22; c1ʳ, line 16).

Reproductions: figs. 1 (lines 3ff.), 3 (lines 3ff.), 5 (lines 2ff.); Götze, pl. 21, lines 1-3; 8.

Type 7
Rotunda text type (M^{88}): 20 lines = 86 mm. Cf. Proctor's survey of types, p. 198, no. vii: 'Basel-Nürnberg text', variant 1 and fig. 36. Proctor does not list it as being used by Dyon, and so far I have found it only in books printed in 1521: as text-type in nos 12 and 13 in my checklist; it is also used for marginal notes in a book by Luther (Benzing/Claus 825 = Burbianka, Dyon 13 (Wrocław BU 461757).

Reproduction: fig. 2 (lines 2ff.).

These types are frequently used in combination with smaller and larger lombard initials and occasionally with chancery initials. For decorative purposes Dyon uses a small number of ornamental blocks and woodcuts, some of which Heyer has described but which, for reasons of space, we cannot discuss here.

Title borders
(a) Complete frames

1. Quarto border with recumbent lions: 166 × 124 mm (text area 66 × 65 mm). Attested 1524-1529
   Reproductions e.g. Johannes Luther, *Die Titeleinfassungen der Reformationszeit.* Mit Verbesserungen und Ergänzungen von Josef Benzing, Helmut Claus und Martin von Hase, (Hildesheim and New York, 1973), pl. 13b; Burbianka, fig. 2.
2. Quarto border, portal with columns and the monogram PV (VP?) in a wreathed shield at the top: 153 × 107 mm (text area 65 × 77 mm). In all known occurrences already cut up into four segments. Attested 1530 (Benzing/Claus 2784 and 2858).
   Reproduction: fig. 3.
3. Octavo border, portal with columns, with an angel's head in the tympanon and St John's head in the shield at the foot: 129 × 88 mm (text area 60 × 45 mm). Attested 1528.
   Reproduction: fig. 5.
4. Octavo border with chubby-cheeked *putti*: 130 × 89 mm (text area 65 × 48 mm). Attested 1529.
   Reproduction: Burbianka, fig. 3.

(b) Single decorative strips

1. With branches, flowers and double-headed bird = Heyer, Orn. 48.1.

2. With bearded man with turban = Heyer, Orn. 48.2.
3. With Virgin and child = Heyer, Orn. 48.3.
4. With three naked boys = Heyer, Orn. 48.4.
   Reproductions of 1-4 in Burbianka, fig. 1.
5. With tendril, squirrel and bird = Heyer, Orn. 48.5.
6. Branches with no other decorative elements. Reproduced in Annerose Klammt, *Flugschriften aus der Reformationszeit (1517-1550) im Bestand der Oberlausitzischen Bibliothek der Wissenschaften zu Görlitz* (Görlitz, 1983), frontispiece, top strip.
7. *ditto*. Reproduced in Klammt, *ibid.*, left-hand vertical strip.
8. *ditto*. Reproduced in Klammt, *ibid.*, right-hand vertical strip.
9. *ditto*. Reproduced in Klammt, *ibid.*, bottom strip.
   6-9 are found in Benzing/Claus *1394a.
10. Horizontal strip with birds and bowls of plants.
11. Vertical strip with column and part of an arch pointing left.
12. Vertical strip with column and part of an arch pointing right.
   11 and 12 were presumably parts of what was originally a complete border, no occurrences of which have yet been discovered.
13. Horizontal strip with mythical creatures fighting, bearded man dressed in leaves and a young mermaid.
   10-13 are found in Benzing/Claus 1921.
14. Vertical strip with an old man and a bishop with a crook.
15. Strip with branches on black background.
   For 13-15 (together with 5) see fig. 1.

Further details worth mentioning with regard to the books which have been identified in addition to those listed by Burbianka and Volz include the fact that, in contrast to what Volz believed, Dyon's press was also active in 1523 and 1528-29 and thus right through until 1531. The great rarity of its products suggests – as in the case of Hans Dorn at Brunswick[9] – that considerable numbers of them have not survived or are still awaiting rediscovery or identification. Amongst other items printed in 1523 is the Breslau edition of Melanchthon's and Luther's *Deuttung der czwo grewlichen Figuren Bapstesels czu Rom vnd Munchkalbs czu Freyberg* (no. 18 and fig. 4), which is unknown to the Weimar edition of Luther's works. That the copy which Michael Pegg found a few years ago in the Stadt- und Universitätsbibliothek at Berne comes from Silesia is immediately evident from the fact that it has an old library stamp on the title page reading 'Doublette der Stadtbibliothek zu Breslau' ('duplicate from the City Library in Breslau').[10] To the year 1528 belong not only the fully signed and dated *Silbenbüchlein* (no. 30 and fig. 5) but also the group of Dyon's

9 See Helmut Claus, 'Hans Dorn, Erstdrucker in Braunschweig', *Basileae Rauracorum. Referate eines informellen ostwestlichen Kolloquiums. Basel und Augst 15. bis 26. April 1991* (Basle, 1991), p. 36f.

10 The Breslau edition is neither listed by Heyer nor is it to be found today in Wrocław University Library (communication of 23.9.1984). The copy in Berne would therefore seem to be unique.

reprints of pieces dealing with the so-called Pack affair.[11] In view of the fact that these booklets were often reprinted by the Catholic side throughout the Empire it would seem wrong to see in them the reason for Dyon's imprisonment by the Bishop of Posen (Poznań) for printing literature deemed undesirable in Poland.

In reconstructing the history of early printing, for which, as we have mentioned, we are largely dependent on what the books tell us about themselves, the changes brought about by the death of the owner of a press and new patterns of ownership always merit particular attention in as much as either the contours are blurred or alternatively there may be a surprising continuity in the use of typographical material. It seems that this phenomenon plays a role in Breslau in the 1530s too.

Dyon's last signed and dated book is still thought to be a broadside of 1531 (Burbianka, Dyon 37; Wrocław BU: Yn 725.1). Since one book printed in 1534 by 'Adam Dyonin' (i.e. the wife of Adam Dyon) is known (Burbianka, Dyon 38; Wrocław BU: 347299), Dyon would seem to have died between 1531 and 1534. At this time the second printer of the Reformation period in Breslau, Kaspar Libisch, was still alive. Little is known about his activities after 1524, and it seems that no signed products of his press have survived. The last book using his type and materials belongs to the first half of 1525.[12]

Nothing changed in the typographical equipment of the Dyon press up to 1534 (thus including the book signed by Dyon's wife). With the sole exception of no. 26 which will be discussed below, all the books from the press printed between 1522 and 1534 employ types 3-5. On the evidence of these three types at least one item from 1532 (no. 36) must be interposed between the books from 1531 and 1534 which were previously thought to be the last two books from Dyon's press. Very probably this appeared while Dyon was still alive. But there is a gap for 1533, which may perhaps be explained by Dyon's death in the meantime. This would mean that in 1534 the widow tried to keep the business going on her own account, as other women had done in other towns.[13] We have

11 On this see Karl Schottenloher, 'Die Druckschriften der Pack'schen Händel', *Zentralblatt für Bibliothekswesen*, 25 (1908), 206-20 and 255-59.

12 It is likely that the following item, hitherto unrecorded in the literature on Breslau printing, is another early book from Libisch's press: *Epistola ... Poggij Florentini ad Leonardû Aretinum ...* (Impressum Vratislavie. Anno M.D.XXIIII.) 4°. 6 fols (printed on the verso of the title-page, last page blank). – Stevenson I, 1960n. – Città del Vaticano BPalat: IV.29(13). The book is set throughout in Libisch's large roman, whose design is reminiscent of models from western Europe such as those used in Paris. See the reduced illustration of this type in Burbianka, illus. 9. This increases the number of Latin books printed by Libisch in the period 1523-1525 to three, a surprisingly small number as Volz (p. 113, note 34) has observed.

13 In this connexion it is worth noting that the book that Dyon's wife brought out in 1534 is a collection of sermons for the succour of people faced with illness and bereavement: *Acht nutzliche vnd fast trostliche predigten, wie sich eyn Christen, ynn kranckens vnd sterbens nöten halten sol*. The anonymous preface ('Dem Christlichen leser', fol. a2^r) is a meditation on dying and death: thus we read '... die weil sichtliche, der tod eyn gemeyne strosse ist, aller lebendige, So wollen wir vnns willig doreyn ergeben, Es mus doch, es were lange, oder kurtz gestorben seyn ...' ('... for whereas it is clear that death is a path to be taken by all living beings, let us

no information about any of Dyon's assistants in the 1520s or 1530s, but some help would have been essential for the widow's venture to succeed.

As long ago as the early nineteenth century Johann Ephraim Scheibel, who carried out a great deal of valuable work on the early history of printing in Breslau, drew attention to an important entry for 15 January 1539 in the Breslau *Libri signaturarum*. This relates to the setting up of a printing house by the learned schoolmaster Andreas Winkler late in 1538 and concerns the setting out of the responsibilities of Kaspar Libisch who was already working as a printer and the new printing house owner, Andreas Winkler. It was agreed that in future Libisch would print only books in German, leaving books in Latin for Winkler. For our purposes it is important to note that Winkler had 'willingly agreed, in consideration of the fact that the worthy Caspar Libisch has already established a press here, that he will not hinder him in its use respecting his privileges'.[14] This agreement was only in force for a short period because Libisch is reported to have died by 19 April 1540. From this Burbianka and Volz assume that, following the death of Dyon, Libisch had started printing again after a break of about ten years and, in the wake of Scheibel, they assign a number of books from the years 1535, 1536 and 1540 to him. These are:

A [SCHEURL, CHRISTOPH:] Keyserlicher Majestat eroberung des Konigreychs Tunisi ... [heraldic woodcut] Gedruckt in der Königlichen stat Breslaw den xxviij. Augusti. 1535. 4° – Scheibel, p. 13. Burbianka: Libisch 30 (no copy located). Volz, p. 116 and note 38 (mentioned). *VD 16* S 2788. – Dresden LB: Hist. Germ. B 180, 33. Wrocław BU: 537836. – See fig. 6.

B Concilium. ... Pauli des dritten ... Bulle, Der Bestimmung vnd ansaczung des heyligen Gemeynen Concilij. – n. pl. [1536]. 4° – Scheibel p. 13. Burbianka: Libisch 31. Volz p. 116 and note 30. – Wrocław BU: 358392 (with the handwritten note: 'Dißes buchlenn ist gedruckt wordenn inn Breßla denn 20 Augustho 1536').

C MOIBANUS, AMBROSIUS: Ueber den 29. Psalm. Breslaw 1536. 8° – Scheibel p. 13. Burbianka: Libisch 32 (no copy located). Volz p. 116 and note 30 (with the remark that the only recorded edition of this work is the Wittenberg one with Luther's preface [Benzing/Claus 3212]).

D Das kleglich ansuchen des ausschus der funff Niderösterreichischen Lande [31.12.1539] ... – (Gedrückt zu Breßlaw, &c. 1540.) 4° – Scheibel p. 14. Burbianka: Libisch 33. Volz p. 117 and note 42 (mentioned). – Wrocław BU: 356052.

Burbianka and Volz did not examine the types used for these editions. We must therefore consider the outward appearance of items A-D and ask whether their attribution to Libisch is justified. In the case of C the question cannot be resolved anyway since no copy has been traced; it is possible that this has been confused with the Wittenberg edition.

accept it willingly, for we all have to die sooner or later ...'). One gains the impression that Dyon's widow published this book less for commercial reasons than as a memorial to her own recent experience.

14 [Johann Ephraim Scheibel,] *Geschichte der seit dreyhundert Jahren in Breslau befindlichen Stadtbuchdruckerey als ein Beitrag zur allgemeinen Geschichte der Buchdruckerkunst* (Breslau, 1804), p. 14.

Items A, B and D fall into two groups. One comprises A and B and represents continuation with Dyon's equipment in that it uses display types 3 and 4 as well as the larger lombard initials. But for the text type there is an innovation inasmuch as we find a form of the 'Wittenberg' type such as had been in regular use elsewhere since 1529 (fig. 6, lines 3ff.). The Schwabacher text type (type 5) is not found in either book. D belongs to the second group. It uses Dyon's type 3 as the larger display type. Beyond that we find a new medium-sized display type, different from the one used in no. 26, with contours reminiscent of those used in the *Theuerdank*, and a Schwabacher text type (20 lines = 93 mm; with a small, shallow comma) which is different from Dyon's type 5. There are also ornamental initials with floral elements on a hatched background of the kind which had become popular in central Germany since the 1530s.

There are a number of further books printed in 1535 and 1537 which bear similarities to features of A and B. All of them are unsigned. A second news-report on events in Tunis in 1535 has the same heraldic woodcut on the title page as A. The edition of Dietrich von Hamburg's *Von der Münsterischen Aufruhr* which was hitherto unknown to bibliographers of the Münster Ana-baptists is not dated but likewise was printed in 1535. Both books share the new 'Wittenberg' text type with the *Sinnreicher Pasquillus* of 1537. On the other hand the 1535 *Rechbüchlein* and the 1537 *Rechtmäßige Ursache*, an anonymous translation of a piece by Melanchthon, use Dyon's old Schwabacher text type and thus are no different from any of the books he printed in the 1520s.

The innovation of the A-B group consists solely in their use of a new text type, attested in books printed in 1535 and 1537. It is unlikely that Dyon or his widow introduced this new type, so that we may assume that a third person was responsible for the innovation, presumably Libisch, as people have thought since Scheibel. But in the last analysis this rests on speculation. The only certain fact is that, if Libisch had started printing in Breslau again after the death of Dyon and had not already been working for him, he did not employ the types and woodcuts he himself had used in the 1520s but instead resorted to using Dyon's equipment. The 'Wittenberg' type cannot have formed part of Libisch's old equipment either because it was not cut until after about 1525.

There are problems over assigning item D of 1540 to a printer. Even if the use of the larger display type suggests a link with Dyon and the Schwabacher represents Libisch's 1520s' type being brought back into use, we have to re-member that Andreas Winkler brought out a signed German book as early as March 1539, that is at a time when, according to the agreement between Winkler and Libisch, vernacular books should have been printed by Libisch. This book, which is not listed in Burbianka's study of Winkler, uses three types, Dyon's old medium-sized display type (type 4), the 'Wittenberg' text type as used in A, and the new *Theuerdank*-style display type found in D.[15]

15 The item in question is: Johann von Bernstein und auff Helffenstein, *Berckfreyheit* ... [woodcut]. (Bresslaw: A. Winckler, den zwelfften Martij 1539.) 4° [8] fols. – Zwickau RSB: 24.8.22(13).

Since Libisch presumably embarked on a career as an independent press-owner in 1539 it is reasonable to suppose that he purchased Dyon's types from his heirs. Whether this could have happened in 1535 at a time when printing in Breslau was being gently if progressively modernized, cannot be determined for sure. Until Libisch's legal dependence on Dyon's heirs is actually proved, it seems reasonable to regard the unsigned books from the period 1535 to 1538 which are entirely or in part printed with Dyon's types as being Kaspar Libisch's work. As there is a book in German with Winkler's impressum dated March 1539 which makes extensive use of Dyon's types but is also linked to D by virtue of its use of the new *Theuerdank*-style display type, we must assume either that Libisch was working for Winkler unofficially or possibly that already at this date Libisch was dead, with the result that Winkler's agreement with him no longer applied. In the circumstances I consider there is a stronger case for assigning the 1540 book (D) to Andreas Winkler.

In the history of printing in Breslau the 1530s represent, in quantitative terms at any rate, a period of gradual transition from early Reformation printing to one of continuous book production based not least on humanist literature of the kind advocated by Philipp Melanchthon. With the death of Libisch the old-fashioned features originally imported from Nuremberg and which had influenced Breslau printing for two decades also recede into the background.

At the end of this brief survey I append a list of those editions which were *not* included by Burbianka or Volz in their respective studies.[16]

I. Adam Dyon

1519

1. (E[2])yn auszug etlicher Practica vnd Propheceyen. Sybille. Brigitte. ... Vnnd Bruder Reinhartz ... [Woodcut illustration] – (Hans Stainberger Buchfurer von Zwicken.) [Breslau: Dyon, *c.* 1519.] 4° – Panzer DA 926e (?). *VD 16* A 4440. Köhler, *Flugschriften* 197. – Munich BSB: 4° Astr. P 510(31.
   The itinerant bookseller from Zwickau named at the end also figures in books printed by Jobst Gutknecht at Nuremberg (*GK* 8.9748) and Erhard Öglin at Augsburg (*VD 16* A 4441). He probably commissioned Gutknecht to print the book whereas the Augsburg and Breslau editions simply reprinted the name. – The full-page woodcut of a horseman on the verso of the title-page was used already by Peter Wagner in Nuremberg in 1500 (Hain 9381). For reproductions see Albert Schramm, *Der Bilderschmuck der Frühdrucke*, vol. 18 (Leipzig, 1935), pl. 69, no. 534; Ferdinand Geldner, *Die deutschen Inkunabeldrucker*, I (Stuttgart, 1968), p. 175. It is also found on fol. c4[v] in the signed book printed on 20 April 1526 (Burbianka, Dyon 29: Wrocław BU: 347831. Another copy in Olomouc SVědKn: 600.983, priv.3; see Pumprla A 452).
2. BOGENTANZ, BERNHARD: Collectanea utriusque cantus. – [Breslau:] Dyon [1519]. – RISM B VI[1], p. 159. – Wrocław BU (mislaid).
3. [EISERMANN, JOHANN:] Encomium Rubij Longipolli apud Lipsim ... [Woodcut illustration] – [Breslau: Dyon 1519.] 4° – Proctor 12003. *Ger STC* 647. Clemen,

16 For details of the bibliographical handbooks referred to see the full list in *VD 16*, vol. i.

Kleine Schriften 1.71. *VD 16* E 879. – Arnstadt K: 652(4). London BL: 3906.i.28(1); Wrocław BU: 400470 (from Brieg, see no. 5); Zwickau RSB: 19.8.32(10).

1520

4. [Prognosticatio astronomica ad annum 1521.] – (Vuratislauie: Dyon 1520.) 4° – Uppsala UB (imperf.).
5. (P)Asquillus. CJRVS PASQVJLLO. [Four distichs] (P)asquilluo [*sic!*] respondet Ciro. [Six distichs] – [Breslau: Dyon, *c.* 1520] 4° – Wrocław BU: 400451. This edition seems not previously to have been described. The edition is the fifth item in a tract volume from the former Royal Grammar School at Brieg (old pressmark: A I f 13) which in addition to Reformation pamphlets (mostly from Leipzig) and hand-written documents from about 1520, contains Burbianka's Dyon nos 2, 5 and 10 and our no. 3.
6. (S^2)Tacion d' Kyrchen czu Rome myt Aplas vnde gnode ym Aduent. – (Bresla: Dyon [*c.* 1520].) 8° – Cf. Volz, p. 108, no. 23a. *VD 16* I 181. – Darmstadt LHB: W 1663/50(2).
   In the secondary literature cited here, which is based on Benzing's record, this item is given a different title and is said to comprise 38 fols. I admit that at the end of this title there is mention of the *Stationes* which, following a woodcut on a verso, seem to begin with a kind of secondary title, but everything which precedes them (presumably 32 rather than 30 fols, collating A-D^8; the Darmstadt copy lacks fols C4-5) is undoubtedly an older, unsigned item printed by Wolfgang Stöckel in Leipzig, probably dating from about 1515, and only the part described above (8 unsigned fols) had been printed using Dyon's three known types. We must therefore be dealing with two sections printed at different times at different places, which have simply been bound together in a mechanical way. – The woodcut at the end of Stöckel's piece, a wonderfully crisp impression showing the characteristic features of the hand of Heinrich Vogtherr the Elder, was later re-used by him many times though its condition was now not so good (for instance, in 1518 in Benzing/Claus 215; *Ger STC*, p. 560 (BL pressmark: 3905.ccc.14); Dommer, *Lutherdrucke* 26, where the woodcut is described as ornament no. 29, with mention of further occurrences in 1519 and 1520).

1521

7. [Bucer, Martin:] (A)yn schoner Dialogus. Vnnd gesprech zwischen aim Pfarrer vnnd aim Schulthayß ... – [Breslau: Dyon 1521.] 4° – Halle ULB: X 5 (77 L 1001/13).
8. Das ist die warhaftige handelung die tzu Kollen ist geschehen ... – ([Breslau: Dyon] 1521.) 4° – Weller 1781. Pegg, SwissL 1884. *VD 16* D 152. – St Gallen Benedikt.
9. Erasmus, Desiderius: Verteutschte aüßlegung vber ... Nemet auff euch mein Joch ... – [Breslau: Dyon] 1521. 4° – Holeczek, *Erasmus deutsch* I.292.45. Bezzel, *Erasmusdrucke* 1225. *VD 16* E 3103. Köhler, *Flugschriften* 1033. – Nuremberg GermanNM: 8° Rl. 3510e: Eduard Schultze; Wolfenbüttel HAB: Yv 2203.8°Helmst.
10. Erasmus, Desiderius: Aüßlegung vber diese wort sanct Paulus tzu den von Corinht ... Vom gesangk. – ([Breslau: Dyon] 1521.) 4° – Holeczek, *Erasmus deutsch* I. 293.57. – Groningen UB.
11. Erasmus, Desiderius: Außlegung vber die wort Christi vnßers lieben herren

vonn den wercken der Phariseyer. ... – [Breslau: Dyon 1521.] 4° – Holeczek, *Erasmus deutsch* I. 295.70. *VD 16* E 3120. – Halle ULB: an 50 B 11/h,53; Wolfenbüttel HAB: Yv 1904.8°Helmst.

12. LUTHER, MARTIN: Copia einer Missiue ... [Breslau: Dyon 1521.] 4° – Benzing/Claus 1041. *VD 16* L 3679. – Hamburg SUB: Inc.App.A/173. – See fig. 2.

13. VULTURINUS, PANCRATIUS: Slesia Bresla. &c. Totius Slesie ... pulcherrima et singularis descriptio ... ([Breslau: Dyon] 1521.) 4° – Wrocław BU: 352857 (probably a unique copy, originally from the library of St Elisabeth's church, Breslau, from which it passed either to the municipal or the university library in Breslau).
On this work, which Vulturinus (Geier), who came from Hirschberg, wrote when he was an Augustinian in Padua in 1506 and which was edited by Michael Schwartzpeck from Neisse, a monk in the same order, see the articles by Paul Drechsler in *Zeitschrift des Vereins für Geschichte und Altertum Schlesiens*, 35 (1901), 35ff. (with a reprint of the text) and Heinrich Meuss in *Mitteilungen der Schlesischen Gesellschaft für Volkskunde*, 28 (1927), 38 ff. (with reprint of the text and German translation).

1522

14. Dialogus von der zwitrachtung des heyligen Christenlichen glaubens ... [Breslau: Dyon 1522.] 4° – Kocher-Benzing 115.(1981).117. 122.(1982).141. – Manchester RylandsUL.

15. LUTHER, MARTIN: (E)Yn Sermon ... [Title border made up from strips 6-9] – [Breslau: Dyon] 1522. 4° – Benzing/Claus *1394a. Klammt 485. *VD 16* L 6100. – Görlitz OLB: A VIII 4°79/12; Wrocław BU.

16. LUTHER, MARTIN: Ain Sermon vonn dem Hayligen Creütz ... – [Breslau: Dyon 1522.] 4° – Weller, *Suppl.* I.231. Benzing/Claus *1464a. *VD 16* L 6378. – Stuttgart LB: Theol. pt K 800.

1523

17. KETTENBACH, HEINRICH VON: Eyn Sermon ... wider die falschen Aposteln ... – [Breslau: Dyon 1523]. 4° – Clemen, *Flugschriften* II, 30.5. *VD 16* K 823. Köhler, *Flugschriften* 2031. – Berlin EKU: Refschr 1345.

18. MELANCHTHON, PHILIPP/LUTHER, MARTIN: Deuttung der czwo grewlichen Figuren Bapstesels czu Rom vnd Munchkalbs czu Freyberg ... – [Breslau: Dyon] 1523. 4° Two woodcuts in text. – Benzing/Claus *1556a. Pegg, SwissL 3966. *VD 16* L 2983. – Berne StUB: AD 230. – See fig. 4.

19. [PERINGER, DIEPOLD:] Ain schone außlegung vber das gotlich gebet. Vater vnser ... – [Breslau: Dyon 15]23. 4° – Claus, *Zwickau* 2, p. 38, no. 78. – Halle ULB: πi 662, RK.

20. TANNEFELD, HANS VON: Durch doctor Martinus Luthers ... – [Breslau: Dyon] 1523. 4° – *VD 16* T 148. – Wrocław BU: 347822.

1524

21. [PERINGER, DIEPOLD:] Ein Sermon geprediget vom Pawren zu Werdt ... [Title woodcut and title border] – [Breslau: Dyon] 1524. 4° – VD *16* P 1405. – In private ownership.

1525

22. Eynn Christlich bekentnus oder beycht auß der Heyligen schrifft getzogenn ... [Title border made up from strips 10, 5, 4, 13].- (Breslaw: Dyon 1525.) 8° – See Scheibel, p. 9, Weller 3487, Burbianka 23, Volz 107.18. Claus/Pegg *2046a =

Benzing/Claus **390/1 (with notes on contents). – Yale U. Beinecke L (with library stamp of the former Stadtbibliothek at Lauban on the title-page).

23. LUTHER, MARTIN: Von B. Henrico ynn Diedmar v'brāt ... [Title border 1] – (Breslaw: Dyon 1525.) 4° – It is unclear whether the variants *Martinus.* (*VD 16* L 7096) and *Martinus* (*VD 16* L 7095) in the title (cf. Claus/Pegg 2111) represent two separate editions.

1527

24. ALBRECHT, *Duke in Prussia*: Christliche verantwortung ... Auff Herr Ditterichs von Clee ... angemoste verunglympffung ... [Ornament] – ([Breslau: Dyon] 1527.) 8° – *VD 16* P 4783. – Wolfenbüttel HAB: 527.107 Quod. (4); Zwickau RSB: 17.8.24(13).

1528

25. ALBRECHT, *Archbishop of Mainz*: Entschuldigung ... Auff die vormeynten vnd ertichtē verbündtnus ... [Ornament] – [Breslau: Dyon 1529.] 4° – Leeds UL: 18.1.

26. GEORG, *Duke of Saxony*: (Z)Vuormergkē mit was betriglicher vnwarheit die Kinder dießer boßhafftigē welt ... sich bearbeitten ... [Breslau: Dyon] 1528. 4°. – Schottenloher, *Pack'sche Händel*, 257.44. – Berlin SB: Flugschr.1528,1cb; Dresden LB: 3 A 8286,11an.
This item is unique among books printed by Dyon. Whereas the text type (type 5, with the rubrum with the x reversed out in white; see above for discussion of this type) clearly points to Dyon, no fewer than three display types are used which are not otherwise known in his work: 1. a large type similar to the so-called *Gebetbuch* type; 2. a striking medium-sized type like the *Theuerdank* type; 3. a medium-sized thick type of the kind used in Augsburg by Hans Froschauer, Johann Schönsperger and others (cf. Proctor's survey, C.b.5: 'Froschauer style', and his fig. 27). These types were in the hands of Simprecht Froschauer who was forced to leave Nikolsburg in Moravia at the latest in the summer of 1528 and worked in Liegnitz for a short period, probably starting in August 1528. I regard this book as evidence that Froschauer's and Dyon's paths may have crossed during this difficult period for Froschauer. It may even indicate that they planned to work together in Breslau. On Froschauer in Liegnitz (1528-32) see Hans Bahlow, 'Die Anfänge des Buchdrucks zu Liegnitz', *Mitteilungen des Geschichts- und Altertums-Vereins zu Liegnitz*, 11 (1928), 1-40.

27. KONRAD, *Bishop of Würzburg*: Entschuldigung ... Vff die vermeynten vnd ertichten verbündtnus ... [Woodcut illustration] – [Breslau: Dyon 1528.] 4° – Uppsala UB.
The title-page woodcut (a bishop = Heyer, Orn. 10) is found already in 1519 in a book by Luther (Benzing/Claus 362 = Heyer 42 = Burbianka, Dyon 8).

28. KONRAD, *Bishop of Würzburg*: Entschuldigung ... Vff die vermeynten vnnd ertichten verbundnus ... [Ornament] – [Breslau: Dyon 1528.] 4° – Schottenloher, *Pack'sche Händel* 257.43. – Berlin SB: Flugschr. 1528,4a.

29. PHILIPP, *Landgrave of Hesse*: Verantwortung ... von wegen etlicher nachrede ... [Ornament] – [Breslau: Dyon 1528.] 4° – Schottenloher, *Pack'sche Händel* 257.42. *VD 16* H 2825. – Berlin SB: Flugschr. 1528,3b; Uppsala UB.

30. Eyn Sylbenbuchleynn ... [Title border 3] – (Breslaw: Dyon 1528.) 8° 2 woodcuts in the text. – Brüggemann / Bruncken I.1191.391 (erroneously states that the last leaf, rather than the last page, is blank). – Vienna NB: 46.V.21. – See fig. 5.

1529

31. Abschidt vnd beschluß des Reichstags zu Speyer. Anno M.D.xxix. gehalten. ... – [Title border 1] (Breslaw: Dyon 1529.) 4° – *GK* 1.4880. – Wrocław BU: 386721.

32. Ordenunge auffm lande. [Title border 1] – [Breslau: Dyon 1529.] 4° – Wrocław BU: 386720.
This item is wrongly entered under 1525 by Burbianka, Dyon 28, and Volz, p. 111, note 24, item b, the description having been taken over from Weller 3597 without further inspection. However, the date given within the work (fol. 2^r: 'Ordenunge Koniglicher Maiestat Stewer vnd hulffgelt Wie es auff dem lande sall gehalten werden angefangen Trinitatis. Anno 1529. ...') shows that it belongs to 1529. In the same way the *Ordnung in Städten* (Weller 3596; Burbianka 27; Volz, p. 111, note 24, item a), of which no copy has yet been traced, must also have appeared in 1529, rather than in 1525.

33. OSIANDER, ANDREAS, *the Elder* [LUTHER, MARTIN *et al.*]: Was zu Marpurgk in Hessen, vom Abendtmal ... vergleicht sey worden. – [Breslau: Dyon 1529.] 8° – Seebaß, *Osiander* 18.3. Benzing/Claus *2743a. – Erfurt WAB: Ts 3411(1).

1530

34. Artickell wie sich die Kriegs lewt Edell vnnd vnedel ym zug widder den Türcken vorhalden sollen ... – [Breslau: Dyon, *c.* 1530.] 4° – Hohenemser 1430. *VD 16* D 858. Claus, *Erfurt*, p. 301. – Frankfurt/Main StUB: G.F. X.85.

35. [Confessio Augustana, *German*] Anzeigung vnd bekantnus des Glaubens vnd der lere ... [Breslau: Dyon] 1530. 4° – CR 26.487.3. Josef Benzing, *Eine unbekannte Ausgabe der Confessio Augustana vom Jahre 1557* (Wiesbaden, 1956), p. 19, no. 3. VD *16* C 4740. W. H. Neuser, *Bibliographie der Confessio Augustana und Apologie 1530-1580* (Nieuwkoop, 1987), p. 52, no. 4. – Lübeck StB: 2 an Theol. 4°2367; Strasbourg BNU (imperf.): R 103253; Wolfenbüttel HAB.

1532

36. JURICIC, NIKOLAUS: Zwen warhafftige Sendtbrieff ... – [Breslau: Dyon] 1532. – Göllner 437. *VD 16* J 1153. – Dresden LB: Hist.univ. A 280,misc.3.

II. Kaspar Libisch

1535

1. (A²)vsczug des vortrags so zwischē der Key. Maiestat vnnd dem Konige vonn Thunis Mulij Alhacen genandt auff den sechsten tag Augusti des M.D.xxxv. ... außgericht worden. [Holzschnitt] – [Breslau: Libisch 1535.] 4° – *GK* 8.9848. – Dresden LB: Hist.Germ. B 180,42.

2. DIETRICH VON HAMBURG: Vonn der Munsterischenn Auffrur, verstockung vnnd iamer, Glaublich anzeyg ... [Woodcut illustration] – [Breslau: Libisch 1535.] 4° – Uppsala UB.

3. [SECKERWITZ, JOHANN (?):] (R)echbuchleyn M.D.xxxv. Ein mol eyns. ... [Headings] – [Breslau: Libisch 1535.] 8° – Wrocław BU: 314408.

1537

4. [MELANCHTHON, PHILIPP:] Rechtmessige vrsach worumb das Concilium von Paulo dē Rom. Bapst des namens dem dritten zu Mantua in Welschen landen zehaltē ... der Kirchen keyns wegs erspryßlich zuachten sey ... [Breslau: Libisch] 1537. 4° – Weimar HAAB: Aut. IV:47

5. Ein sinreicher Pasquillus, der aller erst von Rom kommet, vnd vnser aller Herrn, des Romischen Keisers vnd anderer Potentaten kriegß handlungen vnd andere lauf meldet. – [Breslau: Libisch] Mense Junio. 1537. 4° – Weimar HAAB: Aut. V:65.

DÜRER'S *KLEINE PASSION* AND A VENETIAN BLOCK BOOK

DENIS V. REIDY

WHILE CONSULTING the *Italian STC* of sixteenth century books under the heading Bible, Appendix [Pictorial Illustrations], I noticed an entry which intrigued me: *Opera noua ... laquale tratta de le figure del testamento vecchio ...* printed in Venice by G. A. Vavassore, [1540?], 8°, BL pressmarks C.17.a.11 and 691.a.18, the latter an imperfect copy. The fact that the nineteenth-century British Museum cataloguer had not been able to provide a precise date of printing, always an irritating bibliographical 'loose end', prompted an examination of the two books. The imperfect copy is in a dark blue, grained sheep, blind-tooled nineteenth-century English binding bearing the armorial bookplate of W. Combes. The complete copy (C.17.a.11) is in a late-eighteenth or early-nineteenth-century English gold- and blind-tooled blue straight-grain sheep binding with the crest of the Second Earl Spencer and the binder's label of C. Hering, 10 St Martin's Street, London. The book also has gold-tooled doublures and fly-leaves in green watered silk and also bears an armorial bookplate, that of John Broadley.

The book contains several surprising features. First it is a classic block book consisting of one hundred and twenty illustrations printed entirely from wood blocks together with accompanying xylographic text. The pages are printed on both sides, which indicates that they were produced using a press rather than by rubbing the paper from the back, the method used for most block books. The book is puzzling and intriguing since block books were produced principally in the Low Countries and in Germany in the incunable period.[1] I was not aware that any block book had been printed in Italy in the fifteenth, let alone the sixteenth century – with the possible exception of the 'Passio Christi' in the Kupferstichkabinett in Berlin.[2] I showed the books to Dennis Rhodes and Luigi

1 The current state of scholarship regarding block books is summarized in Sabine Mertens *et al.* (eds), *Blockbücher des Mittelalters. Bilderfolgen als Lektüre* (Mainz, 1991).

2 See Mertens, p. 358. On this item, consisting of nine formerly separate leaves which were assembled into a book in 1989, see the two articles by Paul Kristeller: 'Ein venezianisches Blockbuch', *Jahrbuch der königlich preußischen Kunstsammlungen*, 22 (1901), 132-54, and 'Das italienische Blockbuch des Kupferstichkabinetts zu Berlin', *Monatshefte für Bücherfreunde und Graphiksammler*, 1 (1925), 331-42.

Balsamo, two of the world's leading authorities on Italian printing, but neither had ever seen a copy of the book nor were they aware of its existence. I knew then that if these two experts had never seen the book it might be quite rare. However, in addition to the two British Library copies at least nineteen others are known. In Italy there are copies in the Biblioteca Nazionale at Florence, the Biblioteca Estense at Modena, the Biblioteca Reale at Turin, the Biblioteca Civica at Verona, and the Biblioteca Marciana at Venice. In France there are two copies in Paris (one copy in the Bibliothèque Nationale being from the collection of the bibliophile Ambroise Firmin Didot) and one at Rouen. In Britain, besides the two in London, there are two in the Bodleian Library, Oxford, and one in Birmingham Central Library. In America there are copies at Harvard, Claremont College, California, the Newberry Library, Chicago, Columbia University, New York, New York Public Library (three copies), and Williams College, Williamstown, Mass. There may be others. A second copy once owned by Ambroise Firmin Didot, which formed part of the collection of Andrea Tessier in Venice, was sold in Munich by J. Rosenthal in 1900. This same copy was sold by the Torinese antiquarian bookseller Arturo Pregliasco in 1990 and is now in the private collection of a Parisian bibliophile.

A second interesting feature is the book's similarity to the *Biblia Pauperum*, particularly to the folio edition printed in the Netherlands *c.* 1470 of 40 leaves, 'Schreiber's edition III' (BL pressmark IC.45a.), albeit in a smaller format, octavo. And finally, some of the New Testament woodcuts, particularly that of Christ driving out the money-lenders from the temple, are very reminiscent of similar illustrations by Dürer in his *Kleine Passion* printed in Nuremberg in 1511.

The *Opera nova* measures 15.5 cm × 10 cm and, as one would expect, has a xylographic title-page which is set off by an attractive strapwork border not unlike the one which adorns the *Apocalipsis Iesu Christi*, translated by Federigo da Venezia, also printed in Venice, but by Alessandro de' Paganini in 1516, in folio (B.M. Department of Prints and Drawings). The full title of the work is important for our understanding of how the work is to be used and interpreted and is worth citing in full:

Opera noua contemplativa p*er* | ogni fidel christiano laquale tra | tta de le figure del testamento | vecchio: le quale figure sonno veri- | ficate nel testamento nuouo: con le | sue expositione: Et con el detto | de li propheti sopra esse figure: | Si come legendo trouarete. Et | nota che ciaschuna figura del tes- | tamento nuouo trovareti dua dil te- | stamento vecchio: le quale sonno | affigguratte a quella dil nuouo Et | sempre quella dil nuouo sara posta | nel meggio di quelle dua dil ve- | chio: Cosa belissima da ītēdere | a chi se dilectano de la sacra | scrittura: Nouamente | Stampata.

From this we learn that the printer Giovan Andrea Vavassore intended to show scenes from the Old Testament, on eighty full-page blocks (measuring 135 × 83 mm inclusive of the text above each illustration) in conjunction with scenes from the New Testament, on forty blocks (measuring 106 × 73 mm). These are decorated with attractive side strips and smaller separate blocks at the foot of each of these (measuring 29 × 83 mm) which contain pairs of figures of prophets and relevant quotations from the Old Testament. The blocks are therefore meant to be consulted in groups of three with each New Testament scene (in the middle) flanked by a scene from the Old Testament and a quotation from the prophets which herald and prophesy the New Testament event. The collation of the work is as follows: title-page and blank verso, 64 leaves in 8°, signatures A-H^8, H^8 blank, in gatherings of eight. The colophon (fol. 63^v), which is also xylographic and in gothic characters reads: Opera di Giouãniandrea/Uauassore ditto Uadagni/no: [*sic*] Stampata nouamẽte/ nella inclita citta di/ Vinegia/ Laus Deo. No date is given.

Little is known about the printer Giovanni Andrea Vavassore (Valvassore) except that he was a Venetian, a wood engraver, printer, and bookseller, who was active from *c.* 1520 to *c.* 1572. He began working as a wood engraver from 1522 but the first book signed and printed by him did not appear until 1530. He appears to have printed about 85 separate works as well as a not inconsiderable number of maps. The British Library has in its collections no fewer than 58 separate works printed by him to which have to be added five editions of Ariosto's *Orlando Furioso* printed in 1549, 1553, 1554, 1556-58, 1566 and a reissue in 1567 and an edition of Ariosto's *Satires* printed in 1537 which are also in the British Library.[3] Apart from his maps, one of Vavassore's best known works is the celebrated woodcut book of lace patterns *Esempalrio* [*sic*] *di lauori* Venice, 18 February 1546, 4°, which he produced with his brother Florio Vavassore who signed the border. Given that the gothic lettering of this signature is identical and that the similarity of style and execution between the woodcuts in this latter work and the *Opera nova contemplativa* is very close, it is fairly safe to assume that Florio assisted his brother in producing at least some of the woodcuts for the *Opera nova*.

This is further borne out by the fact that Giovanni Andrea had gone into partnership with his brother Florio. The earliest book which formally acknowledges this partnership is dated 1537 but this does not preclude the possibility that the Vavassore brothers had been working together since the late 1520s or early 1530s. The name of 'Guadagnino' (misspelt in the colophon), which literally means 'a little profit', was often appended to Giovanni Andrea's name almost as a nickname. This practice of using or being referred to by a nickname was not uncommon among Italian printers at the time: one only has to think of the printer Nicolò di Aristotile de' Rossi who was commonly referred to as 'lo Zoppino', literally the 'little lame one'. Rather than being indicative of the fact that Giovanni Andrea was a successful printer – at least 85 editions in 42 years is hardly a very prolific output especially if it is compared with the output of, say, the House of Giunta – it would perhaps rather suggest that Giovanni Andrea Vavassore was also a money-lender, an activity from which he was more likely to earn a 'tidy little profit' than from printing.

3 BL pressmarks: 11426.g.29; Voyn. 32; 11426.g.28 (1); 1073.f.6; 82.g.22; C.28.c.1.

Close study of the British Library copy of Dürer's *Kleine Passion*, or to give the work its correct title *Passio Christi ab Alberto Dürer Nurenbergensi effigíata cū varij generis carminibus Fratris Benedicti Chelidonii Musophílí* ... (Nuremberg, 1511) (pressmark C.44.d.26), revealed that Dürer's woodcut of Christ chasing the money-lenders from the temple was very similar to Vavassore's woodcut of the same scene. Indeed it is far too close a copy of Dürer's original to be merely coincidental. Comparison of other woodcuts in the two books leaves little room for doubt – given the close similarity between some of the New Testament scenes in the two works – that Vavassore had certainly consulted and was greatly influenced by Dürer's *Kleine Passion* when he and his brother Florio produced their woodcuts for the *Opera nova*. Consulting other important works, in particular Essling's 'Princely' magnum opus *Les Livres à figures vénitiens de la fin du XVe siècle, et du commencement du XVIe* (Florence and Paris, 1907) (pt 1, pp. 201-11), it was initially a disappointment to see that the very same woodcuts of Christ and the money-lenders which had led me to make the same link are reproduced (on pp. 204 and 205). Moreover, Eugène Dutuit in his *Manuel de l'amateur d'estampes* (Paris and London, 1884), pp. 95-96, who appears to have been the first to make the link (curiously not referred to by Essling), had anticipated my association and 'discovery' by at least 110 years.

Nevertheless there are still some further points worth making about these two books.

There can be little doubt that Albrecht Dürer (1471-1528) was the most important northern artist of his generation and consequently his work was extremely popular with, and had the greatest influence on, Italian artists. Indeed Dürer's work was so popular that many copies and forgeries of his works were produced from the early sixteenth century onwards. The Italian engraver Marcantonio Raimondi who worked in Venice, to name but one, began to produce engraved copies of Dürer's woodcut series of the *Life of the Virgin* (1504-5) as early as 1506. Giorgio Vasari informs us in his biography of Raimondi (1568) that Dürer made his second trip to Venice in 1506 with the express intention of taking legal action against Raimondi for the production and sale of fakes of his works.[4] Dürer was not all that successful because he could not prevent Raimondi from reproducing his works entirely – he was only able to reach a *modus vivendi* with Raimondi who agreed not to reproduce Dürer's name or monogram. Yet Dürer's works still continued to be copied and forged. Indeed by 1511 Dürer was so incensed that he insisted on including a threatening warning in the colophon of the bound editions of his *Life of the Virgin* and the *Kleine Passion*: 'Heus tu insidiator. ac alíeni laboris. & ingenij. surreptor. ne manus temerarías his nostris operibus inicias. caue.' ('Beware all imitators and thieves of the labour and talents of others, beware of laying your audacious hands on our work!') Dürer's warning had little effect – even in his native

4 On this episode see Jane Campbell Hutchison, *Albrecht Dürer: a biography* (Princeton, NJ, 1990), p. 79.

Nuremberg his works were so frequently forged that the City Council had to issue an edict on 3 January 1512 threatening confiscation and other dire consequences unless Dürer's cipher were removed from forgeries. Needless to say, Raimondi in distant Venice still continued to make copies of the *Kleine Passion* series of 1511 without Dürer's ciphers. It is therefore a possibility, albeit a remote one, that Italian artists, including the Vavassore brothers, could have used Raimondi's excellent piracies of the *Kleine Passion* and of other works by Dürer rather than Dürer's originals. As we shall soon see, there can be little doubt that the Vavassore brothers were familiar with Dürer's works in general and the *Kleine Passion* in particular, whether through Dürer's originals as is most likely, or, more improbably, through Raimondi's forgeries. Incidentally, an Italian edition of the *Kleine Passion* was published in Venice by Daniele Bissuccio as late as 1612, which illustrates the continuing interest in Dürer's work in Venice into the seventeenth century as well.

Turning to four of the New Testament woodcuts common to the *Kleine Passion* and the *Opera nova*, the first thing one notices about them is how exquisite Dürer's woodcuts are compared with the relatively cruder woodcuts by the Vavassore brothers. The very fine detail in Dürer's woodcuts, particularly in the faces of figures, the attention to the folds in clothing and the fine rendering of foliage and architecture, is so precisely executed that one almost disbelieves that these works of art could possibly have been executed in wood. Most of Dürer's original wood blocks of the *Kleine Passion*, incidentally, are preserved in the British Museum (Department of Prints and Drawings). The woodcuts in the *Opera nova* are clearly executed with far less attention to detail and are nowhere near the same level of finish, let alone artistic genius. Another less immediately obvious point of difference between the two works is the absence of halos over the heads of the figures of Christ, the Virgin Mary and the Saints in Dürer's woodcuts and their presence in the woodcuts in the *Opera nova*. The reason for this is probably an attempt by Vavassore to save time and effort in drawing large stylized halos rather than spending considerable time in closely detailed work, as we shall see shortly.

Dürer's woodcut of Christ being laid in the sepulchre by Nicodemus (fig. 1) is clearly the inspiration for the same scene depicted in the *Opera nova* (fig. 2). The general composition of the woodcut, the positioning of the figures in relation to the sepulchre and the cave, the poses of these figures and the reproduction of some of the details in the Dürer woodcut, notably the attention to the folds in the clothing of the figures, the positioning of the crown of thorns and the clothing of Nicodemus and the two figures assisting him, particularly their hats and turban, would all indicate that Dürer's woodcut served as the inspiration for the Vavassore woodcut. The jar of ointment held by the Virgin is also present in the latter woodcut, as is the simplified representation of the foliage in the foreground and background. There are some differences, notably the omission of the third female figure and the figure of St John in the background. The pouch on Nicodemus's belt has also been changed to a hammer. The overall

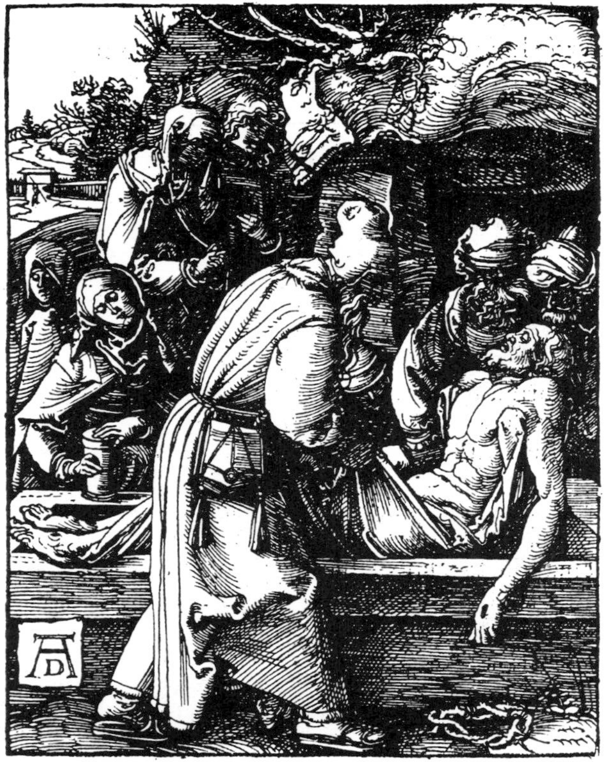

Fig. 1. Christ is laid in the Sepulchre (Dürer).

Fig. 2. Christ is laid in the Sepulchre (block book).

Fig. 3. Christ and Mary Magdalen (Dürer).

Fig. 4. Christ and Mary Magdalen (block book).

E iij

Fig. 5. The Ascension (Dürer).

Fig. 6. The Ascension (block book).

E iiij

Fig. 7. The descent of the Holy Spirit (Dürer).

Fig. 8. The descent of the Holy Spirit (block book).

composition of the Vavassore woodcut without question owes its origins to Dürer's woodcut of the same scene.

Dürer's depiction of Christ's apparition to Mary Magdalen after the Resurrection in the guise of a gardener, a 'Noli me tangere' (fig. 3) with its lavish attention to the folds in the clothing of the two figures, is effectively captured in the same scene in the *Opera nova* (fig. 4). The poses of the two principal figures, particularly Christ's outstretched hand, the position of the spade on Christ's left shoulder and the positioning of Mary Magdalen's left hand on the jar of ointment are very similar in both woodcuts. The general layout of the foliage and the buildings in the background has also been retained in the Vavassore woodcut. The chief differences between the two woodcuts are the omission in the latter of the three female figures in the background, the mark of the nail in Christ's right hand, Mary Magdalen's veil with its many folds, and of course, the powerful depiction of Dürer's sunrise. The omission of these details might indicate an urgency on the part of Vavassore to reproduce his work quickly and with a much reduced artistic input, almost as if he had a self-imposed printer's deadline to meet.

Dürer's woodcut of Christ's Ascension (fig. 5) is also closely reproduced in the woodcut of the same New Testament scene in the *Opera nova* (fig. 6). The overall composition and proportion is very similar, especially the arrangement of the Virgin and the two kneeling saints in the foreground around the rock. The folds in the clothing of the three principal figures are also rendered as are the footprints left by the ascending Christ. The footprints, however, are portrayed on an almost vertical plane in order that the viewer should not overlook them. The fifteen figures in Dürer's woodcut, including that of Christ, have been reduced to ten in Vavassore's – the remaining five have been represented only by their halos, thereby effecting a further economy of effort in reproducing the woodcut. Vavassore departs from Dürer in details of the depiction of Christ's Ascension. In fig. 5 Christ is rising from clouds, in fig. 6 Christ rises from a cloudless sky but rays of light emanate from his feet which not only adds glory and dramatic tension to the event but also imparts more dynamism to the Venetian interpretation.

Similarly Dürer's woodcut of the descent of the Holy Spirit at Pentecost (fig. 7) is clearly the inspiration for the very similar scene depicted by Vavassore (fig. 8). The general poses of the figures in the foreground, especially that of the Virgin Mary with the open book on her lap, flanked by the two apostles, are very similar. There is some attention to Dürer's detail in the folds of the garments of the three figures in the foreground, but this is much more stylized in the *Opera nova*. The number of figures has been reduced from fourteen in fig. 7 to seven in the Vavassore woodcut. The three figures seated on a bench in the background have disappeared altogether in the latter work and four figures have been represented by their halos only, which would indicate a further economy of effort on the part of the Venetian artist. It is also interesting to note that the intricate tongues of fire (fig. 7) have been replaced by halos in the Italian woodcut and one has even been included for the Holy Spirit in the form of a dove.

It should now be possible to date the printing of the *Opera nova* with a little more accuracy. Max Sander, in his *Le Livre à figures italien depuis 1467 jusqu'à 1530* (Milan, 1942), part 1, p. 105, suggests that the *Opera nova* was published *c.* 1510–1512. This would appear to be too early because although Dürer's earliest woodcuts of the *Kleine Passion* can be dated to 1509 and were circulated in loose sheets from that date, the bound editions of his work were not published until 1511. Secondly, there is no evidence as yet to suggest that Giovan Andrea Vavassore was active as a printer before 1530, the year of the first dated book printed by him. It is of course possible that Vavassore did not begin to date his works until 1530 and so a pre-1530 dating is still possible. It is known that there were four issues of the *Opera nova*. Clearly this is one of Vavassore's earliest works and could be dated as early as 1530. The second issue of the *Opera nova* differs from the first in that the first issue consists of xylographic text in gothic letters throughout; the second, however, has a new prophet block containing texts from the Old Testament flanked by two prophets (see the bottom part of figs 2, 4, 6 and 8) on H5^{r} cut in roman letters. The third issue differs in that additional ornamental border strips were provided for the woodcut of the Virgin and Child on fol. H7^{v}. The fourth issue contains two prophet blocks which contain roman text, on fol. E5^{r} as well as fol. H5^{r}, and the border on fol. H7^{v} is different. The copy in the Biblioteca Civica at Verona is a fifth issue, given that the title of the work is composed of larger xylographic characters which were to be read on four separate leaves rather than on a single title-page as is the case with all the other four issues. Since the signatures in this copy are located at the head of each page, it is very likely that this is a unique copy. This book incidentally bears two library stamps of the library of San Nicolò at Verona. The British Library copies are both of the second issue and so a date of 1530 or, more likely, 1531 is a more accurate dating for the printing of the *Opera nova* – nine years earlier than the British Museum cataloguer suggested when he came to catalogue the work last century.

Apart from being able to provide a more accurate dating for the printing of the British Library's copies of the second issue of the *Opera nova* to 1531, there are still some important points to be made about the two books.

In the first place we have seen how the Vavassore brothers were certainly influenced by the work of Dürer, especially by his *Kleine Passion* when they produced and printed their *Opera nova* in about 1530. We have also seen how the Netherlandish edition of the *Biblia Pauperum* (1470?) has also had some influence on the Vavassore version of their blockbook *Biblia Pauperum* which unfortunately space does not permit us to expand on in the confines of this article.[5]

5 See, however, W. L. Schreiber, *Manuel de l'amateur de la gravure sur bois et sur métal au XVe siècle* (Leipzig, 1902), IV, pp. 105–113.

Vavassore's *Opera nova* would also appear to have been influenced by the work of several other Italian artists, particularly the work of Bellini, Carpaccio, Squarcione, Montagna, and Mantegna. Space again unfortunately does not permit us to develop these influences on the Vavassore brothers, although an investigation of them would certainly prove very profitable.[6] Given the obvious influences of the work of Dürer and a northern edition of the *Biblia Pauperum* on Vavassore's *Opera nova* on the one hand, and the influence of other Italian artists on the other, could not Vavassore's *Opera nova* be regarded as a synthesis of art and book production between countries north of the Alps and Italy? Could both the *Kleine Passion* and the *Opera nova* serve as timely reminders that the many facets of the Italian Renaissance, art, painting, printing, architecture, trade – in short what Jacob Burckhardt described as the 'Civilization of the Renaissance in Italy' – did not take place in Italy alone, in splendid isolation, but rather consisted of a two-way exchange of ideas and influences between Italy and other countries north of the Alps? Moreover could not the two works serve as symbols or ciphers of the influence of the book produced north of the Alps, particularly the German book, on the Italian book? The two books are separated in time by just under twenty years. Indeed the *Opera nova* must constitute one of the earliest examples of Dürer's woodcuts being used, copied and adapted by an Italian artist and printer. Could they not help us to pin-point accurately the precise time when the German book influenced the Italian book? The two books are, to my mind, very eloquent and powerful symbols and serve as a timely reminder of the very great debt that the whole continent of Europe in general, and Italy in particular, owes to Germany. Not only is the invention of printing with movable type by Gutenberg in the 1450s a German invention – which played such an important role in disseminating new texts and ideas and also satisfied the ever-increasing demand for the printed word – but we should never forget the very great debt that is owed by Italy to German printers. From the introduction of printing into Italy in 1465 by Konrad Sweynheym and Arnold Pannartz, who worked in partnership to print the *Lactantius* at Subiaco, printing was firmly established in Italy by German printers. Konrad Sweynheym, Arnold Pannartz, Ulrich Han, Sixtus Riessinger, Hans von Laudenbach, Johannes Schurener, Adam Rot, Georgius Lauer, Eucharius Silber, Stephan Plannck, Georg Sachsel, Johannes and Vindelinus de Spira and Bartholomeus Golsch, to name but a few, all assisted in establishing printing on a firm footing on the Italian peninsula. Indeed, as John Flood has pointed out, about two-thirds of the 'printing shops in Rome in the incunable period ... were, not surprisingly, in the hands of Germans'.[7] We should also not forget that a full five years had to elapse between the printing of the first dated book in Italy, the

6 See, however, [L. Cicognara], *Catalogo ragionato dei libri d'arte e d'antichità posseduti dal conte Cicognara* (Pisa, 1821, reprint Bologna, 1987), I, no. 1992.

7 John L. Flood, 'Hans von Laude(n)bach "who printed the first books in Rome"'. In: Denis V. Reidy (ed.), *The Italian Book 1465-1800. Studies presented to Dennis E. Rhodes on his 70th birthday* (London, 1993), pp. 11-19, here p. 15.

Lactantius at Subiaco in 1465, and the appearance of the first book printed by a native Italian printer, Philippus de Lignamine from Messina, who printed his Quintilianus *Institutiones oratoriae* in 1470 (BL 167.i.1; G. 9551).[8] Nor should we forget that in the incunable period printing was first introduced into the major Italian centres of printing, for the most part the larger Italian cities, with the notable exception of the university cities of Bologna and Pavia, by German printers.

8 There is also a claim, made at the time, that Clement of Padua was the first native Italian printer. See Ursula Baurmeister, 'Clément de Padoue, enlumineur et premier imprimeur italien?', *Bulletin du bibliophile*, 1990, no. 1, pp. 19–28.

PHYSICIANS AND PUBLISHERS

The translation of medical works in sixteenth-century Basle[1]

FRANK HIERONYMUS

THE GROWTH OF MEDICAL AND OTHER TECHNICAL LITERATURE is an important part of the intellectual history of early modern Europe, yet it is an aspect which has hitherto been somewhat neglected in the study of the history of the book. As a modest contribution to a re-assessment, I offer a survey of the role played by Basle publishers in encouraging the editing and translating of medical works. Many of these books, copies of which now repose largely undisturbed in the British Library, once represented the leading edge of scientific thought.

Two of the most important translators of Greek medical works in Basle were Albanus Torinus (Thorer, from Winterthur) and Janus Cornarius. Interestingly, both of them also made important contributions as translators of theology, Cornarius, at least, defending himself by maintaining that medicine and theology were related disciplines, both being parts of physics, which had become separated only in recent times. Torinus, who had studied under Paracelsus in 1527, was an advocate of Greek medicine. Although a physician, he prepared the earliest Greek and Latin edition of a work of Bishop Epiphanius of Salamis, which Andreas Cratander published in 1529.[2] In 1530 Cratander also published Torinus's Greek and Latin edition of Theocritus, the first to appear in the German-speaking part of Europe, and in 1542 his translation of Vesalius. As for Cornarius, in 1540 he published a Latin version of the works of Basil the Great with Froben and Episcopius,[3] and in 1543 a translation of the works of Epiphanius who was one of the principal opponents of Origen with Robert Winter.[4]

ALBANUS TORINUS

Torinus and Cornarius distinguished themselves above all as translators of Greek medical texts. Andreas Cratander had already published some older

1 *Editors' note*: This essay is an excerpt from a new, comprehensive study of translations published in Basle in the sixteenth century. Limitations of space have precluded our publishing this study in its entirety, desirable though this undoubtedly would have been.
2 BL pressmark: 487.f.4 (2).
3 BL pressmark: 3670.h.6.
4 BL pressmark: 3835.g.12.

translations of Hippocrates, saying that he felt obliged to bring them out because so few physicians had a command of Greek;[5] these were followed in 1529-1531 by a collection of translations of Galen, some of them previously published, others not yet printed, some the work of the Basle physician Andreas Leennius , others supplied by friends. As early as August 1528, several months before he even finished his studies, Torinus brought out a collection of texts on dietetics, pharmaceutics and surgery by the Greek physicians Soran and Oribasius which were known to him only in Latin translations, together with some texts which had come down under the names of Pliny and Apuleius.[6] In the dedication to Philipp von Gundelsheim, Bishop of Basle, he discusses questions of authenticity, problems of medical terminology, and the provenance of the manuscripts that colleagues in Strasbourg, Frankfurt and elsewhere had given him. Even more important, though to some extent open to debate, are Torinus's achievements as the first modern translator of Paul of Aegina's *Epitome* of Greek medicine, published by Cratander and Johann Bebel in March 1532, as well as of the *Therapeutics*, the principal work of the most important Greek physician after Galen, Alexander of Tralles, published by Heinrich Petri in 1533.[7] According to the dedication in the Paul of Aegina, which is addressed to Archbishop Matthæus Lang of Salzburg, the printer, Bebel, had commissioned him – and paid him – to do the translation. Like Johannes Guinterius in the same year, he bemoans the linguistic defects of his sole source, the less than perfect Aldine of 1528, and apologizes for the clumsiness of his translation by pointing to the difficulty of the content and the short time he had been allowed to prepare the work – he had translated for philologers, not for logophiles, he says. The following year he publishes some amendments (*castigationes*) to his translation in Bebel's edition of Giovanni Bernardino Feliciano's translation of the sixth book, on surgery, which had been lacking in the 1532 edition; he apologizes for the errors, making shortness of time and the poor quality of the original his excuses, remarking that every first foetus runs the risk of being aborted. Then in August 1538 – at the same time as the Basle physician Hieronymus Gemusaeus was bringing out the Greek text of Paul of Aegina with Cratander – Torinus published a thorough revision of his translation, complete with Book VI this time, with Balthasar Lasius.[8] A third edition, revised by Torinus once again, was published in a handy octavo format by Johannes Oporinus in 1546.[9]

5 BL pressmark: 539.a.2.

6 Albanus Torinus, *De re medica insunt Sorani Isagoge ...* (Basle: A. Cratander, 1528). The BL copy, which is imperfect, has the pressmark 541.g.18.

7 The translation by Johannes Guinterius of Andernach appeared at Paris in the same year. Hitherto only the first of the seven books had been available in Latin, in the translation made in 1510 by Guilelmus Copus, the personal physician to King François I. The Greek text had been published at Venice in 1528, and in 1538 Hieronymus Gemusaeus brought out another edition with Cratander.

8 BL pressmark: 540.c.11.

9 BL pressmark: 540.d.24.

In the dedication of his edition of Alexander of Aphrodisias's treatise on fever, published by Robert Winter in 1542, Torinus criticizes the author of the translation he has improved, Giorgio Valla, as being (despite his learning) inexperienced in medical matters.[10] He also adds a treatise on fever by Joannes Damascenus, a manuscript of which he had found in the library of the Bishop of Würzburg, because of its similarity to the Greek ones.[11] If he criticizes Valla's text for being an *ecphrastica interpretatio*, he calls the Spanish physician Gerardus of Cremona, the paraphraser of Jahja Maseweih, a linguistic barbarian, a *metaphrastes*. He says he has endeavoured to improve both of them.

JANUS CORNARIUS

Yet a third physician had translated the *Epitome* of Paul of Aegina by 1531 at the latest, as we learn from the dedication of his translation which was not published until 1556. This was Janus Cornarius, from Zwickau. In a kind of inaugural lecture delivered at Basle in 1528, of which the British Library has three copies,[12] he had dealt with Hippocrates, instead of with Avicenna and other writers of this kind. In August 1529 he had published an anthology of Greek epigrams,[13] partly translated by himself, with Bebel, and in the same month a bilingual edition (with his own Latin version) of Hippocrates's treatise on the climate, with Hieronymus Froben and Johannes Herwagen. As the Polish physician Jan Antonin had already done in a letter to Erasmus in 1527, he criticizes in his dedication the complete translation of Hippocrates made by the philosopher Marcus Fabius Calvus which, though finished in 1515, had not been published until 1525 in Rome. Cornarius considers an accurate translation of one individual treatise to be more valuable than a collection of texts put together in a cavalier fashion. He also provides an amended edition of the original text for the sake of comparison. At the same time we are informed that even at that point he had collated printed editions and manuscripts in Basle in preparation for bringing out a complete edition in Greek and Latin.

His complete Greek edition of the Hippocratic corpus was published by Froben and Episcopius in 1538.[14] He thanks his publishers for their help with obtaining manuscripts from the Augsburg physician Adolph Occo, from the library in Ladenburg, and from the physician Nicolaus Copus (a son of Wilhelm Kopp) in Paris. Two years after publication of Leonhard Fuchs's translation and commentary on Hippocrates's *Aphorisms*, and one year after Fuchs and

10 BL pressmark: 539.b.34.
11 Mesue the Elder, ninth century. Valla's edition is in: Alexander Aphrodisaeus, *De febrium causis et differentijs opusculum. In librum I. Damasceni de febrium curatione diegema A. Torino authore* (Basle: R. Winter, 1542). BL pressmark: 539.b.36.
12 BL pressmarks: 539.e.12 (1); 539.e.13 (1); 542.c.1 (2).
13 BL pressmarks: 1067.i.6. and G.8352.
14 BL pressmark 539.h.1.

Cornarius began to rain polemical tracts down on each other's head, in which their respective translations were one of the points at issue, Cornarius brought out his new complete Latin translation with Froben and Episcopius in March 1546. In the dedication he gives an account of his time as a student and describes conditions at the universities, lamenting the general inadequacy of both texts and medical teaching in contrast to the increasing availability of new, usable translations made by Copus and Leonicenus, though complaining that no one has attempted to translate Hippocrates apart from Calvus. His second, revised and improved complete edition of Hippocrates in Latin was published by the same printers in 1554 and 1558.[15]

Cornarius's translation of the most comprehensive ancient work on medicinal plants, that of Dioscorides, appeared quite late. Published by Froben and Episcopius in 1557,[16] it was the fourth edition of that author's work, having been preceded by Bebel's edition of the Greek text in 1529 and editions of one medieval and three modern Latin translations (Hermolao Barbaro posthumously at Venice in 1516, Jean de la Ruelle at Paris in 1516, and Marcello Virgilio Adriani at Florence in 1518). He still considered it useful to bring out another edition, for he had corrected the text using an old manuscript, looked out parallels in other ancient authors and had examined how their work was reflected in the writings of modern authors, had added guidance from such writers and, finally, instead of providing illustrations he had given the German names for plants as an aid to understanding. Like Dioscorides himself he had not provided illustrations, because the same plants vary too much according to region and season of the year. Furthermore we are treated to his evaluation of the Arabic and Latin translations and his views on the recent spread of knowledge of Greek. It is interesting that he does not regard the contemporary ignorance of Arabic as a deficiency; after all, he says, nobody learns the Indian languages merely on account of a few Indian medicines.

The previous year Cornarius's Latin translation of Paul of Aegina's compendium of ancient Greek medicine in seven books had been published by Herwagen, father and son. This too was only the third edition after those of Torinus and Guinterius of 1532 and reprints of them.[17] In his dedication, written from Zwickau (where he had meanwhile been appointed municipal physician) on 1 April 1555, he gives an account of his early years, once again complaining about the deficiencies of medical education in the universities and telling of how he had discovered the Greek physicians in Aldines at Basle (these probably belonged to Bonifatius Amerbach, for the most part) and of how he has become acquainted with the Basle printers Froben and Herwagen thanks to Erasmus (and doubtless also to Amerbach, who in 1528 had tried to obtain

15 BL pressmark 539.i.1.
16 BL pressmark 456.d.9.
17 The BL has only the following edition: Paul of Aegina, *Medicinæ totius enchiridion*, translated by A. Torinus (Basle: Oporinus, 1546), pressmark 540.d.24.

appointments for him in Basle, Freiburg and Zurich). As in the case of his translation of Dioscorides he also added his own commentary to the compendium.

The first editions of the first translations of the sixteen books of the medical compendium of the Byzantine court physician Aetius of Amida represent an unusual case of long-distance collaboration. In August 1533 Froben and Episcopius published the middle section, books 8-13, the translation being based on a fragment of a Greek manuscript, sent to Cornarius by Matthæus Aurogallus from the library of the Bohemian humanist and statesmen Bohuslaw Lobkowitz of Hassenstein in Komotau which had burnt down in 1525.[18] In the dedication, to Emperor Charles V, Cornarius dwells on the need for the doctor to have specialist knowledge and to be conscientious, while the patient must be able to have confidence in his physician. In September 1534 the first edition of the Greek text of books 1-8 was published by the heirs of Aldus Manutius and Andreas Asulanus at Venice, and in the same year Lucantonio Giunta published the whole work in Latin: books 1-7 and 14-16 is the translation of the renowned Paduan physician Johannes Baptista Montanus, the teacher of Crato von Crafftheim, Vesalius and others, while books 8-13 appeared under the name of Cornarius as translator in the shape of a reprint of the Basle edition of 1533. Finally in August 1535 Froben and Episcopius supplemented their edition of 1533 by adding Montanus's two translations, also giving him credit for the work. The story ends in 1542 when they brought out the entire work in Cornarius's translation.

Cornarius's first translation from Galen appeared in August 1537, published – like his Hippocrates translations – by Froben and Episcopius.[19] In 1536 Cratander had already published a compilation by the Polish physician Joseph Tectander (Zimmermann) of translations, some already published, by other hands, and some, unpublished, of his own. Cornarius's book was a practical pharmaceutical handbook on the preparation of medicines, entitled *Opus medicum practicum ... De compositione pharmacorum localium*. The first 'modern' translation of this had appeared in Paris in 1530 (books 1-7) and in April 1535 (books 1-10). The date of the dedicatory letter prefixed to the commentary, 10 March 1535, indicates that he had probably finished his commentary by then and we may thus assume that the translation had been completed by then too. He suspects, he says, that the translation of this work, which will have formed the basis of all later ones 'right down to the very last dregs', required much more effort on his part than Galen himself expended on the original, for he after all had only had to write down in his own language all the things that his predecessors had taught. A particular problem had been Galen's quotations from older authors which had became difficult to understand as a result of the development of the language and semantic change of some individual words. He

18 BL pressmark 540.h.20 (1).
19 BL pressmark 540.h.11 (1). This copy is imperfect.

says he had not had to work to a deadline (that is, to ensure that the book was ready for the next fair) but had been able to put it aside at times and pick it up again to improve it, unlike other translators who offered their work to booksellers for a pittance who in their turn would sell their shoddy products at a high price. Thus Cornarius works round to Johannes Froben's old motto that a man who buys a good book at a high price gets a bargain, while someone who buys a bad book cheaply makes a loss. Cornarius goes on to say that, in order to establish a sound basis for his translation, he had collated the works of other Greek and Roman physicians, because he had only had the 1525 Aldine of Galen available to him; he has expounded difficult passages and justified his translation of them in his commentary, which he sharply distinguishes from run-of-the-mill medical thesauri, onomastica, and pandects. Cornarius added further translations from Galen in his edition of Marcellus, published by Froben and Episcopius in 1536.

In 1537 he published with Froben and Episcopius his translation of the treatise on agriculture attributed to Constantine the Great, though the authorship was even then regarded as doubtful, and now attributed to Konstantinos VII Porphyrogennetos (10th century).[20] Cornarius had obtained the manuscript from his Bohemian friend Matthæus Aurogallus, the Professor of Hebrew at Wittenberg, who had obtained it from the library of Johannes Alexander Brassicanus. The piece did not appear in Greek until Robert Winter published Simon Grynæus's edition of it in March 1539; it seems that Grynæus used the same manuscript, sent by Brassicanus in Vienna to Basle through the good offices of the Moravian humanist Jan Zvolsky ze Zvole (Volscius).[21] But in 1539 yet another translation by Cornarius appeared with Froben and Episcopius, the first Latin translation of Artemidorus Daldianus's classical work on the interpretation of dreams: *De somniorum interpretatione libri quinque*, the dedication of which contains a defence of the interpretation of dreams against any attacks on the part of the Church.[22] Dreams, he says, should be examined seriously and soberly for unlike nightmares, which it was the physicians' job to treat, they were closely related to prophecies which even in the Bible are held to be a divine gift. Though, as he puts it, the work was not intended for reading by ladies at court, it nevertheless achieved popular success in as much as it gave rise to and formed the basis of vernacular translations: Italian in 1540, French 1555, English 1563, and German 1570, this last the work of the Nuremberg physician and mathematician Walter Hermann Ryff, a man whose pen was never idle. In September 1562 Girolamo Cardano's four books of *Somniorum Synesiorum insomnia explicantes* were published by Heinrich Petri in

20 The BL has a copy of two later editions: *Constantini Cæsaris selectarum præceptionum de agricultura libri viginti*, Basle: H. Froben and N. Episcopius, 1538 (pressmark 7074.b.29), and Basle: H. Froben and N. Episcopius, 1540 (pressmark 967.a.2.).

21 Γεοπονικα. *De re rustica selectorum libri XX*. Basle: [R. Winter], 1539. The BL has four copies: 967.a.8; 234.c.19; G.8900; and 680.b.6.

22 BL copy pressmark 52.a.9.

Basle, with a second edition by his son, Sebastian Henricpetri, in 1585.[23] As early as March 1563 the *Traumbuch Cardani* appeared in German, translated by Johann Jacob Huggelin, a physician in Basle and Professor of Greek who died of the plague in 1564. He, too, justified the professional interpretation of dreams, which had been practised by the Assyrians and in Biblical times right down to the Romans, as being quite in keeping with Christianity, and he recommends the Abbot of Murbach and Lure, Johann Rudolf, to whom the work is dedicated, to find a place for the work in the *Bibliotheck unnd Liberey* which he had arranged on Ptolemaic principles.

In 1543 Cornarius, who had by this time become Professor of Medicine at Marburg where he was still working on his translation of Hippocrates, published with Robert Winter his translation, the first, of the *Physiognomicon* of the fourth-century Jewish physician Adamantios of Alexandria, using a copy of the first printed edition of the Greek text (Paris, 1540) which had been lent to him by his colleague Johannes Dryander, a kindness which he repaid by dedicating the translation to him. He says that the significance of the *Physiognomicon* is evident from the close connexion and mutual dependence of mind and body, body and soul. He supplies the Greek text so that anyone who prefers to do so can read it in the original, and compare and assess his translation.

Cornarius's last translations appeared only after his death, which occurred in Jena on 16 March 1558. He had offered them on 1 September 1557 to Johannes Herwagen the Younger, whose father had published his Zwickau plague treatise in 1551, but in the event they appeared with Froben and Episcopius. They included Plato (1561),[24] the first extensive translation of works of Synesius, the Neo-platonist Bishop of Ptolemais (1560), published as an appendix to the first translation of Georgios Pachymeres's epitome of Aristotle, which had been prepared by Philipp Bächi, the Professor of Greek and Logic in Basle and a Licenciate in Medicine, using a Greek manuscript obtained by Froben and Episcopius from Italy, probably from Arnoldus Arlenius Peraxylus. Cornarius had seen the first complete Greek edition of Synesius (Paris, 1553) in Frankfurt, probably at the book fair, and decided to make the work available to a wider reading public. One wonders whether these translations appeared with Froben and Episcopius because Cornarius's demand for 170 Gulden and 50 Gulden respectively, in four instalments spread over eighteen months, payable at the Frankfurt fairs, with twenty complimentary copies of each, had been too high for Herwagen.

LEONHARD FUCHS

The Tübingen physician and botanist Leonhard Fuchs also had not only his herbals but also his major Latin translations printed in Basle. Thus in 1537,

23 BL pressmarks 719.f.4 (1). and 719.f.5., respectively.
24 BL pressmark G.3034.

even while he was collaborating over the joint enterprise of the Greek edition of Galen in 1538, for the second volume of which he based his recension on the 1525 Aldine, a manuscript from England and the old Latin translation, he published his translation of Hippocrates's *Epidemiorum liber sextus* in partnership with two printers, Johann Bebel and his son-in-law and successor, Michael Isingrin.[25] This translation, which was accompanied by a commentary and an improved Greek text, has a dedication, which, as well as criticizing Calvus's translation (Rome, 1525), reprimands those people who babble on about a knowledge of Greek being superfluous for physicians now that all the writings of the Greek physicians were available in Latin, without realizing that translators are fallible. In August 1544, a good two years after publication of his herbal and just before his quarrel with Cornarius, he published with Oporinus his translation of and commentary on Hippocrates's *Aphorisms*. This was based on lectures which he had held in Esslingen to where the University of Tübingen had moved because of an outbreak of plague. It was the students who had encouraged him to publish them. In March 1549 Oporinus also published Fuchs's new translation of the pharmaceutical writings of Nikolaus Myrepsus ('ointment cook'), the personal physican to the Byzantine emperor in the thirteenth century. An incomplete translation of this by Johannes Agricola Ammonius, with various addenda, had appeared in Ingolstadt in 1541, and an improved reprint of this *germanica editio* had appeared in Venice two years later. For his edition Fuchs replaced the fragmentary work of his friend Agricola with his new, straightforward translation of a Greek manuscript because knowledge and supervision of medicines were then in a parlous state.

Fuchs had quite different aims with his Latin and German herbals. In his brief history of botany in *De Historia stirpium Commentarii* (Basle: Michael Isingrin, March 1542), he had warned against making approximate or forced identifications of local plants with those described by Dioscorides, advising people to call them by native or 'barbarian' names if necessary.[26] At the same time he discussed the plants in alphabetical order under their Greek names, listing them under their 'barbarian' (Vulgar Latin) names only when there was no Greek or Classical Latin name (e.g. *Aquilegia* or *Allaria*), and had the index printed in four parts, in the order Greek, Latin, Vulgar Latin (following the practice of ointment-sellers and contemporary herbals), and German. It is clear from the dedication of his large German *New Kreüterbůch*,[27] in the title of which the names of the plants are listed in the sequence *Teütsche, Lateinische unnd Griechische namen, auch deren sich die Apotecker gebrauchen*, that the work was intended for a different public, being much shorter and containing no scientific or historical discussion. The work was aimed not least at surgeons who had no academic training and in the main did not have a command of Latin, and specifically at laymen with their gardens. Fuchs counselled such people to seek

25 BL copy pressmark 539.h.7 (1).
26 BL pressmarks 450.h.1; 36.h.8; 444.k.6.
27 BL pressmark 450.h.2.

the advice of a doctor before using the herbs he describes for medical purposes. Here too the plants were listed in the same order as in the Latin edition, that is, alphabetically according to their names in Greek, but under their German names, with the Greek names transliterated both in the text (here together with the Latin name printed in Fraktur) and in the Latin index for the benefit of the layman. The original section with the scholarly description (which is often in several parts) headed 'Vires Ex Dioscoride – Ex Galeno – Ex Plinio' was replaced by a single, abridged section headed 'Die krafft und würckung' without specific reference to ancient sources or quotations. The two small editions of 1545 (together with subsequent reprints), which differ from each other only in their preliminaries, the preface to the reader in the case of the German edition of 10 August and to Anton Fugger in the Latin one of 18 August, and their indexes, served different purposes again. The latter did not need a German index, whereas the former has a Latin index preceding the German. The plant illustrations, presumably the work of the same three artists, Füllmaurer, Meyer, and Speckle, are labelled with their usual Latin and German names without descriptions. This means that the illustrations and the Latin index could be printed from the same setting for both editions in a single operation, which would have saved money. One unusual but perfectly understandable feature was the insertion in the privilege against unauthorized reprints granted by Emperor Ferdinand of a total ban on the copying of the illustrations. In the preface Fuchs listed the reasons for bringing out these small editions, though without mentioning a possible subsidiary aim of the publisher: to beat the pirates. He says that the large edition 'is most suitable for use at home and in the house', but anyone needing to have the illustrations with him to identify plants 'when out walking or when making an expedition to find herbs' will find them here 'in a more compact format, but executed with perfect precision', and then launches an attack on copyists like 'the shameless Ryff and Egenolph' and points out that the aim of this edition was to provide painters, goldsmiths 'and similar artists' with an inexpensive handbook that would provide them with all the illustrations they needed.[28] (This last point is, of course, not found in the small Latin edition.) The Dutch *Nieuwe Herbarius* by Isingrin and the Parisian *Commentaires tres excellens de l'hystoire des plantes* by Jacques Gazeau, folios published in 1549, both employ the more economical smaller woodcuts, while the Dutch edition is based on the German text of 1543 and the Paris edition translated from the Latin.

Andreas Vesalius of course had no need to translate the seven books of his *De humani corporis fabrica* (Basle: Oporinus, 1543), which was not his first work to appear in Basle.[29] A digest, more lavish in format and to some extent in regard to illustrations, was translated by Albanus Torinus in the space of a few weeks.

28 Walter Hermann Ryff (Rivius) also translated Vitruvius's *Zehen Bücher von der Architectur*, also published in Basle in 1575, which he then exploited for his *Bawkunst oder Archtectur*. The Frankfurt printer Christian Egenolph brought out Ryff's commentary on Dioscorides's *De medicinali materia libri sex* in 1543 and again in 1549.

29 BL pressmark C.54.k.12.

THEODOR ZWINGER

Theodor Zwinger (born 1533), the most important Basle physician and philosopher of the next generation, whose extensive correspondence with some of the most important people throughout the western world in his day is as yet largely unpublished, no longer translated texts that were already available in more or less satisfactory versions. Rather he fell back on existing translations and brought out commentaries on them, sometimes pointing to the need for a new translation. In August 1566 Oporinus and Eusebius Episcopius published his bilingual edition with commentary on the most important work in ancient ethics, Aristotle's *Ethica Nicomachea*.[30] He made use of the translation and commentary by his Parisian friend Denis Lambinus which had been published in Venice in 1558, edits the Greek text and adds his own, sometimes extensive scholia, incorporates Marc Antoine Muret's commentary on Book V, and, seeing that Aristotle makes frequent allusion to Pythagorean ideas, had a promising young Dutchman Willem Canter[31] make a new translation of and write a commentary on Pythagoras's fragments in Stobaeus's anthology. Canter dedicated his part of the work to his teacher Zwinger, and he in turn dedicated the whole book to Lambinus. A second, completely revised edition was published by Eusebius Episcopius in 1582, after the death of Lambinus in 1572 and the early demise of Canter in 1575. In this case, too, Zwinger supplements the edition with the translation of a piece by another author on a related subject: the *Characteres* of Theophrastus, a disciple and successor of Aristotle. The translation was the work of Claude Aubery, physician and lecturer in Philosophy at Lausanne whom he had probably got to know during his period as a student in Basle in 1573-74 and about which Aubery tells us something in his dedication to the Lausanne patrician Jean Bouvier. Zwinger dedicates this book to Grand Prince Alexander of Lithuania of the Jagellonian House who had visited him in Basle two years earlier when on an educational grand tour.

ADAM VON BODENSTEIN, GERARDUS DORN, AND GEORG FORBERGER AS TRANSLATORS OF PARACELSUS

No survey of the translation of medical works in Basle would be complete without a discussion of the Latin translations of Paracelsus. In his *Bibliographia Paracelsica* Karl Sudhoff lists two hundred and fifty-two editions of his works published during the author's lifetime and before the end of the sixteenth century. Approximately ninety editions, more than a quarter of the total, were published in Basle itself or (in four cases) by people from Basle in nearby Mulhouse, and thirty-seven in Strasbourg. The majority of the first editions

30 BL pressmark 518.m.4.

31 He had published the first translation of Aelius Aristides with Perna and Petri in March 1566 and his translation of Lykophron's difficult *Alexandra* came out with Oporinus and Perna in May.

appeared in these two cities, and the first collected edition in Paracelsus's usual language, German, as well as the first attempt at a collected edition in Latin came out in Basle. But some of his writings came out in print in translation before they appeared in the original, and some of them have in fact come down to us only in translation. With but two exceptions, all the Basle editions were printed or published by Peter Perna, who also acted as publisher for some German editions printed by Apiarius, or by his successor, Conrad Waldkirch.

Paracelsus's main editors and translators in Basle were, first, Adam von Bodenstein, a physician in Basle and son of Andreas Bodenstein von Karlstadt, the Reformer with Anabaptist leanings; secondly, Gerardus Dorn, a man of uncertain origin; and finally Georg Forberger from Mitweida in Meissen. In Strasbourg Paracelsus's books were mainly edited by Michael Toxites (Schütz), a former schoolmaster from Brugg and physician who had studied under Bodenstein. The first Basle edition was *Libri quatuor de vita longa* (1560), which, as we learn from the printer of the 1568 edition, Perna, and the editor of the collected works of 1589–91, Johannes Huser, was translated into Latin by Johannes Oporinus, who later became Professor of Latin and Greek in Basle as well as printer but who, during the months Paracelsus spent in Basle, had been his assistant charged with the responsibility for simultaneous translation of his master's lectures into Latin. Bodenstein, the editor, tells us nothing about the origin of the manuscript he used. The summer of 1562 saw the publication of an edition of *Libri V de vita longa* by Perna, in the dedication of which Bodenstein points out that the manuscript for the earlier edition had been incomplete.[32] But even in the parts which had already been published there are a number of differences between the 1560 and 1562 texts. During the interval between the appearance of these two editions a further six books by Paracelsus had come out; and there were another six first editions in 1562 alone, including the *Libri V de vita longa*, and five of these, whether in German or in Latin, were the work of Bodenstein in Basle and Mulhouse.

When dedicating the first edition of the *Schreiben von den Tartarischen kranckheiten, nach dem alten nammen: Vom griesz sand und stein* (unsigned and undated, but printed by Perna in 1563)[33] to the Colmar apothecary Melchior Dors, who had provided him with printer's copy not only for this work but for others too in the shape of a manuscript from his Paracelsus collection, Bodenstein justified his endeavours to disseminate and promote understanding of the writings of 'the premier and true physician' by saying that many doctors who had acquired books by Paracelsus but found their content too difficult had expressed the wish that he should communicate the contents of the book, or Paracelsus's method, in which all aspects of his practice and the 'new names' might be explained to them. As far as the terminology is concerned, he says, he will try to ensure that 'synonyms' are published, but as regards a book on the method as such, he had no information – it was only several years later that the

32 BL pressmark 1039.d.40.
33 BL pressmarks 7561.a.40 and 773.b.23 (2).

Basle alchemist, physician, geologist, goldsmith and printer Leonhard Thurneysser published an Ερμηνεια: *Das ist ein Onomasticum, Interpretatio oder erklerunge* (Berlin, 1574) and Adam von Bodenstein an *Onomasticon ... eigne Auszlegung etlicher seiner wörter und preparierungen* (Basle: Perna, 1575) as a companion to Paracelsus's writings. In 1563 also Bodenstein prepared the first edition of the *Libri quinque de causis, signis & curationibus morborum ex Tartaro utilissimi* for Perna, a work known to us only from a set of Latin notes on Paracelsus's lectures. In the edition Bodenstein translated into Latin the German words and phrases taken down verbatim at the lectures so that everyone might understand them. In the dedication to Cosimo de Medici he gives a rather highfaluting biographical sketch of his master, claiming that Paracelsus had written a huge number of books in Latin, German and other languages on all branches of philosophy, having demonstrated that truth could be conveyed in any language, as long as one had a proper understanding of it. The transmission of the Latin text of the *Defensiones septem* and of the 1563 German version of *De Tartaro, sive morbis Tartareis* is different again. Both pieces had already been published in the German original together with the *Labyrinthus* in Cologne in 1564 (the *Labyrinthus* having already appeared in Latin in Nuremberg in 1553 and in a Flemish translation based on this in Antwerp in 1563). Here Bodenstein tells the reader that someone had translated these books into Latin many years previously, though that man had been paraphraser rather than a precise translator. This had made it diffcult to improve the translation; if the reader were dissatisfied, he should know that shortness of time was to blame.

The first Paracelsus translation published at Basle by Gerardus Dorn, who already in 1566 had dedicated his *Clavis totius Philosophiae Chymisticae* (Lyon, 1567) to Paracelsus and Adam Bodenstein, was published by Perna in 1568 under the title *Pyrophilia vexationumque liber*.[34] This title was modelled on the *Liber vexationum, Kunst und Natur der Alchimia* which Bodenstein had had printed in Basle early in 1568, as he explained in detail in the preface. He says he was publishing his Latin translation of these together with three further pieces by Paracelsus 'which have been published by Dr Adam von Bodenstein from the author's German manuscript and which subsequently have been translated accurately and faithfully into Latin by Gerardus Dorn'. In the dedication of Paracelsus's *Chirurgia* to Egenolph von Rapoltzstein, Dorn claimed that many important scholars who could discriminate between good and bad had asked him, in view of his experience of translating some of Paracelsus's writings into Latin, to translate all of that author's writings that came into his hands, so that their country too might have a share in this treasure.[35] Since he had perceived that foreigners considered him to be an ornament to Germany, a label he would disclaim, he was inclined to accede to their wishes, for it was not only

34 BL pressmark 1032.b.5 (1).
35 An unknown editor published extracts from the *Grosse Wundartzney* (Ulm, 1536) in Frankfurt (after 1549, and again in 1555 and 1561).

the French but the Belgians and many other nations, too, who desired to read and understand Paracelsus's works. In another publication by Perna in 1570 Dorn brought together his translations of three tracts related in subject matter under the title *De summis Naturae Mysterijs libri tres*:[36] the German original of the first, *De spiritibus Planetarum*, came out only the next year, presumably with Perna, and again in another of Bodenstein's composite volumes in 1572, and, though it appeared on both occasions under the name of Paracelsus, it would seem not in fact to be by him. The second of the three, *De occulta Philosophia*, had been published in German in Strasbourg just in time for the Spring Fair of 1570, and the third, *De Medicina coelesti, sive de signis Zodiaci & Mysterijs eorum*, came out in German only in 1571, together with the first piece.

Early in the 1570s Perna had a row with his translator, Dorn. In 1564 Bodenstein had attempted, misguidedly, to put together the 'five books' that Paracelsus had promised by bringing out under the title *Opus Chyrurgicum, warhaffte unnd vollkomne Wundartzney* the three parts of the *Große Wundartzney* that had appeared in Frankfurt in 1562 and other pieces by him. In 1573 Dorn, apparently commissioned by Perna, had started to translate them into Latin but then, according to Perna at least, had tried to get out of the work, whether out of lack of interest in it or because he hoped to obtain a better reward for his labours from another source. As we discover from Perna's explanation in the dedication, every time Perna enquired about the progress of the translation, Dorn had tried to get other translation work after the contract had been annulled and in the process he had learned of the existence of a private venture, made by a certain Josquin Dalheim for two young people who were besotted with Paracelsus with the deliberate intention of regaining them for traditional medicine by showing them what Paracelsus's fantasies were really like. At Perna's request, he says, Dalheim had agreed to publication of the word-for-word translation after Perna had expressed a wish for a translation that used more familiar medical terms for well-known things than would have been the case if a member of the Paracelsian sect had undertaken the work and, by giving things the names they employed, had shed more dark than light on the tract. And then he quotes what Dalheim says in his covering letter about his approach to translation: that he had paraphrased the author's original at various points, sometimes reproducing not what he in fact said but what he ought to have said or had certainly intended to say. Furthermore, with the aid of a manuscript which he believed was almost certainly in the author's hand, he had translated various things differently from how they appeared in the existing (German) edition. And finally, even though Dalheim seemed to him to have been too pernickety in picking up the mistakes made by others (as often happens in prefaces and epilogues), he had left out unimportant things, which practice Perna defends, even though he expects to be criticized for it.

During the course of 1573 Perna seems to have found another translator

36 BL pressmark 7321.c.49 (3).

in Basle after all, Georg Forberger from Mitweida in Meissen. Forberger is recorded as having registered as a student at the University of Basle as 'Georgius Forberger alias Villanus, Mitweidensis Misnius', in the summer of 1573 and then, in the winter semester 1574-75 at Leipzig. Already in 1570 the Frankfurt printer Georg Rab had printed Forberger's and Hieronymus Halverius's German version of Paolo Giovio's contemporary history for publication by Perna.[37] In 1573-74 Forberger prepared a German version of Curione's Latin translation of Francesco Guicciardini's *Historia d'Italia*, again presumably for publication by Perna. Unlike Dorn, but like Bodenstein, he also prepared a German edition of a work of Paracelsus's for publication by Perna, using a copy he made himself in Silesia from Paracelsus's manuscript and had brought with him to Basle. This was the *Sechstes Buch in der artzney: Von den Tartarischen oder Stein kranckheiten*, printed by Apiarius for Perna in time for the Spring Fair 1574 and dedicated to the Frankfurt councillor Hans Heinrich vom Rhein. In 1572 in Basle Bodenstein had edited the tract *Von den natürlichen Dingen* together with the *Manuale* under a single title, *Metamorphosis*, and, under the title *Drey herrliche Schrifften*, the tracts *Vom geist des lebens und seiner krafft* and *Von krafft innerlicher und leiblicher glider*, along with one further piece, while Toxites in Strasbourg had brought out *Zwen Tractatus: De viribus membrorum spiritualium & De Electro*, in German. Forberger translated both works into Latin using these printed editions and probably manuscript sources as well; they appeared as *De natura rerum libri septem*, *De natura hominis libri duo*, and *Opuscula vere aurea*. To some extent he had rearranged the texts, adding the usual marginal notes detailing the content as expected from a scholarly, Latin edition. This was the first of his Paracelsus editions in which he mentions his name.[38] In the spring of 1575 at the latest Perna conceived the plan of bringing out a collected edition of Paracelsus's works in German for the benefit of those who understood the author's own language and in Latin for foreign readers. The German edition in fact was only completed under his successor, Conrad Waldkirch, in the years 1589-91; it was prepared by Johannes Huser from Waldkirch in the Black Forest, who had studied in Freiburg and Basle and was personal physician and advisor to the Archbishop of Cologne. He undertook this work as a commission – and thus doubtless at the expense – of his lord. The Latin edition started appearing with Perna in 1575, edited by Georg Forberger, but only got as far as the second volume, which nevertheless ran to nearly two thousand octavo pages! In the preface to the first volume Perna not only spelled out the plan for the edition but also drew attention to the editorial and financial problems, especially the difficulty of obtaining texts in the first place because many of these were hidden and retained by Paracelsus's supporters. He pointed

37 *Warhafftige Beschreibunge aller Chronikwirdiger Historien*. BL pressmark 9072.i.8 (1).

38 Sudhoff, *Bibliographica Paracelsica*, p. 205, attributes the Latin translation of the *Liber Paramirum*, published by Perna in time for the Autumn Fair 1570, to Forberger. Support for this view may be seen in the fact that the Giovio translation by Forberger and Halverius was also published by Perna in Frankfurt that year.

out that he tried to arrange in volume one previously printed texts that had not yet come out in Latin in some meaningful order and that volume two would comprise all the theological writings, almost none of which had ever been published in Latin, before going on to say that he was in the process of getting the writings on the practice of medicine ready for the press, not least thanks to the efforts made by Georg Forberger, who made accurate and faithful translations and was engaged in putting the German and Latin texts in order. In the event, the medical writings, which proved to be more numerous and longer than anticipated, filled volume two, and Paracelsus's theological writings are in part still awaiting their editor even today. In the same year as these two volumes appeared, 1575, one of Forberger's translations was published by Perna as an appendix to two alchemistic tracts by Alexander von Suchten and Georgios Phaedros. This was the *Liber de narcoticis aegritudinibus*, which, however, despite the claim on the title page, was not an entirely new translation but a revision made with the help of an additional manuscript of part of the Bodenstein translation of the tract on the Tartar diseases which Perna had published in 1563 and 1570 and to which marginal notes had meanwhile been added. The last piece of work Forberger did for Perna was in 1579, two years after Bodenstein's death, when in response to many requests he was commissioned to arrange for publication such of Paracelsus's writings as had not hitherto been printed. In the dedication he recalled that he had spent the previous winter arranging all of Paracelsus's writings in three volumes. The first would contain the writings on 'medicina physica', that is, internal medicine, the second would deal with surgery, and the third with writings 'die so Astronomiam, Philosophiam und transmutationem oder Alchimiam und verwandlung der metallen betreffen' (that is, writings on astronomy, philosophy, and 'transmutation' or alchemy and the conversion of metals). This was a revival, almost certainly instigated by the publisher himself, of Perna's plan for a complete edition of Paracelsus's German works. But in fact only a volume on surgery came out: *Kleine Wundartzney ... drey Bücher begreiffendt. Deszgleichen auch zwey Fragment ...* Forberger was aware of the existence of yet more texts and expressed a pious hope that one day they would be published. He was aware also that the editions of the *Wundartzney* that had been published hitherto did not correspond to Paracelsus's work.

SIXTEENTH-CENTURY GERMAN BOHEMICA IN THE BRITISH LIBRARY

MIRJAM BOHATCOVÁ

ONE OF THE CHARACTERISTIC FEATURES of the book trade in Bohemia and Moravia in the sixteenth century was the regular use of three languages: Czech, Latin, and German. Latin, as the language of humanistic works, developed such a close link with Czech that books written in Czech often have a preliminary title in Latin or a Latin epigram from the pen of a contemporary poet or a recognized classical author. Little details such as these enhanced the prestige of the author, the printer, or the work itself. German, in contrast, occupies third position in the pecking order, especially in the first half of the sixteenth century, though even then a number of important books were being published in that language.

A number of years ago we attempted on the basis of as yet incomplete information to determine how many books were published in Bohemia and Moravia in the sixteenth century. We concluded that there were at least 4,400 bibliographical entities *in toto*. Of these, books in Czech accounted for more than 2,800, books in Latin for more than 1,400, and books in German (together with a small number in other languages) rather more than 200.[1] These numbers relate to books produced on the territory of Bohemia and Moravia, together with works by Bohemian authors printed elsewhere, and the works of foreign authors printed in Bohemia and Moravia.

The term *Bohemica* can, however, be interpreted in a wider sense, to include foreign books concerned with Bohemian themes, whether religious, social, or political, that is, books by foreign authors printed in foreign countries. An extreme case would be books on a broadly European theme in which the kingdom of Bohemia features somehow. But our scholarly bibliography of Bohemica in foreign languages from the sixteenth to the eighteenth century does not stretch as far as that.[2]

1 Anežka Baďurová, Mirjam Bohatcová and Josef Hejnic, 'Frekvence tištěné literatury 16. století v Čechách a na Moravě' ['The frequency of printed literature in Bohemia and Moravia in the sixteenth century'], *Folia historica Bohemica*, XI (Prague, 1987), 321-42 (with German summary).

2 Josef Hejnic unter Mitwirkung von Anežka Baďurová und Mirjam Bohatcová, 'Fragen der bibliographischen Beschreibung und Bearbeitung der tschechischen und fremdsprachigen bohemikalen Drucke des 16.-18. Jahrhunderts', in: Peter Thiergen (ed.), *Vorträge und Abhandlungen zur Slavistik*, XVII (Munich, 1990).

A. F. Johnson and V. Scholderer listed the Bohemica in the British Library in the *German STC*, while David Paisey has described more recent accessions in his *Supplement*. These lists show that many of these items are chance acquisitions, having been bound up in old tract volumes, while others reflect a sound selection policy on the part of those responsible for building up the collections.

Books printed in Czech were intended primarily for the Bohemian book market, few of them finding their way to the Frankfurt book fair. Yet some Prague printers were the first in Europe to bring out certain important books in German. In particular one thinks of the herbal of Pierandrea Mattioli, the personal physician to Ferdinand of Tyrol, the Habsburg representative in Prague. This was translated by Georg Handsch and the first German edition was published by Georg Melantrich in Prague in 1563 under the title *New Kreuterbuch*.[3] The description in the *German STC* does not make it clear that the book really was printed in Prague and that Mattioli's Venetian printer, Vincenzo Valgrisi, simply had a stake in it as a publisher, as their joint device is meant to indicate. Melantrich's previous work for Mattioli stood him in such good stead that he was entrusted with this German book too, and in the preface to the first Czech version of the herbal (1562) Mattioli praised the printer in the following words:

> Est etiam laudanda sedulitas ac summa quidem diligentia Georgii Melantrichi ab Aventino, calcographi et civis Pragensis, quippe qui tam in opere ipso cudendo, quam in conflandis elegantissimis typis plurimum laboris insumsit, ut eo maior sit operis pulchritudo, quo praestantior fuerit utilitas. ('The assiduity and also the surpassing diligence of George Melantrich of Aventin, a printer and citizen of Prague are to be praised as much for the effort he invested in it as for the elegant types he used, with the result that the attractiveness of the work is matched by its usefulness'.)

Moreover Melantrich had already published in 1561 Mattioli's Latin correspondence with physicians throughout the whole of Europe, an enterprise in which Valgrisi had been a co-publisher also.[4] The second edition appeared at Lyons in 1564. Mattioli's German herbal, edited in 1586 by Joachim Camerarius the Younger (1534-1598), was reissued by Johann Feyerabend at Frankfurt am Main in 1590.[5]

Another technical handbook owned by the British Library is the *Beschreibung Aller fürnemisten Mineralischen Ertzt vnnd Berckwercksarten* by Lazarus Ercker von Schreckenfels, mine-master first in Joachimsthal and then in Kuttenberg and afterwards master of the Prague mint.[6] This was printed in 1574 by Georg Nigrin (Jiří Černý, Georg Schwarz), the leading printer in Prague from 1571-1606 during the reign of Rudolph II. This book contains many illustrations of documentary value, showing how silver, gold and other metals were

3 BL pressmark 450.i.2.

4 Mirjam Bohatcová, 'Prager Drucke der Werke Pierandrea Mattiolis aus den Jahren 1558-1602', *GJ*, 60 (1985), 167-85.

5 BL pressmark L35/145 (see *Ger STC Suppl.*)

6 BL pressmark 443.g.1.

obtained from the ore. Only at the end of the book does the printer reveal that he had commissioned a translation into Czech, which however had not materialized. Ercker's book came out in German again in two Frankfurt editions, one printed by J. Schmidt for Sigmund Feyerabend in 1580, the other by Johann Feyerabend in 1598.[7]

One special group of books comprises the multilingual textbooks produced in Bohemian lands for Czech schoolboys, whose guaranteed sales would have recommended them to almost all Prague printers. Examples in the British Library, all listed in Paisey's *Ger STC Supplement*, include:

M. Collinus, *Nomenclatura rerum familiariorum* (Prague: Jan Kantor Had, 1555) (Latin, Czech and German) (BL: C.114.r.26 (1).)
S. Heyden, *Puerilium colloquiorum formulae* (Prague: Jan Kantor Had, 1557) (Latin, Czech and German) (BL: C.114.r.26 (4).)
V. Makovinus, *Dialogi pueriles* (Prague: Georg Melantrich 1579 (Latin, Czech and German) (BL: C.114.r.27 (4).)
P. Codicilus, *Vokabulář* (Prague: Daniel Adam of Veleslavín, [1586/87]) (in Latin, Czech and German) (BL: C.118.r.27 (3).
M. Bacháček, *Donati declinationum paradigmata* (Prague: Johannes Schuman (Šuman), 1591) (Latin, Czech and German) (BL: C.114.r.27 (1).)

In 1527 Hans Pekk in Pilsen printed the first, anonymous Czech-German conversation guide for merchants, and in 1540 a similar but more compendious work was brought out by Ondřej Klatovský of Dalmanhorst, *Knížka v českém a německém jazyku složená. ... Ein büchlein in Behemischer vnd Deütscher sprach, wie ein Beham Deütsch, deß gleychen ein Deütscher Behamisch lesen, schreiben vnd reden lernen soll.* The British Library has two later editions of Klatovský's book, published by Melantrich (1567) and Daniel Adam of Veleslavín (1595).[8]

Some printers in Bohemia and Moravia originally came from Germany and became fully assimilated in the Bohemian lands. Jan Pekk from Nuremberg married in Pilsen. Another German was Michael Peterle who worked in Prague; he was a very prolific editor of texts and he had originally trained as a cutter of woodcuts. Among his publications were two religious tracts in German by Johann Habermann who was very popular in Bohemia, and in particular a charmingly illustrated little book for ladies in German, Lucas Martini's *Der Christlichen Jungfrawen Ehrenkräntzlein* (1585),[9] which he also brought out in Czech the following year. Peterle also succeeded in gaining a firm foothold in the book market abroad with his many illustrated news-sheets.[10]

7 BL pressmarks 459.a.11 and 444.e.29 (1) respectively.
8 BL pressmarks 12976.aa.6 and 12976.aaa.15 respectively. See Mirjam Bohatcová, 'Unbekannte, in Regensburg entdeckte Pilsner Drucke aus dem 16. Jahrhundert', *Germanoslavica*, n.s. 1 (6) (1994), 11-22.
9 BL pressmarks 1221.a.4 (3), 1221.a.4 (2) and 847.b.5 (1). respectively. See *Ger STC Suppl.*
10 Pravoslav Kneidl, 'Přední pražský dřevorytec a tiskař 16. století. S ilustracemi a se seznamem Peterlových jednolistových tisků' ['The leading sixteenth-century Prague wood engraver and printer. With the illustrations and a checklist of Peterle's pamphlets'], *Bibliotheca Strahoviensis* (at press).

A popular, if often criticized book for many centuries was the *Bohemian Chronicle* (*Kronika česká*), compiled by the enterprising Catholic priest Václav Hájek of Libočany, and printed at Prague in 1541. The British Library has the German version, translated by Johannes Sandel and published in Prague in 1596 by Nikolaus Strauß (Mikuláš Pštros).[11]

Turning now to Moravian books in German, pride of place must be given to the Brno incunable *Von den heissen Bädern*, with its fictitious author's name Clement von Graz, which is in fact the work of the Nuremberg barber-surgeon-poet-printer Hans Folz, printed anonymously in 1495. The British Library's copy (IA 51720) is unique; it was purchased from the library of the eighteenth-century connoisseur J. P. Cerroni.[12]

Johann (Jan) Günther, who had been working as a compositor for Czech with Leonhard Milchtaler in Nuremberg, married his employer's widow and moved with her and her young son to Moravia, first to Prostějov (Proßnitz) and then to Olomouc, where the son eventually founded an important family of printers. One item documenting Günther's work in Prostějov is a textbook in Latin, Czech and German, *Elegantissimae colloquiorum formulae ex Terentij comœdijs selectae*, printed in 1550.[13]

The British Library possesses a number of examples of illegal German imprints produced by the Czech Unity of Brethren (*Unitas Fratrum Bohemorum*). These include not only confessions and catechisms but especially hymnbooks, among which one may single out for special mention Michael Weisse's *Ein New Gesengbuchlen* (Jungbunzlau, 1531) and the *Kirchengeseng, darinnen die Heuptartickel des christlichen Glaubens kurtz gefasset und ausgelegt sind*, which was compiled by Michael Tham, Johann Jeletzký and Peter Herbert from Fulnek and printed on the secret press of the United Brethren at Ivančice (Eibenschitz) in 1566.[14] The latter is a splendid piece of graphic design, with a portrait of Luther in addition to the traditional one of Jan Hus. Furthermore it is the only book produced by the United Brethren with a dedication – to the Emperor and King Maximilian II, to whom the book was officially presented at a formal ceremony on 27 November 1566, to demonstrate that the United Brethren were being unjustly accused of heresy. As the Moravian bishop of the United Brethren Jan Blahoslav put it, *Iste liber profecto vice copiosae apologiae esse poterit* ('This book can truly take the place of copious explanations').

It is not possible here to describe all the German-language Bohemica in the British Library, but, using the index of printers in the *German STC* and its supplement, they are readily identified. Going by place, printer, date and pressmark, they may be summarized as follows:

11 BL pressmark C.185.b.2. See *Ger STC Suppl.*

12 Vladislav Dokoupil, *Počátky brněnského knihtisku. Prvotisky.* [*The beginnings of printing in Brno. Incunabula*] (Brno, 1974), pp. 91–2.

13 BL pressmark C.185.a.21 (1). See *Ger STC Suppl.*

14 BL pressmarks: C.31.f.6 and C.65.gg.4, respectively.

PRAGUE
Unidentified printer 1547: 8073.bb.24 (see *Ger STC*, p. 135: Bohemia – Snem).
Georg Daschitsky (Jiří Dačický) 1570: C.185.a.26 (3) (see *Ger STC Suppl.)*.
Michael Peterle 1576: 1347.a.97 (2); 1576: 1870.d.2 (10); 1577: 1578/393 (see *Ger STC Suppl.)*; 1580: 1221.a.4 (3); 1580: 1221.a.4 (2); 1585: 847.b.5 (1); 1588: 812.f.11 (2).
Michael Peterle the Younger 1592: 812.f.11 (1); 1592: 718.g.8 (2).
Heirs of Michael Peterle the Younger 1595?: 8631.eee.36.
Hans Schuhman (Jan Šuman) 1594: 1312.c.79.
Unidentified printer 1595: 9325.aaa.34 (see *Ger STC Suppl.)*.
Heirs of Schuhman 1599: 9135.de.6 (1).
OLOMOUC (OLMÜTZ)
Unidentified printer 1588: 9476.dd.7 (see *Ger STC*, p. 963, under Pitschen).
Georg Haendl (Jiří Handl) 1598: 4034.c.4 (see *Ger STC*, p. 50, under Auerbacher).

Some of the sixteenth-century German Bohemica emanate from the principal printing centres abroad which often have close connexions with the Bohemian Reformers. Others come from places or printing shops that produced only occasional German Bohemica, at least on the evidence of the British Library's collections. Among the first group are places like Augsburg, Basle, Frankfurt am Main, Leipzig, Nuremberg, Strasbourg, Vienna, and Wittenberg, among the second Altenburg, Cologne, Dillingen, Dresden, Erfurt, Freiberg in Saxony, Hagenau, Hamburg, Heidelberg, Ingolstadt, Königsberg, Magdeburg, Mainz, Speyer, and Zurich. The British Library also has a number of German Bohemica which give no details of their printer.

The earliest book of Bohemian interest in German in the British Library comes from the circle of Bishop Johannes von Neumarkt (Jan ze Středy), the chancellor to Emperor Charles IV. This is the famous *Ackermann von Beheim. Schöne red vnd widerred eins akermans vnd des todes* (Strasbourg, J. Schott, 1500), written by Johann von Saaz (Jan of Žatec, or of Šítbor), the rector of the school in Saaz (Žatec) and later protonotary in Prague.[15]

One of the topics of great interest to people outside Bohemia, and thus to printers throughout Europe, was the burning of Jan Hus and Jerome of Prague at the stake after the Council of Constance in 1415 and 1416. Even a century after his death, Hus's last letters home from his dungeon and some of his writings attracted considerable attention, some of which are found in the British Library. Gabriel Kantz published two short tracts by Hus in Altenburg: *Das die Sekten vnd Menschenleren in der Christenheyt sollen ausgetilget werden* (1525) and *Von Schedlichkeit der menschen satzungen* (1525?).[16] Johann Setzer in Hagenau issued *History wie das heilig Euangelium mit Iohann Hussen ym Concilio zu Costnitz durch den Bapst verdampt ist* (1529).[17] Johann von Eck's *Des heiligen Concilij tzu Costenitz entschůldigung das in Martin Luder mit vnwarheit auffgelegt*

15 BL pressmark IA 2482.
16 BL pressmarks 3905.cc.73 and 3905.cc.74, respectively.
17 BL pressmark 11745.a.50 (2).

Sie haben Huß vnd Hieronymum von Prag wider Bapstlich geleidt, verbrandt (Leipzig: M. Landsberg, 1520),[18] and Johannes Fabri's *Wie sich Iohannis Hußs vnd Iohannis von Wessalia Leren vnd buecher mit Luther vergleichen* (Leipzig: Valentin Schumann, 1528).[19] In Magdeburg Melchior Lotter published Jan Hus, *IIII. Briefe aus dem gefengnis im Concilio zu Costnitz* (1536?),[20] and in Nuremberg Johann Petreius issued *Vier Christliche Briefe so Hus aus dem gefengchnus zu Costentz im Concilio an die Behem geschriben hat* (1536), with a preface by Luther.[21] In Strasbourg J. Schott brought out *Geistlicher Bluthandel Iohannis Hussz zu Costentz verbrannt* (1523?)[22] while Johann Grüninger published Albert Krantz's *Hystoria von den alten hussen zu Behemen* (1523).[23] Joseph Klug in Wittenberg also published Hus's letters from prison, *Etliche Briefe aus dem gefengnis* (1537), with Luther's preface, with another edition, with no printer's name, of the same date,[24] and another Wittenberg printer, Georg Rhau, issued J. Agricola's *Tragedia Iohannis Huss* (1538),[25] of which another edition, whose printer has not been identified, appeared perhaps in 1540.[26]

Among other items of note are the German translations of an account of a recent incident involving a certain Brother Nicolaus: *Eine Lustige Disputation eines vngelerten Bawern B. Nicolaus, in einem Synodo geschehen in Behemen anno 1471 mit den Pfaffen*. Four editions are known: two printed by G. Kreydl in Nuremberg in 1555(?) and 1558, and two unsigned from 1558 and 1560(?).[27] They relate to a certain Nicolaus of Vlásenice near Pelhřimov (Mikuláš Vlásenický, who died in 1495), the founder of a sect (the Mikulášenci, Vláseničtí or Pecinovští), who held a disputation on dogma with utraquist priests in 1471. The sole surviving copy of the Czech edition dates only from the second half of the sixteenth century and is imperfect.[28]

Under the entry 'Peter, Saint and Apostle' in *Ger STC* one will find a curious anti-papal tract entitled *In disem buchlin wirt klärlich bewert das der hailig Apostel Petrus gen Rom nicht kommen*, translated from the Latin of Ulrichus Velenus and printed at Augsburg by Sylvan Otmar in 1521.[29] A Latin edition of this work is thought to have been published also by Andreas Cratander in Basle in 1520: Velenus Ulricus Minhoniensis (*pseud.*): *In hoc libello probatur Apostolum Petrum*

18 BL pressmark 697.h.18 (4).
19 BL pressmark 697.h.18 (1).
20 BL pressmark 697.h.18 (2).
21 BL pressmark 698.e.21 (1).
22 The BL has two copies, pressmarks 4650.c.19 and 697.h.18 (3).
23 BL pressmark 837.e.2 (8).
24 BL pressmarks 3905.f.55 and 3906.cc.49, respectively.
25 The BL has two copies, pressmarks 11745.a.50 (1) and 11517.aa.14.
26 BL pressmark 11748.aa.1.
27 The BL pressmarks are 3905.f.61 and 3908.bbb.41, and 3908.cc.22 and 3907.a.30, respectively.
28 *Knihopis českých a slovenských tisků od doby nejstarší až do konce XVIII. století* [*Descriptive list of Czech and Slovak Imprints from the earliest Times to the End of the Eighteenth Century*]. Edited by Zdeněk Tobolka and (since 1950) by František Horák (Prague, 1925–67), no. 5561.
29 BL pressmark 3906.h.96.

Romam non venisse.[30] Author of this Latin work is the Czech knight, humanist and printer Ondřej Velenský from Mnichov (in Bohemia).[31]

Nicolaus Herman's *Eyn Mandat Ihesu Christi an alle seyne getrewen Christen* aroused great interest both in Bohemia and abroad. Herman, a schoolmaster from Joachimsthal, was a friend of Johannes Matthesius, one of Luther's admirers. In this little treatise Herman uses allegorical devices in a religious counterblast to secular mandates of the kind issued by monarchs. The British Library has the first edition, printed at Wittenberg, without the printer's name, in 1524.[32] Further editions which cannot be assigned to a particular printer came out in 1530 and 1546,[33] and in the latter year it also came out in Czech, followed by a further edition in 1598.[34] Both Czech editions lack details of the printer.

1525 saw the publication of an attractive novelty in German with a fine woodcut illustration, *Ein Wegsprech gen Regensburg zu inß Concilium zwischen eynem Bischoff, Hůrenwirt vnd Kůntzen, seinem knecht.* This is an extremely rare item, with a fictitious imprint, *Gedruckt zu Arnaw* [= Hostinné] *an der Elb in Böhem durch Hans Braun M D XXV.* In *Ger STC* it is entered under 'Ratisbon' and assigned to Amandus Farckall of Hagenau and dated 1525.[35] Josef Dobrovský, on the other hand, considered it the first book in German printed in Bohemia, relying on information from Vienna, where the Austrian National Library has a copy (pressmark 78 D 3).[36] Emil Weller and E. Camillo Rudolphi believed it had been printed by Christoph Froschauer in Zurich, but later investigation of the copy in the Zentralbibliothek at Zurich (pressmark XVIII 65 11) showed that in fact the book was printed by Froschauer's colleague Hans Hager. The author is believed to have been Joachim Vadianus (Joachim von Watt).[37] Froschauer also produced books for the Anabaptists in Nikolsburg (Mikulov).

30 BL pressmark 475.a.19 (1).

31 On this work see Antonie Jan Lamping, *Ulrichus Velenus (Oldřich Velenský) and his Treatise against the Papacy* (Leiden, 1975). The book includes a facsimile of Sylvan Otmar's Latin edition (Augsburg, 1520). We may add that the British Library has a copy of Johannes Cochlaeus, *Ob Sant Peter zu Rom sey geweßen* (Strasbourg: J. Grüninger, [*c.* 1524]), pressmark 3906.f.30.

32 BL pressmark 3906.g.44. On the printer see John L. Flood, 'Lucas Cranach as publisher', *GLL*, n.s. 48 (1995), 241–63, no. 28.

33 British Library pressmarks 1410.c.17 (5) and T.2167 (24).

34 See *Knihopis*, nos. 2955–56.

35 BL pressmark 3906.d.14.

36 Josef Dobrovský, 'Über die Einführung und Verbreitung der Buchdruckerkunst in Böhmen', in: Mirjam Daňková (ed.), *Spisy a projevy Josefa Dobrovského*, XIX (Prague, 1954), pp. 55–6 and 85, plates VI and VII.

37 Emil Weller, *Die falschen und fingierten Druckorte.* 2nd ed. (Leipzig, 1864), I, p. 2. E. Camillo Rudolphi, *Die Buchdruckerfamilie Froschauer in Zürich. Verzeichnis der aus ihrer Offizin hervorgegangenen Druckwerken* (Zurich, 1869). Paul Leemann-van Elck, *Bibliographie der Drucke Hans Hagers* (Berne, 1934). See also his study *Die Offizin Froschauer, Zürichs berühmte Druckerei im 16. Jahrhundert* (Zurich, 1940).

Johannes Fabri, Bishop of Vienna, published his *Vrsach warumb der widertewffer Patron Balthasar Hübmair zu Wien verbrant sey* (Dresden: Wolfgang Stöckel, 1528).[38] The burning of the Anabaptist Hubmair at the stake in Vienna was to spell the end of printing by the Anabaptists in the Moravian town of Nikolsburg (Mikulov) where they had found refuge; in the space of two years they had produced some seventeen books in German there.

Of the many publications by Philipp Melanchthon now in the British Library two deserve special mention here: *Ein Christliche Ermanung an den König Ferdinandum* (Nuremberg: Friedrich Peypus, 1529) and *Die furnemisten vnterschaid zwischen rayner Christlicher Lere vnd der Abgöttischen Papistischen Lere* (Augsburg: Philipp Ulhart [1540?]), for the particular reason that in 1546 the Nuremberg printer Christoph Gutknecht brought out a translation of the second of them: *Naiwetssj ... Rozdjlowe mezy czysteym ... vczenjm Ewangelium Swatého a Mezy tjm modlářským Papežským včenjm.*[39]

The Bohemian humanist Sigismundus Gelenius (Zikmund Hrubý z Jelení), who lived in Basle and had contact with Erasmus and Froben's printing house, made a name for himself through his editing, translating and publishing of classical writers using both printed and manuscript sources. He also made an interesting linguistic experiment, compiling a quadrilingual (Latin, German, Greek, and Czech) dictionary: *Lexicum symphonum quo quatuor linguarum Graecae scilicet, Latinae, Germanicae ac Sclauinicae concordia indicatur* (Basle: H. Froben and N. Episcopius, 1537), with a second edition, Λεξικον συμφωνον, published by R. Winter in Basle in 1544. The British Library has copies of both.[40]

In 1541 Prague suffered a terrible tragedy when the centre of the Lesser Town and the Hradschin Castle were burnt down. The most important source for the laws of the country, the *Desky zemské*, was destroyed. The Augsburg printer Heinrich Steiner rushed out an account of this disaster in his *Newe Zeytung vonn dem erschrockenlichen fewr, so newlich in der klainern statt Prag geschehen ist.*[41]

Christoph Rudolff's book, *Die Coss, mit schönen Exempeln*, published in Königsberg in 1553 or 1554,[42] deserves mention here because its printer, 'A. Lutomyslensis', was a member of an important Bohemian family of printers. He was Alexandr Oujezdecký from Leitomischl who had emigrated for religious

38 BL pressmark 3905.f.56 (2).

39 BL pressmarks 3905.ee.98; 3906.h.83; and 1358.i.10 (2)., respectively. See *Knihopis*, no. 5488, and Mirjam Bohatcová, 'Die tschechischen Drucke des Nürnberger Druckers Christoph Gutknecht', *GJ*, 66 (1991), 249-68, here pp. 252-3.

40 BL pressmarks C.33.f.18 (2) and 12901.c.49, respectively. *Knihopis*, nos. 3218-3219. On this work see Bohumil Ryba, 'Zikmund Hrubý z Jelení – Gelenius'. In: Vilém Mathesius (ed.), *Co daly naše země Evropě a lidstvu* [*What our countries have contributed to Europe and humanity*] (Prague, 1940), pp. 134-7.

41 BL pressmark 8716.bb.19 (see *Ger STC Suppl.*).

42 BL pressmark 8530.c.9.

reasons after the Schmalkaldic War. During his exile he also printed many important works in Polish.

The Czech Unity of Brethren, who were persecuted as an illegal sect of Waldensian or Picard origin, had attracted attention abroad because of their confessions and hymnbooks. As early as 1523 Johann Prüss the Younger, in Strasbourg, had published *Ein Christliche vnderweysung der kleinen Kinder im Glauben* by Bishop Luke of Prague (died 1528),[43] though Müller suggested that the first edition came out with Peypus in Nuremberg in 1522.[44] The *Rechenschaft des glaubens der Brüder in Behemen vnd Mehrern*, with a preface by Luther, was published by Hans Lufft in Wittenberg in 1533.[45] The British Library has a number of Nuremberg editions of books relating to the Brethren: *Artickel vnd vrsprung der waldenser, etc.* (Nuremberg: J. Gutknecht, 1524);[46] *Ein Gesangbuch der Brüder inn Behemen vnnd Merherrn*, edited by J. Horn (Roh) (Nuremberg, Johannes vom Berg and Valentin Neuber, 1544),[47] *Gesangbuch der Brüder in Behmen vnd Merherrn* (Nuremberg: D. Gerlach, 1575),[48] with further editions by K. Gerlachin and the Heirs of Johannes von Berg in 1585 and P. Kauffmann on Gerlach's press in 1594.[49] Michael Weisse (died 1534), the compiler of the 1531 German hymnbook, also published two works in Nuremberg: *Schöne Christliche Gesenge zum Begrebnus der Todten* (Nuremberg: Valentin Neuber, [1555?]) and *Ein schön geistlich Lied vom Leiden Jesu Christi* (Nuremberg: Friedrich Gutknecht, [1555?]).[50]

Finally, the writings of Johann Matthesius, the Lutheran preacher in Joachimsthal who hailed from Saxony and who died in 1565, were read abroad. Caspar Franck edited his *Zwo Trostpredigten* (Leipzig: G. Hantsch, 1556).[51] The British Library's copy of *Ein Trostpredig auß den Worten des Herrn, Matth. IX.* (Nuremberg: Johannes vom Berg and Valentin Neuber, 1561), formerly 4426.df.29 (6), was destroyed during the Second World War. Other books by Matthesius include: *Sarepta, darin von allerley Bergwerck vnnd Metallen guter bericht begeben. Sampt der Joachimsthalischen Chroniken* (Nuremberg: D. Gerlach, 1571), *Bergpostilla* (Nuremberg: K. Gerlach, 1578, and *Diluvium* (Nuremberg: K. Gerlachin, 1587).[52] As late as 1598 T. Wolder published Matthesius's *Oeconomia, das ist Bericht wie man Christlich haußhalten soll* in Hamburg;[53] this popular and useful guide to the conduct of everyday life had appeared in Czech in 1574 and was to do so again in 1615.[54]

43 BL pressmark 1224.a.22 (2).
44 Joseph Th. Müller, *Geschichte der Böhmischen Brüder*, I (Herrnhut, 1922), p. 544.
45 BL pressmark 3910.aaa.9.
46 BL pressmark 4650.c.17.
47 BL pressmark K.2.h.10.
48 BL pressmark 1221.b.55.
49 BL pressmarks C.30.i.9 and 3425.e.5, respectively.
50 BL pressmarks C.175.i.31 (13) and C.175.i.31 (36) (see *Ger STC Suppl.*).
51 BL pressmark 1607/2925 (see *Ger STC Suppl.*).
52 BL pressmarks 443.h.7; 695.k.1 and 1570/863, respectively. (See *Ger STC Suppl.*)
53 BL pressmark C.108.bb.3 (7).
54 *Knihopis*, nos. 5409 and 5410.

The remaining German Bohemica in the British Library can only be dealt with summarily here. I will list their pressmarks by town, printer, and date. In the case of multilingual textbooks and dictionaries it may be assumed that they include Czech.

AUGSBURG
H. Schönsperger 1500: IB.6422; 1504?: C.38.h.13.
E. Öglin 1515?: 1194.d.1; 1516?: IA.8827 (8); 1516: 12901.ccc.8. and 12901.c.11.
H. Steiner 1527: 1315.c.24.
P. Ulhart 1530?: 1312.c.29; 1531: C.33.f.17; 1550?: C..54.g.8 (see *Ger STC Suppl.*).
M. Franck 1560?: C.175.i.31 (25) (see *Ger STC Suppl.*); 1563: 811.d.39.
V. Schönig 1593: 591.c.35 and 168.a.3.

BASLE
S. Henricpetri 1577: 9335.m.8 (1).

DILLINGEN
J. Mayer 1587: 608.i.23; C.48.f.8; and 1328.b.9. (imperfect).

ERFURT
Michael Buchführer 1523: C.190.a.17 (see *Ger STC Suppl.*).
J. Beck 1587: 9475.aaa.18.

FRANKFURT AM MAIN
G. Rabe and S. Feyerabend 1562: 1196.f.43 (14).
Officina Paltheriana sumptibus N. Bassaei 1596: 1568/1358 (see *Ger STC Suppl.*).

FREIBERG IN SAXONY
G. Hofmann 1594: 1312.c.54.

INGOLSTADT
D. Sartorius 1591: 1193.l.42 (1).

LEIPZIG
V. Schumann 1520?: 3906.dd.60.
Heirs of J. Berwald 1577: 1351.a.13 (1).

MAINZ
I. Schöffer 1548: 1347.a.3 (see *Ger STC Suppl.*).

NUREMBERG
A. Koberger 1493: IC.7458.
G. Stuchs 1502: C.38.k.20.
H. Höltzel 1504: C.38.k.22.
J. Gutknecht 1521: 11517.dd.21 (3).
F. Peypus for Lucas Jordanus and Martin of Prague 1534: C.107.a.6. (a unique copy, see *Knihopis*, no. 2984)
J. Daubman 1548: Voyn. 23; 1549: C.33.c.37.
G. Merckel 1553: 11515.c.23 (15).
Printer unknown 1562: 811.c.20 (1).

SPEYER
J. Schmidt 1527: 1570/3461 (see *Ger STC Suppl.*).

STRASBOURG
Bohemians (unidentified) 1485: IA.1834.
G. Husner 1495? IB.2394. (imperfect).
B. Jobin 1571: 1750.c.2. (10).
N. Faber 1582: 9340.c.14.

VIENNA

J. Winterburg 1513: C.18.c.3 (33) (fragment) (see *Ger STC Suppl.*).

J. Singriener 1531: 1315.c.33; 1536: KTC.7.b.5.

Printer unknown 1541: 1235.i.11 (18).

R. Hofhalter 1562: 4034.i.35 (1).

C. Stainhofer 1568: 12903.a.49.

N. Appfel 1572: 4033.bb.43 (1).

WITTENBERG

N. Schirlentz 1524: C.175.b.25 (see *Ger STC Suppl.*).

Printer unknown 1539: 4423.c.14. (destroyed during the Second World War).[55]

UNASSIGNED IMPRINTS (listed by author)

Ferdinand I 1527: 8073.cc.25.

John Frederick of Saxony 1546: T.2167 (27); 1547: T.2167 (28).

Brusch, Caspar 1550?: 1315.c.53 (4).

Welber, Jacob 1553: 9325.c.64; (another edition) 1553: 1315.c.3 (5).

United Brethren 1554: 3505.df.55; 1555: 3505.c.30; 1564: 3506.df.47.[56]

Maximilian II: 1563: 11515.a.49 (2).

Zríny, Miklós (died 1566) 1566?: 1870.d.2 (7) (see *Ger STC Suppl.*).

Kokoschkius, Matthaeus 1577: 11521.ee.29 (7) (see *Ger STC Suppl.*).

Rudolph II: 1594: 9930.ccc.7.

One thing that this survey has revealed to me is the extent of David Paisey's own contribution to enhancing the British Library's holdings of Bohemica. Zdeněk Tobolka, who initiated the bibliography of imprints in Czech (*Knihopis*), did not foresee that it would take so long to appear, from 1925 to 1967. Work on its counterpart, the bibliography of sixteenth to eighteenth-century Bohemica in foreign languages, has already been going on in the library of the Prague Academy for a number of years, and we are optimistic that over the next few years we shall at least get on top of the sixteenth and seventeenth century books. The kind of writing to which we have drawn attention here is so important for the early centuries of the modern period, yet literary scholars devote little space to it in their histories of literature. At least as far as Czech scholars are concerned, critical evaluation of the place of this material in the development of literature so far remains an unfulfilled dream. In conclusion let me draw attention to what may well be the British Library's latest acquisition (in 1993) in the field of German Bohemica, an item brought to my attention by David Paisey himself: it was published in Prague to mark the tercentenary of the invention of printing: Johann G. A. N. Fiebiger, *Das dritte Jubilaeum einer löblichen Buchdrucker-Kunst*, printed by Johann Norbert Fitzky in 1740.[57]

55 Urbanus Rhegius, *Predigt, wie man die falschen Propheten erkennen, ja greiffen mag*. A Czech translation appeared with Jan Olivetský at Olomouc in 1540; see *Knihopis*, no. 14818.

56 This is probably the same as the item mentioned by Joseph Th. Müller, *Geschichte der Böhmischen Brüder*, III (Herrnhut, 1931), p. 417.

57 See Mirjam Bohatcová, 'Die erste offizielle Prager Feier zum Jubiläum des Buchdrucks (1740)', *GJ*, 68 (1993), 159–71.

THE 1576 ANTWERP EDITION OF THE WORKS OF BAPTISTA MANTUANUS AND JOHANNES LUCIENBERGER IN FRANKFURT AM MAIN

ULRICH KOPP

ONE OF THE MOST INFLUENTIAL NEO-LATIN POETS of the years around 1500 was the Carmelite (Giovanni) Battista Spagnoli (Spagnuoli) (1447–1516), generally known simply as Baptista Mantuanus after his place of birth.[1] His poems enjoyed the same esteem as those of classical authors, and they were especially prized because they were on Christian themes. The result was a large number of editions of 'the Christian Vergil' throughout Europe. In the main these were slim brochures, printed with much leading and wide margins so that they might be suitable for use for teaching Latin and poetry.

Edmondo Maria Coccia O.Carm. has provided a valuable survey of these many editions in his *Le edizioni delle opere del Mantovano*. Collectanea bibliographica Carmelitana, 2 (Rome: Institutum Carmelitanum, 1960; reprinted 1977). He lists not only the editions of the separate items but also records the collected editions of Baptista's works, starting with the Bologna edition of 1502 and ending with the Antwerp one of 1576, which is even today the best and most comprehensive edition, in four octavo volumes.

The Herzog August Bibliothek at Wolfenbüttel possesses a copy of this Antwerp edition (Coccia no. 432, p. 88), printed by Joannes I. Bellerus.[2] Turning the pages of the four volumes one is struck by the variety of ornamental initials, types and layouts in the preliminaries and the final sheets as compared with the bulk of the main text. The main text reminds one strangely of Frankfurt am Main, for series of initials are employed which had been used in that city by Peter Braubach since the 1540s. Coccia does not address this problem, and, as far as I can see, it is not mentioned elsewhere in the literature

1 For a brief modern assessment see, for example, the article by Reinhard Düchting, in *Lexikon des Mittelalters*, 1 (Munich and Zurich, 1980), cols. 1424f., and the note on him in Jozef Ijsewijn, *Companion to Neo-Latin Studies*, 1: *History and Diffusion of Neo-Latin Literature*. 2nd ed. (Louvain, 1990), pp. 32 and 59, where particular attention is drawn to the importance of his *Eclogae decem* (sometimes called *Bucolica seu adolescentia*) as a school text.

2 Pressmark 368.7 – 10 Quodlibetica. Basic information about Bellerus may be found in Anne Rouzet *et al.*, *Dictionnaire des imprimeurs, libraires et éditeurs des XVe et XVIe siècles dans les limites géographiques de la Belgique actuelle*. Collection du Centre national de l'archéologie et de l'histoire du livre. Publication 3 (Nieuwkoop, 1975), pp. 8–10.

on the subject, with the single exception of a mention by Christian Daum in 1666, to which I shall return. It thus seems worthwhile to examine the matter more closely. The solution – as is almost always the case in bibliographical matters – is found by means of comparison, in this instance with the 1573 Frankfurt edition in four octavo volumes for Johannes Lucienberger.[3] It may be described, briefly, as follows:

Vol. 1: 8° *^{8}†^{8})(^{8} ¶^{4} A-Z^{8} a-z^{8} Aa-Bb^{8} Cc^{4} = [8], 387, [1] fols;
  Cc4^{r}: publisher's device; Cc4^{v}: blank.
Vol. 2: 8° ***^{8} Aaa-Yyy^{8} Zzz^{4} = [8], 178, [2] fols.
  Zzz3^{r}: publisher's device; Zzz3^{v}-4^{v}: blank.
Vol. 3: 8° **^{8} aa-zz^{8} aaa-ppp^{8} qqq^{4} = [8], 307, [1] fols.
  qqq3^{v}-4^{v}: blank.
Vol. 4: 8° A-Z^{8} AA-FF^{8} = 231 [=230], [2] fols.
  FF7^{r}-8^{v}: blank.

It is this edition which, three years later, supplied sheets for the main part of the new, enlarged Antwerp edition.

I should like now to discuss the links between the two editions, volume by volume, but because Coccia has described the contents of both editions and Cosmas de Villiers those of the 1576 Antwerp edition in detail, I shall concentrate on the way in which the old and the new sheets were brought together as well as on other aspects which are not dealt with adequately by Coccia.[4]

Baptista Mantuanus: *Opera omnia*. Vols. 1-4. Antverpiae: Iohannes Bellerus 1576.

Vol. 1, variant A: 8° [?]^{8}†^{8})(^{8} ¶^{4} Aaa-Zzz^{8} Aaaa-Zzzz^{8} = [28], 375 [= 368] fols.
  Title-page variant: ... quorum Index sequenti pagina ...

Vol. 1, variant B: 8° *^{8} **^{8} †^{8})(^{8} ¶^{4} Aaa-Zzz^{8} Aaaa-Zzzz^{8} = [36], 375 [= 368] fols.
  Title-page variant: ... quorum Index sequentibus paginis ...

As can be seen, vol. 1 exists in two variants, as far as the preliminaries are concerned. Variant A includes a table of contents for all four volumes and a preface by the editor, Laurentius Cupaerus O.Carm., dated Antwerp 1 April 1576.[5] Variant B has the same features, but on fols. **4^{r}-**8^{v} it also contains seven plague poems from 1482 in rhythmic prose, to which is appended 'Threnos, seu Lamentatio'. Coccia records copies of vol. 1 in thirty-five libraries, but he seems to have inspected only variant A personally, for in his commentary on no. 432 on p. 89 he writes:

3 Coccia no. 430, p. 47. See now *VD 16* S7133. Wolfenbüttel copies: 148 Poet [vols. 1 and 2 only]; Alv. Ca 137 and 137a [all four parts], deposited by the von Alvensleben family.

4 Anon [Cosmas de Villiers], *Bibliotheca Carmelitana* (Aurelianis, 1752; reprinted and edited by Gabriel Wessels O.Carm., Rome, 1927), I, cols. 219-32.

5 The table of contents includes folio numbers; it was, therefore, the last part of the work to be printed.

'All' inizio del primo tomo dovrebbero essere i "Psalmi septem, quos Bononiae edidit, dum civitas illa lue pestifera premeretur, anno salutis 1482". Ne parlano, infatti, Petrus Lucius [...]. Poichè in realtà non si trovano in alcun esemplare conosciuto di quest' edizione, si può supporre che del primo tomo siano state fatte due edizioni nello stesso anno e luogo. Probabilmente l'edizione con i salmi andò distrutta nell'incendio ....' ('At the beginning of the first volume we ought to find the "Seven Psalms which he published in Bologna in 1482 when that city was oppressed by plague". They are in fact mentioned by Petrus Lucius ... But whereas they are not actually found in any known copy of this edition one may assume that two editions of the first volume were produced in the same year and the same place. The edition with the Psalms probably perished in the fire ...')

I, on the other hand, know more copies of variant B: there is one in Wolfenbüttel, another in Göttingen (pressmark: 8° Sva. IV, 2500), and two in Cambridge, described by Adams – another good reason to be grateful to him for giving collations.[6] I have also inspected a copy of variant A in the British Library (pressmark: 1213.e.16.).[7]

In variant B the editor's preface has some improved readings. It seems that the text of the 'Psalmi septem' was received at a late juncture while printing was in progress, and so a decision was taken to print two new preliminary sheets.

Sheets Aaa-Yyy in vol. 1 of the Antwerp edition (as far as the middle of the 'Elegia contra amorem') were taken over from vol. 2 of the Frankfurt edition, and sheets †^{8})(^{8} containing the 'Apologeticon in mastigophoros ...' were taken from the first Frankfurt volume. The new elements in the 1576 edition are sheets [?]^{8} and *^{8} **^{8}, discussed above, the half-sheet ¶^{4} (the corresponding half-sheet in the 1573 edition could not be used because it contained a summary of the contents on the last page: 'Quae primo hoc tomo continentur ...'), and twenty-four sheets from Zzz^{8} onwards because extensive new texts were added here.

Vol. 2: 8° †^{8} A-Z^{8} a-z^{8} Aa-Bb^{8} Cc^{4} = [8], 388 fols.
Most of the sheets in this volume are the same as in vol. 1 of the Frankfurt edition. The only parts which have been reset are †^{8} with the title and a further editor's preface, dated Antwerp, 1 February 1576, and minor pieces, and the final half-sheet Cc^{4} with Lucienberger's intrusive publisher's mark.[8]

Vol. 3: 8° *^{8} aa-zz^{8} aaa-qqq^{8} rrr^{4} = [8], 317 [= 316] fols.
This volume is based on vol. 3 of the Frankfurt edition. The parts which have

6 H. M. Adams, *Catalogue of Books Printed on the Continent of Europe 1501-1600 in Cambridge Libraries*. Vol. 1 (Cambridge, 1967), M-390. – After completion of this article a description of both variants of Vol. I was published in Elly Cockx-Indestege, Geneviève Glorieux and Bart Op de Beeck, *Belgica typographica 1541-1600*. 4 vols (Nieuwkoop, 1968-94), III and IV, no. 7843 and 7844, whereas I and II, no. 248 contained no such information.

7 The British Library in fact possesses rather more of the edition than is listed in the *General Catalogue of Printed Books*. It has vols. 1 and 2 (1213.e.16.) and vol. 4 (1213.e.17.).

8 The Wolfenbüttel copy in fact contains the original half-sheet of 1573 at the end of vol. 2; it was this that pointed me in the direction of Frankfurt, too.

been reset are: *8 with the title and another preface by Cupaerus, dated Antwerp, 'in festo S. Mathiae Apostoli' (24 February 1576), and, at the end, sheets qqq^8 and rrr^4 so that some new pieces of Book IV of the *Sylvae* could be inserted. In his commentary to no. 430 (p. 87) Coccia wrongly states that the *Sylvarum libri 4* is identical in the two editions.

Vol. 4: 8° **^{8} a-r^8 S^8 T^8 A-Z^8 AA-FF^8 = [16], 295, [9] pp.; 229, [3] fols.[9] Sheets B-Z^8 AA-EE^8 have been taken over from the Frankfurt edition. The first gathering includes another preface by the editor, dated 1 March 1576, and the nineteen sheets of the first set of signatures contain added prose texts by our author, his brother, Ptolomeo, and Johannes Trithemius. The very last sheet, FF^8, was set in smaller type in 1576 and is able to include an errata list for all four volumes as well as an Antwerp licence to print.

What does the editor, Laurentius Cup(a)erus (Cuypers, 1528/29-1594) tell us in his four prefaces about his work?[10] He devotes not a word to the fundamental fact that the book uses sheets taken from the Frankfurt edition but leaves us with the impression that this is a new edition of the usual kind, prepared by Bellerus and himself. His own assessment of his achievement ranges from the modest formulation that the publisher had had no more suitable editor available to the claim that his own labours as an editor had been comparable with those of the author, Spagnuoli, himself.[11]

From the modern point of view, his principal contribution consists in having expanded the edition by adding material from various printed and manuscript sources. In dealing with the new texts he had the opportunity to ensure that his edition was accurate, but when dealing with the old sheets from the Frankfurt edition the only thing he could do was suggest better reading in the list of errata which take up six closely printed pages at the end of vol. 4. Cupaerus himself mentions the help he had received from a philologically trained assistant with experience in the book trade: a certain Theodorus Pulmannus who had had a great deal of experience in the preparation of printer's copy and in proof-reading had shown himself to be extremely useful.[12]

This man, Théodore Poelman from Cranenburg (1512 or 1513-1581), is

9 Adams says the first sheet is signed *8, but the actual signatures are *2, **3, **4, **5. There are errors in the foliation at the end, but 229 for the last foliated leaf FF5 is correct from the mathematical point of view.

10 Further information about his literary activities and career in the Carmelite Order are supplied by Joannes Franciscus Foppens, *Bibliotheca Belgica ... usque ad annum M.D.C.LXXX.* 2 vols. Brussels 1739, II, p. 806b (following earlier contributors to the *Bibliothecae Belgicae*) and by Cosmas de Villiers, *Bibliotheca Carmelitana*, vol. 2, col. 223f.

11 Vol. 1, p. [?]8^v and **3^v: 'neminem ad manum, ut me Antwerpiae hoc tempore Librarius habuit: quare in restituendo Mantuano non quod volui, sed quod potui feci.' Similarly in vol. 4, p. **7^r. On the other hand, in vol. 4, p. **7^v: 'restitui tomos hosce, ita ut iureiurando asseverare audeam quòd non maiore labore Mantuanus haec scripserit, quam ego restituere studui ...'

12 Vol. 2, p. †4^r: 'Theodorus quidem Pulmannus vir tam in praecastigandis exemplaribus, quàm in formis corrigendis longè solertissimus, magno fuit huic operi adiumento ...'

frequently mentioned in the history of the Antwerp book trade and always with approval.[13] Latin philology was his passion in life; he did a great deal of editing and he collected manuscripts, but he had to earn his living as a fuller and later as a clerk in the Antwerp customs house. He was on friendly terms with Christophe Plantin and his family, worked for him for fourteen years and eventually left his books to him in his will.

We have no first-hand details about the arrangements made for the Antwerp edition, about the acquisition of the 1573 sheets from Frankfurt, about the terms or indeed about the reasons behind it. As we have seen, the editor, Cupaerus, draws a veil over the whole matter. No documentary information of relevance seems to have survived. At the Antwerp end one might have expected Lode van den Branden to have found something during his many years of sifting the archives for information about the Antwerp book trade. His papers are preserved in the Bibliothèque Nationale Albert Ier at Brussels, and he himself almost finished editing the material relating to members of the Bellerus family.[14]

As for the Frankfurt end, it is to be assumed that here too nothing of relevance has survived in the archives since Heinrich Pallmann made no reference to it when he took the opportunity to turn his study of Sigmund Feyerabend into a comprehensive survey of the Frankfurt book trade in the second half of the sixteenth century.[15] Difficult though it is to read, with its many footnotes and documentary appendices, this study contains nearly everything of importance that still survived in Frankfurt archives before the two world wars.[16]

It seems to me that the Frankfurt edition of Baptista Mantuanus sold badly in 1573 because this was a time when the appreciation of religious poetry in Latin was undergoing a change. In Protestant areas of Europe people looked up to new authors – in Germany, for example, Helius Eobanus Hessus (1488-1540),

13 Bibliographical details are given by Alois Gerlo and Hendrik D. L. Vervliet, *Bibliographie de l'humanisme des anciens Pays-Bas. Avec un répertoire bibliographique des humanistes et poètes néo-latins* (Brussels, 1972), p. 432 (nos. 5078-9). For an assessment see Leon Voet, *The Golden Compasses*. 2 vols. (Amsterdam, 1969-72), I, pp. 119, 350, 368, but see also Max Rooses, *Christophe Plantin imprimeur anversois*. 2nd ed. (Antwerp, 1896), pp. 107-09, with an engraved portrait dating from 1572.

14 One of his lectures on the subject was published in the Festschrift for Leon Voet: 'Archiefstukken betreffende het Antwerpse boekwezen in de 15[de] en 16[de] eeuw', *De gulden passer*, 61/63 (1983-85), 169-87. Here he mentions Bellerus's regular visits to the Frankfurt fairs and his collaboration with other printers in Frankfurt. I am grateful to Elly Cockx-Indestege (Brussels) for going through van den Branden's papers for me again.

15 Heinrich Pallmann, *Sigmund Feyerabend, sein Leben und seine geschäftlichen Verbindungen. Nach archivalischen Quellen bearbeitet*. Archiv für Frankfurts Geschichte und Kunst, N.F. 7 (Frankfurt am Main, 1881).

16 The same archive material later formed the basis of Alexander Dietz's more extensive investigations of Frankfurt commerce, *Frankfurter Handelsgeschichte*. 4 vols. (Frankfurt am Main, 1910-25; repr. Glashütten im Taunus, 1970), but he gave less attention to detail. Unfortunately many of his erroneous statements have found their way into more recent literature, including the work of Josef Benzing.

Georg Fabricius Chemnicensis (1516-1571), Johannes Stigel (1515-1562) or, on the wider European stage, the Scot George Buchanan (1506-1582)[17] – whereas Spagnuoli, whose works had still played an important role in the education of Martin Luther and Philipp Melanchthon,[18] now tended to find his readers in Catholic parts. Here the impressum 'Frankfurt am Main' would make the book suspect, whereas 'Antwerp' would offer the prospect of good sales among Catholic readers. While it is true that the Roman indexes did not impose a general interdict on books published in Protestant towns, there is nevertheless a tendency in this direction in the censorship laws of the Dukes of Bavaria, for instance.[19]

The splitting of the original Frankfurt print run into two editions resulted in the survival of relatively few copies of the 1576 *editio optima*, sought after by scholars and bibliophiles. The older bibliographical handbooks, right down to Coccia, have consequently tended to describe this as an *editio rarissima*. Thus, at the beginning of the chain, the Zwickau schoolmaster Christian Daum (1612-1687), in one of his scholarly letters, edited by Johann Andreas Gleich under the title *Epistolae philologicae-criticae* [...] (Chemnitz, 1709), wrote on 28 December 1666: '[Possideo] Et [editionem] Antwerpiensem Anni 1576. quae Francofurdiensem An. 1573. (nec tamen ejus anni, nisi solis titulis tam vorsis quam prorsis operibus) per singulos Tomos adduxit. Unde & hodie rarissima est, nimirum propter incendium eo anno Antwerpiae exortum, quod omnia fere ibi adhuc restantia Exempla sustulit absumpsitque.' What this laconic formulation adds up to is that 'the Antwerp edition of 1576 subsumes the individual volumes of the Frankfurt edition of 1573, for it is only in respect of the title pages of the poetic and prose works that it dates from this year. And it is extremely rare today on account of the fire which broke out in Antwerp that year and destroyed almost all the available copies.' As a trained philologist Daum already anticipated my observation that these two editions are directly linked with one another. But, using a source of information unknown to me, he adds the detail that the stocks of unbound sheets were damaged in a fire. This must be a reference to the three days of plundering, looting and extortion that the Spanish troops indulged in when they succeeded in breaking out of the Antwerp citadel in November 1576, an event which has gone down in the history books as the 'Spanish Fury'. The Bellerus family archives make no mention of this event,

17 On him see *Bibliography of George Buchanan*, by John Durkan (Glasgow, 1994).

18 See Morimichi Watanabe, 'Martin Luther's relations with Italian humanists. With special reference to Ioannes Baptista Mantuanus.' *Luther-Jahrbuch*, 54 (1987), 23-47; Heinz Scheible, 'Philipp Melanchthon, der bedeutendste Sohn der Stadt Bretten,' in: Alfons Schäfer, *Geschichte der Stadt Bretten von den Anfängen bis zur Zerstörung 1689*. Brettener stadtgeschichtliche Veröffentlichungen, 2 (Bretten, 1977), pp. 257-82, where it is mentioned on p. 261 that, as a seven-year-old schoolboy, Melanchthon learnt Latin grammar from analysis of Spagnuoli's verses (Melanchthon's recollection in 1555; see the edition of his works in *Corpus Reformatorum*, XXV, cols. 448f.).

19 For this point I am indebted to John L. Flood, 'Le Livre dans le monde germanique à l'époque de la Réforme,' in: Jean-François Gilmont (ed.), *La Réforme et le livre. L'Europe de l'imprimé (1517 – v. 1570)* (Paris, 1990), pp. 101f.

which must mean that the number of copies still in stock was small. The original edition is divided into Frankfurt copies of 1573, Antwerp copies of 1576, and the copies destroyed in 1576.

I should now like to dwell a little on Johannes Lucienberger and say something about him as a person, his literary endeavours and his role in the Frankfurt book trade. Josef Benzing (1904-1981), who not only published many studies of particular aspects of sixteenth-century German printing history but also attempted a number of comprehensive surveys of the printers and publishers of the period, mentioned Lucienberger only briefly, mainly in his inglorious role as liquidator of Peter Braubach's printing shop, recording that the business was bought by Braubach's second daughter, Agathe, together with her husband Johann Lützelberger (Lucienberg) for 1156 Gulden on 29 April 1570 and saying that they allowed it to decline, eventually winding it up in 1576.[20] The details are taken from Pallmann (and were repeated by Dietz). Pallmann also tells us (pp. 47f. and 69f.) that Agathe Braubach, who on the death of her father in 1567 had received an important inheritance in the form of the business, property and money, married Magister Johann Lützelberger (or Lucienberger) of Frankfurt am Main on 13 August 1568.[21] Their daughter Elisabeth was born in 1570, another, Barbara, in 1572 (d. 1582). Agathe was a spendthrift: two houses had to be sold, and finally she left her husband and daughters and took to a life on the road. In a deposition to the council in Frankfurt in 1586 Lucienberger declares that he had occupied himself 'Jn Studijs et Professionibus vff Vniversitäten, vnd sonsten Jnn andern ehrlichen Herrn Diensten ausserhalb disser löblichen Statt' and describes himself as 'dess Stiffts im Thal Wimpffen Syndicus vndt Advokat'. This is all Pallmann tells us, who gives 1588 as the year of Lucienberger's death. His position in 1586 and presumably at the time of his death in 1588 is sometimes given as '*Syndicus* of Wimpfen', following Dietz, but this is incorrect: Lucienberger was in the service of the collegiate foundation of St Peter at Wimpfen im Tal; the imperial city of Wimpfen am Berg on the opposite bank of the River Neckar was its opponent in a series of long-winded legal cases.

20 Josef Benzing, *Die Buchdrucker des 16. und 17. Jahrhunderts im deutschen Sprachgebiet*. Beiträge zum Buch- und Bibliothekswesen, 12. 2nd ed. (Wiesbaden, 1982), p. 122. Similarly also in his article on Peter Braubach in the *Neue deutsche Biographie*, II (Berlin, 1955), p. 539, quoting the older literature in each case. He also discusses him, on the basis of just one of the books Lucienberger published (the *Collegii Posthimelissaei votum*, 1573), in: 'Die deutschen Verleger des 16. und 17. Jahrhunderts. Eine Neubearbeitung', *Archiv für Geschichte des Buchwesens*, 18 (1977), col. 1207.

21 Pallmann [note 15], p. 47. Pallmann prefers the form Lützelberger (perhaps because he knew of other members of the family from the archives in Frankurt?). The contemporary works generally have the Latin form 'Ioannes Lucienbergius', with a single instance of 'Ioannes de Monte Luciae'. For his dramatisation of the *Aeneid* (*VD 16* L3110) he had a calligraphic woodcut with his name 'Johannes Lucienberger' prepared; this is the decisive form for me. University registers record him as 'Ioannes Lucienberger zu Lucienberg' (Heidelberg 1576) and 'Ioannes Lutzenburger' (Marburg 1561). The editors of *VD 16* have agreed on 'Johannes Lucienberg'.

It is possible to discover further information about Lucienberger's life from his own writings and from his contributions to the works of others. In the dedicatory preface to his treatise on versification, *Methodica instructio componendi omnis generis versus* ...,[22] published in 1576 but dated Frankfurt am Main 10 January 1575 and addressed to Juan Luis de la Cerda the Younger, fifth Duke of Medinaceli (1544-1594) he gives a tongue-in-cheek account of his earlier life, from a distance in time: he says that twenty years before he had gone as a 'puer e patrijs laribus nescio quo fato extrusus'[23] to Belgium, first to Antwerp and then to Brussels where the court of King Philip had made a great impression on him. He found employment for nearly two years with Balthasar Weber who, as far as he could remember, came from Augsburg, and had always been interested in the Spanish language and in Spain itself. In February 1557 he entered the service of Diego de la Cerda, brother of Juan de la Cerda (d. 1575), fourth Duke of Medinaceli, who had just been appointed Viceroy of the Two Sicilies. Don Diego had taken on the 'puer petulans' because he believed he was really of good character. As early as March and April young Johannes's dreams had become true: he was sent with some of Don Diego's entourage on a journey through France to Medinaceli (in Soria, half way between Madrid and Saragossa) where he was well received and even gained access to the viceroy's children in the ducal palace. This idyllic period ended when the family set off to join their father in Italy; Johannes got homesick, asked to be allowed to leave and in 1559 sailed to the Netherlands, whence he returned to Frankfurt. But what was to become of him then? He was too old to take up a trade, in any case the life he had led on the fringes of the court had spoilt him for hard work. His father sought advice and it was eventually decided to let the young man become a student. First he went to Marburg and later to Mainz and other universities.[24] During this time poetry had increasingly become his great passion and, as he self-critically remarks, had led him to neglect other studies, in his case, the law. Yet his studies had borne fruit in the shape of his handbook on metrical quantities and his treatise on

22 *VD 16* L3111, Basle: Samuel König for the author. The date of publication is not actually stated, but on the verso of the title page of his dramatization of the *Aeneid* of 1576 (*VD 16* L3110) there is a brief mention of the fact that his treatise on versfication was due to appear at the spring fair in 1576.

23 It is not clear what 'excluded from my father's house – I know not by what fate' might mean. Did he run away from home, having fallen out with his father? Later he describes the great interest his father had taken in his choice of career. *Puer*, rather than *iuvenis* (and thus still in February 1557) could indicate an age of about twelve years, which would mean that he was born about 1543.

24 He enrolled in Marburg as 'Ioannes Lutzenburger Francofortanus' on 23 December 1561. See Julius Caeser, *Catalogus studiosorum scholae Marpurgensis* ... 4 pts. (Marburg, 1875-87, repr. [with addenda] Nendeln 1980), II, p. 48, col. 2. The intervening period was doubtless necessary for him to complete his preparations. The student records of the old University of Mainz have unfortunately not survived, though towards the end of his life Josef Benzing attempted to reconstruct them: Josef Benzing, *Verzeichnis der Studierenden der alten Universität Mainz*. Beiträge zur Geschichte der Universität Mainz, 13 (Wiesbaden, 1979-82). This does not mention Lucienberger.

versification; with these works he was able to show other young people an easier way to write good poetry.[25]

This is a retrospective account of his early years, studies and literary activities, written in 1575. In the meantime, as we have seen, he had completed his studies in the Faculty of Arts (where is not clear), married in 1568, had acquired the Braubach business, and his children had been born. It is to be assumed that, as the prefaces to his books also indicate, he was living in Frankfurt at this time, though it is possible that he spent some time in Mainz studying law. Lucienberger had a woodcut portrait prepared for use in the *Thesaurus* of 1575. Though not signed, this is almost certainly the work of Tobias Stimmer. If our calculation that he was born around 1543 is correct, this picture shows him as he was at the age of about thirty-two (fig. 1).[26] It is an oval half-length portrait, showing him with a book in his right hand (not a legal folio!), measuring 9.6 × 8.4 cm, in an ornamental frame (with fruit and eight coats-of-arms), measuring 12.6 × 10.6 cm. The subject is not identified, but below the portrait we find his motto: 'After darkness I hope for light, but the Lord is my light, whom I shall revere for evermore'.[27] This portrait has not previously been known to art historians; it is mentioned neither by Andresen or Walter L. Strauss,[28] nor by Paul Tanner who dealt with the portraits for the recent exhibition catalogue *Spätrenaissance am Oberrhein. Tobias Stimmer, 1539-1584. Ausstellung im Kunstmuseum Basel, 23. Sept. – 9. Dez. 1984*. The ornamental frame is rather flatter and less plastic than Stimmer's usual *putti* frames; this is probably a consequence of the need to accommodate eight coats-of-arms in it. Lucienberger seems to have attached importance to these. Reading from left to right, they are: 1 Posthius; 2 von Themar [Dr Adam Werner von Themar was a distinguished sixteenth-century lawyer; his son of the same name was

25 *Thesaurus poeticus in quinque classes divisus ... quibus omnium vocabulorum quantitates ... ostenduntur*. Preface dated Frankfurt am Main 1575. *VD 16* L3113. *VD 16* wrongly gives the printer as Peter Horst in Cologne. The types and layout show that, as with the treatise on versification, the printer was in fact Samuel König in Basle. The phrase 'Eodem Ioanne Lucienbergio Auctore & Collectore' on the title page of the *Methodica instructio* suggests that it had been intended that both works should be published together, but the *Thesaurus* came out in 1575 (as evidenced by the date of ownership in the copy in the Bavarian State Library, Munich (4°L.Lat.303), while the *Methodica instructio* did not appear until the time of the spring fair 1576 (see note 22 above). Peter Horst's Cologne edition of 1588 (*VD 16* L3114) is a reissue of the two hundred sheets of 1575 with a new title page.

26 I am greatly indebted to Irmgard Bezzel (Munich) for having brought this portrait to my attention and for having checked the copies of Lucienberger's books in the Bavarian State Library (note 25 above and 34 below) and for providing information from the as yet unpublished volumes of *VD 16*. The portrait is reproduced from 4°L.Lat.303, fol *2^{v}, by kind permission of the Bavarian State Library. Ilse O'Dell (London) has been so kind as to confirm that it is Stimmer's work, and I am grateful to her for supplying further information.

27 Individual pages with this portrait cut out from copies of the book should show the signature *2 on the other side and the table of contents beginning 'Totum opus in quinque Classes partitum est ... '.

28 Andreas Andresen, *Der deutsche Peintre-Graveur oder die deutschen Maler als Kupferstecher*. 5 vols (Leipzig, 1864-78), III, pp. 7-217; W. L. Strauss, *The German Single-Leaf Woodcut, 1550-1600*. 3 vols (New York, 1975), pp. 985-1057.

Fig. 1. Johannes Lucienberger.

likewise a Doctor of Laws]; 3 not identified; 4 not identified; 5 Grape [an ancient noble family in Pomerania]; 6 von Hattstatt [?, a Rhenish family]; 7 not identified; 8 not identified.

Another of his own works that he published at this time was the stage adaptation of the *Aeneid*, dedicated to princes of the Houses of Habsburg, Saxony, Brunswick, Hesse, Orange, Sayn-Wittgenstein and Nassau, dated

Frankfurt 1 March 1576.[29] In it Lucienberger describes himself as 'Iuris Candidatus'. On 28 April of the same year he is registered as a student at Heidelberg, without mention of any academic degrees but with an expansion of his name which would seem to indicate a claim to an exalted social standing.[30] In 1581 he contributes a poem to Cornelis Loos's catalogue of Catholic writers, and here he calls himself 'Ioannes Lucienbergius zur Lucienburgk/ etc. D. I. [=Doctor Iuris] Professor Moguntinus'.[31] Where and when he had meanwhile taken his doctorate in law we cannot say but it was presumably in Mainz. Two of the works from his pen indicate a connexion with the court of the Elector of Mainz: in 1582 he published poems to mark the death of Bishop Daniel Brendel von Homburg, and the accession of his successor Wolfgang von Dalberg (*VD 16* L3109 and L3112; the copies in the Bavarian State Library were destroyed during the war). In this period such poems were often published, mostly together, with a view to the author's gaining advancement. It seems that Lucienberger, now about forty years old, was seeking a prestigious legal appointment at court, as his choice of addressees in his dedicatory prefaces would also lead us to suppose. But as we have already seen, his future career did not lie in Mainz, a fact in which his disastrous marriage may well have played a part, but rather we find him in the service of 'honourable lords' and finally as *Syndikus* of St Peter's at Wimpfen im Tal until his early death in 1588.

In this account of Lucienberger's life we have left out an episode which led us to him in the first place: his attempt, in 1573, to establish a publishing business of his own in Frankfurt am Main. To be sure, he had been the owner of Braubach's business since 1570, but the details of the contract as given by Pallmann (pp. 47 and 109) seem to imply that Agathe and her husband were mainly to acquire the remaining stocks of books, with the rights to the works of the authors that Peter Braubach had promoted (chiefly the Württemberg reformer Johann Brenz, 1499-1570), so that once stocks had fallen below a certain critical level they had the right to reprint them.[32] It was agreed that the business should be referred to as 'Apud haeredes Petri Brubachij' or 'Bey Peter Brubachs seligen Erben' in German books. Witnesses to the purchase of the

29 *Inclyta Aeneis ... in regiam tragicomoediam, servatis ubique heroicis versibus ... redacta* (Frankfurt am Main: Paul Reffeler, 1576). *VD 16* L3110.

30 See Gustav Toepke (ed.), *Die Matrikel der Universität Heidelberg von 1386-1662*. 3 pts. (Heidelberg, 1884-93; repr. [with a continuation] Nendeln, 1976), pt. II, p. 77, no. 84, where he is listed as 'Joannes Lucienberger zu Lucienberg, patria Francofurdiensis'. Toepke has an appendix on the subject of the award of degrees in law in this period; Lucienberger is not mentioned.

31 *Illustrium Germaniae scriptorum catalogus. ... Quorum potißimùm ope, literarum studia, Germaniae ab Anno M.D. usque LXXXI. sunt restituta: et sacra fidei dogmata à profanis Sectariorum novitatibus ... vindicata*. (Mainz: Kaspar Behem, 1581) (*VD 16* L2478). Loos's preface is dated Mainz, 1 May 1581. The 1582 edition (*VD 16* L2479) simply has a different year on the title page, the books are from the same setting.

32 This was the case, for instance, with Brenz's octavo Latin postil (Gospels and Epistles, *VD 16* B7820 and B7804) which came out in a new edition in 1572 'Apud haeredes honesti Petri Brubachij'.

business, like the hard-headed businessman Sigmund Feyerabend (of whose ruthlessness Pallmann cites various examples) doubtless ensured that the firm did not overstep the mark. It is likely that the printing shop that Peter Braubach had set up in his house, 'Baumeister', on the Liebfrauenberg had ceased to exist as an independent firm with its own employees and technical manager soon after 1567. Already before 25 May 1568 Sigmund Feyerabend and Peter Schmidt acquired 27 and 66 pounds of type respectively (Pallmann, pp. 48 and 179). Nikolaus Basse, who had been running his own printing shop since 1562, rented the premises from Martinmas 1567 until Martinmas 1570, and they were then taken over by a bookbinder and a tailor until 1576 (Pallmann, p. 48). Such ornaments previously used by Braubach as are found in Frankfurt books printed after 1567 are difficult to assign to a particular establishment; to solve the problem a wide-ranging comparative study would be necessary.

Against this background there appeared in 1573 a book signed 'Apud Ioannem Lucienbergium', emanating from the circle of friends of the humanist poets Johannes Posthius (1537-1597) and Paulus Melissus (Schede, 1539-1602), with the somewhat rebarbative title *Collegii Posthimelissaei votum. Hoc est, ebrietatis detestatio, atque potationis saltationisque eiuratio* (*VD 16* C4559, with a summary listing of the contributors). Posthius, personal physician to the Bishop of Würzburg, had had the idea, as an act of self-discipline against the bacchantic tendencies of poets, to swear a solemn oath (*votum sanctum*) to avoid excessive enjoyment of wine. To this end he had made a ring set with an amethyst (the stone of sobriety), engraved on the outside with the words VOTVM SANCTVM DOMINO and 'EN 'OINΩ 'AΣΩTIA (immoderation in wine) on the inside. The first to join him in this campaign was his friend Melissus (1572); among others to join was Lucienberger. This little book contains the poetic invitations to join and declarations of membership of the nineteen people who joined, together with poems in a similar vein by a number of other authors. At the end Posthius and Schede refer explicitly to this being Lucienberger's first product as a publisher, and the book concludes with Posthius's arms.[33]

It would seem that with Posthius and Schede and their circle of poets Lucienberger found a sympathetic audience for his ideas which may be characterized as follows: a high moral regard for the role of the poet, a religious (Catholic) dimension, rejection of poetry of a bacchantic, erotic, playful kind while appreciating the seductive effect of a good poem, conception of the law

33 On Posthius see the recent monograph by Klaus Karrer, *Johannes Posthius (1537-1597). Verzeichnis der Briefe und Werke mit Regesten und Posthius-Biographie.* Gratia. Bamberger Schriften zur Renaissanceforschung, 23. (Wiesbaden, 1993). The *Votum* is described on pp. 400-402 (1573/1), with a detailed list of contents, and the Wolfenbüttel copy Li 7127 is described separately on p. 414 (1574/3) because it is a dedication copy for Canon Neidhard von Thüngen containing manuscript verses by Posthius found nowhere else. In the introduction (pp. 67-70) Karrer states that Posthius was not happy with the second part of the book which had been put together by Schede because of the confessional leanings of the authors; this is confirmed by Wolfenbüttel Li 7127, for here Posthius carefully removed fol. G7 with the list of contributors and gathering F with the worst of the offending poems.

Fig. 2. Lucienberger's devices.

as the foundation of human life. With such opinions he might well refer to the editors as 'amicos suos reverenter colendos' (fol. E2^{v}).[34] His contacts in the Frankfurt book trade gave him the opportunity to show his gratitude by publishing the group's book for them. His next great publishing enterprise was the four-volume edition of Spagnuoli. Even then Lucienberger seems to have been laying plans for the future because he commissioned two publisher's devices: a smaller one (53 × 46 mm) and a larger one in the style of Tobias Stimmer (70 × 54 mm) which would have been eminently suitable for use in quartos. The smaller device is used six times in the Spagnuoli edition, while the larger one appears only on the title page of vol. 4. Since these devices have not been reproduced elsewhere I show them here as fig. 2.[35] The motto 'Servate manibus stateram iustitiae ne sit dolosa' ('Protect the scales of Justice with your hands lest they read false') and the scales extending from Heaven refer to several passages in the Bible, such as Prov. 11,1: Statera dolosa, abominatio est apud Dominum: et pondus aequum, voluntas ejus' ('A false balance is abomination to the Lord: but a just weight is his delight'), and are a link with Lucienberger's profession as a lawyer.

34 The Munich copy of his *Methodica instructio componendi omnis generis versus* (4°L.lat.302) has the handwritten dedication: *D. Paulo Melisso amico & fratri in Christo, Auctor* [*dedicavit*].

35 Not even in Paul Heitz, *Frankfurter und Mainzer Drucker- und Verlegerzeichen bis in das 17. Jahrhundert* (Strasbourg, 1896).

I hope to have shown how Lucienberger's edition of the Christian poet he loved so much could not be expected to be a success; and in the hard, risky business climate in Frankfurt he lacked the confidence to assert himself in the longer term against such rivals as Sigmund Feyerabend. At least, no other book published by him has so far come to light, and after 1575 even his own works were published by other people.[36]

36 In conclusion I should like to thank Martin Boghardt, Wolfenbüttel, for reading a draft of this paper which has benefited from his helpful suggestions.

TWO GERMAN STRAYS IN ITALY

DENNIS E. RHODES

MY STRAYS are not two German hikers who lost their way in the Dolomites or the Apennines. They are two sixteenth-century printed books in the British Library which, for some unaccountable reason, found their way into the British Museum's *Short-Title Catalogue of Italian Books, 1465–1600*, published in 1958, when in my opinion they should instead have been entered in the corresponding German short-title catalogue which followed in 1962. The books are both in Latin and have no imprint. Neither of them, it seems, has anything whatever to do with Italy. They have nothing in common with each other except that, by a coincidence, each is dated 1562. The author of the first was born at or near Bruges, and the second is a declaration by Queen Elizabeth I of England. I will now examine each book in detail, and attempt for the first time to catalogue them correctly.

I

Georgius Cassander was born at Bruges on 24 August 1513 and died at Cologne on 3 February 1566.[1] Having taught theology at Bruges and Ghent, he moved to Cologne about 1544 and seems to have spent the rest of his not very long life there without further travels. He was in Cologne on 18 March 1558, when he wrote the preface to his book *Liturgica de ritu et ordine Dominicae Coenae celebrandae*, which was printed there by the Heirs of Arnold Birckmann in 1558. He was also in Cologne on 1 September 1565 when he wrote the preface to what must have been his last book, *De baptismo infantium*, also issued by the same publishers in 1565, a few months before his death. Since the anonymously

1 P. Larousse, *Grand dictionnaire universel du* XIXe *siècle*, III (Paris, 1867), says that Cassander was born 'on the island of Cadsand in 1518', but I prefer to follow a more reliable and modern source, the *Grote Winkler Prins Encyclopedie*, V (Amsterdam, 1980). Cadsand, which is not really an island, lies down the coast from Flushing, in Zeeuws Vlaanderen, the part of the province of Zealand which geographically is part of Flanders (Belgium), but politically belongs to the Netherlands. Cadsand may have given him his surname of Cassander. In any case, wherever exactly he was born, Bruges is quite near to Cadsand. Miss Anna Simoni kindly supplied me with information on Cadsand.

printed book with which we are here concerned is dated 1562, it is reasonable to suppose that it, too, was printed in Cologne, despite its entry in the British Museum's *Italian STC*, not in the *German STC*. Here is a full description:

DE OFFICIO | PII AC PVBLICAE TRAN- | QVILLITATIS VERE AMAN= | tis uiri, in hoc Religionis | dissidio. | Reperies in hoc scripto, lector, non solùm expeditissimam | controuersiarum, quibus miserè adeò laborat hodie Ecclesia, | componendarum rationem: sed etiam, quo pacto verae pie- | tatis atq; concordiae Christianae ex animo studiosus, | durante isto dissidio, optimè se gerere in | quauis Republica possit | ac debeat. | ADIECTA EST. | Defensio eiusdem libelli, aduersus iniquum & | importunum castigatorem. | AVCTORE *Veranio Modesto Pacimontano.* | *Additur pars illa ex scriptis aduersarijs, cui in hac* | *defensione respondetur.* | Anno M.D. LXII.

4°. 20 leaves. A-E^4. pp. 37 [39]. Capital N on 2^r: 24 mm square; white on dark background, showing a woman with milk (or water?) issuing from her breasts and falling on bodies lying on the ground.

This appears to be the only one of his books which Cassander chose to publish under the pseudonym of Veranius Modestus Pacimontanus.[2]

In my search for the same capital N in other books, I looked carefully through about twenty-five works (some of them large folios) all from the press of the Heirs of Arnold Birckmann, who seem to have been Cassander's regular publishers while he lived in Cologne. Perhaps the book which displays the richest assortment of initial letters from a wide variety of alphabets is the sumptuous edition of William Turner's *Herbal* of 1568. But I did not find the elusive capital N, until I then looked at a few books printed by another member of the same family: Johann Birckmann Junior. Here, in 1559, we find the same capital N used on both p. 367 and p. 571 of the *Opuscula insigniora* of Dionysius Carthusianus. So Cassander did not, after all, have to go beyond the Birckmann firm to find a printer for his little book by 'Veranius Modestus Pacimontanus'; and now that we have established this fact, we can see that the book uses German paper and a roman text-type which is also German.[3] There is no Italian element in this book.

The Bodleian Library, Oxford, has three copies of this text in two editions, both of which are correctly assigned to Cologne as their place of printing.

2 I can offer no satisfactory explanation for his choice of pseudonym. Veranius was a governor of Britain under Nero. The *Defensio libelli De officio pii viri* of Cassander (Cologne, 1564) is in the form of a dialogue between Modestus and Placidius. Two other Germans, of a later age, called themselves Pacimontanus: Balthasar Pacimontanus was Balthasar Hubmeier, and Johannes Pacimontanus was Johann Jacob Zimmermann. But why 'Pacimontanus'? Does it mean 'from Friedberg'? Lastly, a Spaniard named Gregorio Mayans y Síscar used the pseudonym 'Placido Veranio'. These are probably no more than coincidences.

3 At least one of the watermarks in the Pacimontanus is the same as one in *Responsio ad calumnias quibus Georgius Cassander in Germanico quodam libello Viae commonstrator inscripto petulanter impetitur ... A Bartholomaeo Neruio excepta* (Cologne: Heirs of Arnold Birckmann, 1564), showing that the paper stock came from the same source. The roman type of Pacimontanus is the same as that of the *Defensio* of 1564.

The two editions (which Adams calls two issues), are also both in Cambridge: respectively at Peterhouse and the University Library.[4] Both at Oxford and Cambridge the *De officio pii* ... and the *Defensio* are catalogued as one book in two parts, but no attempt has been made to identify their printers. Neither the Bodleian catalogue nor Adams makes the situation immediately clear as to editions. For the purpose of the present contribution I have not thought it necessary to examine and compare all these copies at Oxford and Cambridge; but I am left with the conviction that Georgius Cassander is one of the many important sixteenth-century scholars who obviously need and deserve a new, complete and fully annotated bibliography.

The two 1562 editions are in various German libraries, and are fully described in *VD 16* (nos. C1396 and C1397). I note that they are here attributed to Arnold Birckmann as printer, whereas my researches have led me to Johann the Younger, but in effect the whole Birckmann printing firm may be regarded as one entity for the purposes of the typographical material employed.

II

In September 1562 Queen Elizabeth I of England issued a *Declaration of the Quenes Majestie, Elizabeth ... Conteyning the Causes which have constrayned her to arme certaine of her subjectes, for Defence both of her owne Estate, and of the most Christian Kyng, Charles the Nynth* (Charles IX, son of Henry II and Catherine de Medici, King of France 1560-1574).

This was *Imprinted at London, in Powles Churchyarde, by Rycharde Iugge and Iohn Cawood, Printers to the Quenes Maiestie*, in quarto (STC[2] 9187.3). It is now so rare that only the copy at Lambeth Palace is recorded, but in the eighteenth century a copy was discovered in the library of the late Earl of Oxford (Edward Harley, Second Earl, 1689-1741), and was included by the anonymous editor, William Oldys, in the third volume of the *Harleian Miscellany*, printed in 1745.[5] There was also a Latin version published at the same time *apud Reginaldum Wolfium*, of which copies are now known at Wadham College, Oxford, Corpus Christi College, Cambridge (in MS. 345), and the Folger Library, Washington.[6]

4 H. M. Adams, *Catalogue of Books Printed on the Continent of Europe, 1501-1600 in Cambridge Libraries*. 2 vols (Cambridge, 1967), nos C 844 and C 845. It is interesting to note that Adams also reports at Corpus Christi College (no. C 843) an earlier edition of the *De officio pii* ..., dated August 1561, which he attributes to Basle, printer unknown. I have not seen this book. *VD 16* C1395 ascribes it to the printer Joannes Oporinus. There is also a German translation of 1562 (*VD 16* C1398).

5 I have not thought it necessary for the present article to investigate the possibility that the Lambeth copy is the same copy which was found in the Harleian library in the eighteenth century; but no doubt even by 1745 this English pamphlet of 1562 had already become excessively rare. The Latin versions are not quite as rare, but certainly they are rare enough.

6 STC[2] 9187. Wolfe describes himself as *Regiae Maiest. in Latinis typographus*. Dr Peter Cunich, Fellow of Magdalene College, Cambridge, kindly inspected for me the copy in Corpus Christi College.

EXPOSITIO CAVSA
rum, quibus
ANGLIAE RE-
GINA COMMOVEBATUR, UT
QVASDAM SVBIECTORVM SVORVM
cohortes armis inſtrueret, reſpectu propriæ defen-
ſionis, & Chriſtianiſsimi Regis Caroli No-
ni, fratris chariſsimi & eius
ſubiectorum.

1562.

Fig. 1.

Fig. 2.

There were French and German versions, printed soon after the *Declaration*; but it is with another Latin edition that we are here concerned, since the British Library has a copy which for some unknown reason was included in the *Italian STC* of 1958 (p. 233) under the title: *Expositio causarum quibus Angliae regina commouebatur ut quasdam subiectorum suorum cohortes armis instrueret.* The date 1562 is on the title page, but there is no further imprint. The booklet has eight leaves, the last blank, signed A–B^4, and paginated to p. 14. But this is assuredly not Italian printing, and in my opinion had no claim whatsoever to be entered in the *Italian STC*. It has on the title page a wreath containing a male bust with a halo, and below this an eagle with outspread wings (fig. 1). This is probably metal-cut rather than woodcut. On fol. A2^r is a capital E (29 mm square) containing a very peculiar member of the feline tribe (fig. 2). Neither of these ornaments is Italian in style.

The same round ornament I think we must now term a printer's device, since it is found on the title-page of two other books, and at the end of a third, in the British Library. I found it because one of these books is the German translation of the *Declaration* itself, which was evidently never compared with the Latin version at the time the latter was catalogued either for the *General Catalogue* or the *Italian STC*. If they had been put side by side, the German version would immediately have given the clue to the typographical origin of the Latin. The two books which have the device on the title-page are:

1. Johann Lauterbach, *Epigrammatum libri VI.* Francofurti ex officina Lucij, 1562.
2. *Der Königin zů Engelland Auszschreiben, darinnen sie die vrsachen anzaiget, warumb sie etliche jrer vnderthanen auffgebracht, jre vnd jres vilgeliebten Brüders Carols des Neündten, Königs in Franckreich, vnderthanen damit zů beschutzen. Gedruckt zů Franckfurt durch Ludwig Lücken, im jar nach Christi geburt M.D.LXXIII.*

Could it possibly be that 1573 in the second of these imprints is a mere error for 1563? It would seem strange if the German version appeared eleven years, rather than one year, after the Latin and the English.

There is no doubt that the Latin edition in the British Library was printed at Frankfurt am Main by Ludovicus Lucius, or Ludwig Lücke, a printer of whom the British Library possesses at present only five editions printed in that city, plus nine printed at Basle and five at Heidelberg. According to Benzing, very little is known about Lucius, except that he printed at Basle from 1552 to 1557, at Heidelberg from 1557 to 1562, and at Frankfurt from 1562 until an undetermined date.[7] In August 1560 he is listed in the Heidelberg university records as University Printer, but left there after a quarrel.[8]

Why Lucius interested himself in the *Declaration* of Queen Elizabeth is something of a mystery, but there may have been some connection between him and the man who had already published a Latin version in London: Reyner (Reginald) Wolfe, a German bookseller and printer (from 1542), active in London from *c.* 1530 to 1573.

There is one more book in the British Library collections which is very interesting in this connection. It is by Ioannes Voerthusius, who is described as 'Provost of Deventer', *Academiae veteris et nouae ad Diuum Maximilianum ... legatio*, printed likewise at Frankfurt by Ludovicus Lucius in March 1563. In this case the same round wreath-device is on the verso of the last leaf but one. An even more interesting feature is that at the beginning of this book there is a one-page manuscript dedication in a calligraphic hand to Queen Elizabeth of England. It almost seems as if the printer Lucius had a particular penchant for the British monarch, even though this dedication declares itself to be by the author, Voerthusius.

I have not encountered the same capital E with the strange cat in any other book in the British Library printed by Lucius, but the book by Lauterbach contains an S with a horse, a G with a goose, a C and a Q each with a rabbit but a different rabbit, which may well belong to the same alphabet. In addition, the Lauterbach has a capital I of the same dimensions, without an animal, but simply with a design of branches and leaves. The book by Voerthusius also contains the same capital C as Lauterbach, and furthermore a capital F with a stag.

At this point we must note a most intriguing complication of a kind which is not uncommonly met with in the history of woodcut initials in sixteenth-century books, not only, as here, in Germany, but also in Italy and other countries. They travelled from one city to another. Exactly the same capital E with the cat which we have found in the Latin version of the Queen's *Declaration* now ascribed to Lucius at Frankfurt also occurs on p. 352 of the big folio by John Christopherson (Bishop of Chichester), *Historiae ecclesiasticae scriptores Graeci*, published at Cologne 'apud Haeredes Arnoldi Birckmanni' in 1570. It is the same block, and has the same small breaks. Likewise in the same book we find various other letters of the same zoological alphabet. No doubt the firm of Ludwig Lucius in Frankfurt, always a modest concern, closed down soon after 1563, and this 'animal alphabet' at least was bought up by the

7 Josef Benzing, *Die Buchdrucker des 16. und 17. Jahrhunderts im deutschen Sprachgebiet*. 2nd ed. (Wiesbaden, 1982), p. 40 for Lucius at Basle, p. 124 for Frankfurt, and p. 194 for Heidelberg.

8 'Ludouicus Lucius, Vuetteranus, vniuersitatis typographus', 1 August 1560. See Gustav Toepke (ed.), *Die Matrikel der Universität Heidelberg von 1386 bis 1662*, II (Heidelberg, 1886), p. 21.

enormous Birckmann firm of Cologne. The huge volume of Bishop Christopherson does not say that it was printed by them, only that it was published by them; but even if they gave it to someone else to print, this printer, or these printers, would not be likely to operate outside Cologne.

If the name of Dennis Rhodes is to be as securely linked with the *Italian STC* as that of David Paisey surely is with the *German STC* of 1962 (which was originally compiled by Victor Scholderer who died in 1971 and Alfred Forbes Johnson who died in 1973), then Dennis Rhodes has the following gifts to offer David Paisey:

Italian STC, p. 233:
England. – *Miscellaneous Public Documents.*
Expositio causarum quibus Angliae regina commouebatur ut quasdam subiectorum suorum cohortes armis instrueret. *s.l.*, 1562. 4°. 11403.bb.49 (2).
Correct imprint: [Ludovicus Lucius: Frankfurt am Main,] 1562. 4°

Italian STC, p. 483:
Pacimontanus, Veranius Modestus, *pseud.* [i.e. Georgius Cassander.]
De officio pii ac publicae tranquillitatis uere amantis uiri. *s.l.*, 1562. 4° 3910.bb.76.
Correct imprint: [Johann Birckmann the Younger: Cologne,] 1562. 4°

GERMAN FUNERAL BOOKS AND THE GENRE OF THE FESTIVAL DESCRIPTION

A parallel development

JILL BEPLER

DURING THE EARLY MODERN PERIOD Germany was prominent in the publication of funerary works on a broad scale. It is estimated that as many as 220,000 printed funeral books have survived in the library collections of present-day and former German-speaking territories, a sum which represents only a fraction of the texts presumed actually to have been published.[1] In 1979 David Paisey's contribution to a Wolfenbüttel conference on books and libraries in the seventeenth century, 'Literatur, die nicht in den Meßkatalogen steht',[2] rightly called attention to the need for including such works in any national bibliographic endeavour. Present discussions on the fate and the form of a *VD 17*, a comprehensive catalogue of German imprints of the seventeenth century, in which he has been so closely involved make it clear that this type of literature is still at risk of being passed over and that his warnings retain their urgency. Although, as his contribution argues, the main task of raising consciousness about such neglected forms of literature lies with librarians and bibliographers, there is also a need for scholarly attention to be paid to the neglected genres he enumerates (almanacs, dissertations, newsletters, occasional works) in order to highlight what he terms 'die ganze Literaturwelt der Gesellschaft' (p. 124). Despite various cataloguing projects and conferences over the past fifteen years concerned with the genre *Leichenpredigt* 'funeral sermon', the research interest generated so far has come mainly from social historians interested in using the works for demographic purposes and for obtaining information on the history of

1 See the entry 'Leichenpredigten' by Rudolf Lenz, in: *Handwörterbuch zur deutschen Rechtsgeschichte* (Berlin, 1978), II, cols 1814–18; Rudolf Lenz, *Leichenpredigten. Eine Bestandsaufnahme. Bibliographie und Ergebnisse einer Umfrage* (Marburg, 1980). On the Wolfenbüttel collection see Marina Arnold, 'Die Leichenpredigten der Herzog August Bibliothek und ihre Erschließung', in: *Überlieferung und Kritik. Zwanzig Jahre Barockforschung in der Herzog August Bibliothek Wolfenbüttel*. Wolfenbütteler Arbeiten zur Barockforschung, 21. (Wiesbaden, 1993), pp. 105–12.

2 David Paisey, 'Literatur, die nicht in den Meßkatalogen steht.' In: Paul Raabe (ed.), *Bücher und Bibliotheken im 17. Jahrhundert in Deutschland*. Wolfenbütteler Schriften zur Geschichte des Buchwesens, 6. (Hamburg, 1980), pp. 115–25.

the family.[3] Within the genre as a whole, printed funeral books for princes of the Empire and their female counterparts form a separate group and have in fact attracted even less critical attention than the other groups, mainly because the biographical information contained in them offers nothing new to historians. Besides being devotional works in the *memento mori* tradition, they were also part of the printed political propaganda of the courts for which they were published. In this function they must also be seen in relation to the tradition of the printed festival book which had become common at the courts of the Empire from the second half of the sixteenth century. In his recently published study on the illustrated book in Germany Horst Kunze makes this connection, but immediately dismisses princely funeral publications as unworthy of further attention:

Während Hochzeiten und Kindtaufen Gelegenheit zu allerlei neuartigen Erfindungen und Maskeraden gaben, sind die Kupferstichbände von Leichenfeiern äußerst langweilig. Nur Kostümspezialisten werden ohne weiteres eine niederländische Trauerzeremonie von einer deutschen zu unterscheiden vermögen, und ob die Trauerfeier Ende des 16., 17. oder 18. Jahrhunderts stattfand, spielt dabei nur eine untergeordnete Rolle. (While weddings and christenings afforded opportunities for all kinds of new inventions and masquerades the volumes of funeral sermons with their copper-engravings are exceedingly boring. Only specialists in costume will be able to tell a Dutch funeral from a German one without difficulty, and whether the funeral took place at the end of the sixteenth, seventeenth or eighteenth century is of minimal importance.)[4]

Whereas the royal funerals of France, England and Spain have been the subject of study in recent years, the complexity of the German territories in the Early Modern period has obviously deterred scholars from attempting a survey. The political, ceremonial and artistic aspects of Habsburg state funerals in early modern Germany have received extensive scholarly attention.[5] As yet, however, there has been no comprehensive study of the actual literature published to commemorate funerals of state at the courts of the Empire.[6] I should like to

3 The best summary of this is contained in Rudolf Lenz, *De mortuis nil nisi bene? Leichenpredigten als multidisziplinäre Quelle unter besonderer Berücksichtigung der historischen Familienforschung, der Bildungsgeschichte und der Literaturgeschichte* (Sigmaringen, 1990).

4 Horst Kunze, *Geschichte der Buchillustration in Deutschland. Das 16. und 17. Jahrhundert* (Frankfurt am Main, 1993), p. 506.

5 Michael Brix, 'Trauergerüste für die Habsburger in Wien', *Wiener Jahrbuch für Kunstgeschichte*, 26 (1973), 208-65; Achim Aurnhammer and Friedrich Däuble, 'Die Exequien für Kaiser Karl V. in Augsburg, Brüssel und Bologna', in Paul Richard Blum (ed.), *Studien zur Thematik des Todes im 16. Jahrhundert*. Wolfenbütteler Forschungen, 22 (Wolfenbüttel, 1983), pp. 141-90; Magdalena Hawlik-van der Water, *Der schöne Tod. Zeremonialstrukturen des Wiener Hofes bei Tod und Begräbnis zwischen 1640 und 1740* (Vienna, 1989). Further works dealing with courts and cities within the Empire include: Werner Oechslin and Anja Buschow, *Festarchitektur. Der Architekt als Inszenierungskünstler* (Stuttgart, 1984); Sigrid Metken (ed.), *Die letzte Reise. Sterben, Tod und Trauersitten in Oberbayern* (Munich, 1984); Sebastian Roser and Armin Ruhland, 'Trauerfeierlichkeiten', in Karl Möseneder (ed.), *Feste in Regensburg. Von der Reformation bis in die Gegenwart* (Regensburg, 1986), pp. 57-67.

6 For an examination of two different regions see J. Bepler, 'Das Trauerzeremoniell an den Höfen Hessens undThüringens in der ersten Hälfte des 17. Jahrhunderts', in: J.-J. Berns

examine three of the earliest elaborate funeral publications for princes of the Empire – those for the obsequies held in honour of August Elector of Saxony (1526-1586) in Dresden in 1586, those for William the Rich Duke of Julich (1516-1592) in Düsseldorf in 1592 and those for Moritz the Learned Landgrave of Hessen-Kassel (1572-1632) in Kassel in 1632. All three men were responsible for some of the most splendid court festivities of their era and their courts were cultural centres which attracted scholars and artists from all over Europe. They also represent the three confessions in a divided Germany. August was one of the foremost representatives of orthodox Lutheranism, William of Julich was a Catholic with close ties to the Emperor, and Moritz of Hessen-Kassel was a highly radical Calvinist. The publications and illustrations describing these funerals were of an eminently political nature and are of course also to be read and looked at as political statements by their successors. The difference in the actual presentation of these works – the sheer number published, their format and their degree of illustration – is explained both by confessional considerations and by the local traditions of the courts involved.

The publications issued after the death of the staunch Lutheran August of Saxony in 1586 were legion. The Stolberg collection alone contains 56 different printed texts connected with the funeral.[7] Some emanated from the court in Dresden, others were obviously privately printed by scholars and churchmen both within the Electoral territories and further afield. Places of printing are Dresden, Erfurt, Bautzen, Leipzig, Wittenberg, Freiberg, Eisleben, Lüneburg, Marburg and Schmalkalden. At no point do there seem to have been plans to publish a collection of these works. It is not surprising to find that the most prevalent type of text represented within the over 60 publications discovered so far is the sermon, the core of the Protestant funeral work throughout its development. In addition to the sermons preached for the actual funeral ceremonies, sermons were held throughout the Elector's territories both on the announcement of his death and on the day of the funeral service in Dresden. Neighbouring and related courts such as Hessen and Braunschweig also ordered funeral sermons to be held which found their way into print. Another type of text well represented among those published to commemorate the Elector's death are funeral poems and orations. The remaining publications are works concerned directly or indirectly with the spectacle of funeral itself. This group consists of three texts and an illustrated frieze of the funeral procession. All three texts describe the funeral procession within Dresden and Freiberg in great detail, but only one seems to be a semi-official version of the proceedings. The central text concerning the funeral of August of Saxony, *Historica Narratio*,

and D. Ignasiak (eds), *Frühneuzeitliche Hofkultur in Hessen und Thüringen* (Jena, 1993), pp. 249-65.

7 The Stolberg collection is a private collection of more than 20,000 funerary works, on permanent loan to the Herzog August Bibliothek in Wolfenbüttel. Considerations of space preclude the listing of the titles relevant to the present study here; instead I refer the reader to the catalogue of the collection: Willy Friedrich and Carl Güttich, *Katalog der fürstlich Stolberg-Stolberg'schen Leichenpredigten-Sammlung*, 5 vols (Leipzig, 1927-35).

was written by Bartholomeus Clamorinus and published in two parts.[8] The first deals with the life and the personal and political virtues of the Elector and describes his death in Dresden on 11 February 1586. The second deals with the funeral itself. Clamorinus's modest octavo texts do not in themselves fulfil any representational function (that is, they would hardly be suitable as presentation copies for distribution to neighbouring or related courts). This role seems to have been played by the engraving of the event by Daniel Bretschneider (figs. 1 and 2).[9]

At this early stage in the development of funeral literature the representational potential of the text is neglected. This function is fulfilled by the separately published lavish illustration of the spectacle. The same trend is evident in the publications describing court festivities in Dresden: unassuming printed texts versus lavish illustrations.[10] The works covering the funeral of August of Saxony are closely linked to the publications describing Dresden court festivals. Clamorinus is known to us as a chronicler of tournaments in Saxony in his *Thurnierbüchlein*, a work on the history of tournaments in Saxony published in 1590.[11] Daniel Bretschneider was also the illustrator of festivals in Dresden. In describing the Elector's knightly prowess in the *Historica Narratio*, Clamorinus mentions his love of jousting in his youth, stressing what a serious and dangerous business this was in full battle armour, but commenting that in later years, and indeed up to the end of his life, he had settled for the more decorative pastime of jousting and riding in court festivities.[12] One of the most manifest links between the festivity and the state funeral is to be found in the horses taking part in the funeral procession, especially the charger ridden by a page in August's tournament armour. The tournament horse was an integral part of the state funeral ceremony on a European scale.[13]

At least two Dresden festivities were preserved for a wider posterity in engravings executed by Daniel Bretschneider.[14] As Helen Watanabe has pointed out in her typology of German festival books, early festival engravings follow the pattern set at the beginning of the sixteenth century by the enormous

8 Bartholomeus Clamorinus, *Thurnierbüchlein. Darinne Sechs und dreißig Thurnier/ von Keyser Heinrich dem I. angefangen ... Item/ von zweyen Ritterspielen/ so von Fürsten/ Graffen und Herrn gehalten* (Dresden, 1590), fol. PP4ff. The BL copy has the pressmark 1328.a.5.

9 On Bretschneider see Andreas Andresen, *Der deutsche Peintre-Graveur oder die deutschen Maler als Kupferstecher*. 5 vols (Leipzig, 1864-78), II, pp. 1-9.

10 On court festivities in Dresden see *Zur Festkultur des Dresdner Hofes*. Dresdner Hefte, 21 (Dresden, 1990). On the development of the festival-book as a genre see Helen Watanabe-O'Kelly, 'Festival books in Europe from Renaissance to Rococo', *The Seventeenth Century*, 3 (1987), 181-201.

11 Bartholomeus Clamorinus, *Historia Narratio. Kurtze erzehlunge und betrübte Rede ...* (Dresden, 1586); Bartholomeus Clamorinus, *Altera pars Historicae Orationis luctu plenae ...* (Bautzen, 1586).

12 Clamorinus, *Altera pars*, fol. 17^{v}.

13 Wolfgang Brückner, 'Roß und Reiter im Leichenzeremoniell. Deutungsversuch eines historischen Rechtsbrauches', *Rheinisches Jahrbuch für Völkerkunde*, 15/16 (1964/65), 144-208.

14 These are described in detail by Andresen [note 9].

Fig. 1. Daniel Bretschneider, *Proces vnd Ordnvng des Begenknvs Warhafftige Abcontrafactvr* ... (Dresden, 1585). Herzog August Bibliothek, Wolfenbüttel, Sondersammlung.

Fig. 2. 'Das Freudenpferd'.

engravings executed for Emperor Maximilian such as 'The Triumphal Arch' or 'The Triumphal Procession'.[15] The same principle applies to the engravings dealing with state funerals. Innumerable plates are stuck together to create a panorama of the whole proceedings in an attempt to give the onlooker the sense of a spectacle unfolding. Bretschneider's frieze of the 1582 *Ringrennen* at Dresden consists of 20 plates; in 1584 he used 26 plates to record a second *Ringrennen*. The funeral procession of 1586 occupies approximately 40 plates and is nearly ten metres long. As wall-hangings or scrolls such engravings were usually mounted on canvas to protect them from wear. This is the case with the hand-coloured funeral frieze of the Dresden funeral which has survived in the ducal library in Wolfenbüttel. The engraving probably belonged to Duke Heinrich Julius of Braunschweig-Lüneburg, a son-in-law of August of Saxony.[16] The figures in the funeral procession are labelled in the same way as those participating in the *Ringrennen* entries. The order in which they precede or follow the coffin was, of course, strictly laid down by considerations of rank and representation. The main emphasis in the visual effect of the procession was on the heraldic demonstration of territorial power – the various coats of arms symbolizing the territories over which the Elector had ruled, the insignia of his rank (sword, seal and Electoral hat). For her study of the heraldic and ceremonial aspects of the funeral in Dresden Jutta Bäumel examined the compendious manuscript written at the behest of the marshal's office which sets down the ceremonial plan for the funeral. In comparison to this manuscript account, Clamorinus's description taken together with the engraving give us the published version, the 'media coverage' of the funeral. Manuscripts in Dresden also contain the plans for other court festivities conducted under the auspices of the 'Hofmarschallamt'. These too were made public in modest little volumes and representational engravings which had been separately commissioned.[17]

The next example shows a move in the direction of the compendium funeral book and has the closest links to the tradition of the festival book. In 1587 Theodor Graminaeus, a lawyer and professor of mathematics at Cologne, published his magnificent account of the wedding of Jacoba of Baden and Johann Wilhelm Duke of Julich which had taken place in Düsseldorf in 1585.[18] The account is illustrated with copper engravings which form an integral part of

15 Watanabe-O'Kelly [note 10].

16 Daniel Bretschneider, *Wahrhafftige Abcontrafactur des Durchlauchtigsten Hochgebornnen Fursten und Herrn Herrn Augusti Hertzogen zu Sachssen ... Leiche ...* (Dresden, 1586). The Wolfenbüttel engraving is described in the exhibition catalogue *Sammler, Fürst, Gelehrter. Herzog August zu Braunschweig und Lüneburg 1579-1666* (Wolfenbüttel, 1979), pp. 55-56. Dresden copies of the engraving are discussed in Jutta Bäumel, 'Das Trauerzeremoniell für Kurfürst August von Sachsen 1586 in Dresden und Freiberg', *Dresdner Kunstblätter*, 6 (1987), 208-16.

17 On the close links between archival and printed sources for the tradition of the festival book see Helen Watanabe-O'Kelly, 'Gabriel Tzschimmer's *Durchlauchtigste Zusammenkunft* (1680) and the German festival book tradition', *Daphnis*, 22 (1983), 61-72.

18 Dietrich Graminaeus, *Furstliche Hochzeit ... Anno 1585 am 16. Juni* (Cologne, 1587). On Graminaeus and the Düsseldorf wedding and funeral see Oechslin and Buschow [note 5], pp. 120-23 and 133ff.

the text. In contrast to the octavo unillustrated accounts being put out by the court of Saxony, this fusion of text and illustration represents a first stage in the development of the idea that the printed work commemorating a festival could also contribute to its representational aims. Graminaeus commissioned the engravings for the wedding volume from the Dutch engraver Frans Hogenberg.[19] Five years later Graminaeus and Hogenberg were again responsible for the publication documenting the funeral of William the Rich of Julich who died in 1592.[20] Graminaeus begins his text with general reflections of a moral and theological nature on the theme of death, interpreting and translating the Latin Catholic vigils for All Saints for the lay reader. Like Clamorinus's work on August of Saxony, Graminaeus's funeral book includes a chronicle of the history of the dynasty, stressing its continuity. This is followed by the detailed illustrated description of the funeral ceremony. Even a cursory glance at the festival and the funeral books by Graminaeus and Hogenberg reveals striking similarities in their presentation. The most evident is that they have the same folio format. Another is the title-page engravings (figs. 3 and 4) which have comparable layouts: against an architectural background of columns and pilasters, vignettes form a decorative framework to the actual typography of the title. In keeping with the difference in the actual occasions there is a mixture of mythological and biblical references in the title-page illustrations for the wedding volume whereas the title-page of the funeral description is composed solely of biblical motifs. Both title engravings are accompanied by explanatory poems. The engravings showing the various scenes in the funeral ceremony are integrated into the text as were those in the festival description. In contrast to the illustration of the Dresden funeral which concentrated only on the funeral procession, Graminaeus commissioned engravings by Hogenberg not only of the procession through the streets of Düsseldorf, shown in ten separate plates, but also of the departure of the entourage from the inner courtyard of the castle and of the church. The scene in the interior of the church draped with black cloth shows what seems to be an early precursor of a catafalque. Although it cannot compare with the splendour of the wedding volume, Graminaeus's funeral book is quite obviously outwardly a companion volume to it. There are, however, also similarities in the content of both works. The final 'invention' for the wedding celebrations was a globe illumination depicting the ranks of the angels, the Virgin Mary and the Trinity. This spectacle is described in the festival book with detailed reference to the intercessionary function of the angels and the Virgin. Graminaeus sums up the meaning of the display with an admonition both to participants and reader to consider the vanity of things earthly:

19 On Hogenberg see Friedrich W. H. Hollstein, *Dutch and Flemish Etchings, Engravings and Woodcuts ca. 1450–1700*, IX (Amsterdam, 1949), pp. 50–5.

20 Dietrich Graminaeus, *Spiegel und abbildung der Vergenglichkeit* (Düsseldorf, 1592). The BL copy has the pressmark 9930.g.61.

Fig. 3. Dietrich Graminaeus, *Fvrstliche Hochzeit . . .*

Fig. 4. Dietrich Graminaeus, *Spiegel . . . der Vergenglichkeit*

So hat es dann/ wie vermelt/ die meinung mit vorgedachter zugerichtter Ründe gehabt/ daß man bey angerichter Weltlicher freudt und kurtzweil die betrachtung der Himlischer und ewiger ding nicht underlassen/ noch hindan setzen sol/ sondern das gemüth erheben/ und unzergencklichen eingedenck seyn. (Thus, as I have stated, the meaning of the afore-mentioned globe was that notwithstanding earthly joy and entertainment one ought not to ignore or neglect the contemplation of heavenly and eternal things but lift up one's spirits and be mindful of what is permanent.)[21]

The *Spiegel und abbildung der Vergenglichkeit*, Graminaeus's funeral book, aims likewise to excite the reader to 'gute gedancken/ der Vergengligkeit halben'. His final exhortation here is almost a repetition of the close of the festival book: 'Dan wer den erdischen unnd vergengklichen dingen anhangen wirt/ soll auch mit denselben vergehen und verderben ... ' ('For whoever clings to earthly and transitory things will pass away and perish with them.')[22]

Both Clamorinus in Dresden and Graminaeus in Düsseldorf used their funeral works as vehicles for confessional propaganda. Clamorinus repeatedly praises the harshness with which August of Saxony warded off the threats to orthodoxy from Calvinists and Catholics alike and depicts the imperilled state of the Lutheran cause in the light of his death. Graminaeus is at pains to explain the Catholic liturgical rituals of death in his funeral book. Clamorinus's publication must be seen against the background of the establishment of Lutheran orthodoxy in Saxony and the ensuing witchhunt against Calvinists with the political unrest this had provoked. Graminaeus's work was written at a time when the question of succession in Julich and continued alliance with the Emperor in the face of an increasing move towards Protestantism within the population was, rightly as it transpired, at the forefront of political discussion. Both the funeral ceremonies and the publications issued for them were part of an outward manifestation of political stability and continuity at a moment of potential crisis.

This is true in a particular degree in the case of our third example. The funeral book published in honour of the Calvinist Moritz of Hessen-Kassel was the most extravagant such work to appear in Germany in the first half of the seventeenth century. It is also one of the earliest folio compendium funeral volumes. Like our examples from Dresden and Düsseldorf, the Kassel funeral volume links in with the tradition of festival books at the court. The *Monumentum Sepulchrale* as it is entitled consists of two parts and has a total of 63 copper engravings and 1052 pages.[23] This represents an extraordinary stage in the development of the funeral publication, whereby the book as such outstrips the splendour of the occasion and in itself becomes the act of representation it

21 Graminaeus, *Furstliche Hochzeit*, fol. Aaa3^{v}.

22 Graminaeus, *Spiegel und abbildung der Vergenglichkeit*, fol. T4.

23 *Monumentum Sepulchrale* ... (Kassel, 1638). This work was a joint publication between the printer Johann Saur in Kassel and the publisher Johann Ammon in Frankfurt am Main who supplied the illustrations. Within the volume are two title-pages indicating that poetry for Moritz had been published by Saur in Kassel in 1635. 1639 was the first date of publication for the compendium volume, however. The illustrations were reprinted in 1640.

purports to celebrate, a dynastic statement to be read against the backcloth of the historical situation in which the book was published.

At the turn of the seventeenth century Kassel had been at the forefront in the production of books commemorating 'festivals of the Protestant Union',[24] events such as the christening of Moritz's daughter Elisabeth in 1596 to which her godmother Elizabeth I of England sent the Earl of Lincoln as her representative. The splendour of the proceedings and the tournaments and pageantry, involving scenes from classical mythology were recorded by the Kassel engineer and surveyor Wilhelm Dilich in a book published in 1598.[25] In 1601 the work was reprinted as the first part of a volume issued to publicize another Kassel christening and the accompanying festivities under the joint title *Beschreibung und Abriß dero Ritterspiel ...* (Kassel: Wessel 1601) (fig. 5) and reissued in 1602. These festivities and their iconographical programmes conveyed subtle political and dynastic messages, signalling alliances and claims to political authority and leadership which could not be overtly stated. At the beginning of the century it seemed that Moritz of Hessen-Kassel would play a central role as a focal point of Reformed opposition to Imperial policy, both in the Julich conflict and in the run-up to the Thirty Years' War. Moritz established Kassel as a centre of court culture by staging elaborate festivals, building a theatre, engaging the best Italian musicians and patronizing such men as Heinrich Schütz. He established a Ritterakademie at Kassel and encouraged the learning of modern languages.[26] His own universal intellectual interests and his personal involvement are manifest in the multitude of projects centred on the Kassel court, also a focal point of occult science.[27] When he died at Eschwege in 1632, he was however a broken man.[28] His political demise had occurred five years earlier when with the connivance of his son Wilhelm, his wife Juliane and his own subjects he had been force to abdicate. Besieged by Tilly's forces in Kassel Moritz had been stripped of most of his territorial rights by a decision in the Imperial courts in favour of his Lutheran relatives, the Landgraves of Hessen-Darmstadt.[29] The political situation in Hessen-Kassel

24 Thus the title of a chapter in Helen Watanabe-O'Kelly, *Triumphall Shews. Tournaments at German-speaking Courts in their European Context 1560-1730* (Berlin, 1992), pp. 37-63.

25 Wilhelm Dillich, *Ritterspiele anno 1596* (facsimile), edited by Hartmut Broszinski and Gunter Schweikhart (Kassel, 1986).

26 Gunter Schweikhart, 'Kunst und Kultur in Kassel unter Landgraf Moritz dem Gelehrten (1592-1627)', in: Dieter Berke *et al.* (eds), *Heinrich Schütz. Texte, Bilder, Dokumente* (Kassel, 1985), pp. 13-34.

27 Bruce T. Moran, *The Alchemical World of the German Court. Occult Philosophy and Chemical Medicine in the Circle of Moritz of Hessen* (Stuttgart, 1991).

28 On the history of Hessen-Kassel see Christoph von Rommel, *Geschichte von Hessen*. 9 vols (Kassel, 1836-53), here especially vol. VIII. On Moritz after his abdication and up to his death see Uta Löwenstein, 'Ein Drittel vom Viertel – Hessen-Eschwege in der Quart', *Zeitschrift des Vereins für Hessische Geschichte und Landeskunde*, 94 (1989), 101-23.

29 It is on the funeral book for Ludwig VI of Hessen-Darmstadt that the *Monumentum Sepuchrale* was modelled: *Ehren Gedechtnus Deß Durchleuchtigen ... Herrn Ludwigen Landgraven zu Hessen* ... (Marburg, 1626), with 392 pages and 28 illustrations. On the political and dynastic rivalry expressed in these two volumes see Bepler [note 6].

Das
Ander Buch
Von der Beſchrei-
bung dero Fürſtlichen
Kindtauff Herrn MAU-
RITII des andern / Landgra-
fen zu Heſſen / etc. vnnd von denen dazumals verbrachten
vnd celebrirten Rit-
terſpielen.

Fig. 5. Wilhelm Dilich, *Historische Beschreibung* … (Kassel, 1601). Herzog August Bibliothek, Wolfenbüttel, Gm 4° 411.

on Moritz's death in 1632 was dramatic. Imperial forces had been marauding through the territory since Moritz's abdication. Headed by Gustavus Adolphus, fated also to die in the year 1632 at the battle of Lützen, the Protestant armies were permanently on the move. With the armies was Moritz's successor Wilhelm. Reading of his movements and of the state of his territories it is hard to imagine that there was time or indeed safety enough for the conduct of a funeral on the scale presented to the reader of the *Monumentum Sepulchrale*. The following years brought few positive developments. Driven from his court at Kassel and restlessly involved in military campaigns, Wilhelm died of a fever at Leer in Frisia in 1637. This means that he never actually saw the *Monumentum Sepulchrale* which he had commissioned to glorify his father and further the Protestant cause not just on a national, but on an international scale.

These two aspects of the funeral book for Moritz – the assertion of dynastic and religious continuity and the demonstration of international identification with the Protestant cause – recalled quite consciously the spirit of the festival books and determined both the scale of the enterprise and the calibre of those called upon to execute it. Dilich, estranged from the court, was now in the employ of the Dresden elector. The court of Kassel turned to the local printer Johann Saur who was obviously responsible for setting and printing the texts and to the Frankfurt publisher Johann Ammon who commissioned engravings from the best artists available. Matthäus Merian and his apprentices and Jacob von Heyden engraved the illustrations on the basis of paintings and drawings by the court artist August Erich and the artist and Swedish diplomat Christoph Le Blon.[30] Merian, of course, had a firmly established reputation. He was, however, uniquely qualified to supervise the plates for such an elaborate funeral book, for as an apprentice in France he had worked on one of the most elaborate of European festival books, the exequies for Charles III Duke of Lorraine in Nancy in 1610-11.[31]

The title-engraving of the *Monumentum Sepulchrale* (fig. 6) sets out the programme of Moritz's funeral publication, which is the revival of belief in the capacity of the Kassel dynasty to rally the forces of international Protestantism, especially among Calvinists, against the Habsburg emperor in the Thirty Years' War. The typography of the title is set in an architectural framework with a vignette showing the funeral procession entering Kassel. Moritz is apostrophized in the title as 'true above all to God and the Empire and upholder and protector of the liberty of Germany'. Constancy and religious faith, his two main virtues, flank the monument-like structure in which the title is placed like the inscription on a tomb.

30 On Merian and the *Monumentum Sepulchrale* see Lucas Heinrich Wüthrich, *Das druckgraphische Werk von Matthaeus Merian d. Ä.* 2 vols (Basle, 1966), II, pp. 107ff.

31 *Les pompes funèbres de Charles III, duc de Lorraine* (Nancy: Clause de la Ruelle and Hermann de Loye, n.d.), facsimile: *Denkmäler des Theaters, IV*, edited by Joseph Gregor (Munich, 1925). On the significance of the funeral and the publication for court culture in Nancy see Paulette Choné, *Emblèmes et pensée symbolique en Lorraine 1525-1633: 'comme un jardin au coeur de la chrétienté'* (Paris, 1991), pp. 133-55.

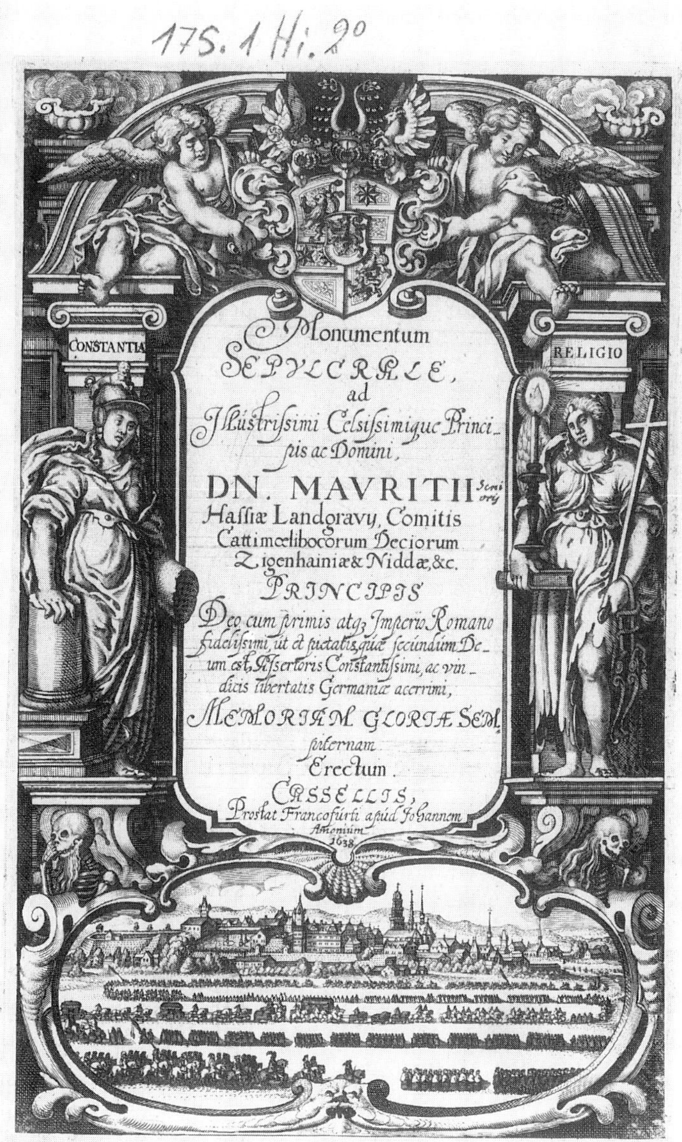

Fig. 6. *Monumentum Sepulchrale* ... (Kassel, 1638). Herzog August Bibliothek, Wolfenbüttel, 175.1 Hist. 2°.

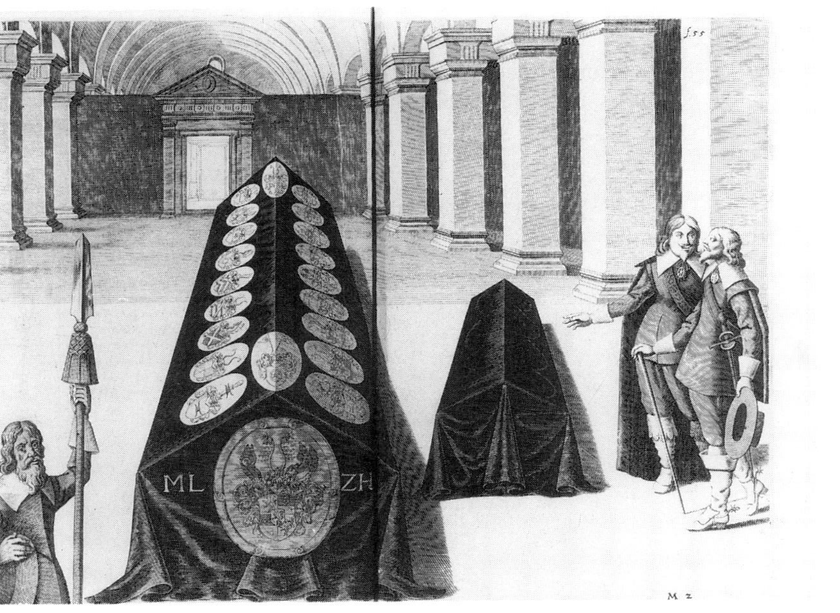

Fig. 7. Chapel in Kassel, from
Monumentum Sepulchrale.

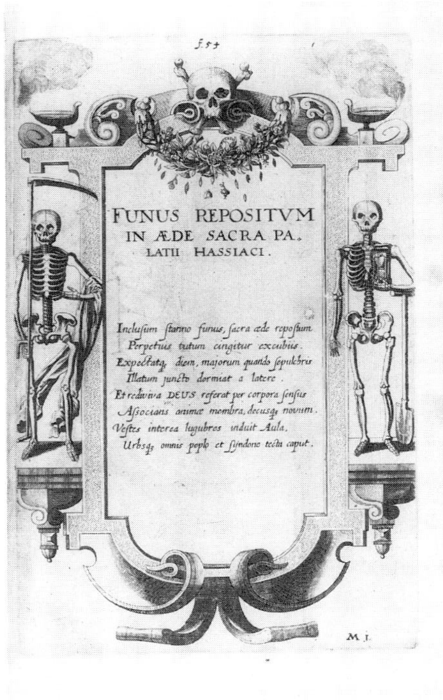

Fig. 8. Explanatory engraving, from
Monumentum Sepulchrale.

The sequence of engravings which follows is unique to the funeral books for Ludwig of Darmstadt (1626) and Moritz, whereby the sixty-three Kassel illustrations far outnumber those in the Darmstadt volume. They consist of a gallery of family portraits, starting with Moritz's grandfather Philipp, a martyr to the Protestant cause and friend of Melanchthon. The family portrait gallery unfolds before the reader's eye and has something of our own taste for a media display of royalty. Moritz is shown both as a young man with his family and again as a mature parent with his second wife – the very Juliane responsible for his abdication. These family portraits, each accompanied by a plate with an explanatory inscription, and the coats of arms for the respective members of the dynasty, account for 44 of the engravings in all. The rest illustrate the actual funeral ceremonies. The first shows the landgrave lying in state on the *lit de parade* in Eschwege. A fold-out engraving then depicts the funeral procession from Eschwege to Kassel. The next scene shows the draped coffin as it stood in the castle chapel in Kassel. Here we note the simplicity of the setting and the fact that the chapel is devoid of any form of decoration beyond the black velvet cloth with its cross of silver on the coffin bearing the Hessen coats of arms (fig. 7). The reality of the funeral ceremony was in full accordance with Calvinist precepts: no images were used. The funeral book, however, compensates for this Calvinist frugality in the accompanying ornamental engravings providing the commentary to each picture. In fig. 8 we have the Baroque imagery of death: the extinguished lamps denoting the fact of death, the Golgotha skull and crossed bones reminding the spectator of the crucifixion, a demi-wreath of flowers shedding their petals symbolizing the transitoriness of human existence, two skeletons holding the familiar symbols of the scythe and the hour-glass. What actually confronts us here is a quasi-emblematic structure: *inscriptio* (*Funus repositum in aede sacra palatii hassiaci*), *pictura* (the landgrave's draped coffin / or the skeletons and apparatus), and *subscriptio* (the explanatory text with its reflections on death and the hope of resurrection). It seems justifiable to assert that at this early stage of *pompe funèbre* at German Protestant courts we do in fact find examples of Ménestrier's *decorations funèbres*,[32] if only on the printed page. The largest engravings come at the end of the series with a panorama of the funeral procession in Kassel approximately one and a half metres long and a depiction of the family tree of the Landgraves of Hessen tracing their ancestry back to Charlemagne.

The enumeration of these illustrations shows that it goes far beyond the limits of a normal funeral work. This also applies to the content, for the work contains twelve sermons preached for Moritz as well as a selection of those held for children who had predeceased him, and the accession-day sermon for Wilhelm from 1627. Three academic orations are then followed by the funeral poetry written in honour of Moritz, grouped according to places of origin. After 45 poems from within the Empire comes an astounding collection of 98 poems sent

32 The most comprehensive contemporary work on the history and etiquette of princely funerals is Claude Ménestrier, *Les décorations funèbres* ... (Paris, 1680).

from abroad – from France, England, Scotland, Bohemia, the Netherlands, Switzerland, Hungary, Silesia, and Moravia. Among the authors of these poems are such prominent men as Jan Amos Comenius, John Dury and Caspar Barlaeus.[33] The universities of Oxford and Cambridge contributed no fewer than 31 poems to the collection.

Not one single poem for Moritz is written in German. Most are in Latin or Greek, a few in Hebrew. The vernacular languages of other countries are represented: French, English, Dutch, even Hungarian and Czech. This was certainly a tribute of the landgrave's gift for languages, it was also a bombastic demonstration of international connections. The only German texts within the funeral work are the sermons; the work's main interest lies clearly in impressing an international audience.

Seen in relation to these earlier publications, the *Monumentum Sepulchrale* is a fascinating example of a representational work produced against a background of chaos which appeared at a time when the fate of the territory of Hessen-Kassel was at its lowest ebb – and is in itself an attempt to constitute dynastic and political representation and continuity on the printed page in the face of its yawning absence in reality. Only when a larger study of funeral works at the courts of the Empire in their historical and political context is undertaken will the role of this neglected genre be fully understood.

33 For a discussion of the poem by Comenius see Leonard W. Forster, 'Unpublished Comeniana II. An unnoticed Czech poem by Comenius', *Slavonic and Eastern European Review*, 39 (1960), 24–30.

A GERMAN-DUTCH TAPESTRY

Some early seventeenth-century Dutch publications with German connections: Henrick van Haestens, Leiden, and Jan Jansz, Arnhem

ANNA E. C. SIMONI

THE FOLLOWING TITLES of books published between 1601 and 1621 by the two publishers Henrick van Haestens and Jan Jansz, themselves interconnected, are with one exception those of books in the British Library, and of that exception the British Library has two editions in French. A comprehensive catalogue of all similar books issued in the Low Countries during this or a longer period and preserved in other libraries as well would make a book in its own right. The strands looked for consist of translations in either direction; French or Latin translations of German texts; reprints of works first published in Germany; or German-made illustrations for books which are Dutch by language or place of publication. Moreover, while several of the books will inevitably already have been described by John Bruckner, pamphlets and single sheets there ignored are included here in so far as applicable.

The pattern is a chronological arrangement under each publisher, with bibliographical references and other observations considered to be of interest added for colour. An alphabetical index of authors' names and anonymous titles will conclude the list.

Abbreviations

Bru: J. Bruckner, *A bibliographical catalogue of seventeenth-century German books published in Holland* (The Hague, 1971) [Anglica Germanica, 13].

Sim: A. E. C. Simoni, *Catalogue of books from the Low Countries 1601-1621 in the British Library* (London, 1990).

A. HENRICK LODEWIJCXSOON VAN HAESTENS, LEIDEN

On Van Haestens and his publications see J. G. C. A. Briels, *Zuidnederlandse boekdrukkers en boekverkopers in de Republiek der Verenigde Nederlanden omstreeks 1570-1630. Een bijdrage tot de kennis van de geschiedenis van het boek* (Nieuwkoop, 1974) [Bibliotheca bibliographica neerlandica, 6], pp. 95, 305-9; A. E. C. Simoni, 'Henrick van Haestens, from Leiden to Louvain via "Cologne"', *Quærendo*, 15 (1985), 187-94; C. Coppens, 'Steadfast I hasten: the Louvain printer Henrick van Ha(e)stens', *Quærendo*, 17 (1987), 185-204; C. Coppens and M. de Schepper, 'Printer to town and university: Henrick van Haestens at Louvain. With a check-list (1621-1628)', in: S. Roach (ed.), *Across the Narrow Seas. Studies in the history and bibliography of Britain and the Low Countries. Presented to Anna E. C. Simoni* (London, 1991), pp. 107-26; and the forthcoming bibliography of the works produced by Van Haestens, by C. Coppens, M. de Schepper and A. E. C. Simoni, with a study of his books on the siege of Ostend by the last-named.

1. 1605: CHRISTOFFEL VAN SICHEM, *Ein Wunderkunstig Schiff, welches vber die gefrohren Wasser vnnd Landt fahret*, etc. Single sheet; obl. fol.

BL: C.18.e.2(106).

An engraving signed: C. V. Sichem sculp. followed by a poem by the artist and bearing the imprint: Zu Leyden, durch Christoffel von Sichem. No doubt Van Sichem owned a plate press and he may also have had a printing press for his woodcuts with or without letterpress text, after he moved to Amsterdam in 1606(?). There are engravings by him dated 1603-6 which bear the imprint of his eldest son, Hans Christoffel. Christoffel himself, a Dutchman by birth, spent a number of years in Basle where he acquired his knowledge of German, such as it was. After his return to Holland he spent the rest of his life in Amsterdam, where his first publication is dated 1607. Although neither Hans Christoffel van Sichem's nor Van Haestens's name appears on this item, the latter had printed earlier material on the same subject, the famous land-yacht invented by Simon Stevin, given a spectacular outing on Scheveningen beach in April 1602, bearing a distinguished company which included Prince Maurice of Orange, the Spaniard Francisco de Mendoza, Admiral of Arragon (taken prisoner at the battle of Nieuwpoort in 1600) and the young Hugo Grotius. The event and the famous print by Jacques de Gheyn, with text by Grotius and printed by Henrick van Haestens in 1603, are discussed in detail in A. Eyffinger, *Grotius Poeta. Aspecten van Hugo Grotius' dichterschap* (The Hague, 1981), pp. 64-77. The present engraving shows the adaptation of the land-yacht for use on ice which was certainly proposed, but does not appear ever to have been executed. The text of the poem was also published in Dutch and French, but no copies of these versions are held by the British Library. Van Haestens and Van Sichem collaborated over several years (cf. no. 3).

Sim S150; L. Forster, *Christoffel van Sichem in Basel und der frühe deutsche Alexandriner* (Amsterdam, etc., 1985) [Verhandelingen der Koninklijke Nederlandse Akademie van Wetenschappen, Afd. Letterkunde, n.r. 131], pp. 65-9, with further literature. An illustration of the engraving serves Forster as frontispiece.

2. 1608: CORNELIS JACOBSZOON DREBBEL, *Ein kurtzer Tractat von der Natur der Elementen vnd wie sie den Windt, Regen, Blitz vnd Donner verursachen, vnd war zu sie nutzen.* 8°; A-B⁸; illus., port. BL: 1033.c.34.

Originally published in 1607 in Haarlem as *Een kort tractaet van de natuere der elementen*, an edition of which no extant copy is known. The translator of this edition is unknown. The original illustrations were woodcuts, the portrait of Drebbel signed: 'CVS', the monogram of Christoffel van Sichem, as used again in the 1621 Haarlem edition (Sim D99). The unsigned engravings in this Leiden German edition are derived from these woodcuts. The German edition was reprinted in Erfurt in 1624, with Latin editions published in Hamburg 1621, Frankfurt 1628 and Geneva 1628. Drebbel was an inventor and probably also what would nowadays be called an eccentric who, among other things, came to England to present James I with a *Perpetuum mobile* and demonstrated a kind of diving suit or bell to him by remaining submerged in the River Thames for three hours. An attempt to demonstrate also an explosive device attached to the bottom of a ship failed, however, but places his ideas far ahead of his time (see Charles van den Heuvel, 'De Huysbou en de Crychconst van Simon Stevin. Nieuwe theorieën van de Hollandse stad en van haar verdediging', *De zeventiende eeuw*, 10 (1994), 79-92, esp. pp. 87, 91).

Bru 5*; Sim D100; W. B. Rye, *England as seen by foreigners in the days of Elizabeth and James the First* (London, 1865), p. 61 and note 84, pp. 232-42, plate facing p. 235; C. C. Gillispie (ed.), *Dictionary of scientific biography*, IV (New York 1971), pp. 183-5; and more literature and bibliographical information in other biographical dictionaries and under his name in the British Library's *General Catalogue of Printed Books*.

3. 1608: [CHRISTOFFEL VAN SICHEM], *Greuwel der vornahmsten Hauptketzeren, So wohl Wiedertauffer, als auch andern ... Zugleich Mitt ihrer Abcontrafaitung, Ihrem Leben, Lher, Anfang vnnd Ende ... beschrieben.* 8°; A-F⁸; illus. BL: 698.a.45(3).

In 1606/7 Van Sichem had issued single sheets bearing portraits of individual heretics and short letterpress text in Dutch or German of which he combined the Dutch versions in bookform in 1608 under the title *Historische beschrijvinge ende afbeeldinge der voornaemste hooft-ketteren.* The engraver-author's name is not mentioned in the German edition any more than it was in the Dutch edition entitled *Grouwelen der voornaemster hooft-ketteren* which Van Haestens had published in 1607 or in the Latin edition entitled *Speculum Anabaptistici furoris*, or in another issue of this, *Apocalypsis insignium aliquot haeresiarcharum*, also published by him in 1608. In all his editions the engravings are copied and the text translated and adapted from Van Sichem's originals. Another Latin edition, brought out by Jan Jansz at Arnhem in 1609 under the title of *Iconica & historica descriptio praecipuorum haeresiarcharum*, reveals the author's name in a laudatory poem and bears the monogram C.V.S. on most of the plates.

Not in Bruckner; Sim S144; F. W. H. Hollstein, *Dutch and Flemish etchings, engravings and woodcuts, ca. 1450-1700* (Amsterdam, 1949-), vol. 27 (by D. de Hoop-Scheffer & G. S. Keys, ed. K. G. Boon), pp. 14-26, nos. 32-50, describes the separate sheets bearing portraits of heretics with German text, without mentioning the book.

4. 1610: SEBASTIAN BRANT, *Aff-ghebeelde Narren-Speel-schuyt, verciert met meer als hondert schoone figueren ... Ghetrouwelick overgheset ... door A.B.* 4°; ff. 109; illus., port. BL: 11511.a.7.

The title-page engraving and 105 woodcut illustrations are based on the original illustrations. The Dutch text is practically the same as that of the first Dutch edition published by Jan van Ghelen at Antwerp in 1584, with only slight adaptations, but the order of 'fools' has been drastically changed. Jan van Ghelen's preface declares him to be the translator: '... soo hebbe ick ... overghestelt ende ghetranslateert wten Latijne ... ende ick hebber af ende toeghedaen, alsoot my oorboorlijck dochte' ('thus I have rendered and translated out of the Latin, and I have taken away from it and added to it as I deemed proper'), but the 'A.B.' of the 1610 edition, who seems to refer to the reviser or alleged new translator, has not been identified. Van Haestens's edition was reprinted by Jan Evertsz Cloppenburgh, Amsterdam, in 1635. The 1608 edition is of particular interest for its additional preliminary matter, contributed by the Leiden scholar Petrus Scriverius who may have had an even greater hand in this publication. A copy of the 1584 Antwerp edition is listed in the auction catalogue of Scriverius's library, *Bibliotheca Scriveriana* (Amsterdam, 1663), 'Miscellanei In Octavo' no. 424: 'Het zotte schip door Seb Brandt tot Antw. by Jan van Geele 1584'. The actual title reads: *Nauis Stultorum... oft, Der sotten schip verciert met hondert ende xv. schoone Figuren ... Eerst Ghemaeckt in Hoochduytsch deur M. Sebastiaen Brandt, Doctoor inder Rechten. THantvverpen. Ghedruckt ... by my Jan van Ghelen. 1584. Met Gratie end Priuilegie.* The illustrations in that edition are copies of those of 1494. Collaboration between scholar and printer is known from other sources: not only did Van Haestens print and publish several of the historical works of Scriverius, he very probably also made use of his patron's library for research on the siege of Ostend on which he wrote and published himself, as shown in the work by Coppens *et al.* mentioned above (p. 162). It is therefore tempting to assume that it was Scriverius who suggested this new edition of Brant to the printer, offered him the use of his copy as a model and promised his cooperation in the introductory pages to lend the new production an extra cachet. They begin with a new text on A3^{v}, 'Vanden Aucteur deses Boecks' ('Of the author of this book'), ending with a reference to Johannes Trithemius. This is taken up on A4^{r} with the quotation itself: 'Iohannes Trithemius Abbas Spanheimensis In Catalogo Illustrium virorum', with a list of Brant's learned works and a special paragraph on 'libellum ... quem Navem Narragoniae appellavit', dated 1495. An engraved portrait of Brant bearing his dates in the margin and an eight-line letterpress Latin poem underneath, signed 'P.S.', fill A4^{v}. Its facing page, B1^{r} = p. 1, bears the 'Sonet op de af-beeldinge, *etc.*' ('Sonnet on the image'), a Dutch poem of the same content as the Latin verses were and equally signed 'P.S.'. Both poems describe the portrait as showing Brant combining the characters of Heraclitus and Democritus, the one known as the laughing, the other as the weeping philosopher, explaining that in this book Brant both castigated and ridiculed mankind. The title of the Dutch poem also discloses the origin of the portrait: it is taken from vol. 2 of J. J. Boissard's 'Icones illustrium virorum', published by Theodor de Bry at Frankfurt. It occurs there, *Icones quinquaginta virorum illustrium doctrina & eruditione praestantium ... Recens in aere ... incisa & publicata a Theodoro de Bry* (Francfordii, 1598), p. 174, in a larger and finer form from which it has been copied in reverse and given its new inscription and verses. De Bry's reference to the *Narrenschiff* on p. 170 reads: '... De stultorum nauicula Satyras plane diuinas carmine latino & Rhitmis etia*m* Germanicis'. But Scriverius does not quote from this, but ends instead with a quotation from 'Paullus Langius in Chronico Citicensi ad Annum M.D.XV.' which he must have found in the compilation by Johann Pistorius of Nidda, *Illustrium veterum scriptorum, qui rerum a Germanis gestarum historias reliquerunt tomus unus* (Francofurti, 1584), pp. 755-907, of which there is a copy in the *Bibliotheca Scriveriana* (see above, p. 164), 'Historici In Folio', no. 164: 'Scriptores Germanici è Bibliotheca Pistorii Nidani typ. Wechelin 1584'. Of the two passages in it dealing with Brant (pp. 886, 893-5) it is the former from which Scriverius has derived his laudatory lines. The latter would have offered him a quotation from a letter by Brant to Pistorius, replying to an enquiry by the latter about a recent burning of heretics in Switzerland, which in a mixed Latin and German verse dialogue includes the happy lines: 'Du bist auch einer, liber Bruder, | Der do zeucht an dem Schelmen Ruder, | Da die Münch angezogen hant, | Die man zu Bern jetzt hat verbrant, *etc.*'

Sim B258. The literature on Brant is vast and the illustrations to the *Narrenschiff* have received particular attention. The Dutch adaptations are however less well known. The 1610 edition is not represented in *NUC*, nor does Brunet know it. On Petrus Scriverius see P. R. Sellin, 'Daniel Heinsius's Nederduytsche Poemata. De uitgaven van 1616 en 1618', *Tijdschrift voor Nederlandse Taal- en Letterkunde*, 78 (1961), 241-46; C. L. Heesakkers, 'Petrus Scriverius as the publisher of the Poemata of Janus Dousa', *Quærendo*, 5 (1975), 105-25; and especially P. Tuynman, 'Petrus Scriverius 12 January 1576-30 April 1660', *Quærendo*, 7 (1977), 4-35.

5. 1612: This would be the place for JAN JANSZ ORLERS and H. L. VAN HAESTENS, *Warhafftige Beschreibung, vnd Eigentliche Abbildung aller Züge vnd Victorien, Zu Wasser vnd zu Landt, Die Gott ... den Hochmögenden Herrn Staten, Der vereinigten Niderlendischen Provintzen verliehen hat*, etc., a work usually referred to by its half-title as *Der Nassawische Loorbeerkrantz Oder Triumph-wagen*, translated from *Den Nassauschen Lauren-crans*. The Dutch edition, two French editions and two German editions were printed by Van Haestens, a third German edition, much altered, appeared in Amsterdam without a date.

Bru 11, 25; Sim 029, 31 (the French editions).

6. 1620: JACOB DIRCXS BOCKENBERG, *Een Pelgerimsche Reyse nae de H. Stadt Ierusalem ... Noch een Pelgerimsche reyse die ghedaen heeft den E. Heer Ieronimus Scheydt van Erffort int iaer 1615 van Ierusalem nae de Iordaen,* ende *voorts nae Sodoma ende Gomorra, ende vvederom door Egypten nae Ierusalem.* Gedruckt tot Coelen, Voor Henrick van Witten ... 1620. 8°; pp. 122, sigg. H6-o8; illus.
BL: 10077.aa.31.

Jacob Bockenberg's pilgrimage took place in 1565-66; Hieronymus Scheydt set out in 1614 and his account was first published by Jacob Singe in Erfurt in 1615 under the title *Kurtze und Warhafftige Beschreibung der Reise, von Erffurdt aus Thüringen nach dem gewesenen gelobten Lande und der heiligen Stadt Jerusalem.* The Dutch translation covers only that part of the pilgrimage which followed on the visit to Jerusalem itself. The book has been given a false imprint. Its whole design and typography relate it to some of the output of Henrick van Haestens and this printer's identity is confirmed by an ornament incorporating his initials. For a full description, reproductions of the title-page and the ornament and a possible explanation for the adoption by Van Haestens of a false imprint, see Simoni, *Quærendo*, 15 (1985), 187-94 (see p. 161).

Sim B196.

B. JAN JANSZ, ARNHEM

Less has been written about Jan Jansz than about Van Haestens. On him and his son, the famous Joannes Janssonius of Amsterdam, see J. Theunisz, 'Het boekdrukkers-geslacht Janssonius', *Het Boek*, 24 (1936-7), 211-15. J. A. Gruys and C. de Wolf, *Thesaurus 1473-1800. Nederlandse boekdrukkers en boekverkopers met plaatsen en jaren van werkzaamheid. Dutch printers and booksellers with places and years of activity* (Nieuwkoop, 1989) [Bibliotheca bibliographica neerlandica, 28], p. 100, assign him to the years 1597-1630.

7. 1604: [WILLEM BAUDAERT], *Af-beeldinge Der Coninghinne Elyzabeth: des Conincks Iacobi .VI. Der Coninginne Annae syner Vrouwe: ende Henrici Frederici des Princen van Wallia. Met een corte beschrijvinghe haerer Stammen, als oock haerer aencompste, tot de Croone van Engelandt ... Wt verscheyden Historien vergadert, ende wtghegheven, Door W. B. Lief-hebber der Historien.* 4°; pp. 32: plates.
BL: G.6182.

One could describe this little book as having three national dimensions and one international one: its Dutch publisher and text, its English subject matter, and – most important here – its German-made illustrations with Latin text. These are the work of Crispijn van de Passe the Elder, then resident in Cologne, but of Dutch origin: born in Arnemuiden he calls himself 'Zeelandus'. The first is an engraved title-page reading *Regiae Anglicae Maiestatis pictura, et Historica declaratio*, with the imprint 'Coloniae apud Crispianum Passaeum'. The words 'Historica declaratio', while agreeing with the Dutch text by 'W. B. Lover of History', point equally well to the Latin text on the plate showing the genealogy

Fig. 1. The genealogy of the English royal family

of the English royal family. This finely engraved plate has the miniature-like oval portrait of Prince Henry at the apex of the double tree (fig. 1). The text reads: 'Habem*us* hic beneuole spectator, duplicem, et, vt sic loquar, coniugale*m* arborem genealogiae Iacobi moderni Regis Britan*n*icarum insularu*m* ... ex hac cognoscere promtum erit qua ratione dict*us* Iacobus maiores suos in regia Angloru*m* stirpe prolixi*us* declarabitur. quae huic tabell*ae* adiunges.' Another, smaller, area holds the regular engraved six-line Latin verses on the same subject and the signature: 'Cris. de. Pas. scul. et ex.' The other portraits bear no prose text and the verses are included on the main copperplates. They are of Elizabeth ('Tantae si vires, virtus mihi quanta Mariana est'), James ('Vt tribus eximijs ornatus dotibus est Rex'), Anne ('Danorum Regis Friderici gnata secundi') and Henry ('Magna quidem res est, Regalis stirpe creari'), the latter's a larger, rectangular version of the same drawing which had served for the miniature on top of the family tree. Some plates bear a further signature reading at its most extended 'Matth. Quad. ludebat', naming the poet. He is, deservedly, better known as an engraver, especially of maps, so much so that P. Meurer (see below), not only assigns to Quad the 'high point' in the development of Cologne atlas production, but connects its decline with his move to Oberursel after 1600. The question arises whether the two components of the book were planned as a unit from the beginning or were only a happy marriage of two hitherto independent publications. There exists in the British Library, and probably elsewhere, an issue of the Dutch text only with the imprint 'T' Amstelredam, By Willem Ianszoon, de Veen Boeckdrukker' (Sim B38). The combined issue is to the best of my knowledge the earliest example of collaboration between the Arnhem publisher and Crispijn van de Passe (first of Cologne, then of Utrecht), a fruitful venture for both, on which see D. Franken, *L'oeuvre gravée des Van de Passe* (Amsterdam and Paris, 1881), pp. 254-65. Indeed, documents quoted by Theunisz, *Het Boek*, 24 (1936-7), 211-15, state that the estate of Jan Jansz still owed a large debt to that of Crispijn Van de Passe and that Jansz and Janssonius were jointly referred to as 'well-known publishers of the works of Crispijn van de Passe'. Separate editions of Baudaert's text and Van de Passe's engravings therefore probably preceded the joint issue of text and illustration. If so, 'Af-beeldinge' in the title of the Dutch text-without-plates must imply verbal portraits only. But then, what a stroke of salesmanship to bring out the two parallel books of such topical interest together! In fact, the format was so successful that in 1610 Jansz published a similar book, this time in German: *Des Fürstlichen Geschlechts und Hauses Gulich, Clef, Berg und Marck, etc. Stammregister* which included the corresponding *Illustriss. Juliacensium ... effigies* with its imprint 'Coloniae Agrippinae. Studio C. P. chalcographi' of which alas the British Library does not own a copy. A. M. Hind, *Engraving in England in the sixteenth & seventeenth centuries*, 2 (Cambridge, 1955), pp. 40-1, reports another, enlarged edition of the English series, published by Crispijn van de Passe at Utrecht in 1613. The copy known to Hind was then in the Huth collection and is now in the Folger Shakespeare Library, Washington.

Sim B39; F. W. H. Hollstein, *Dutch and Flemish etchings, engravings and woodcuts ca. 1400-1700* (Amsterdam, 1949-), XV, p. 288, no. 853, referring the portraits of Elizabeth and James to the numbers of those occurring in Van de Passe's *Effigies regum ac principum ... quorum ... potentia in re nautica ... prae ceteris spectabilis est ... Adjectis in singulas Hexastichis M. Quadi* [Cologne, 1598] – which is true for that of Elizabeth, but James's portrait is different in the two works; R. Strong, *Portraits of Queen Elizabeth I* (Oxford, 1963), p. 113, no. E24 (Elizabeth's portrait only); Hollstein, *op. cit.* (no. 3, p. 164), 15 (by K. B. Boon and J. Verbeek), p. 284 for *Effigies regum*, p. 288 for *Regiae Anglicae Maiestatis pictura*; P. H. Meurer, *Atlantes Colonienses. Die Kölner Schule der Atlaskartographie 1570-1610* (Bad Neustadt a.d. Saale, 1988) [Fundamenta cartographica historica, 1], pp. 197-201, with a biographical sketch and a bibliography of Quad, the former describing him as one-time pupil of Hendrik Goltzius at Haarlem, which makes an early acquaintance with Van de Passe quite possible, the latter listing the *Effigies regum*, but not the *Regiae Anglicae Maiestatis pictura*; I. M. Veldman 'Keulen als toevluchtsoord voor Nederlandse kunstenaars (1597-1612)', *Oud Holland*, 107 (1993), 34-58, referring to Quad as engraver, as author of Latin verses to Van de Passe's prints and as reliable author, especially in his *Teutscher Nation Herligkeitt. Ein ausfuhrliche beschreibung des gegenwertigen, alten, vnd vhralten Standes Germaniae* (Cölln am Rhein, 1609), where Quad's friendship with Van de Passe finds repeated expression: on p. 357, describing Middelburg as the capital of Zeeland, he tells the reader that 'Gegen Oosten ligt das Stettlin Armuien, daraus Crispin de Passe der figurschneider burtig ist', and on p. 432 he mentions him again among the great artists of the Low Countries.

8. 1604: ALBRECHT DÜRER, *Hierinn sind begriffen vier bücher von menschlicher Proportion durch Albrechten Dürer von Nürerberg* [sic] *erfunden vnd beschriben ... M.D.XXViij.* fol.; A-Z^6, last leaf blank, no pagination. BL: C.82.g.9.

This book, a reprint of the original edition of 1528, bears no imprint or date of publication. *Ger STC*, p. 256, describes it: '[*Nuremberg*, 1550?]' which explains its omission from Simoni, but according to H. Bohatta, 'Versuch einer Bibliographie der kunsttheoretischen Werke Albrecht Dürers für das XVI. und XVII. Jahrhundert', *Börsenblatt für den deutschen Buchhandel*, 91 (1928), 530-31, no. 33, this can only be the reissue of his no. 18 (Jan Jansz, Arnhem, 1603), published by Jansz in 1604 as part of Dürer's 'Opera'. Jansz obviously used a copy of the 1528 edition as a model, but incorporated the corrections proposed there on fol. Z6^r. (Readers should be warned here that the facsimile of the first edition (Dietikon-Zürich, 1969), with commentary by Max Streck, made from copies (parts unspecified) in Berne University and Winterthur Municipal Libraries, prints these errata on Z6^v, with another errata list on Z6^r which does not belong to this book.) The British Library copy of the Arnhem edition's binding makes it clear that it belonged to Charles I before his accession, having the Prince of Wales's feathers flanked by the initials C and P and the date 1623 stamped in gold on the covers.

Bru 3 issue B; not in Simoni.

9. 1604: Emanuel van Meteren, *Historia, Oder Eigentliche vnd warhaffte Beschreibung aller fürnehmen Kriegshändel, Gedenckwürdigen Geschichten vnd Thaten, so sich in Niderlandt … Franckreich … zugetragen haben … biss auff diese jetzige gegenwertige zeit* … Durch Emanuel Materanum [*sic*] … jetzo wider auffs new aussgangen, vnd vermehrt. fol., 2 pt.: pp. 878; 876 [238]; illus.
BL: C.47.i.22.

The preface is signed: Emanuel von Meteren, von Antorff. The text ends in August 1604. Among the portraits, which occur in pt. 1 only, are those of Charles V, Philip II, William of Orange, the Earl of Leicester, Queen Elizabeth I, Prince Maurice of Orange. They are crude reversed copies of the round portraits found in earlier German and Latin editions, translated from the *Belgische ofte Nederlantsche historie*, first published, as suggested by J. Verduyn, *Emanuel van Meteren* (The Hague, 1926), p. 171, and confirmed by L. Brummel, *Twee ballingen 's lands. Hugo Blotius (1534-1608), Emanuel van Meteren (1535-1612)* (The Hague, 1972), pp. 87-91, at Oberursel or Cologne in 1596 and the most authoritative work on the Dutch Revolt for many years. The copy in the British Library is bound in blind-stamped pigskin and bears the ownership inscription 'Monasterij Zwifaltens'.

Bru 4; Sim M88; J. F. van Someren, *Beschrijvende catalogus van gegraveerde portretten van Nederlanders*, 1 (Amsterdam, 1888), pp. 31-2, no. 17 and 18 (on the portraits in the earlier German editions); R. Strong, *Portraits of Queen Elizabeth*, p. 113, no. 23 (on the portrait of Queen Elizabeth).

10. 1606: Albrecht Dürer. *Alberti Dureri Institutionum geometricarum libri quatuor versi olim e … Germanicâ in linguam Latinam & nunc iterato editi.* fol., pp. 185; illus.
BL: 530.m.9(1).

A reprint of the edition published by Christian Wechel in Paris in 1535, entitled *Albertus Durerus … ex Germanica in linguam Latinam versus*, with Dürer's monogram on the title-page in place of a device, his dedication to Wilibald Pirckheimer on A2^{r}, a quotation from Erasmus's *De recta Latini Graecique sermonis pronunciatione* referring to Dürer on A2^{v} and with Wechel's dedication to Alcmarius Bouchardus on A3^{r-v}. The illustrations are woodcuts, with one extraneous engraving printed on a separate leaf inserted between pp. 12 and 13. The second work in the volume is a copy of Dürer's *De urbibus, arcibus, castellisque condendis, ac muniendis, rationes … nunc recens e lingua Germanica in Latinam traductae*, published by Christian Wechel, Paris, 1535.

(1) Sim D136; H. Bohatta, art. cit. (no. 8 above, p. 169), p. 441, no. 10 (reissue of Bohatta no. 9, dated 1605 on the title-page, 1606 in the colophon).
(2) *Short-title catalogue of books printed in France and of French books printed in other countries from 1470 to 1600 now in the British Museum* (London, 1924), p. 143; Bohatta, art. cit. (no. 8 above, p. 169), p. 442, no. 16a. The lower case signatures suggest that the sheets bearing this edition were intended as a supplement, and if so, probably to the *Institutiones geometricae*, which explains its presence after the 1606 reprint.

11. 1606: PLUTARCH, [*De educatione puerorum. Greek and Latin*] *Πλουταρχου περι παιδαγωγης. Plutarchi De liberis educandis commentarius ... nunc secunda cura Marci Beumleri ita expolitus vt analysis plané nova, & innumeris mendis purgata proderit.* 8°; pp. 135; few ms. notes. BL: 1030.c.1(2).

A straightforward accurate reprint of the edition 'Spirae, Typis Bernardi Albini' of 1593, but more compressed in its typography.

Sim P151.

12. 1609: GABRIEL HERMANN, *Waerachtighe beschrijvinge: Des gherichtlicken Proces gehouden tot Sursee teghen Martijn van Voysin, Borger ende Passementwercker tot Basel, om de belijdenisse des Evanghelij ... Met noch een Christelick Sermoon vande eere Marie ende voornemelick Jesu Christi onses Heylants. Gedaen tot Basel den neghenden Octobris 1608, door Johannem Jacobum Grynaeum ... Wt de Hoochduytsche sprake in onse Nederlantsche tale getrouwelick overgesedt Door Johannem Coitsium, Dienaer des Godtlicken woorts tot Niemegen.* 4°; A-B[4]
BL: T.2417(16); T.2420(28).

Another highly international booklet. Martin du Voisin or Voysin was of French origin but had settled in Switzerland. He seems to have been an Anabaptist whose anti-Catholic utterances, true or misconstrued, earned him a summary trial followed by immediate execution by first the sword, then fire, at Sursee in the Canton of Lucerne on 3 October 1608. Gabriel Hermann, a school teacher from Berne, and two friends, Hans Jacob Weber and Leonhard Gebhard, happened to be there and witnessed the procedure, to their great indignation. Hermann wrote the story which all three signed as being true. It was printed the following year by Johann Schönfeld at Amberg as *Memoria Martyris Christi. Eine Christliche Predigt, Vber der Gedächtnuss Martins du Voisin ... Gehalten zu Basel im Münster, den 9. Octobris, des gemeldten Jahrs: Durch ... Johannem Jacobum Grynaeum ... Sampt beygefügter vmbständlicher erzehlung, wie es mit solchem erbärmlichen vnnd blutgierigen Prozess zugangen.* Obviously this German edition begins with the text, or rather a summary, of the sermon preached by Grynaeus at Basle: there is in fact very little about the man and his fate to be found in the sermon, beyond a reference near the beginning (p. 4): 'dieweil ... vns seine Witwe vnnd sieben Kinder hertzlich erbarmen', the rest being mainly exegetic on how to honour both the Virgin Mary and Jesus. The real 'Memoria' follows (pp. 17-24): 'Warhafftige History, Von dem Gerichtlichen Process ... dess zu Sursee vnschuldig hingerichten Meister Martin du Voisin, Passamentwebers vnd gewesenen Bürgers zu Basel: auff Montag den 3. Octobris, im Jahr 1608', signed by the three witnesses. But this is not all. In an 'Ode Jambica de Martino Du Voisin ... et Annâ Hoviâ ... Annis 1597, & 1608. Brugis & Surseji, affectorum', signed: C.J.A.P.R.G., with a short Latin prose narrative at the end, a comparison is made between the execution for his faith of our Martin and that of Anneke Wtenhove, eleven years before. The poor woman, a steadfast Anabaptist maid to two ladies who recanted, was buried alive at Brussels and became a potent symbol of Spanish injustice and oppression (cf. A. E. C. Simoni, '1598: an exchange of Dutch pamphlets and their repercussions in England', in: T. Hermans and R. Salverda (eds), *From Revolt to Riches. Culture and history of the Low Countries 1500-1700. International and interdisciplinary perspectives* (London, 1993) [Crossways, 2], pp. 129-62). However, as 'Bruxellis' would not scan, the poet, whoever he was, transferred the event to 'Brugis'. The prose annotation to Anneke's story has a reference to Van Meteren, bk. 18, and Martin is tentatively assigned to Anneke's sect: 'uti accipimus'. Whether it was the Latin text as a whole, too learned for the public to whom the translation was to be presented, or the false statement about the place of Anneke's execution, better known to a Dutch than to a German public, the Ode was omitted from the Arnhem edition. Apart from this and the omission of Gebhard's name from the witnesses' signatures the translation is indeed very accurate. The reference to the widow and orphans is, if anything, heightened: 'Nadermael ... wy hertelijck metlijden hebben met syn Huysvrouwe ende syne Kinderen, die seven int getal syn' ('since we have heartfelt sympathy with his wife and children, of whom there are seven in number'), and there is also an added conclusion after the sermon which here has second place. In it J. Coitsius (cf. *Nieuw Nederlandsch biographisch woordenboek*, 1 (Leiden, 1911), col. 6245; J. P. de Bie and J. Loosjes, *Biographisch woordenboek van protestantsche godgeleerden in Nederland*, 2 (The Hague, n.d.), pp. 164-5), the translator, who does not sign it, but is the only possible writer, piously prays that 'Godt behoet ons voor alle quaet ende voor sulcke bloet dorstighe Surseesche Menschen' ('God preserve us from all evil and from such bloodthirsty Surseeans'). An official Lucerne document, *Warhaffter vnd grundlicher Bericht, Vss was Vrsachen Martinus du Voysin ... in der Statt Surseew, Im Argöw, inn der Catholischen Eydgenossischen Statt Lucern, hohen Oberkeit vnnd Gepiet gelegen, den 13. Tag Octobris dess 1608. Jars, erstlich enthauptet, vnd volgends verbrennt worden. In Namen vnnd Befelch eines Ehrsamen Wolwysen Rhats, derselbigen Statt Lucern, zu Erhaltung der Warheit, wider die Hierumb vnwarhaffte vssgespreittete Bezyhungen vssgangen* (Ingolstatt, 1609), refutes various 'durch Schrifften, Predige*n*, vnnd in offnen Truck vssgespreitete vnwarhaffte bezigk, iniurien, vn*d* schmähungen' (a2^{v}) and ends with 'Beschluss dieses Wercklins, begryffende die Grynaeische Predig' (pp. 10-12). In Holland Du Voysin was later remembered by Willem Baudaert in his *Memoryen ofte cort verhael der gedenckweerdigste ... gheschiedenissen ... van 1603 tot ... 1624*, 1 (Arnhem and Zutphen, 1624), fols 132^{v}-133^{r}.

Sim H88; W. P. C. Knuttel, *Catalogus der pamfletten-verzameling berustende in de Koninklijke Bibliotheek te 's-Gravenhage*, 1/1 (The Hague, 1889, repr. 1978), no. 1509. Strangely, the sermon of 9 Oct. 1608 does not figure in the long list of works by J. J. Grynaeus in Zedler's *Grosses Universal-Lexicon*, vol. 11 (Halle and Leipzig, 1735), cols. 1156-7.

13. 1610: [ZACHARIAS HEYNS], *Jeucht Spieghel door Z.G.H.P.H.S A° 1610. Allerhand Kurtzweilige Stücklein Studenten furnemblich zu lieb das aus Ihren eigenen Stammbuchern* [sic] *zusamen gelesen vnd in diese form gebracht.* obl. 4°; A-D⁴; illus. BL: 555.a.32.

The title-page engraving shows a weeping girl on the left, a young man on horseback, obviously leaving her, on the right, a scene whose relevance to the subject matter of the book is not at all apparent. Indeed, it has been suggested, not unreasonably, that it was taken over from some other book and only had the words replaced. All the plates seem equally to have been either brought together from an earlier publication or to have been carefully copied, but so far any sources remain unknown. The compiler's initials have been explained as 'ZaGarias Pieter Heyns Sone' and the Dutch text is most certainly by Heyns. All the engravings bear Latin or German legends and engraved Latin and German verses, these lower lines at times in a macaroni of both. The versos bear Dutch verses relating to the engraving they face. The scenes and the verses are amusing images of very moral sentiments. For example, on C4^r the scene is of three young men playing skittles in the shape of ladies, one saying 'mich ehrlich halt', the second 'böss woll gestalt', the third 'Reych vnd altt'. One of the young men exclaims: 'Bist eben recht, mich trifft das gluck, ich hab erdapt das rechte stuck' (he has gained the honest girl); one laments: 'O gluck mich von der alten loss' (he has got her!), and the third complains: 'Pfuy Teuffel, mir blibt die böse'. The verses are: 'Qui casu gaudent, casus quo*que* lance reguntur, Cordatis prostant seria nulla loco. – Wie man kuglet so trifft man auch: die framen [*sic* for 'Frommen'] haltu [*sic* for 'halten'] ein andern brauch'. Are these errors, as well as the missing rhyme in the third man's legend which could have been achieved with 'boss' there, or by making the second man say 'löse' rather than 'loss', an indication of copying by an engraver not so sure of his German? D1^r shows a scene of failure; in Dutch 'to fall through the basket' means to come a cropper and once had a German equivalent (cf. J. and W. Grimm, *Deutsches Wörterbuch*, 5 (Leipzig, 1873), cols. 1801-3, on 'Korb' as token of rejection in love also quotes the Dutch idiom 'door de mand vallen', with some applications by German writers not later than the eighteenth century and its modern survival in 'durchfallen' in the sense of failing an examination). Its Latin (!) verses run: 'Armer Mannus ego per Corbem fallere cogor, Cor mócht in tausent springere frusta meum', true schoolboy manufacture. Heyns's Dutch verses are much better, but less fun. My attribution to Jan Jansz as the producer is based on no more than my personal conviction that he was the most, perhaps the only, suitable publisher: he had connections in Germany as well as in the Dutch Republic where the book could well have been sold to what has been termed 'la jeunesse dorée', the children of well-to-do families who relished these pretty oblong books of engravings and poems. I do not know when he and Heyns first met, but in 1615 Jansz published this poet's versions of the Latin verses on Rollenhagen's emblems (cf. no. 16), so why not already in 1610? Confirmation or refutation will be equally welcome. In this copy the engraving on C3^r is the same as that on D1^{r} where it is correctly placed. Was this a mistake, or was it done in some copies to avoid the embarrassingly indecent verses on the correct C3^{r} plate? The text of this, in German only, was most kindly sent me by Mrs E. Cockx-Indestege, copied from the engraving on C3^{r} in the copy now, but not in Van der Haeghen's time, at the Royal Library Albert I, Brussels.

Bru 9; Sim H108; *Bibliotheca Belgica. Bibliographie générale des Pays-Bas. Fondée par Ferdinand van der Haeghen. Réédité sous la direction de Marie-Thérèse Lenger*, 3 (Brussels, 1964), pp. 459-61, H241 (which does not describe the engravings, but is very good on the Dutch texts); C. P. Burger who completed E. W. Moes, *De Amsterdamsche boekdrukkers en uitgevers in de zestiende eeuw*, 4 (Amsterdam, 1915), p. 236, enumerating the works by Heyns after his move to Zwolle where he no longer had a press of his own and where there was no printer who could have done this, referring to the *Jeucht Spieghel* as a forerunner of his emblem books, but without suggesting another printer or publisher.

14. 1610: CAIUS PLINIUS SECUNDUS, *Caii Plinii Secundi. Des wijtberoemden, Hoochgeleerden ouden Philosophi ende Natuyrcondigers, Boecken ende Schriften, in drie deelen onderscheyden, ... Allen Apteeckers, Huysvaderen ende Huysmoederen, oock alle Liefhebbers der Consten, seer dienstelick, profytelick ende vermakelick. Nu nieuwelijck uyt den Hoochduytsche in onse Nederlantsche sprake overgeset,* ende *met schoone Figuren geciert.* 4°; A-4H^{4}, pp. 612; illus. BL: 975.c.13.

The original, a selection from Pliny and other authors, published by Sigmund Feyerabend and Simon Hüter in 1565, by Sigmund and Hieronymus Feyerabend in 1571, Sigmund and Johann Feyerabend in 1584, and Elias Willer, but printed by Sigmund Feyerabend in 1600, all in Frankfurt, was a translation from the Latin by Johann Heyden von Dhaun, with illustrations by Jost Amman. The edition used by Jansz cannot be one earlier than that of 1584 because only then do some of the illustrations appear which were the models for the illustrator of the Dutch edition, e.g. the woodcuts showing single and twin babies in the womb. Though only three parts are named in the title, actually four parts occur as they do in the German original, with the difference that parts 3 and 4 have been transposed. The woodcut illustrations are copies, and not always very skilful ones. Neither translator nor illustrator is named.

Sim P149; A. Geerebaert, *Lijst van Nederlandsche vertalingen der oude Grieksche en Latijnsche schrijvers* (Ghent, 1924), p. 156, no. CXXVII; I. P. de Rynck and A. Welkenhuysen, *De oudheid in het Nederlands. Repertorium en bibliografische gids voor vertalingen van Griekse en Latijnse auteurs en geschriften* (Baarn, 1992), p. 304, note to the entry for the 1617 edition; *VD 16*, P3553-6.

15. 1610? GABRIEL ROLLENHAGEN, *Nucleus emblematum selectissimorum, quae Itali vvlgo impresas vocant priuata industria studio singulari, undique conquisitus non paucis venustis inuentionibus auctus, additis carminibus illustratus* ... E Musaeo coelatorio Crispiani Passaei. Prostant Apud Ioa*nn*e*m* Iansoniu*m* Bibliopola*m* Arnhemie*n*se*m*. 4°; A^{4}; pl. 100; port. BL: 636.a.29.

Following the engraved title-page, on which only the Arnhem details are printed in letterpress, the preliminaries contain, on A2^{r}, the engraved portrait of the author with 4 lines of engraved verse and 4 in letterpress, signed: Valens Cremcovius; on A2^{v}, a longer Latin poem by the same, addressed to Rollenhagen; and on A3^{r}-4^{v} the address to the reader. No place is given for Crispijn van de Passe the Elder's studio on the title-page, but he lived in Cologne until *ca.* 1612 (cf. no. 7 above, pp. 166-9): he must have printed the plates there. The preliminary text was no doubt also printed in Cologne as there is typographical evidence linking it with the 1611 edition described below (no. 16) in which a letterpress title-page bears the imprint of Servatius Erffens in that city. Jan Jansz, named as bookseller, may have financed the whole enterprise or at least assisted Van de Passe. The plates, based on various earlier emblem books, bear mottoes and engraved verses mainly in Latin, but also in Greek, Italian or French. The date of this edition can be inferred from the author's age given on the portrait as twenty-seven years: he was born on 22 March 1583, which dates the portrait in 1610 or very early 1611. The possibility of it being a reissue of a later date is unlikely as there is no sign of the word 'Coloniae', added in 1611 to the engraved title-page (cf. no. 16), having been erased. It seems to be a very rare edition or issue of the book as it is not mentioned in K. Th. Gaedertz, *Gabriel Rollenhagen, sein Leben und seine Werke ... Nebst bibliographischem Anhang* (Leipzig, 1881) nor unequivocally so in any reference book I have seen (but see no. 16). The catalogue of the Bibliothèque Nationale, Paris, lists a copy with only Jansz's name, not the artist's, given for the imprint, but then, all the Rollenhagen entries there are so confused that they are in charity best forgotten. The British Library copy is imperfect, wanting pl. 25-8, 33-6.

Sim R.97.

16. 1611: Gabriel Rollenhagen, *Nucleus emblematum selectissimorum ...* Coloniae e Musaeo coelatorio Crispiani Passaei. Prostant Apud Ioa*nne*m Iansoniu*m* Bibliopola*m* Arnhemie*n*se*m*. 4°; A-B, *A-D*^{4}; pl. 100; port.

BL: C.57.b.24(1).

A new edition of the work described as no. 15 above. Not only has 'Coloniae' been added to the engraved imprint, but the preface has been reset, with differences in spelling, e.g. 'benevole' for 'beneuole', punctuation and typography, e.g. the name 'D. Gabrieli Rollenhagio' is printed in italics where in the earlier edition it was printed in roman. The added gathering B begins with a dedication to Christian William, Margrave of Brandenburg, here addressed as Archbishop of Magdeburg, who had been elected 'Administrator' of the vacant see at the precocious age of ten in 1598 (cf. F. W. Hoffman, *Geschichte der Stadt Magdeburg, nach den Quellen bearbeitet*, III (Magdeburg, 1850), pp. 3-181), which fills B1^{r}-2^{v}. B3^{r-v} repeat this dedication in verse, followed on B4^{r} by a poem addressed to Rollenhagen by the great scholar Janus Gruterus and on B4^{v} an anonymous poem in the engraver's honour. There then follow the two gatherings given signatures in italics, also mainly printed in this face. *A1*^{r} bears a letterpress title-page reading '*Les emblemes de Maistre Gabriel Rollenhague, mis en vers francois par vn professeur de la langue françoise a Colongne*. Coloniae Excudebat Seruatius Erffens: Prostant Apud Ioannem Iansonium bibliopolam Arnheimensem Anno MDCXI.' Its verso is blank. *A2*^{r} has verses entitled 'L'Autheur a ses vers' and *A2*^{v}-*D4*^{r} present the French versions of Rollenhagen's verses to the emblems. These remain unchanged from the preceding (no. 15). The British Library's copy has the bookplate of Syston Park. A second volume, *Gabrielis Rollenhagen selectorum Emblematum Centuria secunda*, dated 1613, bears Van de Passe's Utrecht imprint, together with that of Jansz at Arnhem. Both emblem collections were then reissued at Utrecht and Arnhem in 1615-17, now with Dutch translations of Rollenhagen's verses by Zacharias Heyns in the letterpress preliminaries.

Sim R98; K. Th. Gaedertz, *Gabriel Rollenhagen*, pp. 12-14, 111-2, no. 12; D. Franken, *L'oeuvre gravée des Van de Passe* (no. 7 above, p. 168), pp. 263-4, no. 1334, for the 1613 volume, beginning with a description as if published at the same time of a copy of vol. 1, without a date or any reference to Jansz, though having 'E Musaeo Caelatorio Crispiani Passaei Zeelando Excussori [*sic*]' as imprint of 'Part 1' and containing the plates only, without preliminaries or any letterpress text. This looks very much like an Utrecht reissue of the 1610(?) collection. There is in fact a copy in the British Library (Sim R99) where the deletion of 'Coloniae' and the substitution of Van de Passe's epithet for Jansz's imprint are clearly visible, an issue therefore tentatively dated 1615; M. Praz, *Studies in seventeenth-century imagery* (Rome, 1964), pp. 476-7; J. Landwehr, *Emblem books in the Low Countries 1554-1949. A bibliography* (Utrecht, 1970), no. 573; A. Henke and A. Schöne, *Emblemata. Handbuch zur Sinnbildkunst des XVI. und XVII. Jahrhunderts* (Stuttgart, 1967), pp. LXII-III, describing the copy in the Herzog August Bibliothek, Wolfenbüttel (21.2 Ethica), which seems to be a made-up copy as apparently it lacks the imprint 'Coloniae' on the engraved title-page and has been given that of '[Arnheim 1611]', but not mentioning the French title-page or text, with vol. 2 dated 1613 without the imprint 'Ultraiecti', but said to have the Dutch text by Heyns, which would make it 1617 (nevertheless described as 'Beide Teile Erstausgaben'). In the *Supplement* (Stuttgart, 1976), p. CXCV, the authors describe a copy of vol. 1 found in the Staatsbibliothek Bamberg which might conceivably match the copy described in no. 15 above. A copy in the British Library (Sim R101) consists of a selection of plates from both volumes with neither title-page nor preliminaries. It is impossible to tell whether any or all the plates originally belonging to vol. 1 were printed at Cologne or were reprinted at Utrecht as impressions from suites of engravings could be combined as available for willing buyers.

17. 1613: ALBRECHT DÜRER, *Les quatre livres d'Albert Dvrer, Peinctre & Geometrien tres excellent De la proportion des parties & pourtraicts des corps humains. Tradvicts par Loys Meigret Lionnais, de la langue Latine en Françoise.* fol.; ff. 124; illus. BL: 786.1.44.

If the language of the title seems antiquated for the early seventeenth century, it is in the nature of this edition which is a page-for-page reprint of that of

Charles Perier, Paris 1557. In place of the latter's device of Bellerophon, Jansz's title-page has his own device inscribed 'Constantiam mihi Deus rebus malis des et bonis' around the image of the usual column between scenes of sunshine over inhabited land and a ship tossed by storms on a violent sea, topped by a heart placed there by God's hand (cf. *Bibliotheca Belgica*, IV (Bruxelles, 1964), p. 146, no. 1). Another difference between the original and the reprint is that all the errata which Perier had added to the last page under the title 'Correction des fautes' have here been corrected and this paragraph has of course been omitted, to the great benefit of the appearance of this final page. The German title of the work when first printed in Nuremberg in 1528 had been *Hierin sind begriffen vier bücher von menschlicher Proportion* (see also no. 8 above, p. 169).

Sim D136; H. Bohatta, art. cit. (no. 8 above, p. 169), p. 528, no. 26, followed by a reissue, no. 27, dated 1614.

18. 1616: JOANNES ISAACUS, called HOLLANDUS, *Opera mineralia, et vegetabilia, sive de lapide Philosophico, quae reperire potuimus, omnia. Numquam antehac edita, ac nunc primum ex optimis manuscriptis Teutonicis exemplaribus fidelissime in Latinum sermonem conuersa.* 8°; A-2E[8]; pp. 431; illus. BL: 1033.d.6.

The book contains one anonymous laudatory poem and another one signed: Enoch Sterthemius, who is unknown to the common reference books, but nowhere does it have any indication of the translator or editor or a description of these German manuscripts or their whereabouts. The illustrations are small woodcuts, no doubt also ultimately derived from the manuscripts. The word 'primum' in the title is ambiguous: it may apply to the translation, it certainly does not to the edition, since D. I. Duveen, *Bibliotheca alchemica et chemica* (London, 1949), p. 300, lists one published by Richard Schilders at Middelburg in 1600, with exactly the same title as far as 'translata', but then with the addition of 'a P.M.G.', i.e. the translator's initials, which as yet remain unresolved. Duveen then describes the Middelburg edition as having 431 pages, the same number as Jansz's edition, and containing 'small and curious woodcuts'. Of the Arnhem edition Duveen says that it is largely a reprint of the first. J. Ferguson, *Bibliotheca chemica*, I (Glasgow, 1906), pp. 412-13, describes the Arnhem edition as the earliest. Later editions were all in German. The description in J. H. Zedler, *Grosses und vollständiges Universal Lexicon aller Wissenschaften und Künste*, XIII (Leipzig and Halle, 1735), col. 636, of the only work by him quoted is based on a private library catalogue ('Barberini Bibl.', i.e. the *Index bibliothecae, qua Franciscus Barberinus S. R. E. Cardinalis ... magnificentissimas familiae ad Quirinalem sedes magnificentiores reddidit* (Rome, 1681), in which 'Io. Isaac Hollandus, Theorica Lapidis Philosophici. Bern. 1608' is entered on p. 544 of vol. 1). This text must be identical with *De triplici ordine elixiris et lapidis theoria. Von den drei Ordnungen des Elixirs und Erklärung des Steins* (Berne, 1608), by Isaak Hollandus and (Bernhard) Penot, listed in K. C. Schmieder, *Geschichte der Alchemie* (Halle, 1832), p. 214, no. 3, as having been previously published in Latin together with the *Opera mineralia* in 1600.

The 1608 edition is also listed in F. Ferchl-Mittenwald, *Chemisch-pharmazeutisches Bio- und Bibliographikon* (Mittenwald, 1937), p. 247, *s.v.* Hollandus, Isaac. Both Ferchl and Schmieder, pp. 210-15, *s.vv.* Isaak and Johann Isaak, distinguish father Isaak from son Johann Isaak, who collaborated with each other and are therefore often confused. Their precise dates are unknown, but although C. G. Jöcher, *Allgemeines Gelehrten-Lexicon*, 2 (Leipzig, 1750), col. 1992, says of Joannes that he was a Dutchman living in Amsterdam in the early seventeenth century, a respected physician and physicist, more recent writers like the above place both father and son in the first half of the fifteenth century. There is no mention anywhere of any manuscripts in languages other than Latin or Dutch. The *National Union Catalog Pre-1956 Imprints*, 281 (London and Chicago, 1973), pp. 337-8, *s.v.* Joannes Isaaci, Hollandus, fifteenth century (for both of them), contains a much larger number of editions, some independent, others as parts of Lazarus Zetzner's *Theatrum chemicum* (Argentorati, 1659-61) or of *Alchymia vera* by one I.P.S.M.S. (*s.l.* 1604; 1610?), several of which describe themselves as translated out of Dutch into German and the most recent edition of any works by him listed there is one published in Vienna in 1773. The Bibliotheca Philosophica Hermetica, Amsterdam, to whose assistant librarian Dr C. van Heertum I am greatly indebted for much of the above information, holds a remarkable collection of works by both father and son.

Sim J64.

19. 1617: CAIUS PLINIUS SECUNDUS, *Caii Plinii Secundi. Des Hoochgheleerden ... Natuer-kondighers, Boecken ende Schriften, in vier deelen onderscheyden: ... Allen Apotekers ... liefhebbers der konsten, seer dienstelijck, profytelijck ende vermakelijck. Nu nieuwelijck uyt den Hoochduytsche in onse Nederlantsche sprake overgheset, ende met schoone Figuren verciert.* 4°; A-D⁴, pp. 612; illus.

BL: 461.a.7.

Not a reissue of no. 14 above, which however see for the German edition from which it was translated, except for the fourth part, beginning on p. 515 and the index, now no longer accurate for parts 2 and 3. Not only on the title-page but throughout, spelling and punctuation have been changed and so also have some of the illustrations and their distribution. A shift in pagination became inevitable, starting with bk. 2, and to retrieve pagination for bk. 4 there are no pp. 513-514. This copy came to the British Museum from the library of Sir Joseph Banks.

Sim P150; Geerebaert, *Lijst van Nederlandsche vertalingen* (see no. 14 above), p. 156, no. CXXVII. IIa; De Rynck and Welkenhuysen, *De oudheid in het Nederlands* (see no. 14 above), p. 304.

20. 1618: *Voltolynsche Tyrannye, Dat is: Volcomen ende waerachtige Beschrijvinghe vanden schrickelijcken ende Onmenschelicken Moort inden Lande van*

Voltolijn, den Samptlijcken dry Punten toebehoorende, aende Evangelische Inghesetenen van dien ghedaen door de Barbarische Spaensche macht, de Rebellen ende Banditen, den 9. ende 10. Iul. Anno 1620, Stil. veter. ... Eerstelijck beschreven int Hooch-duytsch, ende tot Zurich ghedruckt. Ende nu tot een Christelijcke Waerschouwinge vertaelt. 4°; A-C⁴ BL: T.2424(7);(25).

Translated from *Veltlinische Tyranney, Das ist: Aussführliche Umbstendliche vnnd Wahrhaffte Beschreibung Dess Grausamen ... Mordts so in dem Landt Veltlin gemeinen dreyen Pündten gehörig ... den 9. Julij ... an den Evangelischen einwohnern daselbsten, dvrch die ... Spanische Macht ... ist gevbet worden* (Zürch, Bey Johann Rudolff Wolffen, 1621), which was one of at least two such reports in German that year (see Knuttel, no. 3131a,b). The Dutch edition, apart from being news in its own right, also served, as the title itself explains, as a warning against the Spaniards and therefore comes within the large number of Dutch pamphlets produced near the end of the Twelve Years' Truce (1609-21) in support of the war party. The Swiss Confederation is often seen in Dutch political literature as a sister republic and the fate of the Valtelline Protestants was bound to move the Dutch public greatly. For the Spaniards the area was a recruiting ground and they wanted it firmly under Catholic control. Of course both parties were equally cruel if given a chance (see H. F. Brown, 'The Valtelline 1603-39', in *Cambridge Modern History*, 4 (Cambridge, 1906), pp. 35-63, esp. pp. 38-9). While more potential soldiers for the war in Flanders boded ill for the Dutch should the war be resumed, yet, considering the alternative as shown here, fighting would be preferable to submission.

Sim V46; Knuttel, *Catalogus der pamfletten-verzameling* (see no. 12 above), no. 3131.

21. 1619: FRANZ KESSLER, *Const-boecxken. Daer in ghevonden worden, Vier onderscheydelijcke secreten oft Konst-stucken, die tot noch toe verborghen ende onbekent zijn gheweest. 1. Om een instrument te maken, daer door men elckanderen zijn meeninghe oft secreten kan doen verstaen, over 't Water oft Landt ende zoo wijt als men malkanderen kan zien. 2. Oock om te maken een Water-Harnas, daer mede men onbeschadicht sommige uren onder 't Water kan zijn ... 3. Noch om een Locht-broeck te maken, met dewelcke men wonderlyck door het Water kan gaen met zijn Gheweyr ende boven-kleederen sonder nat te worden. 4. Met noch eenen Swemriem te maken, dewelcke men kan gebruycken by de voorgaende, ende seer nuttelijck voor Personnen die veel ter Zee oft over andere Wateren reysen ... Beschreven ende in de Hoochduytsche sprake aen den dach ghegeven door Frans Kesseler Conterfeyter van Wetzler. Ende nu uyt den Hoochduytsche overgheset, in onse Nederlantsche sprake, door M.C.H.* 4°; []², A-C⁴ D²; pp. 28; without the engravings mentioned in the preface. BL: 1481.b.27.

Translated from *Unterschiedliche ... Secreta oder Verborgene geheime Künste*, printed by H. Galler and published by J. Th. de Bry at Oppenheim, 1615. For Kessler's work as scientist-inventor see J. C. Adelung, *Fortsetzung und Ergänzung des Gelehrtenlexicons von G. Jöcher*, 3 (Delmenhorst, 1810), cols.

268-9, with a list of his works among which the *Unterschiedliche ... Secreta* is said to have seven plates, whereas J. Benzing, 'Johann Theodor de Bry, Levinus Hulsius und Hieronymus Galler als Verleger und Drucker zu Oppenheim (1610-1620)', *AGB*, 9 (1969), cols. 589-642, lists the same book (col. 612, no. 67) as with three plates in 1615, the same in the reissue of 1616 (col. 614, no. 74), but only one in the new edition of the same year (no. 75). His description as 'Conterfeyter' has earned him a mention in U. Thieme and J. Becker, *Allgemeines Künstlerlexikon*, 20 (Leipzig, n.d.), pp. 211-12.

Sim K8.

22. *Copia Vande Keyserlijcke Achtsverclaringe, tegen pals-Graef Frederick. Ceur-Vorst. Ende te ghelijck, de Copia, Vande Keyserlijcke Achts-verklaringhe, tegen Hans Iorriaen, den Ouden Marck-Grave, van Brandenburgh. Christiaen. Vorste van Anholdt. Ende Iorriaen Frederick, Grave tot Hohenlo.* Na de Copie, Ghedruckt int Iaer... 1621. 4°; AB^4C^2 BL: T.2424(8).

The expression 'Na de Copie' can mean either that this edition is a reprint of one already produced in Dutch, or a direct translation from the German of which the British Library has suitable copies entitled *Copia, Kayserl: Aachts Erklerung, wider Pfaltzgraff Friderich Churfürst* (1621), responsible for the Dutch edition's $A2^r$-$B3^v$, and *Copia, Kayserl: Aachts Erklerung, wider Hanss Georgen den Eltern, Marggraven zu Brandenburg, Christian Fürsten von Anhalt vnd Georg Friderichen Grafen zu Hohenlo*, responsible for $B4^r$-$C2^v$ of the Dutch text. Of course there were many editions of the German documents and as the two described here are without imprint they are certainly not the original official publications, both issued in Vienna on 29 January 1621. The Dutch edition is also without imprint and attributed by me to Jan Jansz on typographical grounds. Frederick's supporters affected by the second document are better known as John George, Margrave of Brandenburg and Jägerndorf, called the Elder to distinguish him from his eleven years younger uncle of the same name – and brother of the Christian William, Administrator-Archbishop of Magdeburg met with in no. 16 above; Prince Christian I of Anhalt; and Count George Frederick of Hohenlohe.

Sim G57; Knuttel, *Catalogus der pamfletten-verzameling* (see no. 12 above), no. 3135; P. A. Tiele, *Bibliotheek van Nederlandsche pamfletten. Verzameling van Frederik Muller te Amsterdam. Naar tijdsorde gerangschikt en beschreven*, 1 (Amsterdam, 1858), no. 1802.

23. 1621: *Dedvctie ofte beleydt, Daer inde* [sic] *Nulliteiten, van de Acht teghen den Ceur Forst Pals-Graven in het Keyserlicke Hof besloten, ende int Rijcke ghepubliceert, nul ende over sulcx crachteloos van onwerden, sonder effect ende nae bedencken te zijn, werden aengewesen. Vertaelt uyt het Latijnsche exemplaer, in s'Graven Hage, by Hillebrant Iocobsz* [sic] ... *gedruckt. Hy is te achten geluck salich ende vroet | Die hem aen een vreemt perickel spiegelen doet.* 4°; pp. 28 BL: T.2424(9).

Although this Dutch translation is only indirectly connected with the German-printed original, entitled *Deductio Nullitatum: quibus proscriptionem in Aulâ Imperatoris contra Electorem Palatinum decretam, et in Imperio evulgatam, scatere; et proinde nullius roboris, valoris, effectûs aut considerationis esse; breviter probatur. Felix quem faciunt aliena pericula cautum* (Haghae Comitis, Ex Officina Hillebrandi Iacobi, 1621), this was itself carefully copied from one of the three editions listed by J. Gebauer, *Die Publicistik über den böhmischen Aufstand von 1618* (Halle, 1892) [Hallesche Abhandlungen zur neueren Geschichte, 29], pp. 67, 114 – and there may have been more (one in the British Library). The parallel German text, *Kurtze Darthuung vnd Bericht: Dass die unlangsten am Kayserl. Hoff erkandte, vnd hernach im Heil. Reich wider die Churfürstl. Pfaltz publicirte Achts-Erklärung, vielen Vnheilbaren Nulliteten vnderworffen, Vnd dahero von keinen Würden oder Kräfften, Weniger bündig vnnd gültig seyn könne, Auch darumb sich niemand dardurch Irr vnd Zweifflich machen lassen soll* (1621), is described by Gebauer (pp. 68, 118) as translated from the Latin (but could it not have been the other way round?), and it too appeared, according to Gebauer, in at least four editions (one in the British Library). The Dutch translation follows its Latin model exactly, even to the moral verse on the title-page, which is also its conclusion. The 'Deductio nullitatum' is directed against the ban declared on Frederick V, Elector Palatine and King of Bohemia, proclaimed, as well as the ban on the German princes who supported him, by the acts of which the translation is given above (no. 22). Gebauer (pp. 68-70) provides a detailed analysis of the text.

Sim D37; Tiele, *Bibliotheek van Nederlandsche pamfletten* (see no. 22 above), no. 1803; J. K. van der Wulp, *Catalogus van de pamfletten, enz. over de geschiedenis van Nederland, aanwezig in de bibliotheek van Isaac Meulman*, 1 (Amsterdam, 1866), p. 258, no. 1758.

24. 1621: Gabriel Bethlen, Prince of Transylvania, *Copia Van een zekere Missive, die Gabriel Koninck van Hungarien, aen den Marck-Grave van Jagerensdorp, nu Koninckliјcke Majesteyts van Bohemen Velt-Overste, geschreven. Waer in hy kortelijck verhaelt, syne wonderbaerlijcke victorie ende ontzettinghe van Nieuheusel die hem Godt teghen syne vyanden verleendt hadde. Wt het Latijn in onse Nederduytsche sprake overgheset.* 4°; A[4] BL: T.2424(22).

Translated from the Latin which the author is said to have spoken fluently. Both writer and recipient were in the most eastern parts of the Empire and it is highly probable that the letter was first printed in that language in Germany. The Dutch translation is without imprint, but attributed by me to Jan Jansz on typographical grounds. C. V. Wedgwood, *The Thirty Years War* (Harmondsworth, 1957), p. 88, describes the writer of this letter as 'a brilliant soldier and a wily diplomat': he certainly proved a slippery ally to the Winter King. The events concerning Neuhäusel are now thought of as so unimportant that even *Der Grosse Brockhaus* does not mention them in its entry for this little town in the Moravian-Hungarian border region. The seven weeks' siege, during which the Duke of Bucquoy met his death, and the surprise of its surrender to Bethlen Gabor are evaluated by A. Gindely, *History of the Thirty Years' War*, 1 (London, 1885), pp. 324-6. The letter, dated 21 July 1621, is addressed to John George, Margrave of Brandenburg and Jägerndorf who, after the ban was declared on him (see no. 22 above) and his appeal for pardon rejected, openly took the side of Frederick and re-engaged the army he had been forced to disband. Bethlen Gabor subsidized him, but also expected him to cooperate, sending him several letters to this effect (cf. Hans Schulz, *Markgraf Johann Georg von Brandenburg-Jägerndorf Generalfeldoberst* (Halle, 1899) [Hallesche Abhandlungen zur neueren Geschichte, 37], p. 114 and passim).

Sim G5; Tiele, *Bibliotheek van Nederlandsche pamfletten* (see no. 22 above), no. 1807.

*

CONCLUSION

This small sample of books produced by just two Dutch booksellers in the course of only seventeen years should be seen in the light of what is generally known of seventeenth-century Dutch booktrade practice. Dutch presses turned out original and reprinted works for export all over Europe, most of them in Latin, but many also in a variety of modern languages. The importation of books into the Netherlands is attested in Frankfurt and Leipzig fair catalogues which Dutch booksellers attended and then referred to in their stock lists. They had an eager reading public at home, supplied again by the local presses as well as by these imports. The twenty-four books described above, a tiny fraction of the whole book production of those years, range over wide fields of interest, from art theory to zoology, from classical antiquity to the hottest of hot news, for the studious and the curious at home and abroad and, preferably, both. Readers of many kinds and in many places would have been thrilled with their purchase, they would have found knowledge and/or pleasure and closed their books, their minds enriched then as ours are still enriched today on being privileged to see them.

LIST OF NAMES AND ANONYMOUS TITLES

(taken from the 24 books only, not their models or the commentaries on them)

WHO PRINTED THE TEXT OF THE *HORTUS EYSTETTENSIS*?

NICOLAS BARKER

IT WAS, I think, in the spring of 1988 that, having become interested in the *Hortus Eystettensis* for other reasons, I began to wonder who had printed the text. The huge copperplates of every tree and plant that grew in and beyond the wonderful garden created by Johann Conrad von Gemmingen (1560/1-1612), Bishop of Eichstätt, have attracted the interest of historians of botany and art, but the printing of the letterpress, some four hundred sheets of royal broadside, was no less substantial a task. The *Hortus Eystettensis* has no imprint, as such, and I had become sceptical, for reasons that will emerge, of the accepted account of the printing of the text. So, like anyone whose path has led to the history of printing in Germany in the seventeenth century, I asked David Paisey how to set about finding out the truth of the matter. It was, he said, difficult: the only real guide was Josef Benzing's *Buchdruckerlexikon des 16. Jahrhunderts (Deutsches Sprachgebiet)*, whose first edition in 1952 had listed not only the names and careers of the printers, but also in summary form such of their works as he had been able to identify; the revised edition, extending to the seventeenth century, did not list works, and it would be a question of following what directions could be found in the work of earlier printers twelve years into *terra incognita* as best one could.[1] His own work was not so advanced that he or it could offer any further help.

The task was too large and too uncertain for me to undertake then, though I was fortunate enough to find another resource, and I was obliged to leave it for the time being, with a footnote recording the views of previous writers.[2] Then I took it up again and had virtually completed the task by 3 October 1994. On that day, however, David Paisey's *magnum opus*, his *Catalogue of Books Printed in the German-Speaking Countries and of German Books Printed in Other Countries from 1601 to 1700 Now in the British Library*, appeared, offering such abundance of

1 The revised edition was published as *Die Buchdrucker des 16. und 17. Jahrhunderts im deutschen Sprachgebiet* (Wiesbaden, 1962; enlarged edition Wiesbaden, 1982).
2 Nicolas Barker, *Hortus Eystettensis: The Bishop's Garden and Besler's Magnificent Book* (London and New York, 1994), p. 16.

new evidence, amply and efficiently indexed, that I have been forced to throw away everything I had written and begin again on 4 October, journeying to Manchester to visit Chetham's Library, the first recorded library in Britain to acquire a copy of the *Hortus Eystettensis*. Many others besides me will experience the same emotions, in which gratitude far exceeds regret, as they too, accepting the wealth that David Paisey has bestowed on them, begin again.

The problem was first essayed by Hans Baier in his pioneering article 'Die Ausgaben des *Hortus Eystettensis*', published in *Aus dem Antiquariat* in 1970.[3] According to him, the letterpress could be attributed to the printer Konrad Bauer or Agricola at Altdorf, now a suburb of Nuremberg, where Basilius Besler (1561-1629), the bishop's confidant and impresario of the whole enterprise, lived. Baier's thesis was based on the similarity of the types found in Bauer's work to those in the *Hortus Eystettensis*, and in particular to the appearance of a large initial C on an arabesque background frequently used in the *Hortus Eystettensis*, which also appeared in Ludwig Jungermann's *Catalogus plantarum, quae circa Altorfium Noricum et vicinis quibusdam locis reperiuntur*, printed by Bauer in 1615.[4] There was more to this argument than mere typographical evidence. Johann Jakob Baier (1677-1735), in his biographical dictionary of his predecessors as professors of medicine at the University of Altdorf, published in 1728, produced contemporary evidence suggesting that Jungermann (1572-1653) had spent months in Besler's house working on the text of the *Hortus Eystettensis*, and might indeed have seen it through the press.[5] What more natural, if so, than that he should take his own little book three years later to the same printer?

Jungermann may well have helped with the text; indeed, Baier quotes a passage to this effect from the manuscript of the introductory commendation provided by the Dean of the Collegium Medicum at Nuremberg for the *Hortus Eystettensis*, which does not appear in print (and may have been suppressed).[6] His own contemporaries detected signs of his hand in it. A letter from Jungermann to Caspar Hofmann, dated 12 December 1614, is contemptuous of Besler: he doubts whether Hofmann will have any better luck in extracting seeds from Besler who refused them to him, thus showing his overweening character; but then he goes on to enquire whether 'opus illud cuius titulo nomen subjectum suum voluit' is yet available for sale.[7] As the *Hortus Eystettensis*, to which Besler had indeed appended his name, clearly as an afterthought (a makeshift perhaps made necessary by the death of Bishop von Gemmingen on

3 Hans Baier, 'Die Ausgaben des *Hortus Eystettensis*, 1613-1750', *Aus dem Antiquariat*, 95 (1970), 273-80.

4 BL pressmarks B.155 (2) and 443.a.34 (1).

5 J. J. Baier, *Biographiae professorum medicinae, qui in Academia Altorfina unquam vixerunt* (1728), pp. 80-92.

6 Baier, p. 82.

7 Hans-Otto Keunecke (ed.), *Hortus Eystettensis: Zur Geschichte eines Gartens und eines Buches* (Munich, 1989), p. 116, note 35.

7 November 1612),[8] had already been available since the autumn of 1613,[9] Jungermann was clearly out of touch with the later stages of its production. It was natural that he should take his own book to a printer at Altdorf, where he was professor; but it does not follow that the *Hortus Eystettensis* had been printed there. If Besler was a long-standing and respected member of the Collegium Medicum of Nuremberg (founded by Joachim Camerarius the Younger in 1592), he had no connection, other than friendship with the members of the university, with Altdorf.

If not Bauer (who cannot be ruled out, as yet, however), what other printers might have undertaken this vast work? A glance at Benzing[10] reveals a number of possible names, with the dates of their activity: Christoph Lochner of Altdorf and Nuremberg (1588-1612) might still have just been able to undertake it, but his son Ludwig (1614-32) is also a possibility; Abraham Wagenmann (1593-1632) was mainly but not exclusively a printer of music books; there is Johann Lantzenberger (1599-1609) whose widow and heirs continued in business until 1617; Johann Lauer (1603-19); Paul Kauffmann (1594-1617), also a music printer, inherited the business of Dietrich Gerlach (1566-75) from his widow Katharina and heirs; Georg Leopold Fuhrmann (1604-16) also inherited the business of his father, the prolific Valentin Fuhrmann (1571-1604), and produced a handsome type-specimen, *Typorum et characterum officinae chalcographiae Georgii Leopoldi Fuhrmanni Descriptio*, in 1616.[11] Other printers seem to be excluded as not practising at or near 1610-13, or as too slight to have undertaken such a work.

What, then, is the typographical material in the *Hortus Eystettensis* on which to base an attribution to one or other of these printers? It consists of four different roman types, a single large italic, and four frakturs. All are easily identifiable by reference to the specimens of sixteenth- and seventeenth-century typefounders, and can be traced back to the business established in 1530 by Christian Egenolff, to which Konrad Berner succeeded in 1591. In addition there are two sets of roman capital initials, both on azured arabesque backgrounds, of different sizes, another from a set with an abstract floral pattern of baroque inspiration, a factotum incorporating two cornucopiae surmounted by a twin-tailed mermaid, and some arabesque headpieces and tailpieces.

8 Barker, [note 2], p. 10.
9 Barker, [note 2], pp. 64-5.
10 Benzing, [note 1], pp. 340-3.
11 Benzing, [note 1], p. 342.

TABLE I
Types, initials and ornaments in the *Hortus Eystettensis*

The roman and italic types are identified by reference to the sheets reproduced in *Type Specimen Facsimiles*, I, edited by John Dreyfus (London, 1963) (= *TSF*), with the names or locations given in the text there, and the source, where known. The fraktur types are identified from the sheets reproduced in Gustav Mori, *Das Schriftgießengewerbe in Frankfurt am Main und Offenbach* (Frankfurt, 1926) (= M).

Types

1. Berner 1592 (*TSF* 2)	2nd line of titling (Jacques Sabon, 1565)
2. Berner 1622 (*TSF* 3)	'Canon' (imitation of 1592 'Canon de Garamond').
3. Voskens *c.* 1660 (*TSF* 6)	2-line Pica (found at Hamburg 1602, and Basle 1603).[12]
4. Fievet 1664 (*TSF* 4)	4th line of titling (in use by Froben by 1517, and in the Petreius specimen, 1525).
5. Berner 1592 (*TSF* 2)	'Parangon' (Robert Granjon, *c.* 1555)
6. Rolloux 1714 (M 19)	'Canon Fractur'.[13]
7. Luther 1678 (M 9)	'Kruas Text Fractur'.
8. Luther 1678 (M 9)	'Tertia oder Bibel Fractur'.
9. Luther 1678 (M 9)	'Mittel Fractur'.

Initials

1. Roman outline capitals, on azured arabesque base, 38 mm.
2. Roman outline capitals, on azured arabesque base, 24 mm.
3. Roman outline capitals, on baroque floral base, 13 mm.
4. Factotum, two cornucopias, mermaid at head, 42 mm.

Head and tailpieces

1. Arabesque headpiece, putto holding wreaths between dogs chasing rabbits, 150 × 36 mm.
2. Arabesque tailpiece, two cornucopias, masks in centre, 107 × 75 mm.
3. Arabesque tailpiece, putto in centre, 107 × 75 mm.

At first sight this might seem a promisingly large selection of material to form a base from which to explore possible identification with the stock of contemporary Nuremberg printers. This is, however, to reckon without two complicating factors. First, the Egenolff-Berner foundry was, at the beginning of the seventeenth century, at the height of its fame and success. Almost all the Nuremberg printers were equipped with its produce, and the frakturs in particular are common to all the printers mentioned above. Secondly, the *Hortus Eystettensis* is by far and away the biggest book produced in Nuremberg (or Europe, for that matter) at this period. Even ordinary folios are rare, and the majority of books recorded as printed by the Lochners, Wagenmann, Lantzenberger, Lauer, Kauffmann, and the Fuhrmanns are small quartos or octavos.

These reflections were first brought home to me at the Stadtbibliothek in Nuremberg where the local imprints are conveniently catalogued in chronological order. Through the great kindness of Frau Elisabeth Beare, I was allowed

12 See A. F. Johnson, 'The "Goût Hollandois"', *Selected Essays* (Amsterdam, 1970), p. 369.
13 The same type, with different capitals and two different forms of 'h', is in Luther 1678.

to examine a number of these, and was able to form the outline of a visual image of the total output of the Nuremberg presses in the first two decades of the seventeenth century, which narrowed the search considerably. I then pursued the recipe recommended to me at the outset by David Paisey. Benzing's citations of the output of the sixteenth-century German presses were based on existing bibliographies, most of them specialist in nature: Ernst Zinner, *Geschichte und Bibliographie der astronomischen Literatur zur Zeit der Renaissance* (Leipzig, 1941), Enrico Stevenson, *Inventario dei libri stampati Palatino-Vaticani* (Rome, 1886-89), Paul Hohenemser, *Flugschriftensammlung Gustav Freytag* (Frankfurt am Main, 1925), Philipp Wackernagel, *Bibliographie zur Geschichte des deutschen Kirchenliedes im 16. Jahrhundert* (Frankfurt am Main, 1855), Emil Weller, *Annalen der poetischen National-Literatur der Deutschen im 16. und 17. Jahrhundert* (Freiburg im Breisgau 1862-64), Gustav Hellmann, *Die Meteorologie in den deutschen Flugschriften und Flugblättern des 16. Jahrhunderts* (Berlin, 1921), Robert Eitner, *Quellen-Lexikon der Musiker und Musikgelehrten* (Leipzig, 1900-04), all provided valuable pointers, but these, with a few scattered references to the *Catalogue générale* of the Bibliothèque Nationale at Paris, were all I had to go on. (I was unable to find a copy of W. Drugulin, *Historischer Bilderatlas: Verzeichnis einer Sammlung von Einzelblättern zur Cultur- und Sittengeschichte vom 15. in das 19. Jahrhundert* (1867).)

The results were inevitably partial, with a strong bias towards almanacs and astronomical literature on the one hand and music on the other, the results of dependence on the two sources that were fullest for the early seventeenth century. Happily, by no means all were in German (and thus in the ubiquitous frakturs); even more fortunately, this bias proves (now that I have David Paisey's magisterial survey of the British Library holdings) not to be untypical of them, and perhaps, therefore, of the total output of the Nuremberg presses in the period.

The most promising candidate appeared to be the press of Georg Leopold Fuhrmann. The 1616 specimen appeared to be the most useful and detailed showing of any of the printers' stock, and much of it corresponded with the

TABLE 2

Types in G. L. Fuhrmann, *Typorum et characterum ... designatio* (1616)

The types as numbered in Table 1 are given with Fuhrmann's names, and the location in the specimen

3. '1. Petit Canon aut typus, quem Garamond vocant', C4.
6. '1. Der grosse Canon',)(4 [with less florid 'h' and different capitals].
6. '2. Der klein Canon', a1 [capitals for the above].
7. '2 [*sic* for 3] Text', a2.
8. '4. *Tertia Fractur*, oder Bibelschrift', a3.
9. '5. Mittel *Fractur*', a4.

types and other material of the *Hortus Eystettensis*. It showed all the frakturs and many of the roman types, and, among a wide range of fine initials (some very like those popularized by Johann Neudorffer) and, among ornaments, the smaller of the two arabesque initial sets.

But it did not show the large titling capitals, or the ancient Froben capitals, or the large arabesque initials, too fine, one would have thought, to be omitted in what was evidently intended to be a full display of available material (the specimen may indeed be a catalogue for the sale of the business, since Fuhrmann had ceased to print by the next year, when the imprint becomes that of his widow and heirs!). Furthermore, the odd and distinctive 'Voskens' 2-line Pica, common to the specimen and to the *Hortus Eystettensis*, also appears in the work of Bauer and Kauffmann, as does the smaller arabesque initial set. The only explanation of the latter is that multiple sets from the original wood blocks must have been made by casting metal from impressions in sand-moulds.[14] There is a further negative piece of evidence against Fuhrmann. After the *Hortus Eystettensis*, the grandest book published in Nuremberg at this time was his *Testudo Gallo-Germanica* (1615), a splendidly printed folio collection of lute music.[15] It is another showcase for Fuhrmann's types, but it does not contain those whose absence is noted above.

On the other hand, the presence in so many other books of the smaller arabesque initials effectively disposes of Baier's argument in favour of Konrad Bauer. Indeed, apart from ornaments, Bauer, Fuhrmann, the Lochners and Wagenmann seem to have had virtually identical supplies of roman type. The Granjon 'parangon' italic is occasionally used, but its large size made it unsuitable for mainly small books. Works as various as *Salviani opera ... curante Cunrado Rittershusio* (1611), *Theses de naturae officio in sanitatis negotio ... praeside Caspare Hofmann* (1613), *Brevis delineatio ingressus ... Matthias ... in urbem Norimbergam* (1614), all printed by Bauer, Melchior Franck, *Viridarium musicum* (1613), J. R. Camerarius, *Sylloges memorabilium et mirabilium* (1614), printed by Fuhrmann, Donatus, *De octo partibus orationis* (1607), one of Wagenmann's non-musical prints, Lauer's J. Marius, *Mundus jovialis anno MDCIX detectus* (1615), and J. Vogel, *Photinismus* (1617), printed by the younger Lochner for S. Halbmayer, all have a very similar appearance.[16]

There remains Paul Kauffmann. At first sight his printing of Caspar Hassler, *Sacrae symphoniae diversorum autorum* (1613), or Georg Gruber, *Reliquiae sacrorum concentuum* (1615)[17] appear little different from Fuhrmann's of

14 The technique is described in Samuel Struck's *Neu-verfasstes Auff der Löbl. Kunst-Buchdrukkerey Nützlich zu gebrauchendes Format-Buch* (Lübeck and Leipzig, 1715), p. 71, under the heading 'Kurtze Nachricht Buchstaben und andere Kleinigkeiten abzuformen'. Examples of its use can, however, be found in the sixteenth century, and the method must long predate the invention of printing.

15 BL Music K.8.h.18.

16 Respectively BL 847.e.10; 1079.k.2 (2); 11403.bb.55; Music C.193j; 1172.e.1 (4); 827.d.13; 531.k.11 (4); and 480.a.7 (8).

17 BL Music B.93b and C.72.

Franck, *Viridarium musicum*. The conventions for music printing were strictly maintained. But Kauffmann's two sets of parts all have a line each of the Sabon large titling capitals and one or more of the large arabesque initial set. If further proof is wanted, it may be found in two books bound together in the British Library, and catalogued under 'Nuremberg: Official Documents' and 'Nuremberg: Collegium Medicum'. The latter is *Dispensatorium pharmacorum omnium ... auctore primo Valerio Cordo, ex tertia editione publicatum*, the former *Leges ac statuta ... senatus Norimbergensis ad medicos, pharmacopoeos & alios pertinentia*.[18] Both were printed by Kauffmann in 1612; both have the full range of roman types and some of both initial sets. The headpieces and tailpieces, of which there are many in the *Dispensatorium*, though similar in style, are different from those in the *Hortus Eystettensis*.

I am sure that Besler's hand can be seen in both these publications, and it confirms the typographic evidence of the other books with Kauffmann's imprint. But whether he actually printed the letterpress pages of the *Hortus Eystettensis* is another matter. None of the books that he printed before 1612 contains all this ample range of material,[19] and the use of the large type and the initials in the later music books is odd: they look rather out of scale. I am inclined to wonder whether the material that Kauffmann used in 1612 and later was actually bought by Besler from the Berner type-foundry specially for the purpose. It is a documented fact that Besler was in negotiations at Frankfurt, in which the printseller and publisher Balthasar Caimox was involved. His petition to the Nuremberg Council, and its verdict, are recorded as follows:

> [31 October 1612] Balthasar Caimox in der canzley gethane aussag und entschuldigung soll man Basilio Peßler, apothecker, furhalten, nachmals der herren hochgelehrten am stattgericht bedencken einnemen, wie solche handlung gegen dem rath zu Franckfurt zu enden.
> [20 November 1612] Basilio Peßler soll man der herren hochgelehrten am stattgericht [bedencken gemes] anzeigen, seine beschwerung wider den rath zu Franckfurt in eine fermbliche supplication bringen zu lassen und dieselbe zu übergeben, so woll man ime fürschrifften mittheilen, damitt er seiner gelaisten caution geledigt werde, sonsten aber soll man auff seinen bericht Balthasar Caimox ferner zu red halten.[20]

We know of no other transaction in connection with the *Hortus Eystettensis* which would have involved Besler with Frankfurt, and it may be that type, as well as plates, were purchased specially for this *magnum opus*. If so, as with the engravers, it may have been not one but many printers who were commissioned to print so many sheets in so short a time, and that Kauffmann, like the engraver

18 BL 777.i.8.
19 The large arabesque initial Q occurs in C. Ritterhusius, *Exequiae Baumgartnerianae* (1604), but the large titling, the lower case of the 'Canon' and even that of the 2-line Pica are not in evidence.
20 Theodor Hampe, *Nürnberger Ratsverlässe über Kunst und Künstler* (Leipzig, 1904), II, nos 2520 and 2528.

Johann Leypolt, was *primus inter pares*. He, at any rate, retained the use of the type and some at least of the ornament stock.

There I must leave this enquiry on a slightly hesitant note. No one will know how many such hesitations, so many of them triumphantly resolved, marked David Paisey's twenty years' pilgrimage through the British Library's German imprints of the seventeenth century, many of them anonymous or imperfectly signed. No one knows this field as he does; the help he has provided and, even more, will provide to workers in it is limitless. I am happy to have this chance of acknowledging my share of the general debt, and to add a small brick to the edifice that will be built on the foundation that he has laid.

CHRISTIAN CUNRAD'S *HIRTEN GESPRÄCH*

LEONARD FORSTER

IN 1975 I bought from from Ludwig Rosenthal's Antiquariaat in Hilversum the small work reproduced here: Christian Cunrad's *Hirten Gespräch.*[1] It was item 128 in their catalogue no. 229. It consists of one quire of six leaves, evidently disbound from a *Sammelband* as the leaves are numbered consecutively 456 to 461 in an early hand. The size is 18.5 × 15 cm. There are library stamps on the verso of the title-page, revealing that the book had been sold as a duplicate by the Stadtbibliothek in Breslau (Wrocław). There is no copy in the British Library. My copy is now in Bristol University Library.

The text consists of 92 alexandrine couplets rhyming feminine and masculine alternately, followed at the end as a space-filler by a sonnet also in alexandrines signed C.C.V. (= Christianus Cunradus Vratislaviensis) rhyming alternately feminine and masculine. The versification is Opitzian throughout, though it does not follow Opitz's rules strictly.

In the text the caesuras are carefully marked throughout by virgulas, even where the syntax does not require it. There are a few misplaced caesuras: *Der durch sein Wigern vnd / Schaumschauben gantz vnd gar*; *Den edlen Musen vnd / Poeten mag gefallen*; *O Gott der Hoffnung / mich* [*mit*] *deiner Freud auch fülle.* Cunrad's use of syncope and apocope is not strictly Opitzian, though he is obviously striving towards it: *richt*, *Bäum*, *in ein' frisch Schatten ort*, *Höh*, *nichtes*, *flamm*, *soltu*, *dein'*, *gnung*, *mein Rede*, *verricht*, *abe thun*, *Gäst*. *Heiligen Geistes Gaben* has one syllable too many.

There are a number of misprints and typographical oddities, including *Schaär*, *Galather* for *Galathee* (rhyming with *Höh*), *saät*.

Cunrad's vocabulary contains a number of rather unfamiliar features. On

1 Max Hippe, 'Christian Cunrad, ein vergessener schlesischer Dichter 1608-1671', in: *Silesiaca. Festschrift des Vereins für Geschichte und Altertum Schlesiens zum sechzigsten Geburtstag seines Präses Colmar Grünhagen* (Breslau, 1898), lists a Latin version: *Gloriosi Jesu Christi Redemptoris ac Salvatoris nostri a morte resurgentis Triumphus per Eclogam decatatus à Christiano Cunrado Vratisl. Phil. et Medicinae Studioso.* Exscriptus Olsnae Silesiorum Typis Johann Bössemesseri MDCXXVIII. The dedication is signed: Breslae ex aedibus Paternis Ao. MDCXXIIX. Kal. Maji. On Cunrad see now the entry by Klaus Garber, in: Walther Killy (ed.), *Literaturlexikon. Autoren und Werke deutscher Sprache*, II (Gütersloh and Munich, 1989), p. 487.

Wigern see Walther Mitzka, *Schlesisches Wörterbuch* (Berlin, 1965), III, map at p. 1498. *Schaumschauben* is not in Mitzka; it is perhaps a misprint for *-schnauben*. *Mantua* is a reference to Virgil, who is closely imitated. *Die eysern Heller* is not found in Mitzka or in Grimms' *Deutsches Wörterbuch*; it is apparently some kind of cutting implement, perhaps a scythe. *seudt* is an old form for *siedet*. *Auf seiner Mutter Pferd* presumably means 'feet', cp. 'shanks's pony'. Other noteworthy items include *zum bestem*, *Nim deines schatzes eins*; *Widerschal* as a verb form.

There are numerous biblical references in the margin, and the sonnet is based supposedly on a biblical text; I have not found it at the place stated in Luther's Bible, the Vulgate, or Tremellius and Beza. Many of the other biblical references are inapplicable and seem to serve a decorative function only. This is the first time such a thing has come to my notice.

The poem is marked out as a learned one by two rather obscure classical allusions in the first couplet, Cynthius – a by-name for Phoebus the sun – and Pyrois, the name of one of his horses. The learned poet goes out into the country near Breslau to a *locus amoenus* and comes upon shepherds who propose a singing-match to be judged by 'der alte Daphnis'. Their names are Corydon and Tityrus. So far everything is completely traditional in the Virgilian mode, though normally Daphnis is the name of a young man. But they decide to sing, not of love and the praises of Galathea but in praise of God, to which Daphnis agrees. This is not a traditional subject; religious eclogues usually deal with pastoral episodes out of the Bible treated in Virgilian style, so that Cunrad shows a certain originality with his 'geistliche Kontrafaktur'. Tityrus and Corydon proceed to sing alternately each eight verses until they go over to longer speeches of 45 lines each, finally terminated by Daphnis who, in 28 verses, declares that both have sung worthily and takes them to his home. The poet sees them off and concludes with the praise of the godly life of the shepherd in a vein reminiscent of Virgil (*Georgic* II, 458-74).

The sonnet *Avari inviti moriuntur* claims to be based on Psalm 49 but, as we saw, the text does not apply. The penultimate line, *Drumb/ wann erst recht gefült/ die eysen Heller kist/*, seems to give no sense.

In 1972 I raised the question of how long the Opitzian verse reform of 1624 propounded in the *Buch von der Deutschen Poeterey* took to become generally accepted.[2] I found no certain answer. It seemed that it was received early in Silesia and became known outside through the work of Silesian students. I was able to point to Christoph Coler writing alexandrines in Strasbourg in 1628 and non-Silesians like Paul Fleming and Georg Gloger elsewhere writing in 1630. 'It seems,' I wrote, 'to have been a matter of local patriotism among young Silesians to write like Opitz.' It apparently took between six and seven years for

2 Leonard Forster, 'German alexandrines on Dutch broadsheets before Opitz', in: George Schultz-Behrend (ed.), *The German Baroque: Literature, Music, Art* (Austin / Texas and London, 1972), pp. 11-64, reprinted in: Leonard Forster, *Kleine Schriften zur deutschen Literatur im 17. Jahrhundert* (Amsterdam, 1977), pp. 119-60.

the reform to become known and generally adopted outside Silesia, and there remained much that we did not know about what was going on in Silesia itself. There the matter rested, though there has been much work done on this early period since then. In 1993 John Roger Paas pointed out that we still 'need to study early German alexandrine poems from the transitional years of 1624 to 1630' and went on to point to a neglected early work by Adam Olearius in 1629.[3] This was particularly interesting because he found two versions, the later one embodying corrections by the author in the direction of Opitz's rules. The work I wish to deal with here is less significant; it represents the sort of work current in Silesia itself in the critical years. The author, Christian Cunrad, was personally acquainted with Opitz (who indeed was to crown him with the poet's laurels in 1629). He was a member of the generation of forward-looking young intellectuals who were soon to take the reform across Germany. He wrote in 1628, when he was twenty years old. Fleming and Gloger were two years older. Coler was twenty-six.

This poem was not Cunrad's first essay in this style. Max Hippe quotes some smooth alexandrines of his from as early as 1624, besides other, later work. It would clearly be worth studying his work in some detail; Reifferscheid observed in 1889: 'Die lateinischen und deutschen Gedichte Christian Cunrad's sind noch nirgends verzeichnet.'[4] This remains true, despite the list made by Hippe, and it is not clear how many of the works mentioned there survived the Second World War; Dünnhaupt does not list them in his *Personalbibliographien zu den Drucken des Barock*. This task could presumably only be undertaken in Poland.

One wonders why this promising beginning was not followed up more fully. Cunrad became a successful medical man and a *poeta laureatus* but published very little in the course of a busy life. (He died in Oppau in 1671, aged sixty-three.) This may have something to do with the demands of a medical career, but also perhaps with the circumstance that he became a Catholic convert and thereby cut himself off from the circle around Opitz. He remains an interesting figure, who deserves more attention than he has received, after the useful account by Max Hippe, not everywhere available, which whets our appetite.

3 John Roger Paas, 'The process of poetic assimilation as revealed in the earliest known German alexandrines by Adam Olearius', in: James Hardin and Jörg Jungmayr (eds), *'Der Buchstab tödt – der Geist macht lebendig' Festschrift zum 60. Geburtstag von Hans-Gert Roloff* (Berne, 1992), II, pp. 761–74.

4 Alexander Reifferscheid, *Quellen zur Geschichte des geistigen Lebens in Deutschland* (Heilbronn, 1889), p. 856.

Hirten Geſpräch
Von
Des Heiligen Geiſtes
Hohen vnd Seeligmachenden
Gaben/
Wie dann auch
Anruffung
Vmb deſſelbigen Heiligen
Beyſtandt:
Getichtet
Von
Chriſtian Cunraden.
Gedruckt zur Olſſe/
Durch Johann Böſſemeſſern.
ANNO 1628.

Denen Edlen/ Ehren-
vesten/ vnd Wolbenahmbten/
Herzen David Albrecht/ Wol-
verordneten Vorstehern des Hospitaals
zu S. Bernhardin.
Hn: Hansen Dobeneckern auff
Stein.
Hn: Christoff Hedwigern auff
Klein Tintz/
Vornehmen Bürgern in Breßlaw:
Meinen Insonders Grossgünstigen/
Hochgeehrten Herzen vnd Föderern.

Nun hatte *Cynthius*, die Rosse köñen fassen/
Vnd seinem *Pyrois*, den Zügel schiessen lassen/
Der durch sein Wigern/ vñ Schaumschaubẽ gantz vñ gar
Erschrecket vnd gedämpfft/ der hellen Sternen schaar:
Als ich mich heute schon / nicht weit von hier befande/
Wo sonst die gröste Stadt/ in diesem vnsrem Lande/
Mein Breßlaw / Hoch empor für allen andern richt/
Ihr groß gethürmtes Haupt/ vnd durch die Wolcken bricht:
Als/ sag Ich / vber Feld Ich etwas gieng spatziern/
Vnd durch die schöne Zeit / so alles jetzt thut Zieren
Vnd frewdig machen / auch erfrewte waß mein Hertz/
Daß sonsten offters doch / auch nagt gemeiner Schmertz/
Den vns der Krieg gebürt; der nun so lange Jahre/
Verwüstet Stadt vnd Dorff / vnd Schulen vnd Altare:
Da ward Ich vngefehr / in einen Ort geführt/
Den Gott vnd die Natur zum vberfluß geziert
Mit vnerschöpffter Lust: der auch für andern allen/
Den Edlen Musen vnd Poëten mag gefallen/
Da Bäum vnd quälle sind / bey welchen kräfftiglich/
Ein Himmlisches gemüth/ kan steigen vbersich.
Da saß Ich nun vnd hört wie durch ihr Musiciren/
Der Vögel leichtes Volck / noch alles mehr thät Zieren;
Da hört ich wie daß Lied der schönen Nachtigal
Weit in dem gantzen Wald' anmutig widerschal
Sih' da! so kommen dort/ Zwey Schäffer her gegangen/
Für welchen Ihre schaar / mit dücker Woll behangen
Vor an lieff vnd das Graß in vollem safft benagt:
Vnd dieses jenes bald/ bald jenes dieses jagt.
Vnd nicht sehr weit von mir da satzten sie sich nieder/
In ein' frisch Schatten ort / bedachten jhre Lieder/
Der Liebsten Freundligkeit/ vnd jhres Schmertzens ruh/
Vnd sahen so mit Lust der Schaffe grasen zu/
Fürwahr/ es wolte mir nicht allerdings gefallen/
Daß hier daß grobe Volck / in diesem Ort solt wallen/
Der *Phœbus* nur gebürt/ vnd wem er zugethan!
So fangen vnter deß sie diß Gespräche an.

A ij Wie

Coridon. Wie steht es *Tityrus*, solln vnsre Waldt Schalmeyen
Mit ihrem süssen Klang nicht wider vns erfrewen?
Wie steht es / wilt du nicht an jetzt der Galathee
Zu Ehren widerumb erheben in die Höh
Ein süsses Buhlen-Lied? Sieh wie mit schwachen Tritten
Auff seiner Mutter pferdt / dort gleich kompt her geritten
Der alte *Daphnis*, der sonst vnser Richter ist/
Vnd nicht ohn vorbedacht / verständig außerkist/
Wer besser singen kan. Nur fort / laß zugefallen
Nun deines Schatzes eins / dein helle Stimm erschallen;
Ich wil auch machen kundt/ daß meiner *Phyllis*, nicht
An Lob der Schönheit auch das wenigste gebricht.

Tityrus. Wie nun mein *Coridon*, waß mag dich doch bethören?
Meinst du das vnsrem Landt/ der Alte zu wird hören/
Vnd zwar zu dieser Zeit? Er weiß ja schon zuvor/
Daß wir sonst nichtes mehr/ gewohnt sein / Hoch empor
Zu führen/ vnd mit Ruhm der Sonnen nah zu setzen/
Als waß wir klagen/ wie vns die vnd die verletzen;
Wie vns so häfftig sehr der Liebe flamm anrennt
Vnd vns nur Safft vnd Krafft auß vnsern Gliedern brennt.
Noch dennoch / wilstu ja jetzt Kämpffen thun mit singen/
Ich schlage dir nichts ab/ Laß nur dein Lied erklingen
Zu Lob dem gutten Geist / Gott/ sag ich/ vnd dem Geist/
Den seinen Hirten / eh vom Himmel zu geweist
PAN vnser grösser GOtt: vnd daß / daß möcht gefallen
Dem *Daphnis* vnd jhm wol für seinen Ohren schallen.
Wo nicht / so laß mich gehn / Ich singe nicht mit dir/
Vnd meine Galathée verdients auch nicht von mir.

Coridon. O grosser Vnbestandt! sind daß die Hohen gaben/
Mit welchen deine Braut du gestern so erhaben?
Ist diß daß alte Lob / daß Ihre Trefflichkeit
Durch dein beredte Zung sonst allen andern weit
Bevor gezogen hat? Ich kan nicht satt belachen/
Daß deiner Liebsten Zorn dich kan so Geistlich machen:
O kähme sie jetzt her / vnd reichte dir die Handt/
Vnd waß dir sonsten / Lieb / wie bald wurd abgewandt
Der Geistlich eyffer sein! doch / diß dein anbeginnen
Ist auch Rühmwürdig: Geh erhebe deine Sinnen/
Geh / laß mit Danckbarkeit / für rinnen deinen Mundt/
Vnd mache Gottes gütt vnd Vaterliebe kundt/

Ich

Ich wil auch mit dir gehn! wie wol mir nicht bewogen
Die *Pierinnen* sein / vnd niemals bin geflogen/
Mit *Mantua* biß auffs *Parnassus* höchste spitz:
Mir ist doch gar gnung / das ich hierunter sitz.

Tityrus. Recht *Coridon*, vnd GOtt / dem thut auch nicht gefallen
Gebette voller Pracht: Er liebet nur für allen/
Ein Hertze das Ihm trawt / vnd schlecht weg Vater heist/
Nicht welches ohne That / mit blossen Worten gleist.
Drumb wil an jetzt Ich nicht zu Ruhm jhm länger schweigen/
Wiewol ich auch nicht kan / biß an die Wolcken steigen
Mit außgeputzten Thon. Ihr aber *Daphnis*, Ihr
Mein Alter gutter Freund / Ich bitte folget mir/
Vnd höret vns doch zu / seidt Richter in den dingen/
Vernehmet / ob wir auch so wol geschickt zu singen
Von gutten Sachen sein / als von der Eytelkeit/
Von *Venus* Wunderthat / vnd Ihres Sohnes streit.

Daphnis. Es ist / O Meine Söhn / gar Löblich diß Fürhaben
Das Ihr jetzt Preisen wolt / des Heyligen Geistes gaben
In dem voll Geistes ist der gantze Kreiß der Welt/ *Sap.2.v.7*
Vnd der die Rede kennt / sich allenthalben helt.
Ihr habet lang genug gerühmet vnd geschmücket

Venus. Der blinden *Venus* werck / vnd wie vns all berücket
Die schöne Zauberey: die Mich auch hart bethört/
Eh dann das Alter mir mein Junges blut versehrt.
Ich hör Euch gerne zu / sitzt her / vnd thut den Sachen
Fort mehr / vnd frölich auch / ein gutten Anfang machen:
Du *Titurus* bevor / weil du der erste bist/
Der diesen gutten Streitt mit *Coridon* erkiest.

Tityrus. O Ewig grosser Geist / O Geist von GOtt gegeben
Vnd selber wahrer GOtt / in Wesen / Standt / vnd Leben/ *Ebræor.9.* *Joh.14.16.*
Du höchster Trost der Welt / du Zuversicht in Noth/
O HErr ohn End vnd Ziel / von Ewigkeit HErr Gott:
Gib meiner Zungen doch / mit deiner Glut zu brennen!
Laß doch mein Hertze dich recht Lieben vnd erkennen!
Regier mein Rede / daß sie innig Preise dich;
Dich nur begehr ich jetzt / von dir nur sing jetzt Ich.

Coridon. O Geist! O heisse Flam des Glaubens / vnd der Liebe! *Rom.5.*
O komm jetzt in mein Hertz / daß es durch dich sich übe/
Zu deinem Lob vnd Preiß / steck an die Flamm in mir/
Mit welcher eh gebrandt / die Hertzen gegen dir

Der

Der vns den Steg zur Thür des Himmels einig zeiget;
Joh.3.v.36. Der vns in Finsternüß allein das Licht zuneiget:
Joh. 12. Steck auch in mir / O Geist desselben Fackel an/
v. 47. Durch Ihn Ich wider Todt vnd Helle Siegen kan.
Tityrus. O Geist der gutten Werck / so auß dem Glauben rinnen!
Johan.14. Durch dein Antreiben wir nur guttes vberkommen/
v. 17. Du richtest vnser Hertz vnd Wercke dahin ab/
Daß an denselben Gott ein Wolgefallen hab.
1. Tim. 6. O gib daß eyfrig Ich dem guttem auch nachsetze!
v. 11. 12. Stets mich in Frömigkeit vnd allem dem ergetze/
So dieser zugethan: Vnd vbe stets den Streit/
Durch welchen mir die Cron des Lebens wird bereit.
Coridon. O Geist / durch den allein / Gottselig sein herühret!
Act.15.v.7. Durch den alleine wird zur Frömigkeit geführet
Ein gläubig Christenhertz; Der bloß allein verricht
Vrspringlich alles diß / was jmmer guts geschicht:
O gib das mich auch mög der grosse Titul ziehren/
Ps.34.v.10. Den Gottes Heilige vnd Liebe Brüder führen:
Gib daß Ich Christum auch mir zum Exempel setz/
Ps.45.v.9. Als meinen Bräutigam mit frôligkeit ergetz.
Tityrus. O Geist / der einig hat in vnser Hertz gegossen/
Rom. 15. Der heissen Liebe brunst: Von dessen quell geflossen
v. 30. Das edle Gutt allein / das alles in sich helt;
1. Cor. 13. Ohn welches alles nichts ist in der gantzen Welt:
v. 2. O gib daß erstlich Gott ich Brünstig such vnd Liebe:
Nach diesem auch die Lieb des Nechsten fleissig vbe:
Lieb gleichsfallß Ihn wie mich ohn angetichten schein:
Matth. 5. Ja selbst die / so mir feind / vnd meine Hasser sein.
v. 44.
Coridon. O Geist des Friedens / vnd der keuschen Liebes flammen/
Halt meine Liebe stets / mit Reinigkeit zusammen/
Das vnbefleckt in mir dieselbe wird gespürt/
Vnd von des Fleisches Lust / mein Hertz bleib vnberührt.
Hebr. 12. Ohn Keuscheit kan niemandt des Herren antlitz schawen:
v. 14. Drumb laß / Laß meine Seel / die Liebe vnterbawen
Mit wahrer Reinigkeit / mit Eintracht vnd bestandt;
Laß allen Halß vnd Neid von mir sein abgewandt.
Tityrus. Mit einem Wort / O Geist / durch den wir alle Gaben
So gut vnd Seelig sein / herab von oben haben!
Du bist der Warheit Brunn / der Hoch versprochen hat
Vns trewe Hülff zuthun / vnd thusts auch mit der that:
Du

Du schaffest alles gutt: Dein Stab der thut vns Leiten;
Du thust zur Weißheit vns vnd vnser Hertz bereiten/ Psalm. 23.
Daß sonst gantz Kindisch ist: machst vnser Wöllen voll:
Vnd Lehrest / wie man Gott mit Furcht erkennen soll:
Du schaffst ein Newes Hertz / das bloß auff Ihn vertrawet/ Psalm. 51.
Ihn Liebet vnd verehret / auff Ihn stets feste bawet:
Mit Kindes Zuversicht Ihn seinen Vater nennt/ Gal. 4. v. 6.
Vnd auch allein vmb Hülff in aller Noth anrennt.
Du thust die Trawrigen / mit reichem Troste laben:
Die Schwachen machstu starck / mit deiner Krafft vnd Gaben;
Die in der Liebe kalt / vnd noch Kleingläubig sein/
Die machstu warm vnd starck / geust jhnen alles ein/
Was jhren Glauben mehrt / vnd vorig Schwaches wissen:
Durch dich / durch dich allein der Warheit sie geniessen/
Du wäschst vnd Heiligst sie / machst sie Gerecht vnd rein/ 1. Cor. 6.
Daß sie in allem Thun gantz Newgebohren sein; v. 11.
Zeuchst sie vom bösen ab / Vernewerst jhre Sinnen/ Joh. 3. v. 5.
So / daß sie nichtes mehr als Frewdig reden können Rom. 8. v. 2.
Von Gott vnd Gottes wort: Du öffnest jhren Mundt/
Vnd machst selbst jhnen dich mit seinen Gaben kundt/ Act. 2. v. 14.
Das sie dich als Ihr Pfandt des Himmels einig Preisen:
Du thust sie vber sich die rechte Strasse weisen
Zum wahren Vaterlandt: Durch dich / durch dich allein/
Durch dich / sag Ich / durch dich sie Kinder Gottes sein.
Vmb daß O werther Geist / mein Gott / mein Schutz vnd Lehrer/
Mein bester Auffenthalt / meins Glaubens grosser mehrer:
O siehe / siehe mich / auch mit Genaden an/
Regier vnd Leite mich auch auff gemelter bahn:
Ich wil / O Trewer Geist! dich wieder Danckbar ehren;
Mein Hirten Lied soll stets dein Gutt vnd Tugendt mehren:
So offt die güldne Sonn vns widerbringen wirdt/
Diß dein so Hohes fest / so lang sich in mir rührt/
Des Athems schwache Lufft: so offte sol für allen
Mir dieser Waldt von dir vernehmlich wiederschallen:
Auch dieser Baum der mich mit seinem Schatten deckt/
Durch mich / zu deinem Lob sol werden auffgeweckt/
Das Er nach meinem Lied mehr hupffen sol vnd springen/
Als dort mein Wieder thut. Ich wil ohn ende singen
Von deinem Gnaden werck / vnd nicht allein nur hier/
Viel mehr in jener Welt; steh du nur steiff bey mir.
Mit

Der Hirten / derer Stäb' uns jetzo noch thun leiten:
Joh.14. O laß jetzt mein Gemüth in deiner Ehr nicht gleiten/
Nihm alle Wort in acht / die ich an jetzo thu;
Dich nur O Trewer Geist/ dich nur erheb' Ich nu.
Tityrus. O Geist der alles schafft! O Geist von GOtt gegeben!
Job.33. O Athem Gottes! der uns aller giebt das Leben/
Treib alle Furcht von mir / die mir das Hertz beschwert/
Das es auff dieser Bahn freymüttig rennt / und fährt.
Durch deine Krafft und Stärck / muß alle Forcht verschwinden/
Du kanst der Zagheit und des Kleinmuths/ uns entbinden/
All' Angst / all Hertz beschwer vergehet bloß durch dich!
O stärcke / grosser Geist / O stärck' auch kräfftig mich!
Coridon. O Geist! O Prediger der alles uns thut Lehren/
Joh. 14. Ohn dich / kan niemandt dich mit rechtem Hertzen ehren/
℣. 17. Ohn dich / weiß keiner nicht / von dir / und deiner gütt/
Mit welcher du erweckst / Zum Glauben das Gemüth.
Joh. 15. ℣. Du nur allein kanst uns in alle Warheit leiten:
16.16. ℣.13. O laß mein bebend Hertz auch kühnlich hierfort schreiten!
Regirest meine Zung / O Geist / du selber nicht/
Gewiß so hüncket sie / ohn dich sie nichts verricht.
Tityrus.
Hebræ: 1. O Geist! O süsses Oel der wahren Himmels frewden!
℣. 9. Der aller Thränen fluß / der alles Trawer-leiden/
Von unsren Augen wischt / der unser mattes Hertz/
Ergäntzet kräfftiglich/ und heilt von allem Schmertz.
O GOtt der Hoffnung / mich deiner Frewd' auch fülle/
Rom. 15. Gib das all Creutz in mir dein Fried im Glauben stille/
℣. 14. Daß meine Hoffnung gantz und völlig durch dich sey:
O Geist du kanst es thun / zu dir ich söhnlich schrey.
Coridon.
Eb. 1. ℣.13. O Geist! Vorsprecher / O du thewres Pfandt der Frommen/
& 14. Der Frommen die zum Erb des Himmels Saal bekommen/
Durch den Versigelt wird die Heilige Zusag/
Die erst Erfüllen soll der grosse Letzte tag.
Job. 5. ℣1. O gib / wann diß mein Hauß / so Irdisch / wird vergehn/
Mir in dem Ewigen mög' eine stell zustehen;
Dem Ewigen / daß Gott / der auff uns alle schawt/
Und keine Menschen hand in Wolcken hat erbawt.
Tityrus. O Geist der Kindschafft / der uns Unbetrüglich lehret/
Rom. 8. ℣. Das alle Dienstbarkeit im grunde gantz Zerstöret
15. 16 17. Und hingeleget sey / daß uns auß aller Welt
Zu seinen Kindern Gott Ihm habe vorgestelt.

O Lehr

O Lehr mich dieses auch mit Danckbarkeit erkennen!
Daß ich mich Gottes Kindt/ und Erben dürffe nennen:
O Salbe / Salbe mich auch zu dem Himmel ein/
Und laß an dessen theil mich ja nicht zweifflig seìn.
O Geist / O Gnaden Geist / durch dessen Krafft und Wercke *Coridon.*
Allein / die Ungenadt verlohren Ihre stärcke/ Heb:2.10.
Und nicht mehr Herscher ist: Der nur alleine gibt/ ℣. 19.
Das Zuvertrawen / daß uns Gott von Hertzen liebt/
Und alle Missethat Sanfftmüttig hat vergeben. Rom. 1. ℣ 4.
O mache weiter rein und Heilig mir mein Leben/
Das nicht durch schwere Sünd und vieler Laster zahl/
Mich Gottes ungnad' und eyffer uberfall.
O Geist der Weißheit! Die sonst alles uberwiget/ *Tityrus.*
Die / welchen sie beziert / auch Gott selbst nahe füget; Esa. 11. ℣. 2.
Der allein Weise ist / von dessen Mundt sie kömbt/ Prov. 2.
O Geist der bloß allein/ waß uns bewust / bestimbt: ℣. 6.
O thue doch uber mich dein Weißheit auch außgiessen! Ephes. 1.
Laß deinen Willen und Geheimnuß mich auch wissen/ ℣. 8. 9.
Lehr auch die Warheit mich die im verborgen ligt/
Und daß / was heimlich ist / was deine Weißheit fügt. *Coridon.*
O Geist der Wissenschafft / der alles Thun erfindet! Eph:3. ℣. 1.
Und auch die Hohe tieff der Gottheit selbst ergründet/ 1. Cor. 2.
Der uns zu einer Speiß / daß Manna zugerüst/ ℣. 10.
Das Ihme nur bekandt / und sonst verborgen ist. Apocal. 2.
℣. 13.
O Laß mich auch mein Heil / und JEsum Christum wissen/ 1. Cor. 2.
Mit seiner heissen Lieb / von welcher nicht gerissen ℣. 2.
Im Leben noch im Todt mein Hertze werden kan/ Rom. 8.
Wo deine Wissenschafft du in mir regest an. v. 38. 39.
O Geist / durch den man lernt Gott fürchten und erkennen/ *Tityrus.*
Durch dessen Wirckung wir gantz unverhindert rennen Ephes. 1.
Mit freyem Zügel / zur Erwegung seiner Macht/ v. 17.
Durch welche Gottesfurcht in uns wird auffgebracht/
So daß wir sein Gebott und Willen steiff bewahren; Joh. 2. v. 3.
O Laß mich deine Gunst bey diesem auch erfahren!
Gib / daß auch meine Seel / Ihn recht mit furcht erkennt/ Joh. 17. v. 3.
Weil Ihn erkennen man alleine Leben nennt.
O Geist des Glaubens / der zum nechsten zu Gott träget/ *Coridon.*
Und die Vereinigung mit Ihm allein erreget; Eph: 1. v. 13.
Durch den man frölich Siegt / der kräfftig umb und an/ Syr. 25. v. 16.
Und frey der Alten Schlang den Kopff zertretten kan: Exod. 17.

Der

Mit einem Wort / O Geist / der alle Tugendt zeuget/
Coridon. Vnd vns von Kindes bein zu allem gutten beuget/
Du bist alleine der/ so vnser Schiff auffricht/
Wann vns im Laster Sée fast Vaß vnd Bodem bricht.
Psalm. 16. Du kanst diß / waß du wilst / in einem Nuh' verrichten;
Ohn deinen weisen Rath / ist vnser Thun vnd Tichten
Vnd alle Wissenschafft nur blosser Narren tandt;
Was vnser Klugheit ist / ist lauter Vnverstandt.
Wo du nicht Schule helst / da kan man nichts verstehen;
Da müssen wir nur blind in allen Sachen gehen:
Da ist kein frey Gemüth / kein Ruh' des Hertzens nicht;
Die Vngenadt nur vns gemein das Vrtheil spricht.
Wer kan ohn deine Hülff vnd güttiges erlauben/
Die grossen Wunderwerck vnd die Geheimnüß glauben
So Gott gesetzet hat? Wen lest die Sünden last/
Das Er mit Glauben Gott / als seinen Retter fast?
Wir bleiben nur vertiefft in Missethaten stecken/
Im fall du vns nicht thust zur Frömigkeit erwecken;
Du nur/ alleine du / bist vnser bestes Heil/
Das vns beschützet/ für des Teuffels Gifft vnd Pfeil.
Du kanst die Schläffrigen zu rechtem ernste bringen;
Die Sünden abe thun / vnd alle Laster zwingen:
Eph:4.℣4. Ziehst vnser Hertz mit Lieb vnd trewer Einigkeit;
Durch dich wird vnser Hertz zum Himmel zubereit.
Joh.6.℣63. Du Lebendig vns machst / führst vns auff rechter Strassen/
Psal.23.℣3. Durch dich den rechten Weg wir wol zu Leben fassen:
Ps 16. ℣.11. Du Lehrest / daß allein die gröste Weißheit ist/
Eph.3.℣19. Für aller Kunst vnd Witz das man Jhm außerkiest
Den HErren Christum frey zu Lieben / zu bekennen:
Du sag ich / machst das wir mit solcher Flamm' entbrennen:
Du gibst vns in den Mundt Bekändtnüß vnd Bericht/
Wann wegen Reiner Lehr vns der vnd der anficht.
Matth.10. Du hilffst vns Noth vnd Todt vnd Teuffel vberwinden;
℣.18.19.20. Durch dich die Leiter wir zu dessen Wohnung finden/
Luc.12. Der vns zu seinem Erb schon lang erwehlet hat/
℣.12. Summ' vnser Seeligkeit ist deine Hülff vnd That.
O Heilig reicher Geist / halt mich bey den Gedancken
Laß meine Schenckel ja auff diesem Pfadt nicht wancken
Laß mich den / den ich schon durch dich einmahl erkennt/
Stets steiff bekennen / auch biß an mein Letztes endt.

Ich

Ich wil hingegen mich auch ernstlich stets bemühen/
Biß selbst zu dir hinauff / von deiner Gütt / zu ziehen
Mit freyem süssen Schall / vnd Hertzens innigkeit
Ein Danckbaren Gesang: so offt ich dieser Zeit
Bey meinen Schaffen hier / auff diesen Platz gestrecket/
Kan Feyerlich begehn: Waß dieser Waldt nur hecket
Bäum / Blumen / Laub vnd Graß / Berg / Thäler / Flüsse/
Soln mir zu meinem Lied einstimmen vberhell. (quälst
Ey nun genug gethan/ genug / genug gesungen/ Daphnis.
Genug auff diesem Sand' gestritten vnd gerungen/
Hört nun mein lieben Söhn / auch endlich wider auff/
Vnd lasset nicht zu weit den Versen jhren Lauff.
Jhr habet Beyde from vnd Geistlich / Euch erweiset;
Jhr habet Beyde wol des HErren gütt gepreiset;
Jhr habet alle beyd Verdient die schöne Croon
Von grünen Lorberbaum/ so Euch *Latonæ* Sohn
Selbst vbergeben sol; drumb last es so bestehen:
Kombt last vns allesambt nunmehr von hinnen gehen;
Die Sonne hat doch gleich des Himmels hertz gefast
Vnd treibt durch jhre Hitz vns selber zu der rast.
Schawt wie die Kräuter jetzt so dürstig nieder sincken
Vnd vns selbst machen Lust zu essen vnd zu trincken:
Die Bach sendt fast für Hitz / vnd schmeckt den Schaffen
Nur Schatten jhnen vnd des Stalles kühle bricht. (nicht
Kombt/ kombt seid meine Gäst. Zwar mein geringe Küchen
Helt keinen hellen Herdt / thut nicht nach Bratten riechen
Doch hab ich gutten Speck / ein frisch gelegtes Ey
Vnd wol mit sambt der Kron die Mutter selbst dabey:
Zu deme kan ich diß / diß *Coridon*, fürsetzen/
Was vber alles dich zum bestem kan ergetzen:
Die *Phyllis* wird auch Heut bey meinem Tische sein/
Vnd jhre Liebes blick gehn dir viel süsser ein/
Als sonst / Jch weiß gewiß / all' andre Lecker bissen.
Nun kombt / wir wollen gehn / vnd vnser Mahl geniessen/
Hernachmahls widerumb erquickt zu Felde ziehn
Mit vnser weissen Schaar / vnd singen wie vorhin.
So eilten Sie nun fort. Vnd Jch war wol zu frieden/
Daß mich zu dieser Zeit / daß Glück hieher beschieden:
Mein Vnwill / der mich kurtz zuvor genommen ein/
Must bald durch diß Gespräch gantz vmbgewendet sein/

O / dacht

O dacht Ich bey mir selbst / O welch ein Seeligs leben
Hat lieben Schäffer Euch der trewe Gott gegeben:
Ihr wüst nichts von der Sünd' vnd vber grossen Schand'
Die in den Städten wohnt / vnd hat die Oberhandt.
Hie thut Euch selbest Gott in seine Schulen führen/
Das Feld vnd die Natur thun selbest Euch Regieren/
Vnd lehren / wie Ihr Gott / vnd nicht das schnöde Goldt/
Das nur der Städte lust / von Hertzen lieben solt.
Hier wohnt Gerechtigkeit vnd Einfalt nah beysammen:
Hier hat die Hoffarth auß / vnd die / mit der die flammen
Von allen Lastern Zeugt / Gottloß- vnd Vppi-keit:
Der Himmel zeuget selbst / daß jhr viel frömer seidt.
Vnd mehr auff Gott gedenckt / als die / die Häuser zieren/
Vnd waß den Leib angeht; Hergegen das verliehren/
Was jhre Seelen zu dem Himmel kleiden sol.
Nun geht / geht glücklich fort / geht vnd gehabt Euch wol.
GOTT der Euch biß hieher zu seiner Ehr geleitet/
Regiere förter Euch / auff daß jhr nimmer schreitet
Vom Zweck der Gottesfurcht/ vnd mich vnd all dazu/
So jhre beste Lust vnd höchste Frewd vnd Ruh'
In Gott ersuchen/ vnd nicht von jhm absetzen:
Ich aber muß jetzt heim / vnd mich mit dir beletzen
Du schöner grüner Waldt / der mir zu keiner Zeit
Mehr Lieblich abgethan das schwartze Trawer kleidt.
Der bleichen Sorgen / als auff dato gleich geschehen/
Ich wil / so offt die Stirn sich runtzelt / dich besehen:
Vnd wünsche nichtes mehr für aller Liebligkeit/
Als daß ein solch Gespräch mir allzeit sey bereit.

SONNET. *Avari inviti moriuntur.* *Psal. 49.*

JE mehr man Holtz vnd Stroh/ des Fewers glut zuleget
Je mehr vnd grösser wird der Flammen Macht gespürt:
Je mehr man Goldt vnd Geldt allhier zusammen führt/
Je mehr man haben wil / je mehr zu hauff man träget.
Der Geitz wird allzeit mehr durch Reichthumb angereget/
Ist schon die Armuth weg / so bleibt doch die begierdt:
Vnd wird zum meisten der mit jhrer Gifft berührt
Der an der Erden klebt / den Tugendt nicht beweget.
Es ist ein Wunderthun! man fraget offt vnd viel/
Warumb doch mancher Mensch so vngern sterben wil/
Da Er doch Alt vnd Schwach mehr jhm es wünschen solte?
Der Geitz gemeiniglich der Alten Kranckheit ist/
Drumb/ wann erst recht gefült/ die eysern Heller kist/
Ein jeder/ ob schon Schwach/ dann gerne Leben wolte.

C. C. V.

A MAN OF MANY PARTS

Some thoughts on the career of Christian Brehme: student, soldier, courtier, librarian, burghermaster, poet

ANTHONY J. HARPER

IN THE COURSE OF THE LAST TWO DECADES literary-historical scholarship has moved beyond the clichés of the histories of literature towards a more firmly established picture of the literary situation of the writers who lived and worked in the various towns and regions of the German-speaking lands in the Early Modern period. Much bio- and bibliographical research into the social conditions and the production of literary works has been necessary to start this trend, which still has a long way to go, but the information which has so far been acquired with the help of archivists and librarians has set a course which will no doubt determine the path of research for some decades to come.[1]

The new breadth of information is not merely to be viewed in a Positivist sense as an accumulation of 'facts' for their own sake, although in the case of the literature of the Early Modern period, where so much remains to be found out, that would not be entirely unwelcome. Rather it enables us to see the work of the writers of the time in a broader context and to evaluate their writings against criteria more appropriate to their period. There was a tendency in the twenties and thirties of this century, and also in the immediate post-war period, to evaluate the poets of the time as writers in the *belles-lettres* tradition of a post-Romantic age. But they were not professional writers – Philipp von Zesen was the first to attempt this role, with little economic success – and to try to establish the spirit of their life and work from their collections of poetry alone leads to eccentric verdicts which need revision. For an age of all-rounders, one needs to attempt the all-round view.

The problems and possibilities become clear if we take the example of the Leipzig writer Christian Brehme, who lived the last decades of his life in Dresden. In most histories of literature Brehme is summarily disposed of as a Leipzig student poet, the author of one, or sometimes to the better-initiated,

1 My warmest thanks are due to David Paisey for his help to me. His generous spending of his own hard-pressed time, the depth of his scholarship and the breadth of his knowledge of the production-methods of the book-trade have been an invaluable source of vital assistance through decades of my research.

more than one collection of vulgar, risqué and often amusing poetry.[2] Little else is said about him in histories of literature and the impression is given that Brehme the writer is thereby sufficiently well served. While his poetry collections are certainly the aspect of his work most likely to interest the modern reader, the breadth of his achievement is worthy of more comment than that and the thrust of his work, even within a few years of his life, is more varied than might be thought. In this essay I propose to use Brehme's life and work as an example of the way in which literary and bio-bibliographical research has opened up broader and more balanced evaluations of writers from the Early Modern period. In particular I want to show how minor and major bibliographical discoveries can modify our picture of the life and work of an individual.

Christian Brehme was born on 26 April 1613;[3] his father was master of works in Leipzig and his mother was the daughter of a Berlin physician.[4] It would appear that his childhood, therefore, was spent in a cultured and reasonably affluent household. Although he lost his father in 1623 and two years later his mother also died, his guardians clearly had some means of supporting the boy's education. After a spell of private tuition at home the young Brehme was sent, probably around 1626, to the little town of Roßleben, about 75 kilometres west of Leipzig.

Although the worst ravages of the Thirty Years' War around Leipzig were still to come, the city was already felt to be at risk and Brehme's guardians probably wanted the boy to be out of harm's way in the country. Roßleben lies in a quiet and charming country area, in the valley of the River Unstrut; even nowadays there is the feeling of being off the beaten track, and in the seventeenth century it must have seemed a safe haven. Possibly there were relatives or friends of the family living there.[5] Originally it seemed that he might have stayed in Roßleben the whole time from around 1626 until the beginning of his

2 Cf. Erdmann Neumeister, *De Poetis Germanicis* (Leipzig, 1695), p. 148; Christian Gottlieb Jöcher, *Allgemeines Gelehrten=Lexikon* (Leipzig, 1750), I, p. 1355; G. G. Gervinus, *Handbuch der Geschichte der poetischen National-Literatur der Deutschen* (Leipzig, 1842), pp. 231-2; August Koberstein, *Geschichte der deutschen Nationalliteratur*, II (5th ed., edited by K. Bartsch, Leipzig, 1872), p. 202; Josef Nadler, *Literaturgeschichte der Deutschen Stämme und Landschaften* (Regensburg, 1913), p. 86; Wilhelm Scherer, *Geschichte der deutschen Literatur* (Berlin, 1905), pp. 365-6; Paul Hankamer, *Deutsche Gegenreformation und deutsches Barock. Die deutsche Literatur im Zeitraum des 17. Jahrhunderts* (Stuttgart, 1935), p. 186 and p. 211; Richard Newald, *Die deutsche Literatur vom Späthumanismus zur Empfindsamkeit 1570-1750* (6th ed., München, 1967), pp. 191-93; Willi Flemming, 'Das Jahrhundert des Barock', in H. O. Burger, *Annalen der deutschen Literatur* (Stuttgart, 1971), p. 358.

3 The details for Brehme's life are based on Christophorus Bulaeus, *Leich= und Trost=Predigt ... An ... Hn Christian Brehmen* (Dresden, 1667), and Georg Beutel, 'Bürgermeister Christian Brehme, ein Dichter des 17. Jahrhunderts', *Dresdner Geschichtsblätter*, 3 (1900), 270-84. These are supplemented by my own research (see note 13).

4 Bulaeus, fols F4^{r}-G1^{r}.

5 Bulaeus, fols G1^{v}-G2^{r}; Beutel, pp. 270-1.

first attested period of university study in Wittenberg in the year 1630, but the discovery of an occasional work in the British Library has opened up an interesting new possibility. As a sixteen-year-old he contributed some Latin verse on 20 April 1629 for the Leipzig wedding of Benjamin Schütz, the younger brother of Heinrich Schütz the composer, to which family the Brehmes were related. This is his earliest known work. It could of course have been sent from Roßleben to Leipzig, something which often happened with occasional poetry at the time; but it also might mean that Brehme was back in Leipzig permanently by this time.[6] If that were the case he may have begun his studies at the University of Leipzig informally as a *non iuratus* by that point. Boys could be enrolled as children by their parents on payment of a fee and many began to study before the age of seventeen, taking the oath and becoming a *iuratus* as soon as possible after that age, as the 1620 university statutes required.[7] If that did happen to Brehme, then his friendship with the famous poet Paul Fleming and with his slightly younger Leipzig contemporary Gottfried Finckelthaus would certainly have begun during this period.

At any rate Brehme then went in 1630 to the University of Wittenberg, to study philosophy, politics and law. The university was best known for theological study, but the Professor of Poetry was Augustus Buchner (1591-1661), who corresponded with many famous writers, including Martin Opitz, and taught many more such as Philipp von Zesen, Johann Klaj and David Schirmer. We do not know whether the young Brehme had any personal acquaintance with Buchner at this stage, but he must surely have been taught by this already famous scholar and he later contributed congratulatory poems for Buchner and for Buchner's most famous pupil Zesen.[8] The period of study will have been productive for the young man. By 1632 he was back in his home town of Leipzig, where he defended a disputation in the University in January, as a recent discovery has revealed.[9] He then remained there as a student until some time in 1633.

We thus find Brehme in his cosmopolitan home town at a time when an exciting group of poets and *literati* were present in the University. For the present purpose a brief roll-call of their names will suffice: Adam Olearius, the assessor of the Faculty of Arts, Paul Fleming, the most famous Saxon poet of his day, well versed in Latin and German poetry, Fleming's older Silesian friends such as Martin Christenius who had made him acquainted with the principles of the Opitzian reform (Georg Gloger, his best friend, had died in 1631), Gottfried

6 In *Pharetra Nuptialis* ... (Leipzig, 1629), C1^r (BL pressmark C.107.e.22 (19)). My thanks are due to David Paisey for drawing my attention to this work and the collection of Leipzigiana in which it stands. Cf. David L. Paisey, 'Some occasional aspects of Johann Hermann Schein', *BLJ*, 1 (1975), 171-80. Cf. Bibliography (see note 13), no. 23 (Dünnhaupt 3).

7 Cf. Georg Erler, *Die Jüngere Matrikel der Universität Leipzig 1559-1634* (Leipzig, 1909; reprint Nendeln, 1976), p. 11.

8 Bibliography (see note 13), nos 18 and 37 (Dünnhaupt 21).

9 Bibliography (see note 13), no. 2.

Finckelthaus from Leipzig, Andreas Hartmann and many others.[10] These poets were increasingly able to write German verse of a high standard and most of them were conscious of the musical tradition of Leipzig with its song-books and its personalities such as the famous cantor of the Thomas-Schule, Johann Hermann Schein, Fleming's teacher, who had died in 1630. The friendships between these poets and writers are reflected in the poems they wrote for Leipzig occasions in the 1630s and later. The students often gathered in the Rosenthal, an attractive valley which provided a *locus amoenus* just outside the city walls, nowadays still a small oasis of green in the centre of the big city.[11] The student background has also to a large extent been held to account for the apparently casual miscellany of their later collections, and for the rough and at times coarse tones in the work of Brehme and others like Finckelthaus.

We know little about Brehme's personal circumstances at this time but the next stage of his career was about to begin, and probably in 1633 he left Leipzig to take up arms as a soldier, first in the Saxon regiment of General Schweidnitz, in which he rose to the rank of ensign, and then later in the service of the Elector of Saxony. He may well have left military service by 1636 or 1637 and returned to Leipzig; at any rate he turned to the Court of the Electors of Saxony in Dresden, and he entered the service of the Kurprinz, the future Johann Georg II, arriving in Dresden on 15 September 1639.[12]

During the 1630s therefore Brehme was studying at Wittenberg and Leipzig, operating for about two and a half years as a soldier, and finally settling for existence as a courtier, which demonstrates his all-round ability up to the age of twenty-six. These years are also characterized by much literary activity; in 1636 he published anonymously the first part of his pastoral novel, the *Winter=Tages Schäfferey*, in Leipzig, and in 1637 his first major collection of poetry, the *Lustige Gedichte*. In 1638 a further anonymously published work, discovered by the present author in 1990, *Thorheit vnd Sünde aller Menschen=Kinder*, also appeared in Leipzig.[13] Literary critics have taken the poetry as the characteristic product of this period. The collection concentrates on the song, on pastoral songs and above all on love songs and humorous songs; of the 89 poems there are 35 songs, and these include most of the substantial items. Many of the remaining poems are short epigrams. Certainly the collection represents a substantial achievement and a cross-section of the poetry of Brehme's formative

10 For a fuller account of this period see Johann Martin Lappenberg, *Paul Flemings Deutsche Gedichte*, II (Stuttgart, 1865, reprint Darmstadt, 1965), pp. 860-8; Hermann Palm, 'Paul Fleming und Georg Gloger', in: *Beiträge zur Geschichte der deutschen Literatur des XVI. und XVII. Jahrhunderts* (Breslau, 1877), pp. 103-12; Georg Witkowski, *Geschichte des literarischen Lebens in Leipzig* (Leipzig and Berlin, 1909), pp. 119-33; Anthony J. Harper, *Schriften zur Lyrik Leipzigs 1620-1670* (Stuttgart, 1985), p. 82f.

11 See Paisey, [note 6], pp. 177-8.

12 Bulaeus, fols G2^r-G2^v; Beutel, p. 271.

13 See Gerhard Dünnhaupt, *Personalbibliographien zu den Drucken des Barock*, II (Stuttgart, 1990), pp. 788-90, which is supplemented by my own bibliography, in: Christian Brehme, *Allerhandt Lustige / Trawrige / vnd nach gelegenheit der zeit vorgekommene Gedichte* (= *Lustige Gedichte*), reprint Tübingen, 1994, pp. 54*-87*. *Thorheit vnd Sünde* is no. 4 in the Bibliography.

years. But Brehme himself may well have seen his years as a soldier as just as important, and certainly he would have regarded the crucial event of the decade as his entry into Court life in 1639, joining the educated middle-class bureaucrats from whom the aristocracy recruited their growing army of administrative officials. And from the literary point of view Brehme may have viewed his pastoral novel of 1636 or the ethical work of 1638 as just as significant as his poetry-collection, especially as *Thorheit vnd Sünde* was successfully dedicated to the Elector of Saxony with the request that the latter look favourably on Brehme's work.

The phase of Brehme's life which began in 1639 was to last until his death in 1667, for he remained in Dresden throughout the whole of that period, first under the Elector Johann Georg I, who was steering his state carefully through the troubles of the Thirty Years' War, and then under his successor Johann Georg II, Brehme's patron, who was more favourably inclined to artistic productions at court and under whom Dresden began its development into the magnificent absolutist centre which was to reach its high point under August the Strong in the eighteenth century.

In the year of Brehme's arrival at court the Librarian Johann Nienborg had died; Brehme applied for the post and was installed as Librarian on 26 August 1640, with a salary of one hundred Gulden. It was not an easy position to take on; the seven thousand or so volumes in the three rooms of the library were already in poor condition on his arrival, and repairs to the roof were necessary as it was already raining in in three places.[14] The Elector was not interested in the library, and the casual attitude of the courtiers towards borrowing and returning books made life very difficult. There were still unbound books and the catalogue did not agree with the actual holdings. Brehme tried to improve the situation and complained several times to the Elector but without success. Finally on 1 June 1654 he asked to be relieved of his post, being succeeded by the younger poet David Schirmer, whom he tried to help; but Schirmer experienced the same problems and was equally unsuccessful, in the end, in solving them. Brehme's years as Librarian can thus hardly be counted a success, although that was not his fault; the impression one gets from the tributes to him is that of a conscientious man who did his best at all times.

From the early 1640s Brehme began to play an important part in the civic life of the town as well as at Court, working in various offices for the Town Council, and in 1657 being elected as ruling burghermaster; between 1657 and his death in 1667 he was four times ruling burghermaster and four times deputy burghermaster, a sign of his reliability and good reputation in civic matters.[15]

During this period Brehme was still active as a writer, although the frequency

14 Friedrich Adolf Ebert, *Geschichte und Beschreibung der Königlichen öffentlichen Bibliothek zu Dresden* (Leipzig, 1822) passim; Beutel, pp. 273-74; Erwin Kunath, *David Schirmer als Dichter und Bibliothekar. Ein Beitrag zur Geistesgeschichte Kursachsens im 17. Jahrhundert* (MS dissertation Leipzig, 1922), pp. 98-106.

15 Bulaeus, fols G3^{r}-H1^{r}; Beutel, p. 274.

of his publications decreased as his court and civic duties increased through the forties and fifties. In 1640 he published his manual of letter-writing, *Art vnd Weise Kurtze Brieflein zu schreiben* along with two small collections of spiritual and secular poetry, a work which shows both his practical bent as well as a wider range of poetic themes than had been apparent in the purely secular poetry of the 1637 collection. He probably brought the bulk of this collection with him in manuscript form from Leipzig. There is also a brief publication celebrating the 200th anniversary of printing and the *Beicht vnd CommunionBüchlein*, a devotional work preparing penitents for the sacraments of confession (still current then in the Lutheran Church) and communion. In the latter work, dedicated to the Electress Magdalene Sybille, Brehme reveals his ability to compose a traditional Christian manual, supplemented by verse from the pens of others, and some translated or composed by himself. It was a politic moment for a work dedicated to the Elector's wife; the all-rounder effect is very visible here. We see in the publications of one single year the wide range of Brehme's activity as a writer.

As Court Librarian Brehme was at last in a secure position in which he could contemplate marriage and on 29 November 1641 he married Anna Margarethe Voigt, daughter of the Elector's Secretary Gabriel Voigt, a marriage into a respected bourgeois family which was on the expected level for Brehme and would have strengthened his position in society by binding him closer to the Court. In the eleven years of the marriage three children were born, two girls and a boy, who all died young. Brehme's wife died in September 1652; on 13 September 1653 he re-married, his bride being Ursula Rosine, daughter of the burghermaster Valentin Schäffer, again a marriage calculated to strengthen his position in middle-class society. This marriage remained childless and his wife later survived him as a widow.[16]

In the 1640s Brehme completed his pastoral novel, the first part of which had appeared in 1636; the *Vier Tage einer Newen und Lustigen Schäfferey* appeared anonymously in Dresden in the year 1647. The complex plot conceals autobiographical references to Brehme's life as a student and soldier in the 1630s. Again we find him composing in a new and fashionable form, and it is no accident that it is this work, along with his first collection of poetry, in other words the two works which most closely adhere to recognized literary forms, that have attracted the most attention from modern critics. No major work appeared from his pen until the years 1659–60, when the two-volume *Christliche Unterredungen* appeared in Dresden; Brehme signs himself in the preface as Councillor and Burghermaster of Dresden. An autographed copy exists in the Sächsische Landesbibliothek, the successor to the Elector's library in Dresden. The work consists of twelve moral and ethical conversations, with women and men taking equal roles as conversation-partners. One model is Georg Philipp Harsdörffer's *Frawenzimmer Gesprächspiele*, which had been appearing during

16 Bulaeus, fol. G3^{r}; Beutel, p. 273.

the previous two decades (Brehme contributed a congratulatory poem to the fifth volume), although Brehme's subject matter is less varied than that of Harsdörffer. Again we see the serious side of Brehme's *œuvre* which appears at odds with the rough songs or the fashionable pastoral, but is one of the many aspects of Brehme and one which had been anticipated in *Thorheit vnd Sünde* of 1638. There are more strands than one might expect in his work.

The last years of Brehme's life were marked by illness, but he remained in his offices at Court and in the town until his death. From 1665 on he suffered from gout and gall-stones which made him very weak. He died on 10 September 1667 at the age of fifty-four, being buried on 15 September in the Frauenkirchhof in Dresden.[17]

This brief biographical sketch has been designed to illustrate the wide range of Brehme's works and the way in which various types of work appear at different stages of his life, without our being able to say that any one type is more characteristic of him than any other. We now wish to return to the ethical work *Thorheit vnd Sünde* for examination in itself, of its place in Brehme's work and of its implications for the evaluation of the work of authors of the Early Modern period more generally.

Die Thorheit vnd Sünde aller Menschen=Kinder was published anonymously in Brehme's home-town of Leipzig in 1638.[18] In the dedication to the Elector of Saxony Brehme himself sets it in the context of his work, mentioning the collection of poetry which he had published in Leipzig the previous year and that he had more such items shut up in his writing desk, an allusion to the poems he was about to publish in 1640. In the preface Brehme, who is not noted for theoretical comments about literature, reminds the reader proudly about the inherent possibilities of the German language, and that there is no need to mix German with Latin in order to make a good impression. The simplicity and directness of these opinions can be related to the simple stylistic recommendation in his manual of letter-writing which appeared two years later.[19]

Thorheit vnd Sünde is a devotional work, and also an examination of contemporary society in the light of Christian ethics. There are twenty chapters on the moral weakness of various social groups. The first five involve general reflections on the lot of man. The bulk of the text, from chapter six to chapter twenty, represents a moral critique of the lifestyle of different groups. Then

17 Bulaeus, fols H1^r-H2^r; Beutel, pp. 276-7.

18 The work was discovered by me in the Herzog August Bibliothek, Wolfenbüttel (pressmark 146.6 Ethica(3)) bound together with two works by Jean Puget de la Serre (see note 22 below). Full title: *Die Thorheit vnd Sünde Aller Menschen=Kinder Jn Vernichtung jhres Lebens/ Dem Todte Zu Liebe vnd Lobe/ erzehlt von C.B.L.G.D.B.* (Leipzig: printed by Gregor Ritzsch, published by Heinrich Nerlich, 1638). The anonymous author signs himself at the end of the dedication to the Elector of Saxony as follows: Jhr. Fürstl. Durchl. Ewiger vnd biß in Todt trewer Knecht C.B.L. genandt der Beständige. The initials G.D.B. are thereby explained ('Der Beständige/ der Bestendige' was a pseudonym much used by Brehme). Thus C.B.L. must stand for 'Christian Brehme Lipsiensis/ aus Leipzig'.

19 Reinhard M. G. Nickisch, *Die Stilprinzipien in den deutschen Briefstellern des 17. und 18. Jahrhunderts* (Göttingen, 1969), pp. 59-69.

from section twenty-one to section thirty-one there is a series of prayers for use directly as a devotional aid.

There is very little quotation from the Bible or Church fathers in the work, although it is clear that many of the general reflections in the first five chapters and in the concluding sections for use as prayer must be commonplaces. The most interesting sections are the central ones describing society. The text vacillates between commonplaces on the one hand, and some strong social criticism, and occasional personal remarks on the other hand, the latter very unusual in the Early Modern period where universality is normally sought and achieved.

In the sixth section on the Emperor and the great nobles, for instance, Brehme produces a large number of platitudes, excusing the lords for their sins on the basis of their many worries. In the following section on the clergy, however, after initially covering himself a little, he launches into an astonishingly strong attack on their sychophancy, their oppression of the poor and their lifestyle: 'Wie kommt's/ daß die Laster bey euch so gemein?' (fol. C11^{r}).

Especially interesting is the condemnation of the sins of the soldiery (section eight), where he mentions his own life:

> Erfahren von dieser Sache zureden/ vnd meine selbsteigene Thorheit mit ein zu mischen/ hat mir die gute Zeit meiner dergleichen Dienste gelernet/ vnd vermag ich noch nicht denenselben wieder zu entgehen/ wiewohl ich mich nicht aller jhrer Laster theilhafftig machen wil (fol. C12^{v}).

This is quite a critical comment, exceeded later by two letters in the manual of 1640 which reveal negative aspects of military life and could be based on Brehme's own life.[20]

In the ninth chapter on the nobles Brehme criticizes their treatment of the peasants, then in the next section on court life he makes a remarkable admission; following the topos of the vices of court life (which can hardly be taken as an attack on this particular court, otherwise Brehme would never have written it in 1638 when hoping for a post there) he speaks with astonishing openness about his own intentions:

> Ich gestehe mein theil/ ob mir wohl wissend/ wie ein schlüppfrig Ding es vmb die Fürsten=Gunst ist/ dennoch strebe ich/ Warheit zu sagen/ nach nichts lieber/ als die zu erlangen (fols D4^{v}-D5^{r}).

Although the criticism of court life is a topos, it is very unusual to find next to such a topos a personal and very materialistic remark which gives away so much, and this in the body of a text devoted to supra-personal ethical comments. Brehme carefully ends positively by saying that not all courts are 'so beschaffen' (fols D7^{v}-D8^{r}).

After attacking other groups such as venal judges and scholars with their very worldly wisdom, Brehme speaks in the fifteenth piece about the life of the

20 *Art vnd Weise*, no. 8 and no. 17; cf. Beutel, p. 272.

peasants. In his poetry the peasant is portrayed as an uncouth figure of fun; but here he speaks about the fate of the peasants during the Thirty Years' War as worthy of compassion, showing that in the appropriate context at least he had an awareness of the appalling inequalities and injustices of the time.[21] Most of the peasants want to die, says Brehme, 'Was kein Mensch in dieser Welt thun wil noch mag/ so heissts/ das thu der Bawer' (fol. E4^{v}). There is no adverse criticism, and the section closes with a moving picture of peasants fleeing from their land into the woods to hide from the marauding armies, something which happened frequently during the course of the Thirty Years' War. This fifteenth section in fact marks a transition in the handling of the social groups; from here to number twenty vulnerable groups are treated – peasants, women, widows and orphans and the very old – in their different ways the underprivileged of society, for whom Brehme clearly has much sympathy.

Brehme's volume fits into a tradition of pragmatic ethical works for which there was a market at the time. A number of works by the Frenchman Jean Puget de la Serre, for example, had been published in the years before 1638; Martin Opitz himself had started the trend with his publication of De la Serre's *Les douces pensées de la mort* (1627) as *Die süßen Todesgedancken* (1632), and in Leipzig itself Henning Grosse had printed and/or published a large number of the Frenchman's works in German translation between 1634 and 1638, ranging from ethical works to practical manuals such as his *Secretaire de la Cour*, which appeared in Leipzig in 1638 as *Allerhand kurtze ... Schreiben* and may have contributed to Brehme's manual of letter-writing of 1640. Since we hear that Brehme knew the works of De la Serre, it is a reasonable assumption that some of them provided sources for him.[22]

Thorheit vnd Sünde of 1638 is located in Brehme's work between two poetry collections, that of 1637 and that of 1640, just after the first part of a pastoral novel (1636) and just before a letter-writing manual and a communion manual, both of 1640. Despite its commonplaces it is the nearest thing in Brehme's *œuvre* to social criticism in the modern sense. There are no grounds for assuming that any one of these types of work was any more important than another from the point of view of Brehme and his contemporaries. Even to the present writer, however, its discovery came as something of a surprise, falling in the middle of a period apparently full of 'creative' works. There should, however, be no surprise. In the Early Modern period writing was an activity associated with

21 *Thorheit vnd Sünde*, fols E4^{r} ff. Examples of poems about peasants from the collection of 1637: *Lustige Gedichte*, fols H4^{v} and K4^{v}.

22 Cf. Renate Jürgensen, *Die deutschen Übersetzungen der 'Astrée' des Honoré d'Urfé*, Frühe Neuzeit 2 (Tübingen, 1990), pp. 163-4 and 358. In a publication for Brehme's second wedding there is a mention that Brehme knew De la Serre's pastoral works (Ratsschulbibliothek Zwickau, pressmark 5.3.26(107), fol. A4^{v}). For works of De la Serre published in Leipzig see the Leipzig book-fair catalogues *Catalogus Universalis* (Leipzig, 1634), fol. F2^{v} and *Catalogus Universalis* (Leipzig, 1638), fol. D2^{v}.

literary ambitions and the mark of a civilized person, not a matter of self-expression in a post-Romantic manner. That activity might take a number of different forms. Perhaps we shall discover more such forms surfacing in the work of the writers of the time as more libraries are explored and research charts the shores of the literary land of the Early Modern period.

ARCADIAN SEMIOTICS

The visual poetry of Sigmund von Birken (1626-81)

JEREMY ADLER

THE PASTORAL ROMANCES of the Pegnitz Shepherds occupy a unique place in the history of the genre. By including figured poetry within the sequential text, they for the first time combine the twinned heritage of the Greek pastoral poets, which had hitherto existed in parallel, namely pastoral and visual poetry. The earliest known figured poems in the western tradition stem from Theocritus, the father of pastoral, to whom a 'Syrinx' is attributed. Simias of Rhodes authored an 'Axe', a pair of 'Wings', and an 'Egg'.[1] Although these *technopaignia* contributed to the rise of medieval figured verse after Porphyrius adopted the genre in the age of Constantine, and they were widely circulated in the Renaissance, when they contributed to the revival of the genre, it appears that the Pegnitz Shepherds were actually the first poets to draw the logical consequence of Theocritus's double legacy by combining figured verse with pastoral. The self-consciousness of this gesture is apparent in Sigmund von Birken's *Fortsetzung der Pegnitz-Schäferey* (1645), where, after Strephon has composed his innovative poem in the form of a 'Garland', Floridan composes one in the rare shape of a 'Syrinx', which recalls the celebrated example by Theocritus. The new marriage of pastoral with figured poetry hereby enacted entails a considerable benefit: the sequential prose creates a context by means of which the writer can construct an interpretative framework for his poems, guiding the reader towards ambiguities, puns, and hidden meanings buried in the figures. In effect, the pastorals become semiotic playgrounds, in which signifiers and signified enter an intricate game, dizzyingly multiplying the meanings of each individual sign. The poet acts as master of signs, determining the transformations by which meaning is engendered and communicated. Just as the Pegnitz Shepherds' pastorals function as 'textual institutions', where

1 For studies of visual poetry that put the Pegnitz Shepherds in context, see Jeremy Adler and Ulrich Ernst, *Text als Figur. Visuelle Poesie von der Antike bis zur Moderne* (Wolfenbüttel, 3rd ed., 1989), esp. pp. 154-67; and Dick Higgins, *Pattern Poetry. Guide to an unknown Literature* (Albany, New York, 1987), esp. pp. 71ff.

Befärbet/
Vm närbet /
Du heitrer Blumen-glanß
Du buntlicher runder KRANTZ/
Artlich gewunden / und zartlich gebunden /
1 Ein Dank Ein Zank 3
2 und Himmelsgabe: der Sinnen-haabe. 4
5 Deine Zier doch dafür 7
6 Ist jetzt ringer worden/ blüht ein schöner Orden 8
9 Es wird noch dieses Riß ein starkes Band gewiß 11
10 beginnen anspinnen: 12
13 und dein Blumbewirken weil die Pegnitz-Hirten 15
14. grünt an Ruhm krönt die Blum. 16
Bezüngtes Gerüchte / Trieb unsrer Gedichte /
Mach unsren Verbindungs-Bund
Kund in dem weiten Rund
Mit Stifften /
in Schrifften.

Fig. 1. Sigmund von Birken, 'Kranz', in *Fortsetzung der Pegnitz-Schäferey* (Nuremberg, 1645), p. 33. Wolfenbüttel HAB, LO 397.

poetry 'does the work of history',[2] the interpolated 'Bilder-Reime', which operate at the interface of visual and verbal, assume a pivotal role in legitimating the pastorals. As telescoped emblems, uniting *pictura* and *subscriptio*, they simultaneously embody the natural, the human, and the Divine, and are therefore essential to the procedures by which the poet establishes his authority as an author of Arcardia. They provide unique evidence of his ability to read the Book of Nature.

It was after Harsdörffer and Klaj had included a poem shaped like an 'Anvil' in their *Pegnesisches Schäfergedicht* (1644)[3] that Birken developed the technique of the interpolated visual poem in his *Fortsetzung der Pegnitz-Schäferey* (1645),[4]

2 See the major analysis of the Pegnitz pastorals, Jane O. Newman, *Pastoral Conventions. Poetry, Language, and Thought in Seventeenth Century Nuremberg* (Baltimore and London, 1990), pp. xi and 2. Still essential and including invaluable bibliographical material is Klaus Garber, *Der Locus Amoenus und Der Locus Terribilis. Bild und Funktion der Natur in der deutschen Schäfer- und Landlebendichtung des 17. Jahrhunderts* (Cologne and Vienna, 1974).

3 Georg Philipp Harsdörffer und Johann Klaj, *Pegnesisches Schäfergedicht* (Nuremberg, 1644). BL pressmark 11408.ee.44(2). For a reproduction of the 'Anvil' see Eberhard Mannack (ed.), *Die Pegnitz-Schäfer. Nürnberger Barockdichtung* (Stuttgart, 1968), p. 35.

4 Sigmund von Birken, *Fortsetzung der Pegnitz-Schäferey* (Nuremberg, 1645).

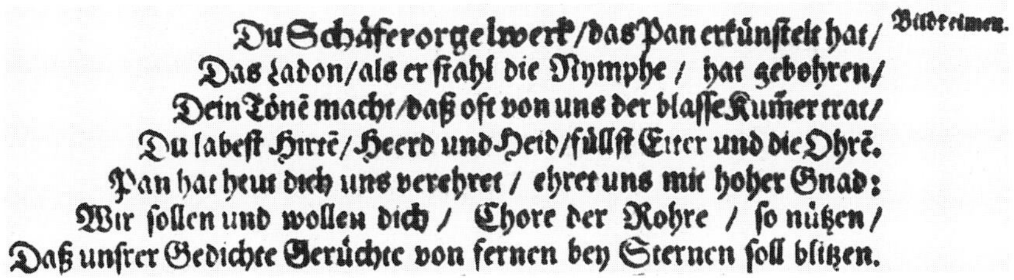

Du Schäferorgelwerk/das Pan erkünstelt hat/ Bildreimen.
Das Ladon/als er stahl die Nymphe / hat gebohren/
Dein Tönē macht/daß oft von uns der blasse Kūmer trat/
Du labest Hirtē/Heerd und Heid/füllst Eiter und die Ohrē.
Pan hat heut dich uns verehret / ehret uns mit hoher Gnad:
Wir sollen und wollen dich / Chore der Rohre / so nützen/
Daß unsrer Gedichte Gerüchte von fernen bey Sternen soll blitzen.

Fig. 2. Sigmund von Birken, 'Pfeiffe', in *Fortsetzung der Pegnitz-Schäferey*, p. 67.

with its 'Garland' (fig. 1) and 'Syrinx' (fig. 2),[5] and this initiated a whole series of pastorals in which several visual poems or 'Bilder-Reime' complement the sequential text. The *technopaignia* are both significantly located within each work, and intertextually, too, by which means Birken constructs an increasingly complex architecture, that also embodies a poetics of the visual poem. Birken's *Guelfis* (1699)[6] contains a 'Heart' (fig. 3), a 'Goblet' (fig. 4), a 'Book' (fig. 5) and a 'Double-Heart' (fig. 6) which were originally published in 1646. His *Pegnesis*[7] reproduces the original *Pegnesisches Schäfergedicht* with a slightly modified 'Anvil' (p. 20), and also includes an innovative poem in the shape of a hat. The technique culminates in *Pegnesis zweyter Teil* (1679),[8] which contains a well-known 'Sceptre' (fig. 7), and a splendid double-page spread comprising a 'Book' (fig. 8), a 'Garland' (fig. 9) and a pair of 'Scales' (fig. 10), first published in 1650, and now exploited to counterpoint the sequence in *Guelfis*. Other poets took their cue from this fecundity. Johann Helwig numerically outdid Birken in *Die Nymphe Noris* (1650), which has no fewer than twelve figured poems, and Johannes Geuder exceeded even that total in *Irene* (1672) with its fourteen figures on the theme of peace. Yet the abundance of Helwig and Geuder notwithstanding, Birken's figures display an artistry that places them among the best that the century produced. The interplay of prose and poetry, and between the poems, is also particularly instructive, as it leads to the handling of visual poetry as a necessary component in a universal sign-system composed of natural objects and language.

The characteristic artifice of Birken's visual poetry is evident from the start, being defined by a play with language not yet attempted in the figured poems of Harsdörffer and Klaj. Whereas their 'Anvil' is a fairly straightforward iconic

5 For reproductions and interpretations of these poems see my 'Pastoral typography: Sigmund von Birken and the "picture rhymes" of Johann Helwig', *Visible Language*, 20 (1986), 121–35, here pp. 122–5; and '*Technopaignia, carmina figurata* and *Bilder-Reime*: seventeenth-century figured poetry in historical perspective', *Comparative Criticism*, 4 (1982), 107–47, here pp. 120, 130–32.

6 Sigmund von Birken, *Guelfis oder NiderSächsischer Lorbeerhayn* (Nuremberg, 1669). BL pressmark 9917.a.11.

7 Sigmund von Birken, *Pegnesis* (Nuremberg, 1673).

8 Sigmund von Birken, *Pegnesis zweyter Teil* (Nuremberg, 1679).

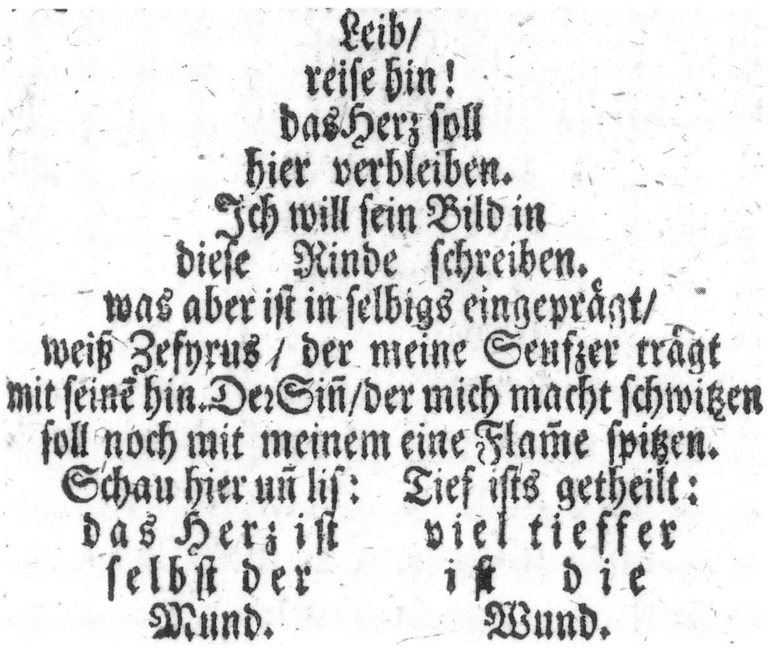
Leib/
reiſe hin!
das Herz ſoll
hier verbleiben.
Ich will ſein Bild in
dieſe Rinde ſchreiben.
was aber iſt in ſelbigs eingeprägt/
weiß Zefyrus / der meine Seufzer trägt
mit ſeinẽ hin. Der Siñ/der mich macht ſchwitzen
ſoll noch mit meinem eine Flam̃e ſpitzen.
Schau hier uñ liſ: Tief iſts getheilt:
das Herz iſt viel tieffer
ſelbſt der iſt die
Mund. Wund.

Fig. 3. Sigmund von Birken, 'Herz', in *Guelfis* (Nuremberg, 1669), p. 23. BL 9917.a.11.

representation of an object, Birken's 'Garland' and 'Syrinx' inaugurate a dazzling textual play on the links and differences between word and object. Although Birken defined visual poetry as 'die Mahlerey der Poeten', his work betrays an interest in the genre that goes beyond the issue of *mimesis*. His practice embodies a more sophisticated understanding of theoretical issues than do his poetics, which have little of interest to say about visual poetry.

The 'Anvil' is almost incidental in *Pegnesis*, but in his *Fortsetzung* Birken places the visual poems into the centre of pastoral. The narrative recounts the founding of the order of the Pegnitz Shepherds, in which a 'Garland' or 'Wreath' and a 'Syrinx' play a crucial role. The garland was the object of friendly strife in a poetic contest between Harsdörffer and Klaj, having been offered as a prize to whichever of the two could produce the best epithalamium. After hanging the garland in a tree (p. 28f.), the pair agree to put the matter to Echo, singing an Echo-poem in the process. As, predictably, the issue remains unresolved, they next unsuccessfully try to separate the flowers of the garland, and then comically try to award it to each other. Finally Strephon (Harsdörffer) hits on a solution. He undoes the garland and takes out two flowers, which symbolize himself and Klajus (Klaj) respectively:

Das übrige fasset er wieder mit dem Faden/ und hengete den entgänzeten Kranz an den nächsten Baum/ ferner also redende: Es soll/ vormahliger der Nymphen Aussag nach/

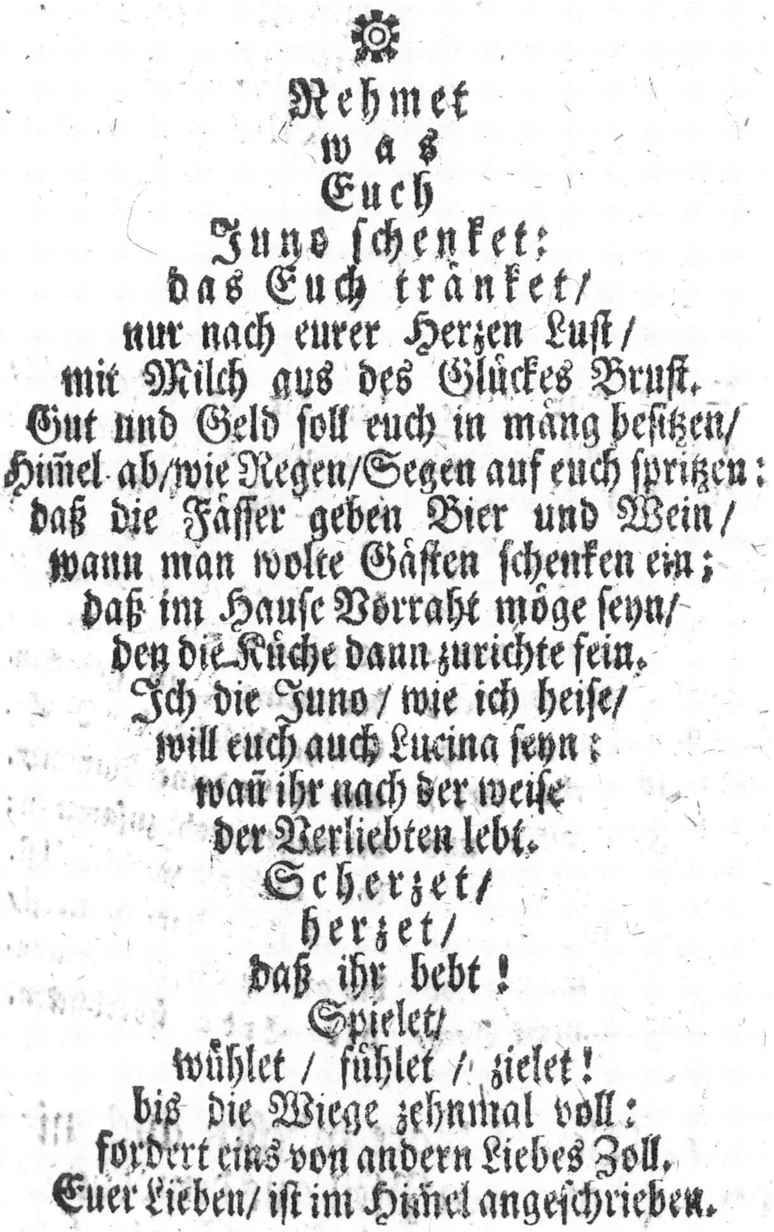

Nehmet
was
Euch
Juno schenket:
das Euch tränket/
nur nach eurer Herzen Lust/
mit Milch aus des Glückes Brust.
Gut und Geld soll euch in mäng besitzen/
Hiñel ab/wie Regen/Segen auf euch spritzen:
daß die Fässer geben Bier und Wein/
wann man wolte Gästen schenken ein;
daß im Hause Vorraht möge seyn/
den die Küche dann zurichte fein.
Ich die Juno/wie ich heise/
will euch auch Lucina seyn:
wañ ihr nach der weise
der Verliebten lebt.
Scherzet/
herzet/
daß ihr bebt!
Spielet/
wühlet/fühlet/zielet!
bis die Wiege zehnmal voll:
fordert eins von andern Liebes Zoll.
Euer Lieben/ist im Hiñel angeschrieben.

Fig. 4. Sigmund von Birken, 'Pocal', in *Guelfis*, p. 35.

36 Bilder-Reimen.

rer Lanze / welche auch ein dichter Demant zu seyn schiene / auf ihre Crystall-Tafel / in der Form eines geöffneten Buches / eingegraben ein Sonnet/ nachfolgenden Innhalts:

Ich Pallas war bisher bey dir in hoher acht/
Fontano! hast du nun die alte Treu gebrochen?
bin ich von Margaris der Schönen abgestochen?
soll ich von meinem Schatz Fontano seyn verlacht?
Ach nein! ich weiß/das noch dein Herz in Liebe wacht/
in Liebe gegen mir: ob schon in dir will pochen
ein neuer Flammentrieb/ der deine Pein gerochen.
Bey Tag behalt ich dich: Sie hat dich bey der Nacht.
Wolan so liebe fort/ und theile deine Flammen.
Wir beyde wollen uns vertragen wohl zusammen:
Wann du mit beyden so den Leibes-wechsel übst.
Und wisse: so du mich nächst ihr beharrlich liebst/
ich will dein Sinnen-Lob bis an die Sterne schicken.
Du solst/von manchē Buch/ die Erde überblicken.

21. Venus ware indessen auch nit faul/ nahme einen Pfeil aus dem Köcher ihres Söhnleins / dessen Spitze sich gleichfalls vornen mit einem Demant endete/ setzte sich auf eine Bank/ die ihr Cupido in eile von Rosen aufgeführet/ und

Fig. 5. Sigmund von Birken, 'Buch' or 'Sonnet', in *Guelfis*, p. 36.

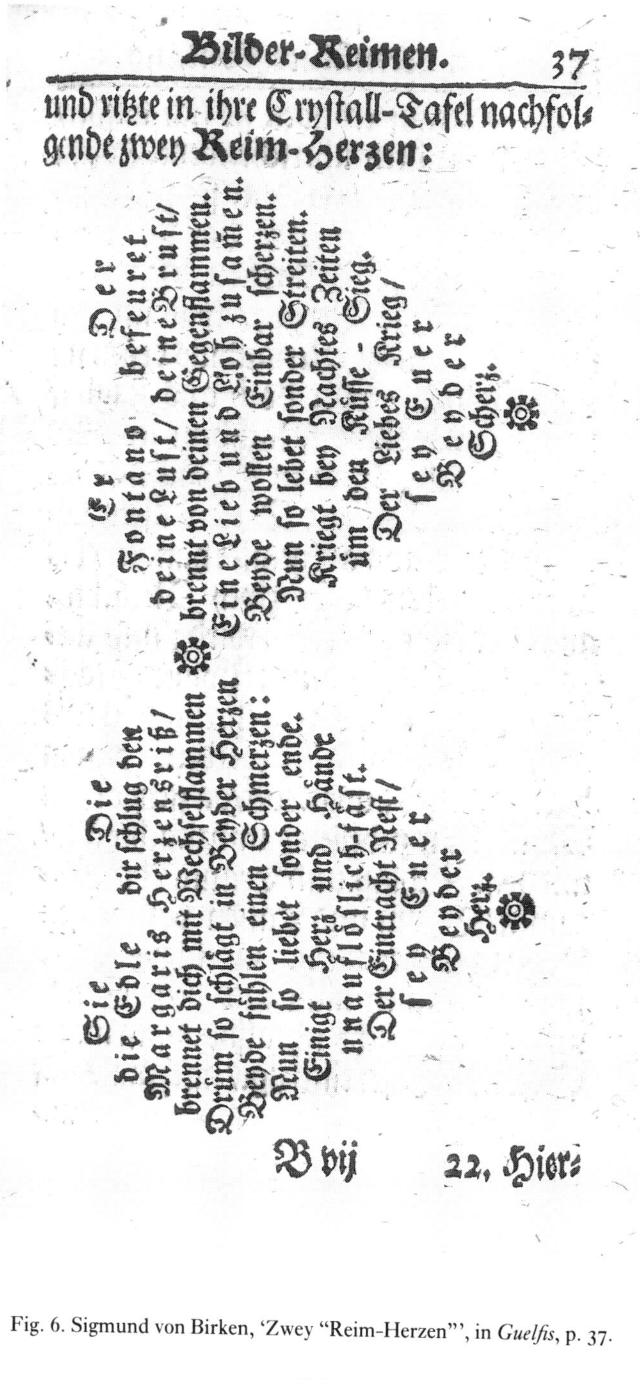

Bilder-Reimen. 37

und ritzte in ihre Crystall-Tafel nachfolgende zwey **Reim-Herzen:**

Sie Die
die Edle dir schlug den
Margaris Herzensriß/
brennet dich mit Wechselflammen
Drüm so schlägt in Beyder Herzen
Beyde fühlen einen Schmerzen:
Nun so liebet sonder ende.
Einigt Herz und Hände
unauflößlich-fäst.
Der Eintracht Nest/
sey Euer
Beyder
Herz.

Er Der
Fontano befeuret
deine Lust/ deine Brust/
brennt von deinen Gegenflammen.
Eine Lieb und Loh zusammen.
Beyde wollen Einbar scherzen.
Nun so lebet sonder Streiten.
Kriegt bey Nachtes Zeiten
um den Küsse-Krieg/
Der Liebes Sieg
sey Euer
Beyder
Scherz.

B vij 22. Hier-

Fig. 6. Sigmund von Birken, 'Zwey "Reim-Herzen"', in *Guelfis*, p. 37.

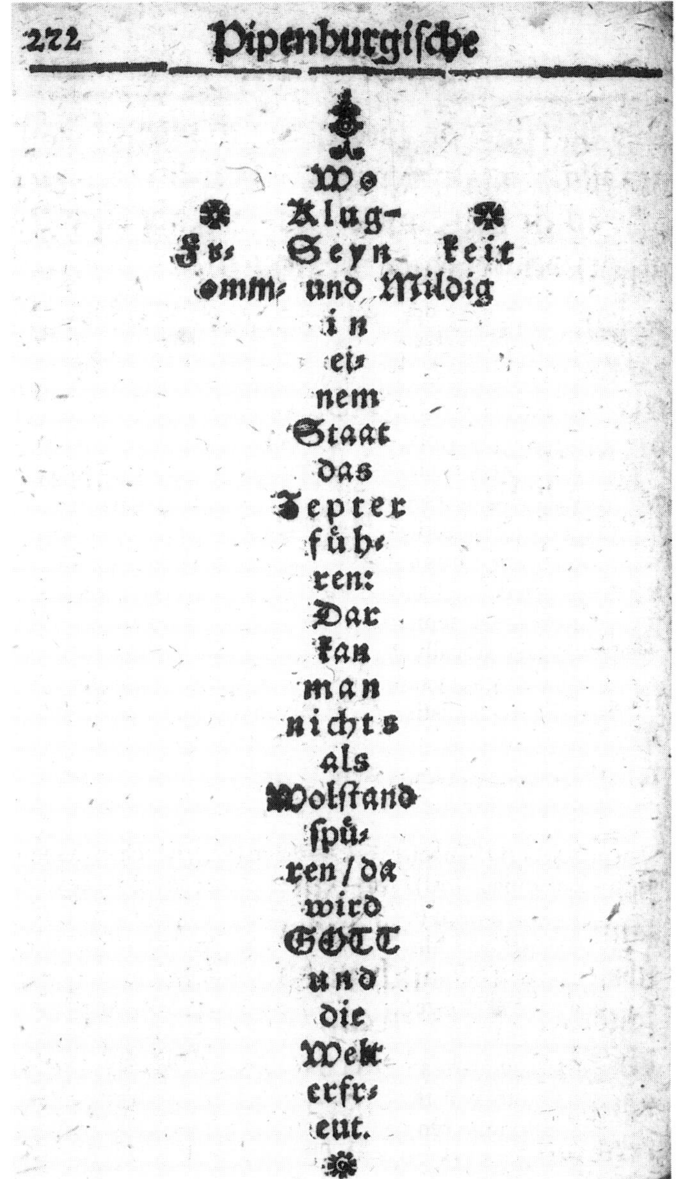

272 Pipenburgiſche

Wo
Klug-
Fr- Seyn keit
omm- und Mildig
in
ei-
nem
Staat
das
Zepter
füh-
ren:
Dar
kan
man
nichts
als
Wolſtand
ſpü-
ren / da
wird
GOTT
und
die
Welt
erfr-
eut.

Fig. 7. Sigmund von Birken, 'Zepter', in *Pegnesis zweyter Teil* (Nuremberg, 1679), p. 224. Wolfenbüttel HAB LO 403.

dieses Kranzes Riß bunt verehren die Hirten. Demnach so behalte Klajus sein Feldkraut/ und ich meine Blum/ und sollen diese Blumen das Bemerke unsrer Hirtengenossenschaft seyn/ welche auch forthin die Gesellschaft der Blumen schäfere heissen mag. (p. 32)

Thus – in a characteristic completion of becoming by onomastics – the Order of Flowers receives its name. In the process, the object becomes a sign ('das Bemerke') laden with meaning. Shortly afterwards, Strephon composes his garland-poem as a further sign of the sign, and cuts it into the branch of the very tree on which the original garland had hung:

und solches schnitte er in eben den Ast/ woran zu vor das Gerüchte den Kranz gehenget. Also ward dieser Schäfergesellschaft (beschlosse Klajus) der Anfang gegeben. (p. 35)

Having once inaugurated the Society with the real garland (p. 32), Klaj reiterates the act by his inscription: only the doubling of the sign in poetry achieves a valid enactment. Crucially, the ceremony concludes by the inscribing of a poem whose shape rehearses the entire procedure. If pastoral is indeed 'synecdoches writ large',[9] then that trope is doubly inscribed into the pastoral *technopaignion*, which represents both the absent garland and the whole Society. But this emblematic method of supplying the world's *pictura* with a *subscriptio* also asks to be understood semiotically.[10] The textual play on the relation between word and image actually depends on the reader apprehending objects and language as belonging to a single system of signs, and can be represented thus, using Charles Peirce's distinction between 'object', 'sign', 'signifier' and 'signified':[11]

$$O^1 \rightarrow PS = Sr \rightarrow Sd \rightarrow O^2 = / \sim O^1$$

The wreath as an object (O^1) inspires a poetic sign (PS), which, as a signifier (Sr) denotes the original object (Sd), but replaces it by being treated as a new, linguistic object in its own right (O^2), both equal to (=) and not equal to ($\sim$) the original (O^1). The relation is almost tautological, except for the fact that the circuit of equivalences is broken ($=/\sim$). The residual but critical *difference* established by the use of language (O^2) occasions the suggestiveness of the visual poem.

By presenting the *writing* of a *technopaignion* in a fictionally real context for the first time in the history of the genre, the Pegnitz Shepherds focus on the moment when the sign undergoes a reversal in character. Here, too, Peirce's

9 Daniel Javitch, *Poetry and Courtliness in the Renaissance* (Princeton, 1978), p. 82.

10 I am here following the pioneering study by John J. White, 'The argument for a semiotic approach to shaped writing: the case of Italian Futurist typography', *Visible Language*, 10 (1976), 53-86.

11 See White, pp. 62ff.

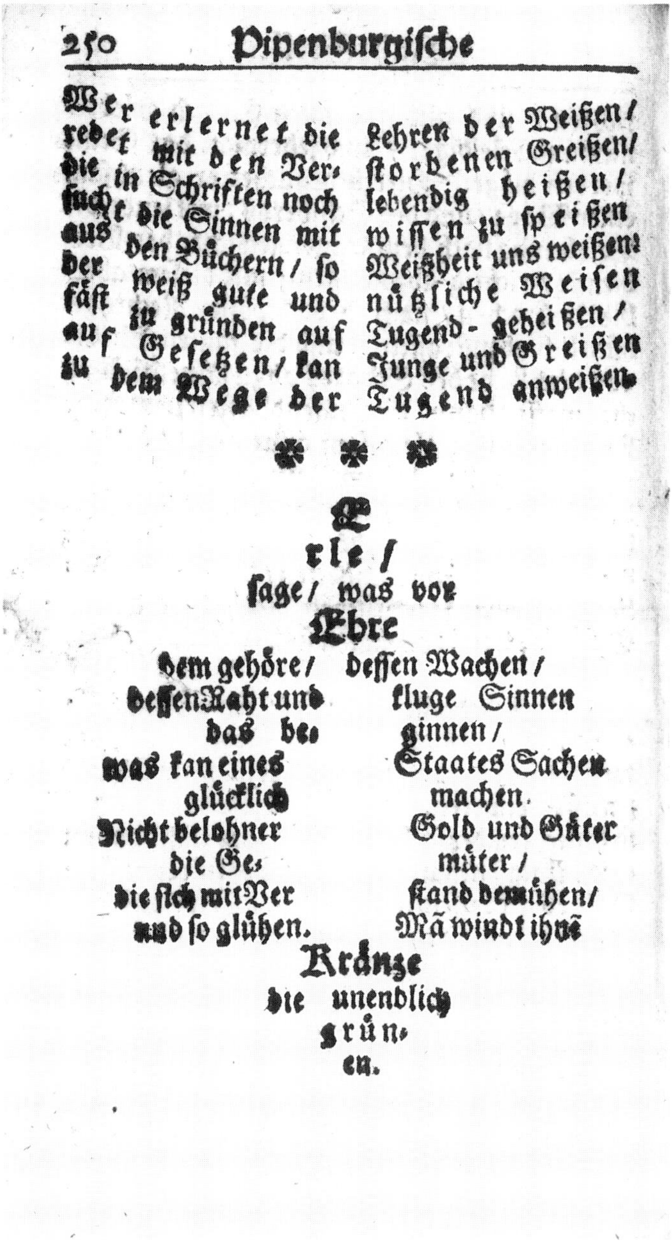

250 Pipenburgische

Wer erlernet die Lehren der Weißen /
redet mit den Ver- storbenen Greißen /
die in Schriften noch lebendig heißen /
sucht die Sinnen mit wissen zu speißen
aus den Büchern / so Weißheit uns weißen:
der weiß gute und nützliche Weisen
fäst zu gründen auf Tugend-geheißen /
auf Gesetzen / kan Junge und Greißen
zu dem Wege der Tugend anweißen.

* * *

E
rle /
sage / was vor
Ehre
dem gehöre / dessen Wachen /
dessenRaht und kluge Sinnen
das be- ginnen /
was kan eines Staates Sachen
glücklich machen.
Nicht belohner Gold und Güter
die Ge- müter /
die sich mitVer stand bemühen /
und so glühen. Mã windt ihnẽ
Kränze
die unendlich
grün-
en.

Fig. 8. Sigmund von Birken, 'Buch', in *Pegnesis zweyter Teil*, p. 250.

Fig. 9. Sigmund von Birken, 'Erle', in *Pegnesis zweyter Teil*, p. 250.

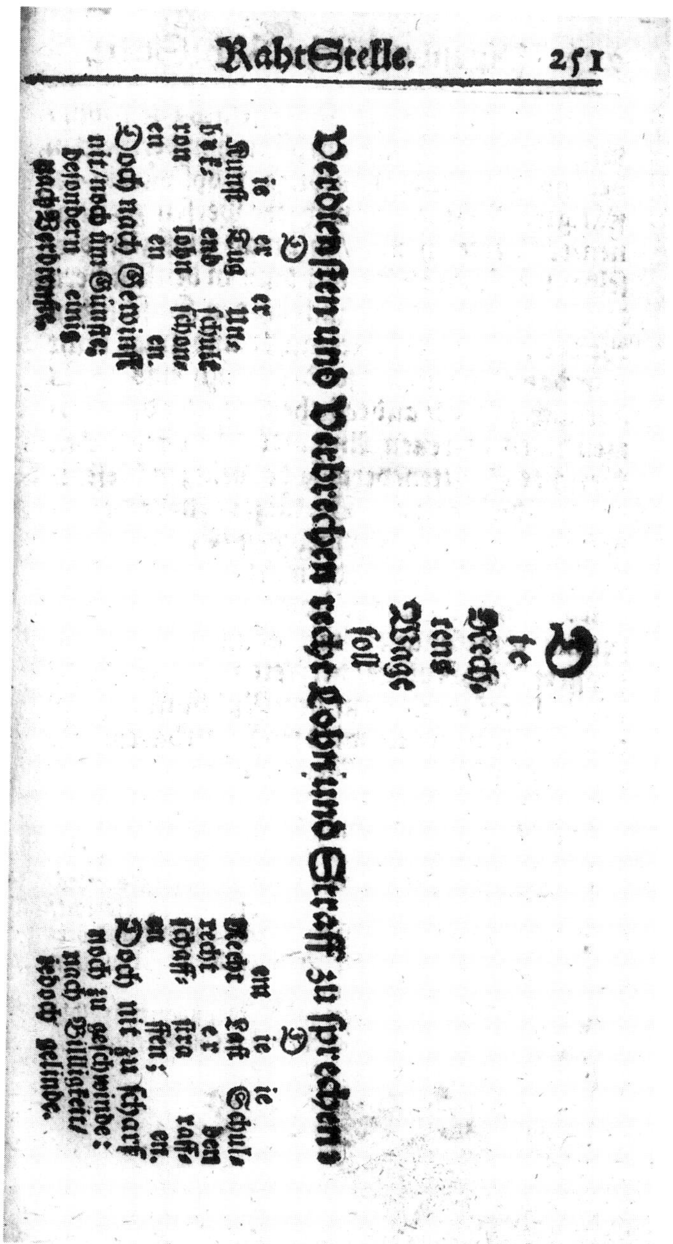

RahtStelle. 251

D
ie
Rech-
tens
Wage
soll

Verdiensten und Verbrechen recht Lohn und Straff zu sprechen:

D
ie er er
Kunst Tug Un-
bek- end schuld
ron lohn schon-
en en en.
Doch nach Gewinst
nit/noch üm Gunste;
besondern einig
nach Verdienste.

D
em ie ie
Recht Last Schul-
recht er den
schaff- stra raff-
en ffen; en.
Doch nit zu scharf
noch zu geschwinde:
nach Billigkeit/
iedoch gelinde.

Fig. 10. Sigmund von Birken, 'Waage', in *Pegnesis zweyter Teil*, p. 251.

vocabulary explains their technique, and specifically that employed by Birken:[12]

There may be a ... relation of reason between the sign and the thing signified; in that case, the sign is an *icon*. Or there may be a direct physical connection; in that case, the sign is an *index*. Or there may be a relation which consists in the fact that the mind associates the sign with its object; in that case, the sign is a *name* (or *symbol*).

These very categories underlie the handling of the 'Garland': in writing the poem of that shape, the linguistic material, as a sign, undergoes a change in character from *symbol* to *icon*; and in being carved in place of the garland, the poem also becomes its *index*. Alternatively, one could say that the poem successively recuperates each of the latter types, to become a triple sign.

A constant tension arises between language and reality, compounded by an ironic awareness that it is a book (the *Fortsetzung*) which authenticates the whole. The tension between word and object is never actually resolved, but rather creates new signs and significations. This can be seen both at the micro- and at the macro-level. Thus, micro-structurally, the 'Garland' is iconic: just as the pattern pretends to imitate a garland, the verse-lines represent individual stalks, for which the printer's ornament (fig. 1) supplies the flowers. Wittily, the floral ornament, normally used decoratively and/or functionally – e.g. as a border – works iconically: the arbitrary sign becomes meaningful. Yet the iconicity of lines, ornament, and shape has its limits. Recognition depends heavily on the verbal signs. One might call this a conventional iconicity – in distinction to a purely symbolic link – which requires the reader to agree with the author, and accept the fiction that his poem looks like a garland. At the same time, the reader is invited to believe that the garland is an icon of a laurel wreath. Reading thus entails entering a conspiracy, accepting the pretence of the author's creation, that language, as a material, can visually represent a physical object. Birken's artifice here entails considerable artful-, not to say archness.

The system is self-perpetuating, and constantly generates new signifiers in order to keep the meaning in play. This, perhaps, provides a key to Birken's own productiveness as an author of pastoral. It can be seen at work in the second visual poem in the *Fortsetzung*, Birken's 'Syrinx' (fig. 3). Again, the poem imitates an object in the text. Two shepherds are led into a grotto where Pyrops takes Pan's original pipe from the wall and addresses them:

[Pyrops ging] zu der Wand/ wo mehrerwähnte des Pans Rohrpfeiffe hienge/ nam dieselbige von dannen/ und nachdem er damit wieder bey den Schäfern angelanget/ fienget er also an gegen ihnen: Wir wissen/ ihr Hirten/ daß ihr unter den löblichen Schäfer-Orden dieses Flusses [= Pegnitz] eure Nahmen gegeben/ so wisset auch ihr/ gestaltsam ihr es zuvor von uns vernommen/ daß der grosse Pan euch und eurer Genossenschaft mehr/ als einiger andern/ geneigt ist: Daher er auch heutiges Tages euch beyden so hohe und grosse Gunst erwiesen/ dergleichen eine keinem vor euch

12 Charles Peirce, *Collected Papers*, I, ed. Charles Hartshorne and Paul Weiss (Cambridge/Mass., 1931), p. 196.

jemahls wiederfahren ist. Nunmehr aber will er auch der gantzen Genossenschaft ein sonderliches Zeichen seiner Gnade darthun/ und lässt derselbigen durch uns verehren gegenwärtige PFEIFFE/ welche ihr eben diese zu seyn wol wisset/ die er das erstemahl aus den Verwandlungsrohr seiner Nymphe geschnitten. So nehmet sie nun (sagete er/ in dem er sie diesen beyden [Schäfern] darreichete) ... (p. 57f.)

Pan pledges to aid the Society, and when the complement of seven shepherds foregathers outside the grotto again, each of them carves a further inscription into the uncomplaining tree, the poems being dedicated to the poet's respective flower (e.g. Alcidor: Veilchen; Montano: Feldnäglein; p. 63f.). After this, Floridan adds the 'Pipe', whose seven reeds recall the seven poets and their flowers (fig.2).

The pipe contains lines of increasing physical length which also grow syllabically from 12 syllables (l. 1) to 18 (l. 7). The rhyme-scheme of ABABACC is enriched by internal rhyme in line 5 ('uns verehret / ehret uns') and by double sets of the same in lines 6 ('Sollen und wollen', 'Chore der Rohre') and 7 ('Gedichte Gerüchte', 'fernen bey Sternen'). Finally, too, the regular alternating rhythm of lines 1-5 makes way for dactyls in lines 6-7. This formal complexity matches a similarly witty sequence of transformations, which can be summarized simply as follows, without taking account of the different types of sign:

$$\left.\begin{array}{l} S^{1} \rightarrow S^{8} \rightarrow S^{15} \rightarrow S^{22} \\ S^{2} \rightarrow S^{9} \rightarrow S^{16} \rightarrow S^{23} \\ S^{3} \rightarrow S^{10} \rightarrow S^{17} \rightarrow S^{24} \\ S^{4} \rightarrow S^{11} \rightarrow S^{18} \rightarrow S^{25} \\ S^{5} \rightarrow S^{12} \rightarrow S^{19} \rightarrow S^{26} \\ S^{6} \rightarrow S^{13} \rightarrow S^{20} \rightarrow S^{27} \\ S^{7} \rightarrow S^{14} \rightarrow S^{21} \rightarrow S^{28} \end{array}\right\} \quad S^{29} \rightarrow S^{30} \rightarrow S^{31} \rightarrow S^{32} \quad \left\{\begin{array}{l} S^{1} \\ S^{2} \\ S^{3} \\ S^{4} \\ S^{5} \\ S^{6} \\ S^{7} \end{array}\right.$$

Key:

S^{1-7}:	Shepherds	S^{29}:	Pipe
S^{8-14}:	Flowers	S^{30}:	Theocritus's Pipe
S^{15-21}:	Lines	S^{31}:	Pipe of Pan
S^{22-28}:	Reeds	S^{32}:	Garland

The individual shepherds (S^{1-7}) represented by the flowers (S^{8-14}) are marked by lines (S^{15-21}) which represent reeds (S^{22-28}) in a pipe (S^{29}) which recalls that written by Theocritus (S^{30}) and that originally created by Pan (S^{31}); finally, when the shepherds elect the pipe as their 'Sinnbild' (p. 67), it comes to equal the original garland (S^{32}) and once again signifies the shepherds (S^{1-7}). By turning the pipe into a second emblem, the shepherds confirm its proven significatory power, and enshrine its value. Once again, Birken's skill lies in unleashing a sequence of significations, by which verbal and visual interact, creating a quasi-tautological structure which actually depends on categorical difference for its success.

'Bilder-Reime' clearly occupy a central place in Birken's Arcadia. As the meeting-ground of the visible and the invisible, they become the poetic space in which the modern shepherd instaurates the Nuremberg Arcady. His ideal is only fully enacted when expressed in this form. Figured poetry therefore serves to legitimate the new Arcadia, and provides a guarantee of meaning; it binds the origin of song (pipe) to the modern myth (garland) and to the timeless accolade (Wreath), thereby assuring the contemporary shepherd a home in the Elysian fields.

Birken's later *technopaignia* extend this self-reflexivity, as is signalled by his inclusion of the book-shaped poems in subsequent collections (figs. 5 and 8). These highly original forms may be understood as synechdoches, which miniaturize the artefacts in which they appear, or as visual metaphors, that turn their primary vehicle into its own tenor: the mere physical carrier of the sign is reproduced as a sign of itself, the printed book joining the pipe of Pan as an emblem of modern pastoral.

Guelfis develops both the handling of the figures and their contextuality. The 'Heart' (fig. 4) enlarges the technical repertory considerably. It introduces a new degree of iconic ambiguity to a genre which, with some notable exceptions, normally consists of unambiguous outlines. But the 'Heart', by reversing the conventional structure of the symbol, and putting the point at the top, enables the pattern to signify a pointed flame (l. 10), the parted lips of a mouth (l. 14a) and a wound (l. 14b): in the act of reading, the verbal text interacts with the visual, enabling successive meanings to unfold:

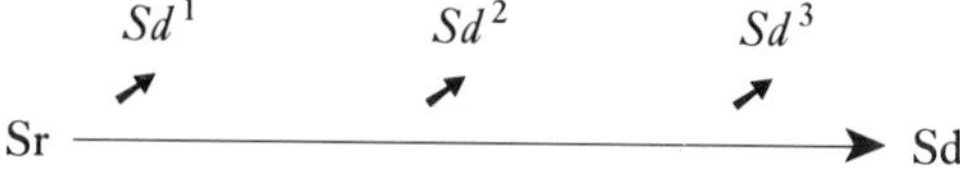

While the icon of the heart remains primary, the three other dependent ones imbue it with suggestive richness. Besides this 'internal' suggestiveness, the pastoral also heightens the contextuality. The poem is to be understood as a kind of literal metaphor, which externalizes Floridan's love of Amaryllis, who is 'inscribed' ('geschrieben', p. 19) on his heart. Then, on the page following the *technopaignion*, an engraving (fig. 11) depicts Filanthon approaching Floridan as he carves the heart into the tree. Thus the pastoral enacts a successive magnification of the original image from the metaphoric and invisible into the iconic and visible, until it finally becomes pictorial; and with each step, the frame is enlarged so that ultimately the poem is reproduced in an image of its pastoral context.

Verbal and numerical ambiguity now become Birken's stock-in-trade. The 'Heart' with three additional significations is echoed by three further figures, that actually comprise a foursome: the 'Goblet' (fig. 4), the 'Book' (fig. 5) and the 'Double-Heart' (fig. 6), whose formal repetition of the first figure concludes the whole sequence. Thus Birken initiates a play on identities based on the numbers one, three and four. Intertextuality increases the mirroring, and heightens the role of the figures. Floridan (Birken) relates that the new visual poems are dedicated to Fontano, i.e. Justus Georg Schottelius who became an early

Fig. 11. Filanthon observes Floridan and his heart-shaped poem to Amaryllis which is inscribed in a tree. In Sigmund von Birken, *Guelfis* (Nuremberg, 1669), facing p. 24.

member of the Pegnitz Shepherds in 1646. To ensure recognition, he adds Schottelius's name as a member of the Fruchtbringende Gesellschaft, i.e. Der Suchende. The poems celebrate his wedding to Margarite Cleve on 8 September 1646. The dedication of no fewer than three figures to Schottelius in *Guelfis* – which celebrates the House of his patron and employer – can perhaps be explained by the importance that his writings possessed for the Shepherds and, not least, for the evolution of their visual poetry. Schottelius included five figured poems in his authoritative *Teutsche Vers- oder Reim-Kunst* in 1641, and these were subsequently reprinted in later editions, and in the *Teutsche HaubtSprache*. His publication of an 'Egg', 'Tower', 'Pyramid', 'Cross' and 'Goblet' lent dignity to a genre which, though listed by Scaliger in his *Poetices*, was passed over in silence by Opitz. So, no doubt, Schottelius contributed to the form's popularity among the Shepherds. Birken's dedication of three figured poems to him may, therefore, be understood as an appropriate act of homage to the great philologist, and – like the echo of Theocritus's pipe in the *Fortsetzung* – assumes a foundational role in *Guelfis*.

The context that Birken creates for his *technopaignia* to Schottelius is among the most remarkable that I have encountered in Baroque figured poetry. It takes the form of a 'poetischer Traum' (p. 48f.), which actually functions as an allegorical poetics. Floridan tells how he fell asleep 'an der Oker/ vielleicht weil etliche Mohnköpfe mein Hauptküssen waren' and dreamt of three enticing ladies, Juno with 'ihr güldnes Krönlein', Pallas with her 'Casquet/ Schild und Lanze', and Venus who was 'halbnackicht'. Lest the reader be in any doubt, Floridan asserts 'mir traumte Poetisch' (p. 34). There follows an allegory of inspiration. Floridan is struck dumb, and rooted to the spot. Juno grants him permission to observe the supernatural act:

> [ich wendete] meine Augen nicht von ihnen/ und verwunderte mich/ daß sie mir also meine Gedanken aus dem Herzen gelesen. Indem naherte sich Juno/ einer Eiche/ und langte von ihrer Zweige einem herab/ drey Täfelein vom reinsten Crystall/ in gold so künst- als köstlich gefasset: von denen sie eines für sich behielte/ die übrige beyde aber ihren Gespielinnen überreichte/ mit diesen Worten sich zu mir kehrend: Hiesige Täfelein/ Schäfer! Sind schon viel Jahre/ zwar unsichtbar/ an diesem Ast gehangen. Du solst aber bald erfahren/ zu was Ende sie jetzund dir sichtbar werden ... (p. 34)

Hereupon, the three goddesses inscribe the figured poems on the crystal tablets using pointed diamonds, Juno drawing the 'Becher' (p. 34f.), Pallas the 'Buch' or 'Sonnet' and Venus the 'Reim-Herzen', choosing her implement 'aus dem Köcher ihres Söhnleins/ dessen Spitze sich gleichfalls vornen mit einem Demant endete' (p. 36). The goddesses hereupon hang 'die drey überschriebene Tafeln an den Baum/ von dem sie solche genommen' (p. 38), whereupon Venus announces:

> Diese Tafeln sollen allhier solang aufgeastet hangen/ bis mit dem Leben dieser zwey Verliebten [= Fontano und Margaris] auch ihre Libe sich enden wird; und alsdann sollen sie/ ihnen zu ewigem Nachruhm/ im Tempel der Ehrengedächtnis verwarlich beygestellet werden. (p. 38)

Floridan's speech is restored:

da fienge mein Munder an zubellen/ und machte also/ mit dem Schlaff und Traum/ die Göttinen/ Baum und Tafeln vor meinen augen verschwinden. Gleichwol hatte ich die Reimen nicht aus dem Sinne verloren/ welche ich alsobald in meine Schreib-Tafel eintruge/ nachmals auf Rinden schriebe und bildete/ und dem edlen Fontano eingehändigte. (p. 38)

Whereas the signs undergo transformation in the *Fortsetzung*, here they remain constant, and attention focuses on the changing vehicles, the mysterious 'Täfelchen' and their various named or implied successors, from the poet's memory to his notepad, an inscription on bark, dedicatory broadsheets for Schottelius, and finally, the book *Guelfis* itself. Ambiguity shrouds the origin of the event. Whereas the action of the goddesses suggests divine inspiration, the fact that Floridan was poetically disposed before his dream (p. 34) offers a psychological dimension, too. The dream models the act of conception in the poet's mind, at which the three chief female deities preside, not to mention Venus's little son, Cupid. Against the standard image of Baroque poetry as predominantly rhetorical, Birken offers a logic of inspiration, a *poetics of the unconscious*. The three *technopaignia* correspond not to physical objects, but emblematically to the goddesses' attributes: the goblet, as a symbol of marriage, is a token of Juno, the Queen of Heaven; the book befits Pallas (as Minerva), patron of the arts; and the double-heart represent Venus, goddess of love and beauty. The meaningful relation between these authors and their texts, confirmed by the shapes, also correlates precisely to the attributes of the addressee, Schottelius, as writer (book), lover (heart), and prospective bridegroom (goblet). Thus Birken creates a stable framework of meanings, grounded in the supernatural, which upholds an absolute correspondence between every element throughout the system of communication, from the identity of the speaker and the constitution of Nature via the character of verbal and visual signs to that of the recipient. Crucially, within this system, it is given to visual poetry to manifest the invisible. In affirming such correspondences, the 'Bilder-Reime' legitimize the project of a divinely ordained Arcadia. And just as these poems enact a bond with the living couple, they also guarantee immortality in Elysium, 'im Tempel der Ehrengedächtnis' (p. 38). The fictional Arcady holds the promise of a real Elysium.

Pegnesis elaborates on the play with meaning, and adds the natural to the supernatural dimension. The second pastoral in the book verbalizes the metaphor which underlies all of Birken's *technopaignia*, the Book of Nature:

[dem Schäfer dünket die Natur] ein stummes Buch zu seyn/ in welches/ der große Baumeister der Welt/ viel tausend Sinnbilder seiner unbeschreiblichen Weisheit und Allmacht gemäl-weis entworfen. In dem Zeitvertreib dieselbe redend zumachen/ suchet er zuweilen seine poetische Wollust/ und schreibet etwan/ an einen Baum/ in dessen Rinden. (p. 63f.)

Although this procedure relates to all poetry, it is particularly applicable to the visual form: the poet deciphers the divine meanings written in Nature, and gives tongue to natural objects. It follows that since the Great Architect has created his meaning 'gemäl-weis', the visual poem offers the most appropriate response to His Creation.

The intricate workings of this method are exhibited in *Floridans mit Lorbeer und Myrtenlaub bekränzter Silvius: samt desselben verliebten Schützen-Geschichte*, included in *Pegnesis*, which contains the 'Doctor-Hut' (fig. 8). The pastoral is dedicated to the theologian Christoph Frank (1642-1704) who became Doctor of Theology (and Professor of Logic) at the new university of Kiel in its foundation year, 1665. It is this event that the hat-poem commemorates. Birken contextualizes it with an allusion to his *Guelfis* 'Bilder-Reime':

> Was ich weiß/ ist dieses/ (erzehlte Rinaldo) daß gleichsam/ unsern wehrten Silvius zu begaben/ die drey Göttinen Juno/ Pallas und Venus/ in Wettstreit begriffen sind. Dann nächstkünftig/ wann der Herbstschein dieses Jahrs in seine Mondsfülle tritt/ werden/ auf dem Cimbrischen Parnaß/ die zwo ersten ihn mit der vördersten *Weißheit-Krone* zieren und beehren/ die dritte aber ihm die edelschöne/ *Catharsis* in die Arme legen/ und also sein Glück vollkommen machen. (p. 390)

The three goddesses now celebrate a double event: Frank's graduation, and his wedding to Catherina Claus. To commemorate the occasion, his friends inscribe sundry poems into the 'Erlenthal', 'weil er diesen Ort geliebet/ und vielen Rinden dieser Eichen und Erlen seine Gedanken zu verwahren gegeben' (p. 391). Among these carvings, various playful forms, such as puzzles, find their way onto the hapless trees. The hat is inscribed onto a piece of bark which is then hung onto the branch of an oak. The simple form takes on a complex of emblematic meanings: apart from suggesting a *hat*, it also physically represents the double-summit of *Parnassus* (l. 1 and 8), which, in the context, takes on other significations: besides the conventional one, as a metaphor of *poetry*, it also represents *learning* and *knowledge* (l. 4). Once again, then, a figured poem occupies a pivotal place in the hermeneutic cycle, depicting in Arcady the visual language of nature and its spiritual signification.

The climax in Birken's handling of visual poems as *natural* – as opposed to supernatural – signs occurs in the *Pipenburgische Rahtstelle* of 1650 included in *Pegnesis zweyter Teil*, where the four 'Bilder-Reime' present an earthly counterpart to the metaphysical quartet in *Guelfis*. Here, too, one encounters the same numerical ambiguity as in the poems for Schottelius. The dedicatee, Joachim Pipenburg, was elected to the Lüneburg Senate in 1649/50, and also became Gerichtspräsident there. It is these events which the visual poems celebrate. The first, a 'Zepter' (fig. 9), is exquisite. It is, apparently, inscribed on one of several 'zusammengerollte Zettel' (p. 223) that fall from the sky onto the unsuspecting Birken whilst he is happily reading the flowers in the Book of Nature ('Das Mahlwerk der Natur', p. 218): the conceit wittily encapsulates a moment of inspiration. The sceptre, representing the three 'vornehmsten Tugenden eines Staatsregierers' (p. 223), numerically anticipates the three following visual poems, and in so doing takes on two additional emblematic meanings: in the context of the 'Wage' of justice (p. 249), the sceptre represents a 'Schwerd' (p. 249), and via this multiplying of meaning also becomes a *cross*, as suggested by the text itself ('Da wird GOTT und die Welt erfreut', l. 20ff.). This visual ambiguity echoes the charming game with the interpreting eye of the reader prompted by the layout: the interplay of short lines, ruptured words, rhyme, and rhythm initiate a physical play in the mind of the reader, and communicate a sense of confident good cheer, reflecting the very virtues enunciated in the text.

The last three figured poems are presented as part of a conscious intellectual process, whereby Floridan/Birken reads the Book of Nature, and deciphers its code. Looking at a tree under which he was sitting:

> ... Ich befande denselben eine Büche zu seyn/ gegen Welchem über eine dick-laubichte Linde/ nahe bey dieser aber eine hochgegipfelte Erle ... also daß diese drey Bäume/ im dreygeecke/ durch zusammenfügung ihrer grünen Arme/ eine schönes Laub-gezelt über mich hergeschlossen hatten. Als ich etwas nachgedacht/ fiele mir ein/ wie daß die Namen der dreyen Zugehörnisse eines Ratsherrn also in Verwandtschaft stünden. (p. 247)

Floridan discovers himself to be in a triangular temple, and in reflecting on its structure, develops a *logic of poetic composition* that provides a rational counterpart to the poetics of the unconscious in *Guelfis*. Everything now depends on the action of his intellect ('als ich etwas nachgedacht'), by means of which he uncovers the emblematic links between the names of the three trees and the virtues of a *Ratsherr*. These emblematic meanings then become the basis for the three visual poems. His interpretations depend on puns, which insinuate the identification of human and natural language. Thus the 'Buche' represents 'Bücher' (fig. 10) which a wise lawyer must read, the 'Erle' the 'Ehre' which he will acquire, signified by the 'Kranz' (fig. 11), and the 'Linde' the 'gelinde Billigkeit' of the just man, signalled by the 'Wage' (fig. 12). By its linking of natural objects, via punning emblematics, to 'Bilder-Reime', *Guelfis* represents the apotheosis of Birken's visual poetry; the poems establish a fictional world which ensnares the reader in a labyrinth of signs, inviting him to interpret everything as expressing a perfect, because utterly meaningful, and therefore Arcadian semiotics.

THE PUBLICATION OF A SEVENTEENTH-CENTURY BESTSELLER

Sigmund von Birken's 'Der Donau-Strand' (1664)

JOHN ROGER PAAS

RECENT TRENDS IN LITERARY STUDIES have led to a decreased emphasis on purely aesthetic considerations and a concomitant growing awareness of the importance of other aspects of literary works. As a consequence of these broadening interests, the works of poets long relegated to the periphery of mainline literary scholarship have come to be appreciated for the new insights they can yield about literary life at the time of their production. One such work is Sigmund von Birken's *Der Donau-Strand*. Bibliographers have traditionally included this historical-topographical work in Birken's *oeuvre*, yet only recently with the discovery of the map that was meant to accompany it has the real nature of this work's original form come to light. Moreover, some of Birken's autobiographical material provides us with a special opportunity to reconstruct the publication of the work, and all this information helps us to understand the process by which a popular baroque work came to appear.

The impetus for Birken's work was the renewed Turkish threat to the empire in the early 1660s. Europe in the seventeenth century was the scene of frequent and violent armed conflict as emerging nation states fought to gain either independence or hegemony, and in the Holy Roman Empire the second half of the century was marked by virtually constant political and military conflict along the middle and lower Danube. Although the Turks had not posed a threat to the empire since the first decade of the seventeenth century this situation changed dramatically as new leaders came to power in mid-century. With the accession of Köprülü Ahmed Paşa (1635-1676) as grand vizier in November of 1661 the Porte adopted an aggressive policy toward the empire. The Turks were once again intent on the destruction of Christianity in the West, and in the summer of 1663 the grand vizier advanced into Hungary and Moravia with a force of 100,000 men. Emperor Leopold I, who had an army of merely 28,000 men, was forced to turn to the princes in the empire and to rulers throughout Europe for support. Not until February of the next year, however, did the imperial diet vote to raise an army to fight the Turks, and by that time a large portion of Hungary was already under Turkish occupation.

Two weeks after the imperial army was able to capture the fortress of Nitra

(Neutra) from the Turks in early May, the grand vizier crossed the Drava with his army and advanced toward Austria. In June, Raimondo, conte di Montecucculi (1609-1680), took over command of the imperial forces in Hungary and went on the offensive. He proved his abilities on the field in July, but it was his brilliant victory over the Turks at Szentgotthard on the Austro-Hungarian border on 1 August that put an end to the immediate danger from the east. With a united force of only 25,000 men he was able to defeat a Turkish force five times that size. Nine days later peace between the empire and the Porte was signed at Vasvár.

During these months of fear and hatred there was naturally a keen interest in German-speaking areas in news and commentary about the Turks and about the Christian campaign against them. Hundreds of works appeared in print, and one of the centers of this production was Nuremberg.[1] Publishers there were quick to realize the potential for profitable sales, and they engaged authors in the city to write works of varying content and length that were then sold in the city and throughout the empire. One of the authors whose work helped to satisfy the public's appetite for information about the Turks in the early 1660s was Sigmund von Birken (1626-1681). His historical-topographical description of the Danube, *Der Donau-Strand*, dealt so successfully with the area where the confrontation between the Turks and the Christians was taking place that this book proved to be one of the bestsellers of the seventeenth century (fig. 1).[2] First published in 1664 in an edition of over two thousand copies, it was updated and reprinted several times into the first quarter of the eighteenth century.[3] Few works in any European country in the latter half of the seventeenth century enjoyed such popularity.

It is not surprising that Birken was capable of producing such a work. For almost three decades in the second half of the century he stood at the centre of the literary scene in Nuremberg, where he acted as an editor and literary manager for others at the same time that he orchestrated the publication of his own works. As a consequence of his wide-ranging literary interests and activities, he maintained contacts with nobles, patricians, and commoners throughout the empire. Although he was admired by his contemporaries for his poetic talent and his elevated literary style, what makes *Der Donau-Strand* especially interesting today is its publication history. Because Birken took more

1 The most complete listing of such works is to be found in Alexander Apponyi, *Hungarica. Ungarn betreffende im Auslande gedruckte Bücher und Flugschriften*, II (Munich, 1903). See also Karl-Heinz Jügelt, *Hungarica-Auswahl-Katalog der Universitätsbibliothek Jena* (Weimar, 1961).

2 *Der | Donau-Strand | mit | Allen seinen Ein- und Zuflüssen/ | angelegenen Königreichen/ Provinzen/ | Herrschaften und Städten/ auch derer- | selben Alten und Neuen Nahmen/ vom | Ursprung bis zum Ausflusse: | in | Dreyfacher LandMappe | vorgestellet* (Nuremberg: Jacob von Sandrart, 1664). This work, which has fewer than 200 pages of text and is embellished with 33 views of cities and fortresses along the Danube, is duodecimo in size.

3 For a complete listing of the various editions, see Gerhard Dünnhaupt, *Personalbibliographien zu den Drucken des Barock*, I (Stuttgart, 1990), pp. 619-23.

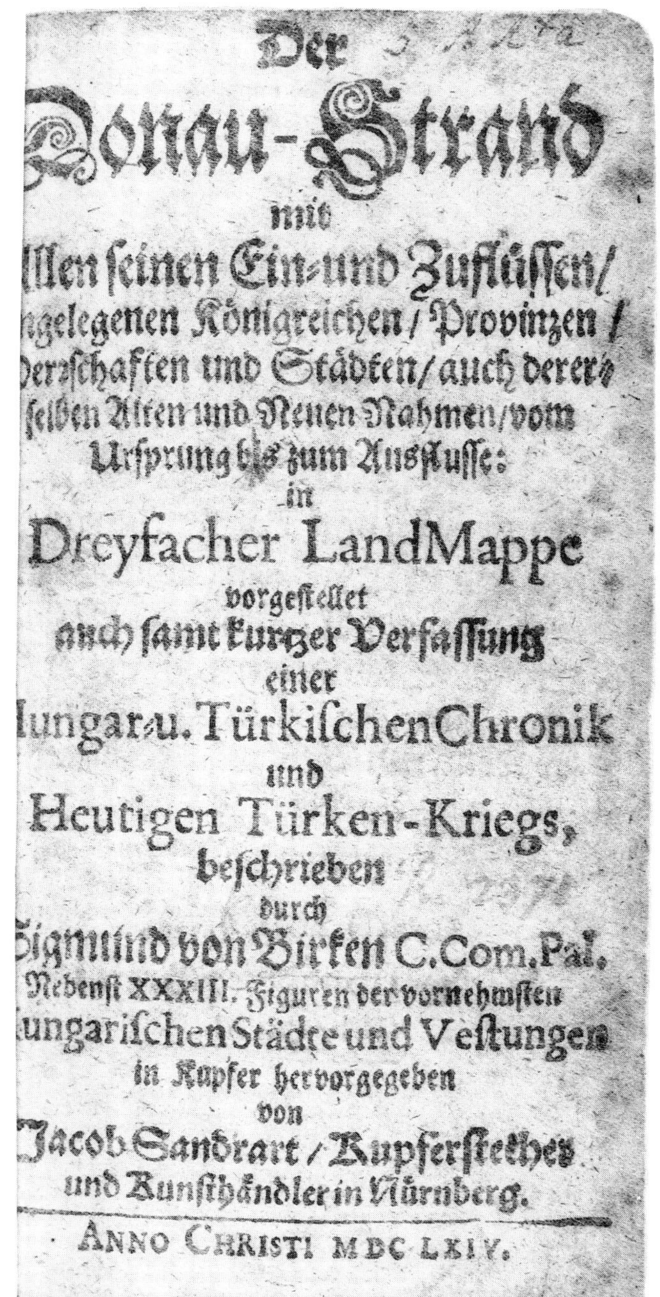

Der
Donau-Strand
mit
llen seinen Ein- und Zuflüssen/
gelegenen Königreichen/ Provinzen/
errschaften und Städten/ auch dererselben Alten und Neuen Nahmen/ vom
Ursprung bis zum Ausflusse:
in
Dreyfacher LandMappe
vorgestellet
auch samt kurtzer Verfassung
einer
ungar- u. Türkischen Chronik
und
Heutigen Türken-Kriegs,
beschrieben
durch
igmund von Birken C.Com.Pal.
Nebenst XXXIII. Figuren der vornehmsten
ungarischen Städte und Vestungen
in Kupfer hervorgegeben
von
Jacob Sandrart/ Kupferstecher
und Kunsthändler in Nürnberg.
ANNO CHRISTI MDCLXIV.

Fig. 1. Title-page to Sigmund von Birken, *Der Donau-Strand* (1664). BL pressmark 573.a.17.

care than any of his contemporaries in documenting his daily activities, we are able with the help of his diary entries for 1664 to follow closely his work on *Der Donau-Strand*.[4] This gives us a special opportunity to follow the process of the creation of a popular work in the early modern period.

As Birken approached this project, his attitude toward the Turks was the one commmonly held by his Christian contemporaries. He interpreted the invasion as God's punishing the Christians for their obdurate sinfulness,[5] and his fear that the invaders would advance at least as far as his homeland in Franconia was real indeed.[6] In writing *Der Donau-Strand* Birken acted primarily as a chronicler and compiler, whose job it was to bring together disparate material about the Danube from a number of sources and to weave it all together into an accurate and readable description. As he himself stated in his introduction: 'Gegenwärtiger Donau-Strand ist/ mit sonderbarem Fleiß/ aus Historischen und Geographischen Schrifften zusammen getragen worden' (fol.)(3^{v}). Behind the façade of scholarly objectivity, however, was the age-old Christian hatred of the Turks. When referring directly to the Turks Birken did not mince words. For him they were, for example, the 'tyrannizing arch-enemy' that had placed a 'barbaric yoke' on the Danube (fol.)(2^{v}) or the 'Mohammedan antichrist' whom he prayed God would obliterate from the face of the earth (p. 177).

The publisher of Birken's book was Jacob von Sandrart, the leading graphic artist in Nuremberg.[7] He is known primarily for his hundreds of printed portraits, but as a publisher of prints and books he was also an able entrepreneur with a solid knowledge of the competitive market. The poet with whom he worked most closely in Nuremberg was Sigmund von Birken, and it was thus natural for the two men to collaborate on this illustrated work. It is unclear when Sandrart first approached Birken about writing *Der Donau-Strand*, but there can be no doubt when work on this project began, for on 18 January 1664 Birken noted in his diary: 'Am Donaustrand Zuschreiben angefangen 1½ pagg[inas]' (*Tagebücher*, p. 94). He continued at this pace for the next few days, but then commitments to other projects forced him to put this work aside. Birken was one of the first German poets to live by his pen, and consequently he was often engaged in several projects at the same time. In addition to composing a number of occasional poems on the same day, Birken was accepting work from the Endters and Felseckers. On 1 February he noted, for example: 'Endter u. Filsecker mir einige TürkenW[erke] einzurichten gebracht; daran Abends

4 Joachim Kröll (ed.), *Die Tagebücher des Sigmund von Birken*, I, Veröffentlichungen der Gesellschaft für Fränkische Geschichte, Series VIII, 5 (Würzburg, 1971). This work is cited below as *Tagebücher*.

5 On 24 February Birken devoted much more space than normal in his diary to summarizing the content of Johann Michael Dilherr's sermon, in which this idea was elaborated upon (*Tagebücher*, p. 106).

6 Joachim Kröll, 'Der Dichter Sigmund von Birken in seinen Beziehungen zu Crueßen und Bayreuth', *Archiv für Geschichte von Oberfranken*, 47 (1967), 262.

7 Sandrart's print *oeuvre* is catalogued in *Hollstein's German Engravings, Etchings and Woodcuts 1400-1700*, vols 38 and 39, ed. John Roger Paas (Roosendaal, 1994).

etwas gethan' (*Tagebücher*, p. 98). One of these works was an account of the Turkish campaign for Michael Endter, which Birken began to write on 4 February and finished the next month.[8] Another was the revision of Simon Wolder's written attack against the Turks (1558), which Birken began to edit on 6 February.[9] In addition to working on these and other small projects he was also engaged in writing articles for newspapers and texts for broadsheets.

At the end of February Birken corrected some of his text for *Der Donau-Strand*,[10] but it was not until the end of April that he began to write once again: 'An dem Donaustr[and] fortgemacht' (*Tagebücher*, p. 118). Yet even then, he continued to have to divide his time between various projects. The most time-consuming of these was his work on *Spiegel der Ehren*, a panegyric history of the House of Habsburg that he began in 1660 and which did not finally appear in print until 1668.[11] It was not until mid-May that Birken was able once again to turn his attention to *Der Donau-Strand* on a sustained basis. By this time he had completed only about one eighth of the book, or the sections on the origins of the Danube (pp. 1-18) and on the Danube in Swabia (pp. 18-25); on 23 May he noted that he was beginning to write the section on the Danube in Austria (pp. 25-48).[12] On the next several days he worked intensively on *Der Donau-Strand*,[13] but after 4 June he interrupted his work once again as he directed his immediate attention toward several other jobs. He was nonetheless making such progress that a date for publication may already have been set, for on 30 June Johann Gebhard, a printer in Bayreuth with whom Birken had long-standing connections, was given an advance payment of 24 florins: 'Gebhardo 24 F[lorin] Zur Angabe auf Künftigen Druck Donaustr[ands]' (*Tagebücher*, p. 127). In early July Birken resumed his work, and on 9 July he made the final corrections on the double-page map that serves as the frontispiece to the book (fig. 2).[14]

In late July Birken began to revise early sections of the book, even though he did not yet have a complete final draft.[15] Although he continued to work

8 He received payment for his work on 16 March (*Tagebücher*, p. 111). This work, which is frequently referred to by Birken as 'der TürkenZug', is a separate work and not, as Kröll assumes, part of *Der Donau-Strand*. One must be especially careful using Kröll's references to specific works by Birken as well as by others, for these references are frequently inaccurate.

9 *Türckischer Untergang* ([Nuremberg: Wolfgang Eberhard Felsecker], 1664). *Tagebücher*, p. 100.

10 'Am Donaustrand 1½ Bogen gemundirt' (*Tagebücher*, p. 107). The verb 'mundiren', which Birken frequently used in connection with his editorial work, means 'to correct'.

11 *Spiegel der Ehren | des | Hochlöblichsten Kayser- und Königlichen | Erzhauses Oesterreich | oder | Ausführliche Geschicht-Schrift | von | Desselben* (Nuremberg: Michael Endter and Johann Friedrich Endter, 1668). BL pressmark 136.c.5.

12 'Am Donaustrand Oesterreich Zu beschreiben angefangen' (*Tagebücher*, p. 122).

13 24 May: 'An der Donau-Beschr[eibung] fortgeschr[ieben]' (*Tagebücher*, p. 122); 25 May: 'An der Donaubeschr[eibung] fortgeschr[ieben]' (p. 122); 26 May: 'Continuatio der Donaubeschr[eibung]' (p. 122); 27 May: 'Eadem Continuatio' (p. 122); 4 June: 'Am Donaustr[and] beschrieben' (p. 124).

14 'Das Titl-Mäpplein Zum Donau-Strand, Zu recht gemacht' (*Tagebücher*, p. 128).

15 22 July: 'Am Donaustr[and] mundirt' (*Tagebücher*, p. 130); 27 July: 'Am DonauStr[and] mundirt' (p. 130); 1 August: 'Am DonauStr[and] geschr[ieben] u. mundirt' (p. 130); 2 August: 'Wiederüm daran gearb[eitet] (p. 130); 10 August: 'Am DonauStr[and] geschrieben' (p. 131).

Fig. 2. Frontispiece to Sigmund von Birken, *Der Donau-Strand* (1664). Etching (10.5 × 11.5 cm) by Jacob von Sandrart. BL pressmark: 573.a.17.

concurrently on a number of projects, he changed his rhythm of work. Instead of splitting his time between several different projects on the same day, as was his normal mode of working, in this stage of his work he appears to have set aside full days to devote himself totally to his work on *Der Donau-Strand*. Birken was so intensively engaged now because Gebhard had begun to set his text in type, and on 11 August Birken corrected the first printed sheet: 'Des DonauStrands 1. Bogen corrig[iert]'.[16] He devoted 14 August to further writing, and three days later he completed the description of the Danube, that is, down to page 120 in the book: 'DonauStr[and] Beschreibung absolviert' (*Tagebücher*, p. 131).

The lengthy description of the course of the Danube is followed by two other sections. The first, entitled 'Kurz-verfasste Hungar- und Türkische Chronik'

16 *Tagebücher*, p. 131. Birken noted on the same day that he wrote a letter to Gebhard, which presumably addressed issues in connection with *Der Donau-Strand*.

(pp. 121–78), is an historical description of the Turkish and Hungarian leaders. The second, entitled 'Türken Kriegs-Verlauf' (pp. 178–84), is an account of the military activities in Hungary from July 1662 to 8 September 1664. Birken began work on these sections on 21 August and had them virtually complete by 7 September.[17] Gebhard was busy setting all of this in type, and the first printed sheet of the Hungarian and Turkish chronicle was probably enclosed in a letter that Birken received from Gebhard on 1 September. That same day Birken corrected the sheet and returned it to Gebhard: 'Schreiben an Gebh[ard] samt 1 Bogen der Chr[onik]' (*Tagebücher*, p. 132). On 17 September he began to compile the index, and on the same day he wrote the titles, captions, and legends for the more than thirty illustrations.[18] His work on the text portion of the book was concluded on 20 September, but he continued to work on the index to the book: 'Den Beschl[uß] des Donauw[erkes] hinzugethan. Am Indice geschrieben' (*Tagebücher*, p. 135). The following day he wrote the dedication and the preface.[19]

Nine months after he had started to write this book, he finished the text. He was, however, not yet finished with the project, for an integral part of this work is a large map of the Danube entitled '*DANUBIUS | FLUVIORUM EUROPÆ PRINCEPS: | cum omnibus | accessoriis Fluminibus, | et quæ alluit | Regnis, Provinciis, Dynastiis, Urbibus: | eorumq[ue] Nominibus | priscis ac recentioribus: | A FONTE AD OSTIA*' (fig. 3).[20] Birken and Sandrart intended readers to use this map and the book together as they studied the course of the Danube from its source near Donaueschingen to its end in the Black Sea, and this connection is clearly stated on the printed title-page to the book, where the words 'Dreyfacher LandMappe' are made to stand out by the use of roman type (see fig. 1). Over the years, however, the map and the book have found their ways into different types of collections because of the difference in their sizes.

17 21 August: 'An der Hung[arischen] Chronik Auszug angefangen und fortgefahren' (*Tagebücher*, pp. 131f.); 27 August: 'Am Hung[arischen] Chronikl fortgeschr[ieben]' (p. 132); 29 August: 'An H[ungarischer] Chron[ik] fortgeschr[ieben]' (p. 132); 30 August: 'An Hung[arischer] Chronik fortgeschr[ieben]' (p. 132); 31 August: 'An Hung[arischer] Chronik fortgeschr[ieben]' (p. 132).

18 *Tagebücher*, p. 134. Birken mentions only three copperplates, which would indicate that several illustrations were etched on the same plate. These were then cut apart and the individual illustrations placed between the appropriate pages in the book.

19 'Die dedication u. praefation Zum Danubio verfärtigt' (*Tagebücher*, p. 135). Birken dedicated this work to Count Gottlieb von Windischgrätz, an official at the court in Vienna who had helped to further Birken's career ever since the early 1650s.

20 Sandrart used three separate plates as he etched this map. The individual printed sections were then glued together to form an oversize oblong map (488 mm × 1173 mm). Impressions of this map are quite rare, and thus references in literary bibliographies are almost non-existent. Richard Mai, who never saw the map himself, gives a cursory description of an impression in Harburg in his 'Bibliographie zum Werk Sigmund von Birkens', *Jahrbuch der Deutschen Schillergesellschaft*, 13 (1969), 602, no. 109. Dünnhaupt, *Personalbibliographien*, mentions the map in his description of *Der Donau-Strand* (no. 127. I), but he assumes that the map is a Latin translation of the work. More complete information on the map is contained in *Hollstein's German Engravings*, vol. 38, no. 23.

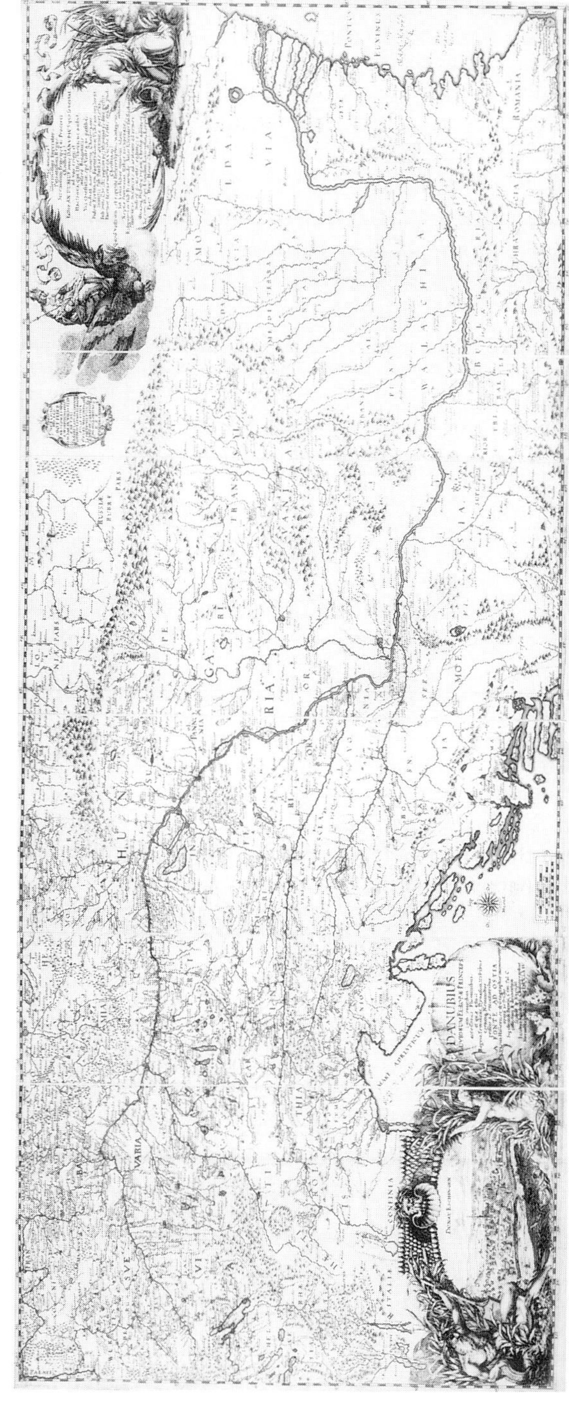

Fig. 3. Map of the Danube (1664). Etching (488 × 1173 mm) by Jacob von Sandrart after a design by Sigmund von Birken. BL Map Room: 27000. (3.).

Separated from the book, the map has been highly susceptible to loss and destruction. Although more copies of the book now survive, statements by Birken in *Der Donau-Strand* indicate that the map was originally considered the more important of the two. In the dedication, for example, he mentioned 'diese Donau-Mappe / samt deren Beschreibung' (fol. A1^r). In his preface he pointed even more clearly to the importance of the map when he referred to the two works as 'diese LandMappe und Werklein' (fol. A2^v). In each instance the map is mentioned first rather than as a simple appendage to the book.

Birken began his work on the map at about the same time he began to write the text for *Der Donau-Strand*. In late January he sent Sandrart an initial sketch,[21] and over the next few months he designed each of the three plates. Birken proceeded to work more quickly on the map than on the book, for already on 18 May he noted that he had completed the third plate: 'Die dridte Mappe Danubij absolv[iert]. d[eo] S[it] G[ratia]' (*Tagebücher*, p. 121). It was not until early September, however, that he and Sandrart met to check the plates carefully for accuracy. This revision was then completed about one week after Birken had finished writing the text.[22] All along Birken must have been revising page proofs, for three days later the first two hundred copies of the book arrived from Bayreuth.[23] The very next day he sent off his first dedication copies: one to Duke Anton Ulrich in Wolfenbüttel, eight to Count Gottlieb von Windischgrätz in Vienna, and one to the imperial historiographer in Vienna, Dr Mannagetta.[24] In the weeks ahead he sent or presented copies to numerous friends and colleagues, among them Catharina Regina von Greiffenberg, Daniel Wülfer, Johann Michael Dilherr, Martin Limburger, Caspar von Lilien, Johann Georg Styrzel, and Jacob Balde.

By the time Birken received the first two hundred copies, Gebhard had virtually finished the print run for the edition, for on 3 October Birken received from Gebhard a barrel weighing 300 pounds and containing 1,600 copies of the book.[25] The entire edition was stored at Birken's home, and periodically

21 27 January: '... ich ihm [i.e., Sandrart] die Erste Mappen-Entwurf des Donaustrands' (*Tagebücher*, p. 96).

22 26 September: 'Die 3 Mappe mit H[errn] Sandr[art] revidirt' (*Tagebücher*, p. 135).

23 29 September: '200 Exempl[are] von Bayr[euth] portorium 44 x [Kreuzer]' (*Tagebücher*, p. 136). On 21 September Birken had received another shipment from Gebhard (*Tagebücher*, p. 135), but the 350 copies he mentions in his diaries were not copies of *Der Donau-Strand*. It is more likely that they were either a printed funeral oration or a separate printing of an occasional poem.

24 *Tagebücher*, p. 136. Birken ultimately sent off a large number of copies, for in addition to twelve copies that Sandrart gave him on 4 October he purchased another 25 on account (*Tagebücher*, p. 137). Because the coinage that Birken mentions often has varying value and because we have no firm information about the selling of the book, the sale price of an individual volume cannot be determined with any accuracy. We do know, however, that on 8 October he sold two copies to an acquaintance for 18 Batzen apiece (*Tagebücher*, p. 137), but this was well below the price Sandrart would have charged. On 21 October Birken paid Sandrart 25 Florins for 300 copies (*Tagebücher*, p. 139), yet this was again a special price per volume.

25 *Tagebücher*, p. 136. Two months later he received a shipment with an additional 350 copies (*Tagebücher*, p. 145). An edition of this magnitude was out of the ordinary. Occasional works

Sandrart would send someone to pick up a hundred copies.[26] Birken acted thus as a clearing house for the edition, and he was careful to keep track of this 'Verlags-Vertrieb'. His calculations indicate that not only did Sandrart periodically have a hundred copies picked up, but also that Michael Endter, who was interested in selling them as part of his own retail book trade, sent for copies. Between 30 September and 13 December Sandrart had six hundred copies picked up, and during that same period Endter picked up three hundred (*Tagebücher*, p. 83).

The sales of *Der Donau-Strand* appear to have been brisk. Of the estimated 2,500-3,000 copies originally printed by Gebhard, over half were sold within the first four months. Birken's calculations on 21 January 1665 indicate that he still had 900 copies in a barrel downstairs and approximately another 300 upstairs (*Tagebücher*, p. 158). In the interim Sandrart had already had 1,200 copies collected. The entire edition was likely sold out in the early spring, and because a demand for additional copies remained, another publisher in Nuremberg, Johann Kramer, decided to issue a new edition. It is commonly assumed that Kramer's edition was a pirated edition, but that is not true since Birken cooperated with Kramer on the publication of the new edition. On 22 April he mentioned working on the new edition,[27] and a week later he completed the financial negotiations with Kramer.[28] Shortly thereafter Kramer had the new edition printed, and on 6 May he had the 1,000 copies collected from Birken's home.[29]

Interest in Birken's book remained strong as a consequence of the continuing volatile military and political situation in Hungary. The peace treaty, which the emperor had signed so hastily with the Porte had caused great dissatisfaction among Hungarian leaders, who had hoped that the emperor would press his advantage against the Turks and drive them completely from Hungary. In their eyes their Austrian overlord was indifferent to the plight of the Hungarians, and in their dissatisfaction with Austrian diplomacy they interpreted the Peace of Vasvár as a treacherous attempt by the Austrians to keep Hungary divided. This dissatisfaction led disillusioned Hungarian Roman Catholic magnates to conspire against the emperor, but in 1670 and 1671 he moved swiftly to crush the conspiracy. Autocratic Habsburg rule over Hungary was established, yet

such as printed funeral orations were frequently printed in editions of fewer than 200 copies, whereas editions of books were commonly limited to 300-500 copies.

26 5 October: H[err] Sandr[art] 100 Exemplare holen lassen' (*Tagebücher*, p. 137); 22 November: H[err] Sandrart - wieder 100 Exemplare abholen lassen' (*Tagebücher*, p. 143).

27 'Den Umlag Bogen Zum Danubio verf[aßt]' (*Tagebücher*, p. 178).

28 29 April: 'Mit H[errn] Joh[ann] Kramern gehandelt, 60 F[lorin] Dr. Dinphiel Bücher, vor 1000 Danubios ...' (*Tagebücher*, p. 179).

29 'H[err] Kramer die 1000 Exempl[are] abholen lassen' (*Tagebücher*, p. 182). Interestingly, Sandrart also sold copies of Kramer's edition. Birken noted, for example, on 16 October that he traded 75 copies of the Kramer edition to Sandrart for 12 copies of the map of the Danube (*Tagebücher*, p. 205). This is further evidence of the importance (and the expense) of the large map.

that was still not enough to guarantee a strong bulwark against the Turks. In 1683 the Turks advanced as far as Vienna, and even after a European coalition had relieved the besieged city, it took another sixteen years to drive them completely from Hungarian soil.

Birken's *Der Donau-Strand* remained thus a very topical work and one that could be updated with little effort. The 1684 edition, for example, is entitled *Der Vermehrte Donau-Strand* and has forty illustrations rather than the original thirty-three (fig. 4). At the end of the book a new section was also added: 'Continuation. Der merckwürdigsten Begebenheiten/ Von An. 1665. bis 1683. Hungarn/ Pohlen/ Candia/ Türckey/ und Tartarey betreffend' (pp. 186-231). The 1686 edition contains a significantly larger number of illustrations (seventy in all), and once again Sandrart modified the title: *Neu-vermehrter Donau-Strand* (fig. 5). At the same time that he was bringing these new editions of the book onto the market, he was also updating the large map and selling it both individually and together with the book. The date on the map was first changed from 1664 to 1683 and then the following year to 1684. That is the last known printing of Sandrart's map of the Danube, but several more editions of the book were published, the last appearing almost four decades after Birken's death.

Der Donau-Strand is a work that only slowly lost its appeal to German readers, and as such it was one of the great publication successes of the seventeenth century. It is a tribute to Birken's ability as a writer that he was able to produce such a well-researched and informative work that could be read and enjoyed by a wide circle of readers. Now that we possess a more thorough understanding of its publication and recognize that the map and the book were meant to be used in conjunction with one another, *Der Donau-Strand* serves as an interesting case study in the literary history of the German baroque period. It also raises a number of significant questions. For example, how typical was Birken's and Sandrart's cooperation in the general publishing history of the baroque? Does *Der Donau-Strand* provide us with insights into the nature of popular literary taste? How widely was this book and others like it read? Is this work evidence for a deepening and broadening of serious interest in the affairs of state? To answer these questions requires that we continue to examine other popular works of the time for their broader contextual importance. Increasingly it is becoming clear that a purely aesthetic measure of their value is an insufficient measure indeed.

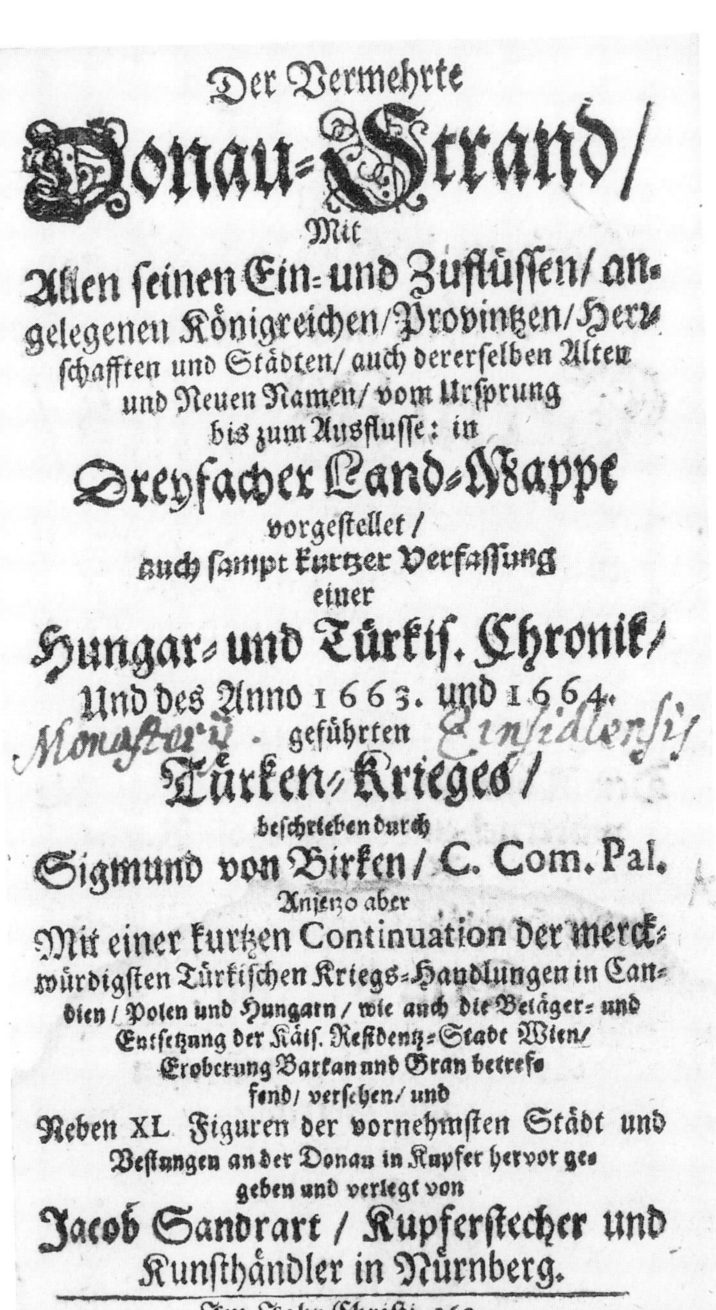

Der Vermehrte
Donau-Strand/
Mit
Allen seinen Ein- und Zuflüssen/ an-
gelegenen Königreichen/ Provintzen/ Herr-
schafften und Städten/ auch dererselben Alten
und Neuen Namen/ vom Ursprung
bis zum Ausflusse: in
Dreyfacher Land-Mappe
vorgestellet/
auch sampt kurtzer Verfassung
einer
Hungar- und Türkis. Chronik/
Und des Anno 1663. und 1664.
geführten

Türken-Krieges/
beschrieben durch
Sigmund von Birken/ C. Com. Pal.
Anjetzo aber
Mit einer kurtzen Continuation der merck-
würdigsten Türkischen Kriegs-Handlungen in Can-
dien/ Polen und Hungarn/ wie auch die Beläger- und
Entsetzung der Käis. Residentz-Stadt Wien/
Eroberung Barkan und Gran betref-
fend/ versehen/ und
Neben XL. Figuren der vornehmsten Städt und
Vestungen an der Donau in Kupfer hervor ge-
geben und verlegt von
Jacob Sandrart/ Kupferstecher und
Kunsthändler in Nürnberg.
Im Jahr Christi 1684.

Fig. 4. Title-page to Sigmund von Birken, *Der Vermehrte Donau-Strand* (1684). BL pressmark 10210.aaa.21.

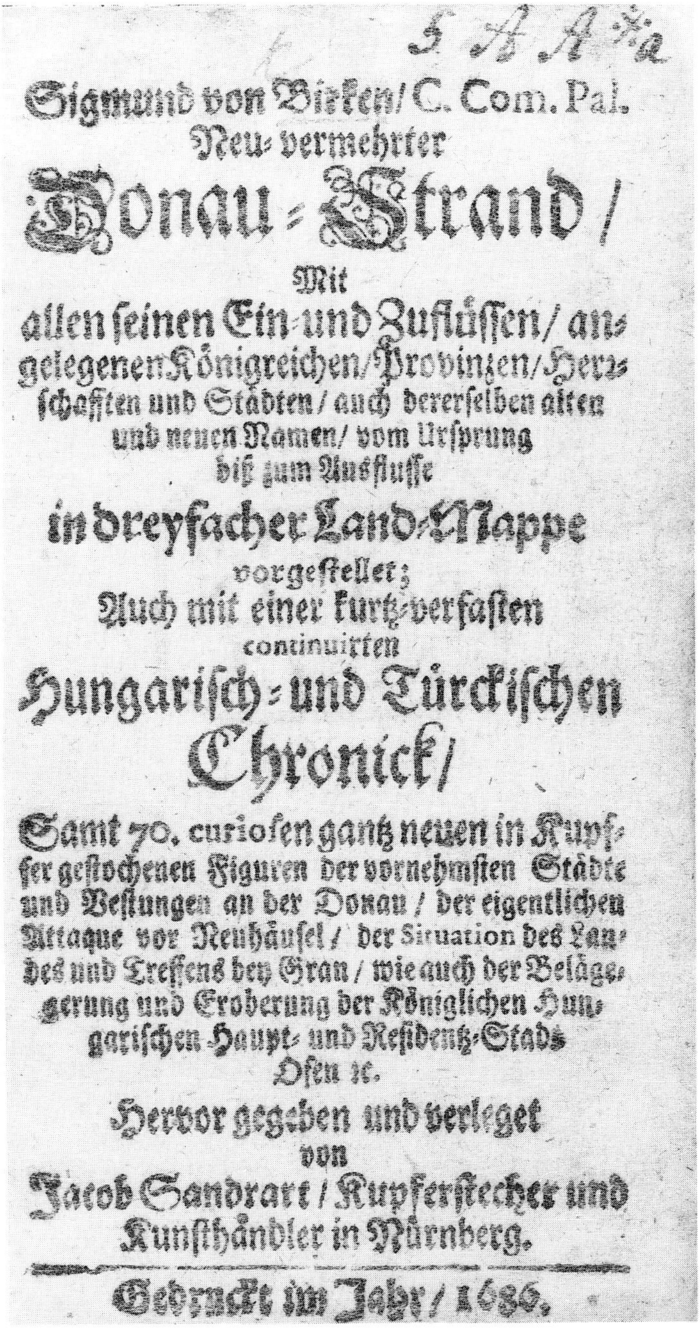

Sigmund von Birken/ C. Com. Pal.
Neu-vermehrter
Donau-Strand/
Mit
allen seinen Ein- und Zuflüssen/ an-
gelegenen Königreichen/ Provinzen/ Herr-
schafften und Städten/ auch dererselben alten
und neuen Namen/ vom Ursprung
biß zum Ausflusse
in dreyfacher Land-Mappe
vorgestellet;
Auch mit einer kurtz-verfasten
continuirten
Hungarisch- und Türckischen
Chronick/
Samt 70. curiosen gantz neuen in Kupf-
fer gestochenen Figuren der vornehmsten Städte
und Vestungen an der Donau/ der eigentlichen
Attaque vor Neuhäusel/ der Situation des Lan-
des und Treffens bey Gran/ wie auch der Belä-
gerung und Eroberung der Königlichen Hun-
garischen Haupt- und Residentz-Stadt
Ofen &c.
Hervor gegeben und verleget
von
Jacob Sandrart/ Kupferstecher und
Kunsthändler in Nürnberg.
Gedruckt im Jahr/ 1686.

Fig. 5. Title-page to Sigmund von Birken, *Neu-vermehrter Donau-Strand* (1686). BL pressmark 573.a.18.

FESTIVAL BOOKS FOR RELIGIOUS OCCASIONS

HELEN WATANABE-O'KELLY

IN THE COURSE of a study of fireworks in the Empire[1] in the Early Modern period I came across a printed and illustrated account in German of the celebrations of the octocentenary of the Augustinian monastery of Ranshoven near Passau in 1699, which included two firework displays.[2] In the Bavarian State Library in Munich, where I located the Ranshoven account, I found two similar works in the vernacular, relating respectively to the quatercentenary of the arrival of the Franciscan Order in Munich in 1684 and the centenary of a Viennese 'Todten-Bruderschafft' in 1738.[3] In the Getty Center in Santa Monica I found another, this time in Latin, of the celebrations in honour of the

1 To appear in *Spectaculum Europaeum. Theatre and Spectacle in Europe 1580-1750 – A Handbook*, edited by Pierre Béhar and Helen Watanabe-O'Kelly and published by Otto Harrassowitz, Wiesbaden, for the Herzog August Bibliothek, Wolfenbüttel.

2 *Acht-tägiger Jubel/ Oder Kurtze/ doch eigentlich= und wahrhaffte Beschreibung Der gantzen acht-täglichen Hoch=feyrlichen Festivitet Wegen deß nunmehro glücklich hinterlegten achten* Saeculi *von erster Erbauung der/ dem heiligen* Phrygis*chen Martyrer uud* [sic] *Blut=zeugen Christi/* Pancratio *Gewidmeten Capellen/ Dan auch Der herrlichen und Freuden=vollen Einbegleitung/ und* Inthronisation *halber/ beeder heiliger Leiber/ der gleichfalls heiligen Martyrer/ und Blut=Zeugen Christi* Marii *und* Caelestini, *Nicht weniger anderer Heiligen vortrefflichen* Reliquien, *Als insonderheit deß heiligen* Felicissimi Martyris *Rippen und Schulter=Blatt/etc. Von denen* Regulierten *Chor=Herren deß H.* Augustini Lateranensis*cher* Congregation *in dem löblichen Stüft und Closter Ranshoven/ Von dem 23. August an bis 31. eiusdem mit sonderbarer Magnificenz und schuldigisten Ehre=Gepräng begangen und gefeyret worden/ Anno Domini M.DC.XCIX.* Augspurg/ gedruckt bey Maria Magdalena Utzschneiderin/ 1702.
The sermons preached on each day of the celebrations were published as: *Abbildung und Beschreibung: Saeculum Octavum, Oder Acht-Tägiges Hoch-feyrliches Jubel=Fest ... Mit ... triumphierlicher Einholung der heiligen zweyen Römischen Martyrer Marii und Caelestini Acht außerlesenen ... Lob= und Ehren=Predigen ... In Ranshoven ... In den 1699. Jahr vom 23. Augustmonats ... gehalten*, Augsburg 1702.

3 *Saeculum, Welt- und Zeit-Lauft deren 400 Jahr von 1284-1684: Acht Lob- und Ehrenreden in der Kirchen S. Antonii de Padua in München gehalten*, Munich 1684; *Hochfeierliches Saeculum, Oder Erstes JahrHundert Einer Hochlöblichen ... Todten-Bruderschafft bey d. WW. EE. PP. Augustinern Barfüßern allhier// Welche Hoche Feyerlichekti In gegenwärtigem Jahr 1738. den 16. Novemb. abends ihren Anfang nehmen/ und die gantze Octav hindurch eyfrigst wird celebriret werden.* Vienna 1738.

canonization of St John of the Cross in Augsburg in 1726.[4] In an anthology of Baroque literature in Bavaria I found four more relating to the translation of the relics of SS. Fortunatus, Laureatus and Candida to the parish church in Biberbach in 1687 and to the anniversaries of the foundation of the monasteries of Tegernsee (1746), Wessobrunn (1753), and Ottobeuren (1766) respectively.[5] Clearly these festival books devoted to religious events constituted a distinct category of material within the extremely numerous and widespread genre of the festival book.[6]

Festival books, defined as official printed accounts of festivals, are often assumed to relate only to courtly occasions. There was a time when I laboured under this misconception myself.[7] It is indeed true that the festival book came into being as an account, usually in the vernacular, of a courtly celebration, held to mark a christening, birthday or nameday, a betrothal, wedding, funeral,

4 *Apparatus sacri honoris primo carmelitarum discalceatorum patenti seraphicae virginis ac matris Theresiae a Jesu filio primogenito S. Joanni a Cruce: post ejus solemnem in Vaticani colle apotheosis, adornatus, a devotissimo filiorum suorum Collegio Augustano.* Augsburg: Sumptibus Joannis Stroetter 1727.

5 Anton Ginther, *Beschreibung vnd Jnhalt Aller Begebenheiten vnd Anstalt/ Bey der Erhaltung/ Uebertragung/ vnd Beysetzung Deren 3. Heiligen Leiber/ Als nämlichen: S. Fortunati Martyris, S. Laureati Martyris, S. Candidae Virginis, & Martyris. Jn der Hoch-Gräfl. Herrschafft Biberbach/ Jn dero Pfarr-Kirchen Bey dem Heiligen vnd Wunderthätigen Creutz.* So alles geschehen im Jahr 1687. den 27. Heumonat. Cum Facultate Superiorum. Augspurg/ Gedruckt bey Simon Utzschneider/ Hoch-Fürstl.: Bischöffl: vnd Stadt-Buchdruckern, 1687;
Michael Wening, *Tausendmahl geseegnete Brünnen Wessonis. Das ist, Zweyfaches Danck-Jubel- Und Freuden-Fest Des Uralt- und befreyten Closters Wessobrunn, Des Heiligen Vatters Benedicti-Ordens in Oberbayrn, GOtt dem Allmächtigen gehalten, Da besagtes Stift zugleich das Tausende von erster Stifftung, und das fünffzigste Jubel-Jahr von erstesmahl abgelegten Ordens-Gelübden Des Hochwürdig, Hochedlgebohrnen Herren Herren Bedae, dermahl würdigst regierenden Abbten ... Jn dem Jahr 1753. von dem 23. Herbstmonaths an, durch fürwährende acht Täg feyerlichst begienge ...* Augspurg, Gedruckt, und zu finden bey Joseph Dominico Gruber, Cathol. Buchdr. Anno 1754;
Castorius Zeitler, *Mille Anni Ante Ocolos. Oder Tausend Jahr Des Uralten und Befreyten GOtts-Hauß Tegernsee Anno M.DCC.XLVI. Als von Einweyhung desselben glorreichen Tausenden Jubel-Jahr Vor Augen gestellet Auf offentlicher Schau-Bühne Jn dem gedachten Stüfft und Closter Tegernsee, nach dessen angefangter Erbauung ebenfahls Jm Tausen siben- und zwaintzigsten Jahr.* Gedruckt im Closter Tegernsee. [1744];
Augustin Bayrhamer, *Das Tausend-jährige/ und durch die Bischöfliche Einweyhung der neuen Kirche geheiligte Ottobeyern: oder Merckwürdige Begebenheiten, welche sich Bey der Feyerlichsten Einseegnung der neu erbauten Kirche/ und dem Tausendjährigen Jubel-Fest Deß befreyten Reichs-Stiffts/ und GOttes-Hauses Ottobeyren/ zugetragen.* Ottobeyern, Gedruckt bey Carl Joseph Wanckenmiller, 1767. Zu finden bey Johann Martin Baader, Buchbinder allda.
The anthology in question is: *Die Literatur des Barock.* Ausgewählt und eingeleitet von Hans Pörnbacher. Bayerische Bibliothek, 2 (Munich, 1986).

6 For general background information on religious festivities see Paulette Choné, *Emblèmes et pensées symbolique en Lorraine (1525-1633). 'Comme un jardin au coeur de la Chrétienté'* (Paris, 1991); Jean-Marie Valentin, *Le théâtre des Jésuites dans les pays de langue allemande (1554-1680)* (Berne, 1978); Ruprecht Wimmer, *Jesuitentheater – Didaktik und Fest* (Frankfurt am Main, 1982).

7 Helen Watanabe-O'Kelly, 'Festival Books in Europe from Renaissance to Rococo', *The Seventeenth Century, 17* (1988), 181-201.

coronation, royal entry, visit by a foreign prince or ambassador, a victory or peace celebration. Such accounts were considered at most European courts during the early modern period to be as indispensable a part of the festivity as the banquet, the firework display or the triumphal arch. Festival books became common after about 1550, grew in number throughout the seventeenth and eighteenth centuries and were still being produced, though more sporadically and often with a historicizing intention, during the nineteenth. In their simplest manifestation they are often no more than unadorned recitals in a few pages of the events of the festival, but as time goes on such unassuming festival books are often replaced by richly illustrated folios with detailed descriptions of every stage of the proceedings. At their most elaborate they are embellished with meditations on the emblematic significance of the events, with verse written for the occasion, with a history or genealogy of the royal or princely house which organized the festivity, with portraits of members of that house and any other material which occurs to the author.[8]

Festival books fulfilled a range of functions, often more than one at once. They could be read by the onlookers while waiting for proceedings to commence, they could be used, as the procession passed by or the allegorical tournament unfolded, to help them understand what they were seeing or tell them what they could not quite see, or explain the emblems, costumes and mythological figures on the floats. Festival books could also serve as substitutes for those who were unable to be present, as souvenirs for those who were, and as models when planning future events. But they always had the function of official propaganda. It was the organizing court which commissioned and paid for them and they were usually written by the court poet or historiographer and illustrated by the court artist. Thus the festival book was expressly designed to emphasize the magnificence of the festival, to bring out the political and dynastic significance of the iconography and in general to promulgate the official view. The accounts were meant to impress on friendly courts the worthiness of their ally and on rivals and enemies the unwisdom of trifling with so splendid and magnificent an adversary. They also served the important function of reminding courtiers that their prestige derived directly from the prince's and subjects in the country at large that the ruler's divinely ordained status precluded any thoughts of rebellion. Thus festival books frequently relate what should have happened rather than what did happen and their value as

8 Two particularly elaborate German festival books which combine narration with reflection are Diderich Graminaeus, *Furstliche Hochzeit So der Durchluchtig hochgeborner Furst und Herr, herr Wilhlem Hertzog Zu Gulich Cleve und Berg ... dem ... hern, her Johann Wilhelm Hertzog Zu Gulich hochermelten Ihrer F.G. geliebten Sohn Und der ... Furstinen Frewlin Jacobae gebornen marggraffinen zu Baden*, Düsseldorf 1585 and Gabriel Tzschimmer, *Die Durchlauchtigste Zusammenkunft/ Oder: Historische Erzehlung/ was der Durchlauchtigste Fürst und Herr/ Herr Johann George der Ander/ ... in ... Dresden im Februario des MDCLXXVII Jahres ... aufführen und vorstellen lassen*, Nürnberg 1680. See Helen Watanabe-O'Kelly, 'Gabriel Tzschimmer's *Durchlauchtigste Zusammenkunft* (1680) and the German Festival Book Tradition', *Daphnis*, 22 (1993), 61–72.

documentary evidence must remain questionable until there is confirmation from other sources. They are, however, an accurate guide to a court's image of itself and how it hoped that image would be perceived.

But were the festival books for religious occasions mentioned at the beginning purely a German phenomenon or was there a body of similar material elsewhere from which they might be derived? Since all the German examples came from Catholic territories, it was obvious that Italy was the first country in which to look for comparable material. The great number of festival books concerned with papal events – entries into Italian cities, so-called *possessi* in which the newly-elected pope formally progressed through Rome from St John Lateran to St Peter's, papal funerals, ambassadorial visits to the Holy See, etc. – turned out on closer scrutiny not to provide a useful comparison, since the events they commemorated related to the pope as head of the church and ruler of the Papal States and, though such events had a religious dimension in that they were concerned with a religious leader, they were used by the pope in the same way as secular leaders used them, that is, for pre-eminently political purposes. Similarly, such celebrations in Protestant territories as those which marked the centenary and bicentenary of the introduction of the Reformation, for instance into Regensburg in 1642 and 1742 respectively,[9] or the various celebrations of the anniversary of the Peace of Augsburg turned out in fact to be civic festivities with a religious dimension.

A search, which by no means claims to be comprehensive, of the British Library, the Piot Collection in the Victoria and Albert Museum, London, the Rondel Collection in the Bibliothèque de l'Arsenal in Paris, the collection in the Getty Center for the History of Art and the Humanities, Santa Monica, and the Lanfranchi Collection, which the Getty Center has recently acquired, yielded, however, about 130 festival books for purely religious occasions from Italy which are comparable with the German material. It was also possible to identify a much smaller but still significant number of religious festival books from Spain, mostly relating to festivals held in Madrid. Systematic searches of Italian and Spanish libraries would undoubtedly yield more.

The occasions celebrated in the Italian accounts are most commonly the canonization or beatification of a saint or saints, the consecration of a new church, the translation of a relic or statue from one church to another, the anniversary of the foundation of a church, monastery or religious order, the devotion of the Forty Hours (*Quarant'ore*), a procession by a confraternity and the feast-day of a saint or of the Virgin Mary. The chronological spread of the accounts would indicate that the form originated in Italy where a festival in honour of the Virgin held in Siena was published in an official account as early as 1546. Italian religious festival books became relatively frequent from the 1580s on, very numerous during the seventeenth century and increased to a flood in

9 See Karl Möseneder (ed.), *Feste in Regensburg von der Reformation bis in die Gegenwart* (Regensburg, 1986), p. 188 and p. 343.

the eighteenth. They describe religious festivals in most important Italian cities, but the overwhelming number relates to festivals held in Rome. Indeed, Rome becomes more and more dominant during the period mentioned, so that in the eighteenth century, most Italian works relate to festivals staged there. It is not surprising that this should be so, since canonizations and beatifications, for instance, had to take place in that city, no matter what the nationality or native city of the saint concerned.

It would appear, therefore, that the religious festival book as defined above is a Catholic and predominantly Italian genre which was imported into the German-speaking territories probably by the religious orders towards the end of the seventeenth century. It is wholly possible that there were many religious festivals in the Catholic territories of the Empire for which there is no published account and only extensive archival research can establish how the number of festival books correlates to the number of actual festivals.

Here I shall concentrate on the relationship between the religious and secular festival book and the religious and secular court festival, taking as my basis Giacomo Certani's *Maria Vergine Coronata*,[10] an account of a Marian festival held in Reggio Emilio in 1674, and the account mentioned above of the festivity held in Ranshoven in 1699.

The festival Certani describes was held in Reggio in Mary's month of May 1674 and concerned a miraculous statue of the Virgin. The statue was finished in 1570 and began quite soon to perform miracles of healing. It even saved the city from the plague in 1630. A grotto and then a church were built to house the statue and in 1674 this image was to be decorated with a magnificent jewelled crown as a thank-offering from the town. It is clear that the possession of such an efficacious image was very good for the local economy. Certani tells us (p. 6) that no fewer than forty thousand strangers came to the town in 1596 for the first solemn festival which commemorated the first miracle. The coronation, therefore, while it may indeed be motivated by religious fervour, is also concerned with advertizing the town and providing a show for the visitors who must have been numerous on this occasion also.

The actual coronation was only the culmination of a highly elaborate procession which was organised like a *trionfo* and divided into groups or 'inventions', each organised by a particular confraternity and consisting of a huge float accompanied by troupes of costumed riders and foot. The floats used the full panoply of triumphal architecture and of sophisticated stage design. The Confraternity of S. Maria del Confalone presented a catafalque surmounted by an empty mausoleum with Mary being assumed into Heaven above it, the Confraternity of the Blessed Sacrament presented a 'Tempio di Gloria' –

10 Giacomo Certani (Abbot), *Maria Vergine Coronata. Descrizione, e Dichiarazione della Divota Solennita fatta in Reggion li 13. Maggio 1674*, Reggio: Prospero Vedrotti, 1675. This account is in the British Library, the Piot Collection at the Victoria and Albert Museum and the J. Paul Getty Center in Santa Monica. The British Library copy (4807.g.3) has two copies of most of the plates bound in with the text.

Fig. 1. Christ crowning the Virgin. From Giacomo Certani, *Maria Vergine Coronata* (Reggio, 1675) (BL pressmark 4807.g.3).

Fig. 2. Moses. From Giacomo Certani, *Maria Vergine Coronata*.

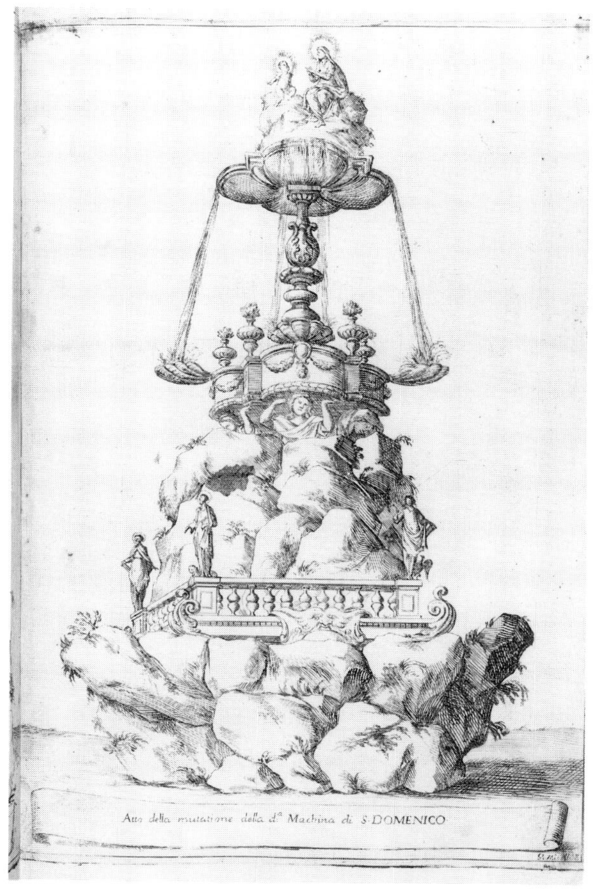

Fig. 3. The Virgin and the Infant Jesus. From Giacomo Certani, *Maria Vergine Coronata*.

a massive architectural structure, in which Christ on a cloud held a crown over Mary's head (fig. 1), the Confraternity of the Blessed Cross presented a huge rock on which Moses stood holding a staff (fig. 2). When he struck the rock, it opened to depict a fountain on top of which Mary and the Baby Jesus were seated (fig. 3). The rock opened again to reveal caryatids holding up the basin. The Confraternity of the Immaculate Conception presented a float containing what the account calls a 'trono glorioso'. This was set under a baldacchino resting on twisted columns. These surmounted a dais with steps leading up to it. The Confraternity of the Visitation of Our Lady presented a 'carro triunfale' pulled by twelve elephants which bears a temple for the Virgin set in a garden. Other inventions contained triumphal arches, obelisks and a tower which opened to reveal Mary holding Jesus and about to be crowned with a laurel wreath. Thus, the full panoply of classical imagery relating to the triumph – arches, thrones, baldachins, temples, obelisks, crowns, victor's wreaths, mausoleums – and which were so familiar from the art of princely glorification are here applied to Mary. Another of those courtly forms which belong to the same art – namely, the opera – was also used here. Each 'invention' presented what almost amounted to a mini-opera, the singers and musicians for which were borne along on the float in question. *Gloria*, *Merito*, *Onore* and *Felicità Publica* – a singularly worldly collection of virtues, one might think – sang a quartet as part of the invention of the Confraternity of the Immaculate Conception, for example. In another invention the singers were the Persian Sibyl, *il Contento* and *l'Allegrezza* and another invention was rounded off by a chorus of angels.

The festival book uses the same techniques of secular glorification as the festival itself. A folio consisting of 137 pages of text, it is adorned with seventeen plates, including an illustrated title-page and a portrait. The other fifteen plates, designed by a group of eight artists but all engraved by Giuseppe Maria Mitelli (1634-1718), are mostly fold-out plates with two lift-the-flap plates of those 'machines' in which a transformation takes place. It is the festival book itself which makes explicit the link between religious festivals and temporal power. Certani dedicates his account to Francesco II d'Este and it is his portrait which precedes the actual account, so that the reader, on opening the work, might imagine that he were about to read of a secular festival in which Francesco played the leading role. Certani, professor of moral philosophy at the University of Bologna, is concerned in his scholarly text to draw out the connection between the religious event he describes and temporal power, for he announces on the first page: 'Vn Cattolico Politico [the marginal note reads: Petri Gregorij de Rep. lib. 22 cap. 14] afferma due soli legami vnire in buona concordia i Cittadini, e renderli in questa maniera padroni della buona fortuna, la Religione cioè, e la Giudizia' ('A Catholic political thinker maintains that there two things only that ensure harmony among the citizens and thus put them in command of good fortune: Religion and Justice'). This point is hammered home later too, for instance in a marginal note on p. 30: 'Felicità civile sussiste nella pietà, e Religione' ('Civic happiness rests on piety and religion'). We are reminded of

Fig. 4. The casket of St Marius at Ranshoven. From *Achttägiger Jubel*... (Augsburg, 1702).

the personified *Felicità Publica* which appeared on one of the floats. So religion and good government, the secular and the ecclesiastical authorities, are complementary forces within the state. The festival book, therefore, must be careful not to make the religious power seem in competition with, still less superior to, the secular power. It must stress the function of the ruler as God's representative on earth and his quasi-divine elevation above his people, while at the same time equipping God, the Virgin Mary and the saints with the trappings of earthly power. The central Christian paradox of God made man is thus transformed into a dual vision of king made God and God made king.

The Ranshoven festivity shows the same stress on the exterior symbols of piety. The skeletons of the martyrs Marius and Caelestinus, together with a rib and shoulder blade from the martyr Felicissimus, have been sent from Rome to Ranshoven, complete with documents of authentication, to be installed in the church of St Pancratius as part of the octocentenary celebrations in 1699 of the foundation of that church and the monastery to which it is attached. The church itself had been redecorated with frescoes, stucco-work and an ornate altar-piece only two years before.[11] The relics have been encased in gold and jewels and each placed in a glass casket, so that they can be venerated (fig. 4). A plenary

11 *Lexicon für Theologie und Kirche*, 2nd ed., VIII, Freiburg/Br. (1963), col. 991.

indulgence has been granted by the pope to all pilgrims to the church who receive the sacraments of Penance and Communion during the octave of the feast. It is as though the Reformation had never happened.

The chief event of the festivities was the triumphal procession of the martyrs to their new resting place. The three martyrs together with another seventeen relics were borne shoulder-high on biers like victors after a battle, accompanied by clergy, local grandees and six floats. The first represents time and history – the seasons, signs of the zodiac, equinoxes and solstices and the eight centuries since the foundation of the monastery – the second honours the founders of the monastery, the third the patron saint of Ranshoven, the fourth depicts Munificence, the fifth salutes those noble families buried at Ranshoven with their coats of arms, and the sixth the Church Triumphant. The procession was accompanied by musket salvos, cannonades and trumpet fanfares. The procession passed through three imposing triumphal arches. The first was devoted to the three martyrs in question, depicting Marius and Caelestinus on one side, Felicissimus on the other. Fame astride a rearing horse crowns the arch, angels blow trumpets at either side and the two martyrs stand like victors under a baldachin. The second arch is devoted to the benefactors and patrons of the monastery and of necessity is a roll call of Bavarian princes and local grandees. The third arch saluted St Pancratius, the patron saint of the monastery, and depicts local parishes and local saints. The church triumphant was thus linked with the Duchy of Bavaria and the region around Passau.

The firework displays were no less striking. In the first, six obelisks on either side receded towards an arch, over which 'Vivat Pancratius' in flaming letters lit up the sky, as all manner of fireworks went off round about. In the second, a model of the monastery was set in a pond (fig. 5) and out of it and round it fireworks exploded, in just the same way that courtly fireworks took a fortress as their centrepiece. The final set piece of the festivities is the catafalque set up in the church so that prayers can be offered for the souls of Ranshoven's benefactors (fig. 6).

Two elements of the festival stand out: the adaptation of secular festival forms, such as the triumphal arch, the triumphal procession, the firework display and even the *castrum doloris*, and the linking of the history of the monastery with the history of Bavaria and of the region. It is particularly this latter which the festival books emphasizes. It too is handsomely illustrated with fifteen fold-out plates and is printed by Maria Magdalena Utzschneiderin[12] of Augsburg, the widow of that Simon Utzschneider who printed Anton Ginther's account of a religious festival in 1687 (see note 5). While the festival book naturally gives an account of the actual events which took place, it devotes most of the text to explicating the emblems on the arches which, given the height at which some of them were placed, must have been virtually indecipherable to the

12 David Paisey, *Deutsche Buchdrucker, Buchhändler und Verleger 1701–1750* (Wiesbaden, 1988), p. 268.

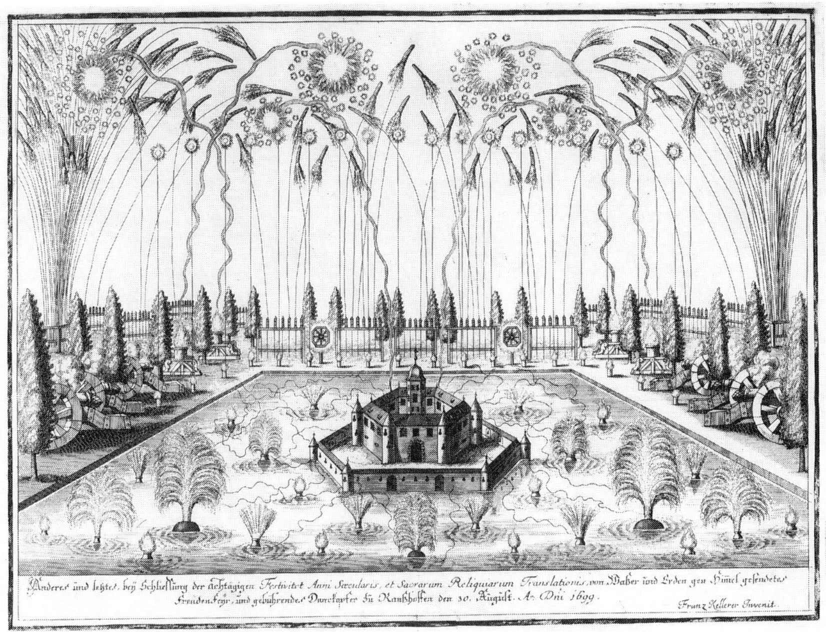

Fig. 5. The fireworks at Ranshoven. From *Achttägiger Jubel* . . .

Fig. 6. The catafalque at Ranshoven. From *Achttägiger Jubel* . . .

naked eye. The text also lays great stress on the history of the monastery which is simultaneously the history of the region and its rulers. A spectator might come away from the week's celebrations in Ranshoven with a clear impression of the Church Triumphant, with a vision of its martyrs as heroes who have vanquished death and with a perception of the monastery itself as an ecclesiastical fortress. The reader of the festival book is left in no doubt that it is the Munificence of secular rulers and patrons which has supported the church and allowed this monastery to flourish.

RESEARCH ON EARLY GERMAN DISSERTATIONS

A report on work in progress[1]

MANFRED KOMOROWSKI

OUR LARGE ACADEMIC LIBRARIES hold enormous quantities of pre-1800 university publications, whose numbers have been estimated conservatively at eighty thousand for the seventeenth century alone in a recent, detailed study.[2] The figure for the eighteenth century must be put even higher, and, if one adds the relatively small numbers of disputations from the sixteenth century, as well as the numerous speeches, programmata and lists of lectures, a total number of two hundred thousand academic publications from the German-speaking area up to 1800 is entirely realistic. Just as at present, the great majority of early academic publications consists of dissertations. In this context the term 'academic publication' is regarded as synonymous with 'university publication', even if the former has a wider compass, in as much as it includes publications issued by institutions which did not enjoy university status.

My purpose in what follows is to present and comment on recent scholarly publications on the genre of early dissertations. In view of the continuing inadequacy of the bibliographical coverage of such works the most important ventures to remedy these deficiencies will be discussed in greater detail.

If large holdings of early dissertations still await cataloguing, the fault lies with the slight attention devoted to them for so long by librarians and academics. Today very large holdings of these materials lie either neglected or barely noticed in the stacks of large libraries, and, as long as this remains the case, numerous bibliographical enquiries will prove fruitless. Accordingly any information on such collections is of fundamental importance for every bibliographer. In recent years access to these source materials has been improved by the regional surveys by Lapp, Vinzent and, above all, in the volumes of the *Handbuch der historischen Buchbestände* published so far,

1 Seventeenth-century university publications are discussed in my essay in the forthcoming volume *Buchdruck im Barockzeitalter*.

2 Wolfgang Müller, *Die Drucke des 17. Jahrhunderts im deutschen Sprachraum* (Wiesbaden, 1990), p. 93.

although they have all revealed how much work there still remains to be done.[3] Together with the more specialized surveys of Ranieri and Marti on legal and philosophical dissertations they have led the researcher to important, though not all the relevant collections.[4] In many cases the researcher on the spot can rely on older or modern special catalogues. The identification of early university publications in traditionally maintained central catalogues in Germany is totally inadequate, though more and more relevant titles are being incorporated in modern union catalogues through retroconversion and the completion of cataloguing projects. The usefulness of the union catalogue in North Rhine-Westphalia for information on early dissertations has now improved radically. The considerable value of regional surveys of important collections cannot be a substitute for the cataloguing of individual dissertations.

Beginning in the latter 1970s, a series of commendable initiatives designed to improve the state of bibliography, which had remained virtually unchanged since the publication in 1904 of Erman and Horn's monumental *Bibliographie der deutschen Universitäten*. However, as even this record of lists of early dissertations and graduation lists and the sale catalogues of booksellers specializing in such material could not inspire academics and librarians to produce modern catalogues, the 1971 edition of Dahlmann/Waitz, incomplete though it is anyway, listed few new entries.[5] There is, however, one exception which needs to be mentioned. In the early 1930s a Leipzig antiquarian bookseller, Erich Carlsohn, acquired from a south German monastery a collection numbering, with duplicates, some seventy-five thousand items, which was partially catalogued by Hermann Mundt. This appeared in fascicles from 1936 to 1942 as *Bio-bibliographisches Verzeichnis von Universitäts- und Hochschuldrucken (Dissertationen) vom Ausgang des 16. bis Ende des 19. Jahrhunderts*, which for the first time gave details of two features, 'dedicationes' and 'gratulationes', which are not only characteristic of dissertations but also contain much of interest to family historians; indeed the catalogue included only dissertations which had these features. It was no accident that this work began to appear at a time when genealogical research received encouragement from the state. Like the *Deutscher Gesamtkatalog* and the *Gesamtkatalog der Wiegendrucke*, Mundt's work was delayed by the war, and did not get beyond the name Ritter. As both the collection and the manuscript entries were burnt, it seemed that the work would remain a torso. However, between 1977 and 1980 Konrad Wickert supplied not

3 Erdmute Lapp, *Katalogsituation der Altbestände (1501-1850) in Bibliotheken der Bundesrepublik Deutschland einschließlich Berlin (West)* (Berlin, 1989); Otwin Vinzent, *Katalogsituation der Altbestände (1501-1850) in Bibliotheken der neuen Bundesländer* (Berlin, 1992); *Handbuch der historischen Buchbestände*, vols. 3-9 (Hildesheim, 1992-94).

4 Filippo Ranieri (ed.), *Juristische Dissertationen deutscher Universitäten 17. und 18. Jahrhundert* (Frankfurt/Main, 1986), pp. 11-24; Hanspeter Marti, *Philosophische Dissertationen deutscher Universitäten 1660-1750. Eine Auswahlbibliographie* (Munich, 1982), pp. 41-51.

5 Friedrich Christoph Dahlmann and Georg Waltz, *Quellenkunde der deutschen Geschichte. Bibliographie der Quellen und Literatur zur deutschen Geschichte.* 10th ed. Vol. II, sect. 44, nos 540-1049 (Stuttgart, 1971).

only the missing part of the alphabet from the holdings of Erlangen University Library but also a general index (Wickert, in contrast to Mundt, generally excluded nineteenth-century dissertations, but he did include ones without dedications or congratulatory verses). For the first time a reader was able to establish the writings of a particular *praeses*. Unfortunately no attempt was made to analyse biographical information in the dissertations, nor is there a break-down of them by university. With its 37,834 titles Mundt/Wickert is the most comprehensive bibliography of early dissertations, but is very far from being complete. For some institutions it is well nigh of no value, e.g. Duisburg, while for others it is moderately useful, e.g. Königsberg, and for yet others it is of extreme importance, e.g. Jena, Leipzig, Halle, Wittenberg.

Against this background some other projects have shown themselves to be absolutely essential. Of special note here is Hermann Schüling, whose university, Giessen, owes him and Franz Kössler[6] a debt 'for the virtually comprehensive information in their catalogues of the early dissertations from the university's foundation in 1607 up to the appearance of the *Jahresverzeichnis der deutschen Hochschulschriften* in 1885. No other institution of higher education in Germany has now had such good bibliographical coverage. Indeed for the nineteenth century alone the few existing lists[7] are entirely outnumbered by the desiderata. Schüling has worked backwards from 1800 to 1607 in three separate works. His *Dissertationen und Habilitationsschriften der Universität Giessen im 18. Jahrhundert* (Giessen, 1976) acted as a spur to similar projects for other universities in the years following its publication. Schüling published a similarly named work covering the years 1650 to 1700 ((Munich, 1982), before rounding off his task with a list for the period 1605-1624, which included other Giessen imprints.[8] The gap for the years 1625 to 1649 in his work is to be explained by the temporary closure of Giessen University during the Thirty Years' War. For relatively poorly attended universities such as Giessen virtually comprehensive lists are more easily achievable than for the much better attended ones in the early modern period. The very different scale of numbers involved may well be the main reason for our not having even today a modern, complete or even partial catalogue of the individual faculties of the universities of Jena, Leipzig or Wittenberg. In spite of Schüling's efforts we still lack a list of the various university speeches and lectures held at Giessen. Resch and Buzas's list for the Catholic University of Ingolstadt, which appeared almost at the same time as Schüling's eighteenth-century list, is purely a register of graduations for

6 Franz Kössler, *Katalog der Dissertationen und Habilitationsschriften der Universität Giessen von 1801-1884* (Giessen, 1971).

7 Wilhelm Erman, *Verzeichnis der Berliner Universitätsschriften 1810-1885* (Berlin, 1899); Fritz Milkau, *Verzeichnis der Bonner Universitätsschriften 1818-1885* (Bonn, 1897); Karl Pretzsch, *Verzeichnis der Breslauer Universitätsschriften 1811-1885* (Breslau, 1905); Wolfram Suchier, *Bibliographie der Universitätsschriften von Halle-Wittenberg 1817-1885* (Berlin, 1953).

8 Hermann Schüling, *Verzeichnis des von 1605-1624 in Giessen erschienenen Schrifttums* (Giessen, 1985).

the period before 1800, which could be of assistance in the next step, that of determining the doctoral dissertations.[9] A partial stop-gap for this continuing lacuna has been supplied by Gerhard Stalla's *Ingolstädter Buchdruck von 1601 bis 1620* (Baden-Baden, 1980), which includes a considerable number of dissertations. By contrast Margarete Anders does not include a single Ingolstadt dissertation in her catalogue of the holdings of the Legal Faculty library in Munich.[10]

However it is not only librarians who have rediscovered early dissertations. At almost the same time more and more university teachers began to take an interest in these long neglected sources. They quickly appreciated that an analysis of these could provide an important foundation for specialized researches. An example is Karl Mommsen's *Auf dem Wege zur Staatssouveranität: staatliche Grundbegriffe in Basler Doktordisputationen, usw.* (Berne, 1970), in which he evaluated and listed a collection of over two thousand legal dissertations, almost all of which had been preserved in Basle, although he had no opportunity to publish the bibliographical part of his study. This was done after Mommsen's death by Werner Kundert, who prefaced the actual catalogue with a closely argued, scholarly introduction, as well as widening the subject approach to the items listed, a feature usually missing from lists drawn up by non-specialists.[11] One must also mention here Kundert's *Katalog der Helmstedter juristischen Disputationen, Programme und Reden 1574-1810* (Wiesbaden, 1984), which is constructed along very similar lines to his Basle catalogue and is based on the relatively complete holdings of the Herzog August Bibliothek in Wolfenbüttel.

It was not only the dissertations of the early legal faculties which quickly attracted greater attention, but also those defended in the arts or philosophical faculties, although at most universities they were not as numerous as the theological, legal and, sometimes, the medical ones. Christoph Daxelmüller's *Bibliographie barocker Dissertationen zu Aberglaube und Brauch* highlighted the fact that early dissertations were not confined to standard, rarified subjects, but on many occasions tackled a variety of real problems.[12] Indeed these works on magic, exorcism, folklore and so on are important contemporary sources for cultural history. The list compiled by Daxelmüller was used by him as the basis of his monograph, *Disputationes curiosae* (Würzburg, 1979), of which a large number were not dissertations, but actually judicial referrals. Hanspeter Marti's

9 Lieselotte Resch, Ladislaus Buzas, *Verzeichnis der Doktoren und Dissertationen der Universität Ingolstadt-Landshut-München 1472-1970*. Vol. 1: *Theologische, juristische, staatswissen. Fakultät*. Vol. 2: *Medizinische Fakultät 1472-1915*. Vol. 7: *Philosophische Fakultät 1750-1950* (Munich, 1975-77).

10 Margarete Anders, *Gesamtkatalog der Dissertationen der juristischen Fakultät der Universität München*. Vol. 1: 1643-1911 (Munich, 1979).

11 Karl Mommsen, *Katalog der Basler juristischen Disputationen 1558-1818*. Aus dem Nachlass herausgegeben von Werner Kundert (Frankfurt/M., 1978).

12 *Jahrbuch für Volkskunde*, N.F., 3 (1980), 194-238; 4 (1981), 225-43; 5 (1982), 213-24; 6 (1983), 230-44; 7 (1984), 195-240.

Philosophische Dissertationen deutscher Universitäten 1660-1750 (Munich, 1982) came about in a very similar way as a by-product of his doctoral dissertation at Basle. Even if, as mentioned above, the dissertations from arts faculties were in the minority at most universities, their numbers still ran into tens of thousands, so that an individual bibliographer can only work on a specific topic. Marti concentrated on philological, historical and philosophical dissertations and less on ones on mathematics and natural sciences. Some of the dissertations defended in an arts faculty could be assigned on a subject basis to one of the higher faculties, for instance those on Biblical matters by the professors of Hebrew and Greek could be assigned to the theological faculty, the works on practical philosophy such as politics or ethics to the legal, or the chemical, biological or pharmaceutical titles to the medical. With his detailed survey of the early dissertations as a genre, his regional descriptions of important library holdings and an interesting bibliographical survey Marti offered much more than a mere list of titles. In addition to the universities he took into consideration many other institutions, the frequency of whose disputations can be ascertained from a list of universities as conveniently as can the subjects of the dissertations from a Latin subject index.

For the small Reformed University of Duisburg the present writer has published a bibliography of all its dissertations based for the most part on the holdings of that institution's library preserved in Bonn University Library since 1818.[13] Unfortunately Duisburg had never comprehensively collected its own dissertations, so that, leaving aside those holdings lost in the Second World War, enquiries have to be made in a number of libraries both in and outside Germany. Given such difficulties, it is not surprising that some two hundred titles can now be added to the seventeen hundred or so listed in the original publication.[14] Duisburg's philosophical and medical dissertations from the seventeenth century have in the meantime been analysed in detail by Francesco Trevisani in his book *Descartes in Germania* (Milan, 1992) where he has used them to show the influence of Cartesianism on the teaching of natural sciences and medicine at Duisburg and thereby has demonstrated its leading role in the spread of Descartes' theories in Germany.

The ground laid by Mommsen/Kundert and Kundert in the investigation of legal dissertations has been built on by the *Juristische Dissertationen deutscher Universitäten. 17. und 18. Jahrhundert* (2 vols. Frankfurt am Main, 1986) produced by a working group of the Max Planck Institute, Frankfurt am Main, under the leadership of Filippo Ranieri. The imprecise wording of the sub-title would lead one to expect a work in ten to fifteen volumes, for the legal dissertations outnumber all the others. It is only in the preface that the

13 Manfred Komorowski, *Bibliographie der Duisburger Universitätsschriften (1652-1817)* (St. Augustin, 1984).

14 Details of these are due to appear under the title 'Duisburger Universitäts- und Personalschriften des 17. und 18. Jahrhunderts' in the proceedings of the conference, 'Stadt und Literatur', which was held in Osnabrück in 1990.

unsuspecting reader first realizes that only the periods 1601-1605, 1651-1655, 1701-1705 and 1751-1755 and respondents' names beginning with the letter E have been included. In view of the necessity of imposing limits on the coverage Ranieri regards the chosen sample survey as an appropriate excuse for making general comments on the nature of legal dissertations and on academic teaching. The majority of reviewers justifiably had some doubts about the work's methodology. A complete listing of easily identifiable holdings, a catalogue of the Max Planck Institute's dissertations or a bibliography of a narrower time span, say 1600-1650, would have been of far greater service to scholarship. In this critique one should not of course forget the many advances achieved. The various access points in the database set up for the project can be accessed without difficulty and printed on demand. Almost all entries are based on personal inspection or on reliable sources. The descriptions of titles lack only details of pagination and, as in almost all bibliographies of dissertations, the names of dedicatees and writers of congratulatory verses. The indexes are very helpful in their ability to answer quickly any enquiries about particular *praesides*, respondents (including their home town), particular legal topics, or dissertations defended at a university. The second, closely related project initiated by Ranieri, his *Biographisches Repertorium der Juristen im alten Reich 16.-18. Jahrhundert* (4 vols. Frankfurt am Main, 1987-1991), an intrinsically highly commendable bio-bibliography of numerous law students with extensive information on the dissertations defended by them, suffered from its ambitious objectives.[15] The work, which tried to achieve too much, was in any case so monumental that even quite a large working group could only cope with the letters A, C, D and E, raising suspicions that no further volumes will appear.[16] It is to be hoped that at the very least the database in Frankfurt will be kept going.

The considerable improvements which could have been achieved in the bibliograpical coverage of early legal dissertations by Ranieri's team have been realized and amplified in Ryuichi Tsuno's catalogue of Chuo University Library in Tokyo. Around 12,500 early legal dissertations principally from Protestant universities in north, central and east Germany are now to be found in a completely unexpected location, having been sold to Japan in the 1980s by Rostock University Library through the Frankfurt antiquarian bookseller Keip.[17] Presumably it was not only duplicates which found their way to Japan. Tsuno's catalogue, the main part of which is arranged alphabetically by respondent, is well served by several indexes. However a serious defect is the lack of standardization of personal and place names which turn up in a confusing variety of forms.

15 See also Barbara Dölemeyer, *Frankfurter Juristen im 17. und 18. Jahrhundert* (Frankfurt/M., 1993), which contains 737 biographies and 571 dissertations by Frankfurt lawyers.

16 Information from F. Ranieri.

17 Ryuichi Tsuno, *Katalog juristischer Dissertationen, Disputationen, Programme und anderer Hochschulschriften im Zeitraum von 1600 bis 1800 aus den Beständen der Universität Rostock*. 2 vols. (Tokyo, 1989).

The importance of the survival of a literary or historical archive *in situ* or in another institution for the success of a bibliography of dissertations can be confirmed by the present writer in respect of Königsberg. The State and University Library at Königsberg as well as the City Library, both of which had extensive, virtually comprehensive holdings of early Königsberg dissertations, went up in flames in 1944/1945. Luckily some of the treasures had been outhoused earlier in East Prussian country houses, where they were examined by Polish and Soviet experts after the war and transferred variously to Torun University Library, the National Library in Warsaw, the State Library in Vilna and the libraries of the Academy of Sciences in Vilna and in St Petersburg. The co-operation of the Soviet locations could not be counted on in preparing the *Promotionen an der Universität Königsberg 1548-1799* (Munich, 1988), so that the identification of the 275 doctoral dissertations in the higher faculties and the names of the 409 Masters of Arts had to suffice. Despite these handicaps the bibliography contains not only dedications and congratulatory verses but also biographical references to almost all candidates. Given that Königsberg was an especially well attended university in the seventeenth century, where disputations were carried on enthusiastically, and that that century has the worst bibliographical coverage, the idea of producing a bibliography of Königsberg dissertations from 1601 to 1700 suggested itself to me. Since 1991 some two thousand titles from German libraries, but particularly from relevant libraries in Eastern Europe, have been gathered.

In most collections of early dissertations those from Catholic universities are in the minority and by and large present more difficulties in their bibliographical recording, a fact which makes it all the more gratifying that catalogues of two such universities, Cologne and Würzburg, have appeared within as many years.[18] Both begin at the end of the sixteenth century – before 1580 there were for the most part relatively few printed dissertations – and list the holdings of dissertations preserved in both locations. In the case of Cologne the holdings are extensive and in that of Würzburg complete, although the description of the dissertations of the latter institution depends only on the large collection of early dissertations in the university library there. A systematic search for dissertations from these institutions in libraries elsewhere would result in some further additions to the 2,300 from Cologne and the 1,600 from Würzburg. It is to the credit of the compilers of the Würzburg catalogue that they have also treated aspects of the printing of dissertations as a genre in an exhibition with an accompanying catalogue.[19] The bibliophilic provision of many Würzburg dissertations with illustrations and fine bindings is hardly representative, as

18 Peter Stauder, *Die Hochschulschriften der alten Kölner Universität 1583-1978. Ein Verzeichnis* (Munich, 1990); *Würzburger Hochschulschriften 1581-1803. Bestandsverzeichnis.* Nach Vorarbeiten von J. A. Brein hrsg. von Gottfried Mälzer (Würzburg, 1992).

19 *Würzburger Dissertationen 1581-1803. Kostbar und schön gebunden, informativ und dekorativ illustriert* (Würzburg, 1992).

such works were printed at the majority of universities in a simple format and frequently to a standard which left much to be desired.

Legal and theological titles dominate all general lists of dissertations, while medical ones sometimes, but not always, outnumber the philosophical, as medical students very rarely accounted for more than ten percent of the university population. Medical dissertations are certainly present in considerable numbers in the *National Union Catalog*, and especially in the monumental holdings of the National Library of Medicine and in David Paisey's catalogue of German imprints of the seventeenth century, where they can be found even more readily, although there are still large gaps in all of these collections. This being so, we are all the more grateful for the catalogue of the private library of Albrecht von Haller (1708-1777), which contains some nine thousand dissertations of the seventeenth and especially the eighteenth century on medicine or natural sciences. The collection is now kept in the Biblioteca Nazionale Braidense in Milan and was fully catalogued some years ago.[20] Dissertations from many European universities, e.g. Paris, Edinburgh, Lund and Leiden among others, are listed there under the *praesides*, but other indexes are lacking. Haller's library is above all a treasure house for the most important universities of the Enlightenment, namely Halle and Göttingen, where the medical giants of the day such as Friedrich Hoffmann, Georg Ernst Stahl and Haller himself taught. Coverage of Göttingen dissertations is especially complete, as Haller lectured there continuously from 1736 to 1753 and up to his death remained in close touch with the university and the Academy of Sciences there. However since 1993 one has not needed the Milan catalogue for Göttingen medical dissertations, as Ulrich Tröhler and Sabine Mildner-Mazzei have demonstrated impressively the usefulness of early dissertations for research on a variety of topics, including social history.[21] They were helped in their work by the fact that neither the university's library nor archives had suffered any losses through war damage to speak of. For this reason they were able to produce not only a catalogue of dissertations but also a large body of documentary evidence on university and family history, which includes supporting details on each candidate's date of matriculation, printed curriculum vitae, formal application to graduate and even the review of his dissertation in the *Göttinger gelehrte Anzeigen*.

Only medical dissertations are recorded in my *Bio-bibliographisches Verzeichnis jüdischer Doktoren des 17. und 18. Jahrhunderts* (Munich, 1991), which contains the titles of some four hundred doctoral dissertations and details of graduation of Jewish medical students at German and Dutch universities. Jews were allowed to graduate at German universities for the first time in 1721, and then only in medicine.

20 *Biblioteca Nazionale Braidense, Milano, Catalogo del Fondo Haller. Pt. 2: Dissertazioni.* A cura di Maria Teresa Monti. 5 vols. (Milan, 1985-87). Pt. 1 is devoted to monographs.

21 Ulrich Tröhler and Sabine Mildner-Mazzei, *Vom Medizinstudenten zum Doktor. Die Göttinger medizinischen Promotionen im 18. Jahrhundert* (Göttingen, 1993).

Relatively little advance has been made in the bibliographical recording of theological dissertations, the first work to follow on from Müller's on Freiburg being Kelly's doctoral dissertation on Helmstedt, the latter incidentally a further example of a fruitful combination of bibliographical research and scholarly analysis of contents.[22] In this connection Hans Burose's *Katalog der Calvörschen Bibliothek* (3 vols. Clausthal-Zellerfeld, 1972-75) deserves to be mentioned as an essential tool for the study of Protestant universities in central Germany.

The listing of dissertations from academic *Gymnasien* is inadequate at the present moment, as a glance at Marti's and Ranieri's index of institutions can quickly confirm. Such lists of the particularly well-known *Gymnasien* such as Bremen, Hamburg or Danzig remain pressing desiderata, even if they would be difficult to compile for the last two towns due to the extensive damage suffered by the considerable holdings of the respective town libraries. In the meantime relevant bibliographies are available for two smaller institutions in Westphalia, Steinfurt and Hamm.[23] As a number of foreign universities on the fringes of the German-speaking areas have great relevance to Germany's intellectual history, the fairly recent lists for Franeker, Harderwijk, Dorpat and Prague enrich not only the history of universities in Germany but also our national bibliography.[24] An important desideratum in research on this subject must still be bibliographies of the dissertations defended at Orléans and Padua, whose well-known legal and medical faculties were attended by many German students, particularly before 1700.

Among dissertations of the early modern period the recording of lists of lectures presents major difficulties, in that these very slim brochures have rarely survived for the period up to 1700 and even for the eighteenth century only in small numbers. Many of these rarities mentioned in Erman/Horn were lost in the Second World War. However as they were often printed in a variety of periodicals, we have an alternative source of information. There is little at present to add to Blanke's lists, if one leaves out the edition of the Königsberg lecture lists of the Kant era, which the present writer has not seen yet.[25]

From the foregoing it is clear that pre-1800 university publications are the

22 Wolfgang Müller, *500 Jahre theologische Promotion an der Universität Freiburg i.Br.* (Freiburg, 1957); W. A. Kelly, *The Theological Faculty at Helmstedt: an outline of its intellectual development as mirrored in its dissertations, together with a chronological catalogue.* Ph.D. thesis, Strathclyde University. 2 vols. 1992.

23 Ingeborg Höting, *Die Professoren der Steinfurter Hohen Schule* (Steinfurt, 1991), which includes details of numerous works written by them; Manfred Komorowski, 'Die Schriften des Akademischen Gymnasiums Hamm/Westfalen (1657-1781). Eine vorläufige Bilanz', *GJ*, 67 (1992), 275-297.

24 Theodorus J. Meijer, *Album promotorum Academiae Franekerensis (1591-1811)* (Franeker, 1973); Matti A. Sainio, *Dissertationen und Orationen der Universität Dorpat 1632-1656* (Stockholm, 1978); Josef Tříška, *Disertace Pražské Univerzity 16.-18. stoleti* (Prague, 1977).

25 Horst Walter Blanke, *Bestandsverzeichnis der in der Universitätsbibliothek Bochum vorhandenen Vorlesungsverzeichnisse deutschsprachiger Universitäten und Hochschulen* (Bochum, 1983); idem, 'Bibliographie der in periodischer Literatur abgedruckten Vorlesungsverzeichnisse

subject of constant searches and analysis, the reasons for which have been illustrated exhaustively by Marti, Kundert and Ranieri in the introductions to their catalogues or have been demonstrated concretely by Trevisani, Kelly and others.[26] Each project to improve the listing of early dissertations is therefore welcome, be it a published catalogue of a large collection,[27] a complete or a partial list of the numerous, still unresearched institutions or a work on a particular academic discipline. Each university should be vitally, intimately interested in recording as completely as possible its own publications and in recreating from its archives an alternative access to the information, especially in those cases where the institution has been closed or where its library has suffered war damage. The most complete recording possible of dissertations is, like the recording of funeral sermons and marriage celebrations, an important task of the German national bibliography of the early modern period. Without these smaller bibliographical items the value of a seventeenth century national bibliography would be greatly reduced. A better survey of the bibliographical output would also put on a much firmer basis the investigation of such topics as early dissertations as a genre, on the theory of disputations in the early modern period, and on the printers of dissertations and their distribution through specialist dealers. Indeed one can start off from the knowledge that the desirable recording of dedications and congratulatory verses in early dissertations will open up a new, extensive body of sources on genealogical research as well as on neo-Latin and German literary studies.

deutschsprachiger Universitäten 1700-1899' *Berichte zur Wissenschaftsgeschichte*, 6 (1983), 205-227; 10 (1987), 17-43; 11 (1988), 105-117. Riccardo Pozzo (ed.), *Vorlesungsverzeichnisse der Universität Königsberg, 1720-1804*. 2 vols. (Stuttgart, 1995).

26 Hanspeter Marti, 'Der wissenschaftsgeschichtliche Dokumentationswert alter Dissertationen', *Nouvelles de la République des Lettres*, 1981, pp. 117-32. Of exceptional importance, particularly for the treatment of the long-running problem of authorship, are the historical contributions of Werner Allweiss and Hans-Joachim Koppitz in *Dissertationen in Wissenschaft und Bibliotheken* (Munich, 1979) and of W. A. Kelly, *Early German dissertations. Their importance for university history* (East Linton, 1992).

27 Typical examples are: *Universitätsbibliothek Tübingen, Dissertationen-Katalog*. 370 microfiches (Munich, 1983); *Universitätsbibliothek der Humboldt-Universität Berlin, Alphabetischer Katalog der Dissertationen*. 510 microfiches (Hildesheim, 1989).

KONRAD PHILIPP LIMMER (1658-1730)

A neglected polymath

WILLIAM A. KELLY

IF I am conscious of the incompleteness of the list of published works of Konrad Philipp Limmer, the long-time holder of the Chair of Medicine and Natural History at the Gymnasium Illustre Anhaltinum, Zerbst, which is offered here as a report of work in progress,[1] I am equally conscious that, in drawing attention to a figure who has been neglected hitherto by scholars, I am paying tribute to two of David Paisey's interests, those of publications not advertized in the regular organs of the book trade and works emanating from towns outwith the main centres of printing.[2]

The majority of the dissertations traced so far have been found among the Dieterichs Collection in the National Library of Scotland, which was bought in 1820 by the Advocates' Library as the remnant of the vast collection of the Regensburg senator Georg Septimus Dieterichs, which had been auctioned at

1 The titles of other dissertations (some with the year of publication) by Limmer will be found in A. G. Schmidt, *Anhalt'sches Schriftsteller-Lexikon* ... (Bernburg, 1830), pp. 212-14, and in J. C. Heffter, *Museum disputatorium physico-medicum tripartitum*. 4 vols (Zittau, 1756-64). I have refrained from including details of those, where I have been unable to verify the details from a located copy. Postal enquiries to a number of libraries in eastern Germany have so far failed to locate any further titles. I would be grateful for details of locations of these other dissertations. Photocopies of the texts located already in Zerbst and Halle have been deposited in the National Library of Scotland and Zerbst now has copies of all those found in Edinburgh. I am grateful to Frau Iruta Völlger, the librarian of the Gymnasium Francisceum, the successor of the Gymnasium Illustre Anhaltinum, for her generous assistance in answering enquiries about the Gymnasium Francisceum's holdings, and to Dr Ursula Perkow of Heidelberg University for supplying details from Zerbst's published matriculation register. I must also thank my colleague, Miss M. Ridley, for her forbearance with my numerous requests for the rather obscure secondary sources on the Gymnasium Illustre Anhaltinum's history, which are listed in notes 5, 7 and 14, through the international lending scheme.

2 There is no mention of Limmer in the medical biographical dictionaries of J. E. Dezeimeris, *Dictionnaire historique de la médecine ancienne et moderne*, [etc]. 4 vols. (Paris, 1828-39); B. Hutchinson, *Biographia medica*, [etc]. (London, 1799); C. W. Kestner, *Medizinisches Gelehrten-Lexicon* (Jena, 1740); idem, *Bibliotheca medica*, [etc]. 2 vols (Jena, 1746); J. J. Manget, *Bibliotheca scriptorum medicorum, veterum et recentiorum*, [etc]. 2 vols (Geneva, 1731); and A. Hirsch (ed.), *Biographisches Lexikon der hervorragenden Ärzte aller Zeiten und Völker*. 6 vols (Vienna, 1884-88).

Leipzig earlier that year.[3] At some time in the 1960s the dissertations were separated from the rest of the collection and given another pressmark, although both parts have been kept together. The dissertations, which number around thirty-five thousand in total, date from the late sixteenth to the very early nineteenth century, but the bulk are from the seventeenth and eighteenth centuries. They rank next after those of the British Library and the Bodleian Library in number, but unlike these have never received the attention from students of German university education which they deserve. Their existence seems to have been unknown to Ritchie and Evans, although this can perhaps be explained by the vast bulk of them still being uncatalogued, a situation unlikely to change in the near future.[4] The majority of the dissertations are from legal faculties, but theological and philosophical faculties are also strongly represented. A very large number come from universities in the eastern part of the Federal Republic of Germany. An interesting feature of the dissertations, like those in the Bodleian Library, is that some are not from universities proper but from institutions of lower status, academic *Gymnasien*, and from Latin schools in various parts of Germany.

Our knowledge of Limmer's life is rather scanty. He was born at Nienburg on the Saale on 28 February 1658. His grandfather, Konrad, had been a pastor in the Upper Palatinate, which his son, Ambrosius Gottfried, also a pastor, abandoned to avoid the troubles of the Thirty Years' War. He found refuge in Anhalt, which belonged to the Reformed confession, eventually finding a benefice at the Jakobikirche in Köthen.[5] Konrad Philipp did not follow the profession of his grandfather or father, preferring to study medicine. On 25 July 1674, at the age of sixteen, he matriculated at the Gymnasium Illustre Anhaltinum at Zerbst, moving over six years later to Leiden University on 16 November 1680 as a student of medicine.[6] In 1685 he was appointed to succeed Jakob Röseler in the Chair of Medicine and Natural History at Zerbst, taking up his appointment the following year. The Gymnasium had been established in 1582 to defend the orthodox purity of true religion, and from its early days attracted many students from outside Germany, but particularly aspiring

3 *Bibliotheca, seu catalogus librorum quibus utitur Georgius Septimus Dieterichs*. 5 vols (Ratisbonae, 1760–63). Cf. also F. K. G. Hirsching, *Versuch einer Beschreibung sehenswürdiger Bibliotheken Teutschlands* (Erlangen, 1786–91), III, pp. 721–23.

4 J. M. Ritchie, 'German books in Glasgow and Edinburgh, 1500–1750', *MLR*, 57 (1962), 523–41; R. J. W. Evans, 'German universities after the Thirty Years War', *History of Universities*, 1 (1981), 169–90. The lack of appreciation of these dissertations can be mirrored, if not excused, in the treatment of similar materials in German libraries. Cf. M. Komorowski, *Die Hochschulschriften des 17. Jahrhunderts und ihre bibliographische Erfassung* [Typescript of a paper read at Wolfenbüttel on 22 Sept. 1993], p. 1.

5 F. Münnich, *Geschichte des Francisceums zu Zerbst 1526–1928* (Zerbst, 1928), p. 132.

6 *Die Matrikel des Gymnasium Illustre zu Zerbst in Anhalt 1582–1797*, ed. R. Specht. Sonderveröffentlichungen der Ostfälischen Familienkundlichen Kommission, 5 (Leipzig, 1930), p. 67; *Album studiosorum Academiae Lugduno Batavae 1575–1875*, [etc.] [compiled by W. N. du Rieu.] (The Hague, 1875).

clergymen from Bohemia, who also received their ordination there.[7] When Johann took over the running of the principality in 1642, he made it his object to return the territory to Lutheranism, which he hoped to gain by the appointment of a staunch Lutheran, Johann Durrius, as superintendent. In spite of this the Gymnasium remained largely Reformed in its staff and outlook.[8] In 1687 Limmer completed his formal education, when on 27 June, ten days after matriculating, he defended a dissertation, *De hydrophobia*, at the University of Altdorf without a *praeses*, as was the custom there for doctoral candidates.[9] Knowing the value of publicity, Limmer supported new, progressive ideas, especially if their consequences would bear fruit, as when he supplemented his lectures on human anatomy with practical classes in dissection, being one of the few in Germany in that century to do so.[10] Limmer was no ivory-towered academic, as he demonstrated in 1693, when he became the town physician, and even more strikingly in 1715, when he succeeded his colleague, Jakob Bernhard Aeplinius, as mayor. These additional offices helped to confirm the reputation for hard work already acquired by Limmer through his numerous dissertations.[11] The variety of subjects covered by these help to show that, for all his showmanship, he was a very competent, versatile scholar, who deserves to be rescued from the oblivion into which he has fallen.[12] Schmidt records the titles and dates of over sixty dissertations written by, and defended under, Limmer up to 1709. The fall in the number of dissertations written by him after 1715 can probably be explained by the fact that his civic duties heavily curtailed the amount of time which he was able to devote to his academic career.[13] He died on 1 January 1730 at the age of seventy three. The Gymnasium, which had an annual average attendance of only 12.6 students throughout its 216-year history, closed in 1798, re-opening in 1803 as a Latin school under the name of Gymnasium Francisceum, which has recently replaced the clumsy and pompous title 'Erweiterte Oberschule' foisted on it by the German Democratic Republic.[14]

The first dissertation prepared under Limmer's supervision for a public

7 H. Becker, *Das Zerbster Gymnasium als anhaltische Universität* (Zerbst, 1903), pp. 1-3. Cf. also F. Kindscher, *Geschichte des hochfürstlich Anhaltinischen academischen Gesammtgymnasiums zu Zerbst* (Zerbst, 1868); W. Sickel, 'Überblick über die Geschichte des Herzoglichen Francisceums', in: *Herzogliches Francisceum zu Zerbst. Bericht über das Schuljahr 1912-1913* (Zerbst, 1913), pp. 1-11; F. Münnich, [note 5], pp. 24-41.

8 Becker, [note 7], pp. 26-7.

9 *Die Matrikel der Universität Altdorf*, ed. Elias von Steinmeyer. Veröffentlichungen der Gesellschaft für fränkische Geschichte. 4. Reihe: Matrikeln fränkischer Schulen. 2 vols (Würzburg, 1912), 1, p. 428. The British Library possesses two copies of the dissertation (pressmarks 1179.k.10(15) and 7306.h.4(14*)).

10 For an earlier instance of practical classes in dissection at an institution of higher learning in Germany see W. A. Kelly, *Hermann Conring (1606-1681): a study in versatility* (East Linton, 1992), p. 6.

11 Schmidt, [note 1].

12 Cf. note 2.

13 Münnich, [note 5], p. 133.

14 F. Sintenis, *Zur Geschichte des Zerbster Schulwesens* (Zerbst, 1853).

disputation at Zerbst was that *De gravitate aëris*, which was defended by J. G. Raumer on 20 March 1686 (no. 1). In this Limmer begins with the obligatory scholarly references to Aristotle before he moves on to demonstrate his acquaintance not only with the experiments on the barometer conducted by the Italian Evangelista Torricelli (1608-1647), but also with the techniques of laboratory science. Any suspicion that the references to Aristotle might show Limmer still tied to rather out-dated patterns of thought is banished by the warm references to Descartes in his *De medio vitandi errores* (no. 3). Indeed Limmer, and possibly some of his other colleagues, may prove on closer examination to have been a hitherto unrecognized element in the reception of Cartesianism in Germany, even if Zerbst's importance was not as great as that of Duisburg University, which also belonged to the Reformed confession.[15] Limmer's interest in philosophy can be seen in another twelve of his dissertations traced so far (nos. 2, 5-6, 10, 16-17, 26-31). The dissertations of a scientific and medical nature described below cover an admirably wide range of subjects, including botany, physiology, the transmission of sound, the circulation of the blood and two interesting investigations, which also demonstrate Limmer's keen interest in local affairs, namely one on the famous Zerbst bitter beer (no. 23), and the other on a case of Siamese twins born the year before in Dessau (no. 24). The latter is especially interesting, not simply for the corroboration of what we know from other sources about Limmer's practical classes on dissection, but also because the dissertation reads in many places very like an autopsy report, which Limmer and the court physician, Dr Euchler, carried out.

CATALOGUE

Reference is made, where appropriate, to J. C. Heffter, *Museum disputatorium physico-medicum tripartitum*. 4 vols (Zittau, 1756-1764). In the notes to the dissertations the following abbreviations are used: *D* to denote the dedicatee; *L* to denote the writer of a dedicatory letter; *V* to denote the writer of congratulatory verses.

(1) 20 March 1686
[roman] DISPVTATIO PHYSICA | [italic] DE | [roman] GRAVITATE AERIS | [italic] QVAM | [...] | [roman] SVB PRÆSIDIO | [roman] CONRADI PHILIPPI LIMMERI, | [...] | [roman] PVBLICO ERVDITORVM EXAMINI SVBJICIT | [roman] JOHANNES GEORGIVS [gothic] Raumer | [roman] DESSAVIENS. ANHALTINVS. | [italic] AD D. XX. MARTII ANNO. M DC LXXXVI. | [roman] HORIS LOCOQVE CONSVETIS. | [line of printer's flowers] | [roman] SERVESTÆ, TYPIS JOH. ERN. BEZELII. ILL. G. A. TYP. |

15 F. Trevisani, *Descartes in Germania: la ricezione del cartesianismo nella Facoltà filosofica e medica di Duisburg (1652-1703)* (Milan, 1992). I am grateful to Dr M. Komorowski of Duisburg University Library for this reference.

A-B⁴[-B3-4]. 4°
V: Immanuel Hoffmeyer
Edinburgh NL

(2) 18 June 1686
[roman] COLLEGII PHYSICI DISPVTATORII | [roman] DISPVTATIO PRIMA | [roman] eaq; Prœmialis | [italic] De | [roman] ORIGINE ERRORVM | [italic] In | [roman] REBVS PHILOSOPHICIS | [italic] Quam | [...] | [roman] SUB PRÆSIDIO | [roman] CONRADI PHILIPPI LIMMERI | [...] [italic] Publicæ Eruditorum Ventilationi | [italic] exponit | [roman] ad d. 18 Jun. M DC LXXXVI. | [italic] h. & l. consuetis. | [roman] CAROLVS [gothic] Gottlieb [roman] WENZLO Servest-Anhaltinus | [roman] Phil. & Medic. Stud. | [line of printer's flowers] | [roman] SERVESTÆ, Typis Joh. Ern. Bezel. Ill. G.A.Typ. |
A-B⁴[-B3-4]. 4°
D: Johann Ernst Schönleben
V: Christian Rudolf Lezius, Johann Friedrich Müller
Zerbst GF

(3) 13 May 1687
[roman] COLLEGII PHYSICI DISPVTATORII | [roman] DISPVTATIO SECVNDA. | [roman] Eaq; Prœmialis | [italic] DE | [roman] MEDIO VITANDI ERRORES | [roman] In REBVS PHILOSOPHICIS | [italic] Quam | [...] | [roman] SVB PRÆSIDIO | [roman] CONRADI PHILIPPI LIMMERI, | [...] | [italic] Publico Eruditorum Examini | [italic] subjicit | [roman] Ad d. 13. Maij M DC LXXXVII. | [italic] h. & l. consuetis, | [roman] JOHANNES CHRISTOPHORVS HEINZIVS, Gernrod- | [roman] Anhaltinus Philos. & Theol. Stud. | [ornament] | [italic] SERVESTÆ, EXCVDIT JOH. ERN. BEZELIVS. |
πA-D⁴[-D4]. 4°
D: Viktor Amadeus & Wilhelm, Counts of Anhalt
V: Christian Heinze
Edinburgh NL

(4) 23 June 1687
[roman] DISPVTATIO CHIRVRGICO-MEDICA | [italic] | DE | [roman] FONTICVLIS | [roman] IN QVA | [roman] Irrationalis eorundem in vulgari Me- | [roman] dicorum Praxi usus ostenditur, nec non ex Fabrica cor- | [roman] poris humani infallibiliter demonstratur, | [roman] ET | [...] | [italic] Publico Eruditorum Examini | [italic] subjicitur | [roman] PRÆSIDE | [roman] CONRADO PHILIPPO LIMMERO, | [...] | [italic] Ad d. 23. Jun. M DC LXXXVII. | [italic] h. & l. consuetis. | [roman] RESPONDENTE | [roman] CAROLO [gothic] Gottlieb [roman] WENZLOVIO, Servest-Anhaltino | [roman] Philos. & Med. Stud. | [ornament] | [italic] SERVESTÆ,

| [italic] Excudit Joh: Ernest: Bezelius, Ill. Gymn. Anh. Typ. |
πA-G^4[-G4]. 4°
D: Wilhelm Heinrich von Freiberg and Friedrich Amadeus Raumer
V: Joh. Georg Michaëlis
London BL: 1179.d.19(2)

(5) 6 April 1688
[roman] DISPVTATIO PHYSICA | [roman] EXTRAORDINARIA | [italic] DE | [roman] VNIONE MENTIS HV- | [roman] MANÆ, | [roman] cum Corpore Organico, | [italic] Quam | [...] | [roman] SVB PRÆSIDIO | [roman] CONRADI PHILIPPI LIMMERI, | [...] | [italic] Publice tueri conabitur | [roman] Ad d. vi. April: M DC LXXXIIX. | [roman] JOH: RVDOLPH: [gothic] Stubenrauch/ [roman] A. Anhalt. | [roman] Philos. & Theol. Studios. | [ornament] | [italic] SERVESTÆ, EXCVDIT JOH. ERN. BEZELIVS. |
A-D^4. 4°
D: Wilhelm Heinrich von Freyberg
V: Joh. Daniel Appel, Augustin Banse (in German)
Edinburgh NL

(6) 6 June 1688
[roman] DISPVTATIO PHYSICA | [roman] EXTRAORDINARIA | [italic] DE | [roman] ORTV MENTIS | [roman] HVMANÆ, | [italic] Quam | [...] | [roman] SVB PRÆSIDIO | [roman] CONRADI PHILIPPI LIMMERI, | [...] | [italic] Publice defendendam suscipiet | [roman] Ad d. vi. Junij M DC LXXXIIX. | [italic] l. & h. solitis antemeridianis | [roman] FRIDERICUS CHRISTOPHORUS STANNIUS, B. A. | [roman] Philos. & Theol. Studios. | [ornament] | [italic] SERVESTÆ, EXCVDIT JOH. ERN. BEZELIVS. |
π^{2}A-B^4[-B4]C^4. 4°
D: Viktor Amadeus, Count of Anhalt
V: Limmer
Edinburgh NL

(7) 10 August 1688
[roman] COLLEGII PHYSICI DISPVTATORII | [roman] DISPVTATIO DECIMA QVINTA. | [italic] DE | [roman] CORPORE PER- | [roman] SPICVO & OPACO. | [italic] Quam | [...] | [roman] SVB PRÆSIDIO | [roman] CONRADI PHILIPPI LIMMERI, | [...] | [italic] Placidæ publicæq; Eruditorum Ventilationi exponet | [roman] Ad d. 10. Augusti M DC LXXXIIX. | [roman] JOHANNES [gothic] Gottlieb Vierthaler/ | [roman] Philos. & L.L. Studiosus. | [ornament] | [italic] SERVESTÆ, EXCVDIT JOH. ERN. BEZELIVS. |
A-B^4. 4°
D: Christoph Vierthaler, Johann Georg Milling

V: Johann Friedrich Müller
Heffter 4211
Edinburgh NL

(8) 8 February 1689
[roman] DISPVTATIO PHYSICA | [roman] EXTRAORDINARIA. | [italic] DE | [roman] CORPORVM NATVRA- | [roman] LIVM PRINCIPIS, | [italic] Quam | [...] | [roman] SVB PRÆSIDIO | [roman] CONRADI PHILIPPI LIMMERI, | [...] | [italic] Publicè Ventilandam proponet | [roman] Ad d. 8. Februar: M DC LXXXIX. | [roman] JOHANNES CHRISTIANVS DARES, Briga-Sil. | [roman] Philosoph. Studios. | [ornament] | [italic] SERVESTÆ, EXCVDIT JOH. ERN. BEZELIVS. |
A-E^4[-E3-4]. 4°
D: Adam Samuel Hartmann, Friedrich Lucas, Johann Dares
V: J.F. Müller
Edinburgh NL

(9) 28 June 1689
[roman] COLLEGII PHYSICI DISPVTATORII | [roman] DISPVTATIO DECIMA SEPTIMA | [italic] DE | [roman] CORPORE CALIDO & | [roman] FRIGIDO, | [italic] Quam | [...] | [roman] SVB PRÆSIDIO | [roman] CONRADI PHILIPPI LIMMERI, | [...] | [italic] Placidæ & publicæ Eruditorum Ventilationi sistet | [roman] Ad d. 28. Junij M DC LXXXIX. | [italic] h. & l. solitis. | [gothic] Gottlieb [roman] EPHRAIM BERNER, Hoym-Anhalt. | [roman] Philosoph. Studiosus. | [ornament] | [italic] SERVESTÆ, EXCVDIT JOH. ERN. BEZELIVS. |
A-C^4. 4°
D: Ernst Friedrich Splithuse, Nathanael Gottlieb Splithuse
V: Johann Friedrich Müller, J.C. Dares (in German), Ephraim Theophil Bobbe (in Greek)
Heffter 4212
Edinburgh NL

(10) 2 August 1689
[roman] DISPUTATIO PHYSICA | [italic] DE | [roman] MENTIS HUMANÆ IM- | [roman] MORTALITATE | [italic] SEU | [roman] PERENNI EJUSDEM DURATIONE, | [italic] Quam | [...] | [roman] SUB UMBONE | [roman] DN. CONRADI PHILIPPI LIMMERI, | [...] | [italic] Publico Eruditorum Examini subjicit | [roman] Ad d. 2. Augusti M DC LXXXIX. | [italic] h. & l. solitis. | [roman] JOHANNES CHRISTOPHORUS HEINZIUS, | [roman] Gernrodâ-Anhaltinus. | [roman] AUTOR. | [ornament] | [italic] SERVESTÆ, EXCVDIT JOH. ERN. BEZELIVS. |
πA-D^4[-D2-4]. 4°

D: Karl Philipp von Beuder, Wolfgang Konrad von Einsiedel
V: Limmer, Christian Heinze
Edinburgh NL

(11) 10 January 1690
[roman] DISPVTATIONEM PHYSICAM | [italic] DE | [roman] ECHO, | [roman] Aspirante Omnipotentis Gratia | [roman] SVB PRÆSIDIO | [roman] DN. CONRADI PHILIPPI LIMMERI, | [...] | [italic] In publico Conflictu tueri conabitur | [roman] Ad d. 10. Januarij M DC XC. | [italic] H. L. Q. C. | [roman] GOTTOFREDUS CHRISTIANUS GOETZIUS, | [roman] Lipsiens. | [roman] AUTOR. | [rule] | [italic] SERVESTÆ, EXCVDIT JOH. ERN. BEZELIVS. |
A-B^4C^2. 4°
D: Johann Bohn, Johann Rudolph
V: Johann Christian Keller
Heffter 4214
Edinburgh NL

(12) 6 June 1690
[roman] DISPVTATIO PHYSICA EXTRAORDINARIA, | [italic] DE | [roman] SENSIBVS INTERNIS, | [italic] Quam | [...] | [roman] SVB PRÆSIDIO | [roman] DN. CONRADI PHILIPPI LIMMERI, | [...] | [italic] Fautoris ac Præceptoris sui debito Reverentiæ cultu ætatem | [italic] prosequendi, | [italic] Publicæ Eruditorum Ventilationi | [roman] Ad d. 6. Junij M DC XC. | [italic] | H. L. Q. C. | [italic] subjicit | [roman] JOHANNES CHRISTIANVS DARES, Briga-Silesius, | [roman] Philosoph. Studiosus. | [roman] Autor & Respondens. | [ornament] | [italic] SERVESTÆ, EXCVDIT JOH. ERN. BEZELIVS. |
πA-C^4D^4[-D3-4]. 4°
V: Martin Gerlach
Edinburgh NL

(13) 20 June 1690
[roman] DISPVTATIO PHYSICA | [italic] DE | [roman] ORTV MVNDI, | [italic] Quam | [...] | [roman] SVB PRÆSIDIO | [roman] DN. CONRADI PHILIPPI LIMMERI, | [...] | [roman] d. 20. Junij M DC XC. | [italic] h. & l. solitis. | [italic] Publicè Ventilandam proponit | [roman] CHRISTIANVS [gothic] Anesorge/ [roman] Cotbusio-Lusatus, | [roman] Philosoph. Studiosus. | [ornament] | [italic] SERVESTÆ, EXCVDIT JOH. ERN. BEZELIVS. |
A-B^4. 4°
D: Town council of Cottbus
V: Joh: Ulrich Vollmar, Joh. Christoph Laurentius (in German)
Edinburgh NL

(14) 12 September 1690
[roman] DISPVTATIO PHYSICA | [italic] DE | [roman] ELEMENTIS | [italic] Quam | [...] | [roman] SVB PRÆSIDIO | [roman] DN. CONRADI PHILIPPI LIMMERI, | [...] | [italic] Publicæ & placidæ Eruditorum Disquisitioni submittet | [roman] d. 12. Septembr: M DC XC. | [italic] H. L. Q. C. | [roman] JOHANNES CHRISTIANUS KELLERUS, | [roman] Servesta-Anhaltinus. | [roman] AUTOR & RESPONDENS. | [ornament] | [italic] SERVESTÆ, EXCVDIT JOH. ERN. BEZELIVS. |
A-D^4. 4°
D: Officials of Wolfgang, Duke of Anhalt
V: J.C. Pauli, G.C. Goez, Christian Anesorge (in German)
Edinburgh NL

(15) November 1690
[roman] DISPVTATIO PHYSICA | [italic] DE | [roman] COMETIS | [italic] Quam | [...] | [roman] SVB CLYPEO | [roman] DN. CONRADI PHILIPPI LIMMERI, | [...] | [italic] Placido ac Publico Eruditorum Examini subjicit, | [roman] Ad d. Novembr: M DC XC. | [italic] H. L. Q. C. | [roman] GOTTLIEB EPHRAIM BERNERUS, | [roman] Hoyma-Anhaltin: Philos. Studiosus. | [roman] AUTOR & RESPONDENS. | [ornament] | [italic] SERVESTÆ, EXCVDIT JOH. ERN. BEZELIVS. |
πA-D^4[-D4]. 4°
D: Nathanael Janus, Johann Ludwig Janus, Johann Ernst Pfau, Andreas Schunck
V: Johann Ernst Bornemann, Johann Ulrich Vollmar, Ephraim Theophil Bobbe, Gottfried Scheurer (in German), Johann Christ. Laurentius (in German), Martin Handt
Edinburgh NL

(16) 6 March 1691
[roman] DISPVTATIO PHYSICA | [roman] EXTRAORDINARIA. | [italic] DE | [roman] PASSIONIBVS ANIMÆ PRIMI- | [roman] TIVIS, EARVNDEMQVE | [roman] EFFECTIBVS, | [italic] Quam | [...] | [roman] SVB PRÆSIDIO | [roman] DN. CONRADI PHILIPPI LIMMERI, | [...] | [italic] Dn. Fautoris ac studiorum suorum Promotoris reve- | [italic] renter colendi, | [italic] Publicæ Eruditorum disquisitioni | [roman] Ad d. 6. Mart. M DC XCI. | [italic] H. L. Q. C. | [italic] sistit | [roman] JOHANNES CHRISTOPHORVS LAVRENTIVS, | [roman] Cothenis-Anhaltinus. | [roman] AUTOR. | [line of printer's flowers] | [italic] SERVESTÆ, EXCVDIT JOH. ERN. BEZELIVS. |
πA-D^4[-D2-4]. 4°
D: Heinrich Hake, Christian Laschke, Johann Sachse, Limmer
Heffter 4216
Edinburgh NL

(17) 12 June 1691
[roman] Favente supremo Musageta DEO | [roman] DISPVTATIONEM HANC PHILOSOPHICAM | [italic] DE | [roman] EXISTENTIA DEI, | [roman] Lumine Rationis demonstranda contra Atheos | [roman] & Scepticos, | [roman] PRÆSIDE | [roman] DN. CONRADO PHILIPPO LIMMERO, | [...] | [italic] Publicæ Eruditorum disquisitioni submittit | [italic] pro ingenii modulo defensurus | [roman] Ad d. 12. Junij: M DC XCI. | [italic] H. L. Q. S. | [roman] ANDREAS OTTOMARUS [gothic] Gölike/ | [roman] Author & Respondens. | [ornament] | [italic] SERVESTÆ, EXCVDIT JOH. ERN. BEZELIVS. |
πA-C[4]. 4°
Edinburgh NL; Zerbst GF

(18) 24 July 1691
[roman] DISPVTATIO MEDICA | [italic] DE | [roman] DYSENTERIA | [italic] Quam | [...] | [roman] SVB PRÆSIDIO | [roman] DN. CONRADI PHILIPPI LIMMERI, | [...] | [italic] Publicæ placidæq; Eruditorum disquisitioni submittit | [roman] JEREMIAS MüLLER. Adorffio-Waldeckus. | [roman] Med: & Philosoph: solidioris Studiosus, | [roman] Author & Respondens. | [roman] XXIV. Julij Anni Currentis M DCLXXXXI. | [italic] Horis locoq; solitis. |
πA-C[4][-C4]. 4°
D: Georg Friedrich, Christian Ludwig, Counts of Waldeck
V: Johann Tiling, Heinrich von Schiffart (in German), Andreas Ottomar Gölike, Melchior Ernst Wagenisius, Heinrich Christian Angelocrator, Ernst Kaspar Kühne, Johann Christian Wolff
Heffter 4213
Edinburgh NL

(19) 14 October 1691
[roman] AVXILIANTE | [roman] Supremo Numine | [roman] DISPVTATIONEM HANC PHYSICAM | [italic] DE | [roman] TONITRU, FVLGVRE | [roman] & FVLMINE, | [roman] PRÆSIDE | [roman] DN. CONRADO PHILIPPO LIMMERO, | [...] | [italic] Dn. Patrono ac studiorum suorum Promotore maxime | [italic] devenerando. | [italic] Publicæ disquisitioni subjicit | [roman] GODOFREDUS SCHEURERUS, Servesta-Anhalt. | [roman] Autor ac Respondens. | [roman] Ad d. 14. Octobr: ANNO M DC LXXXXI. | [italic] Horis consuetis. | [ornament] | [italic] SERVESTÆ, EXCVDIT JOH. ERN. BEZELIVS. |
π[2]A-C[4]. 4°
D: Johann Ernst von Schönleben, Konstantin Konrad Berhold, Karl Friedrich Berhold, Johann Dares, Kaspar Scheurer
V: Christian Friedrich Schwenck, Martin Gerlach, Martin Handt, Lebrecht

Wilhelm Sachse (in German)
Edinburgh NL

(20) 6 November 1691
[roman] DISSERTATIO ANATOMICA | [italic] DE | [roman] CVTE, SIMVLq; INSENSI- | [roman] BILI TRANSPIRATIONE, SV- | [roman] DORIBVS, PILIS, ET ORGANO | [roman] TACTVS, | [italic] Quam | [...] | [roman] SVB VMBONE | [roman] DN. CONRADI PHILIPPI LIMMERI, | [...] | [italic] Dn. Patroni, Præceptoris nullo non tempore maximoperè colendi, | [italic] Publico placidoq; Eruditorum examini | [roman] Ad d. 6. November: ANNO M DC LXXXXI. | [italic] H. L. Q. S. | [italic] exponet | [roman] GEORGIUS GÜNTHER, Badebornâ-Anhalt: | [roman] S.S. Theol. Studios. | [roman] Aut. & Resp. | [line of printer's flowers] | [italic] SERVESTÆ, EXCVDIT JOH. ERN. BEZELIVS. |
πA-B^4. 4°
D: Limmer, Georg Simon Hese, Johann Georg Stann, Georg Friedrich Goth
V: Georg Jakob Löseke, Johann Friedrich Goth
Edinburgh NL

(21) 4 December 1691
[roman] DISPVTATIO BOTANICO-PHYSICA | [italic] DE | [roman] PLANTIS | [roman] In genere, | [[italic] Quam | [...] | [roman] PRÆSIDE | [...] | [roman] DN. CONRADO PHILIPPO LIMMERO, | [...] | [roman] Publicæ & placidæ Eruditorum ventilationi | [italic] submittit | [roman] Ad d. 4. Decembr. ANNO M DC LXXXXI. | [italic] H. L. Q. C. | [roman] MELCHIOR ERNESTUS [gothic] Wagenitz/ [roman] S.A. | [roman] Philos: & Med: Studios. | [roman] Autor & Respondens. | [line of printer's flowers] | [italic] SERVESTÆ, JOH. ERN. BEZELIVS. |
)(^{3}A-C^{4}D1. 4°
L: Wagenitz, undated, to Johann Ernst von Schönleben, Konstantin Konrad Gerhold, Karl Friedrich Gerhold and Melchior Ernst Wagenitz sr.
V: Andreas Ottomar Gölike (in German) and Gottfried Scheurer
Heffter 4655
London BL

(22) 2 September 1692
[roman] SUMMO ADJUVANTE NUMINE! | [roman] DISPVTATIONEM HANC MEDICAM. | [italic] DE | [roman] CHYLIFICATIONE CHYLI- | [roman] QVE ET SANGUINIS IN CORPO- | [roman] RE HUMANO CIRCULATIONE, | [roman] SUB PRÆSIDIO | [...] | [roman] DN. CONRADI PHILIPPI LIMMERI, | [...] | [italic] Domini Fautoris ac Præceptoris sui observantissimè | [italic] colendi. | [roman] Publicæ placidæq; Eruditorum Ventilationi | [roman] d. 2. Septembr:

Anni Currentis | [roman] M DC XCII. | [italic] H. L.Q. C. | [italic] Sistit | [roman] HENRICUS CHRISTIANUS ANGELOCRATOR, | [roman] Serv: Anh: Philos. & Medicinæ Studiosus. | [roman] AUTOR & RESPONDENS. | [line of printer's flowers] | [italic] SERVESTÆ, EXCXVDIT JOH. ERN. BEZELIVS. |
πA-D[4][-D4]. 4°
V: Melchior Ernst Wagenitz (in German), Peter Handt
Heffter 4208
Edinburgh NL

(23a) 6 October 1693
[roman] DISSERTATIO MEDICA | [italic] DE | [roman] CEREVISIA | [roman] SERVESTANA, | [italic] Quam | [...] | [roman] PRÆSIDE | [...] | DN. CONRADO PHILIPPO LIMMERO, | [...] | [roman] Publicæ ac placidæ Eruditorum disquisitioni | [roman] submittit | / [italic] H. L. Q. S. | [roman] MELCHIOR ERNESTUS [gothic] Wagnitz/ [roman] S. A. | [roman] Aut: & Resp: | [roman] Die vi. Octobr: ANNO M DC XCIII. | [line of printer's flowers] | [italic] SERVESTÆ, EXCVDIT JOH. ERN. BEZELIVS. |
πA-G[4]H1. 4°
V: Johann Georg Milling, Andreas Ottomar Gölicke
Heffter 4651
Edinburgh NL

(23b) 6 October 1693
[roman] DISSERTATIO MEDICA | [roman] DE | [roman] CEREVISIA | [roman] SERVESTANA | [roman] QVAM | [...] | [roman] PRAESIDE | [...] | [roman] DN. CONR. PHILIPPO LIMMERO | [...] | [roman] PVBLICAE AC PLACIDAE ERVDITORVM DISQVISITIONI | [roman] SVBMITTIT | [roman] H. L. Q. S. | [roman] MELCHIOR ERNESTVS WAGNITIUS, S.A. | [roman] AVT. ET RESP. | [roman] DIE VI. OCTOBR. ANNO M DC XCIII. | [rule] | [italic] RECVSA SERVESTAE | [roman] prostat apud CHRISTIANVM LAEGELIVM, aulae et regiminis | [roman] typographum. m dcc xlv. |
A-G[4][-G4]. 45[i.e.54]p. 4°
Zerbst GF

(24) 2 March 1694
[roman] DISPVTATIO PHYSICO-MEDICA | [italic] DE | [roman] MONSTROSO ABORTV | [roman] DESSAVIENSI, | [italic] Quam | [roman] JEHOVA JUVANTE, | [roman] PRÆSIDE | [roman] D. CONRADO PHILIPPO LIMMERO, | [...] | [italic] Mæcenate & Studiorum suorum Moderatore perpetuo reverentiæ | [italic] & honoris cultu Venerando. | [roman] Publicæ ventilationi subjiciet | [roman] Ad diem II. Martij Anni M

DC XCIV. | [roman] H. L. Q. S. | [roman] AUTHOR RESPONSURUS | [roman] JOHANNES HENRICVS GRÆTZ, | [roman] Dessa-Anhaltinus, | [roman] Philosoph: & Medicin: Studiosus. | [line of printer's flowers] | [italic] SERVESTÆ, EXCVDIT JOH. ERN. BEZELIVS. |
πA-G⁴[-G4]; [1] leaf of plates. 4°
D: Henrietta Catherina, Duchess of Saxony, Wilhelm Heinrich von Freyberg
V: Limmer, Wilh. Aug. Kindscher, Christian Püschel, A. O. Gölicke (in German)
Heffter 4653
Halle UB

(25) 22 September 1699
[roman] Q. D. B. V. | [roman] DISSERTATIO PHYSICO-MEDICA | [roman] DE | [roman] VERMIUM, seu LUMBRI- | [roman] CORUM in CORPORE HUMANO, | [italic] Ex | [roman] Insectorum Ovis Generatione & Curatione. | [italic] Quam | [...] | [roman] SUB PRÆSIDIO | [roman] DN. CONRADI PHILIPPI LIMMERI, | [...] | [italic] DNI. Patroni ac Præceptoris observantissime semper | [italic] colendi | [roman] Publicæ Eruditorum ventilationi exponet | [roman] Ad Diem xxii. Septembr: Anni M DC XCIX. | [italic] L. horisq; solitis | [roman] AUTHOR ET RESPONDENS. | [roman] JOHANN: LEB: GÖSCHEN, Cotheniensis Anhalt: | [roman] Philosoph: & Medicin: Studiosus. | [line of printer's flowers] | [italic] SERVESTÆ, EXCVDIT JOH. ERN. BEZELIVS. |
A-D⁴[-D3-4]. 4°
D: Emanuel Lebrecht, Duke of Anhalt
V: Limmer, Johann Georg Eltz, Fr. Chr. Pfau (in German), Christian Theophil Göschen, Emanuel Göschen
Heffter 4656
Edinburgh NL

(26) 7 August 1706[?]
[italic] DISPVTATIONVM PHYSICARVM | [italic] HEBDOMATICARVM | [italic] PRIMA | [roman] DE | [roman] PRÆCOGNITIS | [roman] PHILOSOPHIÆ | [roman] NATVRALIS | [roman] QVAM | [...] | [italic] PRÆSIDE | [roman] CONR. PHILIPPO LIMMERO | [...] | [roman] IN AVDITORIO PVBLICO | [roman] D. VII. AVGVST. | [roman] DEFENDET | [italic] ARNOLDVS HEINRICVS DE TRESKOW, | [italic] EQVES MAGDEBVRGICVS. | [rule] | [roman] SERVESTÆ, | [roman] TYPIS JOH. DANIELIS MVLLERI. |
A⁴. 4°
Edinburgh NL

(27) 22 September 1706[?]
[italic] DISPVTATIONVM PHYSICARVM | [italic]

HEBDOMATICARVM | [italic] SECVNDA | [roman] DE | [roman] PRÆCOGNITIS | [roman] PHILOSOPHIÆ | [roman] NATVRALIS | [italic] QVAM | [...] | [italic] PRÆSIDE | [roman] CONR. PHILIPPO LIMMERO | [...] | [italic] IN AVDITORIO PVBLICO | [roman] D. XXII. SEPTEMBR. | [roman] DEFENDET | [roman] ARNOLD. JOHANN. SIGISMUND. [gothic] Rebhun/ | [roman] PHILOS. ET LL. STVD. | [rule] | [roman] SERVESTÆ, | [roman] TYPIS JOH. DANIELIS MÜLLERI, | [roman] ILL. GYMN. ANHALT. TYPOGR. |
b^4. 4°
Edinburgh NL

(28) 27 April 1708
[roman] DISSERTATIO PHILOSO- | [roman] PHICA | [roman] DE | [roman] COGNITIONE | [roman] Et | [roman] CVLTV DEI | [roman] NATVRALI | [roman] PRIMA | [italic] QVAM | [...] | [roman] SVB | [italic] PRÆSIDIO | [roman] CONR. PHILIPPI LIMMERI | [...] | [italic] AD D. XXVII. APRIL. ANNI M DCC IIX. | [roman] LOCO HORISq; SOLITIS. | [roman] PVBLICE DEFENDET | [roman] JOHANN DAVID [gothic] Brodtmann [roman] SERVEST. | [roman] Philos. & L.l. Stud. | [rule] | [roman] SERVESTÆ, TYPIS MULLERI. |
$A^4[B^2]$. 4°
D: Matthias Ludwig Brodtmann
V: Jo. Georg Michael, G.P. de Görne, I.G.B. (in German)
Zerbst GF

(29) 5 May 1708
[roman] DISSERTATIO PHILOSO- | [roman] PHICA | [roman] DE | [roman] COGNITIONE | [roman] Et | [roman] CVLTV DEI | [roman] NATVRALI | [roman] SECVNDA | [italic] QVAM | [...] | [roman] SVB | [italic] ic] PRÆSIDIO | [roman] CONRADI PHILIPPI LIMMERI | [...] | [italic] AD D. V. MAJI. ANNI M DCC IIX. | [roman] LOCO HORISq; SOLITIS. | [roman] PVBLICE DEFENDET | [roman] JOHANN CONRAD [gothic] Limmer/ [roman] SERVEST. | [roman] Philos. Stud. | [rule] | [roman] SERVESTÆ, TYPIS MULLERI. |
$\pi A^4[B1]$. 4°
Zerbst GF

(30) 22 March 1709
[roman] DISSERTATIO PHILOSO- | [roman] PHICA | [roman] DE | [roman] VIRTVTE | [italic] QVAM | [roman] SVB | [italic] PRÆSIDIO | [roman] DN. CONR. PHILIPPI LIMMERI | [...] | [roman] PVBLICAE DISQVISITIONI COMMITTET | [roman] D. XXII. MARTII M. DCC. IX. | [roman] LOCO HORISq; SOLITIS | [italic] AVCTOR ET RESPONDENS | [italic] ANDREAS JOHANNES CHRISTIANVS |

[gothic] Rephun/ [roman] Philos. ac LL. Stud. | [rule] | [roman] SERVESTÆ, TYPIS MULLERI. |
A-C^4. 4°
V: Limmer, J.A. de Treskow, Gurgen Philipp von Görne, Ernst von Steinberg
L: Hunneke
Zerbst GF

(31) 17 April 1709
[roman] DISSERTATIO PHILOSO- | [roman] PHICA | [roman] DE | [roman] AMORE RA- | [roman] TIONIS | [italic] QVAM | [roman] SVB | [italic] PRÆSIDIO | [roman] DN. CONR. PHILIPPI LIMMERI | [...] | [roman] D. XII. APRILIS M.DCC.IX. | [roman] LOCO HORISq; SOLITIS | [roman] PVBLICE DEFENDET | [italic] AVCTOR ET RESPONDENS | [italic] JOHANNES GEORGIVS [gothic] Reineck/ | [roman] Servesta-Anh. Philos. ac LL. Stud. | [rule] | [roman] SERVESTÆ, TYPIS MULLERIANIS. |
A-D^4[-D4]. 4°
V: Limmer, Johann Georg Milling, Johann Konrad Limmer, Johann Georg Michaëlis
Date changed by hand to '17'.
Zerbst GF

(32) 21 June 1709
[roman] DISPVTATIO PHILOSO- | [roman] PHICA | [roman] DE | [roman] FORMIS CORPO- | [roman] RVM NATVRALIVM | [italic] QVAM | [...] | [italic] SVB PRÆSIDIO | [roman] DN. CONR. PHILIPPI LIMMERI | [...] | [italic] D. XXI. JVN. M.DCCIX. | [roman] LOCO HORISq; SOLITIS | [roman] PVBLICE DEFENDET | [italic] GÜRGEN PHILIP DE GÖRNE, | [roman] EQVES MAGDEBVRG. | [rule] | [italic] SERVESTÆ, | [roman] TYPIS JOHANNIS DANIELIS MULLERI. |
π^4. 4°
Zerbst GF

(33) January 1710
[roman] DISSERTATIO PHILOSO- | [roman] PHICA | [roman] DE | [roman] ÆQVALITATE | [roman] ET | [roman] INDIVIDVO VIRTV- | [roman] TVM COMITATV | [italic] QVAM | [roman] VOLENTE DEO | [italic] SVB PRÆSIDIO | [roman] DN. CONR. PHILIPPI LIMMERI | [...] | [italic] DN. FAVTORIS ET PRÆCEPTORIS SVI FIDELISSI- | [italic] MI, OMNIq; HONORE COLENDI | [roman] PVBLICÆ ERVDITORVM SVBJICIT | [roman] DISQVISITIONI | [italic] D. JANVAR. MDCC X. | [roman] HORIS LOCOQVE SOLITIS | [italic] AVTOR DEFENSVRVS | [italic] ERNST de STEINBERG, | [italic] EQVES BRVNSVICENSIS. |

[rule] | [italic] SERVESTAE, [roman] TYPIS JOHANN. DANIELIS MULLERI. |
A-F^4[-F4]. 4°
V: Limmer, Joachim Arndt de Treskow, Johann Konrad Limmer, Johann Georg Michaelis
Wolfenbüttel HAB

THE 'SPLENDID LIBRARY' OF THE COUNTS OF AUERSPERG IN LJUBLJANA

MARTIN BIRCHER

AMONG THE SIGHTS OF LJUBLJANA described by the great scholar and polymath Johann Weikhard von Valvasor (1641-1693) in his compendious survey of his native region, the duchy of Krajina in Croatia, pride of place among the secular buildings is given to the palace of Count Wolfgang Engelbrecht von Auersperg.[1] This princely pile, which was built in 1642 in the Italian style as the residence of Auersperg, the leading citizen of the area, was regarded by his contemporaries as a temple of the muses. It was, according to Valvasor, so spacious and well appointed that it could accommodate three princely establishments, in whose gardens one could admire oranges and lemons. However Valvasor, himself no mean collector of books and curiosities, found Wolfgang Engelbrecht von Auersperg's library and art gallery particularly worthy of praise:

> Überdas ist auch eine treffliche Bibliothec hier anzutreffen: welche, weil sie so überhäuffig mit Büchern versehen, vergrößert, und noch ein Angebäu dazu müssen gemacht werden. Nechst darbei, ist eine schöne Kammer, mit Seltenheiten, kostbarlichen Kunststücken, und köstlichen Gefäßen angefüllt: Unter denen eines, so ziemlich groß, und aus lauter alten Müntzen Römischer Fürsten, zusammengesetzet, nicht sowol wegen der Kostbarkeit, als Alterthums, verehrlicht was: welches aber eine Diebs-Faust entwendet, und dieser Kunst-Kammer entzogen hat.[2]
> (Furthermore there is also a splendid library to be seen here, which, being so crammed with books, will have to be extended by the addition of a new room. Next to this there is a fine room filled with rarities, priceless objets d'art and exquisite pots; of which one is of a considerable size and filled with very old Roman coins, which was admired not so much for its costliness but for its antiquity; however a thief has removed it.)

The collector and owner of these, Count Wolfgang Engelbrecht von Auersperg

1 Johann Weikhard von Valvasor, *Die Ehre des Hertzogthums Crain* (Nuremberg, 1689).

2 Valvasor, p. 671. On the author, his works and his library, which is preserved in the Bibliotheca Metropolitana in Zagreb, see Peter von Radics, *Johann Weikhard Freiherr von Valvasor (1641-1693)* (Laibach, 1910); Branko Reisp, *Kranjski polihistor Janez Vajkard Valvasor* (Ljubljana, 1983), and his *Janez Vajkard Valvasor Slovencem in Evropi* [*Johann Weichard Valvasor to the Slovenes and to Europe*] (Ljubljana, 1989).

(1610-1673) (fig. 1), was a member of an old-established family which had rendered great service to Lutheranism, but by his time had returned to the Roman faith. Its original seat, Auersperg Castle, lay close to Ljubljana. In Valvasor's words, the family gave clear proof that timid animals do not father courageous lions nor cowardly doves quick-tempered eagles.[3] Wolfgang Engelbrecht, whose father, Dietrich, had been a companion-in-arms of Wallenstein at the beginning of the Thirty Years' War, grew up with two brothers, of whom Johann Weikhard, the younger by five years, later rose to a position of pre-eminence at the Imperial court. The three brothers were sent to the courts of Munich, Cleve and Vienna and studied at Graz, where Wolfgang Engelbrecht matriculated in 1627, Vienna, Munich, Padua and Bologna.[4] They had good private tutors in their retinue and enjoyed a careful, humanist education as befitted the leading members of the nobility of the day. Like the old, leading families of the hereditary Habsburg lands the Auerspergs lived at the close of a world in which the aristocracy were a race apart, whose ethos, cultural importance and intellectual view of society continued to live on in Auersperg's thought and scholarly activities. He was imbued with an aristocrat's roots in his region and an attachment to the idea of Europe, of which his library is the finest proof.[5] After his studies abroad Wolfgang Engelbrecht settled down in Krajina, where he rose to the highest position in public life, that of a leading citizen in the region, who needed to be possessed of competence and a position of authority, faced as he was with the imminent threat from the Turks and the difficulties of administering the small region. In Radics's rather flowery description the artists, scholars and lovers of art and learning of the day in Krajina found their way to Auersperg's house, whose apartments, furnished in a mixture of princely pomp and exquisite taste, were the most dazzling proof of the highly educated sense of values of an owner who had attained material success.[6] Wolfgang Engelbrecht devoted his leisure hours to reading and scholarly studies after his father's death in 1634. A particular friend was the historian Johann Ludwig Schönleben (1618-1681) whose father, a journeyman carpenter, had come from Heilbronn to Ljubljana, of which he rose to be mayor on account of his abilities and industry. Schönleben, who had been educated by the Jesuits, graduated with a doctorate in theology at Padua in 1653 before becoming domestic chaplain to Auersperg, who, as his patron, gave him the job of arranging, adding

3 Valvasor, pp. 22-28, with four illustrations.

4 *Die Matrikeln der Universität Graz*, ed. by Johann Andritsch. Vol. 1: 1586-1630 (Graz, 1977), p. 82. In 1657 an obviously distant relative of the same name matriculated at Graz, where he contributed to a work in honour of the Emperor Leopold, *Orbis lusus, pars prima. Seu Lusus geographicus ... ab ... Comite Wolffgango Engelberto ab Auersperg ... praeside, R. P. Matthia Kirchoffer, S.I.* (Graz, 1659).

5 The notion and analysis of this aristocratic world based on an important representative of it derives from Otto Brunner, *Adeliges Landleben und europäischer Geist. Leben und Werk Wolf Helmhards von Hohberg 1612-1688* (Salzburg, 1949).

6 Peter von Radics, 'Die Hausbibliothek der Auersperge', *Neuer Anzeiger für Bibliographie und Bibliothekswissenschaft* (Dresden, 1878), pp. 10-17, 50-55, here p. 11.

Fig. 1. Wolfgang Engelbrecht, Count of Auersperg (1610-1673). Engraving by an unknown artist. (Private collection)

to and cataloguing his library. Schönleben later wrote and published a good number of historical works on the region, for which he undoubtedly made extensive use of Auersperg's library.[7] Little is known of Wolfgang Engelbrecht's life, but it is probable that a biography of him as well as the material still kept in the family's archives at Losensteinleithen Castle in Lower Austria would reveal a thoughtful, learned political scientist of his day. No less a person than the aristocratic Protestant writer Johann Wilhelm von Stubenberg (1619-1663), who managed his estate at Schallaburg in Lower Austria and was a prominent member of the Fruchtbringende Gesellschaft, dedicated to Auersperg his translation of Ferrante Pallavicino, which was published as *Geteutschter Samson* at Nuremberg in 1657. In this he referred to Auersperg as *Hochgeehrter Herr Grafe, und Herr Vetter* ('Honoured Count and cousin') and a *Weltweit-Tugendberuffene Person* ('A man universally known for his virtue'), in whose patronage and encouragement he professed a pride:

Als habe gegenwärtige meine jüngste Dolmetschung E. L. zu einem eigenem Schutzholden und geschwornen Dienstbotten zuuntergeben, ich für eine unumgängliche Pflicht geachtet: in zuversichtlicher Hoffnung, es werde selbige durch diese sonderbare Dienstverpfändung, bey E. L. so Tugend- als Ambt und Geburtshochheit, nicht mindere Gunst und Vertheidigungsschirm zugewarten haben, als dero vorige, anderen gewiedmete Federgeschwisterte.[8]
(Submitting this my latest translation to Your Honour as your protégé and servant I regarded as an essential duty, confidently hoping thereby that no less favour and protection would accrue from this special pledge of my service to Your Honour's high virtue, office and birth than did to those pieces I have previously dedicated to others.)

In the creation of the library as well as in its cataloguing and arrangement Schönleben gave endless help to Auersperg. The Venetian imprints were ordered there directly, while the booksellers of Salzburg and Frankfurt, whose valuable fair catalogues have survived in the collection, were responsible for supplying other works. Auersperg was lucky in acquiring antiquarian books from scholars and clerics in Krajina, for instance numerous legal works from the library of Dr Burchardt Hitzing, the one-time notary of the Bishop of Ljubljana, Thomas Chröe, the leader of the Counter-Reformation in Krajina, as well as volumes left by Sigismund Gall, a student of Slavonic languages and literatures, who had been incumbent of Töplitz, a spa owned by the Auersperg family.[9] At least a copy of Charles Estienne and Jean Liébault's *XV Bücher von dem Feldbaw* (Strasbourg, 1588) from the legendary collection of the Bohemian magnate, Peter Wok von Rosenberg, with his ownership note dated 1609 (two years before his death) came into Auersperg's library, but it is no longer there.[10] Most

7 See the article by Radics in *ADB*, XXXII, 314-15.

8 Stubenberg in the dedicatory letter prefixed to the work.

9 Radics [note 6], p. 13.

10 In catalogue 1 of Sotheby's auction, item 119 (for the title, see note 17); on Wok's library see Klaus Hanson, *Theobald Höck 'Schönes Blumenfeld'* (Bonn, 1975), p. 37f. The British Library has a copy of Estienne's book, pressmark 722.m.7.

of the acquisitions were catalogued in 1655 and 1656, for the most part with Schönleben's manuscript note 'Wolfgangus Engelbertus Comes ab Auersperg Capitanus Carn.' at the top of the title page and 'Catalogo inscriptus' beside the date of publication in the imprint. A larger number of acquisitions came in in 1668 and 1671. Auersperg died on 28 April 1673 at the age of sixty-two without any offspring, his property and library passing to his brother, Johann Weikhard, who survived him by about four years. Johann Weikhard (fig. 2) was one of the most important politicians in the service of the Emperors Ferdinand II, Ferdinand III., and Leopold I.[11] As a diplomat and adviser, and as a tutor to the heir to the throne, Ferdinand IV, who pre-deceased his father in 1654 at the age of twenty-one, Auersperg rose steadily in the court hierarchy. Elevated to the higher nobility, he became a privy counsellor and even set his sights on a cardinal's hat before abruptly falling foul of a cabal in 1669, when he was banished from court without any reasons being given, and forced to return home. In a spirit of fraternal piety he set about adding to the library which he inherited from his brother, although we cannot now ascertain which titles came from his collection. Stubenberg, who had dedicated one of his translations to Wolfgang Engelbrecht in 1657, had three years earlier dedicated to Johann Weikhard his German translation of a work by Francis Bacon, taking the opportunity to praise particularly Auersperg's patronage and his devotion to the noble German language, sentiments which Stubenberg reaffirmed on the admittance of Viennese nobles to the Fruchtbringende Gesellschaft, to whose good health Auersperg passed round a magnificent goblet in 1657.[12] During the next two hundred years the library lay static and unused in the palace at Ljubljana. At the behest of Prince Carlos von Auersperg, the historian Peter von Radics performed a great service in the middle of the nineteenth century in re-arranging, shelving and cataloguing the library; he produced a catalogue which included pressmarks and notes of former owners.[13] In the opinion of Radics, who knew the library better than anyone,

> [sie] stellt ... ein Unicum dar, sie repräsentirt eine in sich abgeschlossene, wohleingerichtete und wohlgewählte Büchersammlung eines österreichischen Cavaliers des

11 The most important work on him is by Grete Mecenseffy, 'Im Dienste dreier Habsburger. Leben und Wirken des Fürsten Johann Weikhard Auersperg (1615-1677)', *Archiv für österreichische Geschichte*, 114 (1938), 296-509. The Auersperg library was not made use of in the monograph and is only mentioned in passing, e.g. p. 299. See also the very short article on him in *ADB*, 1, 640, as well as the recent work by R. J. W. Evans, *The Making of the Habsburg Monarchy, 1550-1700* (Oxford, 1979).

12 *Francisci Baconi ... Fürtrefflicher Staats- Vernunfft- und Sitten-Lehr-Schrifften ... Ubersetzt durch ... den Unglückseligen* (Nuremberg, 1654). Stubenberg dedicated to Ferdinand IV his translation of Bacon's *Getreue Reden*, which appeared in the same year. Neither of these works can now be found in the Auersperg library. See also M. Bircher, *J. W. von Stubenberg (1619-1663) und sein Freundeskreis* (Berlin, 1968), pp. 129, 149, 177.

13 Peter von Radics, 'Die Fürst Carlos Auersperg'sche Hausbibliothek im Laibacher Fürstenhofe', *Oesterreichische Wochenschrift für Wissenschaft, Kultur und öffentliches Leben. Beilage zur k. Wiener Zeitung*, 1863, vol. 2, pp. 624-31.

GIOVANNI WEICARDO DI AVERSPERG PRINCIPE DEL SAC:
R.I. DVCA DI MINSTERBERG, CONTE DI TENGE, PISINO
WELS, E GOTTSCHOE, SIGNORE DI SCHONN, SEISSEMBERG
&. MARESCIALLO, E CAM°. SVPREMO HEREDITARIO NEL
DVCATO DEL CRAGNO, E MARCHESATO DI SCHIAVONIA,
CAV[R]. DEL TOSONE, MAGGIORDOMO MAGGIORE, E PRIMO
MINISTRO DI STATO DI FERDINANDO TERZO IMPERATORE.
&.
F. vanden Sten S.C.M. sculp.

Fig. 2. Johann Weikhard von Auersperg (1615–1677). Portrait engraving by Franciscus van der Steen, with insignia of the Order of the Golden Fleece. (Private collection)

XVII. Jahrhunderts, gleichwie das benachbarte Graz in seinem ständischen Zeughause eine völlständig erhaltene mittelalterliche Rüstkammer bewahrt.[14]
(it is unique in representing the well arranged and well chosen collection, to which no additions have been made, of an Austrian aristocrat of the seventeenth century, in the same way as the complete medieval armoury is preserved in the arsenal at nearby Graz).

Thanks to Otto Brunner's historical and sociological studies we can now appreciate the importance of the library of an Austrian scholar which, built up in the seventeenth century, has been kept intact.[15] It provides us with our most important source for knowing how the nobility used its educational opportunities and what fields its interests covered. All aspects of a broad cultural vision are represented on both the small and the large canvas in Auersperg's library. Besides physical exercise and, most important of course, theological and moral education, the encouragement of the art of speaking well, humanist eloquence both in the vernacular and in Latin, is the basic study of politics as well as of law, which is to be increased through a knowledge of ancient and more modern historians. A nobleman should make himself familiar with the basics of financial calculation as well as with mathematics and its associated studies, and with both civil and military architecture. After Radics arranged and catalogued the library, it sank once more into neglect. Only a handful of readers were able to use it in the following century, and there are very few references to it.[16]

Its later history can be told quickly. In 1895 a severe earthquake led to the loss of the castle in Ljubljana, but the books were undamaged and transferred along with the family's archives to Losensteinleithen Castle in Upper Austria. Eventually the library descended to Senhor D. German Mailhos and Senhora Da Johana Auersperg de Mailhos of Montevideo in Uruguay.[17] The first part of the collection was auctioned in London on 14 and 15 June 1982, the second part on 27 May 1983, since when references to this former aristocratic library, now scattered to the winds for all time, turn up again and again in various dealers'

14 Radics [note 6], p. 13.

15 See Brunner's work mentioned in note 5, to which I am indebted for these details, particularly pp. 158f: 'Das Geistesleben des nieder- und oberösterreichischen Adels im Spiegel seiner Bibliotheken'. Brunner knew the catalogues of only thirteen of these libraries.

16 See for example A. Dimitz, *Geschichte Krains* (Laibach, 1876), II, ch. 6, 'Kunst und Wissenschaft. Schriftsteller. Die Auersperg'sche Bibliothek. Geltung der deutschen Sprache', pp. 473-7. The Auersperg library was 'unfortunately not generally accessible', he says on p. 474. See also F. X. Richter, 'Die Fürsten und Grafen von Auersperg', *Neues Archiv für Geschichte, Staatenkunde, Literatur und Kunst*, 2 (1830), which however does not deal with the library.

17 Sotheby's *Catalogue of valuable printed books and atlases of the fifteenth century formed in the seventeenth century by a Continental nobleman and now the property of Senhor German Mailhos and Senhora Johana Auersperg de Mailhos from Uruguay. 14th/15th June, 1982* (items 1-440) – hereafter cited as Cat. 1, also Sotheby's *Valuable music and Continental printed books ... 26th/27th May, 1983* (items 270-380) – hereafter cited as Cat. 2. It cannot be established that this respresents the entire library catalogued by Radics, as numerous composite volumes are inadequately described. On the Auersperg family see *Genealogisches Handbuch des Adels: Fürsten*, vol. 11, (Glücksburg, 1980), p. 85.

catalogues.[18] While Melitta Pivec-Stelè laid particular stress on the importance of the Auersperg library for medieval sources in a survey of Slovenian libraries published in 1970,[19] twenty years later Véra Deparis failed to allude to it in her survey of Jugoslav libraries.[20] The fullest appreciation of the library was published by Branko Reisp, the Slovenian historian and biographer of Valvasor.[21]

THE ORGANIZATION AND SCOPE OF THE LIBRARY

We are well informed on the scope and importance of the library thanks to the two articles by Peter von Radics, through whose hands each of the 7,000 volumes, representing 3,257 works, passed several times.[22] It was a matter of particular regret that Radics's original plan to produce a printed catalogue of the library was never realised. In his monograph on the library he spoke of what his fellow scholars could expect from the publication of a catalogue such as he envisaged.[23]

In keeping with the seventeenth century's understanding of knowledge, the library was organized into subject groups, as was the custom. Around 1655 Johann Ludwig Schönleben had undertaken the sorting and shelving of the library for the first time, dividing it into nine groups: 1. theology, 2. law, 3. politics and moral philosophy (fig. 3), 4. history, 5. metaphysics, 6. medicine, 7. mathematics and all mechanical arts, 8. humanities (rhetoric and poetry), 9. philology. As a result of the great increase of the library in the 1660s a re-organization was carried out by an unknown librarian, who drew up a manuscript catalogue of the collection with eighteen groups and re-arranged the seven thousand volumes. If one compares the organization of Auersperg's library with that of his contemporary, the bookish Duke August of Brunswick, some parallels are obvious which make the latter's twenty groups still of use to the modern researcher. According to Radics, the Auersperg library's eighteen groups correspond to the respective number of the titles and not of the volumes:

18 See for example Jonathan A. Hill, New York, cat. 11 (1983), 14 items (of which three are important works by Athanasius Kircher, items 90-92); H. Th. Wenner, Osnabruck, cat. 304 and cat. 313 (1982/3), numerous items; H. P. Kraus, New York, several catalogues, of which the most recent is List 208, March 1994, thirteen items. The quality of the details of the titles and the descriptions of the books in the dealers' catalogues for understandable reasons surpasses the minimal ones in Sotheby's auction catalogues.

19 Melitta Pivec-Stelè, 'Mittelalterliche Bibliotheken in Slowenien', in Horst Gericke *et al.* (eds), *Orbis mediaevalis. Festgabe für Anton Blaschka zum 75. Geburtstag.* (Weimar, 1970), pp. 174-91, with the information, on p. 187, that part of the library is in the Library of Congress in Washington.

20 Published in *Préfaces. Les idées et les sciences dans la bibliographie de la France*, 17 (Fév./mars 1990), 77-82.

21 Branko Reisp, 'O nekdanji knjiznici knezov Auerspergov (Turjaskih) v Ljublkani', *Zgodovinski casopis*, 43 (1989), 37-41, with German summary; even Reisp (pp. 42, 46) is unaware of the rumour that the library had gone to the Library of Congress in Washington.

22 Radics [note 6], pp. 10 and 14.

23 Radics [note 6], p. 11.

Fig. 3. Exlibris of the Auersperg library.

Lust-Garten der Weißheit:

Dariñen die vor-
nehmesten der Teutschen Nation bekandte Bäume / sampt anderen
Außländischen / in ihrer Art / Natur vnd Ey-
genschafft: Beneben Hieroglyphischen Bildnussen / Hi-
storien/ Gleichnussen/ Fabeln/ Räthsel / Sprüchwör-
ter vnd Deutungen/ zur Ergetzlichkeit vnd Be-
lustigung des Gemüts / ordentlich ge-
pflantzet vnd gesetzet:

Erstlich von Herzen M. Mylio in Latei-
nischer Spraach beschrieben:

Nun aber dem gönstigen Teutschen Leser / zu Nutz vnd Wolgefallen / in vnser
Mutter-spraach versetzt: Vnd mit einem
außführlichen Register ver-
mehret.

Erstlich gedruckt zu Straßburg / bey
Johann Carolo. Jtzo aber in Ludwig Kö-
nigs selig. Erben Buchladen zu finden,
Anno 1646.

Fig. 4. Martin Mylius, *Lust-Garten der Weißheit*, translated by Wolfhart Spangenberg (Strasbourg, 1646). The only known copy of the second (revised) edition of this important work from the library of Wolfgang Engelbrecht von Auersperg, with his autograph on the title page and the exlibris of the collection, added when Peter von Radics rearranged the library in the 1870s. (Private collection)

1. Theology (1-462), 2. Law (463-967), 3. Politics (968-1619), 4. *Historia spiritualis vel sacra* (1620-1765), 5. *Historia mundana vel prophana* (1766-2426), 6. Medicine (2427-2518), 7. Mathematics (2519-2604), 8. Philosophy (2605-2689), 9. 'Humanistics' (2690-2800), 10. Poetry (2801-2882), 11. Philology (2883-3048), 12. Architecture (3049-3096), 13. Economics (3097-3116), 14. *Venatoria* (3117-3123), 15. Music (3124-3132), 16. 'Romancinos' (3133-3206), 17. Chivalry (3207-3215), 18. *Icones et sculptores* (3216-3257). While a modern appreciation and description of the library after its auction is easier due to a great number of the titles being listed and described in Sotheby's and subsequent dealers' catalogues, it can nevertheless only be taken so far, as we have no details of what titles have been lost or are now in other collections, especially as the volumes themselves cannot now be examined. If one restricts oneself to a consideration of names familiar from the German baroque – doubtless only a modest portion of the overall importance of such an aristocratic library – a whole host of well-known names present themselves:

Ludwig, Prince of Anhalt-Köthen, *Der Fruchtbringenden Geselschaft Nahmen ...* (Frankfurt/M., 1646), with four hundred botanical engravings by M. Merian (Cat. 1, 254). Duke August of Braunschweig-Lüneburg, *Das Schach- oder König-Spiel* (Leipzig, 1616/17) (Cat. 1, 375). T. Garzoni, *Piazza universale: Das ist: Allgemeiner Schawplatz* (Frankfurt/M., 1641) (Cat. 1, 151). G. Greflinger, *Frantzösische Confitirer* (4 pts in 1 vol.) (Hamburg, 1665) (Cat. 1,132); idem, *Der Frantzösische Becker* (3 pts in 1 vol.) (Hamburg, 1665) (Cat. 2, 300). A. Gryphius, *Großmüttiger Rechtsgelehrte ... Aemilius Paulus Papinianus* (Breslau, 1659) (Cat. 2,301). G. Ph. Harsdörffer, *Der grosse Schauplatz jämmerlicher Mordgeschichten* (8 pts in 4 vols.) (Hamburg, 1649-50); vol. 1 is dedicated to the Lower Austrian nobleman, J. W. von Stubenberg, who possibly presented it to Auersperg (Cat. 2, 303); idem, *Mercurius historicus* (Hamburg, 1657) (Cat. 2, 287); Harsdörffer's edition of Daniel Schwenter's *Deliciae physico-mathematicae. Oder mathematische und philosophische Erquickstunden* (Nuremberg, 1636) (Cat. 1, 374), to which he added two parts. A. Kircher: 19 titles (Cat. 1, 201-218; Cat. 2, 314). Kircher's acquaintance with Auersperg is shown by three presentation copies with a note in the latter's hand, 'Ex dono authoris' or 'Donum authoris' in *Diatribe, de prodigiosis crucibus* (Rome, 1661) (Cat. 1, 203), *Itinerarium exstaticum* (Rome, 1656) (Cat. 1, 203) and *Polygraphia nova et universalis* (Rome, 1663) (Cat. 1, 217). J. Klaj, *Irene* (Nuremberg, 1650) 'and another' (Cat. 1,219). G. Neumark, *Der Neu-Sprossende Teutsche Palmbaum* (Nuremberg and Weimar, 1668) (Cat. 2, 329). A. Olearius, *Persianischer Rosenthal* (Schleswig and Hamburg, 1654) (Cat. 1, 177); idem, *Vermehrte newe Beschreibung der Muscowitischen und Persischen Reyse* (Schleswig, 1656) (Cat. 1,286). J. Rist, *Das Friedejauchzende Teutschland* (Nuremberg, 1653). J. B. Schupp, a composite volume containing six works, 1658-59 (Cat. 2, 362). W. Spangenberg, the translation of Martin Mylius's *Lust-Garten der Weißheit* (Strasbourg, 1646), the only copy of the expanded second edition, which is not recorded by Dünnhaupt (fig.4).

Of particular appeal is a composite volume containing 124 German calendars covering the years 1632 to 1699 (Cat. 2, 285),[24] among which is Grimmels-

24 The Herzog August Bibliothek in Wolfenbüttel was later able to acquire eight almanacs from this composite volume for its 'Collection of German imprints, 1601-1700' project (Nuremberg,

hausen's well-known *Des abenteurlichen Simplicissimi ewig-währender Calender* (1670), which the catalogue, faithfully following nineteenth-century ignorance, tentatively attributes to Melchior Sternfels von Fugshaim.

If a student of Romance literatures were to cast an eye over the holdings of contemporary Italian, Spanish and French authors in the library, he would be as delighted and informed as a Germanist on the reception of these literatures by a scholarly, provincial aristocrat. It is also worth noting here that an attractive job lot of 36 works in 48 volumes representing Italian authors such as Luca Assarino, Nicolo Berardi, Maiolino Bisaccioni, Girolamo Brusoni, Carlo de Conti, Giovanni Francesco Loredano, Giovanni Battista Manzini, Ferrante Pallavicino, Francesco Pona and others, who all, as it happened, enjoyed great popularity in the German language areas, was in Auersperg's library and is now in Harvard University's Houghton Library.[25]

Auersperg's library was very well stocked with all sorts of books on contemporary Turkish problems; two copies of a German translation of the Koran (Nuremberg, 1659) have clearly been read. Superb emblem books, particularly from the Roman Catholic areas of the Habsburg Empire, are to be found in the collection. Large quantities of verse and prose eulogies of the Imperial house show the collector's loyalty. Auersperg's library is of course especially important for the geography, indigenous language and history of Krajina. A translation of the Bible into Slovene, published at Wittenberg in 1584, is recognised as a very great rarity. Only the library of Johann Weikhard von Valvasor, already mentioned, which has luckily been preserved in Zagreb, surpasses Auersperg's collection in importance and scope, though we cannot now say where its old, hand-written catalogues, manuscripts and numerous rarities have gone to in the last twenty years.

BOOKS FROM AUERSPERG'S LIBRARY IN THE BRITISH LIBRARY

David Paisey's official duties have included looking after, preserving and adding to the British Library's German holdings. A detailed appreciation of all his activities would require a separate list. However the example of his acquisitions from Auersperg's library can be offered in conclusion as a typical test of his judicious, obvious concern for this particular area, which represents a notable achievement in view of the modest sums of money available to him. It is a stroke of good fortune that at least eight important titles from the Auersperg brothers' collection in Ljubljana, listed below, will for the future be available to scholars in the British Library.[26] These are:

1650; Augsburg, 1651, with a dedication to the assembled lords of Creiina; Nuremberg, 1653; Nuremberg, 1653; Augsburg, 1661; Nuremberg, 1669; Augsburg, 1670; Nuremberg, 1670). Each almanac bears marks of Auersperg's ownership, but there are no entries in his hand.

25 See cat. 2, 309–10; detailed information on this has been kindly supplied by R. Folter of H. P. Kraus, New York.

26 These additions to the British Library's holdings are substantially more important as regards their contents than those acquired by the Herzog August Bibliothek in Wolfenbüttel from

Hans Blum: *Nüzlichs Säulenbuch oder Kunstmässige Beschreibung* ... (Zurich, 1662), a replacement copy for the one destroyed in the Second World War (Sotheby's cat 1, 53, now BL pressmark: 1575/228).

Epithalamium symbolicum conjugibus porphyrogenitis ... Ferdinando III et ... Mariae Reginae Hispaniarum ... cum Vienna Austriae ... Regias nuptias ... agerent (Graz, [1631]), a particularly rare, magnificent emblem book with fifty illustrations on the marriage of the Emperor Ferdinand III (Cat. 1, 116; now BL pressmark: 1572/542).[27]

Johann Praetorius, *Catastrophe Muhammetica: Oder das Endliche Valet, Und schändliche Nativität Des gantzen und nunmehr vergänglichen Türckischen Reichs* (Leipzig, 1664) (cat. 1, 317; now BL pressmark: 1578/5056).

Erhard Weigel, *Speculum Uranicum Aquilæ Romanæ Sacrum, Das ist / Himmels Spiegel* ... (Frankfurt/M., 1661) (cat. 1, 423; now BL pressmark: 1578/5054).

[Rudolf von Dieskau]: 1. Randolphus Duysburgk [pseudonym]: *Legation Oder Abschickung der Esell in Parnassum* (Leipzig, 1638), bound with 2. Damian von Rudelstadt [pseudonym]: *Frühlings-Gedichte / Darinnen auch zugleich mit angeführet wird Wie Ein rechtschaffener / wahrer Christlicher Hoffmann müsse beschaffen seyn* (Altenburg, 1638) (first editions of the two principal works of the early, Dresden-based, member of the Fruchtbringende Gesellschaft, known as 'der Niedrige') (cat. 2, 292; now BL pressmark: 1578/6107).

Johann Lassenius, *Fruchtbringende Gespraech-Spiel darinn vermittelst fünff nicht unangenehmer Unterredungen ... was zum burgerlichen und Stadt-Leben gehöret ... erörtert werden* (Rostock, 1666). (cat. 2, 317; now BL pressmark: 1578/6231).

Jacobus Francus, i.e. Conrad Memmius or Lautenbach, *Relationis historicae semestralis continuatio. Historische Beschreibung aller denckwürdigen Geschichten so sich ... in Europa ... Indien ... Türckey etc. ... zugetragen*, for 1637, 1641, 1649, 1653-58, 1664, 1665, 1667, together 20 vols. (Frankfurt/M., 1637-1667) (cat. 2, 331; now BL pressmark: C.107.bb.73).

Ulrich Zasius, *In usus feudorum epitome* (contemporary German half-pigskin over pasteboards, boards covered with leaves from a thirteenth-century glossed legal manuscript in double column, blind-tooled with a pilaster roll and a roll of four medallion heads and four coats of arms – Saxony, lion, Kursachsen, eagle – each cover decorated with a medallion, red edges. – One of only three recorded German Renaissance bindings with plaquette or medallion ornament.) (cat. 2, 380, with ill.; now BL pressmark: C.183.b.11. See figs. 5a and b.)

various dealers. In addition to the eight almanacs already mentioned Wolfenbüttel has, in chronological order, the following works once owned by Auersperg: 1. A Latin poem on Leopold I's election as Emperor in Frankfurt, *Votiva acclamatio ad ... novae aquilae volatum ...* (Frankfurt/M., 1658). 2. A Roman Catholic memorial on Johann Weikhard von Auersperg's friend, Prince Octavio Piccolomini d'Aragona, the Duke of Amalfi (known as 'der Zwingende' in the Fruchtbringende Gesellschaft), *Elogium sepulchrale excelentissimi herois Octavii Piccolomini* (Vienna, 1656). 3. A Roman Catholic memorial on the death of Archduke Leopold Wilhelm, *Elogium vitae reverendissimi ... Leopoldi Guilelmi Archiducis Austriae* (Munich, 1662). 4. A Latin verse chronicle of all the Emperors from Charlemagne to Leopold from the year of their coronation, *Imperium romano-germanicum, a Carolo Magno ... ad ... Leopoldum* (Vienna, 1658). 5. A Roman Catholic memorial on the death of Archduke Karl Joseph, *Stella matutina in medio nebulae, sive Laudatio funebris ... Caroli Josephi Archiducis Austriae* (Vienna, 1664).

27 See Mario Praz, *Studies in Seventeenth-Century Imagery*, II (Rome, 1974), p. 69.

Fig. 5. Contemporary binding on Ulrich Zasius, *In usus feudorum epitome*. BL C.183.b.11.
(a) front cover (b) back cover

THE HOUSE OF WEIDMANN IN LEIPZIG AND THE EIGHTEENTH-CENTURY IMPORTATION OF ENGLISH BOOKS INTO GERMANY

BERNHARD FABIAN and MARIE-LUISE SPIECKERMANN

I

THE RECEPTION OF ENGLISH CULTURE IN GERMANY in the eighteenth century was, first and foremost, a bookish phenomenon. The primary medium through which the intellectual élite of the country acquired knowledge about England and its literary, scholarly and scientific achievements was the printed page. Translations into German were plentiful and appeared, from the late seventeenth century onwards, in ever larger numbers. Translations into French played a significant role since for the educated German French was the language of social intercourse (and remained so until the nineteenth century). The scholarly reader relied largely on Latin as his language until well into the eighteenth century. He preferred English authors writing in Latin or translated into Latin, whether in Germany or elsewhere.

In this intricate process a matter of key importance was the distribution of original English books. Each translation presupposed the presence in the hands of the translator of a copy of the book as published in England either in English or (less frequently) in Latin. Without it, the receptive process could not be set in motion. Thus, book-trade activities were fundamental in the transmission of intellectual stimuli. The physical conveyance of printed texts from one country to another constituted, as it still does, the basis of the cultural transfer.

Little is known about the presence of English books in Germany in the late seventeenth and early eighteenth centuries – at a time when English was in all respects a foreign language on the Continent and few made an attempt to acquire a rudimentary knowledge of it. David Paisey has been among the first to investigate this presence systematically by studying the early printed catalogues of the university libraries of Heidelberg (1623), Frankfurt an der Oder (1676 and 1706), Wittenberg (1678), Duisburg (1685) and Jena (1746).[1] He found that

1 David Paisey, 'Printed books in English and Dutch in early printed catalogues of German university libraries', in *Across the Narrow Seas: Studies in the history and bibliography of Britain and the Low Countries, presented to Anna E. C. Simoni*, ed. Susan Roach (London, 1991), pp. 127–48).

the English holdings of these libraries were scant, almost negligible. Among roughly 45,000 books/entries in these catalogues there are only 72 in English.

In view of the book-trade situation of the period David Paisey assumes – quite rightly – that these books can hardly be supposed to have 'reached the libraries by way of trade in new publications' or as antiquarian purchases. Most likely, they may have been 'part of private collections given or bequeathed.' Though in the early seventeenth century there was a trade in English books at the Frankfurt Fair, albeit on a limited scale, this trade abated during the Thirty Years' War. The general view is that such trade relations as formerly existed were not again built up until roughly the middle of the eighteenth century when German book production and the German book-trade again reached the level they had attained in the early seventeenth century.

The Fair Catalogues, in general reliable indicators, seem to support this view. For the first three or four decades of the eighteenth century they do not reveal any trade in English books at the Frankfurt or Leipzig Book Fairs. They give the impression that, regardless of the growing number of translations, the presence of English books in Germany remained on the low level identified by David Paisey in the library catalogues.

However, there appear to have been trade channels which are not reflected in the Fair Catalogues, so that the presence of English books in Germany in the 1720s and 1730s was stronger than has hitherto been supposed. In principle, the Fair Catalogues listed new publications, current material published in Germany. Foreign trade at the Book Fairs both in Frankfurt and Leipzig could pass unnoticed and remain undocumented. That English books were exported to Germany is evident from the customs records as examined by Giles Barber.[2] Though Germany does not rank high in early-eighteenth-century British book exports, trade appears to have been continuous, though it did not reach the proportions of the English-Dutch trade.

What happened on the receiving side? How did English books reach Germany, and how were they distributed? Who were the booksellers engaging in the foreign trade? These questions are not easily answered. Some clues are provided by the catalogues of the prominent Leipzig publishers who were also major national and international booksellers. Most of the catalogues are no longer extant but those that survive provide singular information about the early presence of English books in Germany.

II

The house of Weidmann is well known as the *primus inter pares* of eighteenth-century German publishers.[3] Its rise to a pre-eminent position under the

2 Giles Barber, 'Books from the old world and for the new: The British international trade in books in the eighteenth century', in *Studies on Voltaire and the Eighteenth Century* 151 (1976), pp. 185-224. Reprinted in *Studies in the booktrade of the European Enlightenment* (London, 1994).

3 For the history of Weidmann, see Ernst Vollert and W. Joachim Freyburg, *Die Weidmannsche*

direction of Philipp Erasmus Reich (active from 1746 to 1787) is a familiar, though not yet fully explored, chapter in the history of publishing in Germany. Reich was an innovator; he introduced modern business practices into a trade which still operated on late medieval principles.

Among the several hundred publishers who brought out, in the course of the eighteenth century, translations of English authors, Weidmann – in particular under Reich – stands out by the number of titles published and the attention given to the details of production. None published more English works in German translation than Weidmann after about 1760, and none showed more adroitness in selecting successful titles.

Weidmann was also an outstanding bookseller. From the beginning (the business was founded in Frankfurt in 1680 and soon moved to Leipzig), Moritz Georg Weidmann, the founder, took a strong interest in bookselling and kept a superb stock based on the bartering trade then customary among publishers and booksellers. He opened branches in Warsaw and Stockholm and is said to have built up business relations with Holland and France. *Avant la lettre*, he was an international bookseller.

After Weidmann's premature death in 1693 the house was directed by Johann Ludwig Gleditsch until 1717, when Moritz Georg the Younger took over. Gleditsch continued along established lines, and expanded both the publishing and the bookselling business. He trained the younger Weidmann as an international publisher and bookseller by sending him to various places in Germany as well as to Italy, Belgium, France and England. Moritz Georg appears to have been the first German bookman to go to England for his training.

Whether the attention paid to English authors by the house of Weidmann can be attributed to Moritz Georg's personal knowledge of England is a matter of conjecture. At any rate, he seems to have been aware of the growing significance of English authors as early as the 1720s. By the early 1730s he offered English books for sale. In one way or another, the house continued to be a supplier of English books in Germany until the last decades of the century. Weidmann, then, was not only the outstanding publisher of English authors in German translation but also a leading, if not the leading, stockist of English authors in the original language.

Books from England were not the main line business of Weidmann nor of any other Leipzig bookseller – apart, perhaps, from one or two who tried to specialize in English books about the middle of the century.[4] English was the

Verlagsbuchhandlung (Hildesheim, 1983); Adalbert Brauer, *Weidmann, 1680-1980* (1980); Hazel Rosenstrauch, 'Buchhandelsmanufaktur und Aufklärung: Die Reformen des Buchhändlers und Verlegers Ph. E. Reich (1717-1787)', *AGB*, 26 (1986), 1-129; and Mark Lehmstedt, *Philipp Erasmus Reich, 1717-1787: Verleger der Aufklärung und Reformer des deutschen Buchhandels* (Leipzig, 1989).

4 Johann Wendler, who preceded (from 1743 to 1746) Philipp Erasmus Reich as the manager of Weidmann, was the leading supplier of English books at mid-century. See Bernhard Fabian, 'English books and their eighteenth-century German readers', in *The widening circle: Essays on the circulation of literature in eighteenth century Europe* (Philadelphia, 1976), pp. 141f.

'new' foreign language of the eighteenth century, acquired only by an élite. Thus, even for an anglophile bookseller English books could not make up the bulk of his foreign business but, at best, only a smallish portion.

In accordance with the cultural situation in Germany, the earliest Weidmann catalogue to have survived refers to French and Italian books, not to English books, as available at the shop.[5] It was issued in 1709 (still in the Gleditsch period) for a local fair held at Naumburg (in Sachsen-Anhalt). Other extant catalogues, published between 1713 and 1728, are similar to the Naumburg catalogue, though more elaborate. Some bear a French title and suggest that they contained primarily or exclusively books in French.

The early Weidmann catalogues conform to a pattern established among Leipzig booksellers: they were issued in conjunction with the Fairs to attract attention to the central events of the book world. The house of Grosse, for instance, the owner of the Fair Catalogue prior to its acquisition by Weidmann, appended catalogues of books available at their Leipzig shop to the respective Fair Catalogues in the early 1730s.[6] These catalogues usually contain a mixture of new and older books in stock. Occasional English titles are an indication that Weidmann was not the only bookseller to discover a new intellectual territory.

From this conventional type of catalogue Moritz Georg Weidmann departed radically in April 1733, when he began issuing, without reference to a Fair, a weekly catalogue under the title of *Wöchentlicher Catalogus, Alter und Neuer, Frembd- und Einheimischer Bücher*.[7] Obviously intended to appeal primarily to a learned international clientele, it also carried its title in Latin: *Catalogus hebdomadalis, librorum omnium religionum, scientiarum et linguarum, tam veterum quam recentiorum, qui inveniuntur Lipsiæ, in bibliopolio Weidmanniano* (fig. 1). It consisted of four pages in quarto and was continued weekly until May 1735.

This appears to have been the first catalogue issued in Germany to contain English books in appreciable numbers. It includes, as the title suggests, not only recently published works but also older works. That it contains books in 'all' languages is, of course, an exaggeration, unless the announcement is understood to refer to the languages which scholarly or educated readers in Germany and Central Europe would (collectively) command: Latin, German, French, Italian as well as English – if they belonged to the intellectual avantgarde.

5 Early Weidmann catalogues appear to be preserved only in the National Library of Russia in St Petersburg, and were not available for consultation. Our information comes from Karl Baerent, 'Kataloge der Weidmannschen Buchhandlung aus der ersten Hälfte des XVIII. Jahrhunderts', *Zeitschrift für Bücherfreunde* N.F. 5 (1914), 236–41.

6 'Appendix librorum qui præter alios in officina libraria Grossiana venales prostant.' The first was published for the Easter Fair 1733.

7 Two copies of this catalogue appear to be extant: one originally in the National Library of Poland in Warsaw, later in the National Library of Russia in St Petersburg and, since 1926, again in the National Library of Poland. It wants the first two numbers. The other is in the collections of the Buch- und Schriftmuseum of the Deutsche Bücherei in Leipzig. It wants the first number. We are grateful to the Deutsche Bücherei for permission to use their copy. We are grateful to Dr Boris Volodin for supplying information on the catalogue in St Petersburg.

CATALOGUS
HEBDOMADALIS,
LIBRORUM OMNIUM RELIGIONUM,
SCIENTIARUM ET LINGUARUM, TAM VETERUM QUAM RECENTIORUM, QUI INVENIUNTUR
LIPSIÆ,
IN BIBLIOPOLIO WEIDMANNIANO.

Wöchentlicher CATALOGUS,
Alter und Neuer, Frembd- und Einheimischer Bücher,
Von
Allen Religionen, Wissenschafften und Sprachen,
so in Leipzig im Weidmannischen Buchladen
zu bekommen sind.

CATALOGUE DES LIVRES
DE TOUTES LES RELIGIONS, SCIENCES ET LANGUES TANT ANCIENS QUE MODERNES QUI SE TROUVENT
A LEIPZIG chez M. G. WEIDMANN,

EX OFFICINA WEIDMANNIANA,
1735.

Fig. 1

The books from England offered by Weidmann made their appearance in what must be regarded as a new book-trade context. Between roughly 1680 and 1740 business relations between the Dutch and the German trade changed significantly. One of the factors bringing about, or accelerating, this change appears to have been the growing attraction which the scholarly and literary production of England held for various groups of readers on the Continent, however small the trade in English books actually was.

The international relations of Weidmann primarily extended to Holland. Most of the books acquired for trade activities in Germany and Northern and Eastern Europe obviously came from the Netherlands. The elder Weidmann is said to have imported books from France and from Holland. As early as 1693, Johann Friedrich Gleditsch travelled to Holland and reportedly did excellent business with the Dutch trade, presumably in Latin and French books.[8]

The rise in the seventeenth century of the Dutch book-trade to a dominating position in Europe is an established fact, though not a fully explored phenomenon.[9] The Dutch trade extended all over Europe, either through branches established in various places or through its connection with the major Leipzig booksellers who served Germany and Central and Eastern Europe. In this process the flow of books became more and more continuous, and the pattern of the semi-annual Frankfurt Fairs lost its original significance. Frankfurt was ultimately doomed as a book-place – primarily, though not exclusively, it seems, in consequence of the trade between Holland and Leipzig.[10]

A natural corollary of the growing production of books was the increasing demand for current titles. Novelties appear to have reached Leipzig at ever shorter intervals. As a new commodity on the Continental market, books in English (as distinct from English books in Latin, which had long been involved in the scholarly exchange of books in Europe) were absorbed into this pattern. The modern era in publishing and bookselling began to dawn. Thus English books may be said to have helped to speed up the general change in the early eighteenth century which resulted in the establishment of Leipzig as the centre of the German book-world.

As the trade expanded, the relationship between the Dutch trade and the Leipzig trade became more and more ambiguous. On the one hand, the Leipzig booksellers relied heavily on supply from Holland. On the other, they were strongly opposed to the intrusion of the Dutch into what they considered their own territory. Moritz Georg Weidmann the Younger made repeated attempts to prevent Dutch publishers and booksellers from opening branches in Leipzig.

8 See the histories by Vollert and Brauer [note 3].

9 See *Le magasin de l'univers: The Dutch Republic as the Centre of the European Book Trade*, ed. C. Berkvens-Steveling, H. Bots, P. G. Hoftijzer and O. S. Lankhorst (Leiden, 1992).

10 On the Dutch-German trade, see Johann Goldfriedrich, *Geschichte des deutschen Buchhandels vom Westfälischen Frieden bis zum Beginn der Klassischen Litteraturperiode (1648-1740)* (Leipzig, 1908), chapter 5, and Albrecht Kirchhoff, 'Der Zeitpunkt des Wegbleibens der Holländer von der Leipziger Messe', *Archiv für Geschichte des Deutschen Buchhandels* 17 (1894), 363-65.

He failed when Arkstée en Merkus was granted a charter and, in 1737, established a business which was carried on successfully for several decades.[11]

III

It is against this background that the *Catalogus hebdomadalis* must be seen. Its 109 instalments, amounting to about 400 pages, record an exceptionally interesting phase of Leipzig bookselling. There are indications that Weidmann himself only gradually realized that he was doing business on new principles. Towards the end of the catalogue (which is consecutively numbered) he announced that a special title-page would be published, so that the catalogue could be permanently preserved.[12] With it came a short preface in German and Latin in which he pointed out that he regarded his compilation not merely as a sale catalogue but also as a reference manual for the scholar working in the context of *historia litteraria*: it brought to notice rare and useful books 'omnis generis omniumque facultatum'.

At first sight, the *Catalogus* does not appear to be of a new kind. Weidmann had previously issued catalogues of older books which, in retrospect, establish him as one of the founders of the antiquarian book trade in Germany.[13] If not himself a scholar, he was a scholar's bookseller keen on bringing together a well-assorted stock of books which could be regarded as a carefully selected reference collection. But the serial mode of publication and the arrangement of the catalogue indicate a new approach.

The weekly instalments begin with a section of 'Libri Latini'. This ranges from incunables to recently published titles and constitutes the fundamental stratum of Weidmann's stock. Most frequently, the Latin section is followed by a French section. This French section is, on occasion, replaced by a list of books in other vernacular languages: German, Italian, rarely Spanish or Dutch, and – the unexpected feature of the catalogue – English. On the whole, books in Latin dominate and among vernacular titles those in French outnumber all others. The arrangement by language made the catalogue a versatile tool by roughly subdividing it into antiquarian and modern books and it created loose subject categories which must have appealed to different types of readers.

Weidmann's 'antiquarian' books, mostly in Latin and published before 1700, represent a cosmopolitan book world, including exotic places of publication like Constantinople or the fictitious Alethopolis. Predominantly works of historical scholarship, collections of source material or editions of the classics, they were older books which had not yet become obsolete, or modern books which had

11 See Albrecht Kirchhoff, 'Der ausländische Buchhandel in Leipzig im 18. Jahrhundert', *Archiv für Geschichte des Deutschen Buchhandels* 14 (1891), 155-82.

12 See no. XCIX (5 March 1735), p. 392.

13 See Philipp Rath, 'Das Antiquariat des Moritz Georg Weidmann zu Leipzig in der ersten Hälfte des achtzehnten Jahrhunderts', *Börsenblatt für den Deutschen Buchhandel* (11 April 1913).

already made their mark on the world of learning. Frequently in large formats, they were, by and large, standard works for the scholar or the antiquary.

Modern books in French are, in general, recent books published between 1720 and 1735. Again, their authorship ranges widely but, apart from occasional Paris imprints, they are almost invariably published in Holland. By and large, they belong to a different category from that of the Latin books. Though there are French editions of the classics, the majority are books on current affairs, works of minor fiction, periodical essays and accounts of travels or scientific discoveries. They were obviously intended not so much for the scholarly as for the general educated reader.

The books from England which Weidmann offered fit into this pattern. Works in Latin – almost exclusively of a scholarly nature – make their regular, though sparse, appearance in the Latin section. Their total number is small (about 220). More than half of them are seventeenth-century books, published predominantly between 1650 and 1700. Roughly 25 per cent were published after 1700, and about 12 per cent between 1600 and 1650. Only five titles are from the sixteenth century. London and Oxford stand out as places of publication, though Cambridge and Edinburgh are also represented, but Dublin hardly.

Though printed in Britain, Weidmann's English books in Latin (primarily expensive folios) were not necessarily of English authorship. In fact, the number of non-English writers printed before 1710 almost equals that of English writers. There are, of course, ancient classics and Fathers of the Church. There are also, more surprisingly, Continental scholars such as Gerardus Joannes Vossius, or Hiob Ludolf, whose *Lexicon Aethiopico-Latinum* first appeared in London in 1661. Of the *Epistolae omnes* of Jean de Launoy Weidmann offered two Cambridge editions (1689 folio and 1679 quarto), the second of which is either exceedingly rare or a ghost.

In some cases, the first or only edition of a British author was a Continental edition. Robert Fludd's *De natura simia, seu technica macrocosmi*, for instance, was published at Oppenheim. Weidmann's catalogue lists an edition of 1598 and an undated Oppenheim edition of *Utriusque cosmi metaphysica*. All in all, there are about as many Continental editions of British authors as English editions. Two-thirds are seventeenth-century books, nine per cent were printed after 1700, and a few more between 1500 and 1600. The only incunable is William of Ockham's *De potestate Imperatoris & Pontificis* (Lugduni, 1493), marked 'liber rarus'.

Though in the circumstances original editions in Latin, unauthorized reprints and Latin translations of English works were difficult to distinguish, Weidmann generally succeeded in offering the best or most valuable editions. Thus, of Richard Morton's *Phthisiologia seu exercitationes de Phthisi*, then the most influential book on tuberculosis, he advertised the first edition (London, 1689), regardless of two German reprints (Frankfurt, 1690; Ulm, 1714), which might have been easier to obtain. Of Thomas Burnet's *Telluris theoria sacra* the

Amsterdam reprint of 1699 was offered first, and the second London edition (1689) added a few months later. Locke's *Essay concerning human understanding* (1690) is, as one might expect, offered in Latin translation; the London edition (1701) is given preference to a German reprint of it (1709).

A particularly difficult author from the German bookseller's point of view was Robert Boyle. Some of his works were translated into Latin in England. Thus, of *Aerial noctiluca* Weidmann included the London edition (1682), and not the Geneva reprint (1693). Others were only available in Continental Latin translation, so that in order to be able to make the best offer Weidmann had to include the *Opera varia physico-mechanica & chymica* published by Samuel De Tournes in Geneva (1680).

An author conspicuously absent from the catalogue is Isaac Newton. Whether or not Newton in Latin was virtually unobtainable by 1733 is difficult to determine. Weidmann's competitor Grosse offered the Amsterdam reprint of the *Principia*. Weidmann himself had only the French translation of the *Opticks* for sale (Amsterdam, 1720 and Paris, 1722). This presumably appealed both to the scholarly and the general reader. That the French section of the *Catalogus* was in many ways complementary to the Latin section is also obvious in the case of Francis Bacon. Of his works the first complete collection ever made is offered, the Frankfurt edition of the *Opera omnia* (1665). But the *Essays*, a literary work of general appeal, make their appearance in French translation (*Essais de Chevalier Bacon*, Paris, 1735).

English books in English tell a different story from English books in Latin, though not a straightforward one. The *Catalogus* contains about 180 titles both dated and undated. Together with the Latin titles, some 400 books of British authorship are listed – less than five per cent of the total stock. If this seems negligible, it must be remembered that Weidmann was a pioneer and, to a certain extent, experimenting. After all, English books were newcomers in the Continental book world.

The first batch occurs in the third issue (1 May 1733). It consists of ten titles, all akin to Weidmann's Latin-English titles in being works of historical scholarship with a leaning towards (fashionable?) antiquarian studies. An example is John Dart's *History and Antiquities of the Cathedral Church of Canterbury* (London, 1726), advertised as 'cum multis figuris, opus splendissimum'. There are also two seventeenth-century collections of historical source material, Elias Ashmole's *Institutions, Laws & Ceremonies of the Most Noble Order of the Garter* (London, 1672) and Samuel Daniel's *Collection of the History of England* (1653, a reprint of the last revised edition of 1634). Among post-1720 books Weidmann offered as 'liber rarus' the first edition of Alexander Gordon's *Itinerarium septentrionale: Or, a journey thro' most of the Counties of Scotland, and those in the North of England* (1726).

In bringing together works of this kind Weidmann obviously wanted to assemble major, if not classical, works. Judging from the re-appearance of most of them in later catalogues, they were difficult to sell. Was Weidmann out of touch with his customers? Did he overestimate their linguistic proficiency? Were the books too expensive? We do not know. In any case, fewer and fewer of these works were entered in later numbers of the *Catalogus*. George Hughes's *Analytical Exposition of the Whole Book of Moses* (Plymouth, 1710) is one of them. If the imprint is correct, it appears to be so rare that it even escaped the compilers of the *ESTC*.

Lists of books in English are few and far between. If they do occur in later numbers, they usually consist of a medley of titles in which books of entertainment and instruction dominate. Some scientific books are reminiscent of Weidmann's early attempts to provide for the scholar in the first place. More typical lists include books of popular science such as Edward Wells's *The Young Gentleman's Mechanicks* (London, 1713). There are likewise compendia of 'pleasant' instruction, religious books (which reappear later) and, more conspicuous, lives and adventures, memoirs, true stories of extraordinary events, travels and amours, such as 'The velvet coffee-woman: or, the life, gallantries and amours of the late famous Mrs. Anne Rochford, 8, Westmunster 1727'[14] or Penelope Aubin's 'The life of Madam de Beaumont. A French lady; who lived in a cave in Wales above fourteen years undiscovered, being forced to fly France for religion. 12. London, 1728'.[15]

The most striking feature of the *Catalogus* is a long list of nearly 70 plays.[16] With few exceptions, they represent the repertoire of the London stage of the 1720s. Shakespeare is represented by *Henry IV*, *Hamlet*, *Macbeth*, *Julius Caesar* and *Othello*, Ben Jonson by *Volpone*. Of the major Restoration dramatists – Dryden, Wycherley, Otway, Etherege and the Duke of Buckingham – at least one play is included (of Shadwell only two adaptations of Shakespeare). The largest group comprises plays first performed between 1700 and 1725 – from Addison's *Cato* to Young's *Bursiris*. Colley Cibber, Congreve, Rowe, Farquhar and Vanbrugh figure prominently. Even Fielding, whose first play came out in 1727, is on the list. Minor dramatists such as Richard Steele, John Banks, John Crowe, Thomas Killigrew, Joseph Trapp and others are likewise present. *The Beggar's Opera* of 1728 is missing, but Weidmann offered 'Memoirs concerning the life and manners of Captain Makheeth' (London, 1728).[17]

Whether or not Weidmann himself put together this remarkable list cannot be ascertained. If so, he must have been more intimately familiar with the London stage than he can possibly be supposed to have been. Expert advice would seem to have been scarce in Leipzig. Addison's *Cato* was first translated in 1735 by Johann Christoph Gottsched's wife, but it must be doubted whether either the Gottscheds or, for that matter, any other *littérateur* in Leipzig was able to suggest to Weidmann a canon of contemporary English plays.

There is a bibliographical clue to the most likely provenance of the list. Following a common practice, Weidmann listed titles only and omitted authors.

14 *ESTC* lists only an edition of 1728.
15 This edition is not listed in *ESTC*.
16 See no. LXIII (26 June 1734).
17 See no. IX (12 June 1733).

He also omitted dates of publication. This cannot be attributed to sloppy cataloguing since nearly all his other titles carry dates. Moreover, all plays are said to be in octavo, an unusual format for plays of the period. However, uniform octavo editions of Weidmann's plays did exist. Most of them were undated and probably published between 1720 and 1730, many of them with false imprints. Obviously all came from a single publisher: Thomas Johnson in The Hague.

Johnson, possibly a Scot, is known to have been active in The Hague from 1701 to 1728, and afterwards in Rotterdam until his death in 1735.[18] Next to nothing is known about him as a bookseller. As a publisher, Johnson began reprinting English authors around 1710, starting with Shakespeare. His reprints were intended to form a series entitled 'A collection of the best English plays'. In all, it comprised 48 plays, mostly contemporary and all with separate title-pages. The undated plays in Weidmann's *Catalogus* are probably of the second issue (or edition) of the collection, published between 1720 and 1722 and including a number of new titles. Johnson changed the series title slightly and, more important, frequently omitted the dates of publication.

Of the sixty-four plays making up Johnson's collection fifty-eight appear in Weidmann's catalogue. Thus there is sufficient reason to assume that Weidmann did not offer, as he usually did in the case of scholarly works, first or early London editions. His English plays were – in all probability – Dutch reprints. And their provenance would also explain why the latest successes on the London stage – Gay's *Beggar's Opera* (1728) or Lillo's *London Merchant* (1731) – are conspicuously absent. They are not part of Johnson's collection.

Weidmann's business with Johnson was apparently not confined to the plays. There are other Johnson reprints in the catalogue, like Ramsay's *New Cyropaedia* in English and French with a false Edinburgh imprint (n.d.) or Pope's translation of the *Iliad* with the imprint 'London: printed by T. J. for B. L. & Company, 1729' (B.L. refers to Bernard Lintot, Pope's original publisher). As a shrewd bookseller, Weidmann bought from Johnson Swift's *Miscellaneous works* (1720) but abstained from ordering titles difficult to sell in Leipzig, such as a reprint of Pope's *Works* as well as a Dutch tract on the trade of the Dutch East India Company, translated by Johnson into English.

Johnson may have provided Weidmann with current titles from England, and he may also have supplied, wholly or in part, the antiquarian books in Weidmann's catalogue. At any rate, Johnson emerges as an international bookseller of some consequence. On the evidence of Weidmann's catalogue, he may be said to have contributed significantly to the early dissemination of English books in Germany. Johnson died in 1735. Whether his bookselling activities were a sideline to his publishing activities or vice versa remains to be established. Weidmann discontinued his weekly catalogues in the same year.

18 See H. L. Ford, *Shakespeare 1700-1740: A Collation of the Editions and Separate Plays* (1935; reprint New York, 1968), pp. 46-55, and John Feather, 'English books in the Netherlands in the eighteenth century: Reprints or piracies?' in *Le magasin de l'univers* [note 9], pp. 143-54.

IV

In 1745 and 1746 the house of Weidmann published, in two volumes, *Svpellex librorvm praestantissimorvm, compactorvm, qvam collegit et reliqvit Mavritivs Georgivs Weidmannvs ... avctione venalivn.*[19] The title-page (fig. 2) gives the impression that this is the sale catalogue of Weidmann's private library. In a short life in Latin attention is drawn to the honours conferred on him. His achievement as a publisher is commemorated as equal to that of Aldus Manutius, Plantin and others, and important works published by him are duly listed. He is praised as a collector but, significantly, his activities as a bookseller are ignored.

The catalogue lists 6,938 consecutively numbered volumes, mostly with reliable bibliographical data and, in some cases, with notes on bindings. The arrangement is by subject and, within subjects, chronologically by format. 'Literae humaniores' (1,689 volumes) is followed by 'Philosophia' (651 volumes), 'Historia' (1,256 volumes), 'Historia literaria' (677 volumes), 'Medicina' (189 volumes), 'Jurisprudentia' (1,089 volumes) and, finally, 'Theologia' (1,050 volumes) and 'Historia ecclesiastica' (338 volumes).

It is generally agreed that, despite its title, *Svpellex librorvm* is the catalogue not of Weidmann's personal library but of the remaining stock of his bookselling business.[20] At the time of Moritz Georg's death the firm is said to have been in financial difficulties, at least temporarily. It was therefore decided to discontinue the highly original (and in some respects idiosyncratic) bookselling business which Moritz Georg had built up over roughly two decades.[21] Presumably to make the sale attractive to as large a clientele as possible, the catalogue placed, among subjects, theology last and, among formats, duodecimo first. Judging from the upswing of the Weidmann publishing business from the fifties onwards, the sale must have been a success and provided much-needed capital.

Between the earlier catalogue and *Svpellex librorvm* Weidmann's English stock had scarcely increased. *Svpellex librorvm* contains about 480 books from Britain (approximately seven per cent). However, the number of books in English is larger than before. Of books published before 1710, one third is in English, two thirds are in Latin. After 1710, books in Latin drop to 5 per cent. Current books outnumber antiquarian books. Almost 30 per cent of the English titles were published between 1728 and 1742, the year of Weidmann's death.[22]

19 To our knowledge, the only complete copy in Germany is in the Universitätsbibliothek Tübingen. We are grateful to the library for making it available to us. A copy of volume II is also in the Universitätsbibliothek Augsburg. We are grateful to Dr Paul Berthold Rupp of the Universitätsbibliothek Augsburg for supplying information on English imprints in the Augsburg copy.

20 See Baerent [note 5] and Rath [note 13].

21 See Brauer [note 3].

22 *Svpellex librorvm* contains only one title published in 1742.

SVPELLEX LIBRORVM
PRAESTANTISSIMORVM,
COMPACTORVM,
QVAM
COLLEGIT ET RELIQVIT
MAVRITIVS GEORGIVS
WEIDMANNVS,
SERENISSIMO AC POTENTISSIMO
SARMATARVM REGI
AC ELECTORI SAXONIAE
A CONSILIIS AVLAE,
BIBLIOPOLII EIVS OLIM ORNAMENTVM,
NVNC AVCTIONE VENALIVM,
CVIVS
PARS PRIMA
VENDETVR
DIE XXV. IANVARII ANNI MDCCXLV
H. L. Q. C.

LIPSIAE,
IMPRIMEBAT AVG. SAM. CRVCIGER.

Fig. 2

Another 30 per cent bear dates between 1576 and 1700; the rest are scattered evenly over roughly the first three decades of the eighteenth century.

British books in Latin and English, occasionally also in other languages, occur everywhere in the catalogue. Again, not all are by British authors. There is the familiar false imprint 'Londres'. About seventy books by British authors are in French or Latin and were published on the Continent. The number of genuine British imprints among the 'literae humaniores' is small. In theology books in Latin outnumber those in English. Characteristically, English language books are religious books, not theological books. The subsection 'Theologia fanatica et paradoxa' contains, for instance, Richard Baxter's *Right Method for a Settled Peace of Conscience, and Spiritual Comfort, in 32 Directions* (1653) and *The Christian Quaker, and his Divine Testimony, Vindicated by Scripture, Reason and Authorities* (1673-74) by William Penn and George Whitehead.[23] It is also noteworthy that of the nine medical books from Britain only two are in Latin.

In each of the major sections, British books amount to about four or five per cent; in 'historia literaria' there are only 2.5 per cent, and English law books make up one per cent. Surprisingly, the number of British books in 'Literae humaniores' does not exceed three per cent. But 'Literae humaniores' and 'Historia' contain roughly two-thirds of the English imprints in the catalogue. In the subsection of 'Scriptores Magnae Britanniae' eighteen titles are listed, mainly but not exclusively in English. 'Poetae recentiores', a subsection of 'Literae humaniores', boasts 271 English titles. With few exceptions they are plays in duodecimo and octavo, published in London between 1709 and 1741. There is a familiar group of undated plays in octavo, with London imprints. The folio formats include the Duchess of Newcastle's *Poems and Fancies* (London, 1653) in an English binding, John Fletcher's *Fifty Comedies* (London, 1679) and William Killigrew's *Pandora* (Oxford, 1666).

A comparison of *Svpellex librorvm* with the weekly catalogues of 1733-1735 suggests that plays were Weidmann's major English business. The sixteen plays in quarto listed in the weekly catalogues had apparently all been sold by 1745. Of the 58 undated reprints from Johnson's 'Collection of the best English plays' only 20 are still listed. All in all, the number of plays which Weidmann had meanwhile added to his stock was much larger than the number of plays sold. He had bought more of Thomas Johnson's reprints but no longer relied on the 'Collection' as his chief source of supply. But Johnson's canon had served him as a guideline. Reprints which had been sold were replaced by new copies, not necessarily of the latest edition. Of Addison's *Cato*, he had acquired a copy of a 1713 London edition (the first?) to replace the reprint of 1722. Of other authors reprinted by Johnson, Weidmann had tried to obtain plays not included in the 'Collection' – occasionally, as in the case of Dryden and Lee, even the collected plays.

Shakespeare figures prominently. In 1734, Weidmann had advertised John

23 Nos 6538 and 6593.

son's reprints of seven of Shakespeare's plays and of two adaptations by Thomas Shadwell. By 1745 five of these were apparently still on the shelves (or had been replaced by new copies), and as many as 48 editions of single plays had been added. Pope's and Sewell's edition of the *Works* (London, 1728) was also available. Most of the single plays were published in 1734, the year in which 'the output of Shakespeare's plays reached high-water mark'.[24] Weidmann seems to have bought everything by Shakespeare, or attributed to Shakespeare, published in that year. Whether or not Weidmann's acquisition of Shakespeare's plays in bulk made an impact on the early reception of Shakespeare in Germany remains to be established.

For the publication of Restoration and early eighteenth century dramatists 1735 was a peak year. This again is reflected in Weidmann's stock. Nineteen titles are listed in *Svpellex librorvm* – a remarkably large number in view of Weidmann's purchases of other literary and non-literary authors. Most of the dramatists are offered either in first or early or new editions published between 1728 and 1741. Examples are Fielding's *Love in Several Masks* (1728), Gay's *Beggar's Opera* (1728) or Lillo's *London Merchant* (1731). Obviously, Weidmann tried to offer his customers the whole spectrum of eighteenth-century English drama. Allowing for a certain number of titles sold between their acquisition and the publication of *Svpellex librorvm*, Weidmann appears to have bought from ten to fifteen English plays each year – a fraction of the total number published annually but an impressive number in view of the small market he served.

A look at the non-dramatic literature in *Svpellex librorvm* discloses further aspects of Weidmann's business. The stock of antiquarian British books decreased by one third in actual numbers. But here, too, Weidmann kept adding by acquiring new titles or replacing copies sold – not least in the realm of the 'new science' and its popularization. Locke's *Essay* in Latin and Thomas Burnet's *Telluris theoria sacra* were no longer on the shelves in 1745. Gideon Harvey's *De febribus tractatus* (1672) had been sold, while his *Treatise of the Small Pox and Measles* (1696) was newly bought. Less popular were the Fathers of the Church in Latin as well as expensive books with plates. Of Elias Ashmole's book on the Order of the Garter (1672), advertised three times in the weekly catalogues, two copies are offered in different sections of *Svpellex librorvm*, one in a French, the other in an English binding.[25] The historical works in Latin of William Camden and John Selden (*Annales rerum Anglicarum* and *Historiae Anglicanae scriptores*) appear to have been flops.

Generally, British scholarly works in Latin seem to have sold better than works in English, and authors most sought after were evidently those propagating new methods of enquiry or making contributions to the advancement of learning. Weidmann must have been well aware of his customers' preferences.

24 Ford [note 18], p. 41. This was owing to the re-publication of single plays by Johnson and the simultaneous sale of them by Robert Walker.

25 Nos 5454 and 6835.

He appears to have neglected publications in English outside the field of *belles lettres*. An exception is a batch of four books published in 1741, all of which contain accounts of trials.

As a rule, British scholarly books added to the stock after 1735 were antiquarian books. If Weidmann did not buy current British titles in Latin, it was because ever fewer were published. The use of the vernacular in English scholarly publications became more and more common, and Latin translations ceased to be published in England. Foreign scholars had to rely on Latin translations published on the Continent or on translations into vernacular languages. Within two decades after Weidmann's death, the market for translations expanded rapidly.

Though it marked the end of a significant phase of bookselling in Leipzig, the *Svpellex librorvm* also foreshadowed the future of the eighteenth-century German market for English books. Almost until the end of the century, it remained a small market and a market largely confined to literature in the narrow sense. If Weidmann concentrated on plays, he selected a genre particularly suitable for the new reader of English. Plays were relatively short texts, they were entertaining, and they could be used as language learning aids. As the later reprinting of English literary texts in Germany disclosed, the general reader preferred the kind of book which Moritz Georg Weidmann appears to have been the first to introduce in Germany.

V

In the 1750s a new phase began in the importation of English books into Germany. Its beginnings were spectacular but soon subsided into a routine which was to remain characteristic of the second half of the century. After the death of Moritz Georg the Younger the house of Weidmann apparently abstained from trading in foreign books (antiquarian and modern) for some time to concentrate on the publishing side of the business. Meanwhile, other Leipzig booksellers tried to expand their foreign business.

One publisher-bookseller in particular stands out by his attempt to market English books on a large scale: Johann Wendler. Wendler came to Leipzig from Nuremberg and was hired by the heirs of Moritz Georg Weidmann (wife and daughter) as manager of the firm. Whether or not the dispersion of Moritz Georg's antiquarian collection was his idea, he presided over the sale of it. Wendler left in 1746 to open his own business – apparently inspired by the dual activities of the late Moritz Georg Weidmann.

In the autumn Fair Catalogue of 1755 Wendler inserted an unusual block entry consisting of nearly twenty literary titles, ranging from Akenside's *Pleasures of Imagination* to Young's *Love of Fame*. It included Milton and Pope as well as popular novels. Wendler also drew attention to a catalogue of English books available at his shop – the first all-English catalogue issued by a German bookseller. Unfortunately it is not preserved. Over the next decade, Wendler appears to have been the major supplier of English books in Leipzig. He founded a review journal[26] exclusively devoted to English books. His business was taken over by Caspar Fritsch in 1766, and the last catalogue issued by Wendler/Fritsch contains several hundred titles of the late seventeenth and eighteenth centuries from virtually all fields.[27] It is the most comprehensive eighteenth-century German catalogue of books in English.

Throughout the later eighteenth century, English books seem to have been imported into Germany regularly, though in varying numbers, through channels which are difficult to identify. Catalogues or advertisements issued by leading booksellers testify to the availability of a fairly large variety of books in English. Friedrich Nicolai's *Verzeichnis einer Handbibliothek*[28] or Johann Christian Dieterich's insertions in the *Göttingisches Magazin der Wissenschaften und Litteratur*[29] provide evidence, as do the activities of other booksellers.

At the same time, English titles appear again and again in the Fair Catalogues.[30] These annoucements are less sensational than the insertion by Wendler but they appear to be indicative of a new kind of routine business established between English publishers and German publishers and booksellers. It was a routine business in which the house of Weidmann again took the lead. Once more the firm established itself as the *primus inter pares* – this time under Philipp Erasmus Reich, whose business contacts to England were closer and more refined than those of any other publisher in Germany at the time.

Between 1770 and 1790 hardly a Fair Catalogue can be found which does not contain English titles. Some of these are reprints (reprinting increased between 1770 and 1800); the majority, however, are titles published in England but marketed in Germany by Leipzig publishers and booksellers. They were announced, in varying forms, as available from Leipzig (or other places in Central Germany). In many cases, it is difficult to distinguish them from reprints undertaken by German publishers.

Weidmanns Erben und Reich first made their appearance as importers at the autumn Fair of 1770. In established fashion, they announced a number of titles at once. Further titles followed in 1773. The largest number – about thirty - were inserted in the Easter Catalogue for 1778 during the peak period in the reception of English authors in Germany. From the Easter Fair of 1780 (eight titles) the number declined, and the last entry appeared in the Autumn Catalogue of 1787, shortly before Philipp Erasmus Reich died. In all, nearly seventy-five titles were announced. The number is not impressive but it is larger

26 *Brittische Bibliothek*, 1756-1767.

27 'Catalogue of English Books Sold by Caspar Fritsch at Leipzig', appended to the last volume of *Brittische Bibliothek*.

28 Berlin, 1787 and later editions.

29 See, for instance, vols 1 (1780) and 3 (1782-83).

30 See Bernhard Fabian, 'Die Meßkataloge und der Import englischer Bücher nach Deutschland im achtzehnten Jahrhundert', in *Buchhandel und Literatur: Festschrift für Herbert G. Göpfert zum 75. Geburtstag*, ed. Reinhard Wittmann and Berthold Hack (Wiesbaden, 1982), pp. 154-68.

than the number of English books marketed through the Fair Catalogues by any of Reich's colleagues and competitors.

As a general publisher and bookseller, Weidmann offered a large variety of books. There are scholarly and professional works such as Edward Harwood's *View of the Various Editions of the Greek and Roman Classics* or Percival Pott's *Chirurgical Observations* (Easter 1778); technical and practical works such as James Glennie's *History of Gunnery*, Henry Home's *Principles of Agriculture* or John Abercrombie's *Universal Gardener* (Easter 1778, 1780); and books of travel and geographical exploration to satisfy an ever-growing demand for information about foreign countries. Finally, there are literary works both recondite and popular, ranging from the *Additions to the Works of Alexander Pope* to Thomas Vaughan's *Fashionable Follies* (Easter 1778, 1783).

The criteria of selection, if any, are hard to judge. Obviously, the titles announced were intended not only for the local book-buyer in Leipzig frequenting Weidmann's shop but also for the provincial bookseller depending for his supply on the latest Fair Catalogues, if not on the actual Fairs. At any rate, Weidmann is likely to have imported a number of copies (as the firm normally did of French books).

The manner in which these titles were announced suggests that business relations between London and Leipzig were properly established. Various formulas occur: 'to be sold by Weidmann's heirs and Reich', 'London and Leipzig, sold by Weidmann's heirs and Reich' or, even more correct, 'London printed; and Leipzig, to be had of Weidmann's heirs and Reich'. Philipp Erasmus Reich, strongly opposed to reprinting, never reprinted a foreign title. Nor did he present himself, as other Leipzig and Berlin publishers did in their announcements, as a commission agent of foreign publishers. In the tradition of the founder, Weidmann continued to be an international bookseller.

For the most part, the books offered by Weidmann issued from the major London publishers – Cadell, Robinson and Becket-De Hondt. But there were also minor publishers involved, such as Henry Hughes. Strangely enough, the dominant author on the Weidmann list is John Hill, the miscellaneous writer, who accounts for no fewer than ten titles, most of which were 'printed for the author'.

How business was transacted between London and Leipzig remains – after the wartime destruction of the Weidmann archive – largely a matter of conjecture. Philipp Erasmus Reich employed various agents both in Paris and in London. The most active in London was Johann Friedrich Schiller, a cousin of the poet, who acted as Reich's representative between 1776 and 1784, precisely in the period during which about four-fifths of the titles were announced in the Fair Catalogues.[31] Schiller arranged for translations. He is therefore likely to

31 See Karl Buchner, *Aus dem Verkehr einer deutschen Buchhandlung mit den Geschäftsgenossen* (Gießen, 1874), pp. 177f.

have bought the books offered by Weidmann at the Leipzig Fairs. Perhaps he even selected many or most of the titles.

After the death of Philipp Erasmus Reich the English business of Weidmann appears to have rapidly declined and come to an end. A *Catalogus librorum, qvi librariae Weidmannianae Lipsiae svmtibvs svnt vel qvorvm copia svppetit*, published for the Easter Fair in 1793, contains a relatively meagre section of 'Livres françois, anglois et italiens'. The only English title is: 'A Selection of Anthony Wall's Novels; with others of Mr. J. J. Engel's Philosopher for the world. Translated from the German; ... for the Use of those who wish to learn the German language'.

JOSEPH DOWNING AND THE PUBLICATION OF PIETIST LITERATURE IN ENGLAND, 1705-1734

GRAHAM JEFCOATE

SEARCHES of the *Eighteenth-Century Short Title Catalogue (ESTC)* on line for the first four decades of the eighteenth century will retrieve over one hundred bibliographic records for London publications broadly relating to Pietism, that movement within German Lutheranism that arose during the second half of the seventeenth century in opposition to the dogmatism of the Church's established hierarchy. They include translations, reprints and original works in English, Latin and German. Responsibility for publishing the great majority of these lay with just two individuals: Anton Wilhelm Boehme (1673-1722), a Pietist divine, and Joseph Downing (1676-1734), bookseller and printer to the Society for Promoting Christian Knowledge. In addition to Boehme and Downing, Johann Christian Jacobi, another London Pietist, was also associated with a small but significant group of related publications.

Although some Pietist titles achieved a considerable impact, much of the printed evidence for this publishing and bookselling activity is scarce and highly scattered. *ESTC* has recorded relevant material in major research libraries and smaller collections throughout the English-speaking world. Recently, significant finds have also been made in eastern European libraries as they have begun to participate in the project.[1] The *ESTC* file probably now represents the most extensive record of Pietist publishing in England in the early eighteenth century. Even so, while making available a range of valuable archival evidence, neither of the authors of the two most recent studies of London Pietists[2] appears to have made use of this resource. By pursuing the clues provided by the *ESTC* file, and examining some of the printed and archival sources from a somewhat

1 Small collections of London publications in German, for example, have been reported from the Houghton Library at Harvard and the National Library of South Africa. More examples have come to light at the National Library of Estonia and at the Library of the Franckesche Stiftungen at Halle/Saale where I was recently able to record relevant material for *ESTC*.

2 Arno Sames, *Anton Wilhelm Böhme* (Göttingen, 1989); Daniel L. Brunner, *Halle Pietists in England: Anthony William Boehm and the Society for Promoting Christian Knowledge*. Arbeiten zur Geschichte des Pietismus, 26 and 29 (Göttingen, 1993). Neither of these studies is of course specifically concerned with the *publication* of Pietist literature. It seems strange however that the index to Sames's biography of Boehme omits any mention of Downing.

different perspective, it may now be possible to reassess the publication of Pietist literature in England and to re-evaluate the role of Joseph Downing in relation to it.

Joseph Downing was born into a family of London printers in 1676, the second of the four sons of William and Ann Downing.[3] He learnt the trade in the family printing shop, becoming free of the Company of Stationers by patrimony shortly after his father's death in 1703. It was Joseph rather than his elder brother William who then took over the management of the family business in Bartholomew Close near West Smithfield.[4] By 1705 he was binding apprentices in his own right, most of whom went on to become themselves free of the Company and master-printers.[5] Joseph took the Company's livery in 1706 and held minor office in 1713-14 but never became a member of its Court. Of much greater significance in his career was his early involvement with the Society for Promoting Christian Knowledge (SPCK). This association was to enable him to build up a very substantial business, unusually at this period both as a printer and as bookseller.

DOWNING AND THE SOCIETY FOR PROMOTING CHRISTIAN KNOWLEDGE

Since its foundation in 1698, the SPCK had seen as one of its major aims the wide dissemination of religious literature in the form of cheap, improving tracts. The Society did not itself act as publisher; instead it selected 'books and tracts already of proven worth as Christian literature, which it then either had specially reprinted or bought in large quantities, chiefly at this time from its bookseller, Joseph Downing'.[6] Before 1703 books had been printed 'at their own expense and dispersed gratis' to 'residing and corresponding members' as they required them.[7] After that date, members were asked to make contributions towards publication costs. By 1735 about five hundred members were receiving occasional packets of books for distribution among the poor or those in moral danger, many of which contained very substantial numbers of copies. The SPCK also sought to promote its own brand of Christianity by founding charity schools and the well-known parochial libraries associated with Thomas Bray, all of which contained approved titles supplied to order by Downing.

Downing's relationship with the Society may, I believe, have been misunderstood. He was never its servant, nor do his imprints, unlike those of his

3 I am very grateful to Professor Michael Treadwell for providing much of the biographical information about Downing included here from his unpublished notes.

4 Joseph possibly at first shared some of the responsibility for running the shop with his mother. Downing remained at this address until his death in 1734; his wife Martha continued to live there until she died in 1770.

5 Professor Treadwell has counted nine, an unusually high figure. He suggests that Downing's mother's binding an apprentice in her own name as late as 1708 may indicate a need to avoid the Company's limit on the number of apprentices as the business expanded.

6 Leonard W. Cowie, *Henry Newman: An American in London 1708-43* (London, 1956), p. 55.

7 Cowie, p. 56.

successors, ever refer to the SPCK directly. His catalogues make no explicit connection between the publications on offer and the Society, which approved only those it intended to distribute. The most that might be said is that, as Daniel L. Brunner succinctly states, 'to be published by Downing was almost to have the Society's imprimatur, or at least to appear to have it' (p. 131). Much has been made of an incident in December 1703 in which the Society's committee reprimanded Downing for printing a translation from the French[8] 'containing many dangerous points' and threatening to terminate their connection 'if he prints any more such like books'.[9]

This very early incident, however, does not appear to have been typical of the relationship between the Society and its printer as it developed. The minutes of SPCK's twice-monthly committee meetings record relatively few issues of contention between the Society and its printer, although committees occasionally thought it necessary to give Downing advice on where to place advertisements for their publications or which binders to use.[10] It is worth noting, perhaps, that he seems rarely to have appeared before them in person, even when requested to do so, often preferring to send a messenger or sometimes apparently failing to respond altogether. On a number of occasions the committee sought to establish the Society's precise interest in Downing's business.[11] On others he was required to renounce his right to the Society's copies of titles printed by him.[12] What is certain is that his connection with the Society persisted to great mutual benefit until his death in 1734, when the Society reappointed Joseph's widow Martha as their printer despite strong competition from other members of the trade.

Joseph Downing used his role as printer to the Society for Promoting Christian Knowledge (and later to the Society for the Propagation of the Gospel

8 Jeanne Marie de la Motte Guyon: *A short and easie method of prayer* (estc t177419). *ESTC* records only two copies of this edition; another edition with a different imprint (probably a reissue of Downing's) appeared in 1704.

9 SPCK Minutes, vol. 1, pp. 270–74. Downing agreed to 'call in all the copies which were unsold, and to make wast [*sic*] paper of them'. Printing the translation had cost Downing £12. A note showing the Committee had considered compensating him for his loss by giving him three guineas is deleted in the minutes, possibly because it transpired that the translator 'had promis'd to indemnify him as to the charge in case it should not sell'. I am grateful to the Reverend Dr Gordon Huelin, Archivist and Librarian to the SPCK, for his assistance in searching the Society's archives for references to Downing.

10 See for example SPCK Minutes vol. 7, pp. 153, 157; vol. 10, pp. 17, 19.

11 In November 1712 members 'agreed that the Committee be desir'd to consider what copies the Society have a property in, and to treat with Mr. Downing upon such security as shall be thought proper'. The minutes for the meeting held in 12 January 1716 show he was required 'to sign an instrument – as formerly, acknowledging the Society's right to such copies as belong to them, tho published by him.' See SPCK Minutes, vol. 6, p. 179; vol. 7, p. 107 ff. See also vol. 10, p. 59, recording a motion passed on 5 July 1722 that 'the accounts between the Society, their correspondents, and Mr. Downing from the beginning of the new regulation for dispersing books [i.e. since 1703?]' be inspected.

12 Including twenty-two titles in December 1709 and seven in January 1713. Martha Downing was required to sign a similar document relating to some thirty titles in 1735. See SPCK Papers of moment, pp. 4, 16, 140–41.

as well) to establish himself firmly in a specialist but profitable area of the book trade, showing considerable skill in exploiting the possibilities offered by an expanding market. This market depended of course on the spread of literacy, fostered in part by the Society's own charity schools. Most of Downing's publications, however, were not aimed directly at the newly literate, but rather at those 'charitable persons', many of them members of the Societies with which he was connected, who recognized the usefulness of the cheap, improving tract in reaching an increasingly unsettled population. Downing's business was based on the printing of very large quantities of a relatively small number of tracts on topics of particular concern to such people, especially those expected to influence the behaviour of the poor. Swearing, drunkenness, uncleanness, lying and breaches of the Lord's Day were favourite topics, each addressed by a convenient, cheap tract printed by Downing. Others were directed at specific 'problem' groups such as soldiers, prisoners or even London boatmen. The minutes of the Society for Promoting Christian Knowledge contain frequent references to orders for multiple copies of such publications, as well as for 'copy books' for the Society's charity schools.[13]

In 1707 Downing issued an early example of a publisher's catalogue listing titles under topic. As he points out in his advertisement to the reader: 'The following catalogue of books may be very useful to all pious and charitable persons (especially as live in the country) who are religiously disposed to give *any number* of them to their friends, dependants, or others'.[14] Prices are given 'single, and by the hundred, &c.'. Within the catalogue, items in the same format are marked, indicating that they could usefully be bound up together to form a small collection of improving tracts. A second, wholly revised, edition of the catalogue issued in 1708 advises the charitably disposed in some detail about titles proper to be given away on particular occasions, stressing that Downing offered books 'at the lowest rates; *and encouragement given to those who take numbers*'.[15] Interestingly, this edition was issued with a *A Proposal for teaching poor children to read, &c.*, apparently by Downing himself, in which he calculates that a child could be taught to read for an investment of only ten shillings. We should not necessarily conclude from this that Downing's interest here was purely in expanding his market: as well as being a trustee of the London charity schools, his will shows he left £50 to the charity school of his own parish.

13 In June 1713, for example, the Committee 'agreed that Mr. Downing be allow'd to work off 500. copy books from the Society's plates'. SPCK Minutes, vol. 6, p. 83.

14 *A new catalogue of books and tracts, against vice and immorality; and for promoting the knowledge & practice of the Christian religion, collected under particular heads.* London, 1707 (estc t87735). My emphasis. The list includes a few items not printed by Downing himself.

15 *A new catalogue of books and small tracts against vice and immorality.* London, 1708, p. 44 (estc t86715). My emphasis.

PIETAS HALLENSIS

That Downing should not be regarded merely as the purveyor of large quantities of cheap print is evident from his connection with the German Pietists, and especially with Anton Wilhelm Boehme. Their collaboration, which lasted some seventeen years from 1705 until Boehme's death in 1722, shows that Downing was prepared to become involved in printing and selling categories of material not normally associated with the SPCK, nor likely perhaps to produce much immediate profit, including some that might normally be considered the preserve of university presses. Boehme was a pupil and follower of August Hermann Francke (1663-1727), the leading figure in German Pietism at the turn of the eighteenth century. A man of extraordinary energy and pious determination, Francke had founded an orphanage for the children of the poor of his parish at Glaucha near the Prussian town of Halle in 1698. Within a few years this had developed into a complex of charitable and educational institutions enjoying close links with the recently-founded university and encompassing, among much else besides, several schools, a teacher-training college, library, *Kuriositätenkabinett*, centre for bible studies, printing house, farm and an apothecary.[16] Francke had established early links with the Society for Promoting Christian Knowledge in London, sending two emissaries to give a personal account of his foundation to the Committee in May 1699 and becoming a corresponding member himself in 1700.

Boehme arrived in London in 1701, finding a room in Bedfordbury near the Strand, an area already settled by German families, where he started a German-language school.[17] Although his earliest years in England were made difficult by ill health and his lack of English, he soon established links with the SPCK in the person of Frederick Slare, a prominent member and enthusiast for Francke's work, with whom he undertook a tour of English charity schools in 1705. It was Slare's encouragement and practical support that enabled him to translate (with the help of two others) *Die Fußstapfen des noch lebenden Gottes*, Francke's own published account of his foundation at Halle.[18] In a letter to a friend dated 31 January 1705, Francke shows an understanding of the value of the connection with the SPCK in the dissemination of his ideas in England:

Aus Engeland hat H. Böhme geschrieben und berichtet, daß er die Fußtapffen des Waysen-Hauses, so viel davon ediret, ganz ins Englische übersetzt, dieselbe einer gewißen Societaet übergeben, und durch deren recommendation auch einen Verleger

16 The Franckesche Stiftungen zu Halle an der Saale survive at their original location with many of the original buildings and institutions. After years of neglect by the government of the former German Democratic Republic, they were revived by a decree of the *Land* of Sachsen-Anhalt in 1990 as an independent legal entity. See *Die Franckeschen Stiftungen zu Halle an der Saale* (Wolfenbüttel, 1990) and the Foundation's own printed annual programmes (since 1993). I am especially grateful to Dr Penelope Willard and Dr Thomas Müller for their support during my visits to the Stiftungen.

17 Sames, [note 2], p. 111.

18 Brunner, [note 2], pp. 83-4.

dazu gefunden, weil es dieselbe Societaet in ganz Engeland an Correspondenten recommendieren will.[19]
(Herr Böhme has written from England and reported that he has translated as much of the orphanage's *Fußstapfen* as has been issued into English and given it to a certain society and found a publisher for it on their recommendation because the society wishes to recommend it to its members throughout England.)

This publisher was of course Downing, who gave Boehme £1 for the translation and issued the work in the same year under the title *Pietas Hallensis: or a publick demonstration of the foot-steps of a divine being yet in the world: in an historical narration of the orphan-house, ... at Glaucha near Hall in Saxony*.[20] In his 'Preface to the English reader', Boehme begs candid readers to excuse 'Teutonisms or other imperfections', making allowance for 'some little trips in the manner of expression' (p. XLI). The work was reissued in the same year with a cancel title-page omitting from the title the phrase *or a publick demonstration of the foot-steps of a divine being yet in the world*, perhaps because it drew attention to an aspect of Pietism that gave greatest difficulty to some Anglicans, who considered it close to superstition. This issue also bears the imprint 'printed for Joseph Downing, for R. Burrough' and an initial advertisement leaf for Burrough, probably showing that Downing shared the cost of at least part of the edition by involving another bookseller in its publication.[21]

Boehme's translation might have had the general support of the Society for Promoting Christian Knowledge, but an octavo of over three hundred pages was not suitable for distribution in the packets of books sent to corresponding members. On 8 November 1705, the Committee requested Downing to attend its next meeting to discuss the matter. Although he did not in fact appear in person, he was reported on 22 November as agreeing 'to the abridging of the *Pietas Hallensis*, so as that it be done in two sheets & an half'. Slare was asked on 29 November to 'speak to the translator of the Pietas Hallensis to abridge his book'. A Mr Shute reported on 13 December that this abridgement was finished '& will shortly be published'. By 10 January 1706, Slare announced that he and two others had perused and approved the text and the Committee agreed 'that 500 of them be bought, and that 3 of them be putt in to each of the packets that are now about to be sent'. The Treasurer informed the Committee on 24 January that the work 'is printing, & that the price is to be 20s. a hundred, if it come's [sic] within 3 sheets'.[22] This edition duly appeared in the anticipated three sheets duodecimo with the title *An abstract of the marvellous footsteps.*

19 Archiv der Franckeschen Stiftungen C171:18. Printed in: *Der Briefwechsel Carl Hildebrand von Cansteins mit August Hermann Francke*, ed. P. Schicketanz (Berlin and New York, 1972), p. 287.

20 estc t145067. Boehme explains the English title as a rejoinder to Roman Catholic works such as *Pietas Romana* or *Pietas Parisiensis*.

21 estc n37569. This reissue is considerably rarer than the first, although interestingly it is the one held by the Hauptbibliothek der Franckeschen Stiftungen itself. A variant in the Thomas Bray Library now at Birmingham Central Library (estc t221523) apparently has 'J.' for 'Joseph'.

22 SPCK Minutes, vol. 1, pp. 350, 352, 354, 356, 362, 364.

Again, two issues are recorded by *ESTC*, one bearing the imprint 'printed for R. Burrough' and the other 'printed and sold by Joseph Downing'.[23] A second, enlarged edition of the abstract (with the title 'restored' as *Pietas Hallensis: or, an abstract of the marvellous footsteps of divine providence*) was issued in 1707, again partly by Downing and partly by Burrough. This edition also contains a short history of Pietism supplied by Boehme.[24]

Pietas Hallensis, both abridged and 'in large', is listed in the second edition of Downing's *A new catalogue of books* of 1708 under the heading 'Providence'. The full edition is priced at 3*s*. 6*d*. bound in calf, whereas the abridged version might be had for '4d. or 28s. per hundred'. Its publication proved a great success both for Boehme personally and for the links between Francke's foundation and the English-speaking world. Many of the signs of God's providence described by Francke in his book take the form of the timely arrival of substantial cash donations (rather in the manner of some modern evangelism), and the appearance of the *Pietas* in England opened a new channel through which God's providence might flow. The royal consort, Prince George of Denmark, who appointed Boehme a chaplain in his Lutheran chapel at St James's, made the largest single donation (£1,000), but smaller sums continued to be sent by numerous private individuals, encouraged by new editions bringing the story of the *Waisenhaus* up to date.[25] Boehme became a residing member of the SPCK on 3 February 1709 and was taking his turn in chairing meetings of the committee by 1716. The success of the *Pietas Hallensis* also appears to have cemented the working relationship between Boehme and Downing, who began to collaborate closely on what can only be described as a programme of Pietist publications.

DOWNING AS PUBLISHER OF ANTON WILHELM BOEHME

Following the appearance of the *Abstract* in 1706, Boehme and Downing embarked on the publication of further works aimed at a specific readership not normally addressed by the Society for Promoting Christian Knowledge: university students. The imprint of Boehme's edition of Francke's *Manuductio ad lectionem scripturae sacrae*, 'a general practical guide to interpreting the Scripture for his students',[26] reads: 'typis J. Downing, impensis R. Burrough'.

23 estc t114432, t221598. Copies of both issues are scarce, although the 'Burrough' issue is more common; the 'Downing' issue has so far been recorded only at the Hauptbibliothek der Franckeschen Stiftungen.

24 estc t181617 ('printed and sold by J. Downing'); t133491 ('printed for R. Burrough'). The latter is a reissue of the former with the imprint and some signatures reset.

25 For example a Mrs Prigg of Bristol, who 'remitted 5. pounds to be sent to Professor Franck at Hall' in January 1725 (SPCK minutes, vol. 11, p. 114). See also Brunner, [note 2], p. 88.

26 Brunner, [note 2], p. 136. As if to make the publication more acceptable to Anglicans, the edition is equipped with a recommendation by Pierre Allix and an appendix compiled by Francis Fox containing a 'Collection from several eminent English authors, relating to the study of the sacred scriptures'. The *Manuductio* is listed in the term catalogue of 1707 as sold by Burrough, price 2s. 6d (estc t123355). The 1708 edition held by Trinity College, Dublin, with the imprint reading simply 'typis J. Downing, 1708', may well be a reissue of this (estc t171498).

Again, this was issued with an initial advertisement leaf for R. Burrough at the Sun and Moon in Cornhill which allocates *Pietas Hallensis* half the available space. Boehme's translation of Francke's *Nicodemus: or, a treatise against the fear of man*,[27] which followed the *Manuductio* in the same year, was also issued partly by Downing and partly by Burrough. In the following year, as well as the revised edition of the abridged *Pietas Hallensis*, Boehme published the first of his own original works, described as his major treatise, also aimed at a university readership: *Enchiridion precum, ad promovendum solidioris pietatis studium collectum*, with an introduction 'De natura orationis' again printed by Downing but sold 'impensis R. Burrough & J. Baker' (estc n9175).

In the next three years alone (1708-1710) Boehme and Downing collaborated on the publication of about ten further separate editions of Pietist works each year, an extraordinary and probably unsustainable level of output. By 1709, Downing was already able to print three pages of advertisements listing some twelve works written or prepared for publication by Boehme. From 1711 until Boehme's death in 1722, titles continued to appear on average at the rate of three or four a year. This concentrated activity demonstrates a determination to bring the Pietist message to a wide variety of English readers, titles ranging from substantial translations and scholarly editions to brief, improving tracts and sermons. It could only have been achieved by a combination of Boehme's pious energy, the capacity of Downing's printing shop, and his understanding of the market.

After the *Pietas Hallensis*, probably the most influential Pietist text edited by Boehme for English readers was the *Propagation of the Gospel in the east, being an account of the success of two Danish missionaries, lately sent to the East-Indies, for the conversion of the heathens in Malabar*.[28] These 'Danish' missionaries were in fact the Halle Pietists Bartholomaeus Ziegenbalg and Heinrich Plütscho, who jointly wrote the first account of the Lutheran mission at Tranquebar on the Coromandel Coast in south India which had been established under the patronage of the Danish crown. Like the *Pietas Hallensis*, the *Propagation* went through a number of editions bringing the story of the mission up to date and encouraging substantial donations. Subscriptions were invited to pay for a printing press and for 'pious and learned missionaries' to be sent to Tranquebar, or for editions of the gospels in Portuguese, the vernacular of south Indian Christians. The name of 'The Reverend Mr. Boehm, at the Golden Angel in the Strand' (later at the 'Surgeons-Arms near the May-Pole in the Strand') is prominent among the lists of those who took subscriptions in, but Downing's

27 estc t104248 ('printed and sold by Joseph Downing', the more common form); t182179 ('printed for R. Burrough', recorded only in the Thomas Bray Library at Birmingham). Francke's name is spelt 'Franke' on the title-pages of these issues; another rare issue (n51588) has it in the more usual Anglicized form: 'Franck'. In his preface to this work, Boehme responds to those English readers who might consider Francke 'speaks too boldly' by referring them to the *Pietas Hallensis* (p. [6]).

28 estc t42761. See Brunner, [note 2], pp. 103 ff. The Society for the Propagation of the Gospel ordered five hundred copies for distribution in the British Isles and the colonies.

role may have been underestimated. As well as printing the various proposals and editions, it is recorded, for example, that in 1710 Jonas Fincke, a teacher at a German school in London who had volunteered to go to Tranquebar, was placed with him by the committee of the SPCK 'in order to be instructed by him in the art of printing'.[29]

Of particular importance to Boehme were the works of Johann Arndt (1555-1623), described on the title-page of the Latin edition of *Vom wahren Christenthum* of 1708 as 'theologus apud Germanos celeberrimus'.[30] Boehme was clearly determined to disseminate Arndt's work as widely as possible in translation. Characteristically the Latin edition aimed at the university market was followed in 1709 with a duodecimo edition of selections in English intended, as Boehme states in his preface, 'for the use chiefly of the common sort' and therefore more suitable for distribution by the SPCK.[31] The first volume of a full English translation appeared (with three plates engraved by Michael van der Gucht) in 1712. Downing again sought to share the costs of this substantial edition of nearly seven hundred pages with another bookseller, the imprint reading 'printed for D. Brown at the Black Swan and Bible without Temple-Bar; and for J. Downing ...'. Its success was such that Downing felt able to issue the second volume, which appeared in 1714, alone. In his preface Boehme mentions Downing's concern about this second volume, expressing the hope that 'this deservedly applauded treatise may be able to force its way, to the satisfaction of bookseller and reader, now that it appears in English dress'. Some irritation between the two might be read into Boehme's ingenuous complaint at the end of the preface that he is 'here confined by the bookseller, the bulk of this volume [again over six hundred pages] having swelled beyond what was at first designed; I am obliged to break off somewhat abruptly, ...'.[32]

Other publications were intended for a readership rather closer to that usually addressed by Downing and the SPCK. The copy of Francke's *A short introduction to the practice of Christian religion*[33] held by the Franckesche Stiftungen is bound with a number of other duodecimo Pietist tracts in a contemporary English binding with the spine title: 'Lady's libri'.[34] This copy represents a fine example of a custom-made collection of tracts in the same format bound together as Downing recommended. They include works describing extraordinary examples of popular, and especially pre-pubertal, piety, such as Wilhelm Erasmus Arend's *Early piety recommended*, and other

29 Brunner, pp. 105-06. Fincke never reached India, being lost overboard during the outward voyage.

30 estc t127209. Brunner describes this work as 'the book which more than any other reflected Boehme's own style of experiential Christianity' (p. 141).

31 estc t221524. The copy held by the Hauptbibliothek der Franckeschen Stiftungen, 8 H 10 (1), is the first to be recorded for *ESTC*.

32 estc t105557. See especially vol. 2, pp. III-VI. To accommodate Boehme's preface on the sheets available, Downing was forced to reduce the type size on p. XII. See also Brunner, p. 142.

33 A translation of *Der Anfang christlicher Lehre* (estc n36799). See Brunner, pp. 138-39.

34 Hauptbibliothek der Franckeschen Stiftungen 8 H 10.

short treatises by Francke and Boehme himself (or edited by him).[35] A catalogue issued by Downing about 1713 lists them in the section headed 'A catalogue of small tracts, many thousands of which have been dispers'd by charitable and well-disposed persons' at prices ranging from *2d.* to *6d.* each.[36] This catalogue includes in all some thirty works either by Boehme or prepared for publication by him, a small but not insignificant proportion of the total of about one hundred and seventy items advertised. By this time, Boehme's aim to disseminate Pietist literature as widely as possible in England had largely been achieved.

DOWNING AND PRINTING IN GERMAN

Downing's collaboration with Boehme brought him into direct contact with the German-speaking community in London. His role as a printer and bookseller to that community has only now become apparent as the rare printed evidence for this activity is revealed through the *ESTC*. It is not possible to estimate the size of the rather unstable and disparate German population during the first decades of the eighteenth century, however it was clearly smaller than either the French or Dutch-speaking communities. A few Germans were associated with the court, for example, like Boehme himself, with the Lutheran chapel at St James's which continued to function even after the death of Prince George in 1708. Others arrived with the accession of George I in 1714. It is probable, however, that the great majority of Germans in London throughout the period were those involved in trade and commerce, with their families and dependants. The numbers of German speakers in London increased rapidly in the years after 1708 when several thousand Protestant refugees from the Palatinate arrived. Although many of these were *en route* for Ireland or the American colonies, some undoubtedly remained. Small in size and intrinsically unstable as the German community was, institutions specifically intended to serve it were slow to develop. Social life presumably centred around the Lutheran chapels, particularly that in the Savoy, where a charity school 'for the education of children in the German tongue' had been founded by 1718.[37] The existence of a charity school by this date suggests perhaps that the community had grown sufficiently to become of interest to the book trade, and particularly of course to a bookseller such as Downing, who could combine some knowledge of the German community with much experience of publishing for marginal social groups.

35 Examples are *Praise out of the mouth of babes, or a particular account of some extraordinary motions and devout exercises, observ'd of late in many children in Silesia* and *Daily conversation with God: exemplified in the holy life of Armelle Nicolas, a poor ignorant country-maid in France.*

36 Page 8 (estc t186818).

37 Brunner, p. 58. Strype noted the presence of 'High Germans, and Lutherans' among the foreign communities in the Savoy, adding: 'Here also be harbours for many refugees and poor people'. See Katherine Swift, 'The French-booksellers in the Strand', *Proceedings of the Huguenot Society*, 25 (1990), 128-29.

One of the earliest examples of printing in German so far recorded by *ESTC* from this period is a pamphlet addressed to the Lutheran community, written in his own defence by one Christian Gottfried Reinhard, a pastor who had been dismissed from his post at Clausnitz in 1684 for 'improper conduct'.[38] A further example is a *Gebeth-Büchlein: theils aus der englischen Liturgie, theils aus andern geistreichen Gebeth-Büchern zusammengetragen*, printed for use in the chapel at St James's in 1707. Although the work appeared anonymously, the British Library copy (the only one recorded by *ESTC*) bears the manuscript inscription: '... The Gift of the Reverend Mr Behme the Publisher, Chaplain to Prince George &c 31 March 1707'.[39] An *Ausszug geistreicher Lieder*, also intended for the use of the Chapel, was issued in the following year.[40]

There can be no doubt that these works were printed in Downing's shop as the types used (a fraktur, presumably imported) are also found in later works bearing his imprint. These include a bilingual edition of *Der Kirchen-Catechismus ... The church catechism*, translated by Johann Tribbechov, another of the Lutheran chaplains at St James's, which was printed by Downing in 1709 specifically for the use of the Palatines.[41] All of these texts are accurately and neatly set using fraktur types, sometimes mixed with roman, presumably under the supervision of a native speaker of German.

It was clearly the presence of the Palatines in London which led Johann Christian Jacobi, another former student at Halle, to open what was probably the first bookshop in eighteenth-century London with a specifically German character. The Halle bookseller H. J. Elers had apparently considered setting up a branch in London some years earlier,[42] but it was Jacobi who opened a shop in the Strand '... bey kümmerlichen Umbständen u. wenig bücher-Geräthe' ('... in very modest circumstances and with little book-stock')[43] in 1709. A letter preserved in the archives of the Franckesche Stiftungen, apparently overlooked until now, shows he was already despatching books for sale by Elers in Halle in February of that year. These included '40 Exemplaria Arndt [apparently donated by Boehme] ... 5 Piet. Halens. in 8vo. ungeb. ... 2 eiusd. ... gebunden ... 15 Abstracts of Piet. Hal. ... Arndius in 2 vol. for Mr Benson gebunden. ... 6 Funeral sermons of Mr. Tribbecho's' and '15 Exemplaria Enchiridion precum'. As well as bibles and other English books, Jacobi was also supplying Elers with coins and goods such as the '8 yards flannel for Mr Koch Inspect'.[44] All the titles

38 *Aleph: Reinhardus redi-vivus* (estc t213969). The Lambeth Palace copy is bound with a MS. letter from the author to Archbishop Tenison.

39 estc t116541. Brunner, p. 50. 'Behme' appears to have been the form used most frequently by Boehme himself in English.

40 estc t124031. The imprints to both these publications read simply: 'London gedruckt im Jahr ...'.

41 estc t126273. Brunner, p. 60. Lambeth Palace Library holds a copy of a further parallel translation, an edition of the Sermon on the Mount, with an imprint reading simply 'London. An. 1710' (estc t220490).

42 See Brunner, pp. 132-33.

43 Boehme, quoted by Brunner, p. 134.

44 Archiv der Franckeschen Stiftungen A 185(1), dated 21 February 1709.

quoted here, and most of the others in the list I have been able to identify, were of course printed by Downing.

We might reasonably assume that Downing saw in Jacobi, with his direct contacts to the German market both in London and in Halle, a useful addition to his distribution network. *ESTC* brings together for the first time a considerable amount of evidence for Jacobi's bookselling activities and his collaboration with Downing. The close collaboration between them is attested for example by an edition of one of Boehme's sermons which bears the imprint: 'London printed; and are to be sold by Joseph Downing in Bartholomew Close, near West-Smithfield; and by the German booksellers, near Somerset-House in the Strand. 1710'.[45] A similar imprint (reading 'bookseller' rather than 'booksellers') is repeated on other works associated with Boehme or Tribbechov published during the same year, including the second part of *The propagation of the Gospel in the east* (estc t42762). Apart from devotional works, during this period Jacobi also issued an edition of Colsoni's London guide in French (bearing the curious imprint: 'pour le German bookseller-shop'). He may also have been responsible for a primer with parallel English and German texts entitled *A short and easy way for the Palatines to learn English* (estc t56043, t94067).

The evidence of the recorded imprints shows that Jacobi's association with Downing continued through the following year, with a Latin work prepared for publication by Boehme[46] and a translation of a work by Johann Leonhard.[47] Two further titles (a sermon by Boehme and yet another account of pubertal piety[48]), although undoubtedly printed by Downing, omit him from the imprints. The imprint to a Boehme sermon published in 1712 shows that the association was continuing, even if Jacobi had moved to 'Southampton-Court in Southampton-Street, Covent Garden'.[49]

This Jacobi imprint appears to be the latest which links him with Downing directly. Only one further example has so far been recorded by *ESTC*: the Franckesche Stiftungen hold a copy of an extremely curious Pietist tract in English entitled *Comfort and council for persons afflicted on account of their sins* which bears the imprint: 'London: printed for J. Jacobi, bookseller in Exeter-Exchange in the Strand, 1717'.[50] Since the ornament on sig. A3 is one used by Downing in an edition of selected works by Boehme printed in the same year, we may confidently assume that Jacobi's association with Downing had continued at least until that date. More evidence is supplied by the advertise-

45 *The glorious epiphany* (estc t101961).

46 *Christophori Cellarii professoris Hallensis antiquitates Romanae* (estc t165951).

47 *An account of the Grisons* (estc t78291).

48 *Estrid: an account of a Swedish maid* (estc n50163).

49 *The faithful steward* (estc t186180). This may of course simply be a different way of stating more precisely the same rather vague address.

50 Hauptbibliothek der Franckeschen Stiftungen, 83 I b(2). MS. notes in German (estc t221529).

ment on the verso of the final leaf which lists further works sold by Jacobi, including titles by Arndt and Francke, all of which had been published by Downing. Jacobi could also offer 'German bibles in 8vo. at 8s and in 12. at 4s. a piece ... together with other books and treatises in High-Dutch', suggesting that he was importing books presumably supplied by Elers. Exeter Exchange, where Jacobi was now based, was a building on the Strand much frequented by members of the book trade, including Huguenots, who valued the cheap retailing and storage space it offered. By the time Jacobi was using premises there, the Exchange appears to have fallen into decline.[51]

The 1717 imprint is the last bearing Jacobi's name so far recorded by *ESTC*. He may well have abandoned the book trade altogether in this period for the more certain rewards of a post as 'Chapel-Keeper' to the Lutheran Chapel at St James's, although he remained active as a translator.[52] Downing continued to print the texts of Boehme's German sermons until the latter's death in 1722. Seven sermons printed between 1719 and 1722 have so far been recorded by *ESTC*, although copies have been reported from only two collections.[53] Significantly perhaps, these sermons were printed using roman types, with title-pages laid out in the English rather than the German manner. Although the text is accurately set, presumably under Boehme's personal supervision, umlauts are occasionally substituted by circumflexes, in one case even in the author's name on a title-page.[54] No examples of printing in German by Downing from the period after Boehme's death have so far been recorded.

Searches in *ESTC* retrieve fewer than ten further 'Pietist' works (in the broadest sense of the term) printed by Downing between 1722 and his own death in 1734. Apart from a translation of an Easter sermon, the only further substantial work by Francke published by Downing was an edition of the *Christus sacrae scripturae nucleus* issued in 1732. This was translated by an unidentified 'antient doctor of physick'.[55] Even if the publication of new editions of Pietist works largely ceased with Boehme's death, Downing continued to list a selection of the most important titles in his catalogues. One of the last of these includes (apart from the *Nucleus*) Boehme's *Several discourses*, the second edition of Arndt's *True Christianity* and his *The garden of Paradise*, and the *Pietas Hallensis* itself.[56] After Joseph Downing's death it was Richard Ford rather than Martha Downing who, in 1735, issued Jacobi's translation of Johann Jacob Rambach's *Memoirs of the life and death of the late Reverend Mr. Anthony Boehm* (estc t11767).

51 Swift, [note 37], p. 135.
52 Brunner, [note 2], p. 134.
53 At the National Library of South Africa and the Houghton Library at Harvard.
54 *Des Sünders Elend und Trost*, London, 1721 (estc n24796). Reproduced in the RPI microfilm series *The eighteenth century*, reel 3034, no. 9.
55 estc t116432. The preface supplies a biography of Francke and includes information about his Foundation at the conclusion of the year 1731, p. xxxiii.
56 estc t143113. Undated, but issued between 1732 and 1734.

This short essay represents part of a work in progress on the German book trade in eighteenth-century London. I hope that, as well as helping to establish Joseph Downing's role in printing and selling books for the German-speaking community, it might also serve as a stimulus to the more general study I believe he deserves. The picture that has begun to emerge is of a very substantial figure in the contemporary book trade.

ALMANACKS AND POLTERGEISTS

Gottfried Kisling's interleaved 'Oßnabrückscher Stiffts-Calender' (1713-1739)

HORST MEYER

OSNABRÜCK PLAYED A VERY MODEST PART in the history of German printing during the hand-press period. Situated far away from the book-fair centres the city of the Hochstift was unable to provide incentives to publishing activities. The first press established by Martin Mann in 1617 collapsed when Swedish troops captured and devastated Osnabrück in 1633. The heavy loss of life meant that the city declined to little more than a village. It is estimated that the population which ran to some nine thousand in 1618 was reduced to almost a third by the end of the war. The economic resources of the bishopric were exhausted, and the process of regeneration turned out to be extremely slow. It was not until 1790 that the population of the city was restored to the level of 1618. The alternating succession of Protestant and Catholic prince-bishops stipulated by the *Capitulatio Perpetua* of 1650 was an obstacle to the bridging of the gap between the cultural milieus of the rival denominations. While the city remained Protestant, the majority of the population of the bishopric adhered or reverted to the old faith.

Little is known about Tilman Buchholtz who was admitted to the post of episcopal printer in 1657 under the protection of Franz Wilhelm von Wartenberg, an ardent *propagator fidei* who had returned to his bishopric in 1650 after a twenty-year exile. Buchholtz continued to run his workshop when Ernst August I of Braunschweig-Lüneburg succeeded Franz Wilhelm as prince-bishop in 1662, but it appears from his surviving imprints that he had to drop the title of 'Episcopalis Osnabrugensis Typographus'. After his death towards the end of 1670 there was no member of the trade available to carry on his business. For at least two years the bishopric and its city had to do without a local printer's shop.

In February 1673 Johann Georg Schwänder, formerly a bookseller at Halle and since 1666 a chancery clerk in the episcopal administration, obtained permission to purchase and supervise a new press at his own risk. The exclusive privilege, signed by Ernst August I on 7 February 1673, banned any potential competitor from the territory of the Hochstift and exempted Schwänder from municipal taxes. On the other hand he was required to staff his printing shop with experienced men only, to provide for their needs, and to submit the manuscripts of all projected books and pamphlets to the censor. Although the text of the privilege clearly defines his private business as a sideline, he must have spent a lot of time and money in order to build up, within a decade, the impressive list of scholarly and popular books and reprints, a bibliography of which is to be found in Hermann Runge's study of the history of printing in Osnabrück.[1] Towards the end of his life Schwänder was laid low by one illness after another. He succeeded in securing his position in the administration for his elder son, but he lost control of the financial side of his printing business. Only after his death in April 1685 was it discovered that he had gone bankrupt.

His creditors were wise enough to employ Schwänder's printer Johann Wolfgang Distner for a couple of years on their own account until Gerhard Schorlemmer acquired the press in October 1690. From this time the press remained in the hands of the family down to the end of the nineteenth century, protected by a series of exclusive privileges which ended abruptly with the secularization of the Hochstift in 1803.

There are 85 Schorlemmer imprints in the checklist which Runge compiled for the period from 1691 to 1706,[2] but with a few exceptions these are all single-sheet occasional publications. Even if we bear in mind that Schorlemmer printed the Osnabrück almanacks for which the local bookbinders Johann Sebastian Strauff and Peter Andreas Krumbein had obtained a special privilege, we cannot possibly assess the productivity of his press – a dilemma of the historian of printing to which David Paisey has more than once drawn attention in recent years, notably in his pioneering paper on books which are not recorded in the fair catalogues.[3]

While some phases of seventeenth-century printing in Osnabrück will remain obscure because of the loss of archival and library materials, there is a variety of sources relating to the first decades of the eighteenth century which allow us to draw a vivid picture of the privileged printer and the daily routine of his press. When Schorlemmer died in May 1706, his widow Margaretha Elsabein decided to carry on the business for the benefit of her son and daughter who by some ill-luck were to die in their infancy in 1710. On the last day of March 1707 Gottfried Kisling, a native of Eilenburg in Saxony, arrived at Osnabrück as a journeyman printer and was taken on by Margarethe Schorlemmer. They married six months later and had a daughter Anna Maria and a son Johann Wilhelm who was eventually to take over the printing business as late as 1762. Johann Wilhelm's godfather Johann Detleffsen was a printer at Minden for whom Gottfried Kisling occasionally acted as an agent.

1 Hermann Runge, 'Geschichte des Osnabrücker Buchdrucks' [Pt. 1], *Osnabrücker Mitteilungen* 17 (1892), 336-43.

2 Runge, pp. 346-66.

3 David L. Paisey, 'Literatur, die nicht in den Meßkatalogen steht', in: Paul Raabe (ed.), *Bücher und Bibliotheken im 17. Jahrhundert in Deutschland* (Hamburg, 1980), pp. 115-25.

By a lucky coincidence a set of interleaved copies of the quarto *Oßnabrückscher Stiffts-Calender* which Kisling used as notebooks has been preserved in the collection of the local Kulturgeschichtliches Museum. The quarto almanacks were designed as *Schreibkalender*, a kind of desk-diary, set in two columns. Predictably enough Kisling made use of the 'writing' columns as well as the extra leaves. He records private expenses, financial transactions with his business partners and, from time to time, memorable items of local news. The notes are arranged chronologically, but there are many interpolations, cross-references and repetitions. For the numerous calculations recorded in the almanacks the Reichstaler (*Rt*) serves as the basic currency. In the majority of cases Kisling reckons 21 shillings to the Taler and twelve pence to the shilling. In some instances he prefers to return to the local currency of 36 Mariengroschen (*mgl*) to the Taler.

The series of almanacks runs from 1713 to 1739. The copies covering the years 1716, 1719, 1731, and 1734 are missing, and there are no notes in the almanacks for the years 1724, 1727-1730, and 1738. In the 1739 copy a few corrections are found in the calendar of local and regional markets. Runge looked at the interleaved almanacks only sporadically, because he had access to the ledger which Kisling took over from Schorlemmer. This *Geschäftsbuch* was in private hands in the 1880s but is no longer extant. It seems that Kisling used the interleaved *Schreibkalender* as a preliminary journal from which he copied the relevant details into the ledger at a later stage. Of course this does not apply to the private notes which provide us with first-hand information on his domestic affairs.

The house-cum-workshop which Schorlemmer had acquired for his family in the 1690s was known as the Streithorst'scher Hof and must have been a fairly large building. Beside the four members of the family Kisling's unmarried sister-in-law Anna Gertrude Schledehaus lived in it on a permanent basis, and there was a maid in the house who was usually taken on at Michaelmas and had to work for a lump sum of 4 *Rt* to be paid in arrears. Like most of the local 'Ackerbürger' Kisling kept a cow in the shed and at least three pigs next door. As a member of the Martini-Laischaft, one of the four self-help organisations which were responsible for the upkeep of the unfenced grassland and woods outside the city walls, he paid an annual fee of 1 *Rt* for pasturage. This was the same sum as his barber received once a year at Easter.

The maintenance of the large house had its special problems. In February 1713 a heavy storm lifted off part of the roof. The cost of replacing some two hundred tiles and of repairing other damage ran to 18 *Rt* 1*s* 6*d*. Fortunately Kisling owned two pieces of land which he let at an annual rate of 4 *Rt* each. This was welcome regular income which helped him meet unexpected expenses.

As we know from other contemporary sources, good clothes were rather expensive throughout the eighteenth century. In 1721 Kisling had to pay 9½ *Rt* for a black silk dress for his daughter, and a black coat for himself cost him 6 *Rt*

3 *mgl* in 1726. A new *perruque* could not be had for less than 2½ *Rt*. Compared to these prices, expenses for his children's schooling were modest. Anna Maria's elementary school was entitled to an annual fee of 14*s*, while at Gottfried Wilhelm's grammar school 7*s* had to be paid to the Rector and 10*s* 6*d* to the Cantor who probably did most of the teaching. During his anti-authoritarian phase Gottfried Wilhelm was frequently sent to the cell, for which his father had to pay a drastic fine of 1 *Rt* each time.

The major recurrent theme of Kisling's private notes is, however, the long-term arrangements to supply his household with food. He regularly buys an ox at the traditional Oxen Market in mid-October at prices from 23½ *Rt* to 39 *Rt*, and he never fails to record that he recovers a sum of 4 to 5 *Rt* by selling its skin. In the same annual rhythm three pigs find their way into Kisling's pigsty at sums varying from 17 to 22 *Rt*. Somewhat later in the year he buys up large quantities of rye ranging from 12 to 25 bushels at prices from 7½ to 12 *Rt* for the *Malter* (or 3 bushels). In 1715 the high price of rye induces him to turn to barley which is available at a price of 5½ *Rt* a *Malter*. It appears that Kisling was keen on brewing his own beer, for he frequently orders a Taler's worth of hops (usually 21 to 22 pounds) from a local tradesman. More often than not minor debts of his clients were settled by barter, preferably a *Kanne* (or 1.9 litres) of cheap brandy at 4*s*. The only extravagant item in the notes on food and drink is half a pound of 'green tea' on which Kisling was willing to spend 1 *Rt*.

This rough sketch of the cost of living for the Kisling household may serve as an indicator of the level of returns on the printing business needed to support the family. To get the business started on his own account Kisling had to obtain the exclusive privilege which Prince-Bishop Karl von Lothringen granted him in November 1707 at a fee of 30 *Rt* to which were added 3 *Rt* for the secretary and 1 *Rt* for the porter. Like his predecessors Kisling calls himself 'Hoch-Fürstl. Privil. Buchtrucker' in the imprints of all publications ordered by the episcopal authorities. In the imprint of a jocular prothalamium of the 1730s he (or the author) refers to his press as 'Stanno Siliciano', an allusion to *Kieselgur*, the German equivalent of silica. (More recently an oenophilic cataloguer of the BSB-AK at the Bavarian State Library has, by some Freudian slip, chosen to name him 'Rißling'.)

Nothing appears to have changed at the workshop since its establishment in 1691. There was a single press which was worked by Kisling alone, although one may assume that his compositor Johann Henrich Negengert was required to help with the presswork at busy times. Negengert's wages were fixed at 24 *mgl* per week, to be paid in arrears at Easter and Michaelmas. Frequently, though, he received smaller sums on account. As we learn from Kisling's notes, Negengert had a strong penchant for absenteeism. He regularly incurs a deduction of three to seven weeks' wages from the payments for the summer or winter periods. Needless to say, Kisling kept a close eye on him. There are numerous little crosses in his calendars which document the journeyman's 'missing' days. On one occasion he has ticked off three days after the 1714

Christmas Market. At Easter 1714 Johann Christian Molin, a local boy, was taken on to serve a six-year apprenticeship. We do not know if he was formally bound and freed for there were no specific regulations for the Osnabrück privileged press. Molin turned out to be a very reliable workman, and he stayed with his master for at least seven years as a journeyman, although the wages he was offered were not very attractive. He received a weekly payment of 18 *mgl* in his first year as a junior which was raised by 3 *mgl* in the second and third year, but from then on remained at 24 *mgl*. When Negengert was finally dismissed ('cassirt') at Michaelmas 1722, this meant very uncertain times for the compositor's case, and there were many shorter intervals during which Molin was the only journeyman at hand. Kisling was, of course, aware of the efficiency of the young man. At Michaelmas 1726 he silently settled a debt of 50 *Rt* which Molin had incurred elsewhere. Towards the end of the years covered by the notebooks the workshop still had the same minimal level of staffing as it had had twenty years before. In 1720 Kisling had to spend 70 *Rt* on wages. Over the next twelve years an increase of less than one per cent made cost accounting easy. By the end of 1732 the annual figure ran to 77 *Rt*.

There is little information available about Kisling's type stock. In August 1723 he ordered a new Corpus Fraktur and Roman Fraktur as well as some replacements of the Text Fraktur and Antiqua from a type-foundry at Braunschweig, but strangely enough he only notes the cost of transport of 3½ *Rt*. His major paper supplier was the paper-mill at Mettingen in the neighbouring county of Tecklenburg. In later years he bought large quantities of paper from the local paper-maker at Oesede (six miles south of Osnabrück) and from the printers Heinrich Wilhelm and Johann Heinrich Meyer at Lemgo. As his notes document, there was hardly any fluctuation in the price of paper. A *Ballen* (of ten reams) of the low-quality *ordinair Druckpapier* was to be had for 4 *Rt* 6 *mgl*. For the medium-quality *Druckpapier* the Meyers at Lemgo charged 4½ *Rt* per bale. The *groß weiß Druckpapier* Kisling ordered from the Oesede paper-mill was steadily priced at 5 *Rt* per bale. From 1726 onwards he used a sized paper (*geleimbt Papier*) for the quarto *Schreibkalender* which the Oesede paper-mill offered at 7½ *Rt* per bale. The smaller quantities of *Schreibpapier* needed for occasional publications and special copies of a particular book were supplied by the Meyers at Lemgo and the local bookbinder Jobst Linge at steady prices from 9½ *Rt* per bale.

The ingredients for making printing ink, linseed-oil and lampblack, were available from local tradesmen. The prices charged for the oil went up and down as in the case of other agricultural products. In 1714 Kisling paid 5½ *Rt* for a *Blase* containing 49½ pounds. In 1733 a *Blase* containing 42 pounds was offered at the attractive price of 3½ *Rt*, but three years later the autumn price of oil soared dramatically so that Kisling just bought the 15-odd pounds he needed for the rest of the year at 7 *Rt*. The price of lampblack remained unchanged from 1713 to the middle of the 1730s at 1 *Rt* for ten pounds. From the beginning of the 1720s Kisling used to order it from the Meyers at Lemgo as they were able to supply a hundredweight at short notice. Stiff prices had to be paid for *Zinnober* (ground vermilion), the colour ingredient for making red ink. From time to time Kisling ordered half a pound at 20*s* from Jobst Linge, the local bookbinder we have met before.

The most striking feature of the notes and news recorded in the interleaved *Schreibkalender* is the arrival of bale after bale of paper for which there are no contracts for books or almanacks on the printer's agenda. It took me some time to find out that these recurrent large quantities of paper were sent from Mettingen at the order of two tobacco tradesmen, Arning and Kamping (Kisling's supplier of hops), who had their tobacco pouches (*Thobacks-Briefe*) printed at the Osnabrück workshop. These large ephemeral jobs did not require much typesetting, as the pouches would just bear a trade-mark or a note on the different sorts of tobacco (Kisling occasionally refers to 'No. 4' or 'Krüll-Thoback') probably printed from a woodblock, but they kept the press running throughout the year. More often than not the tradesmen paid the paper-maker at Mettingen directly. In these cases Kisling would charge them 1 *Rt* 18 *s* per bale for the press-work. Whenever he bought the *Thobacks-Papier* at 7 *Rt* per bale (the standard price for sized paper), the price per bale his clients were asked to pay went up to 10 *Rt* 5*s* 3*d*. The returns on these long-term ephemeral printing jobs were considerable. In 1713 the annual invoice for Arning amounted to 58 *Rt*. Later on, in the 1720s, Kamping appears to have dominated the market. The annual sums resulting from his orders range from 55 to 77 *Rt*.

Apart from the mass-produced tobacco pouches there was a variety of commercial and non-commercial ephemera which issued from Kisling's press: *Saat-Zettel* for several local seedsmen, *Correspondenz-Zettel* and time-tables (showing the arrivals and departures of the post-chaises) for the postmaster, passports for the city of Osnabrück and the country towns, 'citations' for the lower courts of the bishopric, a sheet of French and Italian poems for the local *Sprachmeister*, and indulgences for the Dominicans on the occasion of the feast of the Holy Rosary. To these we may add the traditional genres of occasional literature, e.g. the prothalamia and the funeral poems. Surprisingly though, there are no references to funeral sermons in the printer's interleaved *Schreibkalender*.

The first entry in the notebooks, an order for two hundred copies of a sheet of funeral poems on the death of Magister Wöbeking may serve as an example of Kisling's pricing policy with regard to occasional jobs. The first hundred copies cost 1 *Rt* 7*s*, the second hundred 'run on' copies 10*s* 6*d* only, so that the author, Johann Westermann, had to pay a sum of 1 *Rt* 17*s* 6*d*. A slight decrease in the price per sheet becomes apparent in another calculation for an edition of five hundred copies: The first hundred copies cost 1 *Rt*, the next hundred copies 10*s* 6*d* and the following 7*s* each. For longer press-runs Kisling used to offer very attractive prices. In the case of an edition of 1,000 copies the price per sheet was fixed at 2 *Rt* 7*s*, i.e. 1 *Rt* 3*s* 6*d* per ream, which was less than half the price based on the calculation for 500 copies. For print-runs of 1,500 or more copies of a given sheet he generally charged 1 *Rt* per ream.

While these minor commercial and private commissions may have yielded an annual profit ranging from 8 to 12 *Rt*, returns on official publications ordered by the municipal and episcopal authorities must have been considerably higher. The number of decrees rose dramatically after the succession of Ernst August II of Braunschweig-Lüneburg in 1716. He was the first resident and 'working' prince-bishop since the Reformation, and he did much to modernize the administration and to improve the economic situation of the bishopric. Unfortunately there are no references to the printing of decrees in the interleaved *Schreibkalender*. It seems that Kisling compiled the annual invoices from the notes in his ledger. From time to time he was asked to print lengthy and long-winded legal treatises. In 1718 the Privy Councillor Christian Wilhelm von Eiben paid no less than 82 *Rt* 10*s* 6*d* via the *Rent-Kammer* for a large treatise of thirty-three sheets, and Dr Mühlenkampf, the secretary of the *Ritterschaft* (the nobility represented the second estate at the *Landtag*), faced an invoice for 79 *Rt* 7*s* for a similar publication. For 160 copies of his shorter tract '*wegen der Jesuiten*' he had to pay another 12 *Rt*. It is perhaps worth noting that even high officials like these two men were not entitled to ask for special rates at the privileged press.

The major event of the printer's year was, however, the production of the almanacks. These were traditionally published in three formats: as a short *Taschenkalender* of two and a half sheets in 16mo, as a quarto *Schreibkalender*, and as a folio broadside wall calendar (which Kisling refers to as *Tafel-Kalender*). The three distinctive issues bear the same main title *Oßnabrückscher Stiffts-Calender Nach der Neuen Zeit Auff das Jahr Christi* ... Except for a serial historical article which is a special feature of the *Schreibkalender*, the contents of the 16mo and quarto almanacks are identical. Each year the 'gentle reader' would find a lunary, the feasts and days of Lenten fasting, the dates of processions, predictions of thunderstorms, and a calendar of the markets in the Hochstift and neighbouring territories. This last item was by any standard a vital source of information for all who wished to buy and sell their commodities at special markets. In a note written in July 1737 Kisling records that he printed 6,500 separate copies of the 1738 16mo market calendars, but he does not specify if this was the first time that separate copies were issued.

Practically nothing is known about Joseph Baumgarten, the author of the almanacks. It seems that he liked the occasional joke. In the title of the *Schreibkalender* for the year 1701 he calls himself 'J. Gartenbaum',[4] and in the issue for the year 1717 we find some lines of harmless poetry to the same effect on the verso of the title-page: 'Unser Baumgart grünt allemahl / Giebet saur und süsse Früchte...'. His serial essays are usually copied from popular books. In the issues for 1701 and 1703 he presents some excerpts from Adam

4 Runge, p. 354.

Olearius's *Muscovitische und Persische Reise*, and in the issues used by Kisling as notebooks he offers the reader a potted history of the lives and deeds of the Roman Emperors of the House of Habsburg taken from an unidentified source.

In July 1700 the local bookbinders Johann Sebastian Strauff and Peter Andreas Krumbein had obtained a publishing privilege for the 16mo and quarto almanacks which they used to the full until the death of Karl von Lothringen in December 1715. Ernst August II did not approve of this monopoly, and that is why from the year 1717 onwards various partnerships of four to eight bookbinders hide behind the imprint formula 'im Verlag und zu finden bey denen Buchbindern'. Throughout the 'Catholic' years of Prince-Bishop Karl the almanacks carried a formal *imprimatur* on the verso of the title-page, signed by the administrator of the *Generalvikariat*. We may assume, though, that only a minority of the readership would be able to make sense of the 1714 Latin approbation 'Auctoritate ordinariâ Nobis delegatâ praesens Calendarium Osnabrugense de anno 1715 visum & approbatum typis mandari ac divulgari concedimus. Datum Osnabrugi ex Vicariatu generali die 12ma Julii 1714'.

It was the common concern of Kisling and the bookbinders to have the 16mo and quarto almanacks ready for distribution at the mid-September Quakenbrück market, an event of regional importance in the north of the bishopric. In most cases the censor's *placet* dates from earlier than the 1714 *imprimatur*. Given the limited capacity of his single press, Kisling had to start the presswork for the 16mos which were printed in runs of from 6,000 to 7,000 copies in the 1710s in mid-July at the latest, as the bookbinders needed some time for the stitching and wrapping of the copies. The printing of the the six sheets of the *Schreibkalender*, whose print-run stagnated at 750 copies for many years, usually began in the last week of August, while the 400-odd folio wall calendars, which appear to have appealed almost exclusively to an urban public, left the Kisling press during the first week of December.

From the early 1720s the 16mo almanacks became a bestselling item, at least from the bookbinders' point of view. In 1725 they sold no fewer than 10,000 copies. A year later they handed in the manuscript of the 1727 almanack on May 28, just in time for an order of 11,000 copies, and by 1733 the annual size of the edition ran to 11,250 copies. The sales figures of the *Schreibkalender* reached 1,000 copies for the first time in 1726, but fell back to an average of 925 copies in later years. The last entry in Kisling's notebook referring to the wall calendars records that 480 copies were printed in 1723.

The spectacular rise of the print-runs of the 16mo almanacks was mainly due to the growing number of partners in the enterprise, but it also reflects the improvement of the economic status of the country and the growth of literacy resulting from the policies adopted by Ernst August II, who died early in 1728. From the printer's point of view the almanack job was by no means a spectacular source of income. In order to print the 28,125 sheets of the 1733 sedecimos, for which he received 56 *Rt* from the bookbinders, he had to purchase 5 bales and

6 reams of *ordinair Druckpapier* at a price of 25 *Rt* 7*s* and cover the corresponding wages of a pressman which amounted to at least 4 *Rt*.

In stark contrast to this laborious secular job the series of liturgical and devotional books and booklets commissioned by the local bookbinders for the benefit of both denominations represented an inexhaustible source of considerable income. As in the case of the almanacks there were numerous partnerships of bookbinders who shared their resources for (and returns on) a publishing project. The major part of this specialized booktrade was in the hands of the Catholics, not only because of the enormous range of their devotional literature, but also as a result of the curious circumstance that part of an edition would always be sold in the neighbouring Niederstift of Münster, even though the Osnabrück Cathedral Chapter had sold the spiritual jurisdiction of the Niederstift to the Bishop of Münster in 1668. In two instances Kisling printed 1,500 and 2,500 copies of the so-called 'Münstersche' catechism for Johann Sebastian Strauff (1713) and a partnership of the widow of the Tecklenburg bookbinder Kallberg with her Osnabrück colleague Levin Voigt (1721). The latter turned out to be a versatile businessman. In 1723 alone he ordered on his own account 1,500 copies of a Catholic prayer-book, the *Großes Tagewerck*, at 24 *Rt*, 2,550 copies of an abridged version of the Lutheran catechism at 21 *Rt*, 1,000 copies of a short Catholic prayer-book, the *Geistliches Räucherwerck*, at 13 *Rt*, 1,500 copies of the Catholic hymn-book at 48 *Rt*, and 1,250 copies of a Lutheran *Hand- und Reise-Büchlein* at 15 *Rt*. Kisling had to cope with similar bulk orders for religious books at frequent intervals. In 1718 he printed 2,500 copies of the Lutheran catechism, 2,500 copies of a Catholic prayer-book, *Morgen- und Abend-Opffer*, and 2.500 copies of the Catholic hymn-book for a sum of 145 *Rt*. In 1733 he delivered to various clients 1,500 copies of the Lutheran catechism, 2,500 copies of the *Morgen- und Abend-Opffer*, and 2,500 Catholic gospel-books for which he received 142 *Rt*. In both cases the total amount may well have been half the annual turnover.

One of the more intriguing episodes in Kisling's business life was his long-term co-operation with the bookseller Michael Andreas Fuhrmann, who, much to the chagrin of the local bookbinders, had opened a bookshop in Osnabrück in 1709. Fuhrmann had a quick sense of the needs of the specialized reader, and he regularly attended the Leipzig book fairs to sell his own new books and to select others for his Osnabrück stock. In 1710 Kisling printed for him Frans Burmann's voluminous *Alle Biblische Wercke*. In 1712 he received an order for a reprint of Samuel Schelwig's *Catechismus-Reinigung* and for a long book of meditations, *Versuchter und treu erfundener Abraham in 12 Andachten*, by the Osnabrück *Pastor primarius* at St Mary's Church, Johann Möser (Justus Möser's grandfather). Both imprints are dated 1713, but the books were ready for the Leipzig Michaelmas book fair in 1712. Fuhrmann makes his first appearance in the interleaved *Schreibkalender* on 3 February 1713, when Kisling agreed to print four hundred copies of Fuhrmann's *Meßsortimentskatalog* in June. Towards the end of August Kisling delivered 1,000 copies of a short legal defence of the marriage of maids, *Die vertheidigte Mägde-Heyrath*, to his partner's bookshop. As a rule Fuhrmann limited an edition of his publications to 1,000 copies, which may be one of the reasons why almost all his books are scarce today.

On 11 September 1713, the printer and the bookseller agreed on a price of 30 *Rt* for a 'Tractätlein in 8vo von den Dortmundischen Polter Geist etc.'. As it turned out, there were two publications on the Dortmund affair in the making, but it was Fuhrmann's book that carried the day. The Rev. Caspar Sparmann of Eicklingshofen had written a report of the doings and undoings of a poltergeist in the house of the Dortmund doctor Barthold Florian Gerstmann (*Eigentlicher Bericht von ... einem Teufels-Engel*) which was printed early in 1714 by Erdmann Andreas Lyce at Idstein with an unsigned preface by the radical pietist Johann Henrich Reitz who used the occasion for a sharp attack on Balthasar Bekker's enlightened critique of the belief in ghosts.[5] It seems that Reitz came across Fuhrmann's book while reading the proofs of the Idstein tract. In a bitter note appended to Sparmann's text he acknowledges the fact that a much fuller report on the Dortmund poltergeist by Dr Gerstmann's own son Florian Barthold had just been published at Osnabrück. Kisling had started printing the *Genaue Vorstellung des Gespenstes und Polter-Geistes ... in der kaiserlichen Reichsstadt Dortmund* on 11 October 1713 and may well have finished the ten sheets of the *Vorstellung* and the additional three sheets of an orthodox commentary by J. D. Brügmann (*Schrifft- und vernunft-mässiger Unterricht*) by the end of the year.[6] Reitz does not fail to criticize the circumlocutary style of the commentator which, he claims, has made the book 'too long and expensive for the gentle reader who likes truth and brevity'.

Surprisingly though, Reitz entrusted Fuhrmann with his next book, an edition of the unpublished manuscript of Henrich Myrike's *Reyse nach Jerusalem und dem Land Canaan* of which the first 613 copies were perfected by Kisling in April 1714 in time for the Easter book fair. The second instalment was delivered to Fuhrmann on 14 June. The book turned out to be a success. In later years it was reprinted at Idstein and other places. Of the Osnabrück *editio princeps* two copies survive.[7]

Throughout the summer of 1714 Fuhrmann kept the Kisling workshop busy with smaller jobs. Early in June 350 copies of an auction catalogue running to five sheets were printed for him. On 16 June Kisling delivered the 350 copies of Fuhrmann's *Meßsortimentskatalog Nr° 2*. A few days later the bookseller received an additional supply of copies and errata sheets for Gerstmann's report of the Dortmund poltergeist, of the *Reyse nach Jerusalem*, and of the legal tract

5 The British Library's copy of the *Eigentlicher Bericht* (pressmark: 3911.aaa.64 (12)) appears to be unique. Balthasar Bekker's treatise, originally in Dutch, was published in German as *Die bezauberte Welt, oder eine gründliche Unstersuchung des allgemeinen Aberglaubens...* (Amsterdam, 1693). BL pressmark: 853.h.15.

6 Two of the 1,000 copies printed have survived: BL 8632.b.29, and Munich BSB Phys.m.87.

7 Göttingen UL: 8 Itin.I.2787, and Harvard UL: Asia 9216.84.

on the marriage of maids. On 27 July Kisling and his partner agreed on the price for a Latin grammatical treatise, *VI. Indices latinitatis corruptae*, by the late Hamburg philologist Gottfried Voigt which was ready for distribution in October although bearing an imprint dated 1715.

In an interesting note of 2 August 1714, Kisling records that he lent his *Format-Buch* to a 'Herr Cunradi' for whom Fuhrmann acted as a guarantor. With the help of David Paisey's never-failing *Deutsche Buchdrucker, Buchhändler und Verleger 1701-1750* I have been able to identify the member of the trade in need of advice as the academic printer of the Gymnasium Arnoldinum at Burgsteinfurt in the neighbouring county of Bentheim.[8]

Meanwhile Fuhrmann continued to build up his list. In October 1714 300 copies of another catalogue of an auction to be held at Münster were printed for him. In the last week of November Kisling started the production of a reprint of Erasmus's *De utraque verborum ac rerum copia libri II*, consisting of twenty duodecimo sheets. As before, 450 complete copies and 50 title-leaves were delivered in time for the Easter book fair, and the rest were perfected in June together with Fuhrmann's *Meßsortimentskatalog Nr° 3*. For printing the Erasmus titles in red and black ('vor das Roth zu drucken') Kisling charged an extra 1 *Rt* 7*s*. In December 1715 the press was started again for a run of 1,000 copies of *Neothea oder neuangerichtete medicinische Theetafel*, a treatise on the medical uses of herbal teas by the physician and writer Johann Heinrich Cohausen. To comply with the author's wish for twenty-five special copies on *Schreibpapier*, Fuhrmann had to pay an extra charge of 14*s* for the re-setting of the outer forme of the first sheet. As Philip Gaskell explains, special-paper copies were printed after the ordinary ones, because 'presswork is better at the end of a run than at the beginning'.[9] To secure a sharp impression of the beginning of the text, the forme including the first columns was usually re-set.

After the publication of *Neothea* in the Spring of 1716 a break occurs in the relationship between Kisling and Fuhrmann. As we know from other sources, the bookseller was involved in quarrels with the local bookbinders who did everything to keep him out of the market for devotional literature. Although he had obtained a privilege from Ernst August II for publishing certain prayer-books in 1716, the bibliopegic fraternity did not let him enter into partnerships with them. This is why Fuhrmann tried to convert his business into an itinerant booktrade which was a much harder job by far. In a report of the Lutheran Consistory to the Privy Council dated 9 February 1719, it is stated that the bookseller left Osnabrück at the beginning of the year to settle at Kleve.

The departure of Fuhrmann was no doubt a loss for Kisling and the press for there was no other bookseller resident in the city until 1766 when Johann Wilhelm Schmid of Hanover opened a branch at Osnabrück. Fuhrmann, however, had at least two more books printed by the Kisling press before he finally

8 David L. Paisey, *Deutsche Buchdrucker, Buchhändler und Verleger 1701-1750* (Wiesbaden, 1988), p. 37.

9 Philip Gaskell, *A New Introduction to Bibliography* (Oxford, 1972), p. 136.

closed his bookshop. In a note in the *Schreibkalender* for 1718 dated 1 October, Kisling records that that day he sent 900 copies of an errata leaf in quarto plus 50 *Schreibpapier* copies to Fuhrmann and another 60 copies to 'Herr Secretarius Göliz'. I have been unable to find out whether these errata belong to Henricus Mascamp's *Tabulae chronologicae* or to Caspar Theodor Summermann's *Praxis Pandectarum*. Both books were published by Fuhrmann in 1717 with the ambitious imprint 'Amstelodami & Lipsiae'. Whether 'Herr Göliz' acted for an institution which had subscribed to sixty copies of one of the books or if he had just volunteered to distribute the errata leaves, remains to be investigated.

Kisling headed the workshop for another four decades, although it is likely that his son took over responsibility for much of the daily routine in the early 1750s. He lived to see the first Osnabrück English-language book come from his press. In 1762 a *Journal of the Allied Army's Marches, From the first Arrival of the British Troops, in Germany, to the present Time* was printed by Johann Wilhelm Kisling for the author, J. Tory, a 'Soldier in the Third Regiment of Guards'. The Department of Printed Books of the Bodleian Library believe they own the only known copy,[10] but there is a second 'unique' copy at the Landesbibliothek Hannover. Neither is recorded in the *ESTC*.

10 Pressmark: Don.e.807. See the note in *Bodleian Library Record*, 9 (1974), 136.

THE BAROQUE SERMON, ILLUSTRATED BY A COLLECTION FROM AUSTRIA AND NEIGHBOURING TERRITORIES

GRAHAM NATTRASS

IN MARCH 1993, the British Library acquired a folio volume of eighteen sermons from the firm of H. P. Kraus in New York.[1] Enquiries have revealed that the late Mr Kraus bought the collection some years before, together with other material relating to Austria, but its earlier provenance is unknown. The sermons come chiefly from Upper and Lower Austria, with a few from other Habsburg lands and from Bavaria, and all are in German. They span the years from 1700 to 1749, and each was delivered to mark a special occasion.

Of the eighteen sermons, six were printed in Vienna, three in Linz, and one each in Prague and Brno. The remainder come from smaller places: Krems, Steyr, Ödenburg, Passau and Burghausen. Passau had seen printing since the incunable period. The earliest Ödenburg imprint in the British Library dates from 1733 – sixteen years earlier than the one in this volume – though David Paisey's *Deutsche Buchdrucker, Buchhändler und Verleger 1701–1750* lists five printers and three publishers in the town. The same work lists four printers in Krems, where printing began in 1676, but all three Krems imprints in this volume are by Ignaz Anton Präxl, third in the chronological succession of printers there. Steyr and Burghausen will be discussed in the appropriate place.

Eleven of the eighteen items, including two with strong Viennese connections (nos. 2 and 6), could not be found in the microfiche catalogue of the Austrian National Library.[2] Each of the sermons will be examined here in turn. The titles are without exception very lengthy, and have been abbreviated in the bibliographical descriptions given. Each item has, however, been fully described in the *Short-title catalogue of German books 1701–1750* which the British Library is compiling, with the exception of no. 5, which is to be found in David Paisey's seventeenth-century *STC*.

1 It has been given the press-mark RB.23.b.656.

2 Österreichische Nationalbibliothek. *Katalog der Druckschriften 1501–1929 (Nominal)*. (Hildesheim, 1982).

(1) BENEDICT FRANCK: *Anmüthiger Liebs-Kampff und hertziger Ehren-Streitt zwischen Gott, und dem heiligen Joannem von Nepomuck.* Crembs, gedruckt bey Ignati Antoni Präxl, Wiennerisch-Universitätischen Buchdrucker, 1736.

The first sermon concerns St John Nepomuk, and was given on his feast-day in the church of Stein, a small town in the Wachau, and printed in nearby Krems. The preacher was a Benedictine from Tegernsee, currently serving as the local priest. He presents the saint as a model of all the Christian virtues, but the reality was rather different. John of Pomuk, Vicar-General of the Archdiocese of Prague and confessor to Queen Joanna, was a proud, obstinate man who resisted the attempts of King Wenceslas to limit the power of the Church. This was not the 'good king' of the Christmas carol, but the son of Emperor Charles IV. In 1393 John was subjected to terrible tortures before being thrown from Charles Bridge into the Moldau. Our preacher, however, prefers a different but widely held version of the story, according to which the saint was murdered in 1383, ten years earlier, for refusing to reveal to his royal master the secrets of the queen's confessional.

In 1736 John Nepomuk was still a very 'new' saint, having been canonised only seven years before. Franck makes clear that his canonisation had followed intense lobbying by Emperor Charles VI and other Catholic princes. He goes on to recount various miracles attributed to the saint, as well as the dire warnings given to those who had tried to desecrate his grave or insult his images. He is hardly exaggerating when he speaks of the saint's enormous popularity in the German-speaking lands, which continued well into the nineteenth century. The composer Hummel, the dramatist Nestroy, the mathematician Bolzano, and Senefelder, inventor of lithography, are just a few of the celebrities who bore the Christian names Johann Nepomuk, though they are not in every case remembered by them.

(2) FRANTZ ANTONI VON SCHMUTZENHAUSS: *Der durch Zahl, Maass, und Gewicht, vielfältiger Wohlthaten bestättigte apostolische Eyfer des Antoni von Padua.* Wienn, gedruckt bey Johann Ignatz Heyinger, Universitäts-Buchdruckern, [1735].

This is another 'Heiligenpredigt', and was likewise given on the saint's feast-day. The setting is the Capuchin church in Vienna, famous for its crypt in which one hundred and thirty-nine members of the House of Habsburg lie buried. The preacher was a secular priest, but he flatters his audience by extolling the achievements of the Franciscan Order, to which St Antony belonged. He concludes by asking the saint to intercede with the Almighty to obtain a male heir for the House of Austria. With hindsight we know that his wish remained unfulfilled, with disastrous consequences for the emperor's successor in the shape of the War of the Austrian Succession.

The volume contains a total of four 'Heiligenpredigten', the others being nos. 4 and 8. All are listed in Werner Welzig's catalogue;[3] he gives locations for all four in Klosterneuburg, but only nos. 1 and 4 are in the Austrian National Library.

(3) DANIEL SCHEÜRING: *Zachaeus favorita Christi Domini Nostri.* Lintz, gedruckt bey Frantz Zachaeo Auinger, 1716.

This takes us to the Cistercian monastery of Baumgartenberg in the Mühlviertel, a district of Upper Austria north of the Danube, for the consecration of the abbey church, following its redecoration in the Baroque style. The preacher compares its new splendour to the rebuilt temple at Jerusalem (Haggai 2, v. 9). The subject-matter of the sermon, however, concerns Zacchaeus and forms a meditation on his character and change of life: in this respect it resembles a 'Heiligenpredigt'. The work is extraordinarily rich in chronograms, and the second page of the Latin dedication contains one on every line (fig. 1). The writer even manages to find a single word to fit the date 1716 – DILVCVLVM, meaning 'dawn' – and his text is 'fILI hoMInIs VIDe oCVLIs' (Ezekiel 40, v. 4). The preacher was Prior of Baumgartenberg, and he dedicates his work to the Abbot, Candidus Pfeiffer.

(4) AUGUSTIN WIDER: *Glorwürdiges Marter-Grab unter dem Heiligen Creutz.* Gedruckt zu Crembs, bey Ignatz Anton Präxl, einer Hochlöbl. Wiennerisch. Universität privilegirten Buchdrucker, [1736].

We remain with the Cistercians for the fourth sermon, which concerns the 'feyerliche Übertragung des zierlich gefasseten gantzen heiligen Leichnambs des glorwürdigen Martyrer ... Justini' to the Abbey of Lilienfeld, in Lower Austria. This is not, as one might think, the early Christian writer Justin Martyr, but another Justin who died in 238 during the persecutions of the first barbarian emperor, Julius Maximinus. Though the abbey already sheltered many other bones and relics, this was the first time it had received the complete body of a saint. Justin's remains had lain in the Roman catacombs until being exhumed at the beginning of the eighteenth century, when they were destined for the Spanish court. For some reason – possibly the War of the Spanish Succession? – the plan failed to materialize, and the body ended up at Lilienfeld instead. The preacher, himself a monk of the abbey, has no doubt this was the work of Providence.

Very little is known about this Justin: we do not know 'wessen Ambts und Stands er gewesen, durch was für eine Art des Todts, an welchen eigentlichen Orth er seinen blutigen und glorwürdigen Marter-Kampff vollbracht'. This does not prevent the preacher from dwelling at length on Justin's virtues. His listeners had before their eyes the shrine containing the relics, placed on a new

3 Werner Welzig, *Lobrede: Katalog deutschsprachiger Heiligenpredigten in Einzeldrucken.* Sitzungsberichte der Österreichischen Akademie der Wissenschaften, Phil.-hist. Klasse, 518. (Vienna, 1989).

AVrora nItens hoDIè perfeCIt Iter, orIebatVr aMICa,
ApparVIt faMa aDVoLans, hæC faLVtat
DILVCVLVM.
PhæbVs gLorIosIor IsIgnI LVMIne CorDa penetrat,
Et noCtVrnas trIftItIæ VMbras repeLLIt ferenIor DIes.
En!
TotVs affVLget CanDIDVs fpLenDor,
Vt CeLebretVr DeVotè nobILe noMen,
CVIVs LaVs DeLata per orbeM,
QVaM DeCenter eXtoLLIt.
AVftrIæSaLoMon egregIâ fapIentIâ,prVDentIâ CLarens haberIs,
â qVo MeDItatô ConsILIô totI patrIæ LIbertas eft ferVata.
VIgILantIa,CVra AtLantIs aDornat AntIftIteM,
BasIs & fortIs CoLVMna DIVæ ReLIgIonI es,
In qVa DIsCIpLIna optIMo VIgore fLoret,
InDefefsVs habItVs Labor paLàM totI orbI InnotesCIt;
NaM ReLIgIofa eXornata BasILICa satIs proDIt.
Cætera taCeo, nè tVa InsIgnIs MoDeftIa IrrItetVr.
Dent SVperI non paVCas gratIas AntIftItI CanDIDo!
Efto nobIs soLaMen, sIs feLICIorI â Deo VItâ sVperftes,
Inftàr AqVILæ (*a*) granDIs fLoresCe MaIorIbVs annIs,
Mors non VenIat, neqVe sIt AbbatIs LILICIDa (*b*)
GratIosâ CLeMentIâ PræsULIs DIgnItas VIgeat.

gLorIofæ patroCInantI AMpLItVDInI TVæ
&c. &c.

(*a*) Infigne Monafterii Aquila.
(*b*) Gentilitium D. Abbatis Lilium.

NoMIne tVI AsCeterII obtVLIt Pr. DanIeL,
PrIor InDIgnVs In ConspICVo PoMœrIo,
non MerItVs De s. CrVCe professVs.

Fig. 1

marble 'Creutz-Altar', above which stood a great cross containing a reputed fragment of the Cross of Christ. Basing himself on a sermon by St Bernard of Clairvaux, in which each of the four corners of the cross symbolizes a virtue of the crucified Christ, namely humility, patience, obedience and love, he applies these same qualities to Justin and endeavours to show how they must have been present in his martyrdom.

(5) CHRISTOPH PLOCHINGER: *Der Allerheiligsten Göttlichen Dreyfaltigkeit über-groſses Gehaimbnuß*. Gedruckt zu Lintz bey Johann Rädlmayr, einer Löblichen Ober-Oesterreichischen Landschafft Buchdr., [1700].

For no. 5 we return to Upper Austria, to the City Church of Linz, for the inauguration of the Brotherhood of the Holy Trinity. The Baroque period saw the foundation of many brotherhoods and congregations throughout southern Germany and Austria, formed mostly of laymen but led by the clergy, especially the Jesuits. Some catered for particular age groups or social classes, or had specific objectives. The Linz brotherhood was dedicated to the service of poor travellers, especially pilgrims, and its aim was to build a hostel for them, where the sick could also be cared for during their convalescence.

The ceremony took place, appropriately enough, on Trinity Sunday, 1700, and was preceded by a procession through the streets of Linz. The Abbot of Garsten (cf. no. 16), who had agreed to become patron of the new brotherhood, took part in the procession and officiated at the service. The sermon was given by a Jesuit, preacher-in-ordinary at the Sunday services. His subject is the Holy Trinity, for which he seeks to find evidence in some unlikely scriptural passages, particularly from the Old Testament. The Baroque mind, still strongly influenced by mediaeval thinking, delighted in the symbolical meaning of numbers, but some of the preacher's conclusions would strike the modern reader as spurious. For example, it is not clear to us why Elijah's act of prostrating himself three times over the widow of Zarephath's son (I Kings 17, v. 21) in order to revive his lifeless body should point to the three-fold nature of God. Perhaps, as the title of the sermon implies, the mystery of the Trinity is indeed 'über-groß'.

(6) FRANZ PEIKHART: *Ehren-Rede, auf das hohe Ehren-Fest, deß wiennerischen zum Ertz-Bistthumb erhobenen Bistthumbs*. Wienn in Oesterreich, gedruckt bey Andreas Heyinger, Universitäts-Buchdruckern, 1723.

This sermon, like the next, was delivered in St Stephen's Cathedral, Vienna. In the early eighteenth century, church jurisdiction over most of Lower Austria still belonged to the Bishop of Passau or the Archbishop of Salzburg; in comparison with these great prelates the Bishop of Vienna seemed fairly small fry. In the eyes of Charles VI, the capital of Europe's greatest dynasty deserved a matching ecclesiastical dignity, and in 1723 he persuaded the Pope to raise it to the status of an archbishopric. This event was celebrated by the Jesuit Franz Peikhart in a sermon which takes as its theme the archiepiscopal vestment known as the pallium and discusses 'its origins, its ancient use, its hidden power and the symbolic meaning of its outward form'.

Peikhart, whose father had been Mayor of Vienna, was considered by his contemporaries to be the greatest homilist of his time (another of his sermons is no. 14 in the collection). As the regular preacher at St Stephen's for a quarter of a century, his services were in demand on great occasions of state, among them the funeral of Charles VI and the coronation of Maria Theresa as Queen of Bohemia. His most famous work, however, is the funeral oration for Prince Eugene of Savoy: not only was it printed in an edition of four thousand copies, which was considered unprecedented for a sermon at the time; it was reprinted in several places and translated into various languages, and read throughout Europe, by Protestants as well as Catholics. The British Library's copy (10703.i.6) is not of the original Viennese edition, but was printed in Stadtamhof, across the Danube from Regensburg.

(7) ANTON STAUDINGER: *Allerschuldigste Ehren-Rede, als Ihro Hoch-Fürstliche Eminenz ... Sigismundus ... von Kollonitz ... die Erstlinge seines fünfftzigjährigen Priesterthums ... hoch-feyerlichst begienge.* Wienn, gedruckt und zu haben, bey Johann Ignatz Heyinger, Hochfürstlich-Ertz-Bischöfflichen Hof-Buchdruckern, in seinem Buch-Gewölb, in der Römer-Strassen, [1749].

Vienna's first archbishop was Sigismund von Kollonitz (Kollonics), a scion of the Hungarian nobility, and the golden jubilee of his ordination to the priesthood is celebrated here. The preacher is another Jesuit, Anton Staudinger, who had succeeded Peikhart at St Stephen's. Though indulging in much exaggerated praise, he manages to give us a rounded portrait of this prince of the Church: a man of prayer, who contrives to remain close to God in the midst of a busy life; a man of discipline, who enforced reverence in the city's churches and prevented their being used for profane, even immoral, purposes, just as he cracked down on the commercial exploitation of feast days; a founder of schools and rebuilder of churches; a generous benefactor of the poor and the sick; an aristocrat who knows how to strike the right note of conversation with all sorts and conditions of men; an intolerant man, who had been put in charge of the Sicilian Inquisition when the island belonged to Austria, and still imposed tight controls on Protestants within his jurisdiction, banning the import of 'poisonous' books.

No tribute to Kollonitz would be complete without mention of his more famous uncle, Leopold, Primate of Hungary, doughty opponent of Protestant and Turk alike, 'den Luther, Calvin und Machomet in seiner Krufften noch förchten' (for 'Krufft' read 'Gruft', or 'burial-vault'). Curiously enough, Leopold's father, Sigismund's grandfather, had been born a Lutheran. In 1749 the archbishop was 73 years of age, but still vigorous in mind and body. The preacher concludes by wishing that he might live to be a hundred, but in fact he died less than two years later. Staudinger never achieved the popularity of Peikhart, but judged by this sermon he was no mean orator.

(8) GYÖRGY PRIMES: *Ehr- und Lob-Rede an dem Fest der heiligen Büsserin Magdalenæ* ... Gedruckt in der Königl. Frey-Stadt Oedenburg, bey Joh. Joseph Sieß, [1749].

This sermon takes us to Hungary itself. Eisenstadt, where the seventeen-year-old Baroness Eleonora von Raizenstain von Beuleviz is taking her vows in the 'Hochfürstlich-Esterhazische' Augustinian convent, was a Hungarian town until 1919. The preacher worked in Sopron (Ödenburg), where the piece was printed. His sermon is a tale of two women: Eleonora, and St Mary Magdalene. Just as the latter turned from a life of sin, and later, according to the legend, retired from the world to live as a penitent in a cave in southern France, so Eleonora is turning her back on wealth and privilege to enter a nunnery. Unlike Mary Magdalene she has no sins to repent of, but has made a spiritual journey of another kind, out of the 'darkness' of Protestantism. The girl's mother, a Lutheran, had entrusted her for a time to the care of Catholics. Imagine her chagrin on learning that her daughter had decided not only to become a Catholic, but to enter a convent. Whilst lamenting the fact that the mother has so far shown no inclination to emulate her daughter's conversion, the preacher does not attempt to hide her grief, which he compares to that of Jephthah (Judges 11, v. 35). He even admits that one of the reasons behind the girl's religious vocation was a desire to escape her family's displeasure. Eleonora was a very gifted child: a beautiful singer, a skilful organist and fluent in several languages. From the standpoint of the present day, this sermon is particularly poignant.

(9) JOHANN STEINER: *Ein Hertz in zweyen Hertzen bey geistlichem Eingang in die Hoch-Löbliche Gesellschafft S. Ursulæ, der hoch- und wohlgebohrnen Fräule Mariæ Josephæ* ... Gedruckt zu Prag im Königs-Hof, bey Johann Norbert Fitzky, Hoch-Fürstl. Ertz-Bischöfflichen Buchdrucker, [1740].

This sermon was written for a similar occasion, but this time the setting is the Ursuline Convent in Prague. The date is 17 May 1740. Fräulein Maria Josepha von Vernier was originally to have taken the veil on 26 April, but her father had died on that very day and the ceremony had been postponed. The mother superior, Maria Anna Přehořovsky, whose name in religion was Maria Anna von dem Herz Jesu, had died shortly before him; in her honour Fräulein von Vernier had adopted the name Maria Anna Josepha von dem Herz Jesu. This no doubt inspired the title of the sermon, 'Ein Hertz in zweyen Hertzen', which also reflects the preacher's text from the Song of Solomon: 'Du hast mir das Hertz verwundet meine Schwester, meine Braut'. The theme is the close union between Christ and his bride, Maria Josepha.

We are not told Fräulein Vernier's age, but we are given plenty of information about her ancestry. Her great-grandmother on her father's side was the sister of Paris Lodron, Archbishop of Salzburg from 1619 to 1653, whilst her mother was a Kaunitz, related to Maria Theresa's great Chancellor, Wenzel Anton von Kaunitz (1711-1794). She was also – though the preacher does not say so – the great-great-granddaughter of Wallenstein. Presumably it would not have been tactful to mention the disgraced commander.

(10) DOMINICUS NEMANIZKY: *Starck-durchtringender Trompeter-Schall* ... Gedruckt zu Brünn, bey Jacob Maximilian Swoboda, [1731].

The scene changes to the Dominican church in Brno for a dazzling ceremony in which the Royal Company of Trumpeters of Moravia celebrate the centenary of the confirmation of their privileges by Ferdinand II. The day is Jubilate Sunday, the third after Easter. The trumpeters are in their full livery, with the military standards of Moravia hanging from their instruments. The preacher takes as his text Hosea 8, v. 1 which begins: 'Set the trumpet to thy mouth'. The remainder of this verse is obscure in the original Hebrew, and has been translated with a variety of meanings; however the Vulgate rendering, 'In guture tuo sit tuba, quasi aquila super domum Domini', fits his purpose admirably by linking the trumpet with an eagle – in this case the Imperial Eagle, as well as the red and gold eagle of Moravia. The Company included drummers as well as trumpeters; its full title was *Landschaffts- Hoff- und Feld-Trompeter, wie auch Heerpaucker.* They had existed long before Ferdinand II's time and had often risked their lives in battle, rallying the troops in times of danger or passing through enemy lines to deliver messages. The preacher, himself a Dominican, concludes his sermon with a reference to the Last Trump, and an exhortation to praise God with the sound of trumpets.

(11) IGNAZ REIFFENSTUEL: *Himmels-geseegnete Ehre- und Tugend-Strasse deß ... Francisci Ferdinandi ... von Rumel.* Gedruckt zu Wienn bey Wolffgang Schwendimann, Univ. Buchdr., 1716.

Sombre by comparison is the setting for no. 11, the funeral oration for Franz Ferdinand von Rumel, Kollonitz's predecessor as Bishop of Vienna. St Stephen's Cathedral is draped in black and lit by burning torches. Rumel was born in the Upper Palatinate in 1642. His parents belonged to the minor nobility, and although ordained priest at an early age, he led a retiring life until the Emperor Leopold chose him as tutor for his eldest son, the future Joseph I. It was an astonishing choice, not only on account of Rumel's obscurity but because it had become customary to entrust the education of Habsburg princes to the Jesuits, who reacted to his appointment with vindictive jealousy. Not surprisingly, Joseph grew up with a very different outlook from his father and younger brother. After he had become emperor he rewarded his former tutor by appointing him Bishop of Vienna. The Jesuits however appear to have had the last word: this oration was given by Ignatius Reiffenstuel, S. J., Peikhart's predecessor on the staff of the Cathedral.

With the exception of no. 13, all the remaining pieces are eulogies of deceased prelates.

(12) JOSEPH SILBERMANN: *Deß Nieder-Altaichischen Josiae ... hönig-süsse, und fröhliche Gedächtnuß*. Gedruckt zu Passau bey Gabriel Mangold, Hoch-Fürstl. Hof-Buchdruckern, [1740].

The monastery of Niederalteich stands beside the Danube between Regensburg and Passau, close to the hills of the Bavarian Forest. Founded in the year 731 on the site of an oak tree where pagan worship had taken place, it rose to become one of the leading Benedictine houses of Bavaria. Joscio Hamberger, the 72nd abbot, died on 4 November 1739, and his funeral oration was delivered on the 24th of that month by Joseph Silbermann, Premonstratensian Abbot of Sankt Salvator, near Ortenburg. It was printed in Passau the following year. With its 36 pages, of which the text of the sermon occupies 32, it is the most substantial piece in the collection.

In the congregation were the Prince-Bishop of Bamberg, Friedrich Karl von Schönborn, and members of his cathedral chapter; the heads of other Bavarian religious houses; representatives of the Estates of Bavaria; secular clergy from the abbey's dependent parishes; ordinary people from the surrounding area and peasants from the abbey estates. As the sermon's title implies, Joscio is compared to King Josiah, of whom it is said: 'Like unto him was there no king before him, that turned to the Lord with all his heart ... neither after him arose there any like him' (II Kings 23, v. 25), and this comparison runs through the text. For example, just as Josiah began to repair the Temple at eighteen, so Joscio took his vows at the same age. (In fact, a more careful reading of the Old Testament would suggest the eighteenth year of his reign, rather than the eighteenth year of his life.)

Abbot Joscio had been born in Munich in 1667. On his election in 1700 he inherited a desperate financial situation caused by the fires of 1671 and 1685, the effects of which were still plain to see. Then came the War of the Spanish Succession, when invading Imperial troops demanded 30,000 Gulden 'protection money'. As with Job, misfortunes were heaped upon him: the abbey and its dependencies were repeatedly struck by lightning, whilst hail ruined the crops; the Danube overflowed, even threatening to change its course and inundate the abbey, causing him to spend vast sums on flood defences; outbreaks of cattle plague caused untold losses; and the east end of the church, which had been rebuilt at great expense, began to collapse. Yet by the time of his death he had doubled the number of monks and completely transformed the abbey church, besides erecting many other new buildings, including the library.

But what sort of man was Joscio Hamberger? First, a man of great simplicity. He dressed like an ordinary monk; his habit was of poor cloth, often patched, and only his pectoral cross distinguished him from his fellows. When the affairs of the Bavarian Diet took him to Munich, he declined to travel around the city in a carriage but walked the streets shabbily dressed, so that people would point him out and say, 'Do you realize who that is? It's the Abbot of Niederalteich!' Though he did much for the material welfare of his monks – for example installing heating in their cells for the first time – he never modernised his own quarters, which were the meanest of all.

He was also a generous man. He assisted the poor, whether his own 'subjects' or not, especially when war or other disasters had robbed them of their homes or livelihood; he channelled alms through the mendicant orders, as well as directly to the hospitals and almshouses; and no pauper ever went away empty-handed from the abbey gates. He opened a school at Niederalteich where all local children of both sexes could be educated free of charge; contributed generously towards the establishment of a botanic garden at Ingolstadt University; and regularly supported the University of Salzburg, which was run by the Benedictines. He was not, however, tolerant of views with which he disagreed, even going so far as to buy up banned books – in at least one case all the copies he could find, at a cost of 150 Gulden – in order to throw them into the fire. In Germany the burning of books has a long history.

The abbot's simple life-style was the outward expression of his personal asceticism, his *Strengheit*. He slept on a hard bed, refused all delicacies, and allowed himself no recreation other than reading in the library. He often spent hours praying alone in the freezing church. After his death scourges, well worn, and tainted with his blood, were found in his room, and the wearing of a hair-shirt had turned his flesh to an open sore. Not surprisingly, his health was bad: he suffered headaches and toothache, and in later life was crippled with arthritis in his hands and feet. He could not raise his voice. As a result of earlier illnesses his stomach was incapable of taking much food, and he appeared as nothing but skin and bone. Yet his official duties as a delegate to the *Landschaft* of Bavaria obliged him to undertake long journeys. Travelling on country roads was difficult enough in those days, much more so for a sick and frail old man. Nevertheless he endured extremes of weather, and all the discomforts of travel, even when so unwell that he had to be lifted into his carriage.

He considered himself unworthy of his high spiritual office, and often asked to be allowed to resign. In a single day he destroyed all his own portraits, believing they did not deserve a place in the abbey. He disliked having books dedicated to him; indeed, when one has seen the dedicatory epistles of the Baroque period with their often fulsome praise, including some in this volume, one can understand why he wrote 'Vanitas vanitatum' (Ecclesiastes I, v. 2) against the offending passages in many a copy belonging to the monastery library. He was convinced that no one would remember him after he was dead. A similar picture emerges from the 'Festschrift'[4] issued to mark the abbey's millennium, in which Placidus Haiden, after devoting nearly two hundred pages to the achievements of all Joscio's predecessors, confesses himself at a loss: 'Zwar solte ich zur Prob den hochgelobten Lebens-Lauff Joscionis

4 *Tausend-jähriges Jubel-Fest des Closters Niederaltaich* (Regensburg, 1732).

wenigstens obenhin berühren, allein die angebohrne Minderträchtigkeit und Demuth dieses Ehr-flüchtigen Herrns entnimmet mir die Feder, die ich auch mit aller Verehrung in so weit zurück halte, daß nur jenes beybringen will, so fast männiglich bekannt, und so gar die stummen Steine und leblose Farben nicht lassen verschwiegen bleiben.' ('To be sure I ought at least to touch on the course of Joscio's laudable life, but the innate modesty and humility of this man who eschewed all honour takes the pen out of my hand, and I hold it back with such reverence that I will only divulge those things which virtually everyone already knows, and which even the mute stones and lifeless colours cannot remain silent about.')

Indeed, Joscio's true memorial is the church of Niederalteich itself, completely remodelled in the years 1718–36.[5] Unusually, in this sermon the preacher takes his hearers round the space they have before their eyes: the high altar, behind its massive iron grille; the new choir, with its great organ and curving rows of stalls;[6] another organ at the west end; the chapels of St Gotthard and Our Lady (both now demolished); the rich furnishings, including the pulpit 'wo ich stehe',[7] and the marble floor; the eight oval openings, cut at regular intervals in the aisle ceilings, which allow sunlight to fall from the gallery windows on to the side altars. 'Wer wird laugnen können,' he concludes, 'daß dise Gedächtnuß nicht Hönig-süß seye?' ('Who will be able to deny that these memories are not as sweet as honey?')

(13) GREGOR SEBASTIAN FRITZ: *Kurtze Cantzel-Rede ... Maximiliano des ... Collegiat-Stiffts ... zu Tiernstein ... erwählten ... Probsten ... zu ... Ehren eingerichtet.* Crembs, gedruckt bey Ignatz Anton Präxl, Wiennerisch-Universität. Buchdr., [1740].

For a complete contrast we turn to no. 13, which marks the installation of Maximilian Leeb as Provost of Tiernstein. For Tiernstein read Dürnstein, a small town in the Wachau where the former Augustinian collegiate church still stands proudly beside the Danube, beneath the ruined castle where Richard the Lionheart was once held prisoner. The religious community was small – there were just twelve canons, including the provost. Maximilian was just thirty-eight years of age, and a very different personality from Joscio Hamberger. The preacher refers to his gentle character, and stresses his sociable nature (*Leuthseeligkeit*). He had not wanted a eulogy on his accession, but the canons had circumvented his objections by inviting the parish priest of Stein to deliver a sermon on his name-day. The oration is relatively short; the occasion is a happy one, and the speaker's warmth and modesty shine through his words. This is perhaps the most pleasing sermon in the volume. It is also attractively

5 The church today is essentially as Abbot Joscio left it; however, damage by lightning in 1813 led to changes in the shape of the towers and the removal of certain other features.

6 These are now in the monastery of Ettal, near Oberammergau.

7 In fact, the pulpit dates from the end of the seventeenth century.

printed in large, clear type. Präxl is described on the title-page as printer to the University of Vienna.

(14) FRANZ PEIKHART: *Trauer-Rede, über dem betrübten Todt-Fall ... Leopoldi des ... Stiffts ... zu Hertzogburg preißwürdigsten Probsten.* Wienn, gedruckt bey Johann Ignatz Heyinger, Hochfürstl. Ertz-Bischöffl. Hof-Buchdruckern, [1740].

The Abbey of Herzogenburg lies a few miles south of the Danube, not far from Dürnstein and Krems. Provost Leopold von Planta, the subject of Peikhart's oration, was descended from the Swiss family of that name which played such a prominent part in the history of the Grisons from the late Middle Ages onwards. One of its members, Joseph Planta, was Principal Librarian of the British Museum from 1799 to 1827. Unlike the Plantas who came to London, Leopold belonged to a Catholic branch of the family; his father had left the canton of Berne to start a new life in Austria, preferring the free exercise of his religion to the advantages of a good position and noble birth. Of all the individuals whom we meet in the pages of these sermons, Planta is almost the only one whose preaching ability is considered worthy of mention. His love of the Eucharist was equalled by his zeal for the ministry of the Word. He gave people, says Peikhart, 'the body of Christ and the Word of God', and loved to go out preaching in the village churches.

(15) VIRGIL HARL: *Der nach dem Wasser-Quell flüchtig-auerische Hirsch.* Burghausen, gedruckt bey Leopold Klatzinger, Churf. Regierungs-Buchdrucker, [1749].

For this sermon we return to Bavaria. The preacher's text is the opening of Psalm 42, the one which begins in the Book of Common Prayer 'Like as the hart desireth the water-brooks', and the 'Auerische Hirsch' of the title is Joachim Böham, Provost of Au am Inn. The text was probably suggested by the stag in Joachim's coat-of-arms, whilst the arms of the monastery conveniently included a representation of the River Inn, 'den fürbeyrauschenden Ynnstrom'. Böham was an able and energetic man, who had brought the rebuilding of his church to a successful conclusion; however his high-handed behaviour and poor financial management had led to his effectual deposition in 1734; he had been allowed to retain the title of provost as long as he lived, but his duties were taken over by an administrator and he was 'banished' to a parish about twenty miles away.[8] In giving his funeral oration, the preacher was thus faced with a ticklish problem. As Dean of the neighbouring Abbey of Gars, and a fellow Augustinian, he was well acquainted with the circumstances, but he alludes only occasionally to the failings of the deceased. He also suggests in his preface that one reason for printing the sermon was the need to rehabilitate the dead man's memory.

8 Peter Schmalzl, *Au am Inn: Geschichte des ehemaligen Augustiner-Chorherrenstiftes* (Au am Inn, 1962).

Burghausen is a small town on the Salzach where printing had only begun in 1735, and Klatzinger was its second printer. This must be the earliest Burghausen imprint in the British Library.

(16) DOMINICUS SEELHAMMER: *Hönig-süsse Gedächtnuß vom Leben und Todt... Ambrosii von Freuden-Pühel.* Steyer, gedruckt bey Joseph Grünenwald, 1730.

Ambrosius von Freuden-Pühel was Abbot of Garsten, a Benedictine house just outside Steyr, that ancient town of Upper Austria which once rivalled Linz in importance. Printing in Steyr began about 1692, and Grünenwald was the third printer to operate in the town, from 1710 to 1733. Seelhammer was Prior of the town's Dominican friary, and tells us that he came from a poor background; as a child he had enjoyed free schooling at Garsten, including free food and clothing and the opportunity to learn Latin, which he describes as 'ein Grundvest so viler herrlicher Wissenschafften' ('the foundation of so many splendid branches of knowledge'). Abbot Ambrose was more than usually interested in education, having studied philosophy and law at the University of Salzburg before becoming professor there. When Ambrose died in 1729 he was only fifty, but his body had been undermined by a whole range of diseases.

Also close to Steyr is the pilgrimage church of Christkindl, where Ambrose received his first priestly charge. Today it is known throughout the world as the place from which hundreds of thousands of goodwill messages are despatched at Christmas time, and to which children from all over Austria write to ask the Christ child for presents.

Reading through the volume one finds a number of statements suggesting, however loosely, that one hour was the normal duration for a sermon on these important public occasions. This sermon however is longer than most. On page 26 the preacher confesses: 'Nunmehro muß ich gestehen, daß die außgesetzte Red-Stund allbereit verflossen, aber ich doch nicht zum Ende meiner Rede gelanget seye' ('I must now admit that the hour allotted for speaking has already run out, but I have not yet reached the end of my address') – and there are still five pages to go ...

(17) ANDREAS PICHLER: *Mausoleum Jonathae Pontificis.* Lintz, gedruckt bey Maria Ursula Freyschmidin, einer Löbl. O. Oe. Landschafft Buchdruckerin, Wittib, [1709].

The subject of this oration is Bernhard Weidner, Abbot of Wilhering, a Cistercian monastery on the south bank of the Danube a few miles upstream from Linz. Unlike most of his fellows in this volume, who are described as 'wohl-edel-gebohrn', 'hoch-edl-gebohrn', etc., Bernhard is referred to on the title-page as 'in Gott geistlich-wol-edlen' – a hint that he was of humble origin. Like his contemporary Leodegar Bürgisser, Abbot of St Gall, who had the distinction of plunging Switzerland into civil war, Bernhard was the son of a shoemaker. His parents were poor,[9] so much so that when Bernhard's father grew too old to work they were compelled to depend on charity; fortunately when their son became abbot he was able to support them from the resources of the abbey. The text of the sermon is taken from a passage in the Apocrypha describing the elaborate mausoleum which Simon the Maccabee constructed following the death of his brother Jonathan the High Priest; it consisted of seven pyramids surrounded by pillars adorned with trophies. The preacher, a Jesuit on the staff of the Stadtpfarrkirche in Linz (cf. no. 5), proceeds to erect an allegorical monument of seven pyramids, or more probably obelisks, each bearing the image of a heavenly body symbolizing one of Bernhard's qualities or a phase of his career.

(18) AEMILIAN DANELI: *Neuer Himmel zu Mölck ... oder Klag-Rede, über den traurigen Todt-Fall ... Herrn Bertholdi ...* Wienn, gedruckt bey Gregori Kurtzböck, Universit. Buchdr. auf dem Juden-Platz neben dem grossen Jordan, [1739].

Our final journey of some sixty miles down the Danube brings us to Melk, where Austria's greatest Benedictine monastery stands on a crag at the entrance to the Wachau. In the eighteenth century there was no bridge at this spot to detract from the wildness of the scene. The abbey took on its present form under the rule of Berthold Dietmair, which lasted from 1700 to 1739 (being exactly contemporaneous with that of Hamberger at Niederalteich), and his funeral oration forms the last item in the collection.

Its title – and the preacher's text – are taken from the passage in Revelation 21, v. 1 which runs 'And I saw a new heaven and a new earth: for the first heaven and the first earth were passed away'. Their significance runs something like this: according to St Bernard, a holy man is a representation of Heaven – *Ego puto omnem animam sanctam, non modo coelestem esse, sed et Coelum ipsum*. Thus the 'new heaven' is none other than Berthold himself. Does not his coat-of-arms, which includes a star, prove as much? But there is more to the metaphor than this; for just as Heaven is the dwelling-place of God, so the abbey of Melk, rebuilt in greater splendour than ever before, had become a dwelling fit for the Almighty on earth. Berthold's death in the early hours of 25 January 1739 coincided with a partial eclipse of the moon, providing the preacher with yet another heavenly association of ideas. It was the lower part of the moon which was obscured; in the same way Berthold's inferior, earthly self is hid in darkness, while his higher being, his immortal soul, is bathed in the light of eternity.

In 1739 the Austrian monasteries were at the height of their wealth and influence. New ones were still being founded, and young men and women were flocking to join the orders. Fifty years later the picture was very different. First,

9 Jodok Stülz, *Geschichte des Cistercienser-Klosters Wilhering* (Linz, 1840).

Maria Theresia's financial reforms took resources away from the big land-owners, including the Church, and concentrated them in the hands of the state, to be spent on the administration and the army. Then came the enlightened despotism of Joseph II, which closed many of the monasteries and scattered their libraries to the winds. Sermons of the type described here were considered old-fashioned and devoid of interest, and very many copies must have been destroyed.[10] Perhaps this explains why they do not seem to come on to the market very often today. The British Library was fortunate, therefore, to acquire this collection.

10 Cf. Walter Zitzenbacher, *Grazer Barockprediger* (Graz, [1973]), p. 99.

PUBLICATIONS BY DAVID L. PAISEY

To the end of May 1995

DENNIS E. RHODES

1 Diction in Gottfried Benn's Poems to 1927. M.A. thesis (unpublished), University of London, 1957, pp. ii, 218.

2 Review: Else Buddeberg, *Gottfried Benn* (Stuttgart, 1961). In: *GLL*, n.s., 15 (1961-62), 324-7.

3 Review: Reinhold Grimm and Wolf-Dieter Marsch (eds), *Die Kunst im Schatten des Gottes. Für und wider Gottfried Benn* (Göttingen, 1962). In: *GLL*, n.s. 17 (1963-64), 177-8.

4 Translation: Lev S. Bagrov, *History of Cartography*. (London, 1964) [Original title: *Die Geschichte der Kartographie*]. (Second edition: Chicago 1986.)

5 'British Germanists and the computer', *GLL*, n.s., 22 (1968-69), 155-61.

6 'Das Schicksal Wole Soyinkas.' In: Tilman Zülch and Klaus Guercke (eds), *Soll Biafra überleben?* 2nd ed. (Berlin, 1969), pp. 209-211.

7 Review: J. Bruckner, *A Bibliographical Catalogue of Seventeenth-century German Books published in Holland* (The Hague and Paris, 1971). In: *The Library*, 5th ser., 27 (1972), 342-4.

8 'Alsatian literature'. In: *Cassell's Encyclopaedia of World Literature* (London, 1973), p. 23.

9 Translation: Tilman Zülch and Herman Womiswor, 'Indonesia abroad. West Papua, the Indonesian skeleton', *Beaver*, no. 132 (London School of Economics, 15 October 1974), 11.

10 'Catalogue of German books of the 17th century', *WBN*, 1 (1974), 46-7.

11 'A collection of German religious songs of the mid-sixteenth century', *BLJ*, 1 (1975), 71-83.

12 'Work in progress: catalogue of German books 1601-1700 in the British Library, Reference Division', *BLJ*, 1 (1975), 105-06.

13 'Some occasional aspects of Johann Hermann Schein [1586-1630]', *BLJ*, 1 (1975), 171-80.

14 [Co-author:] *The arrangement of entries for complex material under headings for personal authors*. (International Federation of Library Associations, London, 1975), pp. viii, 6.

15 'Ein Vorläufer der Pränumerantenverzeichnisse, aus dem Jahre 1684', *WNB*, 1 (1976), 79-80.

16 'Illustrated German broadsides of the seventeenth century', *BLJ*, 2 (1976), 56-69.

17 'Einige Bemerkungen aus Gelegenheitsdichtungen über Wolfgang Endter den

Älteren und sein Nürnberger Unternehmen sowie ein Lobgedicht auf den Buchhandel von Johann Klaj', *AGB*, 15 (1976), 1293-96.

18 'Dating a stock catalogue of Peter Braubach [Frankfurt, 1555]', *GJ*, 51 (1976), 248-53.

19 'A hitherto unattributed German elegy on the death of Simon Dach, 1659 [by Theodor Wolder, printed by Johann Reusner at Königsberg]', *BLJ*, 2 (1976), 177-8.

20 'A new organisation devoted to the history of the book in Germany', *GLL*, n.s. 29 (1976), 228-9.

21 'The first fruits of Johann Friedrich Hager, printer at Göttingen, in 1729: poems for King George II of England', *GJ*, 52 (1977), 170-82.

22 'An unrecorded German periodical from the time of the Napoleonic Wars: *Beyträge zur Geschichte des Krieges der Jahre 1812 und 1813*', *BLJ*, 3 (1977), 129-34.

23 'A "Singballett" from Oels, 1689', *WBN*, 4 (1977), 36.

24 'Catalogue of German Books of the seventeenth century in the British Library.' In: Martin Bircher and Eberhard Mannack (eds), *Deutsche Barockliteratur und europäische Kultur*, Wolfenbütteler Arbeiten zur Barockforschung, 2. (Hamburg, 1977), pp. 317-18.

25 'Deutsche Bücher des 17. Jahrhunderts in der British Library', *Aus dem Antiquariat*, 1977, pp. A 106-A 109.

26 'Zu einer Buchkunstausstellung in London', *Aus dem Antiquariat*, Heft 1, 1978, pp. 21-23.

27 Translation: Hans Henning, 'An addition to the Faust literature: an unknown "Harrowing of Hell" in the British Library', *BLJ*, 4 (1978), 1-7.

28 'La littérature alsacienne.' In: *Histoire des littératures III* ([Paris:] Encyclopédie de la Pléiade, 1978), pp. 1617-24.

29 Review: *Archiv für Geschichte des Buchwesens*, Bd. XVI (Frankfurt, 1976). In: *The Book Collector*, Autumn 1978, pp. 410, 413, 414.

30 'Learning to read: Friedrich Gedike's primer of 1791', *BLJ*, 4 (1978), 112-21.

31 'German newspapers of the seventeenth century in the Public Record Office, London', *GJ*, 53 (1978), 168-72.

32 'Eine Rist-Ausgabe, die es nicht gibt', *WBN*, 5 (1978), 209.

33 'Zum Schlußkapitel des *Simplicissimus*', *WBN*, 5 (1978), 214.

34 'Buchgeschichtliche Zeitschriften in Großbritannien', *Buchhandelsgeschichte* 1978, pp. B 709-B 712.

35 'German popular literature as seen in some recent antiquarian acquisitions', *BLJ*, 5 (1979), 91-101.

36 'The "Officina Poetica" at Leipzig, 1619-1623', *GJ*, 54 (1979), 205-9.

37 *German Books in the British Library* (London, March 1979) [Broadside catalogue of a small exhibition marking the visit to the British Library of the Historische Kommission des Börsenvereins des Deutschen Buchhandels.]

38 Review: Karl Mommsen, *Katalog der Basler juristischen Dissertationen 1558-1818* (Frankfurt am Main, 1978). In: *Buchhandelsgeschichte*, 2, 6 (1980), 349-51.

39 'Acquisitions from the Broxbourne library, 16th century German', *BLJ*, 6 (1980), 104-106.

40 Hans Popst 'Vom "British Museum Catalogue (BM)" zum "British Library Catalogue (BLC)"', *Aus dem Antiquariat*, Heft 2, 1980, pp. A61-A68, [with:] 'Ergän-

zungen von David Paisey', *Aus dem Antiquariat*, Heft 4, 1980, pp. A137-A138.

41 'Literatur, die nicht in den Meßkatalogen steht.' In: Paul Raabe (ed.), *Bücher und Bibliotheken im 17. Jahrhundert in Deutschland*. Wolfenbütteler Schriften zur Geschichte des Buchwesens, 6. (Hamburg, 1980), pp. 115-25.

42 'Some sources of the "Kunstbüchlein" of 1535', *GJ*, 55 (1980), 113-7.

43 Review: *Archiv für Geschichte des Buchwesens*, Bd. XVIII & XIX (Frankfurt, 1977, 1978). In: *The Book Collector*, Autumn 1978, pp. 435, 436, 439, 440, 443.

44 'A German ink-seller of 1621 and his views on publishing.' In: A. R. A. Croiset van Uchelen (ed.), *Hellinga Festschrift / Feestbundel / Mélanges. Forty-Three Studies in Bibliography presented to Prof. Dr. Wytze Hellinga ...* 1978 (Amsterdam, 1980), pp. 403-12.

45 'A Dresden opera-goer in 1756: Johann Christian Trömer, called "Der Deutsch-Franzos".' In: Oliver Neighbour (ed.), *Music and Bibliography. Essays in honour of Alec Hyatt King* (New York, London, etc., 1980), pp. 69-88.

46 'Two Aschaffenburg Meßrelationen, 1628 and 1629', *GJ*, 56 (1981), 210-13.

47 Review: Hans Dieter Gebauer, *Bücherauktionen in Deutschland im 17. Jahrhundert* (Bonn, 1981). In: *The Library*, 6th ser., 3 (1981), 355-7.

48 Review: Leonard Forster, *Iter Bohemicum* (Amsterdam, 1980). In: *Notes and Queries*, 227 (1982), 474-5.

49 Review: Horst Meyer (ed.), *Bibliographie der Buch- und Bibliotheksgeschichte*, 1 (1980/81). In: *The Library Association Rare Books Group Newsletter*, no. 20 (1982), 20.

50 Review: Hartmut Sührig, *Die Entwicklung der niedersächsichen Kalender im 17. Jahrhundert* (Frankfurt am Main, 1979). In: *Zeitschrift für Volkskunde*, 78 (1982), 307-9.

51 Review: *Gutenberg-Jahrbuch* 1981. In: *The Times Literary Supplement*, no. 4,135, 2 July 1982, p. 726.

52 Review: Gerhard Dünnhaupt, *Bibliographisches Handbuch der Barockliteratur* (Stuttgart, 1980-81). In: *The Library*, 6th ser., 4 (1982), 446-50.

53 Review: Werner Arnold, *Eine norddeutsche Fürstenbibliothek des frühen 18. Jahrhunderts. Herzog Ludwig Rudolph von Braunschweig-Lüneburg (1671-1735) und seine Büchersammlung*. Arbeiten zur Geschichte des Buchwesens in Niedersachsen, 3. (Göttingen, 1980). In: *The Book Collector*, 31 (1982), 117-18.

54 Review: K. J. Arndt and May Olson, *German-American Press Research from the American Revolution to the Bicentennial* (Munich, 1980). In: *Library Science Book Distribution Service Quality Monitor*, 4 (1982).

55 Translation: *Johann Wolfgang von Goethe: Rede zum Shakespeare-Tag* (Hamburg, 1982). Also published as: 'Goethe: Speech on the Shakespeare Day. Translated by David Paisey, with an introduction by Berthold Hack', *Comparative Criticism*, 7 (1985), 177-81.

56 Review: Helgard Ulmschneider, *Götz von Berlichingen, Mein Fehd und Handlungen* (Sigmaringen, 1981). In: *The German Quarterly*, 56 (1983), 134.

57 Review: Blake Lee Spahr, *Problems and Perspectives: a Collection of Essays on German Baroque Literature* (Frankfurt am Main, 1981). In: *The German Quarterly*, 56 (1983), 309-10.

58 'Acquisitions, German Section', *BLJ*, 9 (1982), 82-92.

59 Review: *Register zum Gutenberg-Jahrbuch 1926-1975* (Mainz, 1981). In: *The Times Literary Supplement*, no. 4,184, 10 June 1983, p. 612.

60 'Roman type for German text: a proponent in 1733', *GJ*, 58 (1983), 232-40.

61 Review: Franz Blom, *Christoph und Andreas Arnold and England* (Nuremberg, 1982). In: *The Book Collector*, Autumn 1983, pp. 354-6.

62 Review: 1. Georg Jäger and Jörg Schönert (eds), *Die Leihbibliothek als Institution des literarischen Lebens im 18. und 19. Jahrhundert* (Hamburg, 1980); 2. Giles Barber and Bernhard Fabian (eds), *Buch und Buchhandel in Europa im achtzehnten Jahrhundert* (Hamburg, 1981); 3. Paul Raabe (ed.), *Buchgestaltung in Deutschland 1740 bis 1890* (Hamburg, 1980); 4. Paul Raabe (ed.), *Bücher und Bibliotheken im 17. Jahrhundert in Deutschland* (Hamburg, 1980). In: *The Book Collector*, Winter 1983, pp. 484-8.

63 Translation of preface and introduction to: *Verzeichnis der im deutschen Sprachbereich erschienenen Drucke des XVI. Jahrhunderts. VD 16.* Redaktion Irmgard Bezzel. Bd. I (Stuttgart, 1983), pp. VIII, IX, XXXI-XXXVII.

64 'Illustrated books.' In: [Frances Carey and Antony Griffiths], *The Print in Germany 1880-1933: The Age of Expressionism …* . Exhibition catalogue. London: British Museum, 1984.

65 Review: Bernhard Fabian, *Buch, Bibliothek und geisteswissenschaftliche Forschung* (Göttingen, 1983). In: *The Library*, 6th ser., 6 (1984), 299-302.

66 'Blind printing in early Continental books'. In: Anna Laura Lepschy, John Took and Dennis E. Rhodes (eds), *Book Production and Letters in the Western European Renaissance. Essays in Honour of Conor Fahy.* Publications of the Modern Humanities Research Association, 12 (London, 1986), pp. 220-33.

67 *German Studies: British Resources. Papers presented at a colloquium at the British Library 25-27 September 1985.* Edited by David Paisey. British Library Occasional Papers, 8 (London, 1986), pp. XIV, 320.

68 'Nachtrag: Die Sammlung Maltzahn in der British Library', *WBN*, 13 (1986), 74.

69 'Report on a meeting of the Historical Commission of the Börsenverein des Deutschen Buchhandels.' In: *Book Trade History Group Newsletter*, no. 2 (June 1986), 5.

70 Review: John Roger Paas, *The German Political Broadsheet 1600-1700*, vol. 1 (Wiesbaden, 1985). In: *The Library*, 6th ser., 9 (1987), 297-300.

71 *Deutsche Buchdrucker, Buchhändler und Verleger 1701-1750.* Beiträge zum Buch- und Bibliothekswesen, 26 (Wiesbaden, 1988), pp. XI, 361.

72 Review: Werner Welzig (ed.), *Katalog gedruckter deutschsprachiger katholischer Predigtsammlungen.* 2 vols (Vienna, 1984-87). In: *The Library*, 6th ser., 10 (1988), 355-8.

73 'Die deutschen Bestände der British Library', *Zeitschrift für Bibliothekswesen und Bibliographie*, 36 (1989), 495-503.

74 Review: W. Arnold, W. Dittrich and B. Zeller (eds), *Die Erforschung der Buch- und Bibliotheksgeschichte in Deutschland, Paul Raabe zum 60. Geburtstag gewidmet* (Wiesbaden, 1987). In: *The Library*, 6th ser., 11 (1989), 67-71.

75 'German printers, booksellers and publishers of the seventeenth century: some amendments and additions to Benzing,' *GJ*, 64 (1989), 165-79.

76 *World Cup Willie and others. Some German Illustrated Books of the 1960s.* By Rosamond Eden and David L. Paisey. (London 1989) [British Library exhibition notes.]

77 *Short-title Catalogue of Books Printed in the German-speaking Countries and of German Books Printed in Other Countries from 1455 to 1657 now in the British*

Library. Supplement. [Compiled by D. L. Paisey.] (London, 1990), pp. [6], 141.

78 Review: Sibylle Appuhn-Radtke, *Das Thesenblatt im Hochbarock* (Weißenhorn, 1988). In: *Print Quarterly*, 7 (March 1990), 70-1.

79 Review: Werner Welzig (ed.), *Lobrede. Katalog deutschsprachiger Heiligenpredigten in Einzeldrucken aus den Beständen der Stiftsbibliothek Klosterneuburg* (Vienna, 1989). In: *The Library*, 6th ser., 12 (1990), 75.

80 Review: Herbert G. Göpfert and Erdmann Weyrauch, *'Unmoralisch an sich ...' Zensur im 18. und 19. Jahrhundert* (Wiesbaden, 1988). In: *The Library*, 6th ser., 12 (1990), 253-5.

81 Heinrich von Kleist, *On Puppet-Shows* [Über das Marionettentheater]. Translated by David Paisey (Hamburg, 1991).

82 'Printed books in English and Dutch in early printed catalogues of German university libraries.' In: Susan Roach (ed.), *Across the Narrow Seas. Studies in the History and Bibliography of Britain and the Low Countries, presented to Anna E. C. Simoni* (London, 1991), pp. 127-48.

83 Cabal and Love [Unpublished translation by David Paisey of Friedrich Schiller's *Kabale und Liebe*, produced at the Lyric Studio, Hammersmith, March 1992]. British Library, Department of Manuscripts: Playscript no. 5248.

84 'Adressen von deutschen Druckern und Verlegern im 17. Jahrhundert. Eine erste Liste aus den Drucken in der British Library', *WNB*, 17 (1992), 169-76.

85 Translation: Franz Georg Kaltwasser, 'German libraries reunited'. In: *The Times Literary Supplement*, no. 4,669, 25 September 1992, p. 18.

86 'A favourite item [Justus Oldekop, *Warhaffte Beschreibung ...*, Wolfenbüttel, 1664]', *Focus. The British Library Staff Newsletter*, no. 81 (1993), 8.

87 'Decimo. Reflections on some rare formats.' In: Denis V. Reidy (ed.), *The Italian Book 1465-1800. Studies presented to Dennis E. Rhodes on his 70th birthday* (London, 1993), pp. 161-74.

88 *Catalogue of Books Printed in the German-speaking Countries and of German Books Printed in Other Countries from 1601 to 1700 now in the British Library.* 5 vols (London, 1994).

89 Review: *Matthias Merian der Ältere: Zeichner, Stecher und Verleger.* By Wilhelm Bingsohn & others. Frankfurt a.M. 1993. In: *Print Quarterly*, 12 (March 1995), 83-5.

90 *Unbekannte Gedichte des Barock. Anonyme Meisterwerke aus den Schätzen der British Library.* (Darmstadt, 1995).

91 Dieter Breuer, David Paisey and Thomas Bürger (eds), *Buchdruck im Barockzeitalter.* Wolfenbütteler Arbeiten zur Barockforschung. (Wiesbaden, forthcoming).

92 Review: *Handbuch der historischen Buchbestände in Deutschland.* Edited by Bernhard Fabian, Hildesheim, 1992-, Bd. 3-9 (Nordrhein-Westfalen, Hessen, Rheinland-Pfalz, Baden-Württemberg, Saarland). In: *The Library* (forthcoming).

93 Review: Horst Kunze, *Geschichte der Buchillustration in Deutschland. Das 16. und 17. Jahrhundert.* Frankfurt & Leipzig 1993. In: *The Book Collector* (forthcoming).

INDEX